TAKING SIDES

Clashing Views in

Business Ethics and Society

ELEVENTH EDITION

Selected, Edited, and with Introductions by

Lisa H. Newton
Fairfield University

Elaine E. Englehardt
Utah Valley University

Michael S. Pritchard
Western Michigan

Connect
Learn
Succeed™

The McGraw-Hill Companies

Connect
Learn
Succeed™

TAKING SIDES: CLASHING VIEWS IN BUSINESS ETHICS AND SOCIETY,
ELEVENTH EDITION

Taking Sides® is a registered trademark of the McGraw-Hill Companies, Inc.
Taking Sides is published by the **Contemporary Learning Series** group within the McGraw-Hill Higher Education division.

2 3 4 5 6 7 8 9 0 DOC/DOC 10 9 8 7 6 5 4 3 2 1

MHID: 0-07-352731-9
ISBN: 978-0-07-352731-4
ISSN: 95-83859

Managing Editor: *Larry Loeppke*
Production Manager: *Faye Schilling*
Senior Developmental Editor: *Jade Benedict*
Editorial Assistant: *Cindy Hedley*
Production Service Assistant: *Rita Hingtgen*
Permissions Coordinator: *Shirley Lanners*
Senior Marketing Manager: *Julie Keck*
Marketing Communications Specialist: *Mary Klein*
Marketing Coordinator: *Alice Link*
Project Manager: *Erin Melloy*
Design Specialist: *Tara McDermott*
Cover Graphics: *Rick Noel*

Compositor: MPS Limited, A Macmillan Company
Cover Image: © Getty Images/RF

Library of Congress Cataloging-in-Publication Data

Main entry under title:
   Taking sides: clashing views in business ethics and society/selected, edited, and with introductions by Lisa H. Newton et al. 11th ed.

Includes bibliographical references.
1. Business ethics, I. Newton, Lisa H., *comp*. II.
              174.4

Editors/Academic Advisory Board

Members of the Academic Advisory Board are instrumental in the final selection of articles for each edition of TAKING SIDES. Their review of articles for content, level, and appropriateness provides critical direction to the editors and staff. We think that you will find their careful consideration well reflected in this volume.

TAKING SIDES: Clashing Views in BUSINESS ETHICS AND SOCIETY

Eleventh Edition

EDITORS

Lisa H. Newton
Fairfield University

Elaine E. Englehardt
Utah Valley University

Michael S. Pritchard
Western Michigan

ACADEMIC ADVISORY BOARD MEMBERS

Preface

The principle by which we naturally either approve or disapprove of our own conduct, seems to be altogether the same with that by which we exercise the like judgments concerning the conduct of other people. We either approve or disapprove of the conduct of another man according as we feel that, when we bring his case home to ourselves [i.e. when we imagine ourselves into his situation], we either can or cannot entirely sympathize with the sentiments and motives which directed it. And, in the same manner, we either approve or disapprove of our own conduct, according as we feel that, when we place ourselves in the situation of another man, and view it, as it were, with his eyes and from his station, we either can or cannot entirely enter into and sympathize with the sentiments and motives which influenced it. We can never survey our own sentiments and motives, we can never form any judgment concerning them, unless we remove ourselves, as it was, from our natural station, and endeavor to view them as at a certain distance from us. But we can do this in no other way than by endeavoring to view them with the eyes of other people, or as other people are likely to view them.

Adam Smith, *The Theory of Moral Sentiments*,
ed. D.D. Raphael and A.L. Macfie, (Oxford, 1976)

This volume contains 40 selections, presented in a pro and con format, that debate a total of 20 different controversial issues in business ethics. In this book we ask you, the reader, to examine the accepted practices of business in the light of human needs, justice, rights, and dignity. We ask you to consider what moral imperatives and values should be at work in the conduct of business.

This method of presenting opposing views on an issue grows out of the ancient learning method of *dialogue*. Two assumptions lead us to seek the truth in a dialogue between opposed positions. The first assumption is that the truth is really out there and that it is important to find it. The second is that no one of us has all of it (the truth). The way to reach the truth is to form our initial opinions on a subject and give voice to them in public. Then we let others with differing opinions reply, and while they are doing so, we listen carefully. The truth that comes into being in the public space of the dialogue—literally, the space in between the two disputants—becomes part of our opinions on all related matters. We now have more informed opinions, and they are reliably based on the reasoning that emerged in the course of airing those views.

Each issue in this volume has an issue *introduction* that sets the stage for the debate as it is argued in the YES and NO selections. Most issues conclude with a *postscript* that makes some final observations and points the way to other questions related to the issue. The introductions and postscripts do not preempt what is the reader's own task: to achieve a critical and informed view of the issue at stake. In reading an issue and forming your own opinion, you should not feel confined to adopt one or the other of the positions presented. There are positions in between the given views, or totally outside them, and the *suggestions for further reading* that appear in each postscript should help you to continue your study of the subject. At the back of the book is a listing of all the *contributors to this volume,* for further information on the varied backgrounds of the writers represented in this book.

Changes to this edition   This edition represents a change in editors and a substantial revision. Lisa H. Newton continues as the lead editor. We thank Maureen M. Ford for the work she has completed in past editions. Elaine E. Englehardt and Michael S. Pritchard join Lisa H. Newton in presenting four new issues and nine new writings. These issues include: Can Individual Virtue Survive Corporate Pressure? (issue 4); Are the Risks of Derivatives Manageable? (issue 5); Is Price Gouging Morally Acceptable? (issue 6); Are Sweat Shops an Inhumane business practice? (issue 16). We have changed an author on a favorite issue: Is Increasing Profits the Only Social Responsibility of Business? by including an interesting view by Joe DesJardins, (issue 3).

A word to the instructor   An *Instructor's Resource Guide with Test Questions* (multiple choice and essay) is available through the publisher for the instructor using *Taking Sides* in the classroom. A general guidebook, *Using Taking Sides in the Classroom,* which discusses methods and techniques for integrating the pro-con approach into any classroom setting, is also available. An online version of *Using Taking Sides in the Classroom* and a correspondence service for *Taking Sides* adopters can be found at http://www.mhcls.com/usingts/.

Taking Sides: Clashing Views on Controversial Issues in Business Ethics and Society is only one title in the Taking Sides series. If you are interested in seeing the table of contents for any of the other titles, please visit the *Taking Sides* website at http://www.mhcls.com/takingsides/.
ninth edition.

Acknowledgements

We thank our families for their support, patience, caring and spunk. Thanks also to colleagues Matt Holland, Vishal Garg and Caitlin Anderson.

Lisa H. Newton
Fairfield University

Elaine E. Englehardt
Utah Valley University

Michael S. Pritchard
Western Michigan

Contents In Brief

Contents

If we will but leave self-interested people to seek their own advantage, Adam Smith (1723–1790) argues, the result, unintended by any one of them, will be the greater advantage of all. No government interference is necessary to protect the general welfare. Leave people to their own self-interested devices, Karl Marx (1818–1883) and Friedrich Engels (1820–1895) reply, and those who by luck and inheritance own the means of production will rapidly reduce everyone else to virtual slavery. The few may be fabulously happy, but all others will live in misery.

Can moral values be attributed to organizations (as well as to individual persons)? Josef Wieland, director of the German Business Ethics Network's Centre for Business Ethics, argues that they can. After carefully developing a concept of governance ethics for corporations, he argues that the incorporation of moral conditions and requirements into the structures of the firm is the precondition for lasting beneficial effects of the virtues of the individuals within it. We can only be moral persons at work when the workplace, too, is moral. Ian Maitland, professor of Business, Government and Society at the University of Minnesota's Carlson School of Management, here plays his favorite role as Business Ethics Curmudgeon. Changing the rules will have no effect whatsoever on the moral work of the corporation (taking as his example the justice of the distributive mechanisms of the firm) and will succeed, if taken seriously, only in impairing its efficiency.

Friedman argues that businesses have neither the right nor the ability to fool around with "social responsibility" as distinct from profit-making. They serve employees and customers best when they do their work with maximum efficiency. The only restrictions on the pursuit of profit that Friedman accepts are the requirements of law and "the rules of the game" ("open and free competition without deception or fraud"). DesJardins explains that in the early years of the 21st century, we face a set of serious economic, ecological, and ethical challenges that require businesses to accept social responsibilities that support their own environmental sustainability and help meet the real needs of billions of people around the globe. He suggests various ways in which businesses might go about this without sacrificing profitability.

Issue 4.   Can Individual Virtue Survive Corporate Pressure?   78

Joining the long-standing debate on the possibility of free choice and moral agency in the business world, Quincy Lee Centennial Professor of Business and Philosophy at the University of Texas in Austin Robert C. Solomon argues that whatever the structures, the individual's choice is free, and therefore his character or virtue is of the utmost importance in creating a good moral tone in the life of a business. Stuart Professor of Philosophy at Princeton University Gilbert Harman employs determinist arguments to conclude that no individual can of his own free choice make a difference in a group enterprise.

UNIT 2   CURRENT BUSINESS ISSUES   105

Issue 5.   Are the Risks of Derivatives Manageable?   106

In 2008, most of the world watched in horror as the U.S. stock market nearly collapsed, bringing down other monetary world markets with it. Justin Welby contends that derivatives are an important and ethical investment practice, but one that involves risks. He claims that the risks should be understood well before participating in these investment practices. Thomas Bass claims that the market failures were due in large part to mismanagement of these investments he compares to crystal meth. In this 2009 article, he recommends widespread regulation of these instruments or no use of them at all.

Issue 6.   Should Price Gouging Be Regulated?   122

Snyder contends that price gouging conflicts with the goal of equitable access to goods essential to a minimally flourishing human life. Efficient provision of essential goods is not sufficient to prevent serious inequities. Regulations are needed for equitable access. Zwolinski argues that price gouging can be morally permissible, even though this does not mean that price gougers are morally virtuous. Considerations of the availability of institutional alternatives and distributive justice may render price gouging morally acceptable. In any case, regulations cannot be expected to resolve the moral issues more satisfactorily than the market itself.

It seems reasonably clear to Richard Rosen that the disastrous collapse of the Enron energy company—accompanied by soaring prices in California, disruptions of the market here and abroad, and accusations of fraud all around—means we need more government oversight. Not so, say Culp and Hanke; it was the unwise regulation that caused the problem in the first place, and only deregulation will let the market clear up the problems with the industry.

Philosopher Sissela Bok asserts that although blowing the whistle is often justified, it does involve dissent, accusation, and a breach of loyalty to the employer. Robert A. Larmer argues, on the contrary, that putting a stop to illegal or unethical company activities may be the highest type of loyalty an employee can display.

DePree and Jude argue that employers have a right, indeed a duty, to protect the corporation from legal liability incurred by the careless actions of their employees. Unfortunately, the use of e-mail from the employer's computer can get the company into worlds of trouble, and the company must monitor that e-mail. According to the *USA Today* there is apparently a substantial body of opinion in the country that e-mail is like other mail, and no one has the right to read it except the writer and the intended recipient. That goes for employers, too.

Richard Epstein defends the at-will contract as an appropriate expression of autonomy of contract on the part of both employee and employer, and as a means to the most efficient operations of the market. John McCall argues that the defense of the employment-at-will doctrine does not take account of its economic and social consequences and is in derogation of the very moral principles that underlie private property and freedom of contract.

Ira Kay, a consultant on executive compensation for Watson Wyatt Worldwide, argues that in general the pay of the CEO tracks the company's performance, so in general CEOs are simply paid to do what they were hired to do–bring up the price of the stock to increase shareholder wealth. Edgar Woolard, a former CEO himself, holds that the methods by which CEO compensation is determined are fundamentally flawed, and suggests some significant changes.

In this powerful debate, invited by *The New England Journal of Medicine*, two students of current pharmaceutical practices square off: Sidney Wolfe, M.D., of the Public Citizen Health Research Group in Washington, D.C., cites the dangers of overpromoting cures to the consumer. Alan Holmer, J.D., of the Pharmaceutical Research and Manufacturers of America, also in Washington, insists that more information for consumers can only improve the health of Americans.

Mark Dowie's article broke a new kind of scandal for American manufacturing, alleging that Ford Motor Company had deliberately put on the road an unsafe car—the Pinto—in which hundreds of people suffered burn deaths and horrible disfigurement. The accusations gave rise to a series of civil suits and one criminal proceeding, in which Ford was charged with criminal homicide. James Neal, who was chief attorney for the Ford Motor Company's defense against the charge of criminal homicide in connection with the burn deaths, persuaded the jury that Ford could not be held responsible for deaths which were actually caused by others—the driver of the van that struck the victims, for example—and which resulted from Ford's patriotic efforts to produce a competitive small car.

The consumer's interest in knowing where his food comes from does not necessarily have to do with the chemical and nutritional properties of the food. Kosher pastrami, for instance, is identical to the nonkosher product, and dolphin-safe tuna is still tuna. But we have a real and important interest in knowing the processes by which our foods arrived on the table, Bereano argues, and the demand for a label for bioengineered foods is entirely legitimate. Levitt points out that as far as the law is concerned, only the nutritional traits and characteristics of foods are subject to safety assessment. Labeling has been required only where health risks exist, or where there is danger that a product's marketing claims may mislead the consumer as to the food's characteristics. Breeding techniques have never been subject to labeling, nor should genetic engineering techniques.

UNIT 5   GLOBAL OBJECTIVES   311

In the absence of accepted enforcement agencies, there is little probability that any multinational corporation will suffer for violation of rules restricting business for the sake of the common good. Since any business that tried to conform to moral rules in the absence of enforcement would unjustifiably cease to be competitive, it must be the case, Velasquez argues, that moral strictures are not binding on such companies. Velasquez's logic is impressive, replies Fleming, but conditions on the ground in the multinational corporation are not as he describes. Real corporations tend to deal with long-term customers and suppliers in the goldfish bowl of international media exposure and must adhere to moral standards or lose business.

Philosophers Arnold and Bowie argue that managers of multinational enterprises have a duty to ensure that workers in their supply chains are treated with dignity and respect, which includes paying a living wage to those who work in factories with which they contact. Sollars and Englander contend that this work is needed for the very survival of individuals, and the multinational enterprises are not participating directly in the coercion of the workers in sweatshops.

Jeremy Rifkin, a persistent critic of unreflective support of "scientific progress," fears that genetic engineering extends human power over the rest of nature in ways that are unprecedented and whose consequences cannot be known. He urges a halt to research along these lines, especially research whose aim is no more than profit for the company that "owns" the results. William Domnarski, an intellectual property lawyer, finds the patenting of genes or genetic discoveries no different from patenting any other ideas. The purpose of patents is to reward and encourage useful invention, and there is no doubt that the modifications we introduce to the genetic material of plants and animals are useful to feed a starving world.

John Shanahan, vice president of the Alexis de Tocqueville Institution
in Arlington, Virginia, argues that many government environmental policies are unreasonable and infringe on basic economic freedoms. He
concedes that environmental problems exist but denies that there is any
environmental "crisis." Environmental scientists Paul R. Ehrlich and Anne
H. Ehrlich, whose 1974 book *The End of Affluence* first outlined the
consequences of environmental mismanagement, argue that many
objections to environmental protections are self-serving and based on
bad or misused science.

Issue 19.   Is Bottling Water a Good Solution to Problems of Water Purity and Availability?   383

Julie Stauffer presents a good argument for care in the selection and use
of drinking water, while recognizing that guarantees are few and far
between in the bottled water industry. The commonly available information
on bottled water certainly conveys the impression that it is purer and
better than mere tap water; all the ads conjure up a vigorous and healthy
outdoor lifestyle amid forests, lakes, and pure flowing springs. Brian
Howard argues that bottling water is environmentally disastrous because
of the huge drains on scarce aquifers and the haphazard disposal of the
plastic bottles, and that tap water is often superior to bottled in purity.

Issue 20.   Should the World Continue to Rely on Oil as a Major Source of Energy?   402

Red Cavaney, president and chief executive officer of the American
Petroleum Institute, argues that recent revolutionary advances in technology
will yield sufficient quantities of available oil for the foreseeable future.
James Howard Kunstler contends that the peak of oil production, Hubbert's
Peak, was itself the important turning point in our species' relationship to
petroleum. Unless strong conservation measures are put in place, the new
scarcity will destroy much that we have come to expect in our lives.

Correlation Guide

The *Taking Sides* series presents current issues in a debate-style format designed to stimulate student interest and develop critical thinking skills. Each issue is thoughtfully framed with an issue summary, an issue introduction, and a postscript. The pro and con essays—selected for their liveliness and substance—represent the arguments of leading scholars and commentators in their fields.

Taking Sides: Clashing Views in Business Ethics and Society, 11/e, is an easy-to-use reader that presents issues on important topics such as *derivatives, price gouging,* and *CEO compensation.* For more information on *Taking Sides* and other *McGraw-Hill Contemporary Learning Series* titles, visit www.mhhe.com/cls.

This convenient guide matches the issues in **Taking Sides: Clashing Views in Business Ethics and Society, 11/e,** with the corresponding chapters in one of our best-selling McGraw-Hill Business Ethics textbooks by Ghillyer.

Taking Sides: Business Ethics and Society, 11/e	Business Ethics: A Real World Approach, 2/e by Ghillyer
Issue 1: Can Capitalism Lead to Human Happiness?	**Chapter 1:** Understanding Ethics
Issue 2: Can Restructuring a Corporation's Rules Make a Moral Difference?	**Chapter 2:** Defining Business Ethics
Issue 3: Is Increasing Profits the Only Social Responsibility of Business?	**Chapter 4:** Corporate Social Responsibility
Issue 4: Can Individual Virtue Survive Corporate Pressure?	**Chapter 7:** Blowing the Whistle
Issue 5: Are the Risks of Derivatives Manageable?	**Chapter 6:** The Role of Government
Issue 6: Should Price Gouging Be Regulated?	**Chapter 6:** The Role of Government
Issue 7: Does the Enron Collapse Show That We Need More Regulation of the Energy Industry?	**Chapter 6:** The Role of Government
Issue 8: Does Blowing the Whistle Violate Company Loyalty?	**Chapter 7:** Blowing the Whistle
Issue 9: Is Employer Monitoring of Employee E-Mail Justified?	**Chapter 8:** Ethics and Technology
Issue 10: Is "Employment-at-Will" Good Social Policy?	**Chapter 3:** Organizational Ethics
Issue 11: Is CEO Compensation Justified by Performance?	**Chapter 3:** Organizational Ethics

(Continued)

Taking Sides: Business Ethics and Society, 11/e	Business Ethics: A Real World Approach, 2/e by Ghillyer
Issue 12: Is Direct-to-Consumer Advertising of Pharmaceuticals Bad for Our Health?	**Chapter 10:** Making it Stick: Doing What's Right in a Competitive Market
Issue 13: Was Ford to Blame in the Pinto Case?	**Chapter 5:** Corporate Governance
Issue 14: Should We Require Labeling for Genetically Modified Food?	**Chapter 8:** Ethics and Technology **Chapter 9:** Ethics and Globalization
Issue 15: Are Multinational Corporations Free from Moral Obligation?	**Chapter 9:** Ethics and Globalization
Issue 16: Are Sweatshops an Inhumane Business Practice?	**Chapter 9:** Ethics and Globalization **Chapter 10:** Making it Stick: Doing What's Right in a Competitive Market
Issue 17: Should Patenting Life Be Forbidden?	**Chapter 8:** Ethics and Technology **Chapter 9:** Ethics and Globalization
Issue 18: Do Environmental Restrictions Violate Basic Economic Freedoms?	**Chapter 6:** The Role of Government
Issue 19: Is Bottling Water a Good Solution to Problems of Water Purity and Availability?	**Chapter 9:** Ethics and Globalization
Issue 20: Should the World Continue to Rely on Oil as a Major Source of Energy?	**Chapter 9:** Ethics and Globalization

Introduction

An Essay on the Background of Business Ethics: Ethics, Economics, Law, and the Corporation

Philosophy is a conversation; philosophical ethics is a conversation about conduct, the doing of good and the avoiding of evil. Business ethics is a conversation about right and wrong conduct in the business world. This book is aimed at an audience of students who expect to pursue careers in business, who know that there are knotty ethical problems out there, and who want a chance to confront them ahead of time. The method of confronting them is an invitation to join in a debate, a contest of contrary facts and conflicting values in many of the major issues of the millennium. This introductory essay, in effect a short text on the major components of business theory, should make it easier to join in the argument. Managing ethical policy problems in a company takes a wide background—in ethics, economics, law, and the social sciences—that the book cannot hope to provide. But since some background assumptions in these fields are relevant to several of the problems we take on, we will sketch out very briefly the major understandings that control them. There is ultimately no substitute for thorough study of the rules of the game and years of experience and practice, but an overview of the playing field may at least make it easier for a novice to understand the object and limitations of the standard plays.

Business ethics was generally known as the world's most famous oxymoron (a term that contradicts itself into impossibility) until the last thirty years. Then came the alarming newspaper headlines. Foreign bribes, scandals on Wall Street, exploding cars, conflicts over whistleblowers and civil rights in the workplace suddenly came into the headlines and would not go away. Now we know that value questions are never absent from business decisions, and that moral responsibility is the first requirement of a manager in any business. Out of all this has emerged a general consensus that a thorough grounding in ethical reasoning is essential preparation for a career in business.

This book will not supply the substance of a course in ethics. For that you are directed to any of several excellent texts in business ethics (see the suggested readings at the end of this essay), or to any general text in ethics. *Taking Sides* teaches ethics from the issue upward, rather than from the principle downward. You will, however, come upon much of the terminology of ethical reasoning in the course of considering these cases.

Economics: the Capitalist Background

Capitalism as we know it is the product of the thought of Adam Smith (1723–1790), a Scottish philosopher and economist, and a small number of his European contemporaries. The fundamental "capitalist act" is the *voluntary exchange:* Two adults, of sound mind and clear purposes, meet in the marketplace, to which each repairs in order to satisfy some felt need. They discover that each has that which will satisfy the other's need—the housewife needs flour, the miller needs cash—and they exchange, at a price such that the exchange furthers the interest of each. The *marginal utility* to the participant in the free market of the thing acquired must exceed that of the thing traded, or else why would he make the deal? So each party to the voluntary exchange walks away from it richer.

Adding to the value of the exchange is the *competition* of dealers and buyers; because there are many purveyors of each good, the customer is not forced to pay exorbitant prices for things needed (it is a sad fact of economics that to the starving man, the marginal value of a loaf of bread is very large, and a single merchant could become unjustly rich). Conversely, competition among the customers (typified by an auction) makes sure that the available goods end in the hands of those to whom they are worth the most. So at the end of the market day, not only does everyone go home richer (in real terms) than when he came—the voluntariness of the exchange ensures that—but also, as rich as he could possibly be, since he had available all possible options of goods or services to buy and all possible purchasers of his goods or services for sale.

Sellers and buyers win the competition through *efficiency,* through producing the best quality goods at the lowest possible price, or through allotting their scarce resources toward the most valuable of the choices presented to them. It is to the advantage of all participants in the market, then, to strive for efficiency, that is, to keep the cost of goods for sale as low as possible while keeping the quality as high as possible. Adam Smith's most memorable accomplishment was to recognize that the general effect of all this self-interested scrambling would be to make the most possible goods of the best possible quality available at the lowest possible price. Meanwhile, sellers and buyers alike must keep an eye on the market as a whole, adjusting production and purchasing to take advantage of fluctuations in *supply and demand.* Short supply will make goods more valuable, raising the price, and that will bring more suppliers into the market, whose competition will lower the price, to just above the cost of manufacture for the most efficient producers. Increased demand for any reason will have the same effect. Should supply exceed demand, the price will fall to a point where the goods will be bought. Putting this all together, Smith realized that in a system of free enterprise, you have demonstrably the best possible chance of finding for sale what you want, in good quantity and quality, at a reasonable price. Forget benevolent monarchs ordering things for our good, he suggested; in this system we are led as by an *"invisible hand"* to serve the common good even as we think we are being selfish.

Adam Smith's theory of economic enterprise and the "wealth of nations" emerged in the Natural Law tradition of the eighteenth century. As was the fashion for that period, Smith presented his conclusions as a series of iron laws: the Law of Supply and Demand that links supply, demand, and price; the law that links efficiency with success; and ultimately, the laws that link the absolute freedom of the market with the absolute growth of the wealth of the free market country.

To these laws were added others, specifying the conditions under which business enterprise would be conducted in capitalist countries. The laws of *population* of Thomas Malthus (1766–1834) concluded that the supply of human beings would always reach the limits of its food supply, ensuring that the bulk of humanity would always live at the subsistence level. Since Smith had already proved that employers will purchase labor at the lowest possible price, it was a one-step derivation for David Ricardo (1772–1823) to conclude that workers' *wages* would never exceed the subsistence level, no matter how prosperous industrial enterprise should become. From these capitalist theorists alone proceeded the nineteenth-century assumption that society would inevitably divide into two classes, a tiny minority of fabulous wealth and a vast majority of subsistence-level workers.

The Marxian Critique

For Western political philosophy, history emerged as a significant factor in our understanding with the work of the nineteenth-century philosopher G. W. F. Hegel (1770–1831), who traced the history of the Western world as an ordered series of ideal forms, evolving one from another in logical sequence toward an ideal future. A young German student of Hegel's, Karl Marx (1818–1883), concluded from his study of economics that Hegel had to be wrong: The phases of history were ruled not by ideas, but by the *material conditions* of life, and their evolution one from another came about as the ruling class of each age generated its own revolutionary overthrow.

Marx's theory, especially as it applies to the evolution of capitalism, is enormously complex; for the purposes of this unit, it can be summarized simply. According to Marx, the *ruling class* in every age is the group that *owns the means of production* of the age's product. Through the seventeenth century, the product was almost exclusively agricultural, and the means of production was almost exclusively agricultural land: Landowners were the aristocrats and rulers. With the coming of commerce and industry, the owners of the factories joined the ruling class and eventually dominated it. It was in the nature of such capital-intensive industry to concentrate within itself more capital: Its greater efficiency would, as Adam Smith had proved, drive all smaller labor-intensive industry out of business, and its enormous income would be put to work as more capital, expanding the domain of the factory and the machine indefinitely (at the expense of the cottage and the human being). Thus would the wealth of society concentrate in fewer and fewer hands, as the owners of the factories expanded their enterprises without limit into mighty industrial empires, dominated by machines and by the greed of their owners.

Meanwhile, all this wealth was being produced by a new class of workers, the unskilled factory workers. Taken from the ranks of the obsolete peasantry, artisans and craftsmen, this new working class, the "proletariat," expanded in numbers with the gigantic mills, whose "hands" they were. Work on the assembly line demanded no education or skills, so the workers could never make themselves valuable enough to command a living wage on the open market. They survived as a vast underclass, interchangeable with the unemployed workers (recently displaced by more machines) who gathered around the factory gates looking for jobs, *their* jobs. As Ricardo had demonstrated, they could never bargain for any wage above the subsistence level—just enough to keep them alive. As capitalism and its factories expanded, the entire population, excepting only the wealthy capitalist families, sank into this hopeless pauperized class.

So Marx took from Ricardo the vision of ultimate division of Western society under capitalism: into a tiny group of fabulously wealthy capitalists and a huge mass of paupers, mostly factory workers. The minority would keep the majority in strict control by its hired thugs (the state: the army and the police), control rendered easier by thought control (the schools and the churches). The purpose of the "ideology" taught by the schools and the churches—the value structure of capitalism—was to show both classes that the capitalists had a right to their wealth (through the sham of liberty, free enterprise, and the utilitarian benefits of the free market) and a perfect right to govern everyone else (through the sham of democracy and equal justice). Thus the capitalists could enjoy their wealth in good conscience and the poor would understand their moral obligation to accept the oppression of the ruling class with good cheer.

Marx foresaw, and in his writings attempted to help bring about, the disillusionment of the workers: There will come a point when they will suddenly ask, *why* should we accept oppression all our lives? and the search for answers to this question will show them the history of their situation, expose the falsehood of the ideology and the false consciousness of those who believe it, show them their own strength, and lead them directly to the solution that will usher in the new age of socialism—the revolutionary overthrow of the capitalist regime. Why, after all, should they not undertake such a revolution? People are restrained from violence against oppression only by the prospect of losing something valuable, and the industrialized workers of the world had nothing to lose but their chains.

As feudalism had been swept away, then, by the "iron broom" of the French Revolution, so capitalism would be swept away by the revolt of the masses, the irresistible uprising of the vast majority of the people against the tiny minority of industrial overlords and their terrified minions—the armed forces, the state, and the church. After the first rebellions, Marx foresaw no lengthy problem of divided loyalties in the industrialized countries of the world. Once the scales had fallen from their eyes, the working-class hirelings of army and police would quickly turn their guns on their masters, and join their natural allies in the proletariat in the task of creating the new world.

After the revolution, Marx predicted, there would be a temporary "dictatorship of the proletariat," during which the last vestiges of capitalism would be eradicated and the authority to run the industrial establishment returned to the workers of each industry. Once the economy had been decentralized, to turn each factory into an industrial commune run by its own workers and each landed estate into an agricultural commune run by its farmers, the state as such would simply wither away. Some central authority would certainly continue to exist, to coordinate and facilitate the exchange of goods within the country (one imagines a giant computer, taking note of where goods are demanded, where goods are available, and where the railroad cars are, to take the goods from one place to the other). But with no ruling class to serve, no oppression to carry out, there will be no need of state to rule *people;* what is left will be confined to the administration of *things.*

Even as he wrote, just in time for the Revolution of 1848, Marx expected the end of capitalism as a system. Not that capitalism was evil in itself; Marx did not presume to make moral judgments on history. Indeed, capitalism was necessary as an economic system, to concentrate the wealth of the country into the industries of the modern age. So capitalism had a respectable past, and would still be necessary, for a while, in the developing countries, to launch their industries. But that task completed, it had no further role in history, and the longer it stayed around, the more the workers would suffer and the more violent the revolution would be when it came. The sooner the revolution, the better; the future belonged to communism.

As the collapse of the Communist governments in Eastern Europe demonstrates, if demonstration were needed, the course of history has not proceeded quite as Marx predicted in 1848. In fairness, it might be pointed out that no other prophets of the time had any more luck with prognostication; the twentieth century took all of us by surprise. But there is much in Marx's analysis which is rock solid, possibly for reasons, especially ethical reasons, that he himself would have rejected. In any case, since Marx wrote, all participants in the debate on the nature and future of capitalism have had to respond to his judgments and predictions.

Law: Recovering for Damages Sustained

Life is full of misfortune. Ordinarily, if you suffer misfortune, you must put up with it, and find the resources to deal with it. If your misfortune is my fault, however, the law may step in and make me pay for those damages, one way or another. Through the *criminal law,* the public steps in and demands punishment for an offense that is serious enough to outrage public feeling and endanger public welfare. If I knock you on the head and take your wallet, the police will find me, restore your wallet to you, and imprison or otherwise punish me for the crime. Strictly speaking, you should recover from me not only your wallet, but the money to sew up your head and damages for the fright and insult. But the average street criminal does not have the money to make full restitution to his victims; in fact, you'll be lucky to get your wallet back.

Through the *civil law,* if I do you damage through some action of mine, you may take me to civil court and ask a judge (and jury) to determine whether I have damaged you, if so by how much, and how I should pay you back for that damage. There are a number of forms of action under which you may make your claim; the most common for business purposes are *contract* and *torts*. If you and I agree to (or "contract for") some undertaking, and I back out on it, after you have relied on our agreement to commit your resources to the undertaking, you have a right to recover what you have lost. In torts, if I simply injure you in some way, hurting you in health, life or limb, or destroying your property, I have done you a wrong ("tort," in French), and I must pay for the damage I have done. How much I will have to pay will depend (as the jury will determine) on (1) the amount of the damage that has been caused, (2) the extent to which I knew or should have known that my action or neglect to act would cause damage (my *culpability*), and (3) the extent to which *you* contributed to the damage, beyond whatever I did (*contributory negligence*).

In the debates that follow, one (on the Pinto automobile) has to do with suits at law alleging *negligence,* a tort, on the part of a company, in that it made and put up for sale a product known to be defective, and that the defect injured its users. To establish negligence, civil or criminal, four elements must be demonstrated: First, there must have been a *duty:* The party accused of negligence must have had a preexisting duty to the plaintiff. Second, there must have been a *breach,* or failure to fulfill, that duty. Third, the plaintiff must have suffered an *injury.* And fourth, the breach of the duty must have been the *proximate cause* of the injury, the thing that actually brought it about. Where negligence is alleged in a product liability case, it must be established that the manufacturer had a duty to make a product that could not do certain sorts of harm; that the duty was breached, the harm caused, that nothing else was to blame, and that the manufacturer therefore must compensate the victim for the damage done.

There are very similar allegations in other cases here, even when no lawsuit is at issue. In all of these cases one set of claims amounts to an accusation of deliberately damaging innocent consumers, placing them in harm's way for the sake of profit; the other set counters that the company did not know and could not have known that the product was dangerous, and/or that the freely chosen behavior of the consumers contributed in some way to the damage that was done, so the company cannot be held totally responsible. In all cases, *risk* and *responsibility* are the central issues: When a small car explodes and burns when hit by a much larger van, to what extent is the company responsible for the flimsiness of the car and to what extent did the consumer assume the risk of that happening when she bought a small, economical car? (And whatever happened to the responsibility of the driver of the van?) Should companies be ultimately responsible for any harm that comes from the use of the products they so profitably marketed and sold? Or should consumers be content to bear the responsibility for risks they have freely accepted? Our ambivalence on this question as a society mirrors, and proceeds from, the ambivalence of the individual at the two poles of materialization of risk: When we are in a hurry, short of cash, or in need of a cigarette, then risky behavior looks to us to be our right, and we are resentful of the busybodies who would always be having us play it safe and wear our rubbers when it rains. But when the risk materializes—when the accident or the disease happens—the perception of that risk (and the direction of that resentment) change drastically. From the perspective of the hospital bed, it is crystal clear that the behavior was not worth the risk, that we never realized the behavior was risky, that we would never have engaged in the behavior if we had known how risky it was, that we should have been warned about the risks, and that it was someone's duty to warn us. In that instantaneous change of perspective, three elements of negligence come into view: duty, breach, and injury. No wonder product liability suits are so common.

Yet the suit is a relatively recent phenomenon because of a peculiarity in the law. Until the twentieth century, a judge faced with a consumer who had been injured by a product (physically or financially) had to apply the principle of *caveat emptor*—Let the Buyer Beware—and could ask the seller to pay damages only to the original buyer, and only if the exact defect in the product could be proved. For example, a defective kerosene lamp might explode and burn five people, but the exact defect (broken seam or shoddy wick) had to be brought into court or the case would be thrown out. In addition, the buyer could sue only the seller, not the manufacturer or designer, for the right to collect damages rested on the law of *contract,* not torts, and upon the warrant of merchantability implied in the contractual relationship between buyer and seller. The cause of the action was understood to be a breach in that contract.

There matters stood until 1916, when an American judge allowed a buyer to sue the manufacturer of a product. A Mr. MacPherson had been injured when his car collapsed under him due to a defect in the wood used to build one of the wheels, and MacPherson went to court against the Buick Motor Company. The judge reasoned that the action was in torts, specifically negligence, and not in contract, for a manufacturer is under a duty to make carefully any product that could be expected to endanger life, and this duty existed irrespective of any contract. So if MacPherson, or any future user of the product, was injured because the product was badly made, he could collect damages even if he had never dealt with the manufacturer in any way.

In the 1960s the automobile was still center stage in the arguments over the duties of manufacturers. Ralph Nader's book *Unsafe at Any Speed* (1966) spearheaded the consumer rights movement with its scathing attack on General Motors and its exposé of the dangerous design of the Corvair. In response to the consumer activism resulting from that movement, Congress passed the Consumer Product Safety Act in 1972 and empowered the Consumer Product Safety Commission, an independent federal agency, to set safety standards, require warning labels, and order recalls of hazardous products. When three girls died in a Ford Pinto in 1978, the foundations of consumer rights against careless manufacturers were well established. What is new in the Ford Motor Company case is the allegation of *criminal* negligence—in effect, criminal homicide.

At present, product liability suits are major uncharted reefs in the navigational plans of American business. If a number of people die in a fire in a hotel, for instance, their families will often sue not only the hotel, for culpable negligence, but the manufacturers of the furniture that burned, alleging that it should have been fire-retardant; the manufacturers of the cushions on the furniture, alleging that they gave off toxic fumes in the fire; and the manufacturers of the chemicals that went into those cushions, alleging that there was no warning to the consumers on the toxicity of those chemicals in fire conditions. The settlements that can be obtained are used to finance the suit, and the law firm that is managing it, for the years that it will take to exhaust all the appeals. This phenomenon of unlimited litigation is relatively new on the American scene, and we are not quite sure how to respond to it.

The Corporation

The human being is a social animal. We exist in the herd, and depend for our lives on the cooperation of those around us. Who are they? Our anthropologists tell us that originally we traveled in extended families, then settled down into villages of intensely interlocked groups of families. With the advent of the modern era, we have found our identities in family, village, church, and nation. Yet in the great transformation of the obligations of the Western world (see Henry Maine [1822–1888], *From Status to Contract*), we have abandoned the old family-oriented care systems and thrown ourselves upon the mercy of secondary organizations: club, corporation, and State. The French sociologist Emil Durkheim (1858–1917) suggested (in his classic work, *Suicide*) that following the collapse of the family and the church, the corporation would be the association, in the future, that would supply the social support that every individual needs to maintain the moral life.

Can the corporation do that? Or is the corporation merely the organization that implements Adam Smith's self-interested pursuit of the dollar, with no purpose but to maximize return on investment to the investors while protecting them from unlimited liability? The issue of "meaningful work" raises this question in particularly direct form. On the other hand, once formed, and having become a major community figure and employer, does the corporation have a right to exist that transcends at least the immediate pursuit of money? The issue of "hostile takeovers" sends us back to the purpose and foundation of business enterprise in America. Let us review: When an entrepreneur gets a bright idea for how to make money, he secures the capital he will need to run the business from investors (venture capitalists), uses that capital to buy the land, buildings, and machinery he will need to see it through, hires the labor needed to do the work, and goes into production. As the income from the enterprise comes in, he pays the suppliers of raw materials, pays the workers, pays the taxes, rent, mortgages, and utility bills, keeps some for himself (salary), and then divides up the rest of the income ("profit") among the investors (probably including himself) in proportion to the capital they invested. Motives of all parties are presupposed: The entrepreneur wants money, the laborers want money, so do the landlords, and so, of course, do the investors, who are the shareholders in the company. The investors thought that this enterprise would yield them a higher return on their capital than any other investment available to them at the time; that's why they invested. Meanwhile, this is a free country, and people can move around. If the worker sees a better job, he'll take it; if the landlord can rent for more, he'll terminate the lease; and if the investors see a better place to put their capital, they'll move it. The determiner of the flow of capital is the rate of return, no more and no less. "Loyalty to the company," faithfulness to the corporation for the sake of the association itself, is not on anyone's agenda—not on the worker's, certainly not on the landlord's, and *most* certainly not on the shareholder's.

The shareholders are represented by a board of directors elected by them to see that the company is run efficiently—that is, that costs are kept down and income up, to yield the highest possible return. The board of directors hires management—the cadre of corporate officers headed by the president/chief executive officer to do the actual running of the company. The corporate officers thus stand in a *quasi-fiduciary* relationship to the shareholders; that is, they are forbidden by the understandings on which the corporation is founded to do anything at all except that which will protect and enhance the interests of the shareholders. That goes for all the normal business decisions made by the management; even the decision not to break the law can be seen as a prudent estimate of the financial costs of lawbreaking.

Yet our dealings with the business world, as citizens and as consumers, have always turned on recognition and support of the huge, reliable corporations in established industries: not just coal and steel, which had certain natural limitations built into their consumption of natural resources, but the automobile companies, the airlines, the consumer products companies, even the banks. Companies had "reputations," "integrity," cultivated (and bought and sold) "good will," consumers cooperated with the companies that catered to them in developing "brand loyalty." And, most importantly, those working in business cooperated with their employers in developing "company loyalty," which became a part of their lives as loyalty to one's tribe or nation was part of the lives of their ancestors. Is the company that sought our loyalty—and got it—just a scrap of paper, to disappear as soon as return on investment falls below the nearest competition? What part do we want our corporations to play in our associative life? If we want them to be any more than profit maximizers for the investors, what sorts of protections would we have to offer them, and what sorts of limitations should we put on their not-for-profit activities?

Current Issues

Business ethics ultimately rests on a base of political philosophy, economics, and philosophical ethics. As these underlying fields change, new topics and approaches will surface in business ethics. For example, "hostile takeovers" did not take place very often in the regulatory climate that obtained prior to the Reagan administration. The change in political philosophy introduced by his administration resulted in new business practices, which resulted in new ethical problems. Also, the work of John Rawls, a professor of philosophy at Harvard, profoundly influenced our understandings of distributive justice, and therefore our understanding of acceptable economic distribution in the society. The work currently being done in "postmodern" philosophy will change the way we see human beings generally, and hence the activity of business.

No single work can cover all the issues of ethical practice in business in all their range and particularity, especially since, as above, we are dealing with a moving target. Our task here is much more limited. The purpose of this book is just to allow you to grapple with some of the ethical issues of current business practice in the safety of the classroom, before they come up on the job where human rights and careers are at stake and legal action looms outside the boardroom, or factory, door. We think that rational consideration of these issues now will help you prepare for a lifetime of the types of problems that naturally arise in a complex and pluralistic society. You will find here no dogmas, no settled solutions to memorize. These problems do not have preset answers, but require, as Whitehead insisted, that you use your mind, to balance the values in conflict and to work out acceptable policies in each issue. To do business ethics, you must learn to think critically, to look beyond short-term advantage and traditional ways of doing things, to become an innovator. The exercise provided by these debates should help you in this learning.

There is no doubt that businesspersons think that ethics is important. Sometimes the reasons why they think ethics is important have to do only with the long-run profitability of business enterprise. Greater employee honesty and diligence will improve the bottom line, strict attention to environmental and employee health laws is necessary to preserve the company from expensive lawsuits and fines. But ethics goes well beyond profitability, to the lives that we live and the persons we want to be. What the bottom line has taught us is that the working day is not apart from life. We must bring the same integrity and care to the contexts of factory and office that we are used to showing at home and among our friends. The third imperative of business ethics is to make of your business life an opportunity to become, and remain, the person that you know you ought to be—and as far you can, to extend that opportunity to others.

We attempt, in this book, to present in good, debatable form some of the issues that raise the big questions— of justice, of rights, of the common good—in order to build bridges between the workaday world of employment and the ageless world of morality. If you will enter into these dialogues with an open mind, a willingness to have it changed, and a determination to master the skills of critical thinking that will enable you to make responsible decisions in difficult situations, you may be able to help build the bridges for the new ethical issues that will emerge in the century to come. At the least, that is our hope.

Suggested Readings for the Ethics Background for Business Ethics

Beauchamp, Tom L., and Norman E. Bowie. *Ethical Theory and Business*. 8th ed. Englewood Cliffs, NJ: Prentice Hall, 2008.

DeGeorge, Richard T. *Business Ethics*. 7th ed. Englewood Cliffs, NJ: Prentice Hall, 2009.

Donaldson, Thomas, and Patricia H. Werhane. *Ethical Issues in Business: A Philosophical Approach*. 8th ed. Englewood Cliffs, NJ: Prentice Hall, 2007.

Goodpaster, Kenneth, Laura Nash, and Henri-Claude de Bettignies. *Business Ethics: Policies and Persons*. 4th ed. New York: McGraw-Hill, 2005.

Hoffman, W. Michael, and Jennifer Mills Moore. *Business Ethics: Readings and Cases in Corporate Morality*. 4th ed. New York: McGraw-Hill, 2001.

Newton, Lisa H. *Permission to Steal*. Hoboken, NJ: John Wiley and Sons, Inc., 2007.

Pritchard, Michael S. *Professional Integrity: Thinking Ethically*. Lawrence, KS: University of Kansas Press, 2006.

Schmidt, David P., and Lisa H Newton. *Wake-Up Calls: Classic Cases in Business Ethics*. Florence, KY: Cengage, 2003.

Shaw, William, and Vincent Barry. *Moral Issues in Business*. 11th edition. Belmont, CA: Wadsworth, 2009.

Velasquez, Manuel. *Business Ethics: Concepts and Cases*. 6th ed. Englewood Cliffs, NJ: Prentice Hall, 2006.

Internet References . . .

Business Ethics Resources on WWW

Sponsored by the Centre for Applied Ethics, site of business ethics resources links to corporate codes of ethics, business ethics institutions and organizations, and online papers and publications, as well as other elements.

http://www.ethics.ubc.ca/

International Business Ethics Institute

The International Business Ethics Institute offers professional services to organizations interested in implementing, expanding, or modifying business ethics and corporate responsibility programs. Its mission is to foster global business practices that promote equitable economic development, resource sustainability, and democratic forms of government.

http://www.business-ethics.org/

UNIT 1

Capitalism and the Corporation

Given the behavior of the highest officials of the most profitable enterprises in the country in recent years, we might wonder if there is such a thing as ethical business! Where are moral standards to be found in the business enterprise—in the actions of the managers? In the policies, internal and external, of the corporation? Or in the capitalist system itself? How can business itself be encouraged to adopt higher ethical standards than we have seen in operation recently?

- Can Capitalism Lead to Human Happiness?
- Can Restructuring a Corporation's Rules Make a Moral Difference?
- Is Increasing Profits the Only Social Responsibility of Business?
- Can Individual Virtue Survive Corporate Pressure?

ISSUE 1

Can Capitalism Lead to Human Happiness?

YES: Adam Smith, from *An Inquiry Into the Nature and Causes of the Wealth of Nations,* vols. 1 and 2 (1869)

NO: Karl Marx and Friedrich Engels, from *The Communist Manifesto* (1848)

ISSUE SUMMARY

YES: If we will but leave self-interested people to seek their own advantage, Adam Smith (1723–1790) argues, the result, unintended by any one of them, will be the greater advantage of all. No government interference is necessary to protect the general welfare.

NO: Leave people to their own self-interested devices, Karl Marx (1818–1883) and Friedrich Engels (1820–1895) reply, and those who by luck and inheritance own the means of production will rapidly reduce everyone else to virtual slavery. The few may be fabulously happy, but all others will live in misery.

The confrontation of capitalism and communism dominated the twentieth century. In these selections we have the classic defense of the free market and its most powerful opposition. The rationale of capitalism portrays it as an unintended coordination of self-interested actions into the production of the greatest welfare of the whole. The argument is elegant and powerful: As a natural result of free competition in a free market, quality will improve and prices will decline without limit, thereby raising the real standard of living of every buyer. To protect themselves in competition, sellers will be forced to innovate, discover new products and new markets, thereby raising the real wealth of the society as a whole. Products improve without limit, wealth increases without limit, and society prospers.

But how fares the Common Man—the "least advantaged" members of society, as John Rawls would characterize them? Not very well. Only when free competition *fails,* because the economy is expanding so rapidly that it runs out of labor, can the working man's wages rise in a free market. For the most efficient factory will be the one that hires its workers at lowest cost, and if all industry is accomplished by essentially unskilled labor, and every worker can therefore be replaced by any other, there is no reason to pay any worker beyond the subsistence wage. Fortunately for the capitalist, according to the theory, such a market imbalance—too few workers and therefore "artificially" high wages—will rapidly disappear, as greater prosperity causes more of the working-class babies to survive to adulthood and entry into the workforce. Smith and eighteenth-century economists Thomas Malthus and David Ricardo were in agreement: As the society as a whole approaches maximum efficiency, all except the capitalists, the owners, approach the subsistence level of survival. So all the accumulated "wealth" of the nation actually ends up in the hands only of the employers, the factory owners, who enjoy the low prices of bread themselves, and save the money they would have to spend to keep their workers alive if the bread were more expensive. Another way of putting that point: Adam Smith was absolutely correct if he is taken to be describing capital *formation;* but when it comes to the *distribution* of the wealth the free market has created, his mechanisms have no way of ensuring justice.

This is where Karl Marx comes in. He focuses not on the making of the wealth—Adam Smith is quite correct on how wealth is created and accumulated. Instead he asks how the wealth is distributed—who gets it, and gets to enjoy it, when it has been generated by the capitalist process. There is no reason under Heaven that all that money has to languish in the bank accounts of the super-rich, or decorate their houses and their poodles. The welfare of the nation as a whole would be vastly increased if it could be shared systematically with the workers, to allow them to join their employers as consumers of the manufactured goods of the society. Lord John Maynard Keynes would later point out that such distribution would be an enormous spur to the economy; Marx was more concerned that it would be a great gain in justice.

Yes, but if the controllers of the wealth, the capitalists, are required to share it with the workers who produced it, will they not lose motivation to put that money at risk in such productive enterprises? This is one of the empirical questions that surround the issue of social justice in a free market society, often arising when CEO salaries are under discussion. It may seem counterintuitive that CEOs whose salary is reduced from $46.2 million per annum to $24.3 million per annum would suffer a serious loss of incentive to keep working, but that has been argued. Other questions concern entitlement—are not those who control the capital entitled to the entire return on it?—the justice of combination (Adam Smith also had to deal with unions), and the relative importance of liberty and equality as political values. Other questions concern the possibility of "pure" capitalist endeavors. Adam Smith's arguments surely work for small factories and farms, where no producer is big enough to influence the market. These were the only business enterprises he knew. But does it apply to technology-created monopolies and oligopolies? And does it contemplate speculating millions of dollars in foreign currency? Keep in mind, as you read these selections, that the controversy is not bounded by the historical understandings of Marx and his opponents, but goes to the core of our notions of entitlement, social welfare, and justice.

An Inquiry Into the Nature and Causes of the Wealth of Nations

Of the Division of Labour

The greatest improvement in the productive powers of labour, and the greater part of the skill, dexterity, and judgment with which it is anywhere directed or applied, seem to have been the effect of the division of labour.

The effects of the division of labour, in the general business of society, will be more easily understood by considering in what manner it operates in some particular manufactures. It is commonly supposed to be carried furthest in some very trifling ones; not perhaps that it really is carried further in them than in others of more importance: but in those trifling manufactures which are destined to supply the small wants of but a small number of people, the whole number of workmen must necessarily be small; and those employed in every different branch of the work can often be collected into the same workhouse, and placed at once under the view of the spectator. In those great manufactures, on the contrary, which are destined to supply the great wants of the great body of the people, every different branch of the work employs so great a number of workmen, that it is impossible to collect them all into the same workhouse. We can seldom see more, at one time, than those employed in one single branch. Though in such manufactures, therefore, the work may really be divided into a much greater number of parts than in those of a more trifling nature, the division is not near so obvious, and has accordingly been much less observed.

To take an example, therefore, from a very trifling manufacture, but one in which the division of labour has been very often taken notice of, the trade of the pin-maker; a workman not educated to this business (which the division of labour has rendered a distinct trade), nor acquainted with the use of the machinery employed in it (to the invention of which the same division of labour has probably given occasion), could scarce, perhaps, with his utmost industry, make one pin in a day, and certainly could not make twenty. But in the way in which this business is now carried on, not only the whole work is a peculiar trade, but it is divided into a number of branches, of which the greater part are likewise peculiar trades. One man draws out the wire, another straights it, a third cuts it, a fourth points it, a fifth grinds it at the top for receiving the head; to make the head requires two or three distinct operations; to put it on is a peculiar business, to whiten the pins is another; it is even a trade by itself

From Adam Smith, *An Inquiry Into the Nature and Causes of the Wealth of Nations,* vols. 1 and 2b (1869). Notes omitted.

to put them into the paper; and the important business of making a pin is, in this manner, divided into about eighteen distinct operations, which in some manufactories are all performed by distinct hands, though in others the same man will sometimes perform two or three of them. I have seen a small manufactory of this kind where ten men only were employed, and where some of them consequently performed two or three distinct operations. But though they were very poor, and therefore but indifferently accommodated with the necessary machinery, they could, when they exerted themselves, make among them about twelve pounds of pins in a day. There are in a pound upwards of four thousand pins of a middling size. Those ten persons, therefore, could make among them upwards of forty-eight thousand pins in a day. Each person, therefore, making a tenth part of forty-eight thousand pins, might be considered as making four thousand eight hundred pins in a day. But if they had all wrought separately and independently, and without any of them having been educated to this peculiar business, they certainly could not each of them have made twenty, perhaps not one pin in a day; that is, certainly, not the two hundred and fortieth, perhaps not the four thousand eight hundredth part of what they are at present capable of performing, in consequence of a proper division and combination of their different operations. . . .

This great increase of the quantity of work, which, in consequence of the division of labour, the same number of people are capable of performing, is owing to three different circumstances: first, to the increase of dexterity in every particular workman; secondly, to the saving of the time which is commonly lost in passing from one species of work to another; and lastly, to the invention of a great number of machines which facilitate and abridge labour, and enable one man to do the work of many. . . .

It is the great multiplication of the productions of all the different arts, in consequence of the division of labour, which occasions, in a well-governed society, that universal opulence which extends itself to the lowest ranks of the people. Every workman has a great quantity of his own work to dispose of beyond what he himself has occasion for: and every other workman being exactly in the same situation, he is enabled to exchange a great quantity of his own goods for a great quantity, or, what comes to the same thing, for the price of a great quantity of theirs. He supplies them abundantly with what they have occasion for, and they accommodate him as amply with what he has occasion for, and a general plenty diffuses itself through all the different ranks of the society.

Observe the accommodation of the most common artificer or day-labourer in a civilised and thriving country, and you will perceive that the number of people of whose industry a part, though but a small part, has been employed in procuring him this accommodation exceeds all computation. The woollen coat, for example, which covers the day-labourer, as coarse and rough as it may appear, is the produce of the joint labour of a great multitude of workmen. The shepherd, the sorter of the wool, the wool-comber or carder, the dyer, the scribbler, the spinner, the weaver, the fuller, the dresser, with many others, must all join their different arts in order to complete even this homely production. How many merchants and carriers, besides, must have been employed in transporting the materials from some of those workmen to others who often live in a very distant part of the country! How much commerce and navigation in particular, how many ship-builders, sailors, sail-makers, rope-makers, must have been employed in order to bring together the different drugs made use of by the dyer, which often come from the remotest corners of the world! What a variety of labour too is necessary in order to produce the tools of the meanest of those workmen! To say nothing of such complicated machines as the ship of the sailor, the mill of the fuller, or even the loom of the weaver, let us consider only what a variety of labour is requisite in order to form that very simple machine, the shears with which the shepherd clips the wool. The miner, the builder of the furnace for smelting the ore, the feller of the timber, the burner of the charcoal to be made use of in the smelting-house, the brickmaker, the bricklayer, the workmen who attend the furnace, the millwright, the forger, the smith, must all of them join their different arts in order to produce them. Were we to examine, in the same manner, all the different parts of his dress and household furniture, the coarse linen shirt which he wears next his skin, the shoes which cover his feet, the bed which he lies on, and all the different parts which compose it, the kitchen-grate at which he prepares his victuals, the coals which he makes use of for that purpose, dug from the bowels of the earth, and brought to him perhaps by a long sea and a long land carriage, all the other utensils of his kitchen, all the furniture of his table, the knives and forks, the earthen or pewter plates upon which he serves up and divides his victuals, the different hands employed in preparing his bread and his beer, the glass window which lets in the heat and the light and keeps out the wind and the rain, with all the knowledge and art requisite for preparing that beautiful and happy invention, without which these northern parts of the world could scarce have afforded a very comfortable habitation, together with the tools of all the different workmen employed in producing those different conveniences; if we examine, I say, all these things, and consider what a variety of labour is employed about each of them, we shall be sensible that without the assistance and co-operation of many thousands, the very meanest person in a civilised country could not be provided, even according to, what we very falsely imagine, the easy and simple manner in which he is commonly accommodated. Compared, indeed, with the more extravagant luxury of the great, his accommodation must no doubt appear extremely simple and easy; and yet it may be true, perhaps, that the accommodation of an European prince does not always so much exceed that of an industrious and frugal peasant, as the accommodation of the latter exceeds that of many an African king, the absolute master of the lives and liberties of ten thousand naked savages.

Of the Principle Which Gives Occasion to the Division of Labour

This division of labour, from which so many advantages are derived, is not originally the effect of any human wisdom, which foresees and intends that general opulence to which it gives occasion. It is the necessary, though very slow and gradual consequence of a certain propensity in human nature which has in view no such extensive utility; the propensity to truck, barter, and exchange one thing for another.

Whether this propensity be one of those original principles in human nature, of which no further account can be given; or whether, as seems more probable, it be the necessary consequence of the faculties of reason and speech, it belongs not to our present subject to inquire. It is common to all men, and to be found in no other race of animals, which seem to know neither this nor any other species of contracts. . . . But man has almost constant occasion for the help of his brethren, and it is in vain for him to expect it from their benevolence only. He will be more likely to prevail if he can interest their self-love in his favour, and show them that it is for their own advantage to do for him what he requires of them. Whoever offers to another a bargain of any kind, proposes to do this. Give me that which I want, and you shall have this which you want, is the meaning of every such offer; and it is in this manner that we obtain from one another the far greater part of those good offices which we stand in need of. It is not from the benevolence of the butcher, the brewer, or the baker, that we expect our dinner, but from their regard to their own interest. We address ourselves, not to their humanity but to their self-love, and never talk to them of our own necessities but of their advantages. Nobody but a beggar chooses to depend chiefly upon the benevolence of his fellow-citizens. Even a beggar does not depend upon it entirely. The charity of well-disposed people, indeed, supplies him with the whole fund of his subsistence. But though this principle ultimately provides him with all the necessaries of life which he has occasion for, it neither does nor can provide him with them as he has occasion for them. The greater part of his occasional wants are supplied in the same manner as those of other people, by treaty, by barter, and by purchase. With the money which one man gives him he purchases food. The old clothes which another bestows upon him he exchanges for other old clothes which suit him better, or for lodging, or for food, or for money, with which he can buy either food, clothes, or lodging, as he has occasion.

. . . Each animal is still obliged to support and defend itself, separately and independently, and derives no sort of advantage from that variety of talents with which nature has distinguished its fellows. Among men, on the contrary, the most dissimilar geniuses are of use to one another; the different produces of their respective talents, by the general disposition to truck, barter, and exchange, being brought, as it were, into a common stock, where every man may purchase whatever part of the produce of other men's talents he has occasion for. . . .

Of Restraints Upon the Importation From Foreign Countries of Such Goods as Can Be Produced at Home

. . . The general industry of the society never can exceed what the capital of the society can employ. As the number of workmen that can be kept in employment by any particular person must bear a certain proportion to his capital, so the number of those that can be continually employed by all the members of a great society, must bear a certain proportion to the whole capital of that society, and never can exceed that proportion. No regulation of commerce can increase the quantity of industry in any society beyond what its capital can maintain. It can only divert a part of it into a direction into which it might not otherwise have gone; and it is by no means certain that this artificial direction is likely to be more advantageous to the society than that into which it would have gone of its own accord.

Every individual is continually exerting himself to find out the most advantageous employment for whatever capital he can demand. It is his own advantage, indeed, and not that of the society, which he has in view. But the study of his own advantage naturally, or rather necessarily, leads him to prefer that employment which is most advantageous to the society.

First, every individual endeavours to employ his capital as near home as he can, and consequently as much as he can in the support of domestic industry; provided always that he can thereby obtain the ordinary, or not a great deal less than the ordinary, profits of stock.

Thus, upon equal or nearly equal profits, every wholesale merchant naturally prefers the home trade to the foreign trade of consumption, and the foreign trade of consumption to the carrying trade. In the home trade his capital is never so long out of his sight as it frequently is in the foreign trade of consumption. He can know better the character and situation of the persons whom he trusts, and, if he should happen to be deceived, he knows better the laws of the country from which he must seek redress. In the carrying trade, the capital of the merchant is, as it were, divided between two foreign countries, and no part of it is ever necessarily brought home, or placed under his own immediate view and command. The capital which an Amsterdam merchant employs in carrying corn from Konigsberg to Lisbon, and fruit and wine from Lisbon to Konigsberg, must generally be the one half of it at Konigsberg and the other half at Lisbon. No part of it need ever come to Amsterdam. The natural residence of such a merchant should either be at Konigsberg or Lisbon, and it can only be some very particular circumstance which can make him prefer the residence of Amsterdam. The uneasiness, however, which he feels at being separated so far from his capital, generally determines him to bring part both of the Konigsberg goods which he destines for the market of Lisbon, and of the Lisbon goods which he destines for that of Konigsberg, to Amsterdam; and though this necessarily subjects him to a double charge of loading and unloading, as well as to the payment of some duties and customs, yet for the sake of having some part of his capital always under his own view and command, he willingly submits to this extraordinary charge; and it is in this manner that every country which has any considerable share of the carrying trade, becomes always the emporium, or general market, for the goods of all the different countries whose trade it carries on. The merchant, in order to save a second loading and unloading, endeavours always to sell in the home market as much of the goods of all those different countries as he can, and thus, so far as he can, to convert his carrying trade into a foreign trade of consumption. A merchant, in the same manner, who is engaged in the foreign trade of consumption, when he collects goods for foreign markets, will always be glad, upon equal or nearly equal profits, to sell as great a part of them at home as he can. He saves himself the risk and trouble of exportation, when, so far as he can, he thus converts his foreign trade of consumption into a home trade. Home is in this manner the centre, if I may say so, round which the capitals of the inhabitants of every country are continually circulating, and towards which they are always tending, though by particular causes they may sometimes be driven off and repelled from it towards more distant employments. But a capital employed in the home trade, it has already been shown, necessarily puts into motion a greater quantity of domestic industry, and gives revenue and employment to a greater number of the inhabitants of the country, than an equal capital employed in the foreign trade of consumption; and one employed in the foreign trade of consumption has the same advantage over an equal capital employed in the carrying trade. Upon equal, or only nearly equal profits, therefore, every individual naturally inclines to employ his capital in the manner in which it is likely to afford the greatest support to domestic industry, and to give revenue and employment to the greatest number of people of his own country.

Secondly, every individual who employs his capital in the support of domestic industry, necessarily endeavours so to direct that industry, that its produce may be of the greatest possible value.

The produce of industry is what it adds to the subject or materials upon which it is employed. In proportion as the value of this produce is great or small, so will likewise be the profits of the employer. But it is only for the sake of profit that any man employs a capital in the support of industry; and he will always, therefore, endeavour to employ it in the support of that industry of which the produce is likely to be of the greatest value, or to exchange for the greatest quantity either of money or of other goods.

But the annual revenue of every society is always precisely equal to the exchangeable value of the whole annual produce of its industry, or rather is precisely the same thing with that exchangeable value. As every individual, therefore, endeavours as much as he can both to employ his capital in the support of domestic industry, and so to direct that industry that its produce may be of the greatest value, every individual necessarily labours to render the annual revenue of the society as great as he can. He generally, indeed, neither intends to promote the public interest, nor knows how much he is promoting it. By preferring the support of domestic to that of foreign industry, he intends only his own security; and by directing that industry in such a manner as its produce may be of the greatest value, he intends only his own gain, and he is in this, as in many other cases, led by an invisible hand to promote an end which was no part of his intention. Nor is it always the worse for the society that it was no part of it. By pursuing his own interest he frequently promotes that of the society more effectually than when he really intends to promote it. I have never known much good done by those who affected to trade for the public good. It is an affectation, indeed, not very common among merchants, and very few words need be employed in dissuading them from it.

What is the species of domestic industry which his capital can employ, and of which the produce is likely to be of the greatest value, every individual, it is evident, can, in his local situation, judge much better than any statesman or lawgiver can do for him. The statesman, who should attempt to direct private people in what manner they ought to employ their capitals, would not only load himself with a most unnecessary attention, but assume an authority which could safely be trusted, not only to no single person, but to no council or senate whatever, and which would nowhere be so dangerous as in the hands of a man who had folly and presumption enough to fancy himself fit to exercise it.

To give the monopoly of the home market to the produce of domestic industry, in any particular art or manufacture, is in some measure to direct private people in what manner they ought to employ their capitals, and must, in almost all cases, be either a useless or a hurtful regulation. If the produce of domestic can be brought there as cheap as that of foreign industry, the regulation is evidently useless. If it cannot, it must generally be hurtful. It is the maxim of every prudent master of a family, never to attempt to make at home what it will cost him more to make than to buy. The tailor does not attempt to make his own shoes, but buys them of the shoemaker. The shoemaker does not attempt to make his own clothes, but employs a tailor. The farmer attempts to make neither the one nor the other, but employs those different artificers. All of them find it for their interest to employ their whole industry in a way in which they have some advantage over their neighbours, and to purchase with a part of its produce, or, what is the same thing, with the price of a part of it, whatever else they have occasion for.

What is prudence in the conduct of every private family, can scarce be folly in that of a great kingdom. If a foreign country can supply us with a commodity cheaper than we ourselves can make it, better buy it of them with some part of the produce of our own industry, employed in a way in which we have some advantage. The general industry of the country, being always in proportion to the capital which employs it, will not thereby be diminished, no more than that of the above-mentioned artificers, but only left to find out the way in which it can be employed with the greatest advantage. It is certainly not employed to the greatest advantage, when it is thus directed towards an object which it can buy cheaper than it can make. The value of its annual produce is certainly more or less diminished, when it is thus turned away from producing commodities evidently of more value than the commodity which it is directed to produce. According to the supposition, that commodity could be purchased from foreign countries cheaper than it can be made at home. It could, therefore, have been purchased with a part only of the commodities, or, what is the same thing, with a part only of the price of the commodities, which the industry employed by an equal capital would have produced at home, had it been left to follow its natural course. The industry of the country, therefore, is thus turned away from a more to a less advantageous employment, and the exchangeable value of its annual produce, instead of being increased, according to the intention of the lawgiver, must necessarily be diminished by every such regulation.

By means of such regulations, indeed, a particular manufacture may sometimes be acquired sooner than it could have been otherwise, and after a certain time may be made at home as cheap or cheaper than in the foreign country. But though the industry of the society may be thus carried with advantage into a particular channel sooner than it could have been otherwise, it will by no means follow that the sum total, either of its industry or of its revenue, can ever be augmented by any such regulation. The industry of the society can augment only in proportion as its capital augments, and its capital can augment only in proportion to what can be gradually saved out of its revenue. But the immediate effect of every such regulation is to diminish its revenue, and what diminishes its revenue is certainly not very likely to augment its capital faster than it would have augmented of its own accord, had both capital and industry been left to find out their natural employments.

Though for want of such regulations the society should never acquire the proposed manufacture, it would not, upon that account, necessarily be the poorer in any one period of its duration. In every period of its duration its whole capital and industry might still have been employed, though upon different objects, in the manner that was most advantageous at the time. In every period its revenue might have been the greatest which its capital could afford, and both capital and revenue might have been augmented with the greatest possible rapidity.

The natural advantages which one country has over another in producing particular commodities are sometimes so great, that it is acknowledged by all the world to be in vain to struggle with them. By means of glasses, hot-beds, and hot-walls, very good grapes can be raised in Scotland, and very good wine too can be made of them, at about thirty times the expense for which at least equally good can be brought from foreign countries. Would it be a reasonable law to prohibit the importation of all foreign wines, merely to encourage the making of claret and burgundy in Scotland? But if there would be a manifest absurdity in turning towards any employment thirty times more of the capital and industry of the country than would be necessary to purchase from foreign countries an equal quantity of the commodities wanted, there must be an absurdity, though not altogether so glaring, yet exactly of the same kind, in turning towards any such employment a thirtieth or even a three-hundredth part more of either. Whether the advantages which one country has over another be natural or acquired, is in this respect of no consequence. As long as the one country has those advantages and the other wants them, it will always be more advantageous for the latter rather to buy of the former than to make. It is an acquired advantage only which one artificer has over his neighbour who exercises another trade; and yet they both find it more advantageous to buy of one another than to make what does not belong to their particular trades.

**Karl Marx and
Friedrich Engels**

 **NO**

Manifesto of the Communist Party

A spectre is haunting Europe—the spectre of Communism. All the powers of old Europe have entered into a holy alliance to exorcise this spectre; Pope and Czar, Metternich and Guizot, French Radicals and German police-spies.

Where is the party in opposition that has not been decried as communistic by its opponents in power? Where the opposition that has not hurled back the branding reproach of Communism, against the more advanced opposition parties, as well as against its reactionary adversaries?

Two things result from this fact.

I. Communism is already acknowledged by all European Powers to be itself a Power.

II. It is high time that Communists should openly, in the face of the whole world, publish their views, their aims, their tendencies, and meet this nursery tale of the Spectre of Communism with a Manifesto of the party itself.

To this end, Communists of various nationalities have assembled in London, and sketched the following manifesto, to be published in the English, French, German, Italian, Flemish and Danish languages.

Bourgeois and Proletarians

The history of all hitherto existing society is the history of class struggles.

Freeman and slave, patrician and plebeian, lord and serf, guild-master and journeyman, in a word; oppressor and oppressed, stood in constant opposition to one another, carried on an uninterrupted, now hidden, now open fight, a fight that each time ended, either in a revolutionary re-constitution of society at large, or in the common ruin of the contending classes.

In the early epochs of history, we find almost everywhere a complicated arrangement of society into various orders, a manifold graduation of social rank. In ancient Rome we have patricians, knights, plebeians, slaves; in the Middle Ages, feudal lords, vassals, guild-masters, journeymen, apprentices, serfs; in almost all of these classes, again, subordinate gradations.

The modern bourgeois society that has sprouted from the ruins of feudal society, has not done away with class antagonisms. It has but established new classes, new conditions of oppression, new forms of struggle in place of the old ones.

Our epoch, the epoch of the bourgeoisie, possesses, however, this distinctive feature; it has simplified the class antagonisms. Society as a whole is

From Karl Marx and Friedrich Engels, *The Communist Manifesto* (1848).

more and more splitting up into two great hostile camps, into two great classes directly facing each other: Bourgeoisie and Proletariat.

From the serfs of the Middle Ages sprang the chartered burghers of the earliest towns. From these burgesses the first elements of the bourgeoisie were developed.

The discovery of America, the rounding of the Cape, opened up fresh ground for the rising bourgeoisie. The East-Indian and Chinese markets, the colonization of America, trade with the colonies, the increase in the means of exchange in commodities, generally, gave to commerce, to navigation, to industry, an impulse never before known, and thereby, to the revolutionary element in the tottering feudal society, a rapid development.

The feudal system of industry, under which industrial production was monopolized by closed guilds, now no longer sufficed for the growing wants of the new markets. The manufacturing system took its place. The guild-masters were pushed on one side by the manufacturing middle-class; division of labor between the different corporate guilds vanished in the face of division of labor in each single workshop.

Meantime the markets kept ever growing, the demand, ever rising. Even manufacturing no longer sufficed. Thereupon, steam and machinery revolutionized industrial production. The place of manufacture was taken by the giant, Modern Industry, the place of the industrial middle-class, by industrial millionaires, the leaders of whole industrial armies, the modern bourgeoisie.

Modern Industry has established the world-market, for which the discovery of America paved the way. This market has given an immense development to commerce, to navigation, to communication by land. This development has, in its turn, reacted on the extension of industry; and in proportion as industry, commerce, navigation, railways extended in the same proportion the bourgeoisie developed, increased its capital, and pushed into the background every class handed down from the Middle Ages.

We see, therefore, how the modern bourgeoisie is itself the product of a long course of development, of a series of revolutions in the modes of production and of exchange.

Each step in the development of the bourgeoisie was accompanied by a corresponding political advance of that class. An oppressed class under the sway of the feudal nobility, an armed and self-governing association in the medieval commune, here independent urban republic (as in Italy and Germany), there taxable "third estate" of the monarchy (as in France), afterwards, in the period of manufacturing proper, serving either the semi-feudal or the absolute monarchy as a counterpoise against the nobility, and in fact, cornerstone of the great monarchies in general, the bourgeoisie has at last, since the establishment of Modern Industry and of the world-market, conquered for itself, in a modern representative State, exclusive political sway. The executive of the modern State is but a committee for managing the common affairs of the whole bourgeoisie.

The bourgeoisie, historically, has played a most revolutionary part.

The bourgeoisie, wherever it has got the upper hand, has put an end to all feudal, patriarchal, idyllic relations. It has pitilessly torn asunder the motley feudal ties that bound man to his "natural superiors," and has left remaining no other nexus between man and man than naked self-interest, than callous "cash payment." It has drowned the most heavenly ecstasies of religious fervor, of chivalrous enthusiasm, of philistine sentimentalism, in the icy water of egotistical calculation. It has resolved personal worth into exchange value, and in place of the numberless indefeasible chartered freedoms, has set up that single, unconscionable freedom—Free Trade. In one word, for exploitation, veiled by religious and political illusions, it has substituted naked, shameless, direct, brutal exploitation.

The bourgeoisie has stripped of its halo every occupation hitherto honored and looked up to with reverent awe. It has converted the physician, the lawyer, the priest, the poet, the man of science, into its paid wage-laborers.

The bourgeoisie has torn away from the family its sentimental veil, and has reduced the family relation to a mere money relation.

The bourgeoisie has disclosed how it came to pass that the brutal display of vigor in the Middle Ages, which Reactionists so much admire, found its fitting complement in the most slothful indolence. It has been the first to show what man's activity can bring about. It has accomplished wonders far surpassing Egyptian pyramids, Roman aqueducts, and Gothic cathedrals; it has conducted expeditions that put in the shade all former Exoduses of nations and crusades.

The bourgeoisie cannot exist without constantly revolutionizing the instruments of production, and thereby the relations of production, and with them the whole relations of society. Conservation of the old modes of production in unaltered form, was, on the contrary, the first condition of existence for all earlier industrial classes. Constant revolutionizing of production, uninterrupted disturbance of all social conditions, everlasting uncertainty and agitation distinguish the bourgeois epoch from all earlier ones. All fixed, fast-frozen relations, with their train of ancient and venerable prejudices and opinions, are swept away, all newly-formed ones become antiquated before they can ossify. All that is solid melts into air, all that is holy is profaned, and man is at last compelled to face with sober senses, his real conditions of life, and his relations with his kind.

The need of a constantly expanding market for its products chases the bourgeoisie over the whole surface of the globe. It must nestle everywhere, settle everywhere, establish connections everywhere.

The bourgeoisie has through its exploitation of the world-market given a cosmopolitan character to production and consumption in every country. To the great chagrin of Reactionists, it has drawn from under the feet of industry the national ground on which it stood. All old-established national industries have been destroyed or are daily being destroyed. They are dislodged by new industries, whose introduction becomes a life and death question for all civilized nations, by industries that no longer work up indigenous raw material, but raw material drawn from the remotest zones; industries whose products are consumed, not only at home, but in every quarter of the globe. In place of the old wants, satisfied by the productions of the country, we find new wants, requiring for their satisfaction the products of distant lands and climes. In place of the old local and national seclusion and self-sufficiency, we have intercourse in every direction, universal inter-dependence of nations. And as in material, so also in intellectual production. The intellectual creations of individual nations become common property. National one-sidedness and narrow-mindedness become more and more impossible, and from the numerous national and local literatures there arises a world-literature.

The bourgeoisie, by the rapid improvement of all instruments of production, by the immensely facilitated means of communication, draws all, even the most barbarian, nations into civilization. The cheap prices of its commodities are the heavy artillery with which it batters down all Chinese walls, with which it forces the barbarians' intensely obstinate hatred of foreigners to capitulate. It compels all nations, on pain of extinction, to adopt the bourgeois mode of production; it compels them to introduce what it calls civilization into their midst, i.e., to become bourgeois themselves. In a word, it creates a world after its own image.

The bourgeoisie has subjected the country to the rule of the towns. It has created enormous cities, has greatly increased the urban population as compared with the rural, and has thus rescued a considerable part of the population from the idiocy of rural life. Just as it has made the country dependent on the towns, so it has made barbarian and semibarbarian countries dependent on the civilized ones, nations of peasants on nations of bourgeois, the East on the West.

The bourgeoisie keeps more and more doing away with the scattered state of the population, of the means of production, and of property. It has agglomerated population, centralized means of production, and has concentrated property in a few hands. The necessary consequence of this was political centralization. Independent, or but loosely connected provinces, with separate interests, laws, governments and systems of taxation, became lumped together in one nation, with one government, one code of laws, one national class-interest, one frontier and one customs-tariff.

The bourgeoisie, during its rule of scarce one hundred years, has created more massive and more colossal productive forces than have all preceding generations together. Subjection of Nature's forces to man, machinery, application of chemistry to industry and agriculture, steam-navigation, railways, electric telegraphs, clearing of whole continents for cultivation, canalization of rivers, whole populations conjured out of the ground—what earlier century had even a presentiment that such productive forces slumbered in the lap of social labor?

We see then: the means of production and of exchange on whose foundations the bourgeoisie built itself up, were generated in feudal society. At a certain stage in the development of these means of production and of exchange, the conditions under which feudal society produced and exchanged, the feudal organization of agriculture and manufacturing industry, in one word, the feudal relations of property became no longer compatible with the already developed productive forces; they became so many fetters. They had to be burst asunder; they were burst asunder.

Into their places stepped free competition, accompanied by a social and political constitution adapted to it, and by the economical and political sway of the bourgeois class.

A similar movement is going on before our own eyes. Modern bourgeois society with its relations of production, of exchange and of property, a society that has conjured up such gigantic means of production and of exchange, is like the sorcerer, who is no longer able to control the powers of the nether world whom he has called up by his spells. For many a decade past the history of industry and commerce is but the history of the revolt of modern productive forces against modern conditions of production, against the property relations that are the condition for the existence of the bourgeoisie and of its rule. It is enough to mention the commercial crises that by their periodical return put on trial, each time more threateningly, the existence of the entire bourgeois society. In these crises a great part not only of the existing products, but also of the previously created productive forces, are periodically destroyed. In these crises there breaks out an epidemic that, in all earlier epochs, would have seemed an absurdity—the epidemic of overproduction. Society suddenly finds itself put back into a state of momentary barbarism; it appears as if a famine, a universal war of devastation had cut off the supply of every means of subsistence; industry and commerce seem to be destroyed; and why? Because there is too much civilization, too much means of subsistence, too much industry, too much commerce. The productive forces at the disposal of society no longer tend to further the development of the conditions of bourgeois property; on the contrary, they have become too powerful for these conditions, by which they are fettered, and so soon as they overcome these fetters, they bring disorder into the whole of bourgeois society, endangering the existence of bourgeois property. The conditions of bourgeois society are too narrow to comprise the wealth created by them. And how does the bourgeoisie get over these crises? On the one hand by enforced destruction of a mass of productive forces; on the other, by the conquest of new markets, and by the more thorough exploitation of the old ones. That is to say, by paving the way for more extensive and more destructive crises, and by diminishing the means whereby crises are prevented.

The weapons with which the bourgeoisie felled feudalism to the ground are now turned against the bourgeoisie itself.

But not only has the bourgeoisie forged the weapons that bring death to itself; it has also called into existence the men who are to wield those weapons—the modern working-class—the proletarians.

In proportion as the bourgeoisie, i.e., capital, is developed, in the same proportion is the proletariat, the modern working-class, developed, a class of laborers, who live only so long as they find work, and who find work only so long as their labor increases capital. These laborers, who must sell themselves piecemeal, are a commodity, like every other article of commerce, and are consequently exposed to all the vicissitudes of competition, to all the fluctuations of the market.

Owing to the extensive use of machinery and to division of labor, the work of the proletarians has lost all individual character, and, consequently, all charm for the workman. He becomes an appendage of the machine, and it is only the most simple, most monotonous, and most easily acquired knack that is required of him. Hence, the cost of production of a workman is restricted, almost entirely, to the means of subsistence that he requires for his maintenance, and for the propagation of his race. But the price of a commodity, and also of labor, is equal to its cost of production. In proportion, therefore, as the repulsiveness of the work increases, the wage decreases. Nay more, in proportion as the use of machinery and division of labor increases, in the same proportion the burden of toil also increases, whether by prolongation of the working hours, by increase of the work enacted in a given time, or by increased speed of the machinery, etc.

Modern Industry has converted the little workshop of the patriarchal master into the great factory of the industrial capitalist. Masses of laborers, crowded into the factory, are organized like soldiers. As privates of the industrial army they are placed under the command of a perfect hierarchy of officers and sergeants. Not only are they the slaves of the bourgeois class, and of the bourgeois State, they are daily and hourly enslaved by the machine, by the over-looker, and, above all, by the individual bourgeois manufacturer himself. The more openly this despotism proclaims gain to be its end and aim, the more petty, the more hateful and the more embittering it is.

The less the skill and exertion or strength implied in manual labor, in other words, the more modern industry becomes developed, the more is the labor of men superseded by that of women. Differences of age and sex have no longer any distinctive social validity for the working class. All are instruments of labor, more or less expensive to use, according to their age and sex.

No sooner is the exploitation of the laborer by the manufacturer so far at an end, that he receives his wages in cash, than he is set upon by the other portions of the bourgeoisie, the landlord, the shopkeeper, the pawnbroker, etc.

The low strata of the middle class—the small trades-people, shopkeepers, and retired tradesmen generally, the handicraftsmen and peasants—all these sink gradually into the proletariat, partly because their diminutive capital does not suffice for the scale on which Modern Industry is carried on, and is swamped in the competition with the large capitalists, partly because their specialized skill is rendered worthless by new methods of production. Thus the proletariat is recruited from all classes of the population.

The proletariat goes through various stages of development. With its birth begins its struggle with the bourgeoisie. At first the contest is carried on by individual laborers, then by the workpeople of a factory, then by the operatives of one trade, in one locality, against the individual bourgeois who directly exploits them. They direct their attacks not against the bourgeois conditions of production, but against the instruments of production themselves; they destroy imported wares that compete with their labor, they smash to pieces machinery, they set factories ablaze, they seek to restore by force the vanished status of the workman of the Middle Ages.

At this stage the laborers still form an incoherent mass scattered over the whole country, and broken up by their mutual competition. If anywhere they unite to form more compact bodies, this is not yet the consequence of their own active union, but of the union of bourgeoisie, which class, in order to attain its own political ends, is compelled to set the whole proletariat in motion, and is moreover yet, for a time, able to do so. At this stage, therefore, the proletarians do not fight their enemies, but the enemies of their enemies, the remnants of absolute monarchy, the landowners, the non-industrial bourgeoisie, the petty bourgeoisie. Thus the whole historical movement is concentrated in the hands of the bourgeoisie; every victory so obtained is a victory for the bourgeoisie.

But with the development of industry the proletariat not only increases in number, it becomes concentrated in great masses, its strength grows, and it feels that strength more. The various interests and conditions of life within the ranks of the proletariat are more and more equalized, in proportion as machinery obliterates all distinction of labor, and nearly everywhere reduces wages to the same low level. The growing competition among the bourgeoisie, and the resulting commercial crises, make the wages of the worker ever more fluctuating. The unceasing improvement of machinery, ever more rapidly developing, makes their livelihood more and more precarious, the collisions between individual workmen and individual bourgeois take more and more the character of collision between two classes. Thereupon the workers begin to form combinations (Trades Unions) against the bourgeoisie; they club together in order to keep up the rate of wages; they found permanent associations in order to make provision beforehand for these occasional revolts. Here and there the contest breaks out into riots.

Now and then the workers are victorious, but only for a time. The real fruits of their battles lie, not in the immediate result, but in the ever expanding union of the workers. This union is helped on by the improved means of communication that are created by modern industry, and that place the workers of different localities in contact with one another. It was just this contact that was needed to centralize the numerous local struggles, all of the same character, into one national struggle between classes. But every class struggle is a political struggle. And that union, to attain which the burghers of the Middle Ages, with their miserable highways, required centuries, the modern proletarians, thanks to railways, achieve in a few years.

This organization of the proletarians into a class, and consequently into a political party, is continually being upset again by the competition between the workers themselves. But it ever rises up again, stronger, firmer, mightier. It compels legislative recognition of particular interests of the workers, by taking advantage of the divisions among the bourgeoisie itself. Thus the ten-hour bill in England was carried.

Altogether collisions between the classes of the old society further, in many ways, the course of development of the proletariat. The bourgeoisie finds itself involved in a constant battle. At first with the aristocracy; later on, with those portions of the bourgeoisie itself, whose interests have become antagonistic to the progress of industry; at all times, with the bourgeoisie of foreign countries. In all these battles it sees itself compelled to appeal to the proletariat, to ask for its help, and thus, to drag it into the political arena. The bourgeoisie itself, therefore, supplies the proletariat with its own elements of political and general education, in other words, it furnishes the proletariat with weapons for fighting the bourgeoisie.

Further, as we have already seen, entire sections of the ruling classes are, by the advance of industry, precipitated into the proletariat, or are at least threatened in their conditions of existence. These also supply the proletariat with fresh elements of enlightenment and progress.

Finally, in times when the class-struggle nears the decisive hour, the process of dissolution going on within the ruling class, in fact, within the whole range of old society, assumes such a violent, glaring character, that a small section of the ruling class cuts itself adrift, and joins the revolutionary class, the class that holds the future in its hands. Just as, therefore, at an earlier period, a section of the nobility went over to the bourgeoisie, so now a portion of the bourgeoisie goes over to the proletariat, and in particular, a portion of the bourgeois ideologists, who have raised themselves to the level of comprehending theoretically the historical movements as a whole.

Of all the classes that stand face to face with the bourgeoisie today, the proletariat alone is a really revolutionary class. The other classes decay and finally disappear in the face of Modern Industry; the proletariat is its special and essential product. . . .

In the conditions of the proletariat, those of old society at large are already virtually swamped. The proletarian is without property; his relation to his wife and children has no longer anything in common with the bourgeois family-relations; modern industrial labor, modern subjugation to capital, the same in England as in France, in America as in Germany, has stripped him of every trace of national character. Law, morality, religion, are to him so many bourgeois prejudices, behind which lurk in ambush just as many bourgeois interests.

All the preceding classes that got the upper hand, sought to fortify their already acquired status by subjecting society at large to their conditions of appropriation. The proletarians cannot become masters of the productive forces of society, except by abolishing their own previous mode of appropriation, and thereby also every other previous mode of appropriation. They have nothing of their own to secure and to fortify; their mission is to destroy all previous securities for, and insurances of, individual property.

All previous historical movements were movements of minorities, or in the interests of minorities. The proletarian movement is the self-conscious, independent movement of the immense majority, in the interest of the immense majority. The proletariat, the lowest stratum of our present society, cannot stir, cannot raise itself up, without the whole superincumbent strata of official society being sprung into the air.

Though not in substance, yet in form, the struggle of the proletariat with the bourgeoisie is at first a national struggle. The proletariat of each country must, of course, first of all settle matters with its own bourgeoisie.

In depicting the most general phases of the development of the proletariat, we traced the more or less veiled civil war, raging within existing society, up to the point where that war breaks out into open revolution, and where the violent overthrow of the bourgeoisie lays the foundation for the sway of the proletariat.

Hitherto, every form of society has been based, as we have already seen, on the antagonism of oppressing and oppressed classes. But in order to oppress a class, certain conditions must be assured to it under which it can, at least, continue its slavish existence. The serf, in the period of serfdom, raised himself to membership in the commune, just as the petty bourgeois, under the yoke of feudal absolutism, managed to develop into a bourgeois.

The modern laborer, on the contrary, instead of rising with the progress of industry, sinks deeper and deeper below the conditions of existence of his own class. He becomes a pauper, and pauperism develops more rapidly than population and wealth. And here it becomes evident that the bourgeoisie is unfit any longer to be the ruling class in society, and to impose its conditions of existence upon society as an over-riding law. It is unfit to rule, because it is incompetent to assure an existence to its slave within his slavery, because it cannot help letting him sink into such a state that it has to feed him, instead of being fed by him. Society can no longer live under this bourgeoisie, in other words, its existence is no longer compatible with society.

The essential condition for the existence, and for the sway of the bourgeois class, is the formation and augmentation of capital; the condition for capital is wage-labor. Wage-labor rests exclusively on competition between the laborers. The advance of industry, whose involuntary promoter is the bourgeoisie, replaces the isolation of the laborers, due to competition, by their revolutionary combination, due to association. The development of Modern Industry, therefore, cuts from under its feet the very foundation on which the bourgeoisie produces and appropriates products. What the bourgeoisie therefore produces, above all, are its own grave-diggers. Its fall and the victory of the proletariat are equally inevitable.

POSTSCRIPT

Can Capitalism Lead to Human Happiness?

As a society, Americans have always prized liberty over equality. We have always believed what we thought followed from Smith—that the wealth of the society as a whole was the only legitimate goal of economic enterprise as a whole, and that distribution for the sake of equity, or charity, was a side issue, best left to churches and private charity. We Americans have resisted any attempts at socializing such basic needs as medicine, communications (the telephone companies), and economic security for the old, young, and infirm. We have always enjoyed characterizing our business system as one where, as far as your personal income is concerned, "the sky's the limit." We point to the failures of "socialism" in England and Sweden, and cite with particular satisfaction the fall of communism in Eastern Europe and Russia.

We have built some safety nets: Social Security, Medicare and Medicaid, Aid to Dependent Children, and the like. But these and all the other elements of the welfare system have become a major problem and political issue for both parties. People in that system complain about its failure to provide adequately for those in the most need, babies and the infirm elderly. Meanwhile, conservative members of Congress complain that even these modest subsidies are costing the taxpayer too much, and recent modifications to these programs have put firm time limits on our ability to access them.

Why should subsidies to the poor bother us so? We provide price supports to farmers, corporate welfare (bailouts) to businesses, subsidized water and grazing land at public expense to ranchers and farmers, and access to minerals on public land for miners. We have allowed even foreign companies to come into the national forests, to mine and forest for their own profit, even when they leave tailings and barren land for us as taxpayers to clean up and restore. Why, it might be asked, should we subsidize the rich in our tender public compassion, while resenting the poor?

In most of the redistributive activities of the economy, we see the very visible hands of the CEOs and the Wall Street analysts. Where, in all of this, is the Invisible Hand of Adam Smith? Or does the whole arrogant parade of conspicuous billionaires force us to consider the alternatives to Adam Smith? Was Marx's political philosophy persuasive? Should we work to redistribute the productive assets of the country? The last two decades of economic reform have seen a steady redistribution in the other direction, as the richest persons in the country absorb more and more of the wealth and income, as the poorest get poorer. How can this be right?

Suggested Reading

For more information on this subject the following readings may be of help:

Robert L. Heilbroner, *The Worldly Philosophers,* seventh edition (New York: Touchstone, 1999).

Karl Marx, *Communist Manifesto,* New York: Penguin Classics, 2002.

Donald McCloskey, "Bourgeois Virtue," *American Scholar* 63 (1994).

David Schweickart, *Against Capitalism* (Cambridge: Cambridge University Press, l993).

Adam Smith, *The Wealth of Nations,* Selected Edition (Oxford University Press, 2008).

ISSUE 2

Can Restructuring a Corporation's Rules Make a Moral Difference?

YES: Josef Wieland, from "The Ethics of Governance," *Business Ethics Quarterly* (January 2001)

NO: Ian Maitland, from "Distributive Justice in Firms: Do the Rules of Corporate Governance Matter?" *Business Ethics Quarterly* (January 2001)

ISSUE SUMMARY

YES: Can moral values be attributed to organizations (as well as to individual persons)? Josef Wieland, director of the German Business Ethics Network's Centre for Business Ethics, argues that they can. After carefully developing a concept of governance ethics for corporations, he argues that the incorporation of moral conditions and requirements into the structures of the firm is the precondition for lasting beneficial effects on the virtues of the individuals within it. We can only be moral persons at work when the workplace, too, is moral.

NO: Ian Maitland, professor of Business, Government and Society at the University of Minnesota's Carlson School of Management, here plays his favorite role as Business Ethics Curmudgeon. Changing the rules will have no effect whatsoever on the moral work of the corporation (taking as his example the justice of the distributive mechanisms of the firm) and will succeed, if taken seriously, only in impairing its efficiency.

As Wieland points out, the question of whether an organization of some sort, as opposed to its human members, may assume the status of moral agent has been around for a very long time. (It actually goes back to Aristotle, who took up in the *Politics* the question of the conditions under which a government is morally obligated to pay the debts incurred by its predecessor. It is more difficult with organizations than with humans to tell when you're dealing with "the same" entity that undertook the obligation.) New in Wieland's approach is the use of recent economic theory (referred to as "the New Economics of

Organization"). Readers not exposed to the language of this theory may find it rough going at first, but the attempt to reach almost mathematical precision in the language of organizational ethics is a very useful intellectual stretch. We have left out section 4 as peripheral to our purposes; we trust that no confusion will result.

His thesis, again traceable to Aristotle, is perpetually fascinating. To what extent is my ability and inclination to act morally ("cooperate" with others) dependent on the institutional atmosphere, the communication from the highest levels that moral behavior is approved? Approval of being nice won't do it. What the moral agent in the corporation needs is a strong message that moral behavior will be rewarded even if it entails falling short on numerical goals set by the management—even if it cuts into return on investment and the increase of shareholder wealth. That's the only message that matters.

Or does it matter? Ian Maitland addresses himself to a different group of corporate reformers, those who hold that restructuring corporate rules to signal a new concern with morality can make the corporation more willing to take into account stakeholders other than the shareholders—the employees, for instance, or the natural environment. Rules are neutral, Maitland argues, at least as far as morality goes. But they can do a beautiful job of fouling up the corporate enterprise's efficiency, as people who should be worrying about how to get their job done faster and with less consumption of resources find themselves worrying instead about how to create a more moral world.

You'll note that Wieland and Maitland are aiming at slightly different targets, so it should not surprise you if their arrows seem often to fly past each other. Often Maitland sounds simply mischievous, which he is, and often Wieland's article reads like translated German, which it is. But the fundamental conflict is right there, and it is just the conflict that defines business ethics. Should we expect moral behavior of the corporation? Should we hold our corporations to moral standards? Should we engage in moral criticism of the corporation? Or should we recognize, as Milton Friedman, Adam Smith, and so many others have argued, that the corporation is by right and by law no more than a legal device for turning money into money, and to be held to account only insofar as the law specifically requires it to operate within the bounds of the public interest?

Ask yourself, as you read these selections, whether Wieland's conviction that the corporation can be a moral agent, and can make itself more moral if it chooses to, is helped by the theory he brings to bear; ask yourself if Maitland is not simply right in his skepticism about the uselessness of the enterprise.

YES

Josef Wieland

The Ethics of Governance

Introduction: Organization and Ethics

In this [selection] I want to pursue two questions. The first of these is as follows: what is the subject and scope of business ethics?[1] The second question is this: in what way does it make sense to talk about the ethics of the firm-as-an-organization?

The topic of this [selection]—the Ethics of Governance—already implies a connection between corporate governance and business ethics; that is, between the management, governance, and control regimes of a firm and its ethics as an organization. In practice these are interrelated: codes of ethics, ethics management systems, and corporate ethics programs can be understood as governance structures by which firms control, protect, and develop the integrity of their transactions. The theoretical investigation and integration of these ethical systems has hitherto been developed only to a limited extent and has been confined to individual aspects, as far as I can see. There are reasons for this.

The theoretical explanation and integration of codes of ethics, ethics management systems, and other organizational measures for the implementation of moral claims in organizational contexts requires a conceptual distinction between the moral values of an individual person (value ethics), the values of an individual person in a given function or role (management ethics), and the moral values of an organization (governance ethics). This distinction would provide the basis for a better understanding of the trade-offs, conflicts, and dilemmas contained in those distinct levels of business ethics.

In the following discussion I would like to focus my own investigation on just one of the aspects mentioned—i.e., on the moral characteristics of an organization as a distinct moral actor. There has been a lengthy, extensive, and controversial debate on this issue. Its focus is the question of the attribution of moral responsibility to collective actors.[2] Differing viewpoints revolve around the issue as to whether firms as corporate actors are independent action systems or subjects, or whether their status as action systems or subjects is derived from individual actors. Although this discussion has yielded important insights for research on business ethics, the issue remains

From *Business Ethics Quarterly,* vol. 11, no. 1, January 2001, pp. 73–85. Copyright © 2001 by Business Ethics Quarterly. Reprinted by permission of The Philosophy Documentation Center, publisher of Business Ethics Quarterly. References omitted.

unresolved. I believe the reason for this deadlock is to be found in the individualistic notion of action that grounds all the arguments. This emphasis is in full accordance with philosophical tradition. However, business ethics questions are questions about ethics in the context of a functional structure: they cannot be developed by analogy with the ethics of a person, but must be developed out of the characteristics and conditions of the structure itself. Is it then possible to develop a type of business ethics that does not resort to an action-theoretic notion of the person? In the following sections I will argue that this question can be answered affirmatively, and that its answer requires the substitution of the notion of person by that of governance, and of that of action by that of cooperation. . . .

Form and Process of the Organization

In this section, the notions of governance and governance ethics that so far have been introduced in a more intuitive way will be located in theoretical terms and further developed. In accordance with the discussion so far, only one particular form of governance will be the object of this endeavor: governance of the firm. Of course, rules and orders at the level of the state also are governance structures. However, for reasons of precision and simplicity they will not be dealt with systematically here.

Questions regarding the ethics of the firm are questions with regard to an organization. From the point of view of the institutionalist New Economics of Organization,[3] which this [selection] regards as normative, these are questions about the moral characteristics of a governance structure for the execution of economic transactions.

Governance structures are formal and informal arrangements for the "steering" of the different codes of a system or organization. They are a matrix within which distinct transactions are negotiated and executed, completely if possible.[4] For the purposes of this investigation it is useful to distinguish between global and local governance structures. Global governance structures refer to the constitutional parameters of an organization or a system; local governance structures to the micropolitical governance of transactions. State, market, and firms, frameworks, corporate charters, and ethical codes of conduct are global governance structures in this sense. In pursuing the question of business ethics I will interpret global governance structures as firm-specific assets (structures, resources, competences, skills) for the identification and processing of moral problems in the economy. Local governance structures are standard operating procedures, organizational structures, rites, and moral values within the firm that can constitute transaction-specific assets for the identification and processing of problem issues.

Governance structures differ with regard to their ability to support the efficient execution of a given transaction. Efficiency in the context of governance is defined as adaptive efficiency, that is, as comparison of at least two governance structures with regard to their capacity to cope with the uncertainties and contingencies that can occur during the process of transaction. Since such structures usually consist of formal and informal codes of practice, moral ambitions and values can without too much difficulty be interpreted as elements of the governance of economic transactions.

The above argument implies that business ethics is not about the moral standards and behavior of entrepreneurs, management teams, or employees. Those are personal virtues that can be attributed to acting persons, but not to the normativity of organizations. There seems to be general consensus in the literature that the moral constitution of an organization has to be different from the sum of the moral convictions of its members. However, it remains to a large extent unclear how the phenomenon of a structural ethics can be approached at all.[5] In the following I will develop my own views on this topic and locate them in the notion of governance ethics.

First of all it is important to introduce the convention that regarding their normativity organizations are contractually constituted systems of institutionalized behavioral constraints and thus also represent behavioral options.[6] In other words, business ethics cannot be developed based on the notion of action, but must be premised on the characteristics of a global governance structure for economic transactions that limits (and extends) behavioral options. The investigation into the theoretical problems this disposition entails must begin with a differentiated notion of the organization itself. We differentiate as follows: organization denotes the general *process* of organizing, and also the specific *form* within which this process takes place.

The introduction of this distinction between process and form has far-reaching consequences; these can be demonstrated by using the example of the distinction between market and hierarchy[7] common in economic theory. Market and hierarchy represent different global governance structures. As options for the execution of a transaction, e.g., a long-term employment relationship, they are equivalent. But as concrete "form" under whose regime this employment relationship takes place, they are not equivalent. It is precisely because markets and hierarchies have at their disposal different characteristics and capabilities for the governance of economic processes that the problem of cost-efficient assignments of transactions to the most efficient governance structure arises. In the case of a long-term employment relationship governance is optimally organized not via the market but via the hierarchical form of "firm."

The difference between process and form that is inherent in the notion of organization can be used for the theoretical construction of an institutional business ethics. Insofar as the process of organizing involves individual action, virtues and vices matter. But the organizational form within which this process is taking place—the firm—stands outside the realm of traditional value ethics. This decoupling of form and process is rooted in different temporal characteristics. The processual character of the organization called "firm" can in principle be set to infinite duration by the form character of the same organization to the extent that form is based on the exclusion of "human beings," "individuals," or "persons."[8] Because of this, business ethics—if we take the label seriously—has to refer constitutively to the form of a "firm" as a governance structure. It can be systematically developed as governance ethics only under conditions where individual virtues can and must have their effect.

Of course, the analysis and design of governance structures is part of institutional theory. However, it is important to realize that in the theoretical design developed here the notions of "governance" and "institution" are not synonyms. The notion of institution aims at directing behavior via formal or informal behavioral constraints and incentives (utility maximizing). In contrast, the notion of governance emphasizes the integration and interaction of formal and informal constraints with regard to any given problem and focuses on the problem of adaptivity, i.e., the reflexivity and recursiveness of structures. From a governance-theoretic perspective, whereas the notion of institution is more static (goal-oriented directing of behavior via narrowing of options), the notion of governance is dynamic (goal-oriented directing of behavior via adaptivity).

Two conclusions emerge from the foregoing discussion. First, business ethics needs to be developed as governance ethics. Second, the relationship between value ethics and governance ethics is as follows: whereas management virtues belong to the process of the firm, the proper locus of governance ethics is the form of the firm.

Governance Ethics: Contract and Organization

The foregoing argument leads to the consideration that the "shape" of business ethics has to be developed based on the characteristics of a particular form, i.e., that of the firm as organization. The New Economics of Organization, an institutionalist and simultaneously interdisciplinary research program, captures this form in descriptive and explanatory terms in two dimensions—contract and organization.

Contract

From an organization-economic perspective the firm constitutes itself as economic form by means of a constitutional contract, the corporate charter.[9] This establishes not only the goals and policies of the firm, but also the identity of its stakeholders.[10] The process of constitution can be reconstructed in contract-theoretical terms as a "nexus of contracts" between individual resource owners.[11] According to this theoretical architecture, the constituting process of the enterprise (or team) is taking place because the gains of each individual resource owner attainable by cooperation are above the level that could be reached by each alone. The motive for founding the firm is thus not profit making,[12] but the realisation of a cooperation rent. This rent from cooperation, although an organizational collective good, gives a strictly individualist and self-interested motive for the formation of a team.

Now the decisive question is: how can it be possible that actors who are exclusively self-oriented can bind themselves together permanently in an organization in order to produce this collective good? The answer is: by entering into chosen long-term and adaptively designed contractual arrangements in which all partners to the contract commit themselves to agreed contractual provisions. On the one hand they thereby agree to constraints on their present and future behavioral options: only in this way can teamwork among strictly self-interested actors become possible. On the other hand, however, the partners to a contract opt to combine their particular resources and capabilities and thus extend the range of their respective individual behavioral options in a way that is by definition not precisely spelled out by the terms of the contract, but is indicative of the adaptivity of the contractual arrangements. The initial sets of resources of all partners to the contract are not reciprocally known completely, since it is impossible to measure them precisely, nor can future learning processes and the appropriation of implicit knowledge be anticipated. This might be a disadvantage from the performance measurement and marginal productivity point of view. But in this disadvantage lies also the dynamic and adaptive potential of a team.

It is thus the systematic incompleteness of contracts, desired by the contracting parties because of its potential for innovation, that initially leads to a problem of adaptation to newly arising situations and contingencies in the market and organizational environment of a firm. For reasons of adaptivity discretionary behavior has to be acceptable. It would be easy to interpret discretionary behavior as shirking.[13] However, the potential for innovation and productivity, organizational learning, and implicit knowledge; the resources, competences, and skills of an organization and its members for the realization of competitive advantage—all of these can be practically activated and theoretically reconstructed only if incompleteness and uncertainty are allowed to exist in contractual relations. It is the problem of adaptivity that is the source of entrepreneurial dynamic and the origin of novelty. Thus, via incompleteness and uncertainty we reconstruct the firm in contract-theoretic terms as a bundle of resources, skills, and competencies[14] the activation of which is based on implicit contracts.[15]

It is precisely these trade-offs between constraint and extension, performance control and development, contract and resource that characterise the form "firm" as a contractually constituted organization. The constitution of a firm as a network of explicit and implicit contracts codifies behavioral constraints and justified expectations, and thus creates cooperative behavioral options and resource use possibilities. In other words, it is the agreed explicit and implicit contracts of individual resource owners that constitute the collective actor "firm" as a cooperation project, and demarcate the form "firm" from firm-as-process. This interpretation of the form "firm" as a set of constitutional (corporate charter, standards of conduct) and postconstitutional (employment contracts) explicit and implicit contracts between resource owners defines a first interface for questions of morality.

Those questions can be developed on the basis of the problem of cooperation; more precisely, the values "willingness to cooperate" and "capability to cooperate." "Willingness to cooperate" signifies an ability to cooperate successfully, given that cooperation benefits at least one of the partners. The notion thus captures both a resource dimension and a behavioral dimension. The "capability to cooperate" signifies those mental factors that activate the willingness to cooperate. Thus we can formulate more precisely: long-term contracts for the foundation of a cooperation project in and between firms are incomplete[16] regarding the willingness and capability to cooperate, and are therefore characterized by ambiguity and contingency. Their fulfillment thus always raises moral questions. The basis of those moral questions lies in the fact that self-interested actors have a strong incentive to exploit contractual incompleteness, ambiguity, and contingency in an opportunistic way whenever they can do so in a cost-efficient manner. Such behavior by its very nature represents a suspension of the willingness to cooperate and a destruction of the capability to cooperate. On the other hand, the rejection of such behavior on moral grounds and the productive use of incompleteness have the contrary effect. Both types are determinants of the realization of a cooperation rent by the actors, with inverted signs.[17] The governance-theoretic development of questions of morality thus makes it possible to approach business ethics via the values "willingness to cooperate" and "capability to cooperate" as the immanent problematic of the form of a cooperation project.

Organization

It follows from the foregoing that cooperation of self-interested economic actors can attain duration and stability only if conflict, dependence, and order in an organization and between organizations can be balanced and communicated in an appropriate way. In order to generate this balance economic incentive systems and organizational processes and controls are fundamental. However, during the last couple of years the discussion of corporate culture and an "economics of atmosphere"[18] has increasingly made clear that the management of "soft facts," atmosphere, and values is also of crucial importance. The integration of these economic and non-economic incentives and factors is the theoretical and practical core of the ethics of governance.

(i) Conflict in organizations initially and inevitably develops because of the self-interest and opportunism of team members, because of disagreements over the distribution of the cooperation rent, and because of differences in priorities given to the realization of tasks. Technical (procedure, control) and economic (incentives) methods of avoiding or overcoming such conflicts are aggravated by the bounded rationality of actors under conditions of informational, personal, and situational uncertainty and imperfect information. Shared moral values can make a contribution to the handling of conflict.

(ii) Dependency is a basic element in cooperative relationships. It arises from the fact that the success potential of actor A depends on the resources and behavior of actor B and vice versa. If resources were dependent but behavior-predictable, there would be no problem. If resources were independently controlled and behavior-unpredictable there would also be no problem. The problem consists in the exploitability of asymmetric dependencies between the actors by one of the actors via the collective cooperation rent that can be achieved only via this dependency. Shared moral values can make a contribution to containing opportunism.

(iii) Order is manifest in constitutions, standard operating procedures, management principles, guidelines, organizational charts, codes of ethics, ethics management systems, and implicit expectations of performance and behavior, all of which constitute the matrix of globally and locally effective governance structures. For this reason, cooperation projects can be described and analyzed as specific sets of rules and values. In doing so, we must distinguish between performance values (competence), interaction values (loyalty), and moral values (justice) that only together can enable economic cooperation of resource owners and that cannot be reduced to each other. Performance values, interaction values, and moral values form the basis of the two guiding values of firms as cooperation projects, i.e., the "willingness to cooperate" and the "capability to cooperate," and thus determine the number of the chances for cooperation a firm can attain.

(iv) Firms are communication systems. The significance of the role of formal and informal communication in production and cooperation has generated much organizational research in recent years.[19] For our topic it is important to note that firms are polylingual systems. Unlike the market, which has to code every event in prices in order to be able to communicate it, firms have to be able to simultaneously or selectively evaluate and process relevant events in many different "language games"—economy, technology, law, process, morality. The economic code—expenditure/return or cost/profit—has a lead function in the overall bundle of the polylingual resources of the firm when it comes to decisions; this reflects the fact that it is the market system that structures the environment of the firm. Firms are organizations of the economic system: everything relevant in firms has economic relevance or consequence. But not everything in the firm is economic.

We can draw three conclusions from the polylingual character of the firm. In the first place, firms have to build up a comprehensive incentive management that cannot be reduced to economic incentives.[20] In other words, moral values do matter. Secondly, an ethics that aims to achieve something in the firm can be incentive-sensitive and management-oriented without having to become economics. Thirdly, an ethics that seeks to protect itself against this and wants to be undertaken for its own sake is irrelevant in the real-life firms of the economy.

These conclusions follow from the polylingual character of economic cooperation projects, but they also have another basis. From an organizational point of view profits—as mentioned already—are not a maximization goal of firms as cooperation projects, but the inevitable limitation of the relevance of all language games in firms. In other words, profits are the most important, but not the only behavioral constraint of a firm. This methodological rearrangement of profit from a maximization function to a behavioral constraint is an immediate consequence of the rearrangement of the object of the discussion from "firms" to "governance structures for specific transactions." Whereas in the first case the focus of interest is the goal or purpose of the firm, in the second case the focus is on its capacity for adaptivity. A governance structure that would have "profit" as its only adaptive criterion would be inefficient with regard to its adaptive capability.

Moral Communication and Moral Incentives

We must now clarify the status of moral communication in firms. The "moral" does not structure the market environment of the firm, nor is it a behavioral constraint constituting the market. However, via the aspect of comprehensive incentive management and the polylingual character of organization, we have assigned it the status of a behavioral constraint and a resource for firms. Obviously it is relevant to take into account the management context and the way it functions when analyzing behavioral constraints and resources. But what is the role of moral communication in decisions of the firm as a cooperation project? In the economic literature this question often involves a focus on the social and informal character of moral rules and values.[21] These develop in an evolutionary way, exist in society, may well contain both threat and promise, and through these affect decisions of economic actors to a greater or lesser extent. We can accept this analysis, but we do not want to take on the implicit value-ethical interpretation of business ethics that comes with it. We prefer to focus on the ambiguity of evolutionary-derived and non-codified, that is, informal, social moral values. By doing so an interesting characteristic of moral values is exposed. Although in principle it is clear what is meant by moral values, in practice borders between the intended and the approved become fuzzy. Moral values are held in stock communicatively in society, but not in a form that is use-specific.[22] There is thus considerable demand for definition, control, and enforcement of those values that can be met on the level of persons, organizations, and social institutions. Personal societies such as ancient Europe found their moral base in the virtue of actors. Institutionalised societies such as modern Europe make use of specific governance structures for this purpose, e.g., the state or firms.

When firms design an explicit code of ethics,[23] they are attempting to transform moral ambiguity in their environment into organizational self-commitment by rules and values. Those codified rules and values then are firm-specific constitutional global governance structures, idiosyncratic moral resources, competences and capabilities of the organization.[24] From a transaction-cost economics perspective this represents an investment in "asset specificity,"[25] which I would designate "atmospheric specificity" for the execution of transactions. To the extent to which a firm invests in moral specificity and thus builds up a competency for the execution of transactions, it is committed to this investment. The factor-specific implications of moral communication in the firm are thus organizational identity as an economic and moral actor, transparency of claims to action and behavior, and the degree to which these are binding. Furthermore, the moral commitment involved is also an encouragement to a similar commitment on the part of organizational stakeholders (team members, customers, partners, suppliers). The ultimate intention is to attain stable behavioral expectations and control over the organizational and social environment of the firm by committing oneself and thus creating incentives for others to commit themselves as well. Self-commitment and commitment by others thus are the reasons for specific investments in the atmospheric parameters of a transaction.

At this point the significance of genuine moral incentives in polylingual organizations becomes obvious. Firms have economic incentives at their disposal, the relevance and effectiveness of which derive from the economic lead code of organizational systems. However, these have to be distinguished from moral incentives, which cannot be reduced to or transformed into economic incentives. But what do we know about moral incentives? In this investigation we implicitly distinguish between social, personal, and organizational moral incentives. Social moral incentives spring from enculturated moral convictions sanctioned by the majority of the members of society, which are thus intrinsically "intended." Virtues and notions of justice belong to this category. An example of personal moral incentives are lived virtues and credible role model behavior (moral character, charisma) by managers and leaders. Organizational moral incentives are, for instance, codes of ethics, ethics management systems, and ethics audit systems. Neither this characterization nor the examples cited are theoretically elaborated or complete. Their common characteristic, however, seems to be that their relevance depends on the fact that they are valued in themselves and because of their implications. It would be the task of a "theory of moral incentives"—which still needs to be written—to work out and account for these matters in detail.

We now proceed to investigate the specific efficiency of the governance mechanism of moral values. The investigation so far has led to the following conclusions: the economic lead code has a direct and long-acting effect on the cooperation rent achievable in firms via the expenditure/return and cost/profit conditions. The moral encoding works via organizational self-commitment (identity, transparency, binding nature) on the cooperation lead values "willingness to cooperate" and "capability to cooperate," and in this way on the cooperation chances of a firm. Moral self-commitment is activated selectively via reputation capital when transactions can affect this capital. This scheme explains firstly why governance ethics is not and should not be in demand by all firms; after all, manufacturers of screws have a different demand from social service providers. The scheme explains secondly why moral communication always carries a promise of performance that is contingent on self-commitment. We have already explained this in terms of the characteristics of firm- and transaction-specific investments in "atmosphere," but in this context we would like to point out that speech act theory in philosophy has arrived at similar results, in that it has shown that moral communication does have a performative character.[26] Those who talk about morality or codify moral values do not talk about facts but implicitly promise performance. Firms that have codes of ethics are not making statements about existent facts, but promising self-commitment to and self-organization of a performance promise. A firm thus commits itself through its moral communication and the communication's organization in a specific fashion, and thus creates behavioral expectations and behavioral standards for itself and others. If these expectations are disappointed this leads not only to the moral disregard of the collective actors, but also to costs due to loss of reputation or motivation or to political intervention. The reduction of cooperation chances has immediate effects on the level of the cooperation rent attainable. Economic and moral values and incentives thus, in their own distinctively specifiable ways, have an effect on the willingness to cooperate, the capability to cooperate, and the cooperation chances of a firm. Economic and moral values and incentives lose their respective identities only in the cooperation rent.

Definition of Governance Ethics

The differentiation of form- and process-determination of the firm and the ensuing differentiation of the form of the firm in the contract- and organizational relations of a cooperation project has enabled us to develop a view of business ethics on the basis of the governance characteristics of the firm itself. Business ethics, seen systemically, is neither external correction of negative external effects nor external enlightenment of economic stubbornness and blindness. It is rather a constitutive element of the firm itself, mediated by rules and values, governance ethics, and as such it is in every sense part of the economic problem of making possible the cooperation of self-interested actors in and via firms. "In every sense" implies that the economic and organizational relevance of the moral factor parallels its embeddedness in the economic and organizational context.

In conclusion we would like to draw consequences from the theoretical viewpoint outlined here which may be helpful in defining the role of an institutionalist business ethics as governance ethics.

1. The elements of governance ethics are the moral resources and behavioral constraints and extensions deriving from organizational rules and values as well as their communication in and via cooperation projects. Accordingly, it is not the notion of action, but of governance which is its point of reflexion. Governance structures are sets or matrices of communicated formal and informal rules and values that constitute the cooperative actor as constraints and furnish him or her with explicit and implicit rules of the game for contractual and organizational relations for the realisation of specific transactions.

2. Analytically, governance ethics investigates those global and local, formal and informal structures of a firm that constitute and transaction-specifically govern the moral behavior of the individual and collective actors in an organization (intrafirm-relations), between organizations (interfirm-relations), and between organizations and society (extrafirm-relations). The unit of analysis is thus a specific transaction in the context of and in its interaction with the governance structures surrounding it.

3. Methodologically, business ethics compares different structures for the governance of separate economic transactions; it asks which moral and immoral rules, values and incentives they reflect and which kind of economic behavior they reward. It explains the presence, relevance, and the change of moral preferences in the context of the economic and moral incentive structure of a given organization and its economic and social environment. Business ethics as governance ethics thus is a comparative research program.

4. In normative terms business ethics as governance ethics proposes the development and implementation of such ethical systems (e.g., ethics management systems, ethics audit systems[27]) in and by way of organizations. Those organizations—as governance structures for transactions—foster the willingness to cooperate, the capability to cooperate, and the cooperation chances of economic actors. It does this by creating economic and moral certainty of expectations

through providing self-commitment and indirect commitment of others. What is prioritised here is not profit maximization, but rents from the economizing of cooperation.

5. In conclusion: the governance ethics of the firm is the theory of the comparative analysis of a moral-sensitive design and communication of governance structures for specific economic transactions via cooperation.

Notes

1. For the translation of this essay I wish to thank Markus Becker. The original German term is *Unternehmensethik,* which carries the connotation of "corporate ethics."

2. Cf. Donaldson (1982), French (1984), Donaldson/Werhane (1988), Werhane (1985).

3. This research program was initiated by Williamson. For the interdisciplinary intentions connected to it cf. for example Williamson (1990, 1993). In this paper we will make use of contract-based, transaction-cost-based, and organizational (resource-based, economics of competencies; cf. Dosi/ Teece 1998; Teece/Pisano/Shuen 1997) considerations in explaining the role of "soft factors" (culture, communication, morality) in firms. With this, we are continuing our efforts of building an economic theory which is integrating these "soft factors" without dissolving them in the process. Cf. Wieland 1996a.

4. Cf. Williamson 1985, and the 1996 volume edited by Williamson with the telling title *The Mechanisms of Governance.*

5. Contemporary philosophy/ethics has never heard of organization, or at best accepts it as a peripheral phenomenon amongst several other issues. This ignorance as to a central societal actor and addressee of ethical claims is one of the conceptual problems of applied ethics that is blocking its theoretical development in a major way.

6. Cf. Vanberg 1992 and Gifford 1991. For the distinction of the notions of system, institution, and organization cf. Wieland 1997, pp. 62ff. It was Schmoller who made the first institutionalist inspired proposition for a distinction between institution and organization. Whereas institution for him is "the firm container of the action of generations" (Schmoller 1901, p. 61), organization is "the personal side of the institution" (ibid). Organizations are combinations of commodities and persons for a specific purpose. In this distinction, all the problems of contemporary institutionalist theory are already present, i.e., a static notion of institutions and a neglect of the normativity of organizations.

7. Cf. Williamson 1975.

8. In our understanding this insight presents a substantial contribution of German institutionalism to the theory of the firm. Cf. only Sombart (1902–1927/1987, pp. 101ff.), where he states that "the elevation of an independent economic organism over the individual economic human beings is guaranteeing its continual existence over time." Barnard (1938/1968) has shown in systems theoretic terms why precisely it is the exclusion of actors that represents the essence of the firm.

9. This, by the way, is one of the weaknesses of resource based organization theory. It does not treat the process of the constitution of the firm. At this point, contract-based theories are indispensable.

10. For the connection between the management of morality and stakeholders cf. Donaldson/Preston 1995.

11. For an early contribution to that insight cf. Schmoller (1901, pp. 414, 428f, 453). For the relevance of a differentiation of various types of contracts for a theory of the firm cf. Williamson 1991.

12. Of course the resignation from the profit motive is not a new idea, but commences with the development of an independent theory of the firm, independent of the Walrasian equilibrium model and price theory. For this part of the history of ideas cf. the interesting investigation by Krafft/Ravix (1998).

13. Shirking respectively the trade off between performance and control are the central problem of that branch of the theory of the firm that is oriented towards property rights. The classical text is Alchian/Demsetz 1972. However, they already emphasize the potential importance of moral values for the containing of shirking.

14. Cf. Dosi/Teece 1998. They do not take into consideration such a reformulation. They distinguish between theories of firms as production function, as optimal contract, and as organization. As long as this tripartite distinction will remain, there indeed is not much hope for theoretical integration. But contract theories have more to offer than optimal contracts. The theories of incomplete and implicit contracts (cf. Wieland 1996a, pp. 120ff., 158ff.) open the possibility of treating organizational phenomena in organizational terms, and to their own advantage.

15. For an overview cf. Bull 1983.

16. In Wieland 1998 we have pointed out the central sociological and managerial importance of cooperation and a theoretical notion capturing this aspect. This importance forms the basis for the arguments developed here.

17. Hobbes (1651/1914, pp. 68ff.) has described this particularity of contractual cooperation as a game-theoretic dilemma, the only escape from which is represented by rational calculation of advantage plus the power of the state to enforce plus implicit contracts (the covenant in the contract).

18. For the economics of atmosphere cf. Wieland 1996b and the literature referenced there.

19. Cf. Casson 1997 as well as Wieland 1999.

20. This connection has been clear since Xenophon, who in his *Oikonomikos* is building his human resource management and development theory for the *oikos* on this foundation. Cf. Wieland 1989, pp. 196ff.

21. This, by the way, is true for Williamson as well (1985, pp. 44, 271). In this way he is losing the option of a theory-endogenous parameter against opportunism.

22. The ancient Europe has attempted to cope with this characteristic of social moral communication by casuistry with approved exceptions. In functionally differentiated and abstract societies, however, the experience that now exceptions are more or less the rule has led to the situation that moral values have to be kept in stock in an abstractly justified way.

23. For this phenomenon cf. Weaver 1993 as well as Wieland 2001.

24. Cf. the already mentioned paper by Dosi/Teece (1998) as well as Barney 1991.

25. Cf. Williamson 1985, pp. 84ff., which distinguished site specificity, physical assets, human assets, and dedicated assets specificity. We propose an extension of this distinction to the notion of atmospheric specificity. In this way soft factors like culture, communication, and morals can be integrated into the theoretical framework of transaction cost theory.

26. Cf. in particular Searle 1969, chap. 8, and for the pertaining condition of sincerity Searle 1979, pp. 21ff.

27. Cf. the contributions of Center for Business Ethics (1992), Paine (1994), and Weaver/Trevino/Cochran (1999).

Ian Maitland

→ **NO**

Distributive Justice in Firms: Do the Rules of Corporate Governance Matter?

Can we achieve greater fairness by reforming the corporation? Some recent progressive critics of the corporation argue that it is possible to achieve greater social justice both inside and outside the corporation by simply rewriting or reinterpreting corporate rules to favor non-stockholders over stockholders. But the progressive program for reforming the corporation rests on a critical assumption, which I challenge in this [selection],[1] namely that the rules of the corporation matter, so that changing them can effect a lasting redistribution of wealth from stockholders to non-stockholders (for convenience I will refer to non-stockholders as "stakeholders"[2]). This [selection] uses a critique of the progressive reform program to make the case that the rules of the corporation are distributively neutral. The corporation as we know it isn't rigged against stakeholders, and changing its rules will not improve the bargaining power of stakeholders. However, the [selection] will show that while the rules may be epiphenomenal from the standpoint of distributive justice, they can have substantial impacts on the corporation's efficiency. As a result, the proposed reforms of the corporation may hurt its capacity to generate benefits for all the parties concerned.

The Progressive Program for Reforming the Corporation

This [selection] examines some recent "progressive" scholarship on the corporation and proposals for its reform.[3] In many respects, the progressive reformers advocate a model of the corporation strikingly similar to what business ethicists call the "stakeholder corporation." They favor rewriting the rules that govern the relations between stockholders and stakeholders to eliminate what they see as built-in biases in favor of stockholders. And they propose to use reform of the corporation as a vehicle for greater social justice in the work place and the marketplace. They view the rules of a corporation simultaneously as an embodiment of capitalist privilege and as a potential point of leverage for redistributing wealth and power.[4]

From *Business Ethics Quarterly*, vol. 11, no. 1, January 2001, pp. 129–143. Copyright © 2001 by Business Ethics Quarterly. Reprinted by permission of The Philosophy Documentation Center, publisher of Business Ethics Quarterly. References omitted.

It is a key premise of the progressive critique of the corporation that its rules are not neutral between the different constituencies of the corporation. Thus David Millon argues that the important rules that govern the relations between stockholders and stakeholders are systematically biased in favor of stockholders. The rules of the corporation do not simply mirror background inequalities in society but actually create and reinforce those inequalities. As Joseph Singer puts it, "[t]he current legal rules created that imbalance of power [between workers and corporations in the market], and they can be altered to equalize it."[5]

Some of these rules are rules of corporate law, and some are not. As examples of the former, Millon cites voting rights in the corporation, limited liability, and management's fiduciary duty to run the corporation in the exclusive interest of stockholders (the "stockholder primacy principle"). Employment-at-will, on the other hand, is a common law doctrine. All of these rules confer powers and immunities on stockholders while imposing disadvantages on stakeholders or exposing them to certain contingencies or costs.

However, this non-neutrality cuts both ways. If the rules of the corporation are rigged in favor of stockholders, then that bias can be eliminated by simply changing the rules. But why stop there? The reformers want to structure the rules of the corporation to advance the progressive agenda of redistributing power and wealth in the broader society. If the relative power of stockholders and stakeholders is a function (in part) of the current legal rules, then those rules can be rewritten to redress that imbalance or even to tip the scales in favor of stakeholders.

> To a large extent, it is contract and property law that will determine [the parties'] relative bargaining power. If we want to protect the most vulnerable party to the relationship in times of economic stress, we have no alternative but to make them less vulnerable. This means systematically interpreting and changing property and contract principles in ways that effectively redistribute power and wealth to workers.[6]

In summary, the progressives claim that rules matter. Accordingly, the rules furnish a point of leverage for altering the outcomes of the corporation so that they favor stakeholder groups and thereby redistributing power and wealth in society.

Neutrality Thesis

In opposition to the progressive view, this [selection] argues that the rules don't matter. The null hypothesis, or neutrality thesis, proposed here, is that the corporation is distributively neutral. Appearances notwithstanding, the rules don't systematically favor stockholders, and they cannot be manipulated so as to favor stakeholder groups like employees. The corollary is that proposals to change the rules to favor stakeholders will not have any systematic effect on the distributive impacts of the corporation.

This does not mean that existing outcomes are in some way equitable or in conformity with distributive justice. It is simply to say that the rules are neutral, in the sense that they passively pass along or mirror pre-existing inequalities of resources (where resources are to be broadly conceived as wealth, energy, skill, cunning, etc.).

This [essay] does not present a fully rounded or comprehensive account of the progressive critique of the corporation but instead focuses on certain propositions concerning the impact of corporate rules on distributive justice inside the corporation.

The Rules of Corporate Governance

The case for the neutrality of the corporation is rooted in the observation that the rules of corporate governance are essentially voluntary. This claim may seem odd, given the fact that the rules are prescribed by law. But, although we refer to "corporate law," as if the rules were commanded by legislatures or by common law, the reality is that the rules of the corporation are more accurately viewed as being self-imposed. The law does not mandate the rules. Instead, it provides a framework or template of "default" rules, which the parties or groups making up the corporation (stockholders, employees, etc.) remain free to modify or waive by agreement.

Thus nothing in the law stops corporations from accepting unlimited liability for any debts they may incur or from agreeing to override the law's presumption of at-will employment. Nor does the law prevent representatives of employees from sitting on the board of the corporation or from bargaining for the right to have management owe them fiduciary duties. Many progressive scholars concede this point. Millon notes that, "It is true that . . . the affected parties can reverse the assignment of benefit and burden specified by the rule should they choose to do so. Thus, of course, a creditor can bargain for unlimited stockholder liability or for voting rights."[7] Another critic of the corporation, Margaret Blair, notes that, "[b]ecause U.S. corporation law, contract law, and securities law readily accommodate most experiments in new organizational forms, many new governance structures are emerging on their own. This is one of the strengths of the U.S. system."[8]

If the rules are voluntary, then what purpose is served by state law codes or common law rules of corporate governance? The standard answer is that such laws reduce the costs of contracting (or "transaction costs") for the parties by providing a standard contract for governing their relations. That way the parties do not need to re-invent the corporation by explicitly negotiating the whole set of rules from scratch. "[S]hareholders typically contract with management by entering into the standard-form agreement applied by the relevant state law code and corpus of common law. This 'off-the-rack' contract includes a collection of terms that stockholders would typically prefer, so including them greatly reduces transaction costs."[9] Many (though not all) can be modified by express contract if the stockholders so choose.

The fact that the corporate form of organization—with its familiar structure of entitlements and obligations—is the dominant one in our economy may leave the impression that it is somehow mandatory. But the law provides other organizational forms to choose from. These include sole proprietorships, partnerships, cooperatives, trusts, and non-firm relational contracts, such as franchises and long-term supply contracts. In addition, there is an almost infinite variety of arrangements that the parties might conceivably fashion by agreement. Of course, not only are the parties free to take or leave the rules provided by the law, but also nothing prevents them from choosing not to contract with a corporation at all, or from limiting their business to other types of business organization.[10] On this account, then, the corporation is essentially a voluntary association. It exists only because the parties that make it up choose it as a means of governing their relationships.

If the corporation is voluntary, why would some groups agree to terms that seem so clearly inequitable? Why would employees accept, say, rules providing for employment at will or exclusion from voting rights in the corporation? Answers to this question make up the heart of the financial or contractarian theory of the firm developed by Fama and Jensen and others.[11] I won't try to summarize that extensive literature here. But the gist of it is that rights in the firm (say, voting rights) go to the highest bidders. That leaves the question of why stockholders would consistently outbid other groups for management's fiduciary loyalty and for voting control. Contractarian theorists explain that stockholders have the greatest stake in the outcome of corporate decision making because they occupy a peculiarly vulnerable position in the corporation. As "residual claimants" they differ from other groups in that they are not entitled to a guaranteed return. Their share is what is left over (if anything) after every other group's contractually specified claims have been met. That gives stockholders a special interest in the efficient management of the corporation. If efficiency is maximized, then, over the long run, the corporation is better able to provide benefits for all participants.

On this view of the firm, the distribution of rights in the corporation is the outcome of bargaining between the different groups or parties. Since nothing in the law bars it, employees might (and indeed frequently do) contract for protection from arbitrary dismissal. But they have to "buy" that protection with lower wages. Conversely, if stockholders value the right to lay off employees at will more than employees value their job security, they may buy that right with higher wages.

Interestingly, the progressive scholars largely accept the contractarian account of the corporation. Nevertheless they argue that the corporation is rigged against stakeholders. They charge that the corporation does not merely reproduce existing imbalances of social power and wealth but creates and reinforces them. This charge is difficult (if not impossible) to reconcile with the contractarian view of the firm as a voluntary association. It would mean that stakeholders are consistently duped or manipulated by stockholders into accepting bargains that are inferior to the ones they could have achieved.

The thesis of this [selection] is that the rules of the corporation are distributively neutral. If that is the case, then we should observe two things: (a) that existing rules don't discriminate against stakeholders, and (b) that proposed changes in the rules won't make non-stockholders better off. The next section examines specific rules and proposed changes to those rules in order to see if these two predictions hold.

Progressive Proposals for Changing the Rules of the Corporation

Extending Fiduciary Duties

One perennially popular rule change would extend management's fiduciary duties to other parties, like employees. Management would no longer operate the corporation in the exclusive interests of the stockholders but would be required by law to balance the interests of stockholders with those of employees and other stakeholders.[12]

What would be the distributive effects of such a rule change? There could be a once-for-all expropriation of current stockholders. That is, if the law was introduced, enacted, and signed overnight, stockholders would wake up the next day to find that they were no longer the sole beneficiaries of management's fiduciary obligations. They would (literally) be poorer because the anticipated lower returns and increased risk would be reflected in a lower stock market valuation of their shares.

But any benefit to employees would be short-lived as investors would hesitate to buy corporations' shares, would hold off investing, and/or would demand a premium to reflect the added risk and lower return. Investors cannot be compelled to supply capital to American corporations. They can instead buy real estate, gold, Treasury bonds or shares in Japanese corporations, or they can invest in orchards,[13] to mention a few examples. If the risk-adjusted return from owning shares in U.S. corporations falls below that from alternative investments, then we should expect a flight of capital to alternative investments.[14]

In such circumstances, in order to attract the capital necessary to finance their operations, corporations would be forced to take steps to increase the prospective return to stockholders. That would likely require cutting wages, raising prices, laying off workers, etc. In short, it would require changes that would defeat the purpose of changing the fiduciary rule in the first place. Of course, those actions might be complicated—if not barred altogether—by management's new fiduciary duties to stakeholders. In that case, corporations might simply be unable to raise new capital. In due course, this would mean that corporations would find it difficult to expand their operations, there would be a drastic reduction in business start-ups relying on equity capital, and employment would suffer. All the parties to the corporation would be losers from the resulting economic disruptions.[15]

Employment-at-Will

David Millon argues that the employment-at-will rule favors stockholders over employees. It "confers freedom of action on stockholders while imposing costs on employees that would not be present if the default rule were a presumption of employment security."[16] Millon admits that, like other corporate rules, the employment-at-will rule is an optional or default rule, but he claims that even "mere" default rules have distributive consequences. Thus, by replacing the employment-at-will rule by an employment-security rule, we can increase the bargaining leverage of employees and enable them to capture a greater share of the benefits of the corporation. If we reverse the existing biases, "starting points will differ, and outcomes therefore will too."[17]

According to Millon, "a rule like the employment-at-will doctrine makes stockholders wealthier than an employment-security doctrine would." Under employment-at-will, if employees want protection against arbitrary dismissal, they have to *pay* stockholders for it. By contrast, if the rule were reversed, "stockholders would either have to compensate employees following termination of employment or would have to bribe them into giving up a property right in their job. The bias . . . has the potential to affect significantly the respective wealth of stockholders and stakeholders."[18]

Employees are also disadvantaged by the employment-at-will rule in cases where transaction costs prevent the parties from agreeing on trading a wage reduction for job security. There may be substantial, and sometimes prohibitive, costs associated with negotiating and drafting a satisfactory agreement. These "transaction costs" may prevent employees from reaching an agreement even if both sides would gain from it. In such a case, the default rule, viz., employment-at-will, will hold, and employees will find themselves stuck with the *status quo*, namely no job protection.

But Millon's scenario can't withstand close scrutiny. For simplicity, suppose that there are two types of firms, ones that provide job security to their employees and ones that do not. Under an employment-at-will regime, it is reasonable to assume that, other things (like employee characteristics) equal, firms that provide job security pay lower wages than firms that do not. (Otherwise, firms providing job security would have higher labor costs and/or risks which would over time lead to their failure).

Now suppose that we adopt Millon's proposal to replace employment-at-will with employment security as our default rule. Under the new rule, firms that don't provide job security will be required to start doing so *or* to compensate their employees for giving up their right to job security. (Firms that already provide job security will be unaffected.) Recall, however, that firms without job security were *already* paying higher wages. As a result of the rule change, such firms will be faced with a choice between (a) providing job security (*and* continuing to pay the higher wage) or (b) giving employees an additional wage increase (on top of the original premium they enjoy) in return for the right to dismiss at will. In either case, such firms will have unsustainably higher labor costs. Consequently, they will be forced to reduce wages to competitive levels or to go out of business. In either case, of course, there will be no lasting redistribution of wealth from stockholders to employees.

However, while the distributive effect of the initial default rules will be nonexistent or trivial, the real-world efficiency effects might be substantial. By "real-world," I mean that we reintroduce transaction costs into the example. Suppose employees value employment-security guarantees less than stockholders disvalue them, then a rule that provides for employment-security will—in the presence of significant transaction costs—make both stockholders and employees worse off. If the parties are unable to reach an agreement to override the employment-security guarantees in exchange for higher wages, then they will both be poorer than if the rule had been employment-at-will.

This example illustrates why (as economists urge) it is mutually beneficial if default rules are set to reflect the outcomes that the parties *would have* (but for transaction costs) agreed on. That way they can help the parties economize on transaction costs "by supplying standard contract terms the parties would otherwise have to adopt by [expensive] express agreement."[19] In other words, Millon's proposal, by trying to correct an imaginary bias in the rules, will likely make it more difficult for parties to reach a mutually advantageous bargain. As a result, the proposal to flip the rules so that they favor stakeholders may actually wind up hurting the very people it is intended to help.[20]

Limited Liability

Millon also charges that limited liability "benefit[s] stockholders while having a correspondingly negative effect on creditors, who . . . lose a degree of financial security that a rule of unlimited liability would otherwise provide."[21] The rule "limit[s] stockholders' liability to corporate creditors to their capital contribution, leaving creditors to bear the risk of corporate insolvency."[22]

That account is accurate as far as it goes. But Millon is mistaken in thinking that limited liability has any distributive implications. That is because, as Posner has pointed out, creditors are paid to bear this risk. "The lender is fully compensated for the risk of default by the higher interest rate that the corporation must pay lenders by virtue of its limited liability."[23] Furthermore, creditors are "also free to insist as a condition of making the loan that the stockholders personally guarantee the corporation's debts, or insert in the loan agreement other provisions limiting the lender's risk. Any resulting reduction in the risk of default will of course reduce the interest rate."[24]

One risk facing creditors is the possibility of nonpayment because of limited liability. Another risk, according to Easterbrook and Fischel, is the "prospect, common to all debtor-creditor relations, that after the terms of the transaction are set the debtor will take increased risk, to the detriment of the lender."[25] However, as they go on to note,

> As long as these risks are known, the firm pays for the freedom to engage in risky activities. Any creditor can get the risk-free rate by investing in T-bills or some low-risk substitute. The firm must offer a better risk-return combination to attract investment. If it cannot make credible promises to refrain from taking on excessive risks, it must pay higher interest rates (or, when the creditors are employees and trade creditors, higher prices for the work or goods delivered on credit). Although managers may change the riskiness of the firm after borrowing, debt must be repaid; this drives the firm back to the credit market, where it must pay a rate of interest appropriate to the soundness and risk of its current projects. . . . Voluntary creditors receive compensation in advance for the chance that the firm will step up the risk of its projects and later be unable to meet its obligations.[26]

Of course, creditors, too, enjoy limited liability. What is more, in the event of bankruptcy their claims on the corporation's assets outrank the claims of stockholders. Finally, lenders are not compelled to extend credit to the corporation. If limited liability is such a bargain, they are free to use their funds to purchase stock in the corporation instead.

Legal Obligation Arising out of Interdependence

Another proposed reform would change the rules of the corporation to recognize a legally enforceable right to job security arising out of longstanding and/or dependent relationships. Marleen O'Connor advocates that the courts should recognize a right to job security in cases of long-run employment. Joseph Singer proposes that the courts should recognize employees' property rights in longstanding relationships on which they have come to depend. He says "It is morally wrong for the owner to allow a relationship of dependence to be established and then cut off the dependent party."[27]

What would be the distributional impacts of such a rule change? Stockholders would likely be able to defeat or circumvent such a rule or, failing that, shift its cost back to employees. In that event, employees would find themselves forced to purchase a right (job security or severance pay) which they value less than what they would give up (wages and employment opportunities) in exchange for it.[28]

The set of possible responses by stockholders is limited only by the imagination. One obvious move would be to write into all employment contracts a disclaimer by which employees expressly waived their right to such job protection. Of course, the courts might choose to ignore or override such disclaimers.[29] That would still leave stockholders with many options which they might use singly or in combination to get around the rule.

If courts chose to ignore waivers of job security, then stockholders' specific responses would depend on how the rule was framed or interpreted. If courts relied on employees' length of service to determine whether they were owed job security, then the rule would perversely encourage stockholders to dismiss employees shortly before their claims to job security vested. Alternatively, if the courts relied on some measure of dependency or intimacy, stockholders might avoid such relationships with their employees.

Alternatively corporations might develop a two-tier work force with a core of highly skilled workers (who would enjoy job security) and a peripheral floating population of casual or temporary or contract workers (without job security).[30] Only the first would qualify for the legal privileges that come with a long-term relationship with the corporation. In any case, corporations would be cautious about expanding employment because of the legal barriers in the way of lay-offs in the event of a downturn in business. Therefore they would likely respond to increased demand for their products by increasing overtime, speeding up the line or working employees more intensively.

Another possibility is that stockholders might try to offset the expected costs of job security by reducing wages or (if that was impractical) by granting smaller wage increases and/or cutting back on any discretionary benefits (subsidized lunches or parking, pension contributions, etc.). If payroll costs could not be stabilized in this way, stockholders would shift to more capital-intensive production methods, and would reduce employment or increase it more gradually.[31] If the real wages of workers were increased by the implicit cost of greater job security, the stockholders would find it unprofitable to hire "marginal" workers because the value of their marginal product would be less than the cost of employing them.

In the short run, it might be possible for stockholders to pay the higher real wages and pass their cost along to consumers in the form of higher product prices. However, such price increases would not be sustainable in the long run. Of course, any reduced demand as a result of the price increases would mean lower employment. If the stockholders found themselves unable to pass the increased real wages along to consumers or employees, the resulting lower rates of return would eventually cause firms to exit the industry and/or would reduce the flow of investment capital to the industry, thus limiting employment growth. If companies expect to face heavy costs if they have to close a plant, they are going to be more reluctant to open new plants, knowing that the penalty for misjudging the market will be more severe.

One of the ironies of such a rule is that it would impose an implicit "tax" on the very behaviors we would generally wish to encourage—long-term employment relationships, the hiring of marginal workers, and so on. In self-defense, stockholders would avoid relationships with employees that might lock them into an onerous commitment.

Employee Rights in Cases of Plant Closure

The same objections apply to Joseph Singer's proposal to rewrite the rules to give employees a right to purchase their plant for its "fair market value" in the event that the stockholders declare their intention to close it down.

Singer acknowledges that employees might not choose to exercise their right, under such a rule, to buy their plant and keep it in operation. But he says that the rule would be a useful bargaining chip for employees: "[I]f we . . . give workers a right to assert an ownership interest in the plant when the company wants to close it or when the company fails to manage the plant well, then the company would have to offer the workers more than the workers would ask to give up this right. Because the workers would *own* this right, their wealth would be dramatically higher than if the company had the legal liberty to destroy the plant."[32]

As I have noted, employees would get the right to purchase the plant at its "fair market value." That is what Singer says, but it doesn't seem to be what he means. Nothing in the current rules stops employees from banding together and offering to buy the plant. If their bid is higher than the next best alternative bid, then stockholders will presumably accept their offer. That is, employees appear already to enjoy the right that Singer wants to confer on them. What's more, if the employees acquire the plant at its market value, there is no transfer of wealth.

A transfer of wealth from stockholders to employees would happen only if the rules permitted employees to buy the plant at *less* than its market value. But a rule that permitted employees to buy the plant at *less* than what other bidders might pay for it would predictably lead stockholders to take certain actions in their self-defense.[33] Employees would presumably be paid less than they would absent the law. Stockholders would in effect withhold an implicit insurance "premium" from each worker's wage. They might attempt to mitigate the possible additional expense of closure by renting rather than buying plant and equipment. Macey's observations on compulsory plant closing notification apply *a fortiori* to Singer's rule. He says that "if a legislature unilaterally gives rank-and-file workers a right to prior notification of a layoff or a plant closing, the workers will benefit only if, to retain that right, they will not have to give up something worth more than the right itself. The price of the forced 'purchase' of a right to notification may take the form of lower wages, reduced pension benefits, or a reduction in the overall size of the work force."[34]

That is not all. The added difficulty or expense of closing down a money-losing plant would likely make corporations more wary of opening new plants in the first place—especially in marginal areas where alternative employment opportunities are few. As Richard McKenzie has said, restrictions on plant closings are restrictions on plant openings.[35]

In summary, Singer's rule would not have any obvious redistributive effects. But, once again, it might worsen the lot of *both* stockholders and stakeholders by putting obstacles in the way of their agreeing on the optimal contract terms.

Courts as Guardians of Employees' Interests

Some progressive critics of the corporation suggest that the courts should aggressively interpret the law in favor of stakeholders. Singer says that "means systematically interpreting and changing property and contract principles in ways that effectively redistribute power and wealth to workers."[36] O'Connor favors using an expansive interpretation of management's fiduciary duty to tip the scales in favor of the vulnerable. She says that the "courts can use the fiduciary duty to prevent opportunistic behavior even where the terms of the contract explicitly allow the stronger party to engage in this type of conduct."[37] She would have courts to set aside contracts or override contract terms on grounds of distributive justice or "common morality." Although O'Connor invokes supposed "implicit contracts" between stockholders and employees, it is clear that she intends the courts to disregard the actual intentions of the parties (whether express or implicit). The content of the corporations' duties to employees would no longer be defined by the parties' explicit or implicit agreements but by some external standard of social justice or the conscience of the court.

But it is doubtful whether such judicial activism could actually help stakeholders vis-à-vis stockholders. Once again, the crucial point is that investors are not compelled to invest their capital in corporations. If the courts deliberately tilted in favor of stakeholders, then to attract equity capital stakeholders would have to try to devise safeguards to reassure investors.

It is impossible to imagine exactly what forms such safeguards might take. If investors anticipate that the courts will systematically discriminate against them, and disregard the agreements they strike with stakeholders, then they have various (non-mutually exclusive) options. First, they might demand compensation from stakeholders for the additional risk they would have to bear. Second, they might insist on bypassing the courts and resolving their disputes by means of arbitration. (There would be an incentive for workers to band together in "firms" which would seek to acquire a reputation for *not* resorting to the courts in order to opportunistically renege on their agreements with stockholders. That reputation would permit them to lower the cost of capital to themselves.) Third, if it is too costly or impractical for investors to protect themselves by these means (or others), they might simply decide that it is pointless to invest in the stock of U.S. corporations. In that case, all the parties would forgo the benefits that the corporation might have created.

The point is that stockholders and stakeholders alike *need* the courts as a guarantor and/or impartial arbiter of their agreements with one another. Otherwise those (mutually advantageous) agreements may be too risky to enter into in the first place. Consequently, both sides are the losers when the courts define their mission as achieving their own conceptions of social justice in place of giving effect to the intent of the parties. As Easterbrook and Fischel have noted, "future contracting parties, viewing the court's selective enforcement of the present contract, will try to take steps to avoid the disappointment of having their contract selectively enforced. But these steps will cause the parties to incur additional contracting costs, additional over which they would be if the act simply enforced perfect contracts."[38]

Conclusion: How Liberty Upsets Patterns

This [selection] has shown that, on close examination, many corporate rules that appear to be biased in favor of stockholders prove to be neutral and nondiscriminatory. That should not come as a surprise since the rules are essentially voluntary. What would have been surprising would have been the discovery that parties continued to do business with the corporation on terms that are manifestly disadvantageous.

Moreover, precisely because the corporation is a voluntary association, an externally mandated rule change that is intended to achieve greater distributive justice is bound to fail. The parties themselves, including the supposed beneficiaries of the rule, are likely to collude to defeat it, because they all have a stake in maintaining the corporation as a going concern. A rule change that redistributes benefits and costs among the parties without regard to their contributions jeopardizes the carefully constructed bargain on which the corporation is based. If the party that loses from the rule change is not compensated for its loss, then its contribution to the corporation will exceed its benefits, and it will look outside the corporation for returns commensurate with its contribution. Meanwhile, the beneficiary of the rule change will enjoy benefits that exceed its contribution, and it will have to compensate the loser(s) from the rule change in order to retain its cooperation.

Contractarian theorists call the firm a nexus of contracts. If the totality of contracts that make up the corporation (including mandated contract terms or rules) does not accurately value the contributions made respectively by employees, creditors, suppliers, etc. then it is likely to be unstable. In that case, the rules of the corporation cannot be rigged to favor stockholders—or to favor stakeholders either. Therefore the rules can't furnish the point of leverage the progressive reformers of the corporation want in order to implement their program of social reform.

Notes

1. I would like to thank Thomas L. Carson, Alexei Marcoux and Patricia H. Werhane for their comments on an earlier draft of this paper.

2. Strictly, of course, stockholders are stakeholders too, along with employees, customers, vendors, lenders, and, sometimes, local communities.

3. Some of this work is usefully collected in Lawrence E. Mitchell, ed., *Progressive Corporate Law* (Boulder, Col.: Westview Press, 1995). See also Amitai Etzioni, "A Communitarian Note on Stakeholder Theory," *Business Ethics Quarterly* 8 (1998): 679–691.

4. Stakeholder theories also invoke distributive justice. See Thomas Donaldson and L. E. Preston, "The Stakeholder Theory of the Corporation: Concepts, Evidence, and Implications," *Academy of Management Review* 20 (1995): 84.

5. Joseph William Singer, "The Reliance Interest in Property," *Stanford Law Review* 40 (1983): 729.

6. Singer, "Reliance Interest," p. 723.

7. David Millon, "Communitarianism in Corporate Law: Foundations and Law Reform Strategies," in Mitchell, *Progressive Corporate Law,* p. 24.

8. Margaret M. Blair, *Ownership and Control* (Washington, D.C.: Brookings, 1995), p. 277.

9. Millon, "Communitarianism," p. 3.

10. "[N]o one is forced to use the corporate form of organization. . . . Thus, we do not observe all economic activity being carried on through one type of economic activity. Instead, we observe millions of organizations of many types, sizes, and structures" (Henry N. Butler and Larry E. Ribstein, *The Corporation and the Constitution* [Washington, D.C.: AEI Press, 1995], p. 4).

11. Eugene F. Fama and Michael C. Jensen, "Separation of Ownership and Control," *Journal of Law and Economics* 26 (1983): 301–325; Michael C. Jensen and William H. Meckling, "Theory of the Firm: Managerial Behavior, Agency Costs and Ownership Structure," *Journal of Financial Economics* 3 (1976): 305–360. See also Frank H. Easterbrook and Daniel R. Fischel, *The Economic Structure of Corporate Law* (Cambridge, Mass.: Harvard University Press, 1991).

12. Kenneth E. Goodpaster terms this a "multi-fiduciary" theory of managerial responsibility in "Business Ethics and Stakeholder Analysis," *Business Ethics Quarterly* 1 (1991): 53–73. See also Etzioni: "The stakeholder argument . . . accepts the legitimacy of the claim that shareholders have . . . rights and

entitlements, but maintains that the same basic claim should be extended to all those who invest in the corporation. This often includes employees (especially those who worked for a corporation for many years and loyally); the community . . . ; creditors . . . ; and, under some conditions, clients" (Etzioni, "Stakeholder Theory," p. 682, emphasis omitted); and John Orlando, "The Fourth Wave: The Ethics of Corporate Downsizing," *Business Ethics Quarterly* 9 (1999): 295–313.

13. "When we adjust for the risks involved and for various other factors that influence the return to an activity, we see that the returns most firms earn are not excessive compared to what the same resources could have earned in such manifestly non-exploitative alternatives as tree growing" (Robert Frank, *Choosing the Right Pond* [New York: Oxford University Press, 1985], p. 39). See also Easterbrook and Fischel, *Corporate Law,* p. 213.

14. This would not take the form of a "capital strike," as suggested by Lindblom, but would be the result of uncoordinated actions of millions of investors each acting in rational self-defense (Charles E. Lindblom, *Politics and Markets* [New York: Basic, 1977]).

15. The cost of the rule change would be borne by its beneficiaries. "Any legal regime that 'protects' workers by making them the 'beneficiaries' of fiduciary duties will, by definition, make those same workers less valuable (in monetary terms) to their employers. . . . Since workers generally prefer to receive compensation in the form of cash wages rather than in other ways, even the workers themselves will prefer that fiduciary duties not be imposed on employers since such duties will, at the margin, result in lower cash compensation to workers" (Jonathan R. Macey, "An economic analysis of the various rationales for making shareholders the exclusive beneficiaries of corporate fiduciary duties," *Stetson Law Review* 21 (1991): 37–38).

16. Millon, "Communitarianism," p. 24.

17. Ibid., p. 31.

18. Ibid., p. 28.

19. Richard A. Posner, *Economic Analysis of Law* (Boston: Little, Brown and Co., 1977), p. 396.

20. Note that an employment-security rule might be more efficient than an employment-at-will rule. This essay is agnostic on that point. However, the rule change would be neutral from the standpoint of distributive justice.

21. Millon, "Communitarianism," p. 26.

22. Ibid., p. 23.

23. Posner, *Economic Analysis,* p. 395. Posner suggests various reasons why creditors (rather than stockholders) might be better placed to bear the risk of business failure. Assume the lender is a bank. The bank might be in a better position to appraise the risk than is the individual investor who may know little or nothing about the business he has invested in. Then, also, the stockholder is likely to be more risk-averse than the bank.

24. Ibid.

25. *Corporate Law,* p. 50.

26. Ibid., p. 51. "Equity investors and managers have incentives to make arrangements that reduce risk and thus reduce the [interest rate] premium they must

pay to debt claimants" (p. 51). The parties may also purchase insurance. As Easterbrook and Fischel say, "The ability of potential victims to protect themselves against loss through insurance is a strong reason for disregarding distributional concerns in choosing among liability rules" (p. 52).

27. Singer, "Reliance Interest," p. 667. See also Marleen A. O'Connor, "Promoting Economic Justice in Plant Closings: Exploring the Fiduciary/Contract Law Distinction to Enforce Implicit Employment Agreements," in Mitchell, *Progressive Corporate Law*, pp. 224 *et seq.* According to Etzioni, "[a] fair number of court decisions recognize employees' rights to employment by the corporation for which they have been working, based on good faith implied by continuous satisfactory service" ("Stakeholder theory," p. 684).

28. Otherwise why would employees not already have purchased this right in return for lower wages? Or, what is probably the more usual case, why would they have chosen employment in a firm that insisted on its right to dismiss at will?

29. Millon, "Communitarianism," p. 10.

30. New jobs in Europe tend to be temporary or casual owing to the difficulty of firing regular staff. Moreover, in Europe "those out of work for more than a year account for one-third of the unemployed" (Gary Becker, "Unemployment in Europe and the United States," *Journal des Economistes et des Etudes Humaines,* 7 [1996]: 101. Cited by David Schmidtz in Schmidtz and Robert E. Goodin, *Social Welfare and Individual Responsibility* [New York: Cambridge University Press, 1996]).

31. "Laws in many European countries, including Germany, Italy, and France, make it all but impossible to fire people. So companies don't hire—they invest in equipment instead." Thomas K. Grose, "Labor, Social Costs, Taking Toll on Governments," *USA Today,* September 19, 1996, pp. B–1, 2. Cited in Schmidtz and Goodin, *Social Welfare.*

32. Singer, "Reliance Interest," pp. 722–723. See also Orlando, "The Fourth Wave."

33. It also assumes *employees* won't change their behavior. But, as Jonathan R. Macey has pointed out, if employees can acquire the plant at *less* than fair market value, then they will be tempted to sabotage its operations and drive it into bankruptcy. See "Symposium: Fundamental Corporate Changes: Causes, Effects, and Legal Responses: Externalities, Firm-specific Capital Investments, and the Legal Treatment of Fundamental Corporate Changes," *Duke Law Journal,* February 1989, p. 193.

34. Macey, "Symposium," p. 180.

35. Ian Maitland, "Rights in the Workplace: A Nozickian Argument," *Journal of Business Ethics,* 1989, p. 953; Richard B. McKenzie, "The Case for Plant Closures," *Policy Review* 15 (1981): 122.

36. Singer, "Reliance Interest," p. 723.

37. O'Connor, "Plant Closings," p. 233.

38. Easterbrook and Fischel, *Corporate Law,* p. 231.

POSTSCRIPT

Can Restructuring a Corporation's Rules Make a Moral Difference?

Can the corporation live a moral life? For that matter, can *I* live a moral life? This is not the kind of question one can answer in a day, or a week after reading some contrary views on the subject. But it must be answered somehow, and the less we think about it, the more definitively will it be answered by our actions. Corporations have often developed corporate "codes of conduct" or "vision statements," affirming a fundamental recognition of the importance of ethical behavior in business, but just as often they have left us in doubt about the motivation for the code. Was the intention of the "code" to help people live more ethical lives for their own sake? Was it a public relations ploy, to impress neighbors and regulators or to get more favorable treatment from the local zoning board and inspectors? Was it intended as a legal lever, to put corporate officers in a position to fire employees whose aggressive business practices become an embarrassment to the firm, or to get credit for an "ethics program" under the federal sentencing guidelines? Sometimes, corporate executives extol the moral life only, as they will tell us, to keep the lowest-paid workers honest. Where do you stand on the issue?

Suggested Reading

You might want to follow up on this topic, in company with the new literature on the corporate code. The following sources may be of interest:

James Anderson and Elaine Englehardt. *The Organizational Self and Ethical Conduct: Sunlit Virtue and Shadowed Resistance.* (New York: Harcourt Brace, 2001).

D.M. Messick and M.H. Bazerman, "Ethics for the 21st Century: A Decision Making Perspective," *Sloan Management Review* (1996).

R. Murray Lindsay, Linda M. Lindsay, and V. Bruce Irvine, "Instilling Ethical Behavior in Organizations: A Survey of Canadian Companies," *Journal of Business Ethics,* vol. 15, no. 4 (April 1996).

James S. Harvey, Jr., "Reinforcing Ethical Decision Making Through Organizational Structure." *Journal of Business Ethics,* vol. 28, no. 1. November 2000.

O. Scott Stovall, John D. Neill, and David Perkins, "Corporate Governance, Internal Decision Making, and the Invisible Hand," *Journal of Business Ethics,* vol. 51, No. 2, May 2004.

Tracey C. Rembert, "CSR in the Crosshairs: A Broad Counter-Attack Against Corporate Reform Is Growing. (Could That Be a Sign of Progress?)" from *Business Ethics,* vol. 19, no. 1, Spring 2005.

ISSUE 3

Is Increasing Profits the Only Social Responsibility of Business?

YES: Milton Friedman, from "The Social Responsibility of Business Is to Increase Its Profits," *The New York Times Magazine*, September 13, 1970.

NO: Joe DesJardins, "Business and Environmental Sustainability," *Business and Professional Ethics* Vol. 24, nos 1 & 2.

ISSUE SUMMARY

YES: Friedman argues that businesses have neither the right nor the ability to fool around with "social responsibility" as distinct from profit-making. They serve employees and customers best when they do their work with maximum efficiency. The only restrictions on the pursuit of profit that Friedman accepts are the requirements of law and "the rules of the game" ("open and free competition without deception or fraud").

NO: DesJardins explains that in the early years of the 21st century, we face a set of serious economic, ecological, and ethical challenges that require businesses to accept social responsibilities that support their own environmental sustainability and help meet the real needs of billions of people around the globe. He suggests various ways in which businesses might go about this without sacrificing profitability.

Four decades ago, one of the most controversial business ethics statements of the past century was made by economist Milton Friedman when he declared that the only social responsibility of business is to increase its profits. He said that objectives for business such as eliminating discrimination, improving the environment, and providing employment were "pure and unadulterated socialism." Should a company think past the bottom line and try to do good, or at least avoid doing evil in the world? Beyond staying within the boundaries of law and engaging in free and open competition while trying to maximize profits, Friedman's still-popular philosophy says no.

Philosophers such as DesJardins view Friedman's approach to business ethics as being much too narrow. It must be recognized that a discussion of free-market capitalism often includes responsibilities such as sustainability, not just earning financial rewards. DesJardins advocates that businesses replace the neo-classical model of economics as growth with a model that emphasizes ecological considerations, thus making sustainability as well as profitability primary goals. This shift, DesJardins argues, makes room for a much broader notion of social responsibility for business than Friedman's view allows. Not attending directly to environmental and social issues can be a business mistake. For example, if companies are using toxins that pollute their local area, they are probably poisoning their workers and customers. Rather than waiting for regulators to tell them to stop polluting, a more proactive approach would be to seek alternative ways of handling waste products within the company that will save money, at least in the long run—thus benefiting the business, the public, and the environment.

Following Friedman, one might believe that the free market is good, and that profitability as the sole aim of business is not morally problematic so long as it remains within the law and "the rules of the game." However, critics ask, what about exploiting people or polluting in countries where laws may not prohibit these practices?

Some corporate heads see the Friedman style of doing business as unenlightened and unacceptable. In 1979, for example, Quaker Oats president Kenneth Mason, writing in *Business Week*, said Friedman's profits-are-everything philosophy is "a dreary and demeaning view of the role of business and business leaders in our society." Mason continued, "Making a profit is no more the purpose of a corporation than getting enough to eat is the purpose of life. Getting enough to eat is a requirement of life; life's purpose, one would hope, is somewhat broader and more challenging. Likewise with business and profit."[1]

Friedman's philosophy has inspired new management styles that are antithetical to his doctrine. Corporate Social Responsibility (CSR) is one of the most widely discussed issues in business management. Corporate Citizenship and Sustainability are also part of many business management discussions. Stakeholder theories are often seen as fitting better with business profits, employees, customers, and communities. Since the Sarbanes-Oxley act of 2002, companies have been required to show much greater transparency in their responsibilities, first and foremost in their economic activities. However, a 2009 survey of 198 companies by David J. Videl found that most companies—71 percent—report publicly on citizenship and sustainability performance. The majority of these companies believe that corporate citizenship and sustainability must be a major corporate focus.[2]

Is DesJardins correct in his assessment of the corporation's role in society, or is Friedman's philosophy superior in bringing profits to stockholders? Consider what balance between the freedom of the entrepreneur and the protection of the rest of the citizenry would be appropriate in a free and affluent society. How much of the responsibility for the citizenry should be taken on by the corporations themselves?

---

[1] Makower, J. (1995) *Beyond the Bottom Line: Putting Social Responsibility to Work for Your Business and the World.* New York: Simon & Schuster.
[2] Vidal, D. (2006) "Reward Trumps Risk: How Business Perspectives on Corporate Citizenship and Sustainability Are Changing." The Conference Board. Executive Action Reports, November 2006 (online).

YES ⤶   Milton Friedman

The Social Responsibility of Business Is to Increase Its Profits

When I hear businessmen speak eloquently about the "social responsibilities of business in a free-enterprise system," I am reminded of the wonderful line about the Frenchman who discovered at the age of 70 that he had been speaking prose all his life. The businessmen believe that they are defending free enterprise when they declaim that business is not concerned "merely" with profit but also with promoting desirable "social" ends; that business has a "social conscience" and takes seriously its responsibilities for providing employment, eliminating discrimination, avoiding pollution and whatever else may be the catchwords of the contemporary crop of reformers. In fact they are—or would be if they or anyone else took them seriously—preaching pure and unadulterated socialism. Businessmen who talk this way are unwitting puppets of the intellectual forces that have been undermining the basis of a free society these past decades.

The discussions of the "social responsibilities of business" are notable for their analytical looseness and lack of rigor. What does it mean to say that "business" has responsibilities? Only people can have responsibilities. A corporation is an artificial person and in this sense may have artificial responsibilities, but "business" as a whole cannot be said to have responsibilities, even in this vague sense. The first step toward clarity in examining the doctrine of the social responsibility of business is to ask precisely what it implies for whom.

Presumably, the individuals who are to be responsible are businessmen, which means individual proprietors or corporate executives. Most of the discussion of social responsibility is directed at corporations, so in what follows I shall mostly neglect the individual proprietors and speak of corporate executives.

In a free-enterprise, private-property system, a corporate executive is an employee of the owners of the business. He has direct responsibility to his employers. That responsibility is to conduct the business in accordance with their desires, which generally will be to make as much money as possible while conforming to the basic rules of the society, both those embodied in law and those embodied in ethical custom. Of course, in some cases his employers may have a different objective. A group of persons might establish a corporation for an eleemosynary purpose—for example, a hospital or a school. The manager of such a corporation will not have money profit as his objective but the rendering of certain services.

In either case, the key point is that, in his capacity as a corporate executive, the manager is the agent of the individuals who own the corporation or establish the eleemosynary institution, and his primary responsibility is to them.

Needless to say, this does not mean that it is easy to judge how well he is performing his task. But at least the criterion of performance is straightforward, and the persons among whom a voluntary contractual arrangement exists are clearly defined.

Of course, the corporate executive is also a person in his own right. As a person, he may have many other responsibilities that he recognizes or assumes voluntarily—to his family, his conscience, his feelings of charity, his church, his clubs, his city, his country. He may feel impelled by these responsibilities to devote part of his income to causes he regards as worthy, to refuse to work for particular corporations, even to leave his job, for example, to join his country's armed forces. If we wish, we may refer to some of these responsibilities as "social responsibilities." But in these respects he is acting as a principal, not an agent; he is spending his own money or time or energy, not the money of his employers or the time or energy he has contracted to devote to their purposes. If these are "social responsibilities," they are the social responsibilities of individuals, not of business.

What does it mean to say that the corporate executive has a "social responsibility" in his capacity as businessman? If this statement is not pure rhetoric, it must mean that he is to act in some way that is not in the interest of his employers. For example, that he is to refrain from increasing the price of the product in order to contribute to the social objective of preventing inflation, even though a price increase would be in the best interests of the corporation. Or that he is to make expenditures on reducing pollution beyond the amount that is in the best interests of the corporation or that is required by law in order to contribute to the social objective of improving the environment. Or that, at the expense of corporate profits, he is to hire "hard-core" unemployed instead of better qualified available workmen to contribute to the social objective of reducing poverty.

In each of these cases, the corporate executive would be spending someone else's money for a general social interest. Insofar as his actions in accord with his "social responsibility" reduce returns to stockholders, he is spending their money. Insofar as his actions raise the price to customers, he is spending the customers' money. Insofar as his actions lower the wages of some employees, he is spending their money.

The stockholders or the customers or the employees could separately spend their own money on the particular action if they wished to do so. The executive is exercising a distinct "social responsibility," rather than serving as an agent of the stockholders or the customers or the employees, only if he spends the money in a different way than they would have spent it.

But if he does this, he is in effect imposing taxes, on the one hand, and deciding how the tax proceeds shall be spent, on the other.

This process raises political questions on two levels: principle and consequences. On the level of political principle, the imposition of taxes and the expenditure of tax proceeds are governmental functions. We have established elaborate constitutional, parliamentary and judicial provisions to control these functions, to assure that taxes are imposed so far as possible in accordance with the preferences and desires of the public—after all, "taxation without representation" was one of the battle cries of the American Revolution. We have a system of checks and balances to separate the legislative function of imposing taxes and enacting expenditures from the executive function of collecting taxes and administering expenditure programs and from the judicial function of mediating disputes and interpreting the law.

Here the businessman—self-selected or appointed directly or indirectly by stockholders—is to be simultaneously legislator, executive and jurist. He is to decide whom to tax by how much and for what purpose, and he is to spend the proceeds—all this guided only by general exhortations from on high to restrain inflation, improve the environment, fight poverty and so on and on.

The whole justification for permitting the corporate executive to be selected by the stockholders is that the executive is an agent serving the interests of his principal. This justification disappears when the corporate executive imposes taxes and spends the proceeds for "social" purposes. He becomes in effect a public employee, a civil servant, even though he remains in name an employee of a private enterprise. On grounds of political principle, it is intolerable that such civil servants—insofar as their actions in the name of social responsibility are real and not just window dressing—should be selected as they are now. If they are to be civil servants, then they must be selected through a political process. If they are to impose taxes and make expenditures to foster "social" objectives, then political machinery must be set up to make the assessment of taxes and to determine through a political process the objectives to be served.

This is the basic reason why the doctrine of "social responsibility" involves the acceptance of the socialist view that political mechanisms, not market mechanisms, are the appropriate way to determine the allocation of scarce resources to alternative uses.

On the grounds of consequences, can the corporate executive in fact discharge his alleged "social responsibilities"? On the other hand, suppose he could get away with spending the stockholders' or customers' or employees' money. How is he to know how to spend it? He is told that he must contribute to fighting inflation. How is he to know what action of his will contribute to that end? He is presumably an expert in running his company—in producing a product or selling it or financing it. But nothing about his selection makes him an expert on inflation. Will his holding down the price of his product reduce inflationary pressure? Or, by leaving more spending power in the hands of his customers, simply divert it elsewhere? Or, by forcing him to produce less because of the lower price, will it simply contribute to shortages? Even if he could answer these questions, how much cost is he justified in imposing on his stockholders, customers and employees for this social purpose? What is his appropriate share and what is the appropriate share of others?

And, whether he wants to or not, can he get away with spending his stock-holders', customers' or employees' money? Will not the stockholders fire him? (Either the present ones or those who take over when his actions in the name of social responsibility have reduced the corporation's profits and the price of its stock.) His customers and his employees can desert him for other producers and employers less scrupulous in exercising their social responsibilities.

This facet of "social responsibility" doctrine is brought into sharp relief when the doctrine is used to justify wage restraint by trade unions. The con-flict of interest is naked and clear when union officials are asked to subordi-nate the interest of their members to some more general purpose. If the union officials try to enforce wage restraint, the consequence is likely to be wildcat strikes, rank-and-file revolts and the emergence of strong competitors for their jobs. We thus have the ironic phenomenon that union leaders—at least in the U.S.—have objected to Government interference with the market far more consistently and courageously than have business leaders.

The difficulty of exercising "social responsibility" illustrates, of course, the great virtue of private competitive enterprise—it forces people to be respon-sible for their own actions and makes it difficult for them to "exploit" other people for either selfish or unselfish purposes. They can do good—but only at their own expense.

Many a reader who has followed the argument this far may be tempted to remonstrate that it is all well and good to speak of government's having the responsibility to impose taxes and determine expenditures for such "social" purposes as controlling pollution or training the hard-core unemployed, but that the problems are too urgent to wait on the slow course of political proc-esses, that the exercise of social responsibility by businessmen is a quicker and surer way to solve pressing current problems.

Aside from the question of fact—I share Adam Smith's skepticism about the benefits that can be expected from "those who affect to trade for the pub-lic good"—this argument must be rejected on grounds of principle. What it amounts to is an assertion that those who favor the taxes and expenditures in question have failed to persuade a majority of their fellow citizens to be of like mind and that they are seeking to attain by undemocratic procedures what they cannot attain by democratic procedures. In a free society, it is hard for "evil" people to do "evil," especially since one man's good is another's evil.

I have, for simplicity, concentrated on the special case of the corporate executive, except only for the brief digression on trade unions. But precisely the same argument applies to the newer phenomenon of calling upon stockholders to require corporations to exercise social responsibility (the recent G.M. crusade for example). In most of these cases, what is in effect involved is some stock-holders trying to get other stockholders (or customers or employees) to contrib-ute against their will to "social" causes favored by the activists. Insofar as they succeed, they are again imposing taxes and spending the proceeds.

The situation of the individual proprietor is somewhat different. If he acts to reduce the returns of his enterprise in order to exercise his "social respon-sibility," he is spending his own money, not someone else's. If he wishes to spend his money on such purposes, that is his right, and I cannot see that there is any objection to his doing so. In the process, he, too, may impose costs on employees and customers. However, because he is far less likely than a large corporation or union to have monopolistic power, any such side effects will tend to be minor.

Of course, in practice the doctrine of social responsibility is frequently a cloak for actions that are justified on other grounds rather than a reason for those actions.

To illustrate, it may well be in the long-run interest of a corporation that is a major employer in a small community to devote resources to providing amenities to that community or to improving its government. That may make it easier to attract desirable employees, it may reduce the wage bill or lessen losses from pilferage and sabotage or have other worthwhile effects. Or it may be that, given the laws about the deductibility of corporate charitable contributions, the stockholders can contribute more to charities they favor by having the corporation make the gift than by doing it themselves, since they can in that way contribute an amount that would otherwise have been paid as corporate taxes.

In each of these—and many similar—cases, there is a strong temptation to rationalize these actions as an exercise of "social responsibility." In the present climate of opinion, with its widespread aversion to "capitalism," "profits," the "soulless corporation" and so on, this is one way for a corporation to generate goodwill as a by-product of expenditures that are entirely justified in its own self-interest.

It would be inconsistent of me to call on corporate executives to refrain from this hypocritical window-dressing because it harms the foundations of a free society. That would be to call on them to exercise a "social responsibility"! If our institutions, and the attitudes of the public make it in their self-interest to cloak their actions in this way, I cannot summon much indignation to denounce them. At the same time, I can express admiration for those individual proprietors or owners of closely held corporations or stockholders of more broadly held corporations who disdain such tactics as approaching fraud.

Whether blameworthy or not, the use of the cloak of social responsibility, and the nonsense spoken in its name by influential and prestigious businessmen, does clearly harm the foundations of a free society. I have been impressed time and again by the schizophrenic character of many businessmen. They are capable of being extremely far-sighted and clearheaded in matters that are internal to their businesses. They are incredibly short-sighted and muddle-headed in matters that are outside their businesses but affect the possible survival of business in general. This short-sightedness is strikingly exemplified in the calls from many businessmen for wage and price guidelines or controls or income policies. There is nothing that could do more in a brief period to destroy a market system and replace it by a centrally controlled system than effective governmental control of prices and wages.

The short-sightedness is also exemplified in speeches by businessmen on social responsibility. This may gain them kudos in the short run. But it helps to strengthen the already too prevalent view that the pursuit of profits is wicked and immoral and must be curbed and controlled by external forces. Once this view is adopted, the external forces that curb the market will not be the social consciences, however highly developed, of the pontificating executives; it will be the iron fist of government bureaucrats. Here, as with price and wage controls, businessmen seem to me to reveal a suicidal impulse.

The political principle that underlies the market mechanism is unanimity. In an ideal free market resting on private property, no individual can coerce any other, all cooperation is voluntary, all parties to such cooperation benefit or they need not participate. There are no values, no "social" responsibilities in any sense other than the shared values and responsibilities of individuals. Society is a collection of individuals and of the various groups they voluntarily form.

The political principle that underlies the political mechanism is conformity. The individual must serve a more general social interest—whether that be determined by a church or a dictator or a majority. The individual may have a vote and say in what is to be done, but if he is overruled, he must conform. It is appropriate for some to require others to contribute to a general social purpose whether they wish to or not.

Unfortunately, unanimity is not always feasible. There are some respects in which conformity appears unavoidable, so I do not see how one can avoid the use of the political mechanism altogether.

But the doctrine of "social responsibility" taken seriously would extend the scope of the political mechanism to every human activity. It does not differ in philosophy from the most explicitly collectivist doctrine. It differs only by professing to believe that collectivist ends can be attained without collectivist means. That is why, in my book *Capitalism and Freedom*, I have called it a "fundamentally subversive doctrine" in a free society, and have said that in such a society, "there is one and only one social responsibility of business—to use its resources and engage in activities designed to increase its profits so long as it stays within the rules of the game, which is to say, engages in open and free competition without deception or fraud."

→ NO

Business and Environmental Sustainability

Introduction

This paper is about what some have called "the next industrial revolution."[1] My starting assumption is that in the early years of the twenty-first century humanity is faced with a cluster of significant economic, ecological, and ethical challenges. Extreme poverty, exacerbated by a cycle of political repression, war, famine, disease, and natural disasters, confronts hundreds of millions of people on a daily basis. Throughout the world, hundreds of millions of human beings struggle just to get the basic necessities of life: clean water, nutritious food, shelter, health care, education, jobs. Population growth guarantees that these problems will only intensify in the immediate future. Justice and common decency, as well as self-interest, requires that these problems be addressed by those living in the economically developed world. Addressing these challenges will require significant global economic activity, integrated with social and political leadership. However, the earth's biosphere, ultimately the only source for all this economic activity, is already under severe stress from just the type of economic growth that many assume is the solution to these challenges.

These factors will require that business in the twenty-first century be practiced in a way that is *economically* vibrant enough to address the real needs of billions of people, yet *ecologically* informed so that the earth's capacity to support life is not diminished by that activity and *ethically* sensitive enough that the human dignity is not lost or violated in the process.

To get us to the heart of what I would like to say about the role of business in this, I need to take a number of things as given. First, I will assume that, in fact, the earth's biosphere is under significant threat to its ability to support life. A second assumption[2] is that the present configuration of economic and business activity—the reigning paradigm of business and economics—is incapable of adequately addressing these challenges and, in fact, is partially responsible for causing these problems. The failure of this conventional wisdom to address these challenges revolves around two significantly misguided assumptions. The first is that unqualified economic *growth* is the best means for addressing global poverty and the social problems that accompany it. The second

From *Business & Professional Ethics Journal*, Vol. 24, Nos. 1 & 2, 2005, pp. 35–59. Copyright © 2005 by Philosophy Documentation Center. Reprinted by permission.

is that business and economics can operate independently of environmental and ethical concerns. I want to argue for an alternative model for business and economics, what is called the "sustainability" model, which can provide better guidance for creating a world in which we can meet the needs of the present generation without jeopardizing the ability of future generations to meet their own equally valid needs.[3]

Underlying the view I wish to sketch is a shift away from the growth-based model of neoclassical economics to a development-based model of ecological economics. The implications of such a shift for business are substantial. If economic growth is the primary goal of the economic system in which business operates (as it is in the neoclassical model), then the social responsibilities of business are fairly narrow. Business ought to pursue profit within the law and within certain minimal moral constraints. Thus, the primary social responsibility of business is economic, with legal and ethical considerations functioning as side-constraints upon this primary goal. Acting in this way is thought to insure that business activity furthers the overall social goal of economic growth, while respecting other social goals that get reflected in the law. But if this economic model is replaced by one shaped by ecological considerations, then the social responsibilities of business shift substantially. On this new model, corporate social responsibility must be assessed on three criteria: economic, ecological, and ethical. These criteria are commonly referred to as the "triple bottom line" or the "three pillars of sustainability."[4]

What I do hope to do in this paper is to offer some broad categories for how we might conceptualize business and business ethics in a sustainable future. What would sustainable business, and sustainable business ethics, involve? I also want to suggest some directions, for both business practitioners and academics, in which future work in this area might proceed. But first, let me say a few things about the very notion of sustainability.

The Sustainability Paradigm

The concept of sustainability has grown out of the recognition that *economic* development on a global level cannot be separated from questions of social justice and from ecological stability. Part of this new reality is captured in the common phrase: "poverty anywhere is a threat to prosperity everywhere."

The new worldview emerging as an alternative to the reigning paradigm of economic growth and free markets holds that long-term sustainability is the criterion of successful economic and social development. Sustainability, in this sense, is understood to involve three dimensions: economic, ecological, and ethical—the *three pillars of sustainability*. Business, within this conceptualization, is no longer understood as having a primary economic goal, with ethical and environmental consideration functioning as side-constraints. Business has three equally compelling goals that must be balanced over the long-term.

Claiming that economic growth is part of the problem is not to envision a future of economic depression or stagnation. Without significant economic activity, human suffering will get worse, not better. Nor is it to imagine the creation of romantic, bucolic agricultural communities. There are ten urban areas in the world with populations greater than fifteen million, and another fifteen with populations greater than ten million. The people living in each of these urban areas are not likely soon to voluntarily emigrate out into the countryside to start peaceful agricultural communes. There are reasons, after all, why populations have emigrated from the countryside into urban centers. Growth itself is not bad—some things will need to grow to address these challenges. Unqualified and misdirected economic growth is the problem.

Sustainability: Two Caveats

Finally, before turning to a closer look at sustainable business it is worthwhile to issue two caveats concerning the very notion of sustainability. First, we should be clelar that while the concept of sustainability can offer a pragmatic guide for future business directions, it must not be so broadly conceived that just any practice or any business can become sustainable. When we hear talk about "sustainability," we should always be prepared to ask *What* is being sustained?"

Sustainable living and sustainable development will require a changed economy and changed society. There may well be industries and social practices that are incompatible with sustainable development. Sustainability will also require substantially closing the economic gap between wealthy industrialized countries and the poor developing world. We need to be vigilant and not use sustainable development simply as a fashionable way to talk about continued economic growth, consumption, or industrialism. As we learned from the green marketing campaigns of recent years, it will be easy for benign concepts to be co-opted.

Second, the concept of "sustainability" most accurately applies only at more general and systemic levels. An individual firm, for example, may adopt the most ecologically benign and safe practices, but if the economic system or biosphere in which it is embedded collapses, the firm itself will not be sustained. On the other hand, an ecologically destructive practice, such as the creation of nuclear wastes or the destruction of a wetland, can be sustained as long as it occurs as an isolated incident within an otherwise healthy biosphere. An individual business or a particular practice is neither sustainable nor unsustainable in isolation from wider economic and ecological systems. "Sustainability" truly applies only to practices that have an impact, positive or negative, on the broader biosphere. Nevertheless, for convenience sake, we can talk about a sustainable business as a shorthand way of describing practices which, if generalized over an industry or economy, would safeguard the biosphere.

The Business Case for Sustainability

The first topic I would like to address concerns the philosophical implications of the "three pillars" and "triple bottom line" frameworks. The dominant model of economics and business tends to understand the goals of profit and environmental or ethical responsibility as exclusive dualisms. Managers must choose between profit and social responsibility, between their financial duties to their business and their environmental or ethical duties. Cast in these terms, it becomes easy to dismiss both ethical and environmental responsibilities. Pursuing ethical and environmental goals beyond those required by law or minimal moral duties threatens profit, profit is necessary to remain in operation, therefore asking business to pursue environmental goals is unreasonably asking business to jeopardize its very existence.

Both history and ethics can encourage us to think of environmentalism and business in terms of a zero-sum game: environmentally sustainable decision comes at a cost of profitability; pursuing profits requires business managers to forgo environmental responsibility. Historically, most early environmental legislation followed this regulation-and-compliance model. Government passes laws that restrict the freedom of business, and business is forced to comply with such regulation. There is also a long ethical tradition which makes a similar assumption: ethical responsibilities conflict with self-interest. To be ethical, one must forgo self-interest; if one is pursuing self-interest, one is less than ethically praiseworthy. But the possibility exists that what is right in terms of sustainability, may also be right in terms of business performance. Part of the three pillars of sustainability, after all, is economic sustainability. If we expect business to address the significant global economic and environmental challenges of the twenty-first century, we need vibrant and stable, i.e., sustainable, businesses.

Sustainability as the purpose of business provides guidance that creative and entrepreneurial business leaders can follow. As we begin to consider how business might be restructured in order to meet its environmental responsibilities, it is worth emphasizing this point. We should not underestimate the range of managerial discretion. Business executives and managers, rightfully, enjoy a wide range of decision-making discretion. There are many ways to pursue and attain profitability. We must move away from the view of environmental responsibilities as side-constraints on "the" pursuit of profit, as if there is only one way to pursue profits and ethical responsibilities are a barrier to that. Rather, we must recognize that some avenues to profitability can be environmentally risky, others environmentally prudent and sensible.

Barring a catastrophe, society will survive and businesses must play a role in that survival. Models of sustainable business envision a central role for business in a sustainable future. It will be the businesses of the next industrial revolution that meet the real needs of the billions of people living in that sustainable future. The businesses that survive in this sustainable world will be businesses that anticipate this change and adapt to it on their own terms.

The models of sustainable business being developed share common themes that give some indication where these changes will occur. Business products and operations should be modeled on biological processes. "Closed-loop" manufacturing, biomimicry, elimination of wastes and discovering ways to treat wastes as a resource are different ways of emphasizing this point. One implication of these proposals is that new business opportunities exist for realizing new business synergies when the wastes of one firm become the resources of others. Another implication is that great cost savings can be found by looking to reduce and eliminate wastes.

A company that finds ways to turn waste into a new resource will increase its revenues from already existing assets. If the by-products of the production process represent a cost for disposal, then a creative business will search for ways to turn them into revenues.

One practical side of cost savings can be seen with the example of Interface, Inc. The movement towards sustainability initiated by CEO Ray Anderson in the early 1990s did result in increased efficiencies and reduced costs. In the late 1990s however, Interface entered into a three-year period of decreasing sales and lost revenues. Interface's primary market sells carpeting to office and commercial buildings. During the economic recession of these years, office and commercial expansion declined and Interface's business suffered as a result. However, Interface credits the increased efficiencies and reduced costs of their sustainability initiatives with playing a major role in helping to weather the economic downturn. Every business experiences challenging economic periods and, as this Interface example demonstrates, cost savings associated with the move towards sustainability can provide a cushion against economic downturns.

Sustainability also creates opportunities to decrease capital costs in building or remodeling facilities. Buildings designed from the start to be energy efficient, with bright, airy, and well-ventilated space will decrease costs and improve efficiencies over the long term. McDonough and Braungart's work with a new manufacturing plant for Herman Miller, a large office furniture maker, is a case in point. Herman Miller has a long tradition of socially responsible practices and has worked with McDonough and Braungart's cradle-to-cradle design protocol to develop truly sustainable furniture products. But in the early 1990s, Herman Miller also worked with McDonough to design and build their new manufacturing plant in Michigan. The new design has paid dividends in the form of lower energy costs and increased worker productivity. Herman Miller has also been instrumental in creating the United States Green Building Council (USGBC) in 1993. The Council describes itself as "the nation's foremost coalition of leaders from across the building industry working to promote buildings that are environmentally responsible, profitable and healthy places to live and work."[5]

Sustainable companies can also acquire competitive advantages. Not only would increased savings, revenues, and efficiencies place a company in a better position relative to its competitors, but sustainable companies are poised to take advantage of "green" markets. Sustainable practices should not be only a marketing tool, of course, but one should not underestimate the growing consumer market for sustainable and environmentally beneficial products and services. Another aspect of the competitive advantages of sustainability lies in the labor market. Herman Miller discovered that their green building became very popular with employees. Improved morale, increased employee loyalty and, simply, healthier and more attractive working conditions for employees were added benefits of McDonough's sustainable design principles.

Business should recognize the real possibility of future government regulation that may well require steps towards sustainability. The companies already involved in sustainable practices are likely to play leadership roles in fashioning future standards. In the past, many companies waited until environmental regulations coerced them into action. At that point, many were overwhelmed by the costs of clean-up and compensation. Companies that wait and deal with sustainability as a compliance issue take similar risks.

Finally, avoiding future legal liability provides another business reason for the move towards sustainability. There is no better means for managing both regulatory and legal risks than by being proactive in taking steps to prevent problems from occurring. The legal concepts of negligence and forseeability are just waiting to be exploited in holding business liable for the entire life-cycle of its products.

Business Responsibilities in a Sustainable Economy

In this section, I would like to sketch a range of ethical responsibilities facing business during the transition to a sustainable economy. For convenience sake, I will distinguish between responsibilities concerning sustainable consumption and responsibilities concerning sustainable production.

Sustainable Consumption

As business begins to address sustainability concerns, it might seem that consumerism lies beyond what we can reasonably ask business to address. Expecting business to take responsibility, or holding business liable, for the consequences of consumer choice seems unreasonable and unfair. First, what would seem to be the primary alternatives to consumerism—movements such as voluntary simplicity and virtues like frugality and thrift—run counter to business's interests in selling more products. If consumers stop consuming, business loses. If consumers consume less, the economy enters a recession and everyone suffers. Thus, it would seem that asking business to discourage consumption is asking it to put its own survival in jeopardy. Second, consumer demand—the motivating force behind consumerism—seems beyond the scope of business's ethical responsibilities. Business responds to the market after all, it doesn't create the market. If consumers make environmentally bad decisions, the fault should lie with individual consumers not with business.

Nevertheless, I would like to suggest that business has more of a responsibility for consumer behavior and consumption patterns than might first appear. A sustainable business must address the issue of consumption head-on and take responsibility both for the role it plays in shaping consumer demand, and for the choices available to fill that demand. Further, sustainable consumerism can present business with as many opportunities as barriers and managers who miss such opportunities fail all their stakeholders.

If unsustainable consumption is the result simply of autonomously chosen individual desires, then perhaps business has little responsibility for it.

But there is good reason to think that there are other factors involved as well, factors that business can address. Clearly, causal explanations for shopping and consumption are many and varied. But two particular topics are relevant for evaluating the role that business plays in this. First, is the long-debated issue of consumer autonomy. One explanation for why we consume as we do rests with the influence of mass marketing and advertising. Because business is responsible for influencing consumer choice, business is responsible when those choices prove problematic. The second topic concerns certain structural features of our economy. These structural features place individuals in a position in which consumption, and over-consumption, is much more rational that it otherwise would be.

Conventional wisdom teaches us about consumer sovereignty and that supply is a function of demand. Critics claim that consumers are far from sovereign and in control of the marketplace. At one extreme of this debate is the claim that business, through its marketing practices, controls consumer behavior. At the other extreme is the view that business simply responds to pre-existing and independent consumer demand. Surely both extremes are overstated. Human behavior in general is too complex a phenomenon to be controlled by marketing in any straightforward sense. But just as unlikely is the claim that business would spend billions of dollars each year on marketing if it did not have measurable results in changed consumer behavior.

The consumer autonomy debate is complex and well-developed. A full review of that debate is beyond the scope of this essay. But, several points are worth mentioning. First, consumers cannot demand what doesn't exist and what they do not know about. Entrepreneurial businesses often identify consumer needs and desires even before consumers themselves can. They can also identify unmet needs and values that are not addressed in the marketplace. As the personal computer industry so clearly demonstrated, innovative products are very capable of creating their own demand. Few people in the 1970s, both among consumers and industry leaders such as IBM, could even imagine the need for a household computer. Suggesting that Apple Computer simply responded to consumer demand and had no role in creating that demand, is to seriously misunderstand history.

Second, one of the most common counter-arguments to the claim that marketing can influence consumer behavior relies on the failure rates of new products. Estimates vary, but the standard claim is that a very high percentage of new products fail. If marketing can control consumer behavior, so this argument goes, then heavily marketed new products would not fail at such high rates. Since they do, marketing cannot control consumer behavior. But new products failure rates also provide a counter-argument to those who defend consumer sovereignty. If the consumer truly were sovereign, and if business simply responded to consumer demand, then there should be few if any new products that failed. After all, if production responds to demand, only those products for which a market exists would be produced. A high failure rate of new products suggests that business is producing first and trying to find a market afterwards. This, in turn, suggests that many businesses believe that consumer behavior can be influenced by what happens after production.

The second aspect of the explanation of contemporary consumer culture shifts the focus away from the decisions of individuals and looks instead to certain structural features of the society and economy. By "structural feature," I mean those social arrangements, expectations, and norms that provide a context in which individual decisions are made. Our individual choices are shaped to a large degree by how society is arranged. We can only choose from available options, and the options available to consumers are greatly shaped by business and economics. Certain structural features of the present business and economic context can make a choice that is individually rational result in a socially irrational outcome.

In her analysis of why we consume, economist Juliet Shor argues that there are three important structural features of the modern economy that encourage consumers to consume in unsustainable ways.[6] First, Shor points to a "cycle of work and spend" that encourages most individuals to continue working and spending beyond the level that, in some deeper sense, they would prefer. Second, Shor argues that there is a strong "ecological bias" within the economy that discounts the true ecological costs of consumerism. Finally, Shor points to various social meanings given to consumption, particularly "consumption competitions." Each of these structural features encourage individuals to make decisions that lead to over-consumption and its attendant environmental, economic, and ethical difficulties. I want to suggest that business has a role to play in this, especially in respect to the first and third of Shor's structural features.

The conventional wisdom concerning work suggests that market forces tend towards an equilibrium in which individuals balance their desires for income-producing work and leisure. But, present work structures prevent individuals from cutting back work to attain their leisure goals. Such benefits as health insurance, pension, and career mobility and promotion typically are not available to part-time workers. Employers have strong incentives, from tax incentives to the costs of employee benefits, to encourage present workers to work longer hours rather than hiring additional workers. These structural features make it "rational" for individuals to work longer hours than they would prefer, which means that workers have less time to enjoy non-work leisure activities. Further, since they are working longer hours and therefore making more money, yet have less time available for leisure, greater and greater consumption becomes one of the few ways open for an individual to find rewards for their overworked life. In part because of longer work hours, people feel that they deserve extra, and spend the added income on more and more frills. Frills that, perhaps, they don't "really want and value" but which serve as substitutes for other values. The major alternative to this work and spend cycle is to work and spend less. But this option is often unavailable, not the least because only full-time jobs carry health and insurance benefits that would be unaffordable on part-time salaries.

Thus, structural features of the workplace create a cycle of work and spend, a cycle that leads to over-consumption. Businesses have opportunities to change the structure of our working as well as our consuming lives. Here we see opportunities with HR offices to contribute to a sustainable future. Health and other benefits for part-time workers, flexible benefit packages in which workers can trade-off pay and other benefits for more leisure time, and job-sharing opportunities can help workers escape the cycle of work and spend.

Shor's final feature points to the social meanings of consumption as a major factor in explaining why we consume as we do. Social scientists from Thorstein Veblin to the present have described the many roles that consumption plays in establishing our self-image and our social status and identity. In many ways, we are what we own. We shop and buy for entertainment, for therapy, for self-esteem, for status. We have expectations that tell us we can have it all, and we deserve it now. Our mailboxes are flooded with offers for credit cards and retailers offer everyone, including those with bad credit history, easy credit. In a context where positive social meanings are attached to consumption, an ordinarily rational individual is led to act in irrational ways by consuming more than is reasonable.

Business, I believe, has responsibilities derived from the social meaning of consumption. Consumers often buy products for their social meaning, a meaning in part created and encouraged by marketing. Again, contemporary marketing is faced with a choice of what meaning gets conveyed by their marketing campaigns. Let us remember a quote from Theodore Levitt. "The purpose of business is to create and keep a customer." How can business create customers? Two well-known examples can help us understand this claim: GM's marketing of a wide range of automobiles in the mid-twentieth century, and the marketing of home computers in the late twentieth century. Let us look briefly at only the second of these examples.

Consider the creation of the home computing market that exploded in the 1980s and 1990s. As a student in the 1970s, I typed papers on a Smith-Corona manual typewriter. As a young faculty member in the 1980s, I graduated to an IBM electric. At that time, I could not even imagine what I would do with a computer, let alone think I could ever afford one. If Apple Computer and IBM had waited for consumer demand to direct their business, we would all still be typing on electric typewriters, paying bills my mail, and standing in lines in stores and libraries. There simply was no demand for computers, software, MP3 players, video games, on-line banking, virus protection software, search engines, and cable modems in 1980. By 2000, these and other high-tech products and services were driving an unprecedented economic boom.

I suggest that we may be standing at a similar threshold. Consumers are not demanding more sustainable products and services because, like the consumers of 1980, most people have no idea what such a world would look like and what they will need to flourish in a sustainable future. Creative businesses and entrepreneurial individuals will not wait for consumer demand to magically appear. Sustainable products, supported by creative and imaginative marketing, can create their own demand if business is daring enough to try. The social meaning of consumerism is the product of social forces including commercial marketing and advertising. There is no reason to believe that this meaning cannot be shifted towards a more sustainable consumer lifestyle.

The third aspect of the responsibility of business for sustainable consumption: the production of sustainable products. Perhaps most importantly and most directly, businesses ought to produce sustainable goods and services. If consumers over-consume on environmental, social justice, and self-interested grounds, then sustainable products must diminish these harmful consequences. If the food we eat, the homes we live in, the energy we use, the carpets we walk on, are produced in sustainable ways, then the harmful effects of consuming them are greatly reduced. This topic will be examined in more detail in the next section.

Sustainable Products and Production

Let us turn now from the consumer side of the economic equation to the production side. Conventional economic wisdom would place much of the responsibility for products with the consumers who demand them. Supply, we are told, is a function of demand. Thus, from this perspective, the appearance of sustainable products will have to wait for consumer demand or government mandates. But there are good reasons for rejecting this view.

First, as the previous section pointed out, it is a mistake to treat business as a passive spectator responding to, rather than creating and shaping, consumer demand. Consumers are able to demand only what they know about and, to a large extent, only what is available in the marketplace. In 1970 consumers couldn't demand an IBM selectric, in 1980 they couldn't demand a personal computer, in 1990 they couldn't demand an efficient search engine, in 2000 they could not demand an I-POD or Viagra. Business clearly plays an active role in creating both the information consumers use in making demands, and the products available to fulfill those demands. Further, consumer demand is most often generic; consumers want a car, or even more generally transportation, not necessarily a Ford Taurus or an internal combustion engine. Consumers desire headache relief, not necessarily acetaminophen or Tylenol. Consumers demand convenient food, not necessary a fast-food restaurant in a strip-mall. Business thus has options for determining how to satisfy consumer demand and has the ability to help shape that demand.

Second, even if we accept the conventional view that consumers bear primary responsibility for sustainable products, business would not be able to escape significant ethical responsibility for such products. Independent of products themselves is the process by which those goods and services are produced and delivered. Business has wide discretion regarding how their products get designed, manufactured, delivered, and sold. The production process itself creates a challenge, opportunity, and responsibility for creating a sustainable business. Even when consumers demand a specific product, how that product gets designed and manufactured, the working conditions of the people who make it, the resources that go into production, the wastes that are left behind, how the product is transported and retailed are all areas in which business can move towards sustainability.

Third, businesses themselves are consumers relying on other businesses in their supply-chain for a wide range of products for their own operations.

Every business is a consumer and must take responsibility for demanding sustainable products from its suppliers. Business cannot disavow responsibility for sustainable products by allocating that duty to consumers without taking on the same responsibility for itself when it acts as a consumer in purchasing products from other businesses. In recent years business has been held accountable for their supply-chain activities concerning sweatshop working conditions and genetically modified organisms. We have every reason to think that a similar approach will be taken concerning supply-chain responsibility for sustainable products.

We can think about the responsibilities of sustainable production in terms of the two endpoints of the production process: the wastes and pollution that comes out of the process, and the materials and energy that go into the production process.

I won't say much today about the wastes and by-products of the production process. History is a good guide for thinking about business responsibility and liability for the harms caused by the wastes and pollution of production. I believe that society already is moving in the direction of holding business strictly liable for any harms caused by the by-products and wastes of the production process. Many of the very same factors that lead to changes in the regulation of pollution are present today regarding more general sustainability and ecological concerns.

If pollution and waste lie at one side of the production process, resources and materials that go into products lie on the other. Conventional wisdom, represented by Julian Simon's claim that resources are infinite, denies that there is a problem with the supply of resources.[7] What is identified as the *weak sustainability thesis* holds that as long as substitutes exist, any product is sustainable. If this were true, then business would have no responsibility for creating sustainable products. But, to the degree that this is not true, and to the degree that business can foresee the harmful consequences of creating unsustainable products, business does have a responsibility to anticipate and prevent problems by designing and creating sustainable products.

Three trends in production that are likely to follow from this are worth mentioning. First, business should be expected to take responsibility throughout the entire life-cycle of its products. A process called *life-cycle management* entails business accepting stewardship and managing their products throughout their entire life-cycle, including a "take-back" commitment. Second, the liability of business for the materials used in products is likely to result in a movement towards dematerialization. Third, business should anticipate greater responsibility for the type of energy used in its production process.

The concept of life-cycle responsibility holds that business should be responsible for, can be held liable for any harms caused by, a product throughout its entire life-cycle. An ethical case can be made for the claim that when a business chooses to manufacture a product and bring it into the marketplace, it assumes a responsibility for that product that cannot be relinquished simply because someone else has purchased it. The implication is that a business that creates a product must take responsibility for managing its entire life.[8]

Life-cycle management is a tool that has its roots in pollution prevention strategies. Once business recognized that it would be held liable for harms caused downstream by its pollutants, an incentive was created to prevent the harms by reducing pollution upstream at its sources. Life-cycle management is most easily done within firms that are vertically integrated. The very concept of vertical integration, familiar throughout the business management literature, demonstrates that many businesses already do control much of the life-cycle of products. Life-cycle responsibility simply draws out the ethical implications of this fact and acknowledges that where business exercises control, it bears responsibility. I would suggest this is another direction in which future ethics research should move.

The ethics of products liability law offers supporting rationales for such changes. First, business should not assume that it foregoes responsibility whenever it sells a product. As witnessed in the development of products liability law in such cases as asbestos and DES, liability for harmful products is not transferred to a purchaser when the product itself is sold. Second, the negligence standard has always included an element of foreseeability. The law holds individuals and businesses liable for harms that a reasonable person could have foreseen occurring as a result of one's actions. Growing awareness of the ecological and health harms caused by materials used in products virtually guarantees that future businesses will be judged negligent for failing to take steps to prevent easily foreseeable harms.

As part of this life-cycle responsibility, business must begin a process of "dematerialization." Industrial ecologists are looking to dematerialization as an important step in the direction of sustainability. Dematerialization is a process of reducing the material used required for any given product or service. If we start with a standard economic understanding of the value of goods and service in terms of consumer satisfaction, dematerialization is the process of decreasing the amount of material resources that are required to produce a set unit of satisfaction. Dematerialization would aim to decrease both the amount and the rate at which material resources are used.

Business has tremendous opportunities to use dematerialization as a cost cutting and marketing strategy. Dematerialization can involve a wide range of actions, including reducing product size, weight, the amount of packaging, and increasing product life and range of uses. The information technology industry is a model for dematerialization as email replaces physical mail, computers get faster and smaller, and computing services such as printing, fax, copying, and scanning get incorporated into single machines.[9] Hewlett-Packard, for example, is an industry leader in developing opportunities by which information technology creates less demand for physical products. The automobile industry has decreased the average weight of cars, despite the increased popularity of SUVs, by over thirty percent during the last three decades of the twentieth century. The evolution of the music industry from vinyl records to eight-track tapes to cassettes tapes to CDs to digital players is another perfect example of this dematerialization process.

Dematerialization can also involve such practices as reduced fertilizer and pesticide use in agriculture. Many farmers now use global positioning satellite systems to identify more precisely crop areas in need of irrigation or fertilizers, thus using these resources only where and when necessary. Sensors which shut off appliances when not in use, timers aimed at reducing electricity usage, and hybrid technologies in automobiles which shift to battery power when gasoline power is inefficient, would also all be part of a movement towards dematerialization.

Besides materials, energy is the other major factor that goes into the production process. Unquestionably, energy use is at the heart of sustainable business practice. Global energy use at present, with its heavy reliance on fossil fuels and nuclear power, is a major cause of ecological damage. Few believe that fossil fuels and nuclear power are a part of a long-term sustainable energy policy. At best, these energy sources will require significant safeguards and technological improvements to be a part of a transition towards sustainability. Long-term, they will need to be replaced as sources for the energy business requires.[10]

Only solar energy provides new energy input into the earth's biosphere. Solar energy, directly in the form of heat energy absorbed through solar panels or indirectly through wind energy, is the most sustainable long-term energy source. Fuel cells, powered by hydrogen produced through solar and wind power, hold great promise for localized distributed electric power generation. Geothermal, tidal, and some hydro-powered energy sources also have long-term potential. Until such energy sources are more readily available, we might have to rely on technologies to create cleaner and more benign uses of fossil fuels. Hybrid electric and internal combustion engines for automobiles, ultra-clean sulfur-free diesel fuel for truck and heavy machinery, coal gasification, coal-to-liquid, and coal-to-gas technologies can decrease pollution from otherwise unsustainable fossil fuels.

Supply-Chain Responsibility

A third aspect of the production process that certainly will get more attention in the future concerns the responsibility of business for the actions of its supply chain and entire distribution channels. In recent years, public attention has focused on the responsibility of business for the actions of their supply-chain particularly concerning two issues. Food and agricultural businesses have been challenged concerning the presence of genetically-modified organisms in food supply, and retail and textile industries have been challenged regarding sweat-shop working conditions in their supply-chain. In both situations the initial reply of business was to deny responsibility for the actions of their suppliers. In both situations that defense quickly collapsed in the face of public pressure. A strong ethical case can be made for the claim that businesses can be held responsible for the practices of their suppliers.

Ordinarily, we do not hold a person responsible for the actions of someone else. Assuming that the other person is an autonomous agent, we believe that each person is responsible for their own actions. But this is not always the case. For example, we hold parents responsible for the actions of their children. Thus, the ethical and philosophical challenge is to determine exactly when and under what conditions doing so is reasonable.

While it is easy to think of consumers solely in terms of individual human beings, it would be a mistake to do so. In common situations, we think of a consumer as the person who walks into a big-box retail outlet, an automobile showroom, or who stands at the gas pump re-fueling a private car. But as the case of such giant retailers as Wal-Mart has so clearly demonstrated in recent years, retail businesses exercise tremendous control and influence over both their suppliers and the individual consumers who ostensibly make demands on them. If we hold individual consumers responsible for the choices they make in the marketplace, as conventional economic wisdom would have us do, then we must hold individual businesses equally responsible for the choices they make in the wholesale and supply-chain marketplace.

Notes

1. See, for example, William McDonough and Michael Braungart, "The Next Industrial Revolution" *The Atlantic Monthly* (Oct. 1998), vol. 282, No. 4, 88–92.

2. I defend this assumption elsewhere—see *"Business, Ethics, Sustainability: Ethics for the Next Industrial Revolution,"* forthcoming from Prentice Hall.

3. Perhaps the most widely used definition of sustainability comes from the United Nations' Brundtland Commission. The Brundtland Commission published its findings on economic development and the environment in 1987 in a book titled *Our Common Future*. This book offered what has become the standard definition of sustainable development: "sustainable development is development that meets the needs of the present without compromising the ability of future generations to meet their own needs."

4 "Triple bottom line" is a phrase popularlized by John Elkington, *Cannibals with Forks: The Triple Bottom Line of 21st Century Business* Stony Creek, CT.: New Society Publishers, 1998.

5. Information about Herman Miller's long tradition of working towards sustainability can be found on the company's website: . . . . The United States Green Building Council also maintains a helpful website, with links to local affiliates, at: . . . .

6. Juliet Shor, "Why do We Consume So Much?" in *Contemporary Issues in Business Ethics*, fifth edition, Joseph R. DesJardins and John McCall, eds., (Belmont, CA.: Wadsworth Publishing, 2005), 373–381.

7. Julian Simon, *The Ultimate Resource* (Princeton, NJ: Princeton Univ Press 1981).

8. Significant work on life-cycle management is being done by the United Nations Environment Progamme, http://www.uneptie.org/pc/sustain/lcinitiative/.

9. "Sustainability and dematerialization at Hewlett Packard," by David Hudson and Lynelle Preston in *Ants, Galileo, and Gandhi: Designing the Future of Business through Nature, Genius, and Compassion*, Sissel Waage, ed. (Sheffield, U.K, Greenleaf Publishing, 2003), 82–92.

10. A strong case can be made for the claim that world oil production already is at, or has passed, its peak. As early as the 1950s geophysicist M. King

Hubbert formulated an hypothesis concerning a point of maximum production, known as Hubbert Peak, for any resource. Hubbert's hypothesis included the claim that the production peak occurred at the midpoint of the depletion of a resource. Many geologists and oil engineers believe that the world has already hit Hubbert's peak for oil production. A helpful source for pursuing this claim can be found at . . . .

POSTSCRIPT

Is Increasing Profits the Only Social Responsibility of Business?

Friedman and DesJardins agree that corporations wield great power both locally and globally. With power, many hold, comes responsibility. Friedman's view is that the responsibilities entrusted to corporate officers, managers, and employees are to the corporation's owners, its stockholders; and these responsibilities pivot around profit-making. Individuals who work in and for corporations may wish to engage in philanthropic or other endeavors aiming at promoting social good; but, for Friedman, these should be the endeavors of individuals as individuals, not as corporate employees. DesJardins believes that businesses exist in communities where there are special needs and interests, and multinational businesses have a global reach. Given their crucial role in affecting the lives and well-being of people everywhere, and given the dependence that businesses themselves have on being supported by those whose lives and well-being they affect, DesJardins argues for environmental sustainability as a legitimate and fundamental goal for business.

Suggested Readings

Friedman, Milton. "A Friedman Doctrine: The Social Responsibility of Business Is to Increase Its Profits." *The New York Times Magazine* 13 Sept. 1970.

Lantos, Geoffrey P. "The boundaries of strategic corporate social responsibility." *Journal of Consumer Marketing,* vol. 18 no. 7, 2001.

Mackey, John, T.J. Rodgers, "Rethinking the Social Responsibility of Business." *Reason,* Oct. 2005.

Margolis, Joshua D. and James P. Walsh. "Misery Loves Companies: Rethinking Social Initiatives by Business." *Administrative Science Quarterly,* vol. 48, no. 2. June 2003.

Moir, Lance. "What do we mean by corporate social responsibility?" *Corporate Governance,* vol. 1 no. 2, 2001.

ISSUE 4

Can Individual Virtue Survive Corporate Pressure?

YES: Robert C. Solomon, from "Victims of Circumstances? A Defense of Virtue Ethics in Business," *Business Ethics Quarterly* (January 2003)

NO: Gilbert Harman, from "No Character or Personality," *Business Ethics Quarterly* (January 2003)

ISSUE SUMMARY

YES: Joining the long-standing debate on the possibility of free choice and moral agency in the business world, Quincy Lee Centennial Professor of Business and Philosophy at the University of Texas in Austin Robert C. Solomon argues that whatever the structures, the individual's choice is free, and therefore his character or virtue is of the utmost importance in creating a good moral tone in the life of a business.

NO: Stuart Professor of Philosophy at Princeton University Gilbert Harman employs determinist arguments to conclude that no individual can of his own free choice make a difference in a group enterprise.

We have long recognized that the world looks very different from internal and external perspectives.

From the inside, the choices people make are very clearly *their* choices. They wrestle with their fear, they encourage their generosity, they praise themselves for farsightedness and blame themselves for carelessness and haste—and at the end, they choose. "Character" is that foundation in right living that strengthens or enables people to make the right choices by prevailing against the external pressures to make the wrong choices. For example, an athlete is strengthened or enabled to win a contest because he has disciplined himself to exercise regularly.

From the outside, observers can easily explain one's choices by references to the external circumstances and incentives. One may protest that the observers know nothing of one's internal processes, but the standard response is, whatever you may have thought of the situation, given the circumstances, you had no choice but to do what you did.

Philosophically, one notes the difference in perspectives as "free will versus determinism," originally a dispute over whether actions are caused by free choice or by circumstances. Since the philosopher David Hume (1711–1776) explored the subject, we have learned to adopt a more sophisticated analysis of the dispute. One can conclude that, generally, all human actions are determined not just by external circumstances but also by the entire history and upbringing of the agent. One can also conclude that all human actions are free in that the agent, in choosing, builds creatively on that history and upbringing to adapt to the external circumstances.

Robert C. Solomon and Gilbert Harman address a more limited question: If agents (presumably employees in a corporation) are clearly people of good education, sound upbringing, and good character, can one expect that they will act rightly, no matter what external circumstances business life throws at them? Does virtue play a role in the conduct of business? In light of the recent scandals, Enron and all the others, the question becomes very serious indeed.

Certain experiments in social psychology, as mentioned in the selections, suggest that it does not. The Milgram experiments comprised a series of studies of human behavior conducted in several locations in New England, beginning in 1964. Dr. Stanley Milgram invited volunteers from the communities to participate in a "learning" experiment. The purpose, he explained to them, was to find out if negative reinforcement (punishment) speeded up learning of a simple task. Volunteers were directed to man a menacing board of "electrical shock administration" buttons, with one labeled "danger!" The volunteers drew lots to see who would be "student" and who "teacher." As the "teacher," they would administer shocks to the "student." Each time the "student" made a mistake, a higher level of shock would be administered, resulting in the "students" crying out in pain at the higher levels. If a "student" made enough mistakes, the instructions called for the "teacher" to press the "danger!" button; when that happened, there was only an ominous silence from the "student."

Of course the whole thing was a hoax. The lots the volunteers drew were all labeled "teacher." The "student" was an actor employed by Milgram, and the board was a phony. The question Milgram was really trying to answer concerned obedience to authority: Would a normal adult, who knew that it was wrong to inflict pain on another human being and who was given no pressure but the instructions of someone in a white coat, obediently inflict what he had every reason to believe was serious and possibly lethal injury on an innocent stranger? The answer was—an alarming percent of the time—yes, he would.

What does one mean by "character"? Is character supposed to produce virtuous behavior automatically, even when the situation is completely staged and artificial? Is there still room for virtue among the fierce pressures of the business world?

Ask yourself, as you read these selections, just how prepared you are to meet demanding situations as an employee or as a citizen. Is your community of faith or ethics strong enough to enable you to do the right thing in a situation that frightens or constricts you? How would you teach new employees in a company to do the right thing in a difficult situation?

YES

Robert C. Solomon

Victims of Circumstances?
A Defense of Virtue
Ethics in Business

Abstract: Should the responsibilities of business managers be understood independently of the social circumstances and "market forces" that surround them, or (in accord with empiricism and the social sciences) are agents and their choices shaped by their circumstances, free only insofar as they act in accordance with antecedently established dispositions, their "character"? Virtue ethics, of which I consider myself a proponent, shares with empiricism this emphasis on character as well as an affinity with the social sciences. But recent criticisms of both empiricist and virtue ethical accounts of character deny even this apparent compromise between agency and environment. Here is an account of character that emphasizes dynamic interaction both in the formation and in the interplay between personal agency and responsibility on the one hand and social pressures and the environment on the other.

Business ethics is a child of ethics, and business ethics, like its parents, is vulnerable to the same threats and challenges visited on its elders. For many years, one such threat (or rather, a family of threats) has challenged moral philosophy, and it is time it was brought out in the open in business ethics as well. It is a threat that is sometimes identified by way of the philosophical term, "determinism," and though its status in the philosophy of science and theory of knowledge is by no means settled, it has nevertheless wreaked havoc on ethics. If there is determinism, so the argument goes, there can be no agency, properly speaking, and thus no moral responsibility. But determinism admits of at least two interpretations in ethics. The first is determination by "external" circumstances, including pressure or coercion by other people. The second is determination within the person, in particular, by his or her *character*. In the former case, but arguably not in the latter, there is thought to be a problem ascribing moral responsibility.[1]

The argument can be readily extended to business ethics. Versions of the argument have been put forward with regard to corporations, for instance, in the now perennial arguments whether corporations can be or cannot be

From *Business Ethics Quarterly,* January 1, 2003, pp. 43–62. Copyright © 2003 by *Business Ethics Quarterly.* Reprinted by permission of The Philosophy Documentation Center, publisher of *Business Ethics Quarterly.* References omitted.

held responsible.[2] One familiar line of argument holds that only individuals, not corporations, can be held responsible for their actions. But then corporate executives like to excuse their actions by reference to "market forces" that render them helpless, mere victims of economic circumstances, and everyone who works in the corporation similarly excuses their bad behavior by reference to those who set their agenda and policies. They are mere "victims of circumstances." They thus betray their utter lack of leadership. Moreover, it doesn't take a whole lot of research to show that people in corporations tend to behave in conformity with the people and expectations that surround them, even when what they are told to do violates their "personal morality." What (outside of the corporation) might count as "character" tends to be more of an obstacle than a boon to corporate success for many people. What seems to count as "character" in the corporation is a disposition to please others, obey superiors, follow others, and avoid personal responsibility.

In general philosophy, [Immanuel] Kant tried desperately to separate determinism and moral responsibility, defending determinism in the domain of science and "Nature" but preserving agency and responsibility in the domain of ethics. "I have found it necessary to limit knowledge to make room for faith," as he put in one of his most concise but rather misleading *bon mots*. Other philosophers were not so bold. They were willing to accept determinism (even if conjoined with skeptical doubts) and somehow fit agency and responsibility into its domain. David Hume and John Stuart Mill, the two most illustrious empiricist promoters of this strategy, suggested that an act is free (and an agent responsible) if it "flows from the person's character,"[3] where "character" stood for a reasonably stable set of established character traits that were both morally significant and served as the antecedent causal conditions demanded by determinism. Adam Smith, Hume's best friend and the father of not only modern economics but of business ethics too, agreed with this thesis. It was a good solution. It saved the notions of agency and responsibility, it was very much in line with our ordinary intuitions about people's behavior, and it did not try to challenge the scientific establishment. So, too, a major movement in business ethics, of which I consider myself a card-carrying member, is "virtue ethics," which takes the concept of character (and with it the related notions of virtue and integrity) to be central to the idea of being a good person in business. Among the many virtues of virtue ethics in business, one might think, is that, as in Hume and Mill, it would seem to keep at bay the threat of situational ("external") determinism.

Such a solution seems particularly appropriate for business ethics because the concept of character fills the void between institutional behaviorism ("organizational behavior") and an overblown emphasis on free will and personal autonomy that remains oblivious to context, the reality of office work, and the force of peer and corporate pressures. It provides a locus for responsibility without sacrificing the findings of "management science." But I have mixed feelings about the empiricist solution. On the one hand, it seems to me too weak. It does not account (or try to account) for actions "out of character," heroic or saintly or vicious and shockingly greedy behavior, which could not have been predicted of (or even by) the subject. And it does not (as Aristotle does) rigorously hold a person responsible for the formation of his or her character. Aristotle makes it quite clear that a wicked person is responsible for his or her character not because he or she could *now* alter it but because he or she could have and should have acted differently early on and established very different habits and states of character. The corporate bully, the greedy entrepreneur, and the office snitch all would seem to be responsible for not only what they do but who they are, according to Aristotle's tough criterion.

On the other hand, however, the empiricist solution overstates the case for character. (This is what some psychologists, and Gilbert Harman, refer to as the "attribution error.") The empiricists make it sound as if character is something both settled and "robust" (the target of much of the recent psychological literature). Character consists of such traits as honesty and trustworthiness that are more or less resistant to social or interpersonal pressures. But character is never fully formed and settled. It is always vulnerable to circumstances and trauma. People change, and they are malleable. They respond in interesting and sometimes immediate ways to their environment, their peers and pressures from above. Put into an unusual, pressured, or troubled environment, many people will act "out of character," sometimes in heroic but more often in disappointing and sometimes shocking ways. In the corporate setting, in particular, people joke about "leaving their integrity at the office door" and act with sometimes shocking obedience to orders and policies that they personally find unethical and even downright revolting.

These worries can be taken care of with an adequate retooling of the notion of character and its place in ethics, and this is what I will try to do here. But my real worry is that in the effort to correct the excesses of the empiricist emphasis on character, the baby is being thrown out with the bath toys. In recent work by Gilbert Harman and John Doris, in particular, the very notion of character is being thrown into question.[4] Indeed, Harman suggests that "there may be no such thing." Doris entitles his book, tellingly, *Lack of Character.* Both Harman and Doris argue at considerable length that a great deal of what we take as "character" is in fact (and demonstrably) due to specific social settings that reinforce virtuous conduct. To mention two often-used examples, clergy act like clergy not because of character but because they surround themselves with other clergy who expect them to act like clergy. So, too, criminals act like criminals not because of character but because they hang out with other criminals who expect them to act like criminals. Harman argues vehemently against what he calls the illusion of "a robust sense of character." Doris argues, at book length, a very detailed and remarkably nuanced account of virtue and responsibility without character. The conclusion of both authors is that virtue ethics, construed in terms of character, is at best a mistake, and at worst a vicious political maneuver.

It is worth saying a word about this "vicious political maneuver" that is the political target of Harman's and Doris's arguments. I share in their concern, and I, too, would want to argue against those who, on the basis of an absurd notion of character, expect people to "pick themselves up by their own bootstraps," blaming the poor, for instance, for their own impoverishment and thus ignoring social and political (not to mention medical and racial) disadvantages that are certainly not their fault. I, too, reject such a notion of character, but I am not willing to dispense with the very notions of character and the virtues in order to do this.

So, too, in business ethics, there is a good reason to be suspicious of a notion of character that is supposed to stand up to overwhelming pressures without peer or institutional support. I would take Harman's and Doris's arguments as a good reason to insist on sound ethical policies and rigorous ethical enforcement in corporations and in the business community more generally, thus maximizing the likelihood that people will conform to the right kinds of corporate expectations. Nevertheless, something extremely important can get lost in the face of that otherwise quite reasonable and desirable demand. It is the idea that a person can, and should, resist those pressures, even at considerable cost to oneself, depending on the severity of the situation and circumstances. That is the very basis on which virtue ethics has proven to be so appealing to people in business. It is the hope that they can, and sometimes will, resist or even rise up against pressures and policies that they find to be unethical.

So whatever my worries, I find myself a staunch defender of character and the indispensability of talk about character in both ethics and business ethics.[5] To quote my friend and colleague Ed Hartman, "the difference between Peter Hempel [one of the most wonderful human beings we ever met] and Richard Nixon is not just a matter of environment." In both everyday life and in business, there are people we trust, and there are people we do not, often on the basis of a substantial history of disappointments and betrayal. And we trust or distrust those people in much the same circumstances and under much the same conditions. To be sure, character is vulnerable to environment but it is also a bulwark *against* environment. Character supplies that familiar and sometimes uncomfortable or even uncanny resistance to untoward pressures that violate our "principles" or morally disgust us or are damaging to our "integrity." It is character and not God or the Superego that produces that nagging inner voice called "conscience." (It has been suggested that conscience produces character rather than the other way around, but apart from religious predilections there seems to be little sound philosophical argument or empirical research to defend this.) One person refuses to obey a directive to short-change his customers while another refuses to cheat on her expense account despite the fact that everyone around her is doing so. It is character that makes the difference, though not, to be sure, *all* the difference.

Some of my concern with this issue is personal. Like most conscientious people, I worry about my integrity and character, what sorts of temptations and threats I could and would withstand. I feel ashamed (or worse) when I give into those temptations and humiliated when I succumb to (at least some of) those threats. I am occasionally even proud about those temptations and threats I have withstood. Philosophically ("existentially"), I worry about how we view ourselves when the balance of accounts is shifted over to causal and statistical explanations of behavior instead of a continuing emphasis on character, agency, and responsibility. Will that give almost everyone an excuse for almost everything?[6] . . .

The "New Empiricism" Virtue Ethics and Empirical Science

. . . Harman and Doris attack virtue ethics in general and the concept of character in particular on the grounds that they do not survive experimental findings in the past few decades. Exhibit number one for both of them is the infamous Stanley Milgram experiments in which people with supposedly good character performed the most despicable acts when encouraged to do so by an authority (the experimenter). But though empirical research in social psychology can on occasion shock us, surprise us, annoy us, and sometimes burst our illusions, it all gets weighed and accounted for, whether well or badly, in terms of our ordinary folk psychology observations and the ordinary concepts of belief, desire, emotion, character, and interpersonal influences, interactions, and institutions. There are no Copernican revolutions and no Michelson-Morley experiments. The Milgram and other experiments such as those by [J. M.] Darley and [C. D.] Batson that play a central role in Doris's and Harman's arguments get rationalized and explained in all sorts of ways, but none of them in violation of the basic forms of psychological explanation that Aristotle would have found perfectly familiar.[7] Of course, there remains a debate about the relative influence of "external" (environmental) and "inner" factors (character), but the debate, whichever way it goes, remains within the framework of folk psychology and our ordinary psychological concepts.

We might be disturbed, for example, that so many subjects followed the instructions of an authority figure to the point of (what they thought was) the torturing of another human being, but the various explanations in terms of "obedience to authority" or the unusual circumstances of the experiment (how often are most of us told to punish anyone?) do nothing to challenge our ordinary moral intuitions. It just reminds us of something we'd rather not remember, that ordinary people sometimes act very badly in group and institutional situations. This should come as no surprise to those of us who do corporate and organizational ethics. . . .

I have long been an advocate of cooperation between moral philosophy and the social sciences in business ethics. I think that the more we know about how people actually behave in corporations, the richer and more informed our moral judgments and, more important, our decisions will be. In particular, it is very instructive to learn how people will behave in extraordinary circumstances, those in which our ordinary moral intuitions do *not* give us a clue. All of us have asked, say, with regard to the Nazi disease in Germany in the Thirties, how we would have behaved; or how we would behave, think, and feel if we worked for a tobacco company. But even in an ordinary corporation (which is not the same as a university in which there is at least the illusion of individual autonomy and "academic freedom"), the question of "obedience to authority" comes front and center.

Thus an experiment like the Milgram experiment is shocking precisely because it does not seem to presuppose any extraordinary context. Milgram's experiment, which would certainly be prohibited today, has to do with subjects inflicting potentially lethal shocks to victim-learners (in fact the experimenter's accomplices). Even when the victim-learners pleaded for them to stop, the majority of subjects continued to apply the shocks when ordered to do so by the authorities (the experimenters). One could easily imagine this "experiment" being confirmed in any corporation.[8] But I find the use of such research to undermine the notion of character not at all convincing.[9] Harman, for example, argues that

> Empirical studies designed to test whether people behave differently in ways that might reflect their having different character traits have failed to find relevant differences. It is true that studies of this sort are very difficult to carry out and there have been few such studies. Nevertheless, the existing studies have had negative results. Since it is possible to explain our ordinary belief in character traits as deriving from certain illusions, we must conclude that there is no empirical basis for the existence of character traits.[10]

But in addition to leaping from "very few studies" that are "difficult to carry out" to the conclusion that there is "no empirical basis for the existence of character traits," the whole weight of the argument comes to depend on the *possibility* of explaining our ordinary belief in character traits as "deriving from certain illusions." But what would such an explanation consist of? What illusions are we talking about? And what is our "ordinary belief in character"? I will argue that it does not require the "robust" notion attacked by Harman. . . .

What Is a Virtue and Whence Character?

Harman does a nice job of delimiting the ordinary notions of virtue and character, namely those that are most relevant to business ethics. He distinguishes character from various psychological disorders (schizophrenia, mania, depression). More dubiously, he distinguishes character from "innate aspects of temperament such as shyness or being a happy or sad person."[11] Kant, oddly enough, quite correctly insists that being happy (though an "inclination") can be a virtue, as it makes us more inclined to do our duty. But Harman is not just attacking the virtues. He is after character traits in general. Shyness, for example, is a non-moral example of a character trait. Harman considers this a prime example of "false attribution." But I think Jean-Paul Sartre has his eye on something very important when he refers to the citing of such a character trait as "bad faith," namely, where we point to a causal syndrome where we should be talking about decisions and the cultivation (in a very strong sense) of character.[12] There is a certain element of such Sartrianism (an insistence on existential choices rather than robust character) in Harman's argument (with which I quite agree), but this is a very different set of reasons for questioning or qualifying the concepts of character and the virtues.[13] . . .

In the ordinary conceptions of character traits and virtues, Harman and Doris tell us, people differ in their possession of such traits and virtues. People are different, and these differences explain their differences in behavior.

Harman: "We ordinarily suppose that a person's character traits *help* to explain at least some of the things the person does" (italics mine). But, he says, "the fact that people regularly behave in different ways does not establish that they have different character traits. The difference *may* be due to their different situations rather than differences in their characters" (italics mine). But notice that there is no consistency whatever between insisting that a person's character traits *help* to explain their behavior and insisting that a difference in behavior *may* be due to the different situations in which two people find themselves. So, too, Doris's objection to globalism is that people (in experimental situations) fail to display the consistency and stability that explanations in terms of character require. But again, the short-term experiments that he cites do not undermine our more ordinary long-term judgments about personal propensities and dispositions. At best, they force us to face some hard truths about ourselves and consider other propensities and dispositions that may not be virtuous at all.

In our "ordinary conception" two people (one honest, one dishonest) in the same situation (discovering a lost wallet in the street, encountering a person in apparent desperate need, being ordered by an experimenter to "keep on punishing") will very probably act differently. But any philosopher worthy of his or her debating trophies will quickly point out that no two situations are sufficiently similar to make that case. It is only a very thin description of "the situation" (the experimental set-up) that makes it seem so. Subjects come from different backgrounds and different social classes. They are different genders. They may as a consequence have very different senses of the situation. I would not join Joel Feinberg in claiming that those students who do not stop for a stranger in need (in Darley and Batson's much-discussed "Good Samaritan" experiment) have a "character flaw," but neither would I conclude (with Doris) that their behavior is largely "situational."[14] The student's way of seeing and being in the situation may be very different, and this, of course, is just what Aristotle says about character. It is, first of all, a kind of perception, based on good up-bringing. Thus I think Harman is being a bit disingenuous when he argues that "they must be disposed to act differently in the same circumstances (as they perceive those circumstances)." The question of character begins with how they perceive those circumstances.

. . . Corporate managers and employees feel obliged and committed to act in conformity with corporate pressures and policies even when they are questionable or unethical, and they learn to rationalize accordingly. The question is, does any of this imply that we should give up or give in on character? Or should we say that character is both cultivated and maintained through the dynamic interaction of individuals and groups in their environment and they in turn develop those virtues (and vices) that in turn motivate them to remain in the situations in which their virtues are supported, reinforced, and not threatened?

In Milgram's famous "shocking people" experiment in the early 1960s (just as America was getting more deeply involved in the morass of Vietnam), the experimental data were indeed shocking, even to Milgram and his colleagues who expected no such result. In the social context of the times, questions about obedience to authority (left over from the Nuremberg trials not so many years before) had a special poignancy, especially in the face of the soon to be challenged American "innocence" of the time. It was very upsetting to find that good, solid, ordinary middle-class people could be ordered (but not coerced) to act so brutally (whether or not they had severe misgivings about their behavior at the time—a matter of no small importance here). The facts of the experiment are beyond dispute. But what the experiment means remains highly controversial, and it does not deserve the central place in the attack on character that it is now receiving. Doris claims that "Milgram's experiments show how apparently non-coercive situational factors may induce destructive behavior despite the apparent presence of contrary evaluative and dispositional structures." Accordingly, he "gives us reason to question the robustness of dispositions implicated in compassion-relevant moral behavior."[15]

Well, no. The disposition (virtue) that is most prominent and robust in this very contrived and unusual situation, the one that virtually all of the subjects had been brought up with and practiced everyday since childhood, was doing what they were told by those in authority. Compassion, by contrast, is a virtue more often praised than practiced, except on specially designated occasions (giving to the neediest at Christmas time) or stretching the term to include such common courtesies as restraining one's criticism of an unprepared student or letting the other car go first at a four-way intersection. (I would argue that such examples betray a lack of understanding of what compassion is.) Most often, people display compassion by "feeling sorry for" those much worse off than they, a very small expenditure of effort even when it is sincere. It seems to me that what the Milgram experiment shows—and what subsequent events in Vietnam made all too painfully obvious—was that despite our high moral opinions of ourselves and our conformist chorus singing about what independent individuals we all are, Americans, like Germans before them, are capable of beastly behavior in circumstances where their *practiced* virtues are forced to confront an unusual situation in which unpracticed efforts are required. In the Milgram experiment as in Vietnam, American subjects and soldiers were compelled by their own practiced dispositions to follow orders even in the face of consequences that were intolerable. Obedience may not always be a virtue. . . .

In discussions of Vietnam, those who were not there (especially politicians) like to talk about the virtue of courage as the defining trait of the American forces. What they ignore, of course, is the very nature of the war. In several important memoirs by soldiers who served there, Bill Broyles and Tim O'Brien, it becomes clear that courage was just about the last thing on most of the soldiers minds.[16] They were terrified of losing legs and arms. They were moved by camaraderie and a sense of mutual obligation. (The virtue-name "loyalty" misses the mark.) The only discussion of courage in O'Brien's book has to do with a single heroic figure, a Captain Johansen whom he likens to Hector in Homer's *Iliad*. But this one character is exemplary in precisely the fact that he alone talked about and exemplified true courage. But the absence of courage (which is not to imply anything like cowardice on the part of the American troops) had a great deal to do with the nature of this particular war. It lacked any sense of purpose or progress. It lacked any sense of meaning for most of the men. And so, in that moral vacuum, all that was left for most soldiers was the worry about their own physical integrity and their keen sense of responsibility for each other. The atrocities at My Lai and Thanh Phong followed as a matter of course. There was no context in which either character or courage could be exercised.

Which brings us back to the misgivings and feelings of discomfort experienced by some (not all) of the subjects and the "grunts" in Vietnam. Feelings of compassion (and other moral sentiments) may not be definitive in motivating behavior, especially if one has not faced anything like the awful situation in which the subjects and soldiers found themselves. But it does not follow that there is nothing more for virtue ethics to say about such cases. Experiments such as Milgram's are no longer allowed on college campuses, and for good reason. The feelings provoked in the subjects were too painful, and often with lasting damage.[17] And this is nothing, of course, compared to the posttraumatic experiences of many of those who served in Vietnam. The robustness of compassion must be measured not simply in terms of whether the subjects refused to continue with the experiment or not (most did) or whether the soldiers continued to do as they were ordered but by how powerful and upsetting the feelings they experienced both during and after the experiment. It is worth noting that there were a few sadists who actually enjoyed cruelty. There were others that were brutalized by the experiment and many who were brutalized by the war. That, it seems to me, should not be discounted. Bosses today are once again being forced to lay off thousands of their managers and employees. (Market forces is the inescapable explanation.) But there is all the difference in the world between those monsters like the infamous Al "Chainsaw" Dunlap who took such evident pride in cross the board cuts and virtual saints such as Aaron Feuerstein who felt so badly about having to lay off workers (after a fire gutted his factory) that he kept them on the payroll until the company got back on its feet.[18]

The Milgram Experiment Revisited: A Model of Corporate Life?

Is corporate life nothing but the vectors of peer pressures, leaving very little or even no room for the personal virtues? Does social psychology show that this is not the case only for corporate grinds but for all of us? Empirically-minded philosophers love to find a single experiment, or perhaps two, that make this case for them, that is, which provide the basis for speculative excursions that go far beyond the (usually rather timid) findings of the social psychologists themselves. Harman's appeal to the two famous experiments by Milgram and by Darley and Batson are illustrative. Doris takes in a much wider swath of the social science literature, but even he is forced to admit, throughout his admirable book, that there are profound reasons for not generalizing from particular experiments to a good deal of "real life."

Regarding the Milgram experiment, Harman (following Ross and Nisbett) rejects as implausible any explanation in terms of a "character defect" and suggests instead the "step-wise character of the shift from relatively unobjection-able behavior to complicity in a pointless, cruel, and dangerous ordeal." I think that this is indeed part of the explanation. Milgram's subjects needed to have their callousness cultivated even as they dutifully obeyed the authorities (like the proverbial frog in slowly boiling water). The subjects could not have been expected to simply shock strangers on command. But where Harman adds that we are tempted to make the "fundamental attribution error" of blaming the subject's destructive obedience on a personal defect, I would say instead that what the Milgram experiment shows is how foolish and tragic the otherwise important virtues of conformity and obedience can be. There is no "personal defect" on display here precisely because what the experiment shows is the consistency and stability of *that* virtue. And the fact that it is (like all virtues) not always a virtue is no argument against its status as part of the core of the explanation of the subjects' behavior. The rest of the explanation involves not just the incremental but also the disorienting nature of the situation. . . .

The other often-used case for "lack of character" is the case of the "good Samaritan," designed by Darley and Batson. Seminary students, on their way to give an assigned lecture (on "the good Samaritan") were forced to confront a person (an accomplice of the experimenter) on their way. Few of them stopped to help. It is no doubt true that the difference between subjects and their will-ingness to help the (supposed) victim can be partially explained on the basis of such transient variables as the fact that they were "in a hurry." And it is proba-bly true as well (and not at all surprising to those of us who are not pushing "faith-based initiatives" these days) that people who were (or claimed to be) religious or who were about to talk on a religious topic of direct relevance to the experience did not act so differently as they would have supposed. But does it follow that character played no role? I would say that all sorts of character traits, from one's ability to think about time and priorities to one's feelings of anxiety and competence when faced with a (seemingly) suffering human being all come into play. Plus, of course, the sense of responsibility and obligation to arrive at an appointment on time, which once again slips into the background of the interpretation of the experiment and so blinds us to the obvious.

As in the Milgram experiment, how much is the most plausible explana-tion of the case precisely one that the experimenters simply assume but ignore, namely the character trait or virtue of promptness, the desire to arrive at the designated place on time? It is not lack of character. It is a *conflict* of character traits, one practiced and well-cultivated, the other more often spoken of than put in practice. Theology students have no special claims on compassion. They just tend to talk about it a lot. And as students they have had little opportunity to test and practice their compassion in ways that are not routine. . . .

What is not debatable, it seems to me, is that people present themselves differently, whether or not their presentations accurately represent their vir-tues and vices (which longer exposure is sure to reveal). I have long argued that the subject of explanation is not just the behavior of an agent but the behav-ior of an *agent-in-situation* (or some such odd locution). In business ethics, in particular, the behavior in question is the behavior of an *"individual-within-the-organization,"* which is not for a moment to deny that this context may not be the only one of relevance in moral evaluation. Context is essential but it isn't everything. Virtues and vices are important for our explanations of human behavior, but they make sense only in the context of particular situations and cultural surroundings. There is no such thing as courage or generosity in abstraction, but it does not follow that there is no such thing as courage or generosity.

Conclusion: In Defense of Business Virtue Ethics

Virtue ethics has a long pedigree, going back to Plato and Aristotle, Confucius in China, and many other cultures as well as encompassing much of Medieval and modern ethics—including, especially, the ethics of Hume, Adam Smith, and the other "Moral Sentiment Theorists." But we would do well to remind ourselves just why virtue and character have become such large concerns in the world today—in business ethics and in politics in particular. The impetus comes from such disparate sources as the Nuremberg trials and American atrocities in Vietnam, teenage drug use and peer pressure, and the frequently heard rationalization in business and politics that "everyone is doing it." The renewed emphasis on character is an attempt to build a personal bulwark (call it "integrity") against such pressures and rationalizations and (though half-heartedly) to cultivate virtues other than those virtues of unquestioning obedience that proved to be so dominant in the Milgram experiments and in Vietnam atrocities such as My Lai.

. . . If we are to combat intolerance, encourage mutual forgiveness, and facilitate human flourishing in contexts plagued by ethnic hatred, for instance, there is no denying the need for mediating institutions that will create the circumstances in which the virtues can be cultivated. Closer to home, the cultivation of the virtues in much-touted moral education also requires the serious redesign of our educational institutions. And much of the crime and commercial dishonesty in the United States and in the world today is due, no doubt, to the absence of such designs and character-building contexts. (The market, said the late great "Buddhist" economist E. F. Schumaker, "is the institutionalization of non-responsibility."[19]) We need less moralizing and more beneficent social engineering.

I could not agree more with these aims. But the existentialist twist to which Harman alludes (that we *choose* our circumstances) and the postmodern turn encouraged by Doris (that we acknowledge that for the most part our circumstances make us) convince me not that we should eliminate talk of the virtues and character but fully acknowledge both the role of the social sciences (*all* of the social sciences) and stop preaching the virtues without due emphasis upon *both* personal responsibility and the force of circumstances. Like Doris, we should appreciate more such "out of character" heroic and saintly behavior (he mentions Oscar Schindler in particular) and the exigencies of context and circumstances. But we should insist, first and foremost, that people—at any rate, people *like us*—are responsible for what they do, and what they make of themselves.

Notes

1. See, for example, Robert Young, "The Implications of Determinism," in Peter Singer, *A Companion to Ethics* (London: Blackwell, 1991). I am not considering here the post-Freudian complications of determination by way of compulsion or personality disorder.

2. E.g., Kenneth Goodpaster and John B. Matthews, Jr., "Can a Corporation Have a Conscience?" *Harvard Business Review*, Jan–Feb. 1982; John Ladd, "Morality and the Ideal of Rationality in Formal Organizations," *The Monist*, Oct. 1970; Peter A. French, *Collective and Corporate Responsibility* (New York: Columbia University Press, 1984). French, Peter A., "Responsibility and the Moral Role of Corporate Entities," in R. Edward Freeman, ed., *Business as a Humanity* (*Ruffin Lectures II*) (New York: Oxford, 1994); Peter A. French, "The Corporation as a Moral Person," *American Philosophical Quarterly* 16:3 (1979). Manuel G. Velasquez, *Business Ethics* (Engelwood Cliffs, N.J.: Prentice-Hall, 1982 and further editions).

3. David Hume, *An Enquiry Concerning Human Understanding*, 2nd ed. L. A. Sleby; Biggee, ed. (Clarendon: Oxford University Press, 1902). John Stuart Mill, *A System of Logic* 8th ed. (New York: Harper & Row, 1874). Adam Smith, *Theory of the Moral Sentiments* (London: George Bell, 1880).

4. Gilbert Harman, "Moral Philosophy Meets Social Psychology: Virtue Ethics and the Fundamental Attribution Error," *Proceedings of the Aristotelian Society* 99(1998–99): 315–331. Revised version in Harman, G., *Explaining Value and Other Essays in Moral Philosophy* (Oxford: Clarendon Press, 2000), 165–178. See also, "The Nonexistence of Character Traits," *Proceedings of the Aristotelian Society* 100 (1999–2000): 223–226. John Doris, *Lack of Character: Personality and Moral Behavior* (New York: Cambridge University Press, 2002).

5. Two philosophical defenses of character are Joel Kupperman, "The Indispensability of Character," in *Philosophy,* April 2001, 76(2): 239–250, and Maria Merritt, "Virtue Ethics and Situationist Personality Psychology," in *Ethical Theory and Moral Practice* 3 (2000): 365–383.

6. The fight against the pervasiveness of excuses is something I learned early on from Jean-Paul Sartre and pursue in some detail in my series, *No Excuses: Existentialism and the Meaning of Life* (The Teaching Company, 2000).

7. I would plea for something of an exception in the case of the fascinating flow of neuropsychiatric research of the last thirty or so years, which does indeed go beyond folk psychology, not only in its particular findings but in the very vocabulary and structure of its explanations. Nevertheless, what is so dazzling in much of this research is precisely that way in which neurological anomalies violate our ordinary "folk psychology" explanations. I will limit my references to two. The first is a wonderful series of studies published by Oliver Sachs over the years, including *The Man Who Mistook His Wife for a Hat and Other Clinical Tales* (Touchstone, 1998). The second is the recent research of Antonio Damasio, esp. in *Descartes's Error* (Putnam, 1994).

8. Stanley Milgram, "Behavioral Study of Obedience," *Journal of Abnormal and Social Psychology,* vol. 67, 1963; *Obedience to Authority* (New York: HarperCollins, 1983).

9. I have argued with both Harman and Doris that they have made selective use of social science research. In particular, they have restricted their appeals and references almost entirely to social psychology and have been

correspondingly neglectful of counter-arguments in personality theory. The difference in perspective—and consequently the tension—between these two branches of empirical psychology are extremely significant to the argument at hand. See, e.g., Todd F. Heatherton (ed.), Joel Lee Weinberger, (ed.), *Can Personality Change?* [edited book] (Washington, D.C.: American Psychological Association, 1994), xiv, 368. A. Caspi, and B. W Roberts (1999), "Personality Continuity and Change Across the Life Course" in L. A. Pervin and O. P. John (eds.), *Handbook of Personality: Theory and Research,* 2nd ed., (New York: Guilford), 300–326. Thomas J. Bouchard, Jr., "The Genetics of Personality," [chapter], Kenneth Blum (ed.); Ernest P. Noble, (ed.) et al., *Handbook of Psychiatric Genetics* (Boca Raton, Fla.: CRC Press, Inc. 1997), 273–296.

10. Gilbert Harman, "Moral Philosophy Meets Social Psychology" (web version), 1.

11. But see a similar distinction defended by Ed Hartman, "The Role of Character in Business Ethics," in J. Dienhart, D. Moberg, and R. Duska, *The Next Phase of Business Ethics: Integrating Psychology and Ethics* (Amsterdam: JAI/Elsevier, 2001), 341–354.

12. Jean-Paul Sartre, *Being and Nothingness,* trans. H. Barnes (New York: Philosophical Library, 1956), see for instance 104f.

13. An essay that uses the Milgram experiment to talk about "excuses" is A. Strudler and D. Warren, "Authority, Heuristics, and the Structure of Excuses," in J. Dienhart, D. Moberg, and R. Duska, *The Next Phase of Business Ethics,* 355–375. My own view is that "everybody's doing it" is NO excuse, or at best a mitigating one. See my *No Excuses: Existentialism and the Meaning of Life.* See also the now classic essay by Ron Green, "Everybody's Doing It," in *Business Ethics Quarterly* 1(1): 75–94.

14. J. M. Darley and C. D. Batson, "From Jerusalem to Jericho: A Study of Situational and Disposition Variables in Helping Behavior," *Journal of Personality and Social Psychology 27,* 1973.

15. Doris, 69.

16. William Broyles, Jr. *Brothers in Arms* (New York: Knopf, 1986) and Tim O'Brien, *If I Die in a Combat Zone Box Me Up and Ship Me Home* (New York: Delacorte, 1973). Both books are discussed by Thomas Palaima in "Courage and Prowess Afoot in Homer and in Vietnam" in *Classical and Modem Literature,* 20/3/(2000).

17. See Milgram, *Obedience to Authority.*

18. See my discussion in *A Better Way to think about Business* (Oxford, 1999), 10.

19. E. F. Schumaker, *Small is Beautiful* (Harper and Row, 1973).

References

Blackburn, Simon. 1995. *Essays in Quasi-Realism* (New York: Oxford University Press.

Bouchard, Thomas J., Jr. 1997. "The Genetics of Personality" [chapter]. Kenneth Blum (ed.), Ernest P. Noble, (ed.) et al. *Handbook of Psychiatric* Genetics. BocaRaton, Fla.: CRC Press, Inc., 273–296.

Broyles, William, Jr. 1986. *Brothers in Arms.* New York: Knopf.

Carr, Alfred. Jan.–Feb. 1968. "Is Business Bluffing Ethical?" *Harvard Business Review:* 143–153.

Caspi, A., and B. W. Roberts. 1999. "Personality Continuity and Change Across the Life Course" in *Handbook of Personality: Theory and Research* 2nd ed. L. A. Pervin and O. P. John (eds.). New York: Guilford, 300–326.

Damasio, Antonio. 1994. *Descartes's Error.* New York: Putnam.

Darley, J. M., and C. D. Batson. 1973. "From Jerusalem to Jericho: A Study of Situational and Dispositional Variables in Helping Behavior." *Journal of Personality and Psychology* 27.

Doris, John. 2002. *Lack of Character: Personality and Moral Behavior.* New York: Cambridge University Press.

French, Peter A. 1984. Collective and Corporate Responsibility. New York: Columbia University Press.

———. 1979. "The Corporation as a Moral Person." *American Philosophical Quarterly* 16 (3).

———. "Responsibility and the Moral Role of Corporate Entities." 1994. In *Business as a Humanity (Ruffin Lectures II).* R. Edward Freeman (ed.). New York: Oxford.

Funder, David C. 2001. "Personality." *Annual Review of Psychology.* 52:197–221.

Goodpaster, Kenneth, and John B. Matthews, Jr. Jan.–Feb. 1982. "Can a Corporation Have a Conscience? *Harvard Business Review.*

Green, Ronald. "Everybody's Doing It." *Business Ethics Quarterly* 1(1): 75–94.

Griffiths, Paul. 1997. *What Emotions Really Are.* Chicago University of Chicago Press. 1998–99.

Harman, Gilbert. 1998–99. "Moral Philosophy Meets Social Psychology: Virtue Ethics and the Fundamental Attribution Error." *Proceedings of the Aristotelian Society* (99): 315–331.

———. 1999–2000. "The Nonexistence of Character Traits." *Proceedings of the Aristotelian Society* (100): 223–226.

———. 2000. *Explaining Value and Other Essays in Moral Philosophy.* Oxford: Clarendon Press, 165–178.

Hartman, Edwin M., ed. 2001. "The Role of Character in Business Ethics." in *The Next Phase of Business Ethics: Integrating Psychology and Ethics.* J. Dienhart, D. Moberg, and R. Duska (eds.). Amsterdam: JAI/Elsevier, 341–354.

Heatherton, Todd F. and Joel Lee Weinberger (eds.). 1994. "Can Personality Change? [edited book]. Washington, D.C.: American Psychological Association, 368.

Hume, David. 1902. *An Enquiry Concerning Human Understanding,* 2nd ed. L. A. Sleby-Biggee (ed.). Clarendon: Oxford University Press.

Kenrick, D. T., and Funder, D. C. 1988. "Profiting from Controversy: Lessons from the Person-Situation Debate." *American Psychologist* (43): 23–34.

Kupperman, Joel. April 2001. "The Indispensability of Character." *Philosophy* 76(2): 239–250.

Ladd, John. Oct. 1970. "Morality and the Ideal of Rationality in Formal Organizations." *The Monist.*

MacIntyre, Alasdair. 1984. *After Virtue.* Notre Dame: Notre Dame University Press.

Merritt, Maria. 2000. "Virtue Ethics and Situationist Personality Psychology." *Ethical Theory and Moral Practice* (3): 365–383.

Milgram, Stanley. 1963. "Behavioral Study of Obedience." *Journal of Abnormal and Social Psychology* 67.

Milgram, Stanley. 1983. *Obedience to Authority*. New York: HarperCollins.

Mill, John Stuart. 1874. *A System of Logic*. 8th ed. New York: Harper & Row.

Nietzsche, Friedrich. 1954. *Thus Spoke Zarathustra*. Trans., Kaufmann. New York: Viking, 207.

Nisbett and Ross. 1980. *Human Inference: Strategies and Shortcomings of Social Judgement*. Englewood Cliffs, N.J.: Prentice-Hall.

O'Brien, Tim. 1973. *If I Die in a Combat Zone Box Me Up and Ship Me Home*. New York: Delacorte.

Palaima, Thomas. 2000. "Courage and Prowess Afoot in Homer and in Vietnam," in *Classical and Modern Literature* 20 (3): 1–22.

Sachs, Oliver. 1998. *The Man Who Mistook His Wife for a Hat and Other Clinical Tales*. New York: Touchstone.

Sartre, Jean-Paul. 1956. *Being and Nothingness*. Trans. H. Barnes. New York: Philosophical Library.

Schumaker, E. F. 1973. *Small is Beautiful*. New York: Harper and Row.

Smith, Adam. 1880. *Theory of the Moral Sentiments*. London: George Bell.

Solomon, Robert C. 1993. *Ethics and Excellence*. New York: Oxford University Press.

———. 1999. *A Better Way to Think about Business*. New York: Oxford University Press.

Strudler, A., and D. Warren. 2001. "Authority, Heuristics, and the Structure of Excuses" in *The Next Phase of Business Ethics*. J. Dienhart, D. Moberg, and R. Duska (eds.), 355–375.

Velasquez, Manuel G. 1982. *Business Ethics*. Engelwood Cliffs, N.J.: Prentice-Hall.

Young, Robert. 1991. "The Implications of Determinism" in *A Companion to Ethics*. Peter Singer (ed.). London Blackwell.

Gilbert Harman  **NO**

No Character or Personality

Abstract: [Robert] Solomon argues that, although recent research in social psychology has important implications for business ethics, it does not undermine an approach that stresses virtue ethics. However, he underestimates the empirical threat to virtue ethics, and his a priori claim that empirical research cannot overturn our ordinary moral psychology is overstated. His appeal to seemingly obvious differences in character traits between people simply illustrates the fundamental attribution error. His suggestion that the Milgram and Darley and Batson experiments have to do with such character traits as obedience and punctuality cannot help to explain the relevant differences in the way people behave in different situations.

. . . I want to suggest that Solomon underestimates the force of the threat to his version of business virtue ethics and I want to say a bit more about how the evidence from social psychology implies such "fragmentation."

Psychology and Folk Psychology

It is uncontroversial that there is usually a difference between the study of ordinary conceptions of a given phenomenon and the study of the phenomenon itself. We distinguish between folk or common-sense physics, which is studied by certain psychologists, and physics, which is studied by physicists; these are both interesting subjects, but they are different. Similarly, there is a clear difference between the study of conceptions people at a certain time had about witches and witchcraft and the study of what was actually true about people who were taken to be witches and phenomena thought to be witchcraft. We distinguish between the study of how people conceive of God from the study of theology. We distinguish between the study of doctors' views about good medical treatment and an investigation into what sorts of treatment are actually effective. We distinguish interviewers' conceptions of the value of interviewing from whether interviews actually improve selection processes.[1] In the same way, there is a clear conceptual difference between what people generally think about character and personality and what is actually the case; the study of what people think about character and personality (as in "personality theory" or "personality psychology") is part of the study of folk psychology and is not the same as a study of character and personality.

From *Business Ethics Quarterly,* vol. 13, no. 1, January 2003, pp. 87–94. Copyright © 2003 by *Business Ethics Quarterly.* Reprinted by permission of The Philosophy Documentation Center, publisher of *Business Ethics Quarterly.* References omitted.

Surprisingly, Solomon expresses doubts about this sort of difference with respect to the virtues. He says that "there is an easy but wholly misleading analogy with physics." He agrees that "many of our moral intuitions are erroneous or archaic," but insists that "our moral intuitions are not *like* our intuitions in physics. There is no 'matter of fact' independent of our intuitions and attitudes." Furthermore, he says, "*All* psychology, if it is psychology at all, is one or another version of 'folk psychology' ('the only game in town,' according to Jerry Fodor)."

In response, I have to say that, although it has often been argued (e.g., by Dennett, 1981; Fodor, 1987) that psychology has to be belief and desire psychology, I am not familiar with any similar argument that psychology must for that reason also include commitment to character and personality traits. In particular, I do not believe that Fodor has ever made such an argument. Fodor's (1975) "only game in town" is supposed to be a certain sort of computational functionalism involving a "language of thought" with no reference whatsoever to character traits.

Furthermore, whether or not there is a matter of fact about what is right or wrong, it is obvious that many moral judgments presuppose matters of fact. To belabor the point, if I say you were wrong to hit Bob in the nose, I presuppose that in fact you hit Bob in the nose and, if you did not, I am mistaken. Similarly, if I say that you have a certain virtuous character, I presuppose that you have a character. Perhaps, as Solomon believes, it is not a matter of fact whether such a character is virtuous. But it is a matter of fact whether you have the character, and whether there are character traits at all.

In addition to offering these relatively a priori arguments for doubting that social psychology could undermine ordinary conceptions of character and personality traits, Solomon also notes the existence of the field of "personality theory." He has, he says, "long been an advocate of cooperation between moral philosophy and the social sciences in business ethics." But, he says,

> What about that voluminous literature *not* in social psychology but in the (artificially competing) field of personality theory? . . . If we want to play off moral philosophy and virtue ethics against the social sciences, let's make sure that all of the social sciences are represented and not just social psychology.

However, personality theory or personality psychology is in pretty bad institutional shape. Solomon refers to Funder (2001), a bravely upbeat review of the current (utterly dismal) state of personality psychology that nevertheless acknowledges that personality psychology has collapsed as an academic subject. So, Funder revealingly bemoans

> the permanent damage to the infrastructure of personality psychology wreaked by the person-situation debate of the 1970s and 1980s. . . . [O]ne reason for the trend . . . for so much personality research being done by investigators not affiliated with formal programs in personality may be that there are so few formal programs to be affiliated with. The graduate programs in personality psychology that were shrunken beyond recognition or even abolished during the 1970s and 1980s have not been revived. (213)

Why does the critique of virtue ethics appeal to social psychology rather than to personality psychology? Because personality psychology has been concerned with characterizing ordinary folk conceptions of personality. Social psychology is concerned with the accuracy of these conceptions. To the extent that you are interested in the truth and accuracy of claims about character and personality, you need to consult social psychology, not "personality psychology."[2]

What Is the Fundamental Attribution Error?

> The librarian carried the old woman's groceries across the street. The receptionist stepped in front of the old man in line. The plumber slipped an extra $50 into his wife's purse. Although you were not asked to make any inferences about any of these characters, chances are that you inferred that the librarian is helpful, the receptionist rude, and the plumber generous. Perhaps because we do not realize the extent to which behavior is shaped by situations, we tend to spontaneously infer such traits from behavior." (Kunda, 1999, 435)

Psychologists refer to this tendency as "correspondence bias" or "the fundamental attribution error." It is a bias toward explanations in terms of corresponding personality traits, the error of ignoring situational factors. The bias seems to be associated with a perceptual tendency to pay more attention to a figure than to its ground, and there appear to be significant cultural differences in the extent to which people are subject to this tendency and to the fundamental attribution error (Nisbett, 1998).

Having once attributed a trait to a given person, an observer has a strong tendency to continue to attribute that trait to the person even in the face of considerable disconfirming evidence, a tendency psychologists sometimes call "confirmation bias," a bias toward noting evidence that is in accord with one's hypothesis and toward disregarding evidence against it.[3]

Even in a world with no individual differences in character traits or personality traits, people would still strongly believe that there were such differences, as long as they were subject to the fundamental attribution error and to confirmation bias. This means that the apparent obviousness of the claim that people differ in such traits (as in Ed Hartman's comparison, endorsed by Solomon, between Hempel and Nixon) is less evidential than one may think. True, it is "obvious" that, some people have different character and personality traits than others. But our finding this fact so obvious is predicted by our tendency to the fundamental attribution error whether or not there are such differences.

Subtle Situational Effects

Minor and seemingly irrelevant differences in the perceived situation sometimes make significant differences to what people do. Doris (2002) discusses several examples.

Imagine a person making a call in a suburban shopping plaza. As the caller leaves the phone booth, along comes Alice, who drops a folder full of papers that scatter in the caller's path. Will the caller stop and help before the only copy of Alice's magnum opus is trampled by the bargain-hungry throngs? . . . [I]n an experiment by Isen and Levin (1972) . . . the paperdropper was an experimental assistant or "confederate." For one group of callers, a dime was planted in the phone's coin return slot; for the other, the slot was empty. [The results are that, of 16 callers who found a dime, 14 helped and 2 did not; of 25 who did not find a dime, 1 helped and 24 did not.] . . . Finding a bit of change is something one would hardly bother to remark on in describing one's day, yet it makes the difference between helping and not. (Doris, 2002, p. 30)

Whether or not a theology student stops to help someone who seems to be having a heart attack may depend on how much of a hurry the student is to accomplish a comparatively trivial goal (Darley and Batson, 1973). Whether someone in a waiting room will go to the aid of another person who seems to have fallen off a ladder in the next room may depend on whether there is another person in the waiting room who seems unconcerned with the apparent fall (Latane and Darley, 1970).

In the Milgram (1974) experiment, subjects were led by gradual steps to do something they would never have done straight away, namely to administer very severe electrical shocks to another person. The gradualness of the process with no obvious place to stop seems an important part of the explanation why they obeyed a command to shock the other person in that experiment although they would not have done so if directly ordered to give the severe shock at the very beginning.

Similarly, if you are trying not to give into temptation to drink alcohol, to smoke, or to eat caloric food, the best advice is not to try to develop "willpower" or "self-control." Instead, it is best to head the situationist slogan, "People! Places! Things!" Don't go to places where people drink! Do not carry cigarettes or a lighter and avoid people who smoke! Stay out of the kitchen!

Sometimes a person acts well or badly in a seemingly unusual way. Concerning any such case, there is an issue as to what makes the difference that leads to such seemingly unusual behavior. When you perceive or learn about someone you do not know doing such an unusual thing, you have a strong tendency to attribute the behavior to some good or bad trait of the person in question. When you learn that a certain seminary student walked right past someone who seemed to be having a heart attack, actually stepping right over the person, you tend to think of the student as incredibly callous.

The question is what makes the difference that leads to the unusual or surprising behavior. Is it that some theology students are more compassionate than others? Does the Milgram experiment show that almost everyone is basically evil?

Solomon says that certain character traits are relevant in these cases, namely, (1) obedience to (the experimenters') authority and (2) promptness. But relevant to what? Since Solomon thinks that all the experimental subjects had these traits, he does not suppose that these common traits are responsible for the *differences* in helping behavior that were observed. Nor do they account for the difference in obedience between a subject who is commanded to give an intense shock to someone at the very beginning and a subject who starts by giving a little shock and who increases the shock by very small steps.

No one supposes that these two experiments, taken by themselves, show that there are no character traits. What they show is that aspects of a particular situation can be important to how a person acts in ways that ordinary people do not normally appreciate, leading them to attribute certain distinctive actions to an agent's distinctive character rather than to subtle aspects of the situation. In particular, observers [of] some of the events that occur in these experiments are strongly inclined to blame those participants who did not stop to help or who provided intense shocks, thinking that the explanation of these agent's immoral actions lies in their terrible character. But the observers are wrong: that cannot be the explanation.

Near the end of his remarks, Solomon says, "Empirically-minded philosophers love to find a single experiment or perhaps two that . . . provide the basis for speculative excursions which go far beyond the (usually rather timid) findings of the social psychologists themselves." I need to emphasize that the Milgram experiment and others mentioned so far are only a few of the different experiments illustrating subtle effects of situations and the ways in which observers fail to understand those effects, leading observers to make the fundamental attribution error. Furthermore, as I have been insisting, the "speculative excursions" Solomon attributes to Doris and me do not go "far beyond the . . . findings of the social psychologists," but are in fact part of the settled core of the subject of social psychology.

Traits

We must distinguish individual acts of honesty or dishonesty, courage or cowardice, compassion or coldness from the corresponding character traits. The ordinary conception of a character or personality trait is of a relatively broad-based disposition to respond in the relevant way with acts of the corresponding sort. In an important discussion, Merritt (2000) shows that Aristotelian virtue ethics and most contemporary versions of virtue ethics (*but not Hume's theory*) appeal to character traits in this broad sense.

Now, the evidence indicates that people may differ in certain relatively narrow traits but do not have broad and stable dispositions corresponding to the sorts of character and personality traits we normally suppose that people have. Doris's (2002) defense of the fragmentation of character, derided by Solomon, is so widely accepted by social psychologists that a similar account can be found in any introductory textbook in social psychology. This is how Kunda (1999) puts the point:

> Our notion of traits as broad and stable dispositions that manifest themselves to the same extent in a variety of situations cannot hold water. However, this does not mean that there are no enduring and systematic differences among individuals. My intuitions that I am a very different

person from my brother or that my children have predictably different patterns of behavior need not be wrong. Such intuitions may be based on meaningful and stable differences among individuals but not the kind of differences implied by the traditional understanding of traits. . . . [For example,] Carol is extremely extroverted in one-on-one situations, is only moderately extroverted when in small groups, and is not at all extroverted in large groups. She will appear very comfortable and outgoing if you meet with her alone, but will clam up and appear very shy and awkward if you encounter her in a large group setting. Linda has a very different profile. She is extremely extroverted in large groups but not at all extroverted in one-on-one situations. She may appear composed and comfortable when lecturing to a large audience but withdrawn and aloof if you approach her alone. (Kunda, 1999, 443–4)

In conclusion, it appears that we are truly quite consistent in our behavior within each situation, and it is quite appropriate to expect such consistency in others. But we run into trouble when we expect this consistency to extend to other situations as well. Even slight variations in the features of a situation can lead to dramatic shifts in people's behavior. (Kunda, 1999, 499)

Free Will and Responsibility

Solomon worries that in the rejection of the sort of character and personality traits that are accepted in ordinary moral thinking and in his version of virtue ethics,

> something extremely important can get lost. . . . It is the idea that [one] can and should resist [certain] pressures, even at considerable cost to oneself, depending on the severity of the situation and circumstances. That is the very basis on which virtue ethics has proven to be so appealing to people in business.

This is clearly a different issue. Of course, people can and should resist such pressures and we should encourage them to do so. But the point has nothing to do with whether people have character traits. As Solomon would certainly agree, even a person without relevant character traits can and should resist.

Solomon worries about the philosophical consequences of denying the existence of character, because that would be to go "over to causal and statistical explanations of behavior instead of a continuing emphasis on character, agency, and responsibility." But people do not need character traits in order to have agency and responsibility. As Doris (2002, chaps. 7–8) persuasively argues, denying the existence of character traits in no way undermines the notions of agency and of responsibility.

Conclusion

Aristotelian style virtue ethics shares with folk psychology a commitment to broad-based character traits of a sort that people simply do not have. This does not threaten free will and moral responsibility, but it does mean that it is a mistake to base business ethics on that sort of virtue ethics. This leaves open the possibility of Merritt's (2000) Humean style virtue ethics in which virtuous behavior is socially supported and sustained.

Notes

1. For discussion of the well-known "interview illusion," see, e.g., Kunda (1999), 179–89, and references cited there. Interviews are simultaneously very unreliable indicators of later performance and also very vivid. Using interviews adds expensive vivid noise to a decision process. Solomon (who says the Princeton Philosophy Department's practice of not interviewing job candidates is "peculiar") suggests that the point of interviewing is to see how well the candidate will "fit in" with others on the job. The point about expensive vivid noise obviously applies here as well, as is noted in Miller and Cantor (1982), who nevertheless suggest that there is still a point to having a candidate for a teaching position give a talk to members of the hiring department, because these members will almost certainly all have the same impression of the talk, so their decision will tend to be unanimous. (When the Princeton Philosophy Department discussed whether to continue interviewing job candidates, it considered the Miller Cantor point but decided that it did not particularly care about unanimity.)

2. Doris (2002, 67–75) discusses the relation between social psychology and personality psychology in some detail.

3. Confirmation bias is discussed, e.g., in Gilovich (1993), chap. 3.

References

Darely, J. M. 1973. "From Jerusalem to Jericho: A Study of Situational and Dispositional Variables in Helping Behavior." *Journal of Personality and Social Psychology* 27:100–8.

Dennett, D. C. 1981. *Brainstorms: Philosophical Essays on Mind and Psychology.* Cambridge, Mass.: MIT Press.

Doris, J. 2002. *Lack of Character: Personality and Moral Behavior.* New York: Cambridge University Press.

Fodor, J. A. 1975. *The Language of Thought.* New York: Thomas Crowell.

———. 1987. *Psychosemantics: The Problem of Meaning in the Philosophy of Mind.* Cambridge, Mass.: MIT Press.

Funder, D. C. 2001. "Personality." *Annual Review of Psychology* 52: 197–221.

Gilovich, T. 1993. *How We Know What Isn't So: The Fallibility of Human Reason in Everyday Life.* New York: The Free Press.

Harman, G. 1998–99. "Moral Philosophy Meets Social Psychology: Virtue Ethics and the Fundamental Attribution Error." *Proceedings of the Aristotelian Society* 99: 315–31.

———. 1999–2000. "The Nonexistence of Character Traits." *Proceedings of the Aristotelian Society* 100: 223–6.

Isen, A. M., and P. F. Levin. 1972. "Effect of Feeling Good on Helping: Cookies and Kindness." *Journal of Personality and Social Psychology* 21: 384–8.

Kunda, Z. 1999. *Social Cognition: Making Sense of People.* Cambridge, Mass.: MIT Press.

Latané, B., and J. M. Darley. 1970. *The Unresponsive Bystander: Why Doesn't He Help?* New York: Appleton-Century-Crofts.

Merritt, M. 2000. "Virtue Ethics and Situationist Personality Psychology." *Ethical Theory and Moral Practice* 3: 365–83.

Milgram, S. 1974. *Obedience to Authority.* New York: Harper and Row.

Miller, G. A., and N. Cantor. 1982. Review of *Human Inference: Strategies and Shortcomings of Social Judgement.* In *Social Cognition* 1: 83–93.

Nisbett, R. 1998. "Essence and Accident." In *Attribution and Social Interaction: The Legacy of Edward E. Jones,* ed. J. M. Darley and J. Cooper. Washington, D.C.: American Psychological Association.

Solomon, R. 2003. "Victims of Circumstances? A Defense of Virtue Ethics in Business." *Business Ethics Quarterly* 13(1): 43–62.

POSTSCRIPT

Can Individual Virtue Survive Corporate Pressure?

This issue draws on the background of classic behavioral experiments, well known in the field of social psychology. One is often required to master portions of a scientific field in order to understand a question confronting the business world. For example, to understand the Pinto case (Issue 13) one may well have to know a bit of automotive engineering. To understand the dispute over the labeling of genetically modified organisms (Issue 14), one may have to learn how genes can be inserted into reproductive material of plants. Increasingly, business is about information and scientific knowledge, and the corporate officer is expected to be knowledgeable about the fields that interface his or her company's business.

Suggested Readings

John Dalla Costa, *The Ethical Imperative: Why Moral Leadership is Good Business,* (Reading, MA: Perseus Books, 1998).

Kevin T. Jackson, *Building Reputational Capital,* (New York: Oxford University Press, 2004).

Joel Lefkowitz, *Ethics and Values in Industrial-Organizational Psychology,* (Mahwah, NJ: Lawrence Erlbaum Associates, 2003).

Ronald R. Sims, *Ethics and Corporate Social Responsibility: Why Giants Fall,* (Westport, CT.: Praeger, 2003).

Robert C. Solomon, *A Better Way to Think About Business,* (New York: Oxford, 1999).

Internet References . . .

STAT-USA/Internet

This site, a service of the U.S. Department of Commerce, provides one-stop Internet browsing for business, trade, and economic information. It contains daily economic news, frequently requested statistical releases, information on export and international trade, domestic economic news and statistical series, and databases.

http://www.stat-usa.gov/stat-usa.html

PhRMA: America's Pharmaceutical Companies

PhRMA membership represents approximately 100 U.S. pharmaceutical companies that have a primary commitment to pharmaceutical research. Information on the effects of pharmaceutical price controls on research spending is one of the many topics covered at this site.

http://www.phrma.org

NumaWeb

This Numa Financial Systems site calls itself "the Internet's home page for financial derivatives." This site includes a reference index, a discussion forum, and links to many related sites.

http://www.numa.com/index.htm

Current Business Issues

*M*uch as we like profitable businesses, and the benefits and taxes that they bring us, there is always the possibility that the pursuit of profit will go "too far" and negatively affect other valuable parts of our lives—our environment, our future security, the morals of our children (and neighbors), and the reliability of our public utilities. Where is government regulation and limitation of business enterprise needed? appropriate? inappropriate?

- Are the Risks of Derivatives Manageable?

- Should Price Gouging Be Regulated?

- Does the Enron Collapse Show That We Need More Regulation of the Energy Industry?

ISSUE 5

Are the Risks of Derivatives Manageable?

YES: Justin Welby, "The Ethics of Derivatives and Risk Management." *Ethical Perspectives,* 4, 2, 1997

NO: Thomas A. Bass, "Derivatives: The Crystal Meth of Finance." *The Huffington Post,* May 5, 2009

ISSUE SUMMARY

YES: In 2008, most of the world watched in horror as the U.S. stock market nearly collapsed, bringing down other monetary world markets with it. Justin Welby contends that derivatives are an important and ethical investment practice, but one that involves risks. He claims that the risks should be understood well before participating in these investment practices.

NO: Thomas Bass claims that the market failures were due in large part to mismanagement of these investments he compares to crystal meth. In this 2009 article, he recommends widespread regulation of these instruments or no use of them at all.

This business ethics book is filled with a variety of arenas of business ethics. Understanding these issues is vital for individuals to be well educated in both ethics and business concerns. The issue of derivatives is more specific than many of these issues, but in 2009, it is estimated to be one of the largest potential disasters lurking behind the scenes of many business transactions. In examining derivatives, we learn about many of the dangers behind these complex financial investments. Author Thomas A. Bass makes an analogy between derivatives and the "world's biggest betting parlor." Astute businessman Warren Buffett is quoted calling them "financial weapons of mass destruction." It is estimated that in 2009, Buffett may have lost as much as $67 billion in derivative transactions. It is no surprise that Bass can't find any justification for continuing the practice of unregulated derivatives, but he doesn't hold much hope for this conclusion.

Valuing derivatives is generally determined by what someone else is willing to pay for a contract. Imagine the scenario that "A" will be worth "B" if

"C" happens. In some respects, it appears to be financial fantasy. As Justin Welby explains, derivatives are "financial instruments based on other products, whether physical or financial. The other products may themselves be derivative."

Welby is a business scholar and rector, and he finds that with care, derivative contracts can be appropriate with the proper balance of "courage and prudence." Welby calls derivatives powerful and reminds us that "power needs monitoring and controlling." It appears that in today's derivative market, there has been little monitoring, control, or ethical considerations of derivatives.

Derivative contracts are discussed in notional amounts because no one can determine the true values with certainty. Bass and others watching the markets estimate that the outstanding notional value of derivatives is more than $1.144 quadrillion. Quadrillion is probably a number not yet used in any of our readings. Bass explains that currently the U.S. real estate market is valued at $23 trillion, and the stock market is valued at less than $15 trillion. The U.S. gross domestic product is at $14.2 trillion.

YES

Justin Welby[1]

The Ethics of Derivatives and Risk Management

1 Derivatives

Derivatives are financial instruments based on other products, whether physical or financial. The other products may themselves be derivative. Three main forms of derivative exist: futures, options and swaps.

1.1 What Are They?

Futures—Futures originated in the agricultural markets, with the establishment of contracts for future delivery of produce. A farmer might sell next year's potatoes now, thus locking in his return. Derivatives based on physical products remain crucial and enormous markets, covering everything from orange juice to oil. A derivative contract was at this point a contract to take or deliver a given quantity of a specified quality of the product at a particular place and time in the future, and at a price agreed today.

In the 1970s there was a substantial growth in financial derivatives, starting in Chicago, and based on instruments such as US treasury bills and bonds (short or long term promissory notes of the US government). In the 1980s these derivatives spread geographically, with markets opening in London (LIFFE) and France (MATIF), as well as the Far East, in Tokyo, Osaka, Singapore and Hong Kong. All major financial centres now have a derivatives market. They have also spread in form, with new contracts being invented. These have covered all the principal physical products that were freely traded and most financial instruments.

Options—The most important development has been the invention of the option contract. This is fundamentally different from a futures contract in that on the buyer's side a right but not an obligation is obtained (other than the obligation to pay for the option), and on the seller's (technically 'writer's') an obligation but no rights.

Options are based on a complicated mathematical analysis of the volatility of the underlying product. A buyer of an option is making two assumptions at least, (1) that the product will move in value by more than the cost of the option, and (2) that volatility of price movement will at least not decrease. A writer makes one or both of the opposite assumptions. A trader of options should be neutral as to the price but be taking a position on volatility. The

From *Ethical Perspectives*, July 1997, pp. 84–92. Copyright © 1997 by Ethical Perspectives. Reprinted by permission.

earliest option contracts were in the Foreign Exchange (FX) market, on the 'cable' (to be traded internationally using the Atlantic telegraph cable) traded on the Philadelphia stock exchange. The market has developed rapidly so that most large cash contracts and futures contracts now have associated option contracts.

Swaps—The swap market was the last of the major developments in derivatives. It started in the late 1970s. Developing rapidly in size, it is now capable of supporting huge volumes of transactions and underpins a great deal of the activity in the international debt capital markets.

In a swap, two borrowers exchange interest rate obligations. Typically a party with floating rate interest obligation in a currency (e.g. £) undertakes to pay a fixed rate of interest on the same amount of principal to a second party with a fixed rate obligation who pays a rate of interest to the first party based on an agreed floating rate of interest. Each has then effectively exchanged cash flows. Variations on the theme are possible, for example, across two or more currencies. The advantages to each side are considerable. They can manage their exposure to interest rates without needing to raise new loans, and may take advantage of good access to a particular market (e.g., long term fixed interest rate pounds for a large UK company) without being forced to remain exposed to that market if they want a different obligation (for example floating interest rate US$).

1.2 Where Do They Happen?

Derivatives markets usually started as exchange based, linked to a geographical market such as the Chicago Board of Trade (CBOT). However, the financial derivatives (and some others, especially gold and oil) rapidly developed 'over-the-counter' markets (OTC), with no physical location. Major banks act as market-makers and trade the instruments for their own account. This was especially true in the swaps and options markets. It led to a deepening of liquidity and flexibility in the relevant markets and a proliferation of derivatives of derivatives. Examples are 'swaptions', options on swaps, and combinations of different derivatives intended to cause particular cash flow effects. This is where it is easy to lose money!

1.3 Who Uses Them, And Why?

There are three main categories of derivative user:

Producers—Almost all internationally traded commodities have a futures contract somewhere. Whether the producers are nations or companies, they tend to use the derivative markets to hedge price risk, that is, establish a certainty of future prices. This may be to protect a producers' price cartel, or simply as a means of avoiding sudden and unexpected adverse movements. Typically, producers are the most powerful single group in a commodity, but not a controlling group.

Consumers—Consumers are the mirror image of the producers in commodities, or almost any company of medium to large size in the financial derivatives markets. They may be issuers or investors in securities. Again the aim is to prevent surprises, or lock in what is seen as a favourable rate or price of a financial product or security.

Intermediaries—These may be banks, brokers or simply speculative traders. They are likely to provide up to 90% of the volume in any market, but their influence on price is less clear and is the subject of much argument. Their activity provides essential liquidity but also increases volatility. They will often have no underlying interest whatever in the commodity. However, without their participation the markets themselves could not exist. A technical mishap in the North Sea in the 1980s led to one US bank trading in oil futures becoming the proud owner of a physical tanker full of crude oil in a falling market, to the great satisfaction of many oil companies.

2.1 Should We Try to Manage Risk?

The ethical question with regard to financial risk has at its core the ethics of risk management, and the desire for predictability in the future. Risk management involves looking at the justice of the distribution of risk rather than only the relative benefits in a consequentialist manner.[2] In general terms this is obvious in the normal running of life. I should take normal precautions against harm provided that they do not lead to harm to someone less able to protect themselves. It is ethical to test the strength of ice before walking on it, but not to do so by putting my children on it first, on the grounds that their earning power is less than mine and they are therefore more expendable.

In retail finance this is seen in 1980s and 1990s legislation on Investor Protection. The burden of risk in ensuring that a product is suitable for the purchaser has shifted dramatically from a caveat emptor approach to fall squarely on the seller. Thus in any sale of life products the majority of the paperwork is less about the product than whether the purchaser has had all the legal and prudential warnings. It is recognized that a life company is in a far better position to assess risk than an individual, and must make sure that the investor has had the risk management carried out on their behalf. Legislation directs that more weight is given to an ethical than market driven distribution of risk.

2.2 The Risks of Risk Management

All action to resolve risk creates risk. Yet in financial markets inaction is in itself the adoption of a risk profile. As a portfolio manager, to invest or leave reserves in cash are both risk choices. In FX, to engage in the use of option strategies creates many risks, not to do so creates others. Even Boards of Directors have begun to recognize this as the risks of risk management have loomed larger in professional thinking.

In response to the Leeson affair, Proctor & Gamble, Metallgesellschaft, Orange County and lesser known events, the burden of managing risk management has grown, to the point where its consumption of resources in non-financial firms must begin to pose ethical questions even in consequentialist terms.[3]

3 Ethical Perspectives on Risk Management

The question must be asked whether it is ethically justified to use resources in this way. Risk is inherent in life; new financial instruments are often loosely thought of as hedges when they are risk management tools. There is a responsibility for managers who use them to recognize the true nature of what they are doing. Given that most instruments are copious users of energy and other intangible resources of the business, as well as having a risk profile deriving from their use at all, they must be justifiable in terms of consequence, rule or virtue.

3.1 Justifiable in Terms of Consequence

No market is morally neutral.[4] "It both expresses and needs a moral framework which is wider than the market itself. This framework can quite properly justify the basic operations of the system. But because it is a wider moral framework it will also correct and supplement those operations in the light of values to which the market itself appeals."[5]

This is true, but most ethical discourse in finance is essentially a form of debased utilitarianism or consequentialism. The question we ask too often is "does it have good results?", rather than "is it good?" There is a sense in which that is right: any ethical conclusion must have a reason, though the reason may become "God says so." But in business ethics the result has become more and more narrowly defined. One result of this is seen in the common and fallacious argument that ethical behaviour is good because it contributes to the bottom line. The moral framework becomes a subsidiary of the market. Looking at the subject of derivatives has brought this home to me with fresh power. My first thought was "what harm can they do?" I used derivatives for many years, without qualms, as a means of protecting the interests of the company for which I worked. They provide a focused, transparent and efficient method of adjusting price to supply and demand. In the oil industry they were certainly less damaging in their results than the cartel of the 1970s, OPEC, with its indifference to the poorer countries, its corruption and overwhelming greed. At least the derivatives market in oil seems impersonal. The counterparty is invisible.

This is a classically utilitarian argument of the greatest benefit to the greatest number. Similar arguments are ready to hand in other markets. Financial derivatives may lower the cost of capital by allocating it more efficiently to those best able to access it who then pass on some of the benefit through the swaps market. Currency derivatives may ease the risk of cross-currency investment. Some benefit in terms of risk management will at least be intended for all users of derivatives where the use is driven by commercial considerations other than those of trading in derivatives. Within the derivatives markets themselves this issue is extreme. It is a truism to say that a market price cannot be wrong, it is simply a price. In a futures trading pit no ethics exist except performing what you have promised.[6] Inevitably therefore, our comments are from outside the structure of concepts that many practitioners would consider valid.

The consequences of trading in complicated and risky instruments may be more subtle than accounting can reveal. Risk is not always measurable but at times may be inherent in the ethos of an organizational system, part of the culture, like safety. Whatever the controls, a company with a high risk ethos is likely to run high risks. In the early 1980s, at the time of the panic caused by the run on the US bank, Continental Illinois, the Financial Times commented, "Banks should be boring". The use in financial organizations of many of the new financial instruments requires the recruitment of teams whose rewards are usually linked to performance on a profit centre basis. This in itself creates a high risk ethos which is a ratchet that progresses inevitably, and whose culture is often more powerful than all the controls that can be invented.

Although many new financial instruments may benefit many companies and people (look at the example of the new availability of flexible fixed rate mortgages in the UK, all derivative based), like nuclear power, the accidents can have massive fall-out. It is far from clear that the greatest good of the greatest number is the result of the unfettered development of new financial instruments. Even the largest banks seem unable to prevent losses through rash or unauthorized dealing: "banks may have abandoned the safe role of the banker in roulette or the bookmaker at the races in favour of gambling themselves."[7]

3.2 Justifiable in Terms of Rule

The argument so far is that derivatives have their uses but also have a great potential for harm. They concentrate power without accountability. They distance markets from the reality of the people producing. They tend to self-deception about the nature of the world. But they cannot be banned. Nor should they be. Properly used they add flexibility and risk management to investment decisions, and can facilitate wealth creation. Three controls are suggested: capital adequacy, trading restriction and open declaration.

There should be strict limits on the amount of capital (and hence open positions) that any institution can commit to derivatives. This could include step ups in capital allocation once a certain size of position had been reached. There would have to be some concept of concert-party. The explicit aim should be to make it prohibitively expensive, and obviously unacceptable, for a small group of traders to run positions that can control a market. Trading should be restricted so as to prevent excessive volatility. This has worked in New York since 1987. After a certain move, trading must close for a period.

The companies or people who may trade need close regulation. Any use of derivatives over a de minimis level should require regulatory approval. In particular the use of exotics should require evidence of adequate systems to monitor and reveal risk, and a level of independent audit.

Finally, companies using derivatives that are not traders should have to publish a policy, for example after the statement of accounting basis, on the use, limits and intention of derivative involvement.

3.3 Justifiable in Terms of Virtue

3.3.1 *Transparency*

Both in the secular philosophical and the religious traditions of European thought, transparency is thought of as a virtue. Iago may be clever, but is nevertheless a villain because of his dissembling. In the Wagnerian cycle one may feel that Siegfried is a muscle bound idiot, but still a hero because of his transparency. Candide is naïve, but his transparency is seen by Voltaire as virtuous. John's first epistle has the famous exhortation to "walk in the light" with one another and with God. King David's uniqueness is not his moral uprightness but his honesty and openness in his walk of faith, expressed most clearly in Psalm 51. Straightforward dealing is a City virtue ("dictum meum pactum", the motto of the London Stock Exchange, etc.) and is enshrined in legislation and regulation.[8]

The virtue of transparency is not only ethical but a management aim in order to understand risk. Its benefits lie behind reforms in accounting, the break-up of conglomerates, the fashion for mission statements that control priorities, and concern over derivatives. We cannot manage what we cannot see. A recent Accounting Standard Board discussion paper on financial instruments aims for this. "The issue is that, whatever basis [of accounting] is used, it should be unambiguous, universal and simple".[9]

Transparency is not only for self-preservation, in that false information leads to false markets, but applies even when there is no obvious consequential harm, as is often seen in insider trading. Transparency is a virtue even of consenting adults in private, as well as in the open market, and its importance is being reinforced.

3.3.2 *Self-awareness*

Another virtue is self-awareness, considered as such from Aristotle onwards. New financial instruments compel a proper and well balanced view of the nature of the company and its outlook. They increase corporate self-awareness, and encourage a willingness to resist the fatalistic approach to the future that diminishes the significance of human free-will.[10] Like health and safety rules, they encourage the management of risk, and thus focus an organization on its proper objectives. They encourage a proper balance between prudence and risk, leading management to take the risks it should, and transfer others to those better able to carry them. An oil exploration and production company may hedge interest rate and foreign exchange risk, buying certainty in contrast to the vagaries of the drill-bit.

3.3.3 *Between Recklessness and Immobility*

An ethics of virtue raises questions when risk management becomes obsessive, and behaviour such as cowardice is first held in contempt and then treated as pathological in extreme cases. It is recognized that an obsession with risk paralyses action, and that there is a proper balance between recklessness and terrified immobility. An honest living with the fact of risk and its consequences is seen as a good. This is a view deeply rooted in all human ethical traditions, and in the European seen at its most sophisticated in the Stoics.

The same balance is reflected in the Judaeo-Christian tradition. Within the Bible there is a tension between faith in the ultimate goodness of God in all circumstances[11] and an avoidance of recklessness that tests providence and faithfulness.[12] This same tension is reflected in common law in the Anglo-Saxon tradition with the tests of reasonable care and contributory negligence. The search for a risk free life is seen in such absurdities as the famous McDonald's coffee lawsuit in the US, where a jury initially awarded damages of $2,000,000 (reduced on appeal) to a woman who was scalded while simultaneously driving and trying to drink a hot cup of coffee. In legal ethics such cases are seen as increasingly indefensible. The opposite extreme is found at the Pont du Gard, near Nîmes, an unrailed and crumbling Roman aqueduct with a vertical drop of over 100 feet. Anyone can walk across, if they dare, the only caution being a rusty sign saying "Les vents puissent s'enlever", perhaps translatable as "gone with the wind!".

If one takes the three main approaches to ethics, the consequentialist, deontological and virtue based, it is clear that the last two place risk management as one sensible preoccupation among others, without giving it primacy.

Conclusion

The widespread and elaborate use of new financial instruments among corporate entities and financial institutions requires justification. It faces the charge of increasing both the level and complexity of risk in the financial system under the pretext of reducing it. It is a prodigious user of management resources and IT. It obscures the integrity of the nature of the non-financial user.

It is not mere academic argument to question the ethics of certain instruments. Both in the US and the UK certain forms of financial instrument are deemed too risky to be used by all and sundry.[13] Other forms of instrument may be banned outright, even though many financial professionals will be perfectly capable of measuring the risk involved.[14] The force of this attack is recognized in the financial industry. One defence frequently put forward is similar to that of the National Rifle Association in the US about guns. It is the users, not the product, that are the problem. "One misconception is that derivatives are risky instruments that are used for speculation. It is more accurate to say that derivatives are instruments that can be used to alter risk profiles".[15] The mere fact of an instrument existing is no reason to use it. The biggest advocates of exotic options are bankers. Practising Treasurers spend much time seeking to distinguish between the fascinating idea which the bank's rocket scientist wants to try, and the derivative that will genuinely benefit the company. The fact that many of these instruments are harmful or spurious does not mean they should be banned, but neither does the absence of a ban make them ethical.

The ethical question to ask for the non-financial corporation has to do with the proper balance of courage and prudence. Will this instrument enable the company to carry out its proper task with more focus and self-awareness, or is it an attempt to neutralize the proper risks that we are paid to take? For financial corporations the inevitable presence of derivatives poses two issues.

First, are they intrinsically valuable or simply so complicated that no client could use them and monitor the new exposures involved? Secondly, will the active management of our positions created by this activity result in a change in the nature of our business, and if so, has this been clearly communicated to the world around?

On reading this again I am once more struck by a remark made to me by a clergyman long before I was ordained. "What is an ethical Treasurer?" One of the major challenges in the field of financial ethics is the development of an adequate, and clearly communicated, measure of the intrinsic ethics of finance.

This paper is not arguing that derivatives are wrong, but that they are powerful, and power needs monitoring and controlling. The events of October 1987 are often referred to as the meltdown of the markets. My clear memory is of the whole executive board of directors standing in my office gazing in awe at a Topic Screen (showing FTSE prices) as waves of red chased across the screen. The use of nuclear metaphors was apt. A system that seemed safe had assumed a life of its own. There is little doubt that derivatives fuelled the reaction.

Notes

1. Justin Welby has been Rector of St. James's Anglican Church, Southam in Warwickshire, England, a small market town, since 1995. Before that he was assistant minister (curate) in a depressed urban industrial parish in the Midlands of England from 1992. Before being ordained he worked in the oil industry, first for Elf Aquitaine in Paris, and then as Group Treasurer of Enterprise Oil in the UK. During that time he had experience of projects throughout the world, especially in Nigeria and the North Sea. He is a member of the British Association of Corporate Treasurers, and is still involved in aspects of finance work. He holds degrees from Cambridge and Durham universities.

2. 'Risk' in *New Dictionary of Christian Ethics*. SCM, p. 557, see also *The Common Good*, Catholic Bishop's Conference 1996, § 77, p. 19.

3. Stewart Hodges, Director, Financial Operations Research Centre at the University of Warwick, pointed out, in a complicated article dealing with the effects of delta hedging using the Black-Scholes model, that "the risk exposure is constantly adjusted in response to market movements" and that this leads to very high turnover (thus costs and transaction risks); "in fact the expected level of turnover is proportional to the square root of the number of revisions [of the hedge following market movements], becoming unbounded in the limit". Cf. 'Current Research on Derivative Products' in *Treasurer*, November 1991, p. 6 and 9.

4. Dr Robert Song, at Cranmer Hall, Durham University, has been very helpful in discussing this.

5. Richard HARRIES, *Is There a Gospel for the Rich?* Mowbray, 1992, p. 95.

6. The film 'Trading Places', with Eddie Murphy, is an enjoyable and generally accurate way of understanding this.

7. 'Editorial' in *Treasurer*, April 1995.

8. Stock exchange listing regulations, especially obligations on disclosure of material facts, insider trading legislation and Takeover Panel rules about concert parties, would be three examples.

9. David CREED (Group Treasurer Tate & Lyle PLC), 'A personal view of the ASB's Financial Instruments Discussion Paper' in *Treasurer*, October 1996, p. 16.

10. The basic argument in an article by Gay EVANS (Chairman International Swaps and Futures Association), 'The Great Contradiction' in *Treasurer*, October 1996, p. 30.

11. e.g. Daniel 3:17–18 and Romans 8:28.

12. e.g. Deuteronomy 6:16 and Matthew 4:7.

13. Investing in private placements in the US, and the 'sophisticated investor' test under the FSA.

14. Pyramid selling schemes.

15. Gay EVANS, *op. cit.*

Thomas A. Bass

→ **NO**

Derivatives: The Crystal Meth of Finance

In May 2008, Warren Buffett, the great "value" investor from Omaha and America's second-richest man, announced on the eve of his annual shareholders' meeting that he had lost $1.6 billion in bad bets on derivatives. Most of this loss came from shorting put derivatives on Standard and Poor's Index of 500 leading stocks and on three other foreign stock indexes in Europe and Japan. In laymen's terms, Mr. Buffett had placed a bet—a very large bet, which wiped out 64% of Berkshire Hathaway's profits—that global stock markets would rise instead of fall.

Preparing for this year's shareholders' meeting, Mr. Buffett announced in February 2009 that his gambling on derivatives had resulted in an "accounting loss" of $14.6 billion, with $10 billion of this loss coming from his wrong-way bet that global stock prices would rise. On the eve of the meeting itself, on May 2nd, the *New York Times* reported that Buffett's "worst-case exposure" had risen to $67 billion. After the company's fourth quarter net income fell 96%, Berkshire was stripped of its triple-A debt rating by both Fitch and Moody's, and this was in spite of the fact that Buffett owns twenty percent of Moody's parent company.

How could the Oracle of Omaha be getting burned by derivatives? Was this the same Warren Buffett who in 2002 warned that "Derivatives are financial weapons of mass destruction, carrying dangers that, while now latent, are potentially lethal"? Buffett had promised his shareholders that he would avoid these "time bombs . . . for . . . the economic system," but here he was, seven years later, announcing that the crystal speed of derivatives had got a fearsome hold on him.

Derivatives have got a fearsome hold on all of us, but my fellow journalists, who missed the story in the first place, are still avoiding the subject. They file an avalanche of twitters describing every move made by someone like Bernie Madoff, because this is a story anyone can understand. "I trusted the guy. I gave him my money. He stole it." Camera cues to tears glistening on cheeks. It's a wrap.

But derivatives? Financial weapons of mass destruction? Shorting puts on the S&P 500? *Whoa, man, how am I going to get my mind around this story?* How am I going to explain the exquisite pleasure that comes from using this crystal meth of finance? Why do derivatives exist in the first place, and why have they become the world's biggest betting parlor, in spite of the fact that no one understands the size or nature of these bets?

As the Oracle of Omaha confessed in his recent "letter to shareholders,"

"Improved 'transparency'—a favorite remedy of politicians, commentators and financial regulators for averting future train wrecks—won't cure the problems that derivatives pose. I know of no reporting mechanism that would come close to describing and measuring the risks in a huge and complex portfolio of derivatives."

Buffett goes on to say,

"Auditors can't audit these contracts, and regulators can't regulate them. When I read the pages of 'disclosure' in 10-Ks of companies that are entangled with these instruments, all I end up knowing is that I don't know what is going on in their portfolios (and then I reach for some aspirin)."

By now the entire world is joining Mr. Buffett in reaching for some aspirin. Why, for example, did AIG, the biggest financial meth freak on the street, refuse for six months to report on what it had done with the $200 billion that the United States Treasury has dumped into its coffers, and why is there still no public disclosure of the company's assets and liabilities? The answer to the first question is that both AIG and the U.S. government were too embarrassed to announce, in this age of global markets, that much of the bailout money has gone overseas, with sixteen of the top twenty-two recipients being foreign banks. And how much more money will be required to keep AIG in the game? No one knows the answer to this question, or, to quote the great physicist Neils Bohr, "Prediction is difficult, especially of the future."

So why have derivatives got such a fearsome hold on our financial system? What is this speedy form of finance, and why, assuming that we will not be setting the clock back to Year Zero, will derivatives be around—transformed and traded differently, perhaps, but around—for the foreseeable future?

A derivative is something that takes its value from something else. It is a bet on a bet, a second order gamble that General Motors stock will rise or fall or that the S&P Index of 500 stocks (which includes General Motors) will rise or fall. As the Oracle of Omaha wrote in his 2002 letter to Berkshire Hathaway shareholders:

"derivatives . . . call for money to change hands at some future date, with the amount to be determined by one or more reference items, such as interest rates, stock prices, or currency values. If, for example, you are either long or short [on] an S&P 500 futures contract, you are a party to a very simple derivative transaction—with your gain or loss derived from movements in the index."

These deals get more complicated when you start betting on household mortgages or car or student loans. The underlying transactions are sliced and diced into financial securities that are tied to interest rate fluctuations or some other aspect of currency or financial futures.

The key word here is "future." If I sell you a share of General Motors stock, you pay me, and the deal is done. If I sell you a derivative contract with General Motors sliced into it, I am selling you a contingent future payment for which I could be liable twenty years down the road.

This is why my friends in finance *like* derivatives. They see them as a kind of voting system, where today's prices reveal people's expectations about the future. But this is also why Warren Buffett calls derivatives "financial weapons of mass destruction." Given the boom and bust nature of capitalism, betting that the markets will not explode twenty years down the road is a matter of faith, not finance.

Exploded derivatives contracts are called toxic waste, and the institutions holding these bad bets are called zombies, because they would be bankrupt and buried save for the public handouts that keep them among the "living dead." We have borrowed these terms from epidemiology and Afro-Caribbean voodoo because the situation is really quite terrifying.

Let's start with a simple question. How big is the market in derivatives? No one knows, because no one has been recording or regulating these contracts, many of which are traded over-the-counter via telephone calls or electronic signals from one banker or hedge fund trader to another. Derivatives are a kind of "shadow banking system" because the black box trading systems that deal in them can easily shade into black market operations good at money laundering, tax evasion, or outright theft.

Tom Foremski, a former reporter for the *Financial Times*, and British analyst D. K. Matai, using data compiled in 2007 by the Bank for International Settlements in Basel, Switzerland, estimate that the outstanding notional value of derivatives is $1.144 quadrillion. To help you get your mind around this number, we are talking about more than a thousand trillion dollars. This sum is made up of $548 trillion in listed credit derivatives and $596 trillion in over-the-counter derivatives, which includes trading on interest rates ($393 trillion), credit default swaps ($58 trillion), foreign exchange ($56 trillion), and commodities ($9 trillion).

These numbers indicate the face value of contracts currently traded, but if any of these contracts were to default, which has been happening recently with some frequency—either because the financial markets have frozen up or the financial institutions trading these contracts have gone belly up— then the numbers would be discounted. So instead of saying that the world is currently on the hook for a quadrillion dollars in derivatives, let's cut the number in half and say that the world's derivative bubble is only $500 trillion.

How big is $500 trillion?

The gross domestic product of the United States is $15 trillion. The money supply of the United States—all the greenbacks currently in circulation—is also about $15 trillion. The gross domestic product of the entire world is $50 trillion. The total value of the world's real estate is $75 trillion. The value of the world's stock and bond markets is about $100 trillion.

As you can see, the world's derivative markets—even with a "half-price" sticker of $500 trillion—are huge, and if somebody as smart as Warren Buffett can get burned by trading derivatives then imagine how the rest of us suckers are faring. Lest you think that you, oh, virtuous reader, would never dabble in derivatives, stand warned that TIAA-CREF, Fidelity, and other guardians of your financial futures are big players in the world's derivative markets. As the

Oracle of Omaha wrote in 2002: "The range of derivative contracts is limited only by the imagination of man (or sometimes, it seems, madmen)."

Again, I hate to disabuse any of you readers who are Marxists, Maoists, anarcho-syndicalists, or goldbugs, but, unless we crank the clock back to Year Zero and bring Pol Pot out of the jungle to reorganize our financial system, derivatives are here to stay. A few flavors might disappear off the menu. One example is the formerly-trendy product known as "portfolio insurance," which blew up during the crash of 1987, when the markets began gapping downward so fast that the "insurance" written against this risk proved worthless.

The market in mortgage-backed securities—frozen last fall but thawed this spring with TARP money—will return. The market in asset-backed securities (covering things such as student loans), which was dead in its tracks last fall, until being resurrected with TALF money, will return. The market in credit default swaps (CDSs), which was suffering from an absence of liquidity that resulted in hair-raising volatility, will return. Foreign exchange rate derivatives, commodity derivatives, equity-linked derivatives, all will be with us next year.

And why is this? Derivatives are fun. Trading shares in G.M. is grandad's game. Trading puts on the FTSE with a LIBOR chaser is the hepped up work of testosterone-driven bonus boys. Derivatives are useful. They speed up the velocity with which money changes hands, and increased velocity means more volume. Playing the overnight float in the Asian markets and then zipping your money back for a day's work at the Merc effectively doubles your bank, even before you get the mojo going that allows you to leverage your investment ten-fold.

Derivatives fill out the mathematical space of financial markets (an argument made best by quants and computers). They lay off risk—or so say my financial friends, when they are not being blown up by bad bets. Derivatives do the work of Adam Smith's invisible hand. They transmogrify individual greed into the collective good. They exist not because they are complicated, but because people find them useful—and I am not talking merely about the dealers who profit from them.

The world economy sits on top of the world financial markets, and there is no hope of engineering an economic recovery without a functioning financial system. This is why the government is printing money and pumping it as fast as possible into TARPs, TALFS, and other bailouts designed the get the markets back in business—not the markets that deal in stocks and commodities, but those that operate in the high-speed world of derivatives. This is the big financial story of the day, and any journalist interested in doing more than compiling an updated version of Gustave Flaubert's *Dictionary of Received Ideas* should be covering this story.

POSTSCRIPT

Are the Risks of Derivatives Manageable?

In the fall of 2008, the housing market in the United States and worldwide took a nosedive. But government bailouts haven't done much to bring the prices of these homes back. Mortgages were sold off to secondary buyers, and then a variety of derivative securities were devised based on those mortgages. Next the securities were traded on something else—maybe A, B, or C. However, the original value of the real estate may have no relevance to the determination of the current value of A, B, or C. (Justin Welby explains in a detailed footnote the derivative real estate problem in Europe.)[1]

To be well educated in today's business and ethics climate, a student, investor, politician, or ordinary citizen needs to know about derivatives and weigh in on solutions for the future.

Perhaps it is time for a slightly contrarian view and an attempt to suggest ways in which ethical finance is more than an oxymoron. First, arguably ethical aims do not of themselves make actions ethical. It is possible to do the right thing in such a wrong way that it becomes the wrong thing. Especially in the sub-prime market it is arguable that in many ways the aims were good. Home ownership brings a level of security and commitment to an area, tends to reduce crime and vandalism and promotes good citizenship. Enabling low income families to own homes is good. The fact that banks sought to make money out of doing so is also perfectly reasonable. Even the packaging of loans and selling them on can be portrayed as reasonable and prudent balance sheet management. But in all the activity any potential virtue was lost in poor execution.

Loan making pushed the boundaries of what was wise and prudent by allowing (in the UK) self certification of income, developing products that had hidden and unsustainable costs and losing sight of the interests of the client borrower. Profit was maximized through excessive slicing of risks and the use of instruments of such complexity that they could not be tracked or valued. At the heart of the whole complexity was the steady and then rapid distancing of the original product and the final investor. Disintermediation began with investors and clients separated through exchanges or trading of an asset. Once the risk began to be sliced, in the end all that is left is a financial flow, or even an off balance sheet exposure.

---

[1] Welby. J. (12/1/2008). The European Weekly: New Europe. "Ethics Finance and the Human Factor." Issue: 810.

ISSUE 6

Should Price Gouging Be Regulated?

YES: Jeremy Snyder, "What's the Matter with Price Gouging?" *Business Ethics Quarterly*, 19:2 (April 2009)

NO: Matt Zwolinski, "Price Gouging, Non-Worseness, and Distributive Justice." *Business Ethics Quarterly*, 19:2 (April 2009)

ISSUE SUMMARY

YES: Snyder contends that price gouging conflicts with the goal of equitable access to goods essential to a minimally flourishing human life. Efficient provision of essential goods is not sufficient to prevent serious inequities. Regulations are needed for equitable access.

NO: Zwolinski argues that price gouging can be morally permissible, even though this does not mean that price gougers are morally virtuous. Considerations of the availability of institutional alternatives and distributive justice may render price gouging morally acceptable. In any case, regulations cannot be expected to resolve the moral issues more satisfactorily than the market itself.

Price gouging is often associated with notions like the powerful harming the needy. Often a natural disaster of some type occurs and people are in extreme need of goods. Suddenly, supply is short and demand is intense. In this condition, prices go up. The law of supply and demand is one of the staples of the business world. This law would allow for price gouging, but eventually, as supply and demand adjust to one another, the price will go down. Price gouging is probably as old as the business market itself.

Some business ethicists believe that during times of extreme need, prices should be regulated by the government to bring about stability to the disaster area more rapidly. For example, gas companies should be held to a standard price in the aftermath of a hurricane. Grocers or merchants should keep prices fair and stable in an effort to alleviate some of the pain during a disaster.

Thomas Aquinas, in *Summa Theologica*,[1] brings up the notion of the "just price." In essence, the notion of the just price says that the seller must not sell

---

[1] Aquinas, Saint Thomas (1991) In: T. McDermott (Trans.), *Summa Theologiae: A Concise Translation*. Allen, Texas: Christian Classics.

something for a higher price simply because the buyer is in a needy condition. But how does a merchant in a position of holding the goods that others need utilize self-control and keep prices at a normal rate? "Savvy" might be the term some would use in characterizing an individual who raises prices on needed goods during a disaster, thereby making a large profit. "Unethical" might also be a term for this type of behavior. Adam Smith is known as a defender of the free market. In his *Wealth of Nations*,[2] he explains how famines intensify when the government enforces a "just price" during a period of "scarcity or dearth." Smith explains that it is unacceptable for the government to impose prices on merchants during a time of "dearth." He believes that the artificial regulation increases the length of the famine because of the withholding of produce by merchants or farmers. For Smith, the price-gouging traders are working to control mass starvation. These merchants might be derided for their "gouging," but Smith explains that they merely offer the supply to meet the demand. They save the hungry from starving.

Many economists have commented on price gouging since the time of Smith, including our two authors.[3] What really is price *gouging*? Is it fair? Is it an acceptable practice?

[2] Smith, A. (2009) *The Wealth of Nations*. New York: Classic House Books.

[3] William Sundstrom introduced us to the price gouging writings by Aquinas and Smith. Sundstrom, an economist, contributes to the Web site for the Markkula Center for Applied Ethics at Santa Clara University.

YES ←

What's the Matter with Price Gouging?

PRICES FOR ESSENTIAL GOODS are likely to increase when a disaster strikes, should that event decrease available supplies of these goods, increase demand, or both.[1] Sometimes these price increases are condemned as 'price gouging' or 'profiteering.' Such labels are not intended as simply descriptions of price increases; rather, they carry a strong negative moral valence. In many cases, the moral wrong of these price increases is identified as wrongfully gaining from another's misfortune. Consider the common view that "[t]hings like selling generators for four and five times their cost is not free enterprise, that's taking advantage of other people's misery" (Rushing 2004, A-l). In other cases, price gouging is condemned as unfairly taking advantage of others' needs, language that is often associated with exploitation.[2]

But it isn't clear from these kinds of sentiments when a price increase amounts to price gouging or why, if at all, certain price increases following disasters are morally worrisome. Moreover, there are many reasons to think that price increases can create a net benefit for a community following a disaster. As one critic of anti-price gouging legislation puts it:

> Price to the left of the intersection of the supply-and-demand curve and you are guaranteed to vaporize whatever you are attempting to keep inexpensive. . . . The reason that gasoline is disappearing from service stations across the nation is because station owners aren't gouging with sufficient gusto. Whether out of a misguided sense of kindness, concern about what politicians might think, fear of bad press, or the desire to keep customers happy, they are pricing below what the market would otherwise bear and, as a result, their inventory has disappeared. Now, how are the poor being helped by service stations closing down for lack of fuel? Gas at $6 a gallon, after all, is better than gas unavailable at any price. (Taylor 2005)

Price increases lead to rationing by consumers and encourage increased production of scarce goods. If the aim of anti-gouging legislation is to prevent vendors from profiting too much from a supply disruption, then achieving this aim may come at the cost of a swift return to normal market conditions.

From *Business Ethics Quarterly*, April 2009, pp. 295–302. Copyright © 2009 by Business Ethics Quarterly. Reprinted by permission of The Philosophy Documentation Center, publisher of Business Ethics Quarterly. References omitted.

In this paper, I discuss what moral wrongs, if any, are most reasonably ascribed to accusations of price gouging. This discussion keeps in mind both practical and moral defenses of price gouging following disasters.[3] In the first section of this paper, I examine existing anti-gouging legislation for commonalities in their definitions of gouging. I then present arguments in favor of the permissibility of gouging, focusing on the economic benefits of price increases following disasters. In the third section I present a critique of gouging based on specific forms of a failure of respect for others. This critique is followed by a discussion of means for avoiding gouging in practice and responses to objections to my view. As I will argue, even when morally defensible anti-gouging legislation is not in place, individual vendors will have a duty not to gouge their customers.

Price Gouging in the Law

At present, thirty-two states and the District of Columbia have passed some form of anti-gouging legislation. Although there is no federal anti-gouging law in the US, a bill targeting fuel price increases passed the House of Representatives in 2007. In order to develop a better sense of what actions raise worries about price gouging, I will briefly examine this body of legislation.

Anti-gouging legislation is typically triggered by the declaration of a state of emergency or disaster. This declaration may be made by the state governor, local officials, or even the President. In substantially fewer cases, anti-gouging legislation requires a declaration by public officials in addition to a declaration of emergency. The duration of the activation of anti-gouging controls can vary from the length of the declaration of a disaster to a fixed length of time or some mix of the two.[4]

Laws against price gouging limit price increases for goods during their period of activation. For the most part, price increases are allowed when they reflect increases in the cost of doing business following the disaster and, to some extent, changes in the market. For example, the Federal Trade Commission defined price gouging as occurring when "a firm's average monthly sales price for gasoline in a particular area is higher than for a previous month, *and* where such higher prices are not substantially attributable to *either* (1) increased costs, or (2) national or international market trends" (Federal Trade Commission 2006, 137). In many cases, these caps seek to factor in changes in the market and costs by allowing the price of goods to increase a certain percentage above the pre-disaster price. Otherwise, vague language prohibiting "unconscionable" or "gross" increases in prices is used.[5] At their most extreme, anti-gouging legislation may forbid *any* increase in the prices of goods beyond those justified by higher business costs. These more extreme restrictions are unusual and at present limited to Georgia, Louisiana, Mississippi, and Connecticut.[6]

Anti-gouging laws can be tied to all goods and services following activation of anti-gouging statutes[7] or limited to specific, essential goods. What counts as an essential good is often left undefined but can explicitly include dwelling units, gasoline, food, water, supplies for home repair, and pharmaceuticals.[8]

Despite many broad commonalities in state anti-gouging legislation, this overview reveals four key areas of disagreement and vagueness in determining what constitutes price gouging. First, there is disagreement as to how much of a price increase, particularly beyond what can be justified by increases in business costs, is allowable. Second, state legislatures disagree as to whether prohibitions of price increases should be extended to all goods and services or limited only to certain exchanges, although most favor the latter. Third, when legislation is limited to certain exchanges, there is disagreement as to what goods and services should be covered. Fourth, and most importantly from the perspective of this paper, when anti-gouging legislation uses moral language to justify itself, this language tends to be vague.[9]

In Defense of Price Increases

Anti-gouging legislation and charges of price gouging are common. While the precise nature of the moral wrong associated with gouging is unclear, there is widespread agreement that *something* is wrong about these price increases. Yet, there are many reasons to think that price increases condemned as gouging are morally innocent at worst and, more often, create a positive and morally praiseworthy benefit for all concerned.

In a gouging situation following a disaster, both vendor and customer understand the exchange to be to their advantage. Since the good being exchanged is likely to be something essential to the well-being of the customer (e.g., food, water, shelter), the exchange is actually likely to provide proportionally greater utility to the customer than the vendor even at the higher than usual price. While the vendor may stand to clear a larger than normal profit as a result of the disaster, the essential nature of the goods mean that they will be of enormous, possibly even life saving, benefit to the consumer. Despite the harms to the consumer and possibly vendor as a result of the disaster, the high price exchange does no harm in itself when compared to the welfare of each person following the disaster. Rather, the exchange will provide the customer with essential goods that increase her welfare.

While disasters create a temporary increase in the pricing power of vendors, this shift can easily be explained and justified by the rules of the market. A disaster is likely to cause a reduction in essential supplies. For example, fuel may no longer be able pass through ruptured pipes or closed roads. These disasters—or even the threat of one—may also create an increase in demand for essential goods, such as plywood for protecting homes. The resulting shift in the equilibrium point between supply and demand predictably creates an increase in prices for goods, especially for essential goods that have inelastic demand, without any untoward manipulation of the market. From the standpoint of the dynamic functioning of the market, these higher prices should be allowed and the market can be trusted to maintain itself (Jacoby 2004).

Not only are price increases explainable as a result of the natural functioning of the market, it is argued, they serve a beneficial purpose. High prices for essential goods have the effect of helping the market to return to pre-disaster prices. These prices achieve a signaling effect for both vendors and consumers (Hayek 1945). The high prices charged by vendors will lure other suppliers into the market, quickly increasing supplies of essential goods. An increase in supplies will meet increased demand and help move prices toward pre-disaster levels. Without these price increases, vendors may lack both the information and motivation necessary to enter the post-disaster market and increase supplies.

Defenders of price gouging argue that higher prices also aid in the conservation of scarce goods by making it more likely that they will be purchased by those who place the greatest value on them. These high prices also tend to ensure that scarce essential goods will be used sparingly. While ice might be valuable to those seeking to keep their beer cold following a hurricane, higher prices will tend to ensure that those purchasing ice put it to more highly valued uses such as preserving medicine and scarce food. This efficiency of allocation is coupled with a rationing effect created by higher prices. When fuel prices spike, generators that might have been used to power the air conditioning in an entire house will instead be limited to cooling a single room. As a result, fuel supplies that would have been exhausted quickly at pre-disaster prices are now prolonged (*Wall Street Journal* 2005).

The promise of price increases following a disaster can also help increase supplies of essential goods prior to the event. If the disaster is foreseeable (as in the case of a hurricane), suppliers can pre-position goods in the area likely to be affected. The prospect of higher prices encourages such preemptive actions and acts in the long run to keep prices relatively low, meeting the needs of far more people than otherwise would have been the case.

Some extra profit following a disaster can also serve as a fair reward for the efforts and risks undertaken by vendors. Vendors of scarce goods may go to extraordinary lengths to get goods to the market following a disaster. A vendor might pre-position goods in a likely disaster area at considerable cost to himself and at considerable risk if the disaster destroys these stocks or strikes too far away for the supplies to be of use. Vendors in the affected area might act to protect existing stocks of supplies from damage at great expense to themselves and perhaps at some sacrifice to their own safety. If some of these supplies are lost, the local vendor, too, will be a victim of the disaster. Those who bring needed goods into the affected area after the event may also forgo opportunities for profit at home, face high costs in transporting the goods to the affected area, and may be subjected to bodily danger if the disaster is still ongoing or law and order have broken down.

Given these positive economic effects, price increases following a disaster need not be morally troubling. In fact, it could be argued, given that the needs of the affected population are especially strong, the so-called gouger might even deserve special praise for her efforts. At the very least, her self-interested motives in the post-disaster market are not obviously different from those typically judged to be morally innocent in a normal market.

Price Gouging and Respect for Others

If there is something morally wrong with price gouging, it is not that gouging causes direct harms or economic inefficiency. In fact, a critique of price gouging will need to confront the positive moral value of the efficiencies and rationing effect created by price increases.

As I have noted, many anti-gouging laws are limited to price increases on certain goods that are tied to basic human needs. I believe that this characteristic of anti-gouging legislation offers an important insight regarding what is morally objectionable about price gouging. As not all types of price increases trigger the worry about gouging, it is not price increases themselves that motivate this concern. Rather, I would like to argue, it is price increases that undermine equitable access to certain, essential goods that motivate the worry about price gouging.

Put another way, worries about price gouging are engaged when price increases cut off poor consumers from necessary goods, not when price increases are unfair. We might think that price increases following a disaster are unfair in the sense that they allow for a large shift in the social surplus of the interaction in the favor of the vendor. If the normally functioning market serves as a benchmark for a fair transaction and fair distribution of the social surplus generated by that transaction, then the disaster shifts the equilibrium point between supply and demand in such a way that the vendor can now charge unfair prices for her products (Wertheimer 1996).

To see that it is not fairness, *per se,* that motivates concerns over price gouging, consider an example. An avalanche outside of an exclusive ski resort blocks the only road to the resort on New Year's eve. Because this road is blocked, a group of wealthy revelers at the resort no longer have access to a resupply of champagne that was to be used to celebrate the new year. While there is food, drink, and shelter to meet everyone's essential needs until the road is cleared, there is far too little champagne on hand to ensure that everyone will be able to make a toast at midnight. Because of the high value placed on participating in the midnight toast by the resort's wealthy patrons, the owners of the limited remaining supply of champagne are able to clear unusually high profits by selling their supplies.

The actions of these vendors could certainly be considered unfair by the lights of the normally functioning market. But to label these actions as a case of price gouging strains the normal use of the term.[10] Consider that the language surrounding gouging typically focuses on the vulnerability created by the disaster and the desperation of consumers to meet their basic needs. As the Attorney General of Texas put it, following gouging accusations in the wake of hurricane Ike, "They took advantage of the fear and the needs of people who were evacuating the Gulf Coast region, and they jacked up prices" (Elliott 2008). Price hikes for gasoline following that same hurricane again focus on the absolute needs of consumers: "It's sad to think that merchants would take advantage of people who are already struggling to fill their gas tanks just to get from home to work or from home to church and back" (*Jackson Sun* 2008). While the would-be champagne drinkers may be desperate to participate in the New Year's toast and willing to pay unusually high prices to do so, their desperation is of an entirely different kind than that which normally motivates the charge of gouging. It is the desperation of individuals for essential goods, rather than simply the unfairness of the transaction, that motivates accusations of price gouging following a disaster.

Having located the wrongness of price gouging in access to essential goods, we can now say more about the duty that price gouging violates. To be specific, I would like to argue that price increases following a disaster can undermine equitable access to the goods essential to minimal human functioning. When price increases do so, they violate the norm of equal respect for persons. Respect for persons is often understood in terms of a duty to treat others as ends in themselves. More specifically, this respect is expressed both through recognizing that human animals are capable of forming and acting on a conception of the good life but need material support in order to do so (Hill 1991).[11]

Proponents of various ethical theories can agree that basic respect for human persons will entail two components: Negatively, we should not interfere with others as they live out their conception of the good life given reciprocal respect and non-interference. Positively, we should aid others in forming and living out their conception of the good life, particularly by ensuring that they have the minimal means of developing such a conception. An attitude of respect for others will be expressed through our actions, including non-interference, positive support, and other expressions of the equal value of all human persons (Anderson 1993).

At first glance, it would seem that placing limits on the functioning of the market through anti-gouging legislation would run counter to the goal of respecting others' freedom to pursue their conception of the good life. In the first place, I have discussed how price increases efficiently bring new supplies of essential goods into the market and help ration existing supplies. In this way, free markets serve as a means of supplying the goods essential to forming and acting on a conception of the good life.

Secondly, in their ideal form, markets carry their own value as institutions that protect and enlarge human freedom.[12] By offering a space in which consumers can freely negotiate, consummate, and exit exchanges, markets ensure that consumers are not beholden to any particular vendor in their pursuit of the good life.[13] Adam Smith specifically defends markets in terms of their historical role in undermining the oppressive feudal system of production (Satz 2007). Under a feudal system, serfs are tied to single masters and denied the freedoms of movement and exit created by a well-functioning market. Without the freedom to exit from the feudal relationship, the serf is condemned to take whatever terms of exchange are offered by her master. In a market, on the other hand, the "tradesman or artificer derives his subsistence from the employment, not of one, but of a hundred or thousand different customers. Though in some measure obliged to them all, therefore, he is not absolutely dependent on any one of them" (Smith 1976, 420). Markets guarantee legal protections for persons so that the equal right to make exchanges is enshrined as an entitlement, creating political equality between richer and poorer (Anderson 2004). The moral concern that justifies the idealized institution of the market, then, is an interest in providing the material means to and institutional protection of individual freedom.

Conditions following a disaster can be highly non-ideal for a market, however, at least from the perspective of a stable balance between supply and demand. A disaster potentially results in a reduction of supply and spike in demand for some or all essential goods. While price increases reflect a new, post-disaster balance between supply and demand, over the short-term this new equilibrium point can be particularly disruptive to the lives of the poorest members of a community. Until the pricing signals created by the new equilibrium increase supplies of essential goods, prices will remain high and supplies may be insufficient to meet demand. This gap between supply and demand is morally troubling because the goods in question are essential to minimal human functioning and may be out of reach for the poorest members of the affected community. While price increases in a free market represent one means of restoring supplies and rationing existing stocks of essential goods, anti-gouging legislation offers an alternative approach to this problem.

There are many good reasons to think that, following a disaster, an unfettered free market does not best serve the freedom-enhancing purpose by which it is morally justified. While unfettered price increases work toward *efficiently* promoting increases in the supply of essential goods following a disaster, the concern that motivates price gouging laws is that an unfettered market in these goods runs counter to the goal of *equity*, a key component of respect for persons. This failure of equity takes place in terms of the distribution of scarce essential goods within the affected community.[14]

While price increases can decrease consumption rates of essential goods, they do so at the cost of giving the wealthiest members of a community the greatest access to limited supplies. This access is created in two ways. First, and most obviously, wealthy persons will have greater financial means with which to bid on scarce resources when they have been located (Ramasastry 2005).[15] Second, these persons will likely have greater access to the information and transport needed to locate and reach scarce resources. In an idealized market, free competition lowers prices in order to put essential goods into the hands of all but the poorest members of a community. Following a disaster, free competition gives greater access to these goods to those who have the greatest resources within a community.

Avoiding Price Gouging in Practice

A vendor concerned about the effects of unconstrained price increases on equitable access to essential goods might respond by retaining pre-disaster prices for his poorest customers while allowing price increases for the remainder. That is, instead of allowing price increases according to the market, a vendor might adjust prices according to each consumer's ability to pay. This response would have the benefit of protecting the vendor against committing the moral wrongs I have described while preserving some of the price signaling and rationing effects of price increases.

In practice, vendors will face a range of difficulties should they attempt to price goods according to consumers' ability to pay. A great deal of information will often not be available to the merchant, particularly the means available to customers for purchasing essential goods. While some vendors in smaller communities will be intimately familiar with the needs and vulnerabilities of their customers, typically this will not be the case, particularly if the vendor enters the market from outside of the community in response to a disaster.

Given this problem, legislators and vendors can take two steps in order to avoid the moral wrong that I have argued is associated with price gouging. First, legislators can adopt a typical strategy found in existing state price gouging legislation and limit price increases to the going market rate prior to the disaster, plus increases for additional costs and risks to the vendor. When legislation of this kind has not been enacted within a community, individual vendors should still take it upon themselves to moderate their price increases. The aim of this moderation is to prevent vendors from receiving windfall profits in the face of the desperate need of their individual customers. By raising prices only to reflect changes in costs and risks in the post-disaster market, vendors maintain their own access to essential goods without unduly worsening others' access.

This strategy presumes that the going fair market price enabled members of the community generally to meet their essential needs prior to the disaster. Of course, this is an imperfect strategy since some persons will be priced out of competitive markets for essential goods even under normal conditions. If the local market prior to the disaster does not provide access to essential goods for a large portion of the community prior to the disaster, then this benchmark for setting prices should be discarded. This problem demonstrates that pre-disaster prices can serve as a useful shortcut under conditions of uncertainty only; these prices do not carry normative weight of their own. Nonetheless, a competitive market, in conjunction with a social safety net to make up for those priced out of the market, will serve as a useful mechanism for distributing goods essential to basic functioning.

Because the exchanges under discussion are mutually advantageous, there is good reason to allow for prices to exceed slightly the pre-disaster rate. As I have noted, price increases following a disaster have the positive effect of increasing supplies, encouraging rationing, and discouraging waste. Insofar as the prices charged by merchants aim at these goals, they can also serve the goal of equitable access to essential goods. Therefore, limited price increases even beyond those justified by increased costs and risks can be justified. Otherwise, price increases merely promote the vendor's self-interest at the cost of the basic needs of those around her.

While even limited price increases achieve a rationing effect, they will typically need to be supplemented with non-price rationing mechanisms, such as caps on purchases. As a second step, legislators should impose caps on the purchase of essential goods in order to ration these goods without distributing them according to ability to pay. When these caps are not mandated by law, individual vendors should impose caps on the sale of their own stocks of essential goods. The limits placed by these caps should depend on supplies and demand for essential goods following a disaster and the needs of the local population. For example, rationing of generators will not be necessary in a post-disaster setting where ample electricity remains available. Therefore, attention to the context in which the disaster takes place will be essential to the proper execution of this step.

Caps on purchases retain some of the rationing effect of unlimited price increases without rationing according to ability to pay. Instead of distributing scarce goods to those with the greatest financial resources in a community, caps on purchases mimic a lottery for essential goods, treating all persons as equally deserving of the goods essential to basic human functioning. In practice, those individuals with the greatest resources within a community will retain some advantage in obtaining scarce goods under a system of purchasing caps. Well-off members of a community may be better able to obtain information about the location of scarce goods, to travel to the location of these goods, and to have the time to wait in line to obtain these goods compared to less well-off persons.

A coordinated, community-wide cap on purchases of essential goods would seemingly reduce this problem. A central authority could distribute equal numbers of vouchers for essential goods to each member of the community, and vendors would be required to sell essential goods only to those customers holding a voucher. Moreover, these vouchers could be accepted in lieu of payment, with the local government repaying vendors at a later time for their goods. This policy would limit all members of the community to the same numbers of essential goods with the added benefit of ensuring that even very poor persons would have an equal opportunity to access essential goods.

However, the level of coordination between vendors required for a community-wide cap is likely to be impractical given the disruption created by the disaster, at least over the short-term.[16] A system of caps on purchases enforced by individual vendors represents a compromise between achieving a rationing effect that is to the benefit of all persons within a community and ensuring that this benefit is spread evenly throughout the community. Insofar as the state and federal government are able to distribute supplies, those supplies should be distributed on a lottery basis.

Both of the steps I have recommended are restricted to essential goods. Since the moral concerns facing price increases are triggered by the capacity of customers to engage in minimal human functioning, those goods not necessary to this purpose may be given whatever price the post-disaster market will bear. Following a disaster, for example, an individual might desperately wish to replace a damaged wide screen, high definition television. If many other persons in the local community share this desire and supplies of the product have been disrupted by the disaster, we can expect that the market price of high-end televisions will rise substantially. But, because this product is non-essential, television vendors can ethically charge whatever price the market will bear for their products.[17] While would-be customers might resent this situation, by the standards of price gouging the merchant does not act unethically.

Recall that state price gouging legislation is divided on what price increases were acceptable following a disaster and on what goods should be covered by the legislation. My account suggests that, for the vendor operating under conditions of uncertainty, equal respect for all members of a community will require: 1) Limited price increases beyond those justified by increases in costs and risk; and 2) Caps on purchases of essential goods in order to ration supplies of these goods. Neither of these restrictions should apply to persons selling non-essential goods. These guidelines will be most relevant when the pre-disaster market is reasonably successful at meeting the basic needs of all members of the community. Therefore, contextual factors make these guidelines defeasible.

Objections

Matt Zwolinski (2008) argues against both the effectiveness of price gouging legislation and the immorality of price increases that are typically condemned as gouging. His positive argument hinges largely on the benefits created by price increases, which I have largely granted in this paper.[18] In order to strengthen my argument as to the immorality of these price increases, I will respond to two of Zwolinski's central arguments. First, I will address the 'non-worseness claim' (NWC) that it cannot be morally worse to engage in a voluntary and mutually beneficial exchange than no exchange at all. Second, I will consider Zwolinski's argument that price increases do not exhibit a failure of respect for consumers.

Zwolinski asks how we can criticize vendors who engage in voluntary and mutually beneficial exchanges while we ignore those who do nothing to help the needy in disaster areas:

> On the one hand, to the extent that we hold that price gougers are guilty of mutually beneficial exploitation, we hold that they are acting wrongly even though their actions bring *some* benefit to disaster victims. On the other hand, many of *us* do *nothing* to relieve the suffering of most disaster victims, and we generally do not view ourselves as acting wrongly in failing to provide this benefit—or, at least, we do not view ourselves as acting *as* wrongly as price gougers. (Zwolinski 2008, 356–57)

This "non-worseness claim" asks why we should condemn those who help bring needed supplies into disaster areas as "gougers" when we do not condemn those who stay home, helping no one.[19] That is, how can it be morally worse to engage in a voluntary and mutually beneficial interaction than to do nothing at all?[20]

In response, I believe that we must take the long view when assessing the moral principles underlying our actions. Individual actions, such as charging high prices for essential goods or sitting on one's couch in response to a disaster, may not tell the full story as to one's responsiveness toward the basic needs of others. One is not required to respond to every disaster nor every needy person in order to live a morally praiseworthy life. However, a *pattern* of failure to respond to the needs of others can exhibit a greater level of indifference toward the basic needs of others than is exhibited through a single instance of price gouging.

Zwolinski is right to note that some of those who charge market clearing prices following a disaster might be motivated both by self-interest and the benefits created for some consumers (Zwolinski 2008, 337–68). These motives may be morally superior to those of the person motivated to enter the disaster zone purely by self-interest. My point is that the person who chooses not to enter the disaster zone may be motivated purely by self-interest or have other, morally laudable responses toward the basic needs of her fellow humans. As the non-gouger's duty of beneficence has not been specified in the way that, as I have argued, the gouger's duty has been specified, she retains leeway as to how she will discharge this duty.

In order to assess a non-gouger's underlying moral motivation, we must consider her responsiveness to others who lack access to essential goods. For example, does the non-gouger rise from her couch to help some other persons in situations of desperate need? Or is she solely moved to maximize her own welfare? In the latter case, the non-gouger can be accurately assessed as being guided by more morally problematic principles than those that guide a gouger who is motivated both by self-interest and the needs of others. The NWC, then, is false when motivations are assessed through sets of actions rather than single, morally ambiguous actions.

A second concern raised by Zwolinski also hinges on the positive consequences created by price gouging. Given that the exchanges I have been discussing are mutually beneficial and voluntary, Zwolinski questions whether placing limits on these exchanges is in keeping with respect for others:

> Exploitation might plausibly be argued to manifest a lack of respect for the personhood of the exploitee. But laws against price gouging both manifest and encourage similar or greater lack of respect. They manifest a lack of respect for both merchants and customers by preventing them from making the autonomous choice to enter into economic exchanges at the market-clearing price. They send the signal, in effect, that *your* decision that this exchange is in your best interest is unimportant, and that the law will decide for you what sorts of transactions you are allowed to enter into. (Zwolinski 2008, 352–53).

That is, if consumers are not forced into these exchanges—and in fact they desperately seek them out—how can it be consistent with respect for others' choices to rule them out of bounds?

I have argued that proper respect for the needs of others demands that vendors moderate their price increases and engage in non-price rationing. This argument does not hold that agreements between vendors and consumers at market clearing prices are coercive. Rather, vendors ought to limit their price increases and legislators ought to pass laws requiring vendors to do so. These restrictions aim to aid the entire post-disaster community while distributing essential goods more equitably. My claim is not that individual freedom is unimportant, but that the market may not support freedom equitably following a disaster.

Zwolinski defends his position by noting, "Price gougers treat their fellow human beings as traders, rather than as brothers and sisters in the Kingdom of Ends. But to treat someone as a trader is still a far cry more respectful than treating him as an object" (Zwolinski 2008, 359). Perhaps so, but I have argued that a disaster disrupts the market in a way that makes it *inappropriate* to treat one's fellow human beings as traders. When the market is functioning under normal conditions, it can be appropriate to treat one's fellow humans as traders in market transactions, especially in the presence of an adequate social safety net. This is so because the institution of the market creates a space in which self-interest and hard bargaining enhances the freedom of all persons. Following a disaster, however, the market fails to behave in this way over the short-term, pricing the poorest members of the community out of the market for essential goods.

Conclusions

If my account of the wrongness of price gouging is correct, it supports three major conclusions. First, the moral wrongs associated with price gouging should be understood generally as failures of respect for others. Vendors who ration scarce essential goods according to ability to pay undercut the goal of equitable access to essential goods within their community. This failure of respect takes place in a setting where the vendor owes a specified duty of beneficence to her customers and alternative means of achieving price signaling (through modest price increases) and rationing (through purchasing caps) are available.

Second, price gouging is only possible in transactions involving some good essential to living a distinctly human life. Price increases for diamonds, for example, are not instances of price gouging under my account. Moral wrongs, such as unfairness, may accompany price increases for non-essential goods. These wrongs, however, are distinct from the wrongs I have ascribed to price gouging.

Finally, the potential for price gouging will depend on the extent and strength of non-market social institutions for distributing essential goods. If these institutions are in place prior to a disaster and survive that event, price gouging is unlikely to occur even if vendors freely raise their prices in the post-disaster market. Individuals are more highly susceptible to price gouging in communities where entitlements to essential goods are weak or non-existent. Therefore, the moral wrong of price gouging cannot be reduced merely to price increases for essential goods following a disaster, even if these prices cannot be justified by increased costs.

The general shape of anti-gouging legislation gives a good rule of thumb for avoiding gouging. Price gouging legislation should allow for price increases justified by changes in the costs and risks of doing business. Otherwise, price increases should be limited and vendors should be required to ration their goods by placing caps on the number of purchases of essential goods. These limits on the market should be triggered by declarations of a state of emergency and limited to essential goods. Price controls should be restricted to the area affected by the disaster rather than entire states (Rapp 2005/2006). If price gouging legislation along these lines should prove to be deeply impractical or has not been enacted in a community, vendors should still constrain their market transactions along these lines.

Many cases of what are sometimes popularly called gouging are not morally problematic under my account nor considered cases of gouging. We should expect price increases on many goods following a disaster and many, if not most, of these increases will be justified by increases in cost, supply disruptions, and increased risk. However, in the most egregious cases, price increases cannot be justified in these ways, giving justification to the charge of price gouging as representing a kind of moral wrong.

These observations depend on an account of price gouging as a kind of failure of respect for others, but I hope to have shown that this account tracks well with widespread intuitions as to when and why certain price increases are morally problematic while revealing where those intuitions are unjustified. In practice, determining whether gouging has taken place will require great attention to local context, as shaped by the goal of equitable access to goods that meet the essential needs of consumers.

Notes

1. I am grateful to Robert Leider, Maggie Little, Daniel Levine, Leigh Anne Palmer, David Skarbek, Justin Weinberg, and Matt Zwolinski for their extensive comments on earlier versions of this paper. I am also thankful to the participants in a presentation of an earlier version of this paper at the 2008 APA Pacific Division Annual Meeting.

2. For example, a proposed federal anti-gouging law bans "taking unfair advantage of the circumstances related to an energy emergency to increase prices unreasonably." See . . . (accessed May 28, 2008). New York's anti-gouging law (NY GEN BUS S 396-r) is justified by the need to prevent vendors "from taking unfair advantage of consumers during abnormal disruptions of the market." In broader terms, USA Today condemns gougers as 'Vultures' (McCarthy 2004). Similarly, Florida Governor Charlie Crist complained that "It is astounding to me, the level of greed that someone must have in their soul to be willing to take advantage of someone suffering in the wake of a hurricane" (Jacoby 2004, F11).

3. I will use the term "disasters" to include any event that creates physical damage to a discrete area, disrupting the normal functioning of the market. These events include both natural disasters such as hurricanes and man-made disasters such as terrorist attacks.

4. For a helpful summary of US anti-gouging laws, see Skarbek & Skarbek 2008.

5. See, for example, Michigan (Mich. Stat. Ann. §445.903(z)), Missouri (15 CSR §60-8.030), and Texas (Tex. Bus & Com. Code §17.46(b)(27)).

6. See Geoffrey Rapp (2005/2006).

7. For example, California, Connecticut, the District of Columbia, Hawaii, and Mississippi make general prohibitions against price increases. California prohibits price increases generally for consumer goods and services (Cal. Pen. Code §396), Connecticut includes any item (Conn. Gen. Stat. §42-230), DC any merchandise or service (D.C. Code §28.4101 to 4102), Hawaii any commodity (Haw. Rev. Stat. §209-9), and Mississippi all goods and services (Miss. Code Ann. §75-24-25).

8. See generally the American Bar Association's summary of state legislation at: . . . (accessed May 28, 2008).

9. When explicit justification for anti-gouging legislation is given, references to 'unfair' prices is most common. The language of unconscionable and gross price increases, drawn from the common law tradition, are frequent as well (Rapp 2005/2006).

10. If one feels that 'price gouging' can appropriately apply to the champagne example, we can discriminate between two senses of price gouging. 'Fairness gouging' can apply to price increases on all goods following a disaster or other market disruption while 'needs gouging' will be limited to price increases on essential goods. As I argue, 'needs gouging' is at the heart of the moral wrong that is typically associated with gouging.

11. The goods essential to minimal human functioning are supported through various non-essential goods. For this reason, I will also discuss non-essential goods like electrical generators, gasoline, and ice that are, in many communities, instrumental to the durability of essential goods such as food, water, and adequate shelter. Insofar as the essential goods are relevant to the wrongness of gouging, these non-essential goods will be relevant as well.

12. Of course, disagreement will take place as to what corresponding regulatory environment best supports this freedom-enhancing function.

13. This point has been made by authors as diverse as Milton Friedman (1962) and Amartya Sen (1999).

14. There is a long history within Judeo-Christian and Islamic thought condemning excessive price increases against vulnerable populations. These restrictions are motivated by concerns about oppression of the weak. Consider, for example, Leviticus 25:14: "And if thou sell ought unto thy neighbor, or buyest ought of thy neighbor's hand, ye shall not oppress one another." More generally, see Brewer 2007, 1104–06.

15. In some cases, even wealthy persons following a disaster may not have the immediately available resources to afford price increases on essential goods. When referencing 'the wealthy' I intend those with the resources available to afford price increases rather than those with the greatest savings and assets within a community. My thanks to an anonymous reviewer for pointing out this ambiguity.

16. Moreover, such a system, even if it could be established, would likely create or exacerbate a black market in essential goods (Rockoff 2002). See also Abhi Raghunathan (2005).

17. By the standards of fairness, the price *might* be morally problematic. At the least, however, the vendor does not gouge his customer by the standard I am proposing.

18. There is some disagreement on this point, however. Geoffrey Rapp (2005/2006, 553–59) argues that anti-gouging laws are economically justified in two ways. First, they help preserve hard currency reserves when a disaster or terrorist attack disrupts electronic payment systems such as ATMs. Second, they counteract the effects of pricing irrationality that prevent efficient pricing during market disruptions.

19. Zwolinski discusses price increases among vendors who bring goods into the post-disaster market whereas I have focused my discussion on vendors with goods already in the market. The risks and opportunity costs faced

by outsiders may be different from those of locals, meaning that outsiders and locals may be justified in offering different prices for their goods based on different levels of risk and cost. I discuss the relevance of vendors' risks and costs to post-disaster prices in the previous section. The source of these goods, however, is not relevant to the basic moral wrong of price gouging.

20. Alan Wertheimer (1996, 289–93) describes the non-worseness claim as holding that an interaction Y between A and B cannot be morally worse than no interaction at all if Y makes both A and B better off when compared to a baseline of no interaction. In other words, the NWC denies the possibility that a mutually beneficial exploitative interaction can be morally worse than no interaction at all.

Bibliography

Anderson, Elizabeth. 1993. *Value in ethics and economics*. Cambridge, MA: Harvard University Press.

———. 2004. Ethical assumptions in economic theory: Some lessons from the history of credit and bankruptcy. *Ethical Theory and Moral Practice,* 7: 347–60.

Brewer, Michael. 2007. Planning disaster: Price gouging statutes and the shortages they create. *Brooklyn Law Review,* 72: 1101–37.

Elliott, Janet. 2008. Two hotels face lawsuits for raising rates. *The Houston Chronicle* (October 3).

Federal Trade Commission. 2006. *Investigation of gasoline price manipulation and post-Katrina gasoline price increases. . . .*

Friedman, Milton. 1962. *Capitalism and freedom*. Chicago: University of Chicago Press.

Hayek, Friedrich. 1945. The use of knowledge in society. *American Economic Review,* 35(4): 519–30.

Hill, Thomas. 1991. *Autonomy and self-respect*. New York: Cambridge University Press.

Jackson Sun. 2008. Go after those who may be price gouging. *The Jackson Sun* (September 17).

Jacoby, Jeff. 2004. Bring on the 'price gougers.' *The Boston Globe* (August 22): F11.

Kittay, Eva. 1999. *Love's labor: Essays on women, equality, and dependency*. New York: Routledge.

McCarthy, Michael. 2004. After the storm come the vultures. *USA Today* (August 20): 6B.

Nussbaum, Martha. 2000. *Women and human development*. New York: Cambridge University Press.

Page, Edward, & Cho, Min. 2006. Price gouging 101: A call to Florida lawmakers to perfect Florida's price gouging law, *Florida Bar Journal,* 80: 49–52.

Raghunathan, Abhi. 2005. South Florida shortages fuel black market. *St. Petersburg Times* (October 29): 1B.

Ramasastry, Anita. 2005. Assessing anti-price-gouging statutes in the wake of hurricane Katrina: Why they're necessary in emergencies, but need to be rewritten. *Findlaw* (September 15). Available at. . .

Rapp, Geoffrey. 2005/2006. Gouging: Terrorist attacks, hurricanes, and the legal and economic aspects of post-disaster price regulation. *Kentucky Law Journal*, 94: 535–60.

Reader, Soran. 2003. Distance, relationship and moral obligation. *The Monist*, 86: 367–81.

Rockoff, Hugh. 2002. Price controls. In David R. Henderson (Ed.), *The Concise Encyclopedia of Economics*. Indianapolis: Liberty Fund, Inc. Available at. . .

Rushing, J. Taylor. 2004. Storms stir up price gouging. *Florida Times-Union* (September 18):A-1.

Satz, Debra. 2007. Liberalism, economic freedom, and the limits of markets. *Social Philosophy and Policy*, 24: 120–40.

Sen, Amartya. 1992. *Inequality reexamined*. Cambridge, MA: Harvard University Press.

———. 1999. *Development as freedom*. New York: Knopf.

Skarbek, Brian R., & Skarbek, David B. 2008. The price is right: Regulation, reputation, and recovery. *Dartmouth Law Journal*, 6(2): 235–76.

Smith, Adam. 1976 (1776). *An inquiry into the nature and causes of the wealth of nations*. Ed. R. H. Campbell, Andrew Skinner, and W. B. Todd. Oxford: Oxford University Press.

Snyder, Jeremy. 2008. Needs exploitation. *Ethical Theory and Moral Practice*, 11: 389–405.

Taylor, Jerry. 2005. Gouge on. *National Review Online* (September 2). . . .

Treaster, Joseph. 2004. With storm gone, Floridians are hit with price gouging. *New York Times* (August 18): A1.

Waldron, Jeremy. 2003. Who is my neighbor?: Humanity and proximity. *The Monist*, 86: 333–54.

Wall Street Journal. 2005. In praise of 'gouging.' *Wall Street Journal* (September 7): A16.

Wertheimer, Alan. 1996. *Exploitation*. Princeton, NJ: Princeton University Press.

Zwolinski, Matt. 2008. The ethics of price gouging. *Business Ethics Quarterly*, 18: 347–78.

Matt Zwolinski   → **NO**

Price Gouging, Non-Worseness, and Distributive Justice

PRICE GOUGING tends to evoke from humane and decent people an immediate and overwhelming sense of repugnance.[1] Most people have a strong sense that price gouging involves a kind of predatory behavior—a ruthless satisfaction of individual greed at the expense of the vulnerable—and that it must therefore constitute a serious moral wrong. Indeed, recent research in moral psychology suggests that this kind of "gut" reaction against price gouging might be very deeply rooted in us indeed. Instinctive and powerful reactions against the exploitation of the vulnerable may have served our early ancestors well by promoting the cohesion and survival of the small groups in which they lived.[2] But while reliance on automatic emotional reactions might have worked well for our primitive ancestors, such reactions are of little help in coming to a sophisticated and subtle understanding of the many and varied questions bearing on the morality of price gouging.[3] For such an understanding requires us to do more than simply decide whether "price gouging" is "good" or "bad." It requires us to discriminate among the many forms price gouging can take—between, for instance, an established merchant's raising prices to cover increased costs of supplies and risk, and a low-level entrepreneur who is drawn by the lure of high profits to begin selling items for the first time in the wake of a disaster. And it requires us to discriminate between the many different kinds of moral evaluations we can make of price gouging—whether it ought to be morally permissible or impermissible; whether it is morally praiseworthy, morally blameworthy, or merely morally tolerable; whether we have good moral reasons to prohibit it by law or by social pressure; and so forth. Each of these questions in turn raises a host of differing and difficult subsidiary questions that require both careful empirical research and thoughtful philosophical analysis to fully address.

Fortunately, Jeremy Snyder's paper on the subject contains no shortage of precisely this sort of thoughtful analysis.[4] Although his conclusions differ in some ways from my own,[5] he nevertheless provides a carefully argued case for the immorality of price gouging, while at the same time demonstrating an admirable sensitivity to the many morally attractive features of a free-market price system. Still, in spite of its many strengths, there are some points at which Snyder's position is less clear or less well-defended than it might be. Rather

From *Business Ethics Quarterly*, April 2009, pp. 303–306. Copyright © 2009 by Business Ethics Quarterly. Reprinted by permission of The Philosophy Documentation Center, publisher of Business Ethics Quarterly. References omitted.

than continuing to sing the praises of what is generally a very fine piece of work, then, I shall focus my comments on what I take to be two problematic areas of his paper—first, Snyder's rejection of the non-worseness claim appears to be based on a misunderstanding of the kind of moral objects to which that principle is meant to apply; and second, Snyder's appeal to considerations of distributive justice and equal respect for persons is flawed insofar as it rests on two false assumptions—that price gouging undermines equitable access to vital goods, and that a regime in which price gouging is banned promotes equitable access. I will conclude with some brief comments on how Snyder's evaluation of price gouging compares with my own.

1. The Non-Worseness Claim

One of Snyder's major objections to my argument stems from my use of the "nonworseness claim" (NWC) to defend price gouging against the charge that it is wrongfully exploitative. NWC, as I described it, holds that "in cases where *A* has a right not to transact with *B*, and where transacting with *B* is not worse for *B* than not transacting with *B* at all, then it cannot be seriously wrong for *A* to engage in this transaction, even if its terms are judged to be unfair by some external standard" (Zwolinski 2008: 357). If the NWC is true, then it is hard to see how standard cases of price gouging can be serious moral wrongs. After all, most of us would think that an individual who could sell generators to victims of a disaster but chose not to do so would be acting within his rights (even if we also believe that she would be acting less than fully virtuously), and it also seems clear (Snyder himself concedes this [Snyder 2009: 277–78]) that those who buy from price gougers at inflated prices are nevertheless better off as a result than they would have been had the transaction not taken place at all. So, since gouging someone is better for them than neglecting them, and we have a moral right to neglect them, must we not therefore have a moral right to gouge them as well? How could gouging possibly be worse than neglect?

Snyder takes issue with this argument by holding that it fails when "motivations are assessed through sets of actions rather than single, morally ambiguous actions" (Snyder 2009: 288). Price gougers might indeed be acting in ways that help their customers, Snyder concedes, but they might be doing so only out of the vicious motive to extract as much profit as possible out of people in desperate need. Of course, they *might* be doing it out of a sense of morally virtuous beneficence as well. We can't tell just by looking at one action in isolation. To determine whether a person is properly motivated by a responsiveness to the needs of others, we need to look at their pattern of action as a whole, and not just one isolated instance.

This reasoning seems correct, as far as it goes. But it is not clear what lesson Snyder thinks he can draw from it. At times, Snyder writes as though he is making a point about the *moral character* of the price gouger and what it takes to lead a "morally praiseworthy life" (Snyder 2009: 287). With this point I am in full agreement—indeed it is one which I tried to make myself in part five of my paper (Zwolinski 2008: 366–68). One's moral character is a matter of one's general disposition to see the needs of others as reason-giving and to respond appropriately to those reasons. And the act of price gouging is too morally ambiguous for us to read this disposition (or its absence) off of it. But NWC is not a thesis about moral character, it is a thesis about the wrongness of moral *acts*. And this is importantly different. Vicious people can perform morally permissible actions. Think, for instance, of Kant's shopkeeper who returns the correct change to a naïve customer *only* out of a selfish concern for his own reputation and long-term profit. If he could be sure he could steal a penny from a child's change and get away with it, he would, but prudence dictates restraint. Such a person has a bad moral character. But the act he is performing—giving the child back her correct change—is perfectly innocent. The distinction between these two moral assessments becomes clear, and especially important to recognize, when we think about their respective implications for third parties. If we see a person—vicious or innocent—performing a morally *impermissible* action then, all else being equal, we should try to stop him, either as individuals or perhaps through the collective institutions of the state. But there is no comparable reason for us to try to stop someone from doing that which it is morally permissible for her to do, even if the person doing it is morally vicious. Her moral viciousness might give us *other* kinds of reason for action. We might have reason to censure her and get her to see the intrinsic value of all persons. And, in the case of Kant's shopkeeper, we might be very hesitant to patronize her store for fear that circumstances in the future will *not* always tip the scales of self-interest toward the side of honesty. But we do not have reason to interfere with her performance of a morally permissible act, or even to morally condemn the act, though we might have reason to morally condemn the agent.

Thus, Snyder's concerns about NWC do not give us reason to prohibit price gouging, or even condemn it. For all his arguments show (correctly, I think) is that price gouging can sometimes be done by morally vicious people. They do not show that the act of price gouging itself is morally impermissible. And that is all that my use of NWC was ever meant to deny.

2. Distributive Justice

One of the most common criticisms of price gouging, and one which is central to Snyder's argument as I understand it, is that it leads to vital resources being distributed in a morally objectionable way. Because price gouging involves charging a higher than normal price for goods, it disadvantages those who are poor relative to those who are well off. According to Snyder, price gouging thus undermines equitable access to essential goods, and thereby manifests a lack of equal respect for persons (Snyder 2009: 280).

However, the claim that price gouging undermines equitable access to goods is problematic for two reasons. First, it is the *emergency* that undermines equitable access, not whatever price gouging may occur in response to that disaster. Prior to the emergency, there is generally a well-functioning market in food, water, and other vital goods that generally ensures that all who need these goods will be able to purchase them. Emergencies lead to either a sharp increase in the demand for, or a sharp decrease in the supply of, these goods, and it is *this fact* that undermines equitable access. When supply and demand are radically altered so that there are not enough goods to go around, *no* method of distribution will produce equitable access—at least not at levels sufficient to meet people's needs.[6] Some people will get the goods, and others will not.

This is true of all methods of distribution, including Snyder's proposed method involving legislatively imposed caps on both the price of essential goods and on the amount of those goods that any consumer can purchase. Such a method of distribution, Snyder says, "mimic[s] a lottery for essential goods, treating all persons as equally deserving of the goods essential to basic human functioning" (Snyder 2009: 285). But the lottery metaphor, while apt in its characterization of a system of this sort, is puzzling as a way of highlighting the alleged distributive justice of such a system. For a lottery has seemed to many—most memorably to John Rawls—the paradigm case of moral arbitrariness (Rawls 1971: 74). In a lottery, some will obtain goods, some will not, and the difference between the two is nothing more than brute luck. In Snyder's lottery-like system, people will likewise be divided into "Haves" and "Have-Nots," and the difference between them will be based on who manages to get in line before supplies run out. This may not be *entirely* a matter of luck—perhaps it gives an edge to the perceptive, or those with a lot of time on their hands to stand in line. But it can hardly be said to be a system that distributes in accordance with any characteristic of great moral significance.

Furthermore, the sense in which it can be said to be a system that treats people as "equals" is at best a highly attenuated one. Because the context in which such a system operates is one where demand greatly exceeds supply, it is highly unlikely that the result of such a system will be equal units of vital goods being distributed to each person. For non-divisible goods like generators and radios, there will simply be no alternative to some people getting the good while others go away empty-handed. Other goods like ice could theoretically be divided into equally sized units for each person. But such a proposal is rife with practical difficulties. What if the portions of the good, once equally divided, are too small to be of any practical use? A bag of 300 ice cubes equally divided among 300 people is almost infinitely less useful than the same bag of ice in one person's hands. How is the relevant 'community' among which equal distribution is to take place to be defined? How are shopkeepers to determine what an equal unit of the good should be? And, most significantly, what sort of restrictions are to be put on the use to which people's shares of the good may be put? Will people be allowed to sell their goods to others—even though this would be certain to undermine equitable access?[7] Or will such secondary markets be prohibited?

The only kind of equality that Snyder's system can hope to achieve, then, is equality of *opportunity* to access vital goods. But this too, on closer examination, turns out to be less satisfying from a moral perspective than we might have hoped for. For in reality, opportunity under Snyder's proposed system will *not* be equal. Even if the system runs perfectly, those who show up first to a vendor will have a better opportunity than those who show up later. And in reality, rationing systems like the one proposed are often subject to corruption that favors 'insiders'—those with a personal, religious, ethnic, or other connection to those with resources or the power to affect their distribution.[8] It is true that nothing in Snyder's proposed system directly makes access to vital goods contingent on wealth, so with respect to *that* variable opportunity may be said to be equal. But in reality, and with respect to other equally if not more arbitrary variables, opportunity will not be equal.

Finally, it is worth noting that while Snyder's proposed distributive mechanism seeks to mimic while improving upon the *allocative* function of prices, it makes *no* effort to mimic their equally if not more important *signaling* function.[9] Prices that increase and decline in response to changes in supply and demand are important not only to allocate scarce resources among competing uses, but to signal when too much or too little social resources are being invested in a particular activity. In particular, the high prices that vital goods like water, sandbags, and hotel rooms command in the wake of a disaster signal to entrepreneurs to provide *more* of these goods, and indicate that larger-than-normal profits can be made by doing so. Post-disaster high prices thus convey both the *information* that increased supply is needed, and the *incentive* to provide that additional supply. But in so doing, high prices provide their own best corrective—as profit-seeking entrepreneurs rush to reap the windfall profits that the radically altered balance of supply and demand makes possible, they increase supply and in doing so drive the price down to something approximating its pre-disaster equilibrium. This means that the window of opportunity during which price gouging can occur is narrow, *but only if individuals are free to set prices as they see fit.*

This point is crucial. No one, not even those of us who argue that price gouging is morally permissible, thinks that price gouging is unqualifiedly *good* in the sense of being something that would occur in an ideal world. Cases of price gouging occur in circumstances of desperate need and terrible suffering. And in the short run, price gouging is just one more allocative mechanism among others, with the result that some people's needs—often the needs of the poorest and most vulnerable—will go unmet. But policies and moral injunctions that prevent prices from rising freely in the wake of a disaster do not diminish the desperation of the short run; they simply make it harder to move past that short run into a period of recovery. This might not be the case if we could rely on all people to act on the principles of beneficence that Snyder enjoins. And indeed, one of the most heartening aspects of some of the recent natural disasters in the United States has been the extent to which beneficence *has* been effective in delivering vital goods and services to those who so desperately need them. But it is probably a permanent feature of the human condition that there will always be less beneficence to go around than is needed. And in such a condition we would do well to take as much advantage as we can of the market's ability to channel individual self-interest toward socially desirable ends. In some cases, as is demonstrated in the response of Wal-Mart and Home Depot to Hurricane Katrina, even narrow self-interest will not lead to price gouging, and this is a happy result.[10] But where it does, we should recognize that gouging ought to be tolerated not as an end in itself, but merely as a method of making a very bad short-run situation less bad (by conserving scarce resources and allocating them effectively) and also of making that short run as short as possible (by providing incentives to increase supply).

3. Conclusion

Despite the concerns raised above, Snyder's ultimate position on the morality of price gouging does not seem to be too distant from my own. We both believe that price increases in the wake of a disaster can, in some circumstances, be not only morally permissible but positively morally desirable insofar as they serve to promote the interests of those suffering in the wake of a disaster. And we both believe that under other circumstances, price gouging can be wrongfully exploitative. The main differences between our views seem to be two: we differ regarding the precise conditions under which price gouging becomes wrongfully exploitative, and we differ regarding the desirability of the legal regulation of price gouging.

On the first of these differences, Snyder's position is somewhat unclear. He states that some "price increases condemned as gouging are morally innocent at worst and, more often, create a positive and morally praiseworthy benefit for all concerned" (Snyder 2009: 277). They do this, he notes, in many of the ways I discussed in my own paper: they aid "in the conservation of scarce goods by making it more likely that they will be purchased by those who place the greatest value on them" (Snyder 2009: 278), they send signals which lead "other suppliers into the market, quickly increasing supplies of essential goods" (Snyder 2009: 278), they provide an incentive to merchants to "increase supplies of essential goods prior to the [disaster]" (Snyder 2009: 278), and they serve as a "fair reward for the efforts and risks undertaken by vendors" (Snyder 2009: 278). And Snyder seems to indicate that insofar as price increases are necessary to serve these morally praiseworthy goals, they are morally permissible, as when he writes that "price increases even beyond those justified by increased costs and risks can be justified" insofar as they increase supplies, encourage rationing, and discourage waste (Snyder 2009: 285).

The question this raises, then, is under what conditions price gouging *will not* be morally acceptable on Snyder's account. The only clue Snyder provides to an answer is that price increases will be unacceptable when they "undermine equitable access to certain, essential goods" (Snyder 2009: 279). But this is puzzling, since price increases can presumably serve the morally praiseworthy goals described above (e.g. increasing rationing, discouraging waste) while *at the same time* undermining the equitable access of individuals to those goods. Indeed, it seems likely that the only way that price increases *can* promote goals like allocative efficiency and signaling new supply is by undermining equitable access, since these price increases will operate in a context in which individuals will face dramatically different budget constraints. This suggests that we cannot hope for both equitable access and the morally attractive benefits of price increases, and it is not clear which of these Snyder's account counsels us to choose in the (possibly ubiquitous) cases of conflict.

The second difference between Snyder's account and my own is that I favor the repeal of all laws prohibiting or regulating price gouging, whereas Snyder thinks some regulation is appropriate. Here, again, it is easy to overstate the differences between our accounts. We both think, as far as I can tell, that current laws are a bad idea insofar as they prohibit many mutually beneficial exchanges that would not be objectionably exploitative. But Snyder does seem to suggest that there is some role for the legal regulation of price gouging, and that it will involve limiting permissible price increases to those necessary to promote allocative efficiency, signal new supply, and compensate for increased risk and costs to merchants (Snyder 2009: 285). Now, I actually think that Snyder provides a fairly exhaustive list of the morally praiseworthy aspects of price increases, such that somebody who knowingly increased her price beyond this level could properly be described as satisfying her individual greed with no morally redeeming side-effects. So as an account of the conditions under which price increases are *morally praiseworthy,* I don't have much to disagree with in Snyder's proposal. But as a proposal for the *legal regulation* of price gouging (or even the social regulation of price gouging in the forms of boycotts/social pressure), I have a serious problem with it. The problem is that by Snyder's standard, it is virtually impossible to know whether any given price increase is moral or immoral.[11] What percentage price increase is necessary to encourage the optimal level of rationing among one's consumers? In trying to answer this question, the merchant at least has the advantage of observing the behavior of her customers and seeing who responds in what way to a certain rate of price increase. But how will the merchant know who *should* be buying less, and who *should* be buying more? How would legislators know this? And what hope does a merchant or a legislator have—even if she is lucky enough to have a PhD in econometrics—of predicting the level of price increase necessary to attract sufficient supply to where it is needed?[12]

Thus, even if Snyder's list of morally relevant criteria is complete, it is useless as a standard of regulation because we cannot ever know if we are satisfying it. My contention is that the best hope we have of finding a price that approximates the satisfaction of these criteria is to let that price emerge through the free choices of numerous individuals in the market. This, too, is an imperfect mechanism, since actual prices do not always and necessarily reflect a proper balance of supply and demand, nor do they even purport to approximate "fair rewards" for risk and effort. Market prices, in other words, are not a perfect measure of moral significance. My claim, though, is that given the constraints in knowledge faced by those who would be charged with regulating prices, reliance on market prices in post-disaster contexts does a better job at promoting our moral values than any feasible alternative mechanism.

Notes

1. For a discussion of the role of repugnance as a reaction to price gouging and other forms of market exchange, see Roth 2007: 43–44.
2. For an overview of the possible evolutionary origins of "deontic" moral intuitions, such as those which tend to be invoked against the permissibility of mutually beneficial exploitation, see Greene 2007; Haidt 2001; Prinz 2008.

3. They may also be less helpful in a world in which distant, impersonal relationships have replaced close-knit societies as the locus of interpersonal interaction, and in which the distant indirect and non-obvious effects of our actions have an increasingly great relative causal significance on human well-being as the direct and visible ones. On this point, see Hayek's discussion of the extended order in Hayek and Bartley 1988: chap. 1, but also the concluding sections of Greene 2007.

4. Snyder 2009.

5. See Zwolinski 2008. See also Zwolinski forthcoming.

6. Of course, one could guarantee equity of a sort with a policy that bans distribution of the good altogether. Such a policy, if effectively enforced, could result in each person getting an equitable share of nothing.

7. Here we face a problem similar to that illustrated by Robert Nozick's famous Wilt Chamberlain example (Nozick 1974: 160–64). The maintenance of an initially equal distribution will require either a prohibition on trades or continual redistribution. And since Snyder's proposal is not to initially distribute *all* resources equally, but only to provide equal access to certain vital resources, the difficulty of maintaining equality will be even greater.

8. See, for a discussion, Alchian and Allen 1968: 95–99.

9. On this distinction, see Zwolinski 2008: 360–64.

10. Steven Horowitz has documented the response of the private sector to Hurricane Katrina, noting that in the two weeks following the disaster Wal-Mart shipped over 2500 truckloads of needed goods to Louisiana, a substantial portion of which was given away free. This quick response time was made possible by Wal-Mart's elaborate mechanisms for tracking storms before they hit in order to ensure that its stores are well stocked prior to the time that demand increases. Neither Home Depot nor Wal-Mart engaged in price gouging in the aftermath of Katrina. And while it is possible that this restraint was at least partly motivated by altruistic concerns, no doubt a large part of it was motivated by the recognition that their behavior during this highly public and emotionally charged disaster situation would affect consumers' future willingness to give them their business. For established retailers, post-disaster deals are but one move in a long series of iterated prisoners' dilemmas with customers, and in such contexts mutual cooperation is often the strategy best in accord with individual self-interest (Axelrod 1984). Or, as one Home Depot executive put it, "I can't think of a quicker way to lose customers than price gouging." See Horowitz 2008; Horowitz forthcoming.

11. The problem is that no individual or group of individuals has sufficient information to know what price would be necessary to satisfy the criteria Snyder sets out. This problem is essentially just a specific instance of the more general knowledge problem discussed by Friedrich Hayek in Hayek 1937, 1945; and elsewhere.

12. There is strong evidence that even well-trained economists are severely limited in their ability to predict how actual markets will respond to events like a change in the general price level, much less a change in the price charged by one particular merchant. See, for a discussion, Gaus forthcoming; Gaus 2007.

Bibliography

Alchian, A., and W. Allen. 1968. *University Economics,* 2nd ed. New York: Wadsworth.

Axelrod, R. 1984. *The Evolution of Cooperation.* New York: Basic Books.

Gaus, G. F. 2007. "Social Complexity and Evolved Moral Principles," in *Liberalism, Conservatism, and Hayek's Idea of Spontaneous Order,* ed. P. McNamara. London: Palgrave Macmillan.

———. Forthcoming. "Is the Public Incompetent? Compared to Whom? About What?" *Critical Review.*

Greene, J. 2007. "The Secret Joke in Kant's Soul," in *Moral Psychology, Vol. 3: The Neuroscience of Morality: Emotion, Disease, and Development,* ed. W. Sinnott-Armstrong. Cambridge, Mass.: MIT Press.

Haidt, J. 2001. "The Emotional Dog and Its Rational Tail: A Social Intuitionist Approach to Moral Judgment," *Psychological Review* 108: 814–34.

Hayek, F. A. 1937. "Economics and Knowledge," *Economica* 4: 33–54.

———. 1945. "The Use of Knowledge in Society," *American Economic Review* 35(4): 519–30.

Hayek, F. A., and W. W. Bartley III. 1988. *The Fatal Conceit: The Errors of Socialism.* Chicago: University of Chicago Press.

Horowitz, S. 2008. *Making Hurricane Response More Effective: Lessons from the Private Sector and the Coast Guard During Katrina.* Washington, D.C.: Mercatus Center.

———. Forthcoming. "Wal-Mart to the Rescue: Private Enterprise's Response to Hurricane Katrina," *The Independent Review* 13(4).

Nozick, R. 1974. *Anarchy, State, and Utopia.* New York: Basic Books.

Prinz, J. 2008. *The Emotional Construction of Morals.* Oxford: Oxford University Press.

Rawls, J. 1971. *A Theory of Justice,* 1st ed. Cambridge: Belknap Press.

Roth, A. 2007. "Repugnance as a Constraint on Markets," *Journal of Economic Perspectives* 21(3): 37–58.

Snyder, J. 2009. "What's the Matter with Price Gouging?" *Business Ethics Quarterly.* 19(2) (April): 275–93.

Zwolinski, M. 2008. "The Ethics of Price Gouging," *Business Ethics Quarterly* 18(3): 347–78.

———. Forthcoming. "Price Gouging and Market Failure," in *New Essays on Philosophy, Politics & Economics: Integration and Common Research Projects,* ed. G. Gaus, J. Lamont, and C. Favor. Stanford, Calif.: Stanford University Press.

POSTSCRIPT

Should Price Gouging Be Regulated?

Consumers are thinking about the people who make the products they purchase and the conditions in which they work. American retailers and name brands have produced clothing, shoes, toys, and more. Store shelves are filled with merchandise made in sweatshops where often the workers conduct their labor in unsafe conditions with little pay. Many of these retailers say there are strict codes of conduct and on-site monitoring. However business ethicists believe that some factories have found ways to conceal abuses and to keep double sets of books to fool auditors. At some factories individuals are tutored with a script to recite to auditors. The script is different than the real conditions at the sweatshop. What can Americans ethically believe about what they wear and use? Is a Kantian ideal being followed in the production of these goods?

Will the poorest in society still be able to purchase the goods and services they need in times of disaster? Probably not, and they could very well perish. The invisible hand of the market (the law of supply and demand) may seem harsh in times such as these.

Society could strive to reduce situations in which buyers or sellers are desperate. Warding off natural disasters is impossible, but perhaps better preparation for any disaster might keep members of a society more in line with the free market in times when price gouging seems savvy.

A reply by Matt Zwolinski is also found in Business Ethics Quarterly 19:2 (April 2009), pp. 303–308, in which he answers some of Snyder's concerns, and clarifies his points that it is not morally justified to have laws prohibiting price gouging; that it is morally permissible behavior to engage in price gouging; and that price gouging doesn't reflect badly on the moral character of those who participate in it.

Suggested Readings

Henry Altman, "Who's Gored by Gouging?" *Nation's Business,* June 1987.

Mark Kahler, "Fight Price Gouging," September 1, 2009. Budgettravel. about.com/od/cheapgroundtransportation/a/price_gouging_2.htm.

Miranda Okker, "Bad-business Ethics/Price Gouging," Ad Traps, April 25, 2005. http://www.marketingprofs.com/

Harris R. Sherline, "Price Gouging and Excess Profits," May 24, 2008. http://www.articlesbase.com/ethics-articles/price-gouging-and-excess-profits-425486.html.

ISSUE 7

Does the Enron Collapse Show That We Need More Regulation of the Energy Industry?

YES: Richard Rosen, from "Regulating Power: An Idea Whose Time Is Back," *The American Prospect* (March 25, 2002)

NO: Christopher L. Culp and Steve H. Hanke, from "Empire of the Sun: An Economic Interpretation of Enron's Energy Business," *Cato Policy Analysis No. 470* (February 20, 2003)

ISSUE SUMMARY

YES: It seems reasonably clear to Richard Rosen that the disastrous collapse of the Enron energy company—accompanied by soaring prices in California, disruptions of the market here and abroad, and accusations of fraud all around—means we need more government oversight.

NO: Not so, say Culp and Hanke; it was the unwise regulation that caused the problem in the first place, and only deregulation will let the market clear up the problems with the industry.

Everyone since Adam Smith has acknowledged that no matter what the virtues of the free market—and they are many—there are areas where the public needs protection. For an obvious instance, the state, to be called a state, must assert and maintain an absolute monopoly on the use of force, not just force that would deprive of life, health, or liberty, but any force at all (there are towns that forbid parents to spank their children). Force, therefore, or the threat of violence, cannot be part of any legal negotiation. For another instance, there are products so dangerous to human health and welfare that by law we forbid them to be sold on the open market under any circumstances, even though a high demand and lucrative trade could be predicted—hand grenades, crack cocaine, and canisters of poison gas come to mind. (After that, there are the flotillas of restrictions on open trade—drugs available only by prescription, bans on the sale of wild or endangered animals or their parts, bans on pesticides that endure in the environment—the list goes on.) The state creates such restrictions in the exercise of its inalienable "police power," the responsibility to protect the health, welfare, and morals of the people. The exercise of that responsibility in most developed nations includes the provision of a free educational system and free health care for all citizens; the United States, as a matter of policy, has exempted itself from the latter and seems to be aiming at phasing out the former.

At least since the beginning of the twentieth century, state monopoly and regulation have been extended to a large variety of "utilities"—public goods that cannot fall into private hands without putting the public at serious risk of exploitation. These include transportation corridors (including roads, railways, all waterways), communications pathways (airwaves, telegraph lines, telephone services), and all provision of water and energy (heat and light). For most of that period, at least a portion of most of those services has been in private hands, but all were subject to the regulation of rates, the regulation of the choice of services to provide and areas to be served, and the expectation that they would serve the public interest (evidence to the contrary could result in government intervention at any time).

Deregulation began as part of the antiregulatory climate during the Reagan administration, during the period when companies were led by the mergers and acquisitions departments. At that time Kenneth Lay took over the Enron company from his predecessor and rapidly picked up several more unexciting pipeline companies. He cultivated friends in high places, and furthered his deregulation agenda all through the Clinton administration. (In 1993, for instance, Wendy Gramm, wife of Senator Phil Gramm, ushered a ruling exempting futures contracts from government oversight through the Commodity Futures Trading Commission, which she chaired. Shortly thereafter, she left that post and accepted a position on Enron's board of directors.) Lay, and Enron generally, spent a very large amount of money on contributions to political campaigns, including at least $6 million to federal candidates and parties as well as $1.8 million or more to candidates for state office. Very large contributions went to George W. Bush's presidential campaign. By the time Bush attained the White House, Lay was his close friend ("Kenny Boy," as he was known to the president). Enron was the most persistent and loudest voice for deregulation.

Was it a good idea? In California, deregulation led to skyrocketing prices, draining the state's coffers. Enron made out very well. Is this just free enterprise at work? Would it have all steadied eventually? There are two sides to this dispute, which were both silenced on October 18, 2002, when Enron officers pleaded guilty to conspiracy to manipulate energy prices in California. Maybe the damage to California was due to regulation, maybe it was due to deregulation, but probably it was due to criminal conspiracies undertaken by criminals under cover of the deregulation agenda. We will have to await a more honest trial of deregulation to discover the public's real best interest.

Ask yourself, as you read these brief selections, what we expect the free market to provide and to refrain from providing, and what we expect government, in the exercise of its police power, to ensure for our common life. The questions are not simple, and there is no national consensus.

YES ↰   Richard Rosen

Regulating Power: An Idea Whose Time Is Back

Ignored in the scandal about Enron's off-the-books deals is the fact that Enron's core businesses—trading and selling energy—made little economic sense. Starting in the early 1990s, Enron claimed it could make electricity generation more efficient through a system to trade more electric power than regulated utilities. To that end, the company urged the Federal Energy Regulatory Commission (FERC) to promote the deregulation of wholesale electric markets.

But whenever there was an opportunity to reduce consumers' electric rates by trading power at the wholesale level, the old regulated electric utilities had always done so. Indeed, most electric utilities had already grouped themselves into "power pools" or other voluntary energy-swapping systems set up to trade power at its cost of production—the cheapest approach for consumers. If we calculate the relative costs of producing and selling electricity, new wholesale traders like Enron could have reduced our national average electric rates by perhaps 1 percent, if that.

So most of the supposed efficiencies of deregulation were already being realized by regulated utilities. To the extent that Enron could reap large profits, it was only by amassing market power, monopolizing transmission lines, and taking advantage of temporary scarcity—thus raising prices and frustrating the whole supposed point of deregulation. Any efficiency gains were more than wiped out by the cost of administering a new, complex trading system pursuing its own quest for profit.

When it lobbied state legislatures and public-utility commissions to deregulate electric utilities, Enron promised to sell retail electricity to all types of customers. Instead, because it was too costly to compete with traditional utilities for small customers, Enron wound up selling retail electricity primarily to large industrial and commercial companies under long-term contracts. Because government takes ultimate responsibility for the power supply, even in states that have deregulated generation, utilities will remain providers of last resort for at least the next few years. Regulated retail rates, meanwhile, have always been a fallback option for large and small consumers. Enron and other similar companies could seldom beat the regulated price.

From *The American Prospect*, vol. 13, no. 6, March 25 2002, pp. 22. Copyright © 2002. Reprinted with permission from Richard Rosen and The American Prospect, Boston, MA. All rights reserved.

Ultimately, Enron never made a profit in its retail business. The costs of gaining market share were just too high—and they were probably hidden by some of Enron's now famous off-balance-sheet debt. In some cases, very large customers saved a few percentage points on their electricity bills, but often only until wholesale prices rose, forcing them to turn back to the regulated utilities for the best rates.

The small savings that deregulation might deliver to some customers must be weighed against the higher costs to others—and against the huge risks of overcharges like those seen during the California debacle, well before Enron's collapse. Analysts who deny that Enron was a failure of deregulation, or who paint Enron as just an isolated case of corporate mismanagement, forget that the firm never realized its original promises—even though deregulated electricity sales, at both the wholesale and retail levels, were its primary reason for being.

How, then, should we regulate electricity? Contrary to the current fashion, our old system—state regulation of vertically integrated electric utilities—makes sense. Regulators need to stress state-of-the-art, "least cost" planning for new investments in generation and transmission. Traditional regulation means that utilities charge consumers their costs plus a reasonably low regulated return on equity.

Utilities should be grouped into power pools—like those we've had in the Northeast—in order to make possible economically efficient sharing of their generating plants. Under a regulated system, concentrated market power is a strength, not a threat, because utilities are prohibited from gouging consumers.

It turns out that it is not economically efficient to divide electric-utility services and create an unregulated market for each. We probably don't even need a competitive wholesale power market. Ironically, by the early 1990s many state regulatory commissions were getting quite good at keeping electric rates in check, thanks in part to growing investments in energy conservation. It was the big industrial customers who thought that they could get better deals in a deregulated market for electricity. On the whole, they didn't. While co-generation and other energy-saving technology surely make sense, deregulation doesn't.

Christopher L. Culp
and Steve H. Hanke

➡ **NO**

Empire of the Sun: An Economic Interpretation of Enron's Energy Business

Executive Summary

The collapse of Enron Corporation has been portrayed as the result of accounting fraud and greed. Not everything that Enron did, however, was wrong or fraudulent. Fraud contributed to the timing of Enron's failure but was not the root cause of that failure. In analyzing Enron, it is critically important to distinguish what Enron did wrong from what it did right.

Enron's basic business strategy, known as "asset lite," was legitimate and quite beneficial for the marketplace and consumers. By combining a small investment in a capital-intensive industry such as energy with a derivatives-trading operation and a market-making overlay for that market, Enron was able to transform itself from a small, regional energy market operator into one of America's largest companies.

Enron contributed to the creation of the natural gas derivatives market, and, for a while, it was the sole market maker, entering into price risk management contracts with all other market participants. Its physical market presence, as a wholesale merchant of natural gas and electricity, placed the Houston-based company in an ideal position to discover and transmit to the market relevant knowledge of energy markets and to make those markets more efficient.

When Enron applied that same strategy in other markets in which it had no comparative informational advantage or deviated from the asset-lite strategy, it had to incur significant costs to create the physical market presence required to rectify its relative lack of market information. The absence of a financial market overlay in several of those markets further prevented Enron from recovering its costs. It was at that point that Enron abused accounting and disclosure policies to hide debt and cover up the fact that its business model did not work in those other areas.

For its innovations, Enron should be commended; for their alleged illegal activities, Enron's managers should be prosecuted to the full extent of the law. But under no circumstance should Enron's failure be used as an excuse to enact policies and regulations aimed at eliminating risk taking and economic failure, because unless a firm takes the risk of failure, it will never earn the premium of

From *Policy Analysis*, no. 470, February 20, 2003, pp. 1–19. Copyright © 2003 by Cato Institute. Reprinted by permission.

success. As was demonstrated in the case of Enron, markets—not politicians—are the best judges of success and failure.

Introduction

By the time the Enron Corporation filed for Chapter 11 bankruptcy protection on December 2, 2001, virtually everyone with a television set knew that things were not as they had once seemed in Houston. How could a company go from a market capitalization of more than $100 billion and being ranked fifth in the *Fortune 500* list to bust within two years? How could a stock that had seen highs of nearly $90 per share become a penny stock in record time? How could the six-time consecutive winner (1996–2001) of *Fortune*'s "most innovative company in the United States" have engineered its own financial destruction? *And more important, what can be done to make sure this never happens again?*

One must be careful, however, when defining "this" in the phrase "make sure this never happens again." Not everything Enron ever did, after all, was illegal, unethical, or even questionable. In fact, what actually caused Enron to fail is still subject to contentious debate. It is clear, however, that Enron did not fail because it was engaged in commercial and merchant commodity businesses.[1] Nor did a "rogue trader" or Enron's use of creative and sometimes-complex financial contracts bring Enron to its knees. Nor, finally, did Enron's corrupt financial activities—concealing its true indebtedness, lining the pockets of select senior managers at the expense of shareholders, hiding major losses, and the like—cause Enron to fail.[2] Enron's financial deception undoubtedly allowed it to remain in business longer than an otherwise similar firm engaged in accurate financial disclosures might have, but that is a question of timing alone and not causality.

This [selection] argues that Enron's ultimate financial failure most likely occurred for the very same reason that WorldCom, Global Crossing, and many other firms periodically have gone bankrupt or run into trouble. In short, those firms all lacked the ability to identify their true comparative advantage. In some cases that meant Enron overinvested in new markets and technologies that never took off; in other cases it simply meant that the company overestimated the value that it could add. But is *that* something that new policies and regulations should strive to ensure "never happens again"? Or, as argued in this study, is this aspect of Enron's failure simply a testimonial to the fact that competitive markets are effective judges of success and failure?

This study begins with an overview of Enron to stress that it was first and foremost an energy business that employed an innovative "asset-lite" strategy that accounted for many of its genuinely successful years. A discussion of those businesses in which Enron failed follows because it is in those areas where Enron departed from the successful asset-lite strategy employed in the energy business. The next section formally frames Enron's asset-lite strategy in the context of competitive economic theory. Standard "neoclassical" economic models do not explain firms such as Enron, and consequently a more "disequilibrium-oriented," or "neo-Austrian," approach is required. The [selection] concludes by considering whether Enron's failure *as a business* either offers lessons for other firms or provides a proscriptive case for greater regulation.

Neoclassical vs. Neo-Austrian Economic Theory

In addition to providing an analysis of Enron's business strategy through the lens of economic theory, this study illustrates the limitations of the traditional neoclassical theory of the price system for explaining entrepreneurship and innovation—terms that, despite Enron's illegal and fraudulent activities in some areas, nevertheless do describe that company in other areas. The neoclassical perspective views markets as existing in a stationary state in which the relevant knowledge about demand and supply is known; market prices are static, or given; and data are available to be used by individuals and firms. In this world without change, there is no need to ask how that stationary state came about. That knowledge simply falls into the category of irrelevant bygones.

Neoclassical economics does, of course, also deal with change. It does so by employing comparative statistics. For example, we can conceive of a quasi-stationary state in which changes in the relevant knowledge in a market are few and far between, and analysis of the full repercussions is dealt with by evaluating and comparing the stationary states before and after changes in relevant knowledge occur. In the neoclassical world, prices act as signposts, guiding consumers to substitute goods for one another and producers to learn which lines of production to abandon or toward which to turn. In this neoclassical conception, the price system acts as a network of communication in which relevant knowledge is transmitted at once throughout markets that jump from one stationary state to the next.

In the neo-Austrian, or disequilibrium-oriented, context, by contrast, the market is viewed as a process that is in a constant state of flux.[3] In consequence, there are no stationary or quasi-stationary states. Indeed, expectations about the current and future state of affairs are always changing because the state of relevant knowledge is always changing. And with changing expectations, market prices are also changing. In consequence, the price system functions as a network for communicating all relevant knowledge. It is also a discovery process that is in continuous motion, working toward creating unity and coherence in the economic system. The speed of adjustment and of the dissemination of knowledge in the price system depends on the scope and scale of the markets, however.

As it relates to the discussion here, the full force of market integration is realized when both spot and forward markets exist. Indeed, the function of forward, or derivatives, markets is to spread relevant knowledge now about what market participants think the future will be. Forward markets connect and integrate those expectations about the future with the present in a consistent manner.[4] Although the future will always remain uncertain, it is possible for individuals to acquire information about the expected future and to adjust their plans accordingly. In addition, they can—via forward markets—express their views about the future by either buying or selling forward. Forward markets, then, bring expectations about the future into consistency with each other and also bring forward prices into consistency with spot prices, with the difference being turned into "the basis."

In a neo-Austrian world, relevant knowledge and expectations are in a constant state of flux. And not surprisingly, spot and forward prices, as well as their difference (the basis), are constantly changing, too. Individuals' ever-changing expectations, therefore, keep the market process in motion. In consequence, disequilibrium is a hallmark of the neo-Austrian orientation. While the neo-Austrian market process is in a constant state of flux, it is working toward integrating and making consistent both spot and forward prices.[5]

As the analysis in this [selection] will demonstrate, the explicit incorporation of neo-Austrian variables such as time, knowledge, and market process into the traditional price-theoretic framework for microeconomic analysis is fundamental to understanding fully the financial and commercial market strategies of a company such as Enron.

Enron's Energy Business

Understanding Enron's business model for its core activities requires a brief explanation of how commodity markets function. The usefulness of many physical commodities to producers (e.g., wheat that can be milled into flour) and consumers (e.g., bread) depends on the "supply chain" through which the commodity is transformed from its raw, natural state into something of practical use. Figure 1 shows a typical supply chain for a variety of commodities.

When a commodity moves from one part of the supply chain to the next, transportation, distribution, and delivery services are almost always involved. Those services are the glue that keeps the supply chain linked. To put it simply, Enron was a firm that specialized in those transportation, distribution, and transformation services—often called "intermediate supply chain," or "midstream," services. Accordingly, Enron acted as a wholesale merchant. It acquired the latest information about alternative sources of supply and set

Figure 1

The Supply Chain

prices for goods in a process that would maximize Enron's turnover. Enron was therefore an ideal vehicle for the discovery and transmission of relevant knowledge.

In its *2000 Annual Report*, Enron described itself as "a firm that manages efficient, flexible networks to reliably deliver physical products at predictable prices."[6] This involved four core business areas for the firm: wholesale services, energy services, broadband services, and transportation services.

Enron Wholesale Services was by far the largest—and generally the most profitable—operation of Enron Corp. The bulk of that business involved the transportation, transmission, and distribution of natural gas and electricity. On a volume basis, Enron accounted for more than twice the amount of gas and power delivery of its next-largest competitor in the United States.[7] In addition, Enron maintained an active (and, in several cases, growing) market presence in the supply chains for other commodities, including coal, crude oil, liquefied natural gas, metals, steel, and pulp and paper. Enron Wholesale Services' customers were generally other large producers and industrial firms.

Enron Energy Services dealt mainly at the retail end of the energy market supply chains. Enron Wholesale Services' operation might deliver electrical power to a utility, for example, whereas Enron Energy Services might contract directly with a large grocery store chain to supply their power directly.

Enron Broadband was focused on the nonenergy business of broadband services, or the use of fiber optics to transmit audio and video. Capacity on fiber-optic cables is known as "bandwidth." Enron Broadband had three business goals. The first was to deploy the largest open global broadband network in the world, called the Enron Intelligent Network and consisting of 18,000 miles of fiber-optic cable. The second commercial objective in broadband was for Enron to dominate the market for buying and selling bandwidth. Finally, Enron sought to become a dominant provider of premium content, mainly through streaming audio and video over the worldwide web.

Enron's fourth operating division was Enron Transportation Services, formerly the Gas Pipeline Group. Enron Transportation Services concentrated on operating interstate pipelines for the transportation of natural gas, long a core competency of Enron. Albeit highly specialized and narrowly focused, gas transportation was perhaps the core brick on which the Enron Corp. foundation was laid.

The Houston Natural Gas Production Company was founded in 1953 as a subsidiary of Houston Natural Gas [HNG] to explore, drill, and transport gas. From 1953 to 1985, the firm underwent a slow but steady expansion, respectably keeping pace with the gradual development of the gas market.

Natural gas was deregulated in the late 1980s and early 1990s. During that time, supplies increased substantially, and prices fell by more than 50 percent from 1985 to 1991 alone. As competition increased, the number of new entrants into various parts of the natural gas supply chain grew dramatically, and many existing firms restructured.

One such restructuring was the acquisition in 1985 of HNG by Inter-North, Inc. The takeover of HNG was largely the brainchild of Kenneth Lay, who had joined HNG as its CEO in 1984. Working closely with Michael Milken,

Lay helped structure the InterNorth purchase of HNG as a leveraged buyout relying heavily on junk-bond finance.[8] Lay wrested the position of CEO of the merged firm from InterNorth CEO Samuel Segnar in 1985.

In 1986 InterNorth changed its name to Enron Corporation and incorporated Enron Oil & Gas Company, reflecting its expansion into oil markets to supplement its gas market presence. By then, most firms active in oil markets were also involved in gas—and conversely—given complementarities in exploration, drilling, pumping, distribution, and the like. With the exception of a brief hiatus toward the end, Kenneth Lay remained CEO of Enron Corp. until the firm failed.[9]

In 1985 the Federal Energy Regulatory Commission allowed "open access" to gas pipelines for the first time. In consequence, Enron was able to charge other firms for using Enron pipelines to transport gas, and, similarly, Enron was able to transport gas through other companies' pipelines.

Around that time, Jeffrey Skilling, then a consultant for McKinsey, began working at Enron. He was charged with developing a creative strategy to help Enron—recall, it had just been created through the InterNorth-HNG merger—leverage its presence in the emerging gas market. Skilling argued that the benefits of open access might well be more than offset by the decline in revenues associated with the general decline in prices and margins that greater competition would bring. Add to that Enron's mountain of debt, and Skilling maintained that Enron would not last very long unless a creative solution was identified.

Skilling argued, in particular, that natural gas would never be a serious source of revenues for the firm as long as natural gas was traded exclusively in a "spot" physical market for immediate delivery. Instead, he argued that a key success driver in the coming era of post-deregulation price volatility would be the development of a "derivatives market" in gas in which Enron would provide its customers with various price risk management solutions—forward contracts in which consumers could control their price risk by purchasing gas today at a fixed price for future delivery, and option contracts that allowed customers the right but not obligation to purchase or sell gas at a fixed price in the future.

Viewed from a neo-Austrian perspective, Skilling was functioning as a classic entrepreneur. Once FERC changed the rules of the game and natural gas became deregulated, Skilling spotted an entrepreneurial opportunity, literally, to develop new forward markets. Once forward markets were introduced, individuals could acquire information and knowledge about the future and express their own expectations by either buying or selling forward. Moreover, with both spot and futures prices revealed, "the basis"—the difference between spot and futures prices—could be revealed, and a more unified and coherently integrated natural gas "market" could be created. Although such a new setup would not eliminate risk and uncertainty, it promised to allow much more relevant knowledge to be discovered and disseminated, allowing firms to adjust their expectations and plans accordingly and to manage their risk more effectively.[10]

To create that market in natural gas derivatives, Skilling urged Enron to set up a "gasbank." Much as traditional banks intermediate funds, Enron's GasBank intermediated gas purchases, sales, and deliveries by entering into long-term, fixed-price delivery and price risk management contracts with customers. Soon thereafter, other natural gas firms began to offer clients similar risk management solutions. And those producers, in turn, also came to Enron for their risk management needs—that is, to "swap" the exposure to falling prices they created by offering fixed-price forwards to customers back into the "natural" exposure to price increases those producers had before offering their customers fixed-price protection.

Enron acted as a classic market maker, standing ready to enter into natural gas derivatives on "both sides of the market"—that is, both buying and selling gas (or, equivalently, buying and selling at both fixed and floating prices or swapping one for the other). Enron thus became the primary supplier of liquidity to the market, earning the spread between bid and offer prices as a fee for providing the market with liquidity. And in a broader sense, Enron was functioning to spread knowledge about what market participants expected prices to be.

Did that mean Enron was exposed to *all* of the price risks that its trading counter parties were attempting to avoid? No. Many of the contracts into which Enron entered naturally offset one another. True, a consumer seeking to lock in its future energy purchase price with Enron would create a risk exposure for Enron. If prices rose above the fixed price at which Enron agreed to sell energy to a consumer, Enron could lose big money. But that might be offset by a risk exposure to *falling* prices that Enron would assume by agreeing to *buy* that same asset from a producer at a fixed price, thus allowing the producer to hedge its own price risk.[11] Enron was left only with the *residual* risk across all its customer positions in its GasBank, which, in turn, Enron could manage by using derivatives with other emerging market makers, generally known as "swap dealers," or on organized futures exchanges such as the New York Mercantile Exchange.[12]

For a long time, Enron was not merely a market maker for natural gas derivatives—it was *the* market maker. Having virtually created the market, Enron enjoyed wider spreads, higher margins, and more revenues as the sole real liquidity supplier to the market. But that also meant few counterparties existed with which Enron could hedge its own residual risks.

Here is where Enron's physical market presence comes back into the picture. In addition to allowing Enron to discover and reveal a great deal of "local" knowledge, Enron's presence in the physical market meant that it could control some of the residual price risks from its market-making operations. That could be accomplished because of *offsetting positions in its physical pipeline and gas operations*. Consider, for example, a firm that is buying natural gas in Tulsa, Oklahoma, from a pipeline with a supply source in San Angelo, Texas. If that firm seeks to lock in its future purchase price for gas to protect against unexpected price spikes, it might enter into a forward purchase agreement with Enron, thus leaving Enron to bear the risk of a price increase. But if Enron also *owns the pipeline* and charges a price for distribution proportional to the spot price of gas, then the net effect will be roughly offsetting.

Operating that kind of a gas bank also gave Enron very valuable information about the gas market itself. Knowing from its pipeline operations that congestion was likely to occur at Point A, for example, Enron could anticipate price spikes at delivery points beyond Point A arising from the squeeze in available pipeline capacity. And Enron could very successfully "trade around" such congestion points. Conversely, when prices in derivatives markets signaled surplus or deficit pipeline capacity in the financial market, Enron could stand ready to exploit that information in the physical market.

Gradually, thanks to Enron's role as market maker, the natural gas derivatives market became increasingly standardized and liquid. Accordingly, relevant knowledge was spread more rapidly and the natural gas market became more integrated and coherent. Enron still offered customized solutions to certain consumers and producers, but much of the volume of the market shifted to exchanges like the NYMEX that began to provide standardized gas futures. Nevertheless, Enron's role as dominant market maker left the GasBank well placed to profit from supplying liquidity to those standardized markets, as well as from retaining much of the custom over-the-counter derivatives-dealing business.

The Enron GasBank division eventually became Enron Gas Services, and later Enron Capital and Trade Resources. In 1990 Jeff Skilling left McKinsey to become a full-time Enron employee, and he later became CEO of both EGS and EC&TR. In early 2001 Skilling replaced Lay as CEO of the whole firm, marking the only time in the history of Enron that Lay was not at the helm.

Asset Lite as a More General Business Strategy

When Skilling formally joined Enron in 1990, he maintained that the future success of the firm would be in repeating the GasBank experience in other markets. To accomplish that, Skilling developed a business concept known as "asset lite" in which Enron would combine small investments in capital-intensive commodity markets with a derivatives-trading and market-making "overlay" for those markets. The idea was to begin with a small capital expenditure that was used to acquire portions of assets and establish a presence in the physical market. That allowed Enron to learn the operational features of the market and to collect information about factors that might affect market price dynamics. Then, Enron would create a new financial market overlaid on top of that underlying physical market presence—a market in which Enron would act as market maker and liquidity supplier to meet other firms' risk management needs. As Skilling described it: "[Enron] is a company that makes markets. We create the market, and once it's created, we make the market."[13] Needless to say, that encapsulates the essence of one of the central roles of an Austrian entrepreneur.

One reason for the appeal of asset lite was that it enabled Enron to exploit some presence in the physical market without incurring huge capital expenditures on bulk fixed investments. Enron quickly discovered that this was best accomplished by focusing on investing in *intermediate* assets in commodity supply chains. In natural gas, this meant that Enron could get the biggest bang for its buck in midstream activities such as transportation, pipeline compression, storage, and distribution. In fact, Enron's Transwestern Pipeline Company eventually became the first U.S. pipeline that was exclusively for transportation, neither pumping gas at the wellhead nor selling it to customers.[14]

Other markets in which Enron applied its asset-lite business expansion strategy with a large degree of success included coal, fossil fuels, and, to some extent, pulp and paper. But after its successful experience with gas, Enron remained much more interested in markets that were being deregulated. Electricity thus became a major focus of the firm in the mid-1990s and was a key success driver for Enron.[15]

Oil and Water Do Not Mix

Throughout its history, Enron's consistent financial and market successes occurred in the energy sector. On more than one occasion, however, Enron tried to expand its business outside the energy area, albeit rarely with any success.

Asset Heavy at Enron International

When it became clear that Kenneth Lay was preparing to turn over the reins in the latter half of the 1990s, an extremely contentious struggle for the leadership of Enron ensued.[16] That occurred in no small part because of the success of Enron GasBank and the power-marketing operations of EC&TR. When the dust settled, Lay named EC&TR CEO and asset-lite inventor Jeff Skilling as the new CEO of Enron Corp. in February 2001. That Skilling would rise to this level, however, was not at all a foregone conclusion. Right up to the announcement date, debates over whose shoulder Kenneth Lay would tap were popular coffee shop banter. Skilling's chief competitor was Rebecca Mark.

In 1993 Mark prevailed upon Lay to establish Enron International, of which she became the first president. Mark did not adhere to an asset-lite strategy. Instead, she pursued an "asset-heavy" strategy of attempting to acquire or develop large capital-intensive projects *for their own sake*. In other words, there was no financial-trading activity overlay component for most of her initiatives. She tried instead to identify projects whose revenues promised to be sizable based purely on the capital investment component with no need for a market maker component. Unlike asset lite, that did not prove to be an area in which Enron Corp. had much comparative advantage.

Water-Trading Rights

The EI operations delved into the asset-heavy water-supply industry. At least here there was some pretense of eventually developing a "water rights trading market," but that possibility was so far down the road that the firm's water investments have to be regarded as largely self-contained capital projects, the largest of which was Azurix and its Wessex Water initiative.

In 1998 Enron spun off the water company Azurix. Enron retained a major interest in the firm, which focused its efforts on water markets in a single purchase—the British firm Wessex Water, for which Enron paid about $1.9 billion. But in this case, deregulation did not help Enron. There was no market-making function and no trading overlay—there was only a British water company serving a market with plummeting prices. (That experience also underscores the fundamentally correct view that Skilling advanced when he was still at McKinsey—namely, that expanding in a deregulating market makes little sense if you are limited to selling a commodity whose price is falling sharply in the spot markets.)

At the same time that the falling prices caused by deregulation in Britain were eating away Wessex's margins, Azurix itself was hit with staggering losses on several of its other operations, mainly in Argentina. In light of that failure, as well as the spectacular failure of EI's Dhabhol, India, power plant project, which may have cost Enron as much as $4 billion, Mark resigned as CEO of Enron International in the summer of 2000. Enron eventually sold Wessex in 2002, about three years after financing its acquisition by Azurix, to a Malaysian firm for $777 million, or $1.1 billion less than it paid for the firm.[17]

The Broadband Black Hole

Like its forays into the water industry, Enron's broadband efforts were plagued with problems from the start. In gas and power markets, Enron acquired its physical market presence by investing in assets sold mainly by would-be competing energy companies. It then used those investments to help create and develop a financial market, the growth of which, in turn, helped *increase* the value of Enron's physical investments. But that increase did not come at the expense of Enron's competitors, which in turn were benefiting from the new price risk management market. In broadband technologies, by contrast, Enron's asset-lite effort required the firm to acquire assets not just from competitors but from the *inventors* of the technology. Even then, Enron was paying for a technology that was essentially untested with no guarantee that the "emerging" bandwidth market would bolster asset values. Enron therefore had to pay dearly to acquire a market presence from firms that viewed Enron's effort not as a constructive market-making move but as essentially an intrusive one.

Several other drags on Enron's broadband expansion efforts contributed to its ultimate failure. One was that demand for the technology failed to materialize as expected. Enron is also alleged to have been using the "bandwidth market" to mislead investors—and possibly certain senior managers and directors—about its losses on underlying broadband technologies. On the one hand, Enron was optimistic about the eventual success of the broadband strategy; it "pointed at" significant trading in the bandwidth market. On the other hand, few other market participants observed any appreciable trading activity, and Enron was openly disclosing millions of dollars of losses on its quarterly and annual reports on its broadband efforts. Much of that "market activity" now seems to have come from Enron's "wash," or "roundtrip," trades or transactions in which Enron was essentially trading with itself.[18] To take a simple example, a purchase and sale of the same contract within a one- or two-minute period of time in which prices have not changed will show up as "volume," but the transactions wash out and amount to no real bottom-line profits.

In addition to apparently using wash trades to exaggerate the state of the market's development, Enron was also alleged to have used some of its bandwidth derivatives for "manufacturing" exaggeratedly high valuations for its technological assets. Specifically, Enron and Qwest are under investigation for engaging in transactions with one another that are alleged to have been designed specifically to create artificial mark-to-market valuations. Enron and Qwest engaged in a $500 million bandwidth swap negotiated just prior to the end of the 2001 third-quarter financial reporting period. Many observers would argue that Enron and Qwest were swapping one worthless thing for another worthless thing, given the lack of a market for bandwidth and the lack of *interest* in bandwidth. Nevertheless, both firms apparently used the swaps to justify having acquired a much more valuable asset than the one of which they were getting rid. With essentially no "market," no market prices were available for evaluating the validity of those claims at the time.

The Economics of Asset Lite and "Basis Trading"

Through its investments in the underlying commodity supply chains, the trading-room "overlay" on the physical markets allowed Enron to generate substantial revenues as a market maker. But that was not the only source of profits associated with the asset-lite strategy of combining physical and financial market positions. Specifically, Enron engaged in significant "basis trading." Understanding what that is and when a company might be able to do it profitably is essential for recognizing the differences between businesses on which Enron "made money" and those on which it did not.

To understand the economics of basis trading (sometimes called spread trading), one must first recognize the important finance proposition that commodity derivatives—contracts for the purchase or sale of a commodity in the future—are economic substitutes for physical market operations.[19] Buying a forward oil purchase contract, for example, is economically equivalent to buying and storing oil.[20] In a competitive equilibrium of the physical and derivatives markets, the forward purchase price—denoted $F(t,T)$ and defined as the fixed price negotiated on date t for the purchase of a commodity to be delivered on later date T—can be expressed using the famed "cost of carry model" as[21]

$$F(t,T) = S(t)[1 + b(t,T)]$$

Where $b(t,T)$ $r(t,T) + w(t,T) - d(t,T)$
and $S(t)$ = time t spot price of the commodity to be delivered at T
             $r(t,T)$ = the interest rate prevailing from t to T
             $w(t,T)$ = the cost of physical storage of the commodity from t to T
             $d(t,T)$ = the benefit of holding the commodity from t to T

such that w and d are expressed as a proportion of $S(t)$ and are denominated in time T dollars.

The term $b(t,T)$—the "basis"—is also often called the "net cost of carry," to convey the fact that its three components together make up the cost of "carrying" the commodity across time and space to the delivery location on future date T. The term $d(t,T)$ that reflects the benefit of physical storage is called the "convenience yield," a concept developed by John Maynard Keynes, Nicholas Kaldor, Holbrook Working, Michael J. Brennan, and Lester G. Telser.[22] The convenience yield is driven mainly by what Working calls the "precautionary demand for storage," or concerns by firms that unanticipated shocks to demand or supply could precipitate a costly inventory depletion.[23] Airlines store fuel at different airports, for example, to avoid the huge costs of grounding their local fleets in the case of a jet fuel outage. Gas pipeline owners store gas to help ensure that there is always an adequate supply of gas in the lines to maintain the flow and avoid a shutdown.

Keynes, Working, and others have observed how the "supply of storage" (i.e., the amount of a commodity in physical storage) is related to the convenience yield and, by extension, to the "term structure of futures prices."[24] That relation defines the economic linkage between derivatives, physical asset markets, and the allocation of physical supplies across time. Specifically, the supply of storage is directly related to the premium placed on selling inventory *in the future* relative to selling spot *today*. When inventories are high, the *relative* premium that a commodity commands in the future vis-à-vis the present is reasonably small; plenty of the commodity is on hand today to assure producers and intermediaries that a stock-out will not occur, leading to a very low convenience yield. As current inventories get smaller, however, the convenience yield rises (at an increasing rate) and the spot price rises relative to the futures price in order to induce producers to take physical product out of inventory and sell it in the current spot market. A high spot price *alone* would not do that. But a high spot price *relative* to the futures price signals the market that inventories are tight *today* relative to the future.

We can now see more meaningfully where cost-of-carry pricing comes from. Namely, it is the condition that must hold in equilibrium to make market participants indifferent toward physical storage or "synthetic storage" using forwards or other derivatives. Here's how it works. Suppose a firm borrows $S(t)$ in funds at time t and uses the proceeds to buy a commodity worth $S(t)$. At time T, the firm is holding an asset then worth $S(T)$ and repays the money loan. In the interim, the firm incurs physical storage costs w but earns the convenience yield d. Table 1 shows the net effect of this physical storage operation.

In turn, a short position in a forward contract involves no initial outlay and has a time T value of $F(t,T) - S(T)$. From the last line of Table 1, it should be clear that physical storage plus borrowing can be used to hedge the short forward contract (or vice versa). The net of the hedged position is then just $F(t,T) - S(t)[1 + r(t,T) + w(t,T) - d(t,T)]$, all of which is known at time t and thus is riskless. If all market participants are price takers and face identical benefits and costs of storage, cost-of-carry futures pricing thus holds purely through the mechanism of arbitrage.

Table 1

Physical Commodity Storage		
	t	**T**
Money loan		
Borrow dollars	$S(t)$	-
Repay dollars and interest	-	$-S(t)[1 + r(t,T)]$
Buy and store the asset		
Buy commodity	$-S(t)$	-
Pay storage costs	-	$-S(t)w(t,T)$
Earn convenience yield	-	$S(t)d(t,T)$
Still own the commodity	-	$S(T)$
Net	0	$S(T) - S(t)[1 + r(t,T) + w(t,T) - d(t,T)]$

Because not every firm has the same convenience yield or storage costs, however, commodity forward prices are driven to the cost-of-carry expression instead by the dynamics of a competitive equilibrium.[25] To see how it works, suppose the forward purchase price is

$$F° = S(t)[1 + b°(t,T)]$$

where $b°(t,T)$ denotes any arbitrary net cost of carry. All firms for which $S(t)[1 + b(t,T)] < F°$ can earn positive economic profits by going short the forward and simultaneously buying and storing the commodity. They will continue to do this until the forward price falls and $S(t)[1 + b(t,T)] = F°$. As long as any firm can make positive profits from this operation, the selling will continue, until

$$S(t)[1 + b(t,T)] = F*$$

where $F* = S(t)[1 + b*(t,T)]$ and where $b*(t,T)$ denotes the marginal net cost of carry from t to T for the marginal storer. This marginal entrant earns exactly zero economic profits since its own net cost of carry is equal to $b*$.

Things work in the other direction for any firms for which $S(t)[1 + b(t,T)] > F°$. Those firms will go long the forward and then engage in a commodity repurchase agreement (i.e., lending the commodity at time t and repurchasing it at time T).[26] Again, entry occurs until $F°$ exactly equals $F*$ and reflects the marginal basis of the marginal storer.

In the short run, the basis $b*$ thus reflects the marginal cost of carrying an incremental unit of the commodity over time. In the long run, $b*$ will also correspond to the minimum point on a traditional U-shaped long-run average-cost curve.[27] Suppose all firms have $b*$ below this minimum long-run average cost. In this case, at least one firm will expand output until the marginal cost rises to the minimum average cost and equals the marginal price of the cost of carry and the new $b*$ will also be reflected in the forward price.

The process by which commodity derivatives and the underlying asset market simultaneously grope toward a competitive equilibrium helps illustrate an important point: namely, the relation between forward and spot prices—the "basis"—is really a "third market" implied by the prices of the two explicit ones.[28] In the example above, the two explicit markets are the spot and forward markets, and the relation between the two implicitly defines *the price of physical storage.* Such "third markets" are also called "basis" or "spread" relations. The implicit market for storage over time is called the "calendar basis or spread," the implicit market for transportation is called the "transportation basis or spread," and so on.

Firms can also use derivatives *based on different assets* in order to conduct spread trades to synthesize a third market. Going short crude oil and simultaneously long heating oil and gasoline, for example, is called trading the "crack spread" and is economically equivalent in equilibrium to synthetic refining. Short soybeans and long bean oil and meal are likewise "synthetic crushing." And trading the "spark spread" through a short position in natural gas and a long position in electricity is called "synthetic generation" because the derivatives positions replicate the economic exposure of a gas-fired electric turbine.

A Neo-Austrian Explanation for Basis Trading

Armed with an understanding of how commodity derivatives are priced in equilibrium, we want now to consider the economic rationale for why Enron and firms like it sometimes dedicate substantial resources to "basis trading." We want to recognize what can happen out of *equilibrium*—a state of affairs that typically prevails. Indeed, expectations and relevant knowledge (data) are in a constant state of flux. Accordingly, a neoclassical stationary state—one that treats the data as constant—is of limited use in explaining the market process.[29]

We have seen how equilibrium emerges from the interactions of numerous firms competing to drive prices to their marginal cost. Specifically, suppose b^* reflects the marginal net cost of carry reflected in the prevailing natural gas forward price. This is the price of transportation and delivery in equilibrium. The net cost of carry b^* may only conform to the actual physical and capital costs of carry less the convenience yield for one firm—the marginal entrant into the gas transportation market. Or b^* may be shared by all firms in the short run, but aggregate output may need to adjust in the long run if b^* does not also reflect the minimum average long-run cost of carry. The point is this: the cost of carry reflected in the forward price may or may not be the optimal cost of carry for any given firm at any given time. As is standard in neoclassical microeconomic theory, the price that "clears the market" in the long run will equal the short-run marginal cost for any given firm only by pure coincidence.

Suppose we begin in a situation where b^* is the cost of carry reflected in the forward price and is equal to the short-run marginal costs of all market participants at their production optima. Now consider a new entrant into the market and suppose that new entrant is Enron with its large amount of pipelines and strong economies of scale that lead to a cost of distributing and transporting natural gas at some point in time of $b^e < b^*$, where b^e is Enron's marginal cost of carry. In this case, Enron can physically move gas across time and space at a lower cost than gas can be moved "synthetically" using derivatives.

By going short or selling gas for future delivery using forwards, or futures, Enron is selling gas at an implied net cost of carry of b^*. But its own net cost of carry—a cost that is quite relevant to Enron's ability to move the gas across time and space in order to honor its own future sale obligation created by the forward contract—is less. Accordingly, in *disequilibrium*— or, more properly, on the way to equilibrium—Enron can make a profit equal to the difference between its own net cost of storage and the cost reflected in the market.

The reason that that profit is a short-run profit inconsistent with a long-run equilibrium is that Enron's sale of the forward contract drives the b^* reflected in forward prices closer to b^e. If Enron is the lowest-cost producer and other firms can replicate its production techniques (i.e., Enron owns no unique resources), ultimately b^* will become b^e, which will also eventually approach the long-run minimum average cost of carry. Enron's capacity to earn supranormal profits will vanish in this new equilibrium—in fact, zero economic profits earned by every producer is basically the very meaning of a long-run equilibrium.

Because markets are constantly adjusting to new information, new trading activity, and new entrants, however, it is quite hard to determine when a market actually is in some kind of "final equilibrium resting state," as opposed to when it is adjusting from one state to another. The inevitability of a long-run competitive equilibrium in which profits are not possible thus must be considered relative to the inability of market participants to identify slippery concepts such as "long-run" and "in equilibrium." Strictly speaking, a market is "in equilibrium" as long as supply equals demand. But the term is used here in a more subtle fashion, where "equilibrium" refers to the steady state in which firms earn zero supranormal economic profits in the long run. Accordingly, firms may engage in basis trading to try and exploit the differences in prices reflected in derivatives and their own ability to conduct physical market "pseudoarbitrage" operations that are economically equivalent to those derivatives transactions.[30]

Now consider a situation in which the market is *always* adjusting and never reaches a long-run competitive equilibrium.[31] In this situation, the tendency is still toward the archetypical neoclassical long-run competitive equilibrium, but we never quite get there. Why not? Certainly economic agents are responding in the manner here described, and their behavior should ultimately lead to a steady-state long-run equilibrium. The only reason it does not is, quite simply, that too much is happening at any given moment to make the leap from "short run" to "long run."

In that situation, all firms are always, by definition, inframarginal in some sense of the term. The kind of "pseudoarbitrage" between physical and synthetic storage described above thus can be expected to occur *quite regularly*. And at least some firms will earn supranormal profits quite regularly. Those profits are not riskless, but at least some firms are sure to be right at least some of the time.

Does that mean that physical and synthetic storage are not really equivalent? Technically, it does. But it was never said otherwise. It was only claimed that the two are equivalent in *equilibrium*. When a market is in disequilibrium, what you actually pay to store a commodity physically may well differ from what you actually pay to store it synthetically. But that is not important.

What is important is that, even if new information and other market activities drive a wedge between $b°$ and $b*$, maximizing decisions by firms *always* lead *toward* the convergence of the two prices of storage. Conversely, the price mechanism *never* sends a signal that will lead maximizing firms to engage in physical or derivatives transactions that drive $b°$ and $b*$ further apart. The very fact that maximizing firms are constantly seeking to exploit differences between $b°$ and $b*$ itself is what gives the theory meaning. That the two might never end up exactly equal is not very relevant because, as explained below, information changes before the long-run equilibrium is ever reached.

Asymmetric Information

Now suppose that the net cost of storage is a random variable about which some firms are better informed than others—for example, the impact of supply or demand shocks on particular locational prices, the impact of pipeline congestion on the transportation basis, and the like. Suppose further that we assume a competitive long-run equilibrium *does* hold. Because of the information asymmetry, a rational expectations equilibrium (REE) in which expected supranormal profits are zero in the long run will result. But *expected by whom?*

In that case, firms such as Enron may engage in basis, or spread, trading in an effort to exploit a perceived comparative informational advantage. If a firm owns physical pipelines, for example, it may have a superior capability for forecasting congestion or regional supply-and-demand shocks. That creates a situation quite similar to a market that is out of or on the way to equilibrium— that is, the net cost of carry that the *firm* observes may be *different* from the net cost of carry market participants expect, given the different information on which the two numbers are based. Just as in the disequilibrium case, firms may engage in basis trading to exploit those differences.

In a traditional REE that type of behavior is akin to inframarginal firms attempting to exploit their storage cost advantage relative to the marginal price of storage reflected in forward markets. And as noted, that cannot go on for very long, because the trading actions of the lower-cost firm eventually lead it to become the marginal entrant, thus driving $b*$ to $b°$ for that firm. The same is true in a REE, where trading *itself* is informative. Every time a well-informed trader attempts to exploit its superior information through a transaction, it reveals that superior information to the market. So, the paradox for the firm with better information is that the firm must either *not trade* based on that information in order to preserve its informational advantage, or it must *give away* its informational advantage while simultaneously trying to exploit it in the short run through trading.

In a study written with the late Nobel laureate economist Merton H. Miller, one of this paper's authors argues,[32] however, that that sort of classic equilibrium assumes that the trading activities of the better-informed firm are, indeed, informative. But what if other market participants cannot see all the firm's trades? And what if the trades are occurring in highly opaque, bilateral markets rather than on an exchange? In this case, better-informed firms can profit from their superior information without necessarily having all of their valuable information reflected in the new marginal price. Anecdotal evidence certainly seems to support this in the case of Enron, given how heavily the firm focused on less-liquid and less-transparent markets.

Why Not Speculate Outright?

Trading to exploit disequilibrium, market imperfections, or asymmetric information is hardly riskless. On the contrary, it can be quite risky. That helps explain why many firms engaged in such trading do so with *relative*, or *spread*, positions in third markets rather than take outright positions in one of the two explicit markets. Suppose, for example, that a firm perceives the "true" net cost of storage of gas to be b^* (which is equal to the firm's own net cost of carry) but that the current net cost of carry reflected in listed gas futures prices is $b' > b^*$. It is a good bet that b' will fall toward b^*. In that case, an outright short position in forward contracts would make sense. But that is *extremely risky*.

A position that exploits the same information asymmetry without the high degree of risk is to go short futures and *simultaneously* buy and hold gas. In this manner, the firm is protected from wild short-term price swings and instead is expressing a view solely on the *relative* prices of storage as reflected in the futures market and storage by the firm itself.

In essence, asset lite is a basis-trading or "third-market" trading strategy in which physical assets are traded vis-à-vis derivatives positions. A physical market combined with the *residual risk* of a market-making function is essentially one big spread trade.

Putting Enron in Context

Reading the marketing and business materials of Enron's energy business lines is eerily similar to reading an example of a firm putting all the theories of basis trading just discussed into practice. And in that sense, Enron was hardly the first firm to leverage its physical market presence into financial- and basis-trading opportunities. Perhaps the best-known example of a firm engaged in the same practice is Cargill.[33] Cargill is the largest private company in the world, with $50 billion in annual sales and 97,000 employees deployed in 59 countries. For 137 years, Cargill has employed an asset-lite strategy that has allowed it to basis trade and manage risks for a wide variety of agricultural commodities, among other things. For the commodities it deals in, Cargill is involved in every link of the supply chains. As a result of its commodity trading, processing, freight shipping, and futures businesses, Cargill has been able to develop an effective intelligence network that generates valuable information. Indeed, via its people on the ground, Cargill knows where every ship and rail car hauling commodities is in real time and what that implies about prospective prices over time and space. By being able to ferret out valuable local information, Cargill has been able to obtain an edge, one that accounts for much of its success.[34]

Basis trading can make economic sense to a firm *ex ante* without making profits *ex post*. The key driver underlying most basis traders' behavior is the *perception* that they have some comparative informational advantage about some basis relation. But perception need not be reality. Markets are, after all, relatively efficient. Indeed, most of the inefficiencies that give rise to profitable trading opportunities can be linked to taxes, regulations, and other institutional frictions that essentially prevent markets from reflecting all available information at all times.

Enron did indeed attempt to focus its efforts on markets riddled with inefficiencies, often created by overregulation, poorly defined property rights, or a slow deregulation process. But that did not mean Enron had a comparative informational advantage in all of those markets.

Structural inefficiencies that prevent prices from fully reflecting all available information are only part of what it takes to run a successful basis-trading operation. The other requisite component is for a firm to perceive itself as (and, it is hoped, actually be) *better informed*. In oil and power, Enron achieved that informational superiority like many other firms do in their own industries—by dominating the financial market. That allowed Enron to develop informationally rich customer relationships that in turn could be extrapolated into superior knowledge of firm-specific supply-and-demand considerations, congestion points along the supply chain, and other important factors.

Now consider, by contrast, a market such as broadband in which Enron was *not* the primary inventor of the technology, *not* the primary buyer or seller of the supply chain infrastructure, and *not* a regular player in the consumer telecommunications arena. The mere existence of market frictions in broadband attracted Enron, but without the requisite information, Enron could not achieve the market dominance required to make asset lite in that market profitable.

Buying Time and the End of Enron

As Culp and Miller explain,[35] firms best suited to the asset-lite kind of strategy that Enron pursued typically require fairly significant amounts of capital—not invested capital assets necessarily but *equity capital* in a financial market sense. Equity capital is a necessary component of successful basis trading and the asset-lite strategy for several reasons. First, equity is required to absorb the occasional loss inevitably arising from the volatility that basis trading can bring to cash flows. Second, maintaining a strong market-making and financial-market presence requires at least the perception by other participants of financial integrity and credit worthiness. Especially in long-dated, credit-sensitive over-the-counter (OTC) derivatives, financial capital is essential to support the credit requirements that other OTC derivatives users and dealers demand.[36]

Unfortunately, Enron's cash management skills were no match for its apparent trading savvy. Despite being "asset lite," Enron's expenditures on intermediate supply chain assets were still not cheap. Add to this EI's asset-heavy investment programs and a corporate culture under Skilling and Lay that emphasized high and stable *earnings* often at the expense of high and stable *cash flows*,[37] and the net result was financial trouble for the firm.[38]

Enron's Deceptions

Much of the public controversy about Enron focuses on how Enron abused accounting and disclosure policies. In short, Enron's abuses in those areas included the following:

- Using inappropriate or aggressive accounting and disclosure policies to conceal assets owned and debt incurred by Enron through special purpose entities (SPEs);[39]
- Using inadequately capitalized subsidiaries and SPEs for "hedges" that reduced Enron's earnings volatility on paper, despite in many cases being dysfunctional or nonperforming in practice;[40] and
- Allegedly engaging in "wash trades" with undisclosed subsidiaries designed to increase trading revenues or mark-to-market valuations artificially.[41]

At first, Enron's abuses of those structures seem to have been driven more by a desire to manage earnings than by anything else. But as time passed, Enron used aggressive accounting and disclosure policies to "buy time" for itself. Especially as Enron moved into new markets in which its comparative advantage was more questionable (e.g., broadband) or in which Enron's success depended strongly on the rate of government deregulation (e.g., water), Enron's financial shenanigans amounted to "robbing Peter to pay Paul." In other words, as Enron's cash balances got lower and lower, concealing its true financial condition was the only way that Enron could sustain itself long enough to hope that its next big investment program would pay off. That might have worked had Enron stuck to markets in which its success with asset lite was more assured. Unfortunately, as has been argued, the firm's end became inevitable once it decided to start moving into areas that deviated from its core business strategy.

There is also the question of whom Enron was actually deceiving with its accounting and disclosure policies. Over the course of many years, one could argue that Enron seduced investors, monitors (e.g., rating agencies and accounting firms), creditors, and even its own employees into believing that the firm was stronger financially than it actually was through a mixture of aggressive marketing, cultural arrogance, and, in some cases, outright deception. But especially as the end of Enron neared, many institutions had begun to view the company with deepening suspicion.[42] By the time Enron failed, a surprisingly large number of firms dealing with Enron commercially had come to fear that the worst for Enron might lie ahead.[43] In the end, those who seem to have been the most deceived—and for the longest time—were Enron's own employees, who, unlike other firms dealing with Enron, had more cause to be inherently optimistic and were doubtless taken almost completely off-guard.

Conclusion

Enron's main business was asset lite—exploiting the synergies between a small physical market presence, a market-making function on derivatives, and a basis-trading operation to "arbitrage" the first two. Many observers have questioned the wisdom of Enron's asset-lite strategy. Most of the criticisms are hard to address without getting into deeper details of Enron's financial situation. In short, people argue that although asset lite did not require a lot of capital *expenditures* and investments in fixed capital, the strategy *did* require Enron to have a fairly large chunk of equity capital—enough to convince its numerous financial counterparties that it was creditworthy. If indeed Enron was camouflaging its capital structure to hide a massive amount of debt, then Enron probably *was* undercapitalized to exploit asset lite effectively. But that is not a criticism of asset lite—it is a criticism of Enron.

In fact, asset lite has become a very common practice for many firms engaged in energy market activities, especially at intermediate points along the various physical supply chains—transmission and distribution of power and midstream transportation and distribution of oil and gas, to name two. One firm that has been consistently successful at playing the asset-lite game, for example, is Kinder Morgan, founded by Enron's former president Richard Kinder when he left Enron in 1996. Kinder Morgan was started in part by Kinder's successful acquisition from Enron of Enron Gas Liquids, for which he outbid six other firms, including Mobil Oil.[44]

In nonenergy markets, firms such as Cargill have also long practiced their version of asset lite, often going the way of Enron in electricity and becoming asset heavy over time. The key common denominators are two: the use of a physical market presence to acquire specific information about the underlying market and the use of a financial-trading operation to make markets and engage in basis trading to leverage off that underlying asset infrastructure.

Unfortunately, there is no exact answer to the question of when asset lite and basis trading might work for a firm versus when they might fail dismally. The comparative informational advantage that allows some firms to earn positive economic profits is exceedingly hard to analyze or identify except through trial and error. That process of trial and error is what Austrian economist Joseph Schumpeter meant by the "creative destruction" of capitalism, and great economists such as Frank H. Knight and Keynes went on to emphasize further that the success or failure of a given firm cannot ever really be predicted. "Animal spirits," as Keynes put it, ultimately dictate the success or failure of a business as much as any other variable.

Economists are uneasy with that notion. As noted earlier, the neoclassical model postulates that markets tend to be "in equilibrium," whereas the neo-Austrian perspective merely argues that markets "lean in that direction." To be in equilibrium implies some steady state of profits resting on an identifiable cost advantage or structural informational asymmetry. But concepts such as "information asymmetry" are completely nontestable. That makes theoretical economists nervous because it means that the success or failure of a firm cannot be related to a defined set of assumptions and parameters *ex ante*. And empirical economists get even more disgruntled because the success or failure of a firm cannot be explained *ex post*.

Nevertheless, that is the state of affairs. Economic theory merely says that firms will strive to exploit perceived comparative informational advantages in disequilibrium situations where prices do not reflect every market participant's information equally. Theory says nothing about firms being correct in their perceived advantages, nor does theory help us pinpoint precisely what those advantages are. Those things are what *the market* is for.

Can Enron's experience be generalized to suggest a "failure" of the theory underlying basis trading? In fact, Enron cannot be generalized at *all*. Looking purely at the firm's *legitimate* business activities, Enron perceived a comparative informational advantage, pursued it, and was wrong. That does not make the underlying economic model wrong, nor even Enron's managers and shareholders. If we could generalize the economic factors that explain why one firm succeeds and another fails, then competition in the open market would serve no purpose. Instead, competition and the market are both judge and jury to a company's perceived informational advantage. And unless a firm takes the risk of failure, it will never earn the premium of success.[45]

There can be little doubt that Enron did a lot wrong. Indeed, where it deviated from its asset-lite strategy, Enron tended to engage in businesses that were unprofitable. In addition, many of the firm's senior managers were basically unethical. But amid all those legitimate criticisms of Enron, we must be careful not to indict everything the firm did. In some instances, Enron got it right. And at a minimum, the firm moved entrepreneurially into new areas and put itself to the ultimate test of the market. Finally, Enron failed that test, but we must at least tip our hats to that part of Enron that was willing to try. Without that spirit of innovation, the process of capitalism would grind to a screeching halt.

Notes

1. See *Corporate Aftershock: The Public Policy Lessons from the Collapse of Enron and Other Major Corporations*, ed. Christopher L. Culp and William A. Niskanen (New York: John Wiley and Sons, forthcoming 2003), part I.

2. See ibid., part II.

3. The Austrian school of economics was developed in the 19th and 20th centuries by a group of principally Austrian economists in response to several noted shortcomings in the neoclassical theory of the price system. The approach adopted here, however, is more properly called *neo-Austrian*. Following Sir John Hicks's use of the term, a neo-Austrian approach recognizes some of the deficiencies of the neoclassical school and seeks to address those problems from a more Austrian perspective. We do not consider, as some do, the pure Austrian school to be a viable stand-alone theory of the price system. Rather than forcing a choice of theories in either/or fashion, the neo-Austrian approach recognizes instead that a little bit of Austrian insight can go a long way toward salvaging the neoclassical paradigm. For an example of this theoretical approach, see John R. Hicks, *Capital and Time: A Neo-Austrian Theory* (1973; reprint, Oxford: Oxford University Press, 2001).

4. That does not require that forward prices always be unbiased expectations of future spot prices, although they frequently are, especially for physical commodities. But even if forward prices are not unbiased predictors of future spot prices, as in some currency markets, there is still a strong and

consistent relation between spot and forward prices—just not an unbiased one. For further discussion of this issue, see Christopher L. Culp, *Risk Transfer: Derivatives in Theory and Practice* (New York: John Wiley and Sons, forthcoming 2003).

5. For a full elaboration of these concepts, see Ludwig M. Lachmann, *Capital and Its Structure* (Kansas City, Mo.: Sheed Andrews and McMeel, 1978).

6. See Enron Corporation, *2000 Annual Report*, 2001, cover page.

7. Ibid., p. 9.

8. A typical use of junk bonds during this period was providing funds to companies with otherwise questionable access to capital, given their credit risk. Highly leveraged transactions like leveraged buyouts were thus a natural candidate for junk-bond financing.

9. EOG continued for two decades to spearhead all of Enron Corp.'s exploration and production activities in oil and gas. In 1999, EOG exchanged the shares in EOG held by Enron for its operations in India and China. In so doing, EOG became independent of Enron Corp. and, in fact, changed its name the same year to EOG Resources, Inc. This firm still exists today.

10. See Lachmann.

11. For more discussion of these different types of contracts, see Andrea M. P. Neves, "Wholesale Electricity Markets and Products after Enron," in *Corporate Aftershock*; and Barbara T. Kavanagh, "An Introduction to the Business of Structure Finance," in *Corporate Aftershock*.

12. In the huge interest rate swap market, dealers did essentially the same thing as the Enron GasBank—they used other swaps and futures contracts to manage the *residual* risks of running a dealing portfolio, called a "swap warehouse."

13. Quoted in Joel Kurtzman and Glenn Rifkin, *Radical E: From GE to Enron—Lessons on How to Rule the Web* (New York: John Wiley & Sons, 2001), p. 47.

14. See Ronnie J. Clayton, William Scroggins, and Christopher Westley, "Enron: Market Exploitation and Correction," *Financial Decisions* (Spring 2002): 1–16.

15. See Neves.

16. See Peter C. Fusaro and Ross M. Miller, *What Went Wrong at Enron?* (New York: John Wiley & Sons, 2002).

17. Ibid.

18. This can be accomplished in various ways. For examples, see Andrea S. Kramer, Paul J. Pantano, and Doron F. Ezickson, "Regulation of Electricity Trading after Enron," in *Corporate Aftershock*; and Paul Palmer, "The Market for Complex Credit Risk," in *Corporate Aftershock*.

19. Early discussions of the economic rationale for basis, or spread, trading can be found in L. Leland Johnson, "The Theory of Hedging and Speculation in Commodity Futures," *Review of Economic Studies* 27, no. 3 (1960): 139–51; Holbrook Working, "Theory of the Inverse Carrying Charge in Futures Markets," *Journal of Farm Economics* 30 (1948): 1–28; Holbrook Working, "The Theory of Price of Storage," *American Economic Review* 39

(1949): 1254–62; and Holbrook Working, "New Concepts Concerning Futures Markets and Prices," *American Economic Review* 52 (1962): 432–59.

20. See, for example, Jeffrey B. Williams, *The Economic Function of Futures Markets* (New York: Cambridge University Press, 1986); Culp, *Risk Transfer*; and Steve H. Hanke, "Backwardation Revisited," *Friedberg's Commodity and Currency Comments* 8, no. 11 (December 20, 1987).

21. Alternative versions of this rely on different types of discounting and compounding assumptions, as well as allowing certain variables in the equation to be stochastic (i.e., subject to random variation). But the spirit of all versions of the model is well captured by the representation here. See Culp, *Risk Transfer*, for more detail.

22. See John Maynard Keynes, *The Theory of Money*, vol. II, *The Applied Theory of Money* (London: Macmillan, 1930); Nicholas Kaldor, "Speculation and Economic Stability," *Review of Economic Studies* 7 (1939): 1–27; Working, "Theory of the Inverse Carrying Charge in Futures Markets"; Working, "The Theory of Price of Storage"; Michael J. Brennan, "The Supply of Storage," *American Economic Review* 48 (1958): 50–72; and Lester G. Telser, "Futures Trading and the Storage of Cotton and Wheat," *Journal of Political Economy* 66 (1958): 233–55.

23. See Working, "New Concepts Concerning Futures Markets and Storage."

24. See Keynes; Working, "The Theory of Price of Storage"; Culp, *Risk Transfer*; and Hanke.

25. Cost-of-carry pricing for forwards on financial assets, by contrast, is enforced by direct "cash-and-carry" arbitrage because financial assets pay *observable* and *explicit* dividends that are the same regardless of who holds the asset. See Culp, *Risk Transfer*.

26. Commodity lending does occur, so this example is in no way unrealistic. See Williams.

27. The classical U-shape is consistent with a production technology that demonstrates increasing returns to scale up to b^* and diminishing returns thereafter.

28. See Williams.

29. For a more general discussion, see John H. Cochrane and Christopher L. Culp, "Equilibrium Asset Pricing: Implications for Risk Management," in *The Growth of Risk Management: A History* (London: Risk Books, 2002).

30. This is pseudoarbitrage because it has the flavor of an arbitrage transaction but is far from riskless.

31. This seems heretical in the neoclassical microeconomic paradigm, but is typical of the notion of "equilibrium" developed by economists in the "Austrian" and "neo-Austrian" tradition, such as Carl Menger, *Principles of Economics* (1871; reprint, Grove City, Pa.: Libertarian Press, 1974); F. A. Hayek, "Economics and Knowledge," *Economica* 4 (1937): 33–54; F. A. Hayek, "The Use of Knowledge in Society," *American Economic Review* 35, no. 4 (1945): 519–30; F. A. Hayek, "The Meaning of Competition," in *Individualism and Economic Order* (1948; reprint, London: Routledge and Kegan Paul, 1978), pp. 92–107; F. A. Hayek, "Competition as a Discovery Procedure," in *New Studies in Philosophy, Politics, Economics, and the History of Ideas* (Chicago: University of Chicago Press, 1978), pp. 179–91;

F. A. Hayek, "The New Confusion about 'Planning,' " in *New Studies in Philosophy, Politics, Economics, and the History of Ideas*, pp. 232–49; Hicks; and Lachmann.

32. See Christopher L. Culp and Merton H. Miller, "Hedging in the Theory of Corporate Finance," *Journal of Applied Corporate Finance* 8, no. 1 (Spring 1995): 121–27.

33. See, for example, Wayne G. Broehl Jr., *Cargill: Trading the World's Grains* (Hanover, N.H.: University Press of New England, 1992).

34. See, for example, Neil Weinberg and Brandon Copple, "Going against the Grain," *Forbes*, November 25, 2002, pp. 158–68.

35. See Culp and Miller, "Hedging in the Theory of Corporate Finance"; Christopher L. Culp and Merton H. Miller, "Metallgesellschaft and the Economics of Synthetic Storage," *Journal of Applied Corporate Finance* 7, no. 4 (Winter 1995): 62–76; and Christopher L. Culp and Merton H. Miller, "Introduction: Why a Firm Hedges Affects How a Firm Should Hedge," in *Corporate Hedging in Theory and Practice: Lessons from Metallgesellschaft*, ed. Christopher L. Culp and Merton H. Miller (London: Risk Books, 1999).

36. See David Mengle, "Do Swaps Need More Regulation?" in *Corporate Aftershock*; and Christopher L. Culp, "Credit Risk Management Lessons from Enron," in *Corporate Aftershock*.

37. See Richard Bassett and Mark Storrie, "Accounting at Energy Firms after Enron: Is the 'Cure' Worse than the Disease?" in *Corporate Aftershock*.

38. Cash flow mismanagement was not always the norm at Enron. Jeffrey Skilling's predecessor Richard Kinder was actually known for being a cash flow "tightwad" and kept the firm's financial health relatively strong during his tenure at the operational helm of Enron.

39. See Bassett and Storrie; Kavanagh; and Keith A. Bockus, W. Dana Northcut, and Mark E. Zmijewski, "Accounting and Disclosure Issues in Structured Finance," in *Corporate Aftershock*.

40. See Bassett and Storrie; and Kavanagh.

41. See ibid.; Neves; Kramer, Pantano, and Ezickson; John Herron, "Online Trading and Clearing after Enron," in *Corporate Aftershock*; and Bockus, Northcut, and Zmijewski.

42. See Bassett and Storrie.

43. See Culp, *Risk Transfer*.

44. See Fusaro and Miller.

45. See Frank H. Knight, *Risk, Uncertainty, and Profit* (Boston: Houghton Mifflin, 1933).

POSTSCRIPT

Does the Enron Collapse Show That We Need More Regulation of the Energy Industry?

The Enron case is in many ways a poor exemplar for any discussion of business activity, since it contains so many activities that were clearly criminal! Had the officers of the corporation been honest men (they were all men except the vice president, Sherron Watkins, who finally blew the whistle on the whole affair), what would we have found out about the operations of deregulated markets in public utilities?

Suggested Reading

For more on the Enron case, and on the energy industry generally, you might wish to consult the following readings:

Michael K. Block, "Energy Deregulation: Moving Ahead Quickly (and Wisely), The Progress and Freedom Foundation (mail@ppf.org).

Peter Behr and April Witt, "Visionary's Dream Led to Risky Business," *Washington Post,* July 28, 2002 (p. A1).

Allan Sloan, "Who Killed Enron?" *Newsweek,* January 21, 2002 (pp. 22–23).

Brian Cruver, *Anatomy of Greed: The Unshredded Truth from an Enron Insider* (New York: Caroll and Graff, 2002).

Kurt Eichenwald with Floyd Norris, "Early Verdict on Audit: Procedures Ignored," *The New York Times*, June 6, 2002 (C5).

Kurt Eichenwald, "Flinging Billions to Acquire Assets That No One Else Would Touch," *The New York Times,* October 18, 2002 (pp. C1 and C9).

Rural Utilities Service, *Connecting Rural America*, RUS Press Releases and Official Statements: 2002. www.usda.gov/rus/index2/press.htm

Internet References . . .

Workplace Fairness

Workplace Fairness is a nonprofit organization that was founded to assist individuals, both employed and unemployed, in understanding, enforcing, and expanding their rights in the workplace.

http://www.nerinet.org

WorkNet@ILR

The School of Industrial and Labor Relations at Cornell University offers this site consisting of an index of Internet sites relevant to the field of industrial and labor relations; a list of centers, institutes, and affiliated groups; and an electronic archive that contains full-text documents on the glass ceiling, child labor, and more.

http://www.ilr.cornell.edu/

WorkNet: Alcohol and Other Drugs in the Workplace

This site of the Canadian Centre on Substance Abuse provides news, databases, bibliographies, resources, and research on alcohol and other drugs in the workplace.

http://www.ccsa.ca/ccsa/

Employee Incentives and Career Development

This site is dedicated to the proposition that effective employee compensation and career development is a valuable tool in obtaining, maintaining, and retaining a productive workforce. It contains links to pay-for-knowledge, incentive systems, career development, wage and salary compensation, and more.

http://www.snc.edu/socsci/chair/336/group1.htm

Executive PayWatch

Executive PayWatch, sponsored by the American Federation of Labor—Congress of Industrial Organizations (AFL-CIO), is a working families' guide to monitoring and curtailing the excessive salaries, bonuses, and perks in CEO compensation packages.

http://www.aflcio.org/corporateamerica/paywatch/

UNIT 3

Human Resources: The Corporation and Employees

*W*hat is a just wage—for a worker near the poverty line, or for a multimillionaire corporate executive? What is a just employment policy? What rights does the employer have to limit employee privacy for company interests? And what right does an employee have to denounce an employer publicly for wrongdoing? The limits of employer and employee rights are never fixed, but require repeated examination and balancing.

- Does Blowing the Whistle Violate Company Loyalty?
- Is Employer Monitoring of Employee E-Mail Justified?
- Is "Employment-at-Will" Good Social Policy?
- Is CEO Compensation Justified by Performance?

ISSUE 8

Does Blowing the Whistle Violate Company Loyalty?

YES: Sissela Bok, from "Whistleblowing and Professional Responsibility," *New York University Education Quarterly* (Summer 1980)

NO: Robert A. Larmer, from "Whistleblowing and Employee Loyalty," *Journal of Business Ethics* (vol. 11, 1992)

ISSUE SUMMARY

YES: Philosopher Sissela Bok asserts that although blowing the whistle is often justified, it does involve dissent, accusation, and a breach of loyalty to the employer.

NO: Robert A. Larmer argues, on the contrary, that putting a stop to illegal or unethical company activities may be the highest type of loyalty an employee can display.

The whistleblower is a nearly mythical character—the brave, lonely person who exposes evil in the corporate or governmental bureaucracy. Since the readings are very general, some specific cases might be useful. In a fascinating treatment of the phenomenon, N. R. Kleinfeld portrays five of the early whistleblowers, some of whom have become famous as case studies in business schools across the country. Each one has an interesting story to tell; each claims that if he had it to do over again he would, for he likes living with a clear conscience. But each has paid a price: great stress, sometimes ill health, career loss, financial ruin, and/or loss of friends and family. Worst of all is the universal suspicion of anyone who can be characterized as a "snitch" or a "tattletale."

Charles Atchison, for example, blew the whistle on the Comanche Park nuclear plant in Glen Rose, Texas, a power station that was clearly unsafe. It cost him his job, plunged him into debt from which he is still trying to recover, and left emotional scars on his family, but he says he would do it again. Kermit Vandivier, the man who blew the whistle on the B.F. Goodrich Aircraft Brakes scandal, also lost his job; he has a new career as a journalist. James Pope claimed that the Federal Aviation Administration had found in 1975 an effective device that would prevent midair crashes, known as an airborne collision avoidance system, but chose to pursue an inferior device they had had a hand in developing. Mr. Pope was "retired" early by the F.A.A. And A. Ernest Fitzgerald (*The High Priests of Waste; The Pentagonists*), most famous of them all, was an Air Force cost analyst who found huge cost overruns on Lockheed cargo planes being developed for the Air Force. After his revelations, he was discharged from the Air Force, but fought for thirteen years to be reinstated; he was, at full rank, in 1982. The common thread of these hero stories is that when a wrong was seen, and properly reported, the reporters were all demoted, labeled as troublemakers, disciplined, and/or fired even when the evidence was very much in their favor. All of them, incidentally, initially believed in their organizations and acted explicitly out of loyalty. They were sure not only that they were acting in an ethical manner, but that they would be thanked for their efforts and diligence.

Professors Myron and Penina Glazer tell the story of fifty-five whistleblowers, why they did what they did, and what the consequences were for them and their families. The Glazers found their dominant trait to be a very strong belief in individual responsibility. One of the spouses of a whistleblower stated it very clearly: "A corrupt system can happen only if the individuals who make up that system are corrupt. You are either going to be part of the corruption or part of the forces working against it. There isn't a third choice. Someone, someday, has to take a stand; if you don't, maybe no one will. And that is wrong."

The Glazers write that a strong belief in individual responsibility that drives ethical resisters is often supported by professional ethics, religious values, or allegiance to the community. But the personal costs of public disclosure have been high, and the results have been less than satisfactory. In some cases no change in the corrupt system occurred. But the whistleblowers had to re-create careers, relocate, and settle for less money in a new job. For most resisters, the worst part was the devastating months or even years of dislocation, unemployment, and temporary jobs. In a response to a question posed by the Glazers, twenty-one of the whistleblowers advised potential whistleblowers to "forget it," or "leak the information without your name attached," or if you must blow the whistle, "be prepared to be ostracized, have your career come to a screeching halt and perhaps even be driven into bankruptcy." Such outsized punishments must dampen the most heroic. Does it have to be this way?

As you read the debate that follows, think of these cases, and think of others you have known. What would you do if confronted with the challenge to blow the whistle? Then turn it around. How would you react if someone blew the whistle on *you*? Does the role reversal change your weighting of the values at stake in this dilemma?

YES ⬅   Sissela Bok

Whistleblowing and Professional Responsibility

Whistleblowing is a new label generated by our increased awareness of the ethical conflicts encountered at work. Whistleblowers sound an alarm from within the very organization in which they work, aiming to spotlight neglect or abuses that threaten the public interest.

The stakes in whistleblowing are high. Take the nurse who alleges that physicians enrich themselves in her hospital through unnecessary surgery; the engineer who discloses safety defects in the braking systems of a fleet of new rapid-transit vehicles; the Defense Department official who alerts Congress to military graft and overspending: all know that they pose a threat to those whom they denounce and that their own careers may be at risk.

Moral Conflicts

Moral conflicts on several levels confront anyone who is wondering whether to speak out about abuses or risks or serious neglect. In the first place, he must try to decide whether, other things being equal, speaking out is in fact in the public interest. This choice is often made more complicated by factual uncertainties: Who is responsible for the abuse or neglect? How great is the threat? And how likely is it that speaking out will precipitate changes for the better?

In the second place, a would-be whistleblower must weigh his responsibility to serve the public interest against the responsibility he owes to his colleagues and the institution in which he works. While the professional ethic requires collegial loyalty, the codes of ethics often stress responsibility to the public over and above duties to colleagues and clients. Thus the United States Code of Ethics for Government Servants asks them to "expose corruption wherever uncovered" and to "put loyalty to the highest moral principles and to country above loyalty to persons, party, or government."[1] Similarly, the largest professional engineering association requires members to speak out against abuses threatening the safety, health, and welfare of the public.[2]

A third conflict for would-be whistleblowers is personal in nature and cuts across the first two: even in cases where they have concluded that the

From *New York University Education Quarterly*, Vol. 11, Summer 1980, pp. 2–7. Copyright © 1980 by Sissela Bok. Reprinted by permission of the author.

facts warrant speaking out, and that their duty to do so overrides loyalties to colleagues and institutions, they often have reason to fear the results of carrying out such a duty. However strong this duty may seem in theory, they know that, in practice, retaliation is likely. As a result, their careers and their ability to support themselves and their families may be unjustly impaired.[3] A government handbook issued during the Nixon era recommends reassigning "undesirables" to places so remote that they would prefer to resign. Whistleblowers may also be downgraded or given work without responsibility or work for which they are not qualified; or else they may be given many more tasks than they can possibly perform. Another risk is that an outspoken civil servant may be ordered to undergo a psychiatric fitness-for-duty examination,[4] declared unfit for service, and "separated" as well as discredited from the point of view of any allegations he may be making. Outright firing, finally, is the most direct institutional response to whistleblowers.

Add to the conflicts confronting individual whistleblowers the claim to self-policing that many professions make, and professional responsibility is at issue in still another way. For an appeal to the public goes against everything that "self-policing" stands for. The question for the different professions, then, is how to resolve, insofar as it is possible, the conflict between professional loyalty and professional responsibility toward the outside world. The same conflicts arise to some extent in all groups, but professional groups often have special cohesion and claim special dignity and privileges.

The plight of whistleblowers has come to be documented by the press and described in a number of books. Evidence of the hardships imposed on those who chose to act in the public interest has combined with a heightened awareness of professional malfeasance and corruption to produce a shift toward greater public support of whistleblowers. Public service law firms and consumer groups have taken up their cause; institutional reforms and legislation have been proposed to combat illegitimate reprisals.[5]

Given the indispensable services performed by so many whistleblowers, strong public support is often merited. But the new climate of acceptance makes it easy to overlook the dangers of whistleblowing: of uses in error or in malice; of work and reputations unjustly lost for those falsely accused; of privacy invaded and trust undermined. There comes a level of internal prying and mutual suspicion at which no institution can function. And it is a fact that the disappointed, the incompetent, the malicious, and the paranoid all too often leap to accusations in public. Worst of all, ideological persecution throughout the world traditionally relies on insiders willing to inform on their colleagues or even on their family members, often through staged public denunciations or press campaigns.

No society can count itself immune from such dangers. But neither can it risk silencing those with a legitimate reason to blow the whistle. How then can we distinguish between different instances of whistleblowing? A society that fails to protect the right to speak out even on the part of those whose warnings turn out to be spurious obviously opens the door to political repression. But from the moral point of view there are important differences between the aims, messages, and methods of dissenters from within.

Nature of Whistleblowing

Three elements, each jarring, and triply jarring when conjoined, lend acts of whistleblowing special urgency and bitterness: dissent, breach of loyalty, and accusation.

Like all dissent, whistleblowing makes public a disagreement with an authority or a majority view. But whereas dissent can concern all forms of disagreement with, for instance, religious dogma or government policy or court decisions, whistleblowing has the narrower aim of shedding light on negligence or abuse, or alerting to a risk, and of assigning responsibility for this risk.

Would-be whistleblowers confront the conflict inherent in all dissent: between conforming and sticking their necks out. The more repressive the authority they challenge, the greater the personal risk they take in speaking out. At exceptional times, as in times of war, even ordinarily tolerant authorities may come to regard dissent as unacceptable and even disloyal.[6]

Furthermore, the whistleblower hopes to stop the game; but since he is neither referee nor coach, and since he blows the whistle on his own team, his act is seen as a violation of loyalty. In holding his position, he has assumed certain obligations to his colleagues and clients. He may even have subscribed to a loyalty oath or a promise of confidentiality. Loyalty to colleagues and to clients comes to be pitted against loyalty to the public interest, to those who may be injured unless the revelation is made.

Not only is loyalty violated in whistleblowing, hierarchy as well is often opposed, since the whistleblower is not only a colleague but a subordinate. Though aware of the risks inherent in such disobedience, he often hopes to keep his job.[7] At times, however, he plans his alarm to coincide with leaving the institution. If he is highly placed, or joined by others, resigning in protest may effectively direct public attention to the wrongdoing at issue.[8] Still another alternative, often chosen by those who wish to be safe from retaliation, is to leave the institution quietly, to secure another post, and then to blow the whistle. In this way, it is possible to speak with the authority and knowledge of an insider without having the vulnerability of that position.

It is the element of accusation, of calling a "foul," that arouses the strongest reactions on the part of the hierarchy. The accusation may be of neglect, of willfully concealed dangers, or of outright abuse on the part of colleagues or superiors. It singles out specific persons or groups as responsible for threats to the public interest. If no one could be held responsible—as in the case of an impending avalanche—the warning would not constitute whistleblowing.

The accusation of the whistleblower, moreover, concerns a present or an imminent threat. Past errors or misdeeds occasion such an alarm only if they still affect current practices. And risks far in the future lack the immediacy needed to make the alarm a compelling one, as well as the close connection to particular individuals that would justify actual accusations. Thus an alarm can be sounded about safety defects in a rapid-transit system that threaten or will shortly threaten passengers, but the revelation of safety defects in a system no longer in use, while of historical interest, would not constitute whistleblowing. Nor would the revelation of potential problems in a system not yet fully designed and far from implemented.[9]

Not only immediacy, but also specificity, is needed for there to be an alarm capable of pinpointing responsibility. A concrete risk must be at issue rather than a vague foreboding or a somber prediction. The act of whistleblowing differs in this respect from the lamentation or the dire prophecy. An immediate and specific threat would normally be acted upon by those at risk. The whistleblower assumes that his message will alert listeners to something they do not know, or whose significance they have not grasped because it has been kept secret.

The desire for openness inheres in the temptation to reveal any secret, sometimes joined to an urge for self-aggrandizement and publicity and the hope for revenge for past slights or injustices. There can be pleasure, too—righteous or malicious—in laying bare the secrets of co-workers and in setting the record straight at last. Colleagues of the whistleblower often suspect his motives: they may regard him as a crank, as publicity-hungry, wrong about the facts, eager for scandal and discord, and driven to indiscretion by his personal biases and shortcomings.

For whistleblowing to be effective, it must arouse its audience. Inarticulate whistleblowers are likely to fail from the outset. When they are greeted by apathy, their message dissipates. When they are greeted by disbelief, they elicit no response at all. And when the audience is not free to receive or to act on the information—when censorship or fear of retribution stifles response—then the message rebounds to injure the whistleblower. Whistleblowing also requires the possibility of concerted public response: the idea of whistleblowing in an anarchy is therefore merely quixotic.

Such characteristics of whistleblowing and strategic considerations for achieving an impact are common to the noblest warnings, the most vicious personal attacks, and the delusions of the paranoid. How can one distinguish the many acts of sounding an alarm that are genuinely in the public interest from all the petty, biased, or lurid revelations that pervade our querulous and gossip-ridden society? Can we draw distinctions between different whistleblowers, different messages, different methods?

We clearly can, in a number of cases. Whistleblowing may be starkly inappropriate when in malice or error, or when it lays bare legitimately private matters having to do, for instance, with political belief or sexual life. It can, just as clearly, be the only way to shed light on an ongoing unjust practice such as drugging political prisoners or subjecting them to electroshock treatment. It can be the last resort for alerting the public to an impending disaster. Taking such clear-cut cases as benchmarks, and reflecting on what it is about them that weighs so heavily for or against speaking out, we can work our way toward the admittedly more complex cases in which whistleblowing is not so clearly the right or wrong choice, or where different points of view exist regarding its legitimacy—cases where there are moral reasons both for concealment and for disclosure and where judgments conflict. . . .

Individual Moral Choice

What questions might those who consider sounding an alarm in public ask themselves? How might they articulate the problem they see and weigh its injustice before deciding whether or not to reveal it? How can they best try to make sure their choice is the right one? In thinking about these questions it helps to keep in mind the three elements mentioned earlier: dissent, breach of loyalty, and accusation. They impose certain requirements—of accuracy and judgment in dissent; of exploring alternative ways to cope with improprieties that minimize the breach of loyalty; and of fairness in accusation. For each, careful articulation and testing of arguments are needed to limit error and bias.

Dissent by whistleblowers, first of all, is expressly claimed to be intended to benefit the public. It carries with it, as a result, an obligation to consider the nature of this benefit and to consider also the possible harm that may come from speaking out: harm to persons or institutions and, ultimately, to the public interest itself. Whistleblowers must, therefore, begin by making every effort to consider the effects of speaking out versus those of remaining silent. They must assure themselves of the accuracy of their reports, checking and rechecking the facts before speaking out; specify the degree to which there is genuine impropriety; consider how imminent is the threat they see, how serious, and how closely linked to those accused of neglect and abuse.

If the facts warrant whistleblowing, how can the second element—breach of loyalty—be minimized? The most important question here is whether the existing avenues for change within the organization have been explored. It is a waste of time for the public as well as harmful to the institution to sound the loudest alarm first. Whistleblowing has to remain a last alternative because of its destructive side effects: it must be chosen only when other alternatives have been considered and rejected. They may be rejected if they simply do not apply to the problem at hand, or when there is not time to go through routine channels or when the institution is so corrupt or coercive that steps will be taken to silence the whistleblower should he try the regular channels first.

What weight should an oath or a promise of silence have in the conflict of loyalties? One sworn to silence is doubtless under a stronger obligation because of the oath he has taken. He has bound himself, assumed specific obligations beyond those assumed in merely taking a new position. But even such promises can be overridden when the public interest at issue is strong enough. They can be overridden if they were obtained under duress or through deceit. They can be overridden, too, if they promise something that is in itself wrong or unlawful. The fact that one has promised silence is no excuse for complicity in covering up a crime or a violation of the public's trust.

The third element in whistleblowing—accusation—raises equally serious ethical concerns. They are concerns of fairness to the persons accused of impropriety. Is the message one to which the public is entitled in the first place? Or does it infringe on personal and private matters that one has no right to invade? Here, the very notion of what is in the public's best "interest" is at issue: "accusations" regarding an official's unusual sexual or religious experiences may well appeal to the public's interest without being information relevant to "the public interest."

Great conflicts arise here. We have witnessed excessive claims to executive privilege and to secrecy by government officials during the Watergate scandal in order to cover up for abuses the public had every right to discover. Conversely, those hoping to profit from prying into private matters have become adept at invoking "the public's right to know." Some even regard such private matters as threats to the public: they voice their own religious and political prejudices in the language of accusation. Such a danger is never stronger than when the accusation is delivered surreptitiously. The anonymous accusations made during the McCarthy period regarding political beliefs and associations often injured persons who did not even know their accusers or the exact nature of the accusations.

From the public's point of view, accusations that are openly made by identifiable individuals are more likely to be taken seriously. And in fairness to those criticized, openly accepted responsibility for blowing the whistle should be preferred to the denunciation or the leaked rumor. What is openly stated can more easily be checked, its source's motives challenged, and the underlying information examined. Those under attack may otherwise be hard put to defend themselves against nameless adversaries. Often they do not even know that they are threatened until it is too late to respond. The anonymous denunciation, moreover, common to so many regimes, places the burden of investigation on government agencies that may thereby gain the power of a secret police.

From the point of view of the whistleblower, on the other hand, the anonymous message is safer in situations where retaliation is likely. But it is also often less likely to be taken seriously. Unless the message is accompanied by indications of how the evidence can be checked, its anonymity, however safe for the source, speaks against it.

During the process of weighing the legitimacy of speaking out, the method used, and the degree of fairness needed, whistleblowers must try to compensate for the strong possibility of bias on their part. They should be scrupulously aware of any motive that might skew their message: a desire for self-defense in a difficult bureaucratic situation, perhaps, or the urge to seek revenge, or inflated expectations regarding the effect their message will have on the situation. (Needless to say, bias affects the silent as well as the outspoken. The motive for holding back important information about abuses and injustice ought to give similar cause for soul-searching.)

Likewise, the possibility of personal gain from sounding the alarm ought to give pause. Once again there is then greater risk of a biased message. Even if the whistleblower regards himself as incorruptible, his profiting from revelations of neglect or abuse will lead others to question his motives and to put less credence in his charges. If, for example, a government employee stands to make large profits from a book exposing the inequities in his agency, there is danger that he will, perhaps even unconsciously, slant his report in order to cause more of a sensation.

A special problem arises when there is a high risk that the civil servant who speaks out will have to go through costly litigation. Might he not justifiably try to make enough money on his public revelations—say, through books or public speaking—to offset his losses? In so doing he will not strictly speaking have *profited* from his revelations: he merely avoids being financially crushed by their sequels. He will nevertheless still be suspected at the time of revelation, and his message will therefore seem more questionable.

Reducing bias and error in moral choice often requires consultation, even open debate[10]: methods that force articulation of the moral arguments at stake and challenge privately held assumptions. But acts of whistleblowing present special problems when it comes to open consultation. On the one hand, once the whistleblower sounds his alarm publicly, his arguments will be subjected to open scrutiny; he will have to articulate his reasons for speaking out and substantiate his charges. On the other hand, it will then be too late to retract the alarm or to combat its harmful effects, should his choice to speak out have been ill-advised.

For this reason, the whistleblower owes it to all involved to make sure of two things: that he has sought as much and as objective advice regarding his choice as he can *before* going public; and that he is aware of the arguments for and against the practice of whistleblowing in general, so that he can see his own choice against as richly detailed and coherently structured a background as possible. Satisfying these two requirements once again has special problems because of the very nature of whistleblowing: the more corrupt the circumstances, the more dangerous it may be to seek consultation before speaking out. And yet, since the whistleblower himself may have a biased view of the state of affairs, he may choose not to consult others when in fact it would be not only safe but advantageous to do so; he may see corruption and conspiracy where none exists.

Notes

1. Code of Ethics for Government Service passed by the U.S. House of Representatives in the 85th Congress (1958) and applying to all government employees and office holders.

2. Code of Ethics of the Institute of Electrical and Electronics Engineers, Article IV.

3. For case histories and descriptions of what befalls whistleblowers, see Rosemary Chalk and Frank von Hippel, "Due Process for Dissenting Whistle-Blowers," *Technology Review* 81 (June–July 1979); 48–55; Alan S. Westin and Stephen Salisbury, eds., *Individual Rights in the Corporation* (New York: Pantheon, 1980); Helen Dudar, "The Price of Blowing the Whistle," *New York Times Magazine,* 30 October 1979, pp. 41–54; John Edsall, *Scientific Freedom and Responsibility* (Washington, D.C.: American Association for the Advancement of Science, 1975), p. 5; David Ewing, *Freedom Inside the Organization* (New York: Dutton, 1977); Ralph Nader, Peter Petkas, and Kate Blackwell, *Whistle Blowing* (New York: Grossman, 1972); Charles Peter and Taylor Branch, *Blowing the Whistle* (New York: Praeger, 1972).

4. Congressional hearings uncovered a growing resort to mandatory psychiatric examinations.

5. For an account of strategies and proposals to support government whistle-blowers, see Government Accountability Project, *A Whistleblower's Guide to the Federal Bureaucracy* (Washington, D.C.: Institute for Policy Studies, 1977).

6. See, e.g., Samuel Eliot Morison, Frederick Merk, and Frank Friedel, *Dissent in Three American Wars* (Cambridge: Harvard University Press, 1970).

7. In the scheme worked out by Albert Hirschman in *Exit, Voice and Loyalty* (Cambridge: Harvard University Press, 1970), whistleblowing represents "voice" accompanied by a preference not to "exit," though forced "exit" is clearly a possibility and "voice" after or during "exit" may be chosen for strategic reasons.

8. Edward Weisband and Thomas N. Franck, *Resignation in Protest* (New York: Grossman, 1975).

9. Future developments can, however, be the cause for whistleblowing if they are seen as resulting from steps being taken or about to be taken that render them inevitable.

10. I discuss these questions of consultation and publicity with respect to moral choice in chapter 7 of Sissela Bok, *Lying* (New York: Pantheon, 1978); and in *Secrets* (New York: Pantheon Books, 1982), Ch. IX and XV.

Robert A. Larmer

NO

Whistleblowing and Employee Loyalty

Whistleblowing by an employee is the act of complaining, either within the corporation or publicly, about a corporation's unethical practices. Such an act raises important questions concerning the loyalties and duties of employees. Traditionally, the employee has been viewed as an agent who acts on behalf of a principal, i.e., the employer, and as possessing duties of loyalty and confidentiality. Whistleblowing, at least at first blush, seems a violation of these duties and it is scarcely surprising that in many instances employers and fellow employees argue that it is an act of disloyalty and hence morally wrong.[1]

It is this issue of the relation between whistleblowing and employee loyalty that I want to address. What I will call the standard view is that employees possess *prima facie* duties of loyalty and confidentiality to their employers and that whistleblowing cannot be justified except on the basis of a higher duty to the public good. Against this standard view, Ronald Duska has recently argued that employees do not have even a *prima facie* duty of loyalty to their employers and that whistleblowing needs, therefore, no moral justification.[2] I am going to criticize both views. My suggestion is that both misunderstand the relation between loyalty and whistleblowing. In their place I will propose a third more adequate view.

Duska's view is more radical in that it suggests that there can be no issue of whistleblowing and employee loyalty, since the employee has no duty to be loyal to his employer. His reason for suggesting that the employee owes the employer, at least the corporate employer, no loyalty is that companies are not the kinds of things which are proper objects of loyalty. His argument in support of this rests upon two key claims. The first is that loyalty, properly understood, implies a reciprocal relationship and is only appropriate in the context of a mutual surrendering of self-interest. He writes,

> It is important to recognize that in any relationship which demands loyalty the relationship works both ways and involves mutual enrichment. Loyalty is incompatible with self-interest, because it is something that necessarily requires we go beyond self-interest. My loyalty to my friend, for example, requires I put aside my interests some of the time. . . . Loyalty depends on ties that demand self-sacrifice with no expectation of reward, e.g., the ties of loyalty that bind a family together.[3]

From *Journal of Business Ethics*, Vol. 11, 1992, pp. 125–128. Copyright © 1992 by Springer Science and Business Media. Reprinted by permission via Rightslink.

The second is that the relation between a company and an employee does not involve any surrender of self-interest on the part of the company, since its primary goal is to maximize profit. Indeed, although it is convenient, it is misleading to talk of a company having interests. As Duska comments,

> A company is not a person. A company is an instrument, and an instrument with a specific purpose, the making of profit. To treat an instrument as an end in itself, like a person, may not be as bad as treating an end as an instrument, but it does give the instrument a moral status it does not deserve . . . [4]

Since, then, the relation between a company and an employee does not fulfill the minimal requirement of being a relation between two individuals, much less two reciprocally self-sacrificing individuals, Duska feels it is a mistake to suggest the employee has any duties of loyalty to the company.

This view does not seem adequate, however. First, it is not true that loyalty must be quite so reciprocal as Duska demands. Ideally, of course, one expects that if one is loyal to another person that person will reciprocate in kind. There are, however, many cases where loyalty is not entirely reciprocated, but where we do not feel that it is misplaced. A parent, for example, may remain loyal to an erring teenager, even though the teenager demonstrates no loyalty to the parent. Indeed, part of being a proper parent is to demonstrate loyalty to your children whether or not that loyalty is reciprocated. This is not to suggest any kind of analogy between parents and employees, but rather that it is not nonsense to suppose that loyalty may be appropriate even though it is not reciprocated. Inasmuch as he ignores this possibility, Duska's account of loyalty is flawed.

Second, even if Duska is correct in holding that loyalty is only appropriate between moral agents and that a company is not genuinely a moral agent, the question may still be raised whether an employee owes loyalty to fellow employees or the shareholders of the company. Granted that reference to a company as an individual involves reification and should not be taken too literally, it may nevertheless constitute a legitimate shorthand way of describing relations between genuine moral agents.

Third, it seems wrong to suggest that simply because the primary motive of the employer is economic, considerations of loyalty are irrelevant. An employee's primary motive in working for an employer is generally economic, but no one on that account would argue that it is impossible for her to demonstrate loyalty to the employer, even if it turns out to be misplaced. All that is required is that her primary economic motive be in some degree qualified by considerations of the employer's welfare. Similarly, the fact that an employer's primary motive is economic does not imply that it is not qualified by considerations of the employee's welfare. Given the possibility of mutual qualification of admittedly primary economic motives, it is fallacious to argue that employee loyalty is never appropriate.

In contrast to Duska, the standard view is that loyalty to one's employer is appropriate. According to it, one has an obligation to be loyal to one's employer and, consequently, a *prima facie* duty to protect the employer's interests. Whistleblowing constitutes, therefore, a violation of duty to one's employer and needs strong justification if it is to be appropriate. Sissela Bok summarizes this view very well when she writes

> the whistleblower hopes to stop the game; but since he is neither referee nor coach, and since he blows the whistle on his own team, his act is seen as a violation of loyalty. In holding his position, he has assumed certain obligations to his colleagues and clients. He may even have subscribed to a loyalty oath or a promise of confidentiality. Loyalty to colleagues and to clients comes to be pitted against loyalty to the public interest, to those who may be injured unless the revelation is made.[5]

The strength of this view is that it recognizes that loyalty is due one's employer. Its weakness is that it tends to conceive of whistleblowing as involving a tragic moral choice, since blowing the whistle is seen not so much as a positive action, but rather the lesser of two evils. Bok again puts the essence of this view very clearly when she writes that "a would-be whistleblower must weigh his responsibility to serve the public interest *against* the responsibility he owes to his colleagues and the institution in which he works" and "that [when] their duty [to whistleblow] . . . *so overrides loyalties to colleagues and institutions,* they [whistleblowers] often have reason to fear the results of carrying out such a duty."[6] The employee, according to this understanding of whistleblowing, must choose between two acts of betrayal, either her employer or the public interest, each in itself reprehensible.

Behind this view lies the assumption that to be loyal to someone is to act in a way that accords with what that person believes to be in her best interests. To be loyal to an employer, therefore, is to act in a way which the employer deems to be in his or her best interests. Since employers very rarely approve of whistleblowing and generally feel that it is not in their best interests, it follows that whistleblowing is an act of betrayal on the part of the employee, albeit a betrayal made in the interests of the public good.

Plausible though it initially seems, I think this view of whistleblowing is mistaken and that it embodies a mistaken conception of what constitutes employee loyalty. It ignores the fact that

> the great majority of corporate whistleblowers . . . [consider] themselves to be very loyal employees who . . . [try] to use 'direct voice' (internal whistleblowing), . . . [are] rebuffed and punished for this, and then . . . [use] 'indirect voice' (external whistleblowing). They . . . [believe] initially that they . . . [are] behaving in a loyal manner, helping their employers by calling top management's attention to practices that could eventually get the firm in trouble.[7]

By ignoring the possibility that blowing the whistle may demonstrate greater loyalty than not blowing the whistle, it fails to do justice to the many instances where loyalty to someone constrains us to act in defiance of what that person believes to be in her best interests. I am not, for example, being disloyal to a friend if I refuse to loan her money for an investment I am sure will bring her financial ruin; even if she bitterly reproaches me for denying her what is so obviously a golden opportunity to make a fortune.

A more adequate definition of being loyal to someone is that loyalty involves acting in accordance with what one has good reason to believe to be in that person's best interests. A key question, of course, is what constitutes a good reason to think that something is in a person's best interests. Very often, but by no means invariably, we accept that a person thinking that something is in her best interests is a sufficiently good reason to think that it actually is. Other times, especially when we feel that she is being rash, foolish, or misinformed we are prepared, precisely by virtue of being loyal, to act contrary to the person's wishes. It is beyond the scope of this paper to investigate such cases in detail, but three general points can be made.

First, to the degree that an action is genuinely immoral, it is impossible that it is in the agent's best interests. We would not, for example, say that someone who sells child pornography was acting in his own best interests, even if he vigorously protested that there was nothing wrong with such activity. Loyalty does not imply that we have a duty to refrain from reporting the immoral actions of those to whom we are loyal. An employer who is acting immorally is not acting in her own best interests and an employee is not acting disloyally in blowing the whistle.[8] Indeed, the argument can be made that the employee who blows the whistle may be demonstrating greater loyalty than the employee who simply ignores the immoral conduct, inasmuch as she is attempting to prevent her employer from engaging in self-destructive behaviour.

Second, loyalty requires that, whenever possible, in trying to resolve a problem we deal directly with the person to whom we are loyal. If, for example, I am loyal to a friend I do not immediately involve a third party when I try to dissuade my friend from involvement in immoral actions. Rather, I approach my friend directly, listen to his perspective on the events in question, and provide an opportunity for him to address the problem in a morally satisfactory way. This implies that, whenever possible, a loyal employee blows the whistle internally. This provides the employer with the opportunity to either demonstrate to the employee that, contrary to first appearances, no genuine wrongdoing had occurred, or, if there is a genuine moral problem, the opportunity to resolve it.

This principle of dealing directly with the person to whom loyalty is due needs to be qualified, however. Loyalty to a person requires that one acts in that person's best interests. Generally, this cannot be done without directly involving the person to whom one is loyal in the decision-making process, but there may arise cases where acting in a person's best interests requires that one act independently and perhaps even against the wishes of the person to whom one is loyal. Such cases will be especially apt to arise when the person to whom one is loyal is either immoral or ignoring the moral consequences of his actions. Thus, for example, loyalty to a friend who deals in hard narcotics would not imply that I speak first to my friend about my decision to inform the police of his activities, if the only effect of my doing so would be to make him more careful in his criminal dealings. Similarly, a loyal employee is under no obligation to speak first to an employer about the employer's immoral actions, if the only response of the employer will be to take care to cover up wrongdoing.

Neither is a loyal employee under obligation to speak first to an employer if it is clear that by doing so she places herself in jeopardy from an employer who will retaliate if given the opportunity. Loyalty amounts to acting in another's best interests and that may mean qualifying what seems to be in one's own interests, but it cannot imply that one take no steps to protect oneself from the immorality of those to whom one is loyal. The reason it cannot is that, as has already been argued, acting immorally can never really be in a person's best interests. It follows, therefore, that one is not acting in a person's best interests if one allows oneself to be treated immorally by that person. Thus, for example, a father might be loyal to a child even though the child is guilty of stealing from him, but this would not mean that the father should let the child continue to steal. Similarly, an employee may be loyal to an employer even though she takes steps to protect herself against unfair retaliation by the employer, e.g., by blowing the whistle externally.

Third, loyalty requires that one is concerned with more than considerations of justice. I have been arguing that loyalty cannot require one to ignore immoral or unjust behaviour on the part of those to whom one is loyal, since loyalty amounts to acting in a person's best interests and it can never be in a person's best interests to be allowed to act immorally. Loyalty, however, goes beyond considerations of justice in that, while it is possible to be disinterested and just, it is not possible to be disinterested and loyal. Loyalty implies a desire that the person to whom one is loyal take no moral stumbles, but that if moral stumbles have occurred that the person be restored and not simply punished. A loyal friend is not only someone who sticks by you in times of trouble, but someone who tries to help you avoid trouble. This suggests that a loyal employee will have a desire to point out problems and potential problems long before the drastic measures associated with whistleblowing become necessary, but that if whistleblowing does become necessary there remains a desire to help the employer.

In conclusion, although much more could be said on the subject of loyalty, our brief discussion has enabled us to clarify considerably the relation between whistleblowing and employee loyalty. It permits us to steer a course between the Scylla of Duska's view that, since the primary link between employer and employee is economic, the ideal of employee loyalty is an oxymoron, and the Charybdis of the standard view that, since it forces an employee to weigh conflicting duties, whistleblowing inevitably involves some degree of moral tragedy. The solution lies in realizing that to whistleblow for reasons of morality is to act in one's employer's best interests and involves, therefore, no disloyalty.

Notes

1. The definition I have proposed applies most directly to the relation between privately owned companies aiming to realize a profit and their employees. Obviously, issues of whistleblowing arise in other contexts, e.g., governmental organizations or charitable agencies, and deserve careful thought.

I do not propose, in this paper, to discuss whistleblowing in these other contexts, but I think my development of the concept of whistleblowing as positive demonstration of loyalty can easily be applied and will prove useful.

2. Duska, R.: 1985, 'Whistleblowing and Employee Loyalty,' in J. R. Desjardins and J. J. McCall, eds., *Contemporary Issues in Business Ethics* (Wadsworth, Belmont, California), pp. 295–300.

3. Duska, p. 297.

4. Duska, p. 298.

5. Bok, S.: 1983, 'Whistleblowing and Professional Responsibility,' in T. L. Beauchamp and N. E. Bowie, eds., *Ethical Theory and Business,* 2nd ed. (Prentice-Hall Inc., Englewood Cliffs, New Jersey), pp. 261–269, p. 263.

6. Bok, pp. 261–2, emphasis added.

7. Near, J. P. and P. Miceli: 1985, 'Organizational Dissidence: The Case of Whistle-Blowing', *Journal of Business Ethics* 4, pp. 1–16, p. 10.

8. As Near and Miceli note 'The whistle-blower may provide valuable information helpful in improving organizational effectiveness . . . the prevalence of illegal activity in organizations is associated with declining organizational performance' (p. 1).

The general point is that the structure of the world is such that it is not in a company's long-term interests to act immorally. Sooner or later a company which flouts morality and legality will suffer.

POSTSCRIPT

Does Blowing the Whistle Violate Company Loyalty?

Whistleblowers are hard role models. What would you do in their shoes? The corporation, incidentally, is not the only setting for whistles. Would you tell about a friend's drug abuse, cheating on exams (or on his wife), stealing just a little bit of money? How do you weigh the possibility of damage done to the community against the security of your own career (some damage done to many people versus much damage done to a few people)? If you can see nothing but painful consequences all around if you blow the whistle, does that settle the problem—or does simple justice and fidelity to law have a claim of its own, as Ernest Fitzgerald argued? At what point do you decide that you cannot survive as a moral person unless you take action to end an evil that is being concealed—that the value of your own integrity outweighs the certain penalties of honesty?

Should we, as a society, protect the whistleblower with legislation designed to discourage corporate retaliation? Richard De George and Alan Westin, the earliest business ethics writers to take whistleblowing seriously, agree that the best policy is one that precludes the need for such heroics. "The need for moral heroes," De George concludes, "shows a defective society and defective corporations. It is more important to change the legal and corporate structures that make whistle blowing necessary than to convince people to be moral heroes" (*Business Ethics*, 2nd edition, 1986, p. 236). "The single most important element in creating a meaningful internal system to deal with whistle blowing is to have top leadership accept this as a management priority," says Westin, "This means that the chief operating officer and his senior colleagues have to believe that a policy which encourages discussion and dissent, and deals fairly with whistle-blowing claims, is a good and important thing for their company to adopt. . . . They have to see it, in their own terms, as a moral duty of good private enterprise" (*Whistle-Blowing!* 1981, p. 141). He cites Alexander Trowbridge, former secretary of commerce, on the importance of creating the proper organizational climate within the corporation: "It must be one that fosters the development of discipline in response to strong leadership and yet creates an atmosphere in which the individual, when confronted with something clearly illegal, unethical or unjust, can feel free to speak up—and to bring the problem to the attention of those high enough up in the corporation to solve it" (Ibid., p. 142). We need clear policies that permit and encourage the employees to communicate their doubts, and we need to train our managers to be responsive instead of punitive when the doubts are communicated.

But these are not enough. "Even the best drafted policy statements and management training programs will not resolve all the questions of illegal, dangerous, or improper conduct that might arise," Westin concludes. "There has to be a clear process of receiving complaints, conducting impartial investigations, defining standards of judgment, providing a fair-hearing procedure, and reaching the most objective and responsible decision possible. Such a procedure has to be fair both to the complaining employee and to company officials if morale is to be preserved and general confidence in management's integrity is to be the general expectation of the work force" (Ibid., p. 143). The company can "establish channels whereby those employees who have moral concerns can get a fair hearing without danger to their position or standing in the company," suggests De George, "Expressing such concerns, moreover, should be considered a demonstration of company loyalty and should be rewarded appropriately" (De George, p. 237). Possibilities for appropriate mechanisms include company ombudsmen, employee advocates, and committees of the board of directors.

Yes, but suppose that *these* are not enough. We run a moral company, we think; we have mechanisms in place to receive and process complaints, we think; but it will still happen that under the pressure of competition, company policies may bend, and the ombudsmen and advocates may become co-opted into the company agenda. At this point, do we as a society have any remaining interest in protecting the whistleblower? Laws are already in place protecting those who expose their companies' illegal activities; but we have always had protections for those who help the authorities bring lawbreakers to justice, so those laws are nothing novel. The question is really, does the society as a whole have any collective interest in the monitoring of private organizations in the economic sphere? And if it does, and it seems that it does, is the legal protection of the whistleblower the appropriate way to express that interest?

Suggested Reading

Roberta Ann Johnson, *Whistle Blowing: When It Works and Why*, New York: L. Reinner Publishers, 2002.

Wim Vandekerchkhove and M.S. Ronald Commers, "Whistle Blowing and Rational Loyalty," *Journal of Business Ethics*, vol. 53 no. 1–2, August 2004.

Colin Grant, "Whistle Blowers: Saints of Secular Culture," *Journal of Business Ethics*, vol. 39 no. 2, September, 2002.

A. Bather & M. Kelly (2005). "Whistleblowing: The Advantages of Self-regulation." Department of Accounting Working Paper Series, Number 82. Hamilton, New Zealand: University of Waikato.

ISSUE 9

Is Employer Monitoring of Employee E-Mail Justified?

YES: Chauncey M. DePree, Jr., and Rebecca K. Jude, from "Who's Reading Your Office E-Mail? Is That Legal?" *Strategic Finance* (April 2006)

NO: *USA Today*, from "E-monitoring of Workers Sparks Concerns," *USA Today* (May 29, 2001)

ISSUE SUMMARY

YES: DePree and Jude argue that employers have a right, indeed a duty, to protect the corporation from legal liability incurred by the careless actions of their employees. Unfortunately, the use of e-mail from the employer's computer can get the company into worlds of trouble, and the company must monitor that e-mail.

NO: According to the *USA Today* there is apparently a substantial body of opinion in the country that e-mail is like other mail, and no one has the right to read it except the writer and the intended recipient. That goes for employers, too.

Is privacy a "right" for the worker? If history is to be our guide, absolutely not. Dictatorial employers of the 19th century had no qualms about making and enforcing rules governing not only job performance but dress and personal behavior on the job; many also had rules for off-the-job behavior. But Americans do not take easily to such governance, and with the advent of organized labor, the freedom of the employer to dictate the employee's lifestyle off the job almost disappeared. On-the-job requirements also ceased to be absolute; although certain obvious safety rules could be enforced, the presumption was that rules should not be extended beyond necessity and that that necessity had to be job-related.

The last generation's privacy issue turned on the employee's use of recreational drugs outside of business hours. Few employees openly snorted cocaine at their desks, but an employee could stay pleasantly elevated all day with doses in the morning and lunch hour. Employers frowned on such use, partly out of fears of liability should the company's premises be used for drug consumption, or should any product made by the employee turn out badly flawed because of the drugs, but mainly because of the loss of productivity resulting from the impairment and the ever-present threat of drug-induced behavior, bizarre or violent, that would impact the other employees and the workplace as a whole. Drugs were worse than alcohol, if only because any experienced foreman or supervisor can spot drunkenness, which manifests itself in the employee's gait, his speech, and on his breath. But drugs hid themselves, and therefore had to be tested for.

This generation's issue is the monitoring of employee computer use. There are uses of the employer's computer that can raise the same liability issues for the employer as employee drug use: If someone is harmed by the employee's nonbusiness use of the computer on the employer's premises, how shall the employer answer the complaint? The question is not hypothetical: According to the American Management Association (AMA), 13 percent of employers who responded to its survey on the subject had had to battle lawsuits triggered by employee e-mail. Of even more concern to employers is inappropriate surfing of the Internet; 65 percent of employers surveyed now use software to block connections to websites whose images have no place in the workplace; similarly, 900 numbers cannot be accessed from office phones. It is also possible to monitor keystrokes—to find out if a secretary, say, is apparently writing more letters than her productivity would indicate. The AMA insists that employers for the most part give the employees fair warning about all monitoring and surveillance and that it is done with their consent.

Employees understandably object to being watched all the time, down to the least detail of documents stored in their computer files, all e-mail correspondence, and all use of the Web. Of course they "consented," signed a document as they started work, but consent has a strange heft when the alternative is unemployment.

Part of the problem, of course, stems from the semiprivate nature of the cubicle and the sense of invisibility that it conveys. Workplaces traditionally have been open floors for all but the top executives, floors in which work was carried on in full view of everyone, in which the physical products were immediately visible to all, and in which the modes of communication were oral and very audible, or in black and white for several sets of eyes to read before they landed in the company's outgoing mail box. Now the worker seems to have the entirety of the office equipment at his sole command, including the mailroom, and the sense of anonymity is very tempting.

Bear in mind as you read these selections that the requirements that work get done and inappropriate behavior be avoided in the workplace have not changed for hundreds of years and are affirmed by employer and employee alike. But the technology has changed the workplace setting beyond recognition, and many of our previous assumptions about monitoring and freedom will have to be renegotiated.

YES ↵

**Chauncey M. DePree, Jr.,
and Rebecca K. Jude**

Who's Reading Your Office E-Mail?
Is That Legal?

Yesterday, as you sat working at your desk, you checked your e-mail and spotted a note from a friend. The message was an off-color joke complete with graphic illustration. Sure, some stick-in-the-mud might find it offensive, but it was awfully funny. So, without thinking, you clicked on the forward button, typed in an e-mail address or two or three, and hit the send button. No big deal, right?

You don't give the e-mail another thought until this morning when a somber supervisor invites you to her office. She hands you a letter of reprimand along with a copy of the e-mail. She tells you that as a matter of office policy, employee e-mails are monitored. Copies are placed in your file, and, in the event it happens again, she warns that you'll receive a termination letter.

It simply never occurred to you that someone might be monitoring your e-mail. What about your right to privacy?

What Happened to Privacy?

As an employee, the idea of being monitored may trouble you. As an employer, the idea of monitoring employees may be equally distasteful. The right to privacy is so thoroughly ingrained in most of us that we take it for granted—especially in a peaceful environment when we're sitting alone, typing into a computer. We may be lulled into a false sense of isolation and freedom from observation. But even if the technology is available, aren't there simply too many e-mails and too much Internet use to review effectively? After all, the Internet is so big and so anonymous. No one can really track everybody's e-mail or Internet surfing. Besides, it's probably an invasion of privacy and illegal.

Wrong on both counts. To quote Scott McNealy, CEO of Sun Microsystems, on the issue of Internet privacy: "You have zero privacy anyway. Get over it." McNealy's rather abrupt observation and admonition are particularly true in the work environment.

The simple fact is that monitoring employee e-mail and Internet usage is legal under almost all circumstances. As a general rule, when an employee enters the workplace, an employer may monitor and record communications, including e-mail and Internet use, without any notice to the employee. In *Fraser v. Nationwide Mutual Insurance Co.*, 352 F. 3d 107 (3rd Cir. 2003), the court specifically held that The Electronic Communications Privacy Act, 18 U.S.C.§2701, didn't apply to an employer's search of e-mail stored on its own system.

But in some instances, simple facts tend to beget complicated, counterintuitive consequences. For example, an employer repeatedly assured its employees that e-mail communications would remain confidential. As it turned out, the assurance wasn't a guarantee that the employees' e-mails wouldn't be used as a basis for discharge. In *Smyth v. The Pillsbury Company*, 914 F. Supp. 97 (ED Pa. 1996), a supervisor e-mailed inappropriate comments to an employee at home, and the employee responded in kind. The e-mails were communicated over the company system. Regardless of the company's assurances, the employee was terminated for communicating "inappropriate and unprofessional comments" via the company system. The Court held that "once plaintiff communicated the alleged unprofessional comments to a second person over the e-mail system that was apparently utilized by the entire company, any reasonable expectation of privacy was lost."

Employee e-mail habits have developed over time, but, as the *Pillsbury* decision exemplifies, employers' practices also can change—sometimes quickly and unpredictably. The Pillsbury case wouldn't be the last surprise for employees. Employers can review e-mail at any time and with lightning speed. Dow Chemical took a "snapshot" of a day's worth of employee e-mails and then systematically sorted through them. Some 254 employees had saved, filed, or sent sexually related, violent, and other inappropriate e-mails. The actual participation and involvement of the employees varied considerably. Dow created a set of criteria so that discipline taken, if any, could be based on each employee's participation. The criteria included offensiveness; what the employee did with the material, such as circulating the materials within Dow; and the frequency of the conduct. Dow discharged 20 employees and disciplined others. The court, although recognizing that Dow was probably employing a union-busting tactic, upheld the company's review and use of its employees' e-mail (*Dow Chemical v. Local No. 564, Operating Engineers*, 246 F. Supp. 2d 602 (SD Texas, 2002)).

Is Monitoring E-Mail and Internet Use Necessary?

Despite the near cultural aversion to intruding on communications, growing numbers of companies and managers record, review, and monitor telephone and computer activities of their employees. According to the American Management Association (AMA) 2005 Electronic Monitoring & Surveillance Survey, 76% of employers monitor website connections, "26% have fired workers for misusing the Internet," and "another 25% have terminated employees for e-mail misuse." Inexpensive software packages facilitate these decisions, and the overriding reason is compelling—it has become a business necessity.

An inescapable consequence of employee e-mail and Internet use is that the employer is responsible for illegal, discriminatory, or offensive communications that are transmitted over the system or viewed by others from a company computer screen. Sexually explicit, graphically violent, or racially inappropriate websites open to view by co-workers may be used to support claims of discriminatory behavior or a hostile work environment. E-mails containing such inappropriate materials that are circulated around the office or forwarded to others have the same effect.

But so there's no misunderstanding, employers and managers can get into just as much trouble with their e-mail as employees. E-mails sent by managers can be used by employees to prove claims of corporate misconduct. For example, the characterization of an employee as "ready for the bone yard" may be evidence of age discrimination. The simple truth is that e-mails containing potentially libelous or defamatory content should *not* be sent or forwarded— even internally. Not only can they easily get away from managers with a click of a button, but they also may become—in a stored capacity on the server or archive—the target of discovery in litigation.

Because e-mails can seem so informal, managers and employees are more likely to say things in them they would never put in a letter. Unlike letters, e-mails can be forwarded over and over to thousands of people with the touch of a button. Impulsive and thoughtless comments can travel the world over. Often overlooked is the liability with regard to foreign laws. Because e-mails can be transmitted anywhere and may then be forwarded practically *ad infinitum,* an employer may be responsible for content based on the laws of the country in which the e-mail ultimately arrives. Electronic communications originating in the company office may have far-ranging legal consequences.

An Easy Prediction and Another Surprise

Some potential liabilities are much better known and may occur with considerable frequency. For example, an employee might use office computers to wrongfully appropriate other people's intellectual property from the Internet, leaving the employer responsible. One of the most popular forms of this activity is file sharing—downloading copyrighted music or movies without payment. Or an employee might copy and paste copyrighted material from someone else's website onto the employer's without the knowledge or consent of any manager or supervisor. The company may be responsible for the copyright infringement.

Other kinds of e-mail-facilitated problems might not be easily anticipated. For example, an employee can enter into a contract with the click of a mouse. This was our firm's first e-mail surprise. An employee took it upon himself to purchase CDs containing copies of documents that we already had in our possession. It was easy. An e-mail arrived asking if he would be willing to share the cost of obtaining copies of documents. All he had to do was return an e-mail agreeing to participate in the project. Seemingly out of the blue, at least from our perspective, a half dozen CDs and an invoice for several thousand dollars arrived at our office. There was no correspondence in the files authorizing the purchase. Ultimately, though, we found a brief e-mail from our employee responding to the inquiry. The reply e-mail simply said "count us in." Of course, the company that provided the service wanted its money. After all, they had spent time and effort preparing the materials for us. We were stuck. If our office had monitored e-mails, we could have caught this and stopped the expensive and wasteful process before the vendor incurred its costs.

From Top to Bottom Line

Even when a company gets lucky and avoids civil or contractual liability, employees will still take time for personal communications, e-mails, and Internet surfing instead of working. This could cost the company a fortune in lost productivity and lost dollars. Time away from work also translates to poor client service. Poor service may lose clients. Consequently, as unappealing as it is, monitoring employee communications is increasingly viewed as a business necessity.

For our firm, a good place to start was to develop a policy to educate employees in the use of company e-mail and the Internet. We believed, as do other employers, that to avoid any potential gray areas in the law, and in the interest of fairness, employers should advise managers and employees of e-mail or Internet monitoring as part of their employment agreement, and it should be included in the employee handbook. We breathed a sigh of relief after we disseminated the policy to all employees and confirmed that everyone understood the importance of compliance.

We weren't so naïve as to believe it would solve our Internet and e-mail problems, but we had no idea just how difficult it would be to change habits. As unbelievable as it may sound, the very next day after the Internet and e-mail policy was communicated, it was completely ignored by a professional employee. He thoughtlessly e-mailed his latest "joke" far and wide, even though it could easily be construed not only as racist but salacious as well. It was forwarded as cavalierly as if he had never read the policy or studied the law. And that's right, he is a lawyer!

USA Today

E-monitoring of Workers
Sparks Concerns

Employee privacy in the United States is under siege as old rules for what employers can and cannot monitor give way to a regime of everyday observation, patchy legal protections and conflicting business priorities.

Software that pours over intimate e-mail correspondences, tracks worker performance or thwarts employee theft has narrowed the realm of privacy for employees in offices, factories, on the road or telecommuting from home.

Three-quarters of U.S. businesses now electronically monitor employees in some fashion, double the rate of just five years ago, according to a recent study by the American Management Association, a New York-based corporate training and consulting group.

Meet the downside of the low-cost, easy-to-use technologies that have powered the technology revolution of recent years.

"As the work has been automated, so also has the watching been automated," said Eric Rolphe Greenberg, director of management studies at the AMA.

"Now that the nature of the work has changed, so also has the nature of the supervision," said Greenberg, the author of the AMA's annual study of electronic workplace monitoring.

Vague policies allow Web and e-mail monitoring software not only to track when an employee views sexually explicit material but potentially any intimate subject. Voice mail retrieval software does the same. Keystroke and screen-capture software can check what you are working on at any moment in time.

Punching the time clock takes on new meaning when every movement can be traced. Field sales representatives have their movements tracked by location-based tracking systems in new wireless phones. Some hospitals now require nurses to wear badges on their uniforms so they can be located constantly.

Managers, business consultants and legal experts say this rise in corporate curiosity is required to keep pace with free-wheeling communications technologies in the Internet age.

Electronic Monitoring Now a Fact of Workplace Life

The AMA's survey of major U.S. firms found that 77.7% now record and review some sort of employee communications and activities on the job.

For example, Internet connections were monitored by 63% of the more than 1,600 companies responding to the survey. Telephone use was tracked by 43%. Computer use such as time logged on or keystroke counts was monitored by 19%. Video surveillance for security purposes was used by 38%.

In addition, the annual survey found that more than a quarter of respondent companies fired people for misuse of company technology and three-quarters have disciplined people.

"People act as if they have privacy protection. They don't stop to think they are under scrutiny," said Stewart Baker, head of the technology law practice at Washington, D.C.-firm Steptoe & Johnson.

"Surprisingly for such a law-happy society, there are few limits on what employers can do in the electronic age with respect to the privacy of their employees," said Baker, a cyber-law expert who was former general counsel of the U.S. National Security Agency.

While federal laws against wiretapping prevent monitoring of employee conversations under most circumstances, there are few limitations on monitoring such things as voice mail, e-mail or Web monitoring—any information that is stored and retrieved instead of directly intercepted, as live phone calls must be.

"Work-place privacy is a contradiction in terms. It's an oxymoron," the AMA's Greenberg said. "I know the illusion of privacy is there, but you are not using your own stuff. The phone, the keyboard, the connections, the job itself—they don't belong to you; they belong to the company, legally."

Most management and legal experts agree that simple prior notice to employees that their activities will be watched give employers wide freedom to monitor. Consultants advise companies to use notice as a way to "get over employees' expectations of privacy," which is an issue of social etiquette rather than a legal one.

Struggle to Balance New Technology, Individual Rights

The Internet has given a powerful window on the world to every office worker with a personal computer and a Web connection. It has also proven to be a powerful distraction, as the spike in usage of sites ranging from eBay to E-Trade during work hours reveals.

The very definition of what is private is up for grabs as lines blur between working hours, personal time and home life. What privacy rights do employees have when working on employer-supplied laptops from home, for example?

Meanwhile, the porous nature of electronic mail communications makes it quick and easy for employees to gossip with friends or business associates outside the organization.

The informality of the medium lends itself to the rapid transfer of a company's trade secrets outside the organization. What they don't send via e-mail angry employees can carry on a floppy disk in their shirt pocket as they walk out the door.

"Employers are much more aware and much more nervous about productivity, legality and security, and these issues are behind the increase," Greenberg said of the spiraling use of monitoring.

But it's a far cry from a century ago when Ford Motor used its Sociological Department to ensure that employees lived "unblemished" personal lives at home, the outgrowth of the intrusive management practices of 19th century industry.

Between productivity issues and competitive threats lie a wasp's nest of potential employer liability if computer systems are not policed for off-color jokes, mean-spirited gossip, or sexual harassment that show a pattern of discrimination.

E-mails and voicemails are frequently the smoking guns in corporate litigation. Standard operating procedure for any plaintiff's attorney in a corporate legal battle is to demand production of electronic records.

Big Brother Does Rest

Still, most monitoring is directed at specific job roles and not done around the clock, Greenberg said.

Because of obvious limitations on time and financial resources the watching is not perpetual and can't be. It mostly consists of keyword searches on Web use and e-mail, just as companies have looked over telephone bills for decades.

"Big Brother is snoozing more often than he's watching," Greenberg said.

POSTSCRIPT

Is Employer Monitoring of Employee E-Mail Justified?

This pair of selections marks a first for this series: While the YES article is from a standard opinion piece from a standard publication, the NO is a contribution from We the People, the general opinion as reported by a news agency. We think that this is significant. It is too early for much official reflection to have taken place on this subject; the technology is new, it changes by the day, the general goals of surveillance remain the same, but the means are very frightening. Technology changes our environment, announces itself, strides forward, and dictates how we will live our lives. (Under surveillance, I may do exactly what I did before, but now I know I am not doing it *in private,* and that changes my perception of what I am doing.) Technology is thought out and intentional. Our reaction to the technology, blindsiding us at least once a week, is inchoate for a while, expressed as fears, rejections, often turning into legal or political action before it can be fully formulated. Be impressed: We are present at the creation of a controversy that will be with us for a long time.

Suggested Reading

Stephanie Armour, "Employers Look Closely at What Workers Do on Job," *USA Today Newspaper,* November 8, 2006.

Corey Ciocchetti, "Monitoring Employee E-Mail: Efficient Workplaces vs. Employee Privacy," *Duke Law and Technology Review,* Feb. 6, 2008.

Robert Downes, The Spy Who Employed Me, September 27, 1997. HYPERLINK "http://web.cln.com/archives/atlanta/newsstand/092797/cover2.htm" http://web.cln.com/archives/atlanta/newsstand/092797/cover2.htm Laura Hartman, The Rights and Wrongs of Workplace Snooping, HYPERLINK "http://www.depaul.edu/ethics/monitor.html" http://www.depaul.edu/ethics/monitor.html Dewey Poteet, Employee Privacy in The Public Sector, HYPERLINK "http://www.akingump.com/labor/publications/att_art1.html" http://www.akingump.com/labor/publications/att_art1.html Privacy in America: Electronic Monitoring, HYPERLINK "http://www.aclu.org/library/pbr2.html" http://www.aclu.org/library/pbr2.html Privacy Rights Clearinghouse, Fact Sheet # 7: Employee Monitoring: Is There Privacy in the Workplace?, HYPERLINK "http://www.privacyrights.org/FS/fs7-work.htm" http://www.privacyrights.org/FS/fs7-work.htm

ISSUE 10

Is "Employment-at-Will" Good Social Policy?

YES: Richard A. Epstein, from "A Defense of the Contract at Will," *University of Chicago Law Review* (Fall 1984)

NO: John J. McCall, from "In Defense of Just Cause Dismissal Rules," *Business Ethics Quarterly* (April 2003)

ISSUE SUMMARY

YES: Richard Epstein defends the at-will contract as an appropriate expression of autonomy of contract on the part of both employee and employer and as a means to the most efficient operations of the market.

NO: John McCall argues that the defense of the employment-at-will doctrine does not take account of its economic and social consequences and is in derogation of the very moral principles that underlie private property and freedom of contract.

How can there possibly be any objection to freedom? If I want to make a deal with my neighbor that I will help him move some boxes on Saturday, and he will pay me $20, what could be wrong with that? Suppose I do a really good job moving his boxes. It turns out that he runs an appliance store, and he wants to hire me to move boxes every day. I have the time, the pay's all right, but I have one problem—suppose something better comes along, and I want to up and leave, no offense? Maybe he has a problem, too: There's machinery out there that might make my job unnecessary, and he might want to invest in it next year. So we make a further stipulation: I can leave on thirty days' notice, he can terminate my job on thirty days' notice. We've both bought ourselves more freedom in the future. What's wrong with that?

Note that we don't have to do it that way. I could have said no, I have better things to do Saturday, and no, I don't want to move boxes every day, at least not at that pay. Or, on the other hand, either one of us might be coming off a really bad experience with unreliable bosses or employees, and we might decide to write restrictive terms into the contract—we might make it a five-year contract, with strong penalties on both sides for premature termination, or, as a college professor, I might insist on lifetime tenure in the job before I'll take it. (He might change his mind about hiring me at that point.) If one of those alternatives looks better to us, we can go that way—the law allows us a wide range of freedom in forging our own contracts. But if we choose the first way, what's wrong with it?

Epstein is in the stronger position here, for he only has to say, over and over again, that freedom is good, that autonomy is morally preferable to servitude, and that intelligent people should therefore be free to decide the terms of their own contracts on the basis of their own perceived interests. But the story above is not the situation that raises the question of just-cause dismissal. The story that raises that question is of the employee who took the job in the shop right out of high school, or in the office right out of college, and has now been a faithful employee for twenty-two years. A new boss comes in and decides that the productivity of the shop is not high enough, or the office doesn't look smart enough, so she fires most of the older employees to hire new young people who will look better and work harder. Should she be able to do that?

The point is, as McCall points out, that after twenty-odd years of work, it doesn't seem fair to be tossed out on your ear with only thirty days' notice, too late in your life to make a new career or, often, even to get another job, after all those years of making it to work through rain and snow, loyal to the company, assuming that you'd be at the company working hard for the rest of your life. Contract or no contract, it is not in accordance with justice to reciprocate an effective lifetime of labor with a thirty-day termination. When your employer hired you year after year, wasn't he entering into some kind of super-contract with you, that you would always be there for him and he would always be there for you? If your boyfriend hangs out with you for twenty years, you can call yourself married in the common law, and you can get a financial award from the man if he walks out on you. Shouldn't employment be bound by the same presumptions?

Ask yourself, as you read these selections, what you will expect of an employer. If you're doing your job, shouldn't you be allowed to keep it? If times change and the employer wants something else, shouldn't you have the opportunity to upgrade yourself before your employer upgrades for you?

YES ↵

Richard A. Epstein

In Defense of the Contract at Will

. . . The persistent tension between private ordering and government regulation exists in virtually every area known to the law, and in none has that
tension been more pronounced than in the law of employer and employee
relations. During the last fifty years, the balance of power has shifted heavily
in favor of direct public regulation, which has been thought strictly necessary
to redress the perceived imbalance between the individual and the firm. In
particular the employment relationship has been the subject of at least two
major statutory revolutions. The first, which culminated in the passage of the
National Labor Relations Act in 1935,[1] set the basic structure for collective
bargaining that persists to the current time. The second, which is embodied
in Title VII of the Civil Rights Act of 1964,[2] offers extensive protection to
all individuals against discrimination on the basis of race, sex, religion, or
national origin. The effect of these two statutes is so pervasive that it is easy
to forget that, even after their passage, large portions of the employment relation remain subject to the traditional common law rules, which when all was
said and done set their face in support of freedom of contract and the system
of voluntary exchange. One manifestation of that position was the prominent place that the common law, especially as it developed in the nineteenth
century, gave to the contract at will. The basic position was well set out in an
oft-quoted passage from *Payne v. Western & Atlantic Railroad:*

> [M]en must be left, without interference to buy and sell where they
> please, and to discharge or retain employees at will for good cause or
> for no cause, or even for bad cause without thereby being guilty of an
> unlawful act *per se*. It is a right which an employee may exercise in the
> same way, to the same extent, for the same cause or want of cause as
> the employer.[3]

The survival of the contract at will, and the frequency of its use in private
markets, might well be taken as a sign of its suitability for employment relations. But the contract at will has been in retreat even at common law, as the
movement for public control of labor markets has now spilled over into the
judicial arena. The judicial erosion of the older position has been spurred on by
academic commentators, who have been almost unanimous in their condem-
nation of the at-will relationship, often treating it as an archaic relic that should
be jettisoned along with other vestiges of nineteenth-century laissez-faire.[4] . . .

. . . The contract at will is not ideal for every employment relation. No court or legislature should ever command its use. Nonetheless, there are two ways in which the contract at will should be respected: one deals with entitlements against regulation and the other with presumptions in the event of contractual silence.

First, the parties should be permitted as of right to adopt this form of contract if they so desire. The principle behind this conclusion is that freedom of contract tends both to advance individual autonomy and to promote the efficient operation of labor markets.

Second, the contract at will should be respected as a rule of construction in response to the perennial question of gaps in contract language: what term should be implied in the absence of explicit agreement on the question of duration or grounds for termination? The applicable standard asks two familiar questions: what rule tends to lend predictability to litigation and to advance the joint interests of the parties?[5] On both these points I hope to show that the contract at will represents in most contexts the efficient solution to the employment relation. . . .

I. The Fairness of the Contract At Will

The first way to argue for the contract at will is to insist upon the importance of freedom of contract as an end in itself. Freedom of contract is an aspect of individual liberty, every bit as much as freedom of speech, or freedom in the selection of marriage partners or in the adoption of religious beliefs or affiliations. Just as it is regarded as prima facie unjust to abridge these liberties, so too is it presumptively unjust to abridge the economic liberties of individuals. The desire to make one's own choices about employment may be as strong as it is with respect to marriage or participation in religious activities, and it is doubtless more pervasive than the desire to participate in political activity. Indeed for most people, their own health and comfort, and that of their families, depend critically upon their ability to earn a living by entering the employment market. If government regulation is inappropriate for personal, religious, or political activities, then what makes it intrinsically desirable for employment relations?

It is one thing to set aside the occasional transaction that reflects only the momentary aberrations of particular parties who are overwhelmed by major personal and social dislocations. It is quite another to announce that a rule to which vast numbers of individuals adhere is so fundamentally corrupt that it does not deserve the minimum respect of the law. With employment contracts we are not dealing with the widow who has sold her inheritance for a song to a man with a thin mustache. Instead we are dealing with the routine stuff of ordinary life; people who are competent enough to marry, vote, and pray are not unable to protect themselves in their day-to-day business transactions.

Courts and legislatures have intervened so often in private contractual relations that it may seem almost quixotic to insist that they bear a heavy burden of justification every time they wish to substitute their own judgment for that of the immediate parties to the transactions. Yet it is hardly likely that remote public bodies have better information about individual preferences than the parties who hold them. This basic principle of autonomy, moreover, is not limited to some areas of individual conduct and wholly inapplicable to others. It covers all these activities as a piece and admits no ad hoc exceptions, but only principled limitations. . . .

II. The Utility of the Contract At Will

The strong fairness argument in favor of freedom of contract makes short work of the various for-cause and good-faith restrictions upon private contracts. Yet the argument is incomplete in several respects. In particular, it does not explain why the presumption in the case of silence should be in favor of the contract at will. Nor does it give a descriptive account of *why* the contract at will is so commonly found in all trades and professions. Nor does the argument meet on their own terms the concerns voiced most frequently by the critics of the contract at will. Thus, the commonplace belief today (at least outside the actual world of business) is that the contract at will is so unfair and one-sided that it cannot be the outcome of a rational set of bargaining processes any more than, to take the extreme case, a contract for total slavery. While we may not, the criticism continues, be able to observe them, defects in capacity at contract formation nonetheless must be present: the ban upon the contract at will is an effective way to reach abuses that are pervasive but difficult to detect, so that modest government interference only strengthens the operation of market forces.[6] . . .

In order to show the interaction of all relevant factors, it is useful to analyze a case in which the problem of bilateral control exists, but where the overtones of inequality of bargaining power are absent. The treatment of partnership relations is therefore very instructive because partners are generally social and economic equals between whom considerations of inequality of bargaining power, so evident in the debate over the contract at will, have no relevance. To be sure, the structural differences between partnership and employment contracts must be identified, but these will in the end explain why the at-will contract may make even greater sense in the employment context. . . .

The case for the contract at will is further strengthened by another feature common to contracts of this sort. The employer is often required either to give notice or to pay damages in lieu of notice; damages are traditionally equal to the wages that the employee would have earned during the notice period. These provisions for "severance pay" provide the worker with some protection against casual or hasty discharges, but they do not interfere with the powerful efficiency characteristics of the contract at will. First, lump-sum transfers do not require the introduction of any "for cause" requirement, which could be the source of expensive litigation. Second, because the sums are definite, they can be easily computed, so that administrative costs are minimized. Third, because the payments are unconditional, they do not create perverse incentives for the employee or heavy monitoring costs for the employer: the terminated employee will not be tempted to avoid gainful employment in order to run up his damages for wrongful discharge; the employer, for his part, will not have to monitor the post-termination behavior of the employee in order to guard against that very risk. Thus, provisions for severance pay can be used to give employees added protection against arbitrary discharge without sacrificing the advantages of a clean break between the parties. . . .

The contract at will is also a sensible private adaptation to the problem of imperfect information over time. In sharp contrast to the purchase of standard goods, an inspection of the job before acceptance is far less likely to guarantee its quality thereafter. The future is not clearly known. More important, employees, like employers, *know what they do not know.* They are not faced with a bolt from the blue, with an "unknown unknown." Rather they face a known unknown for which they can plan. The at-will contract is an essential part of that planning because it allows both sides to take a wait-and-see attitude to their relationship so that new and more accurate choices can be made on the strength of improved information. ("You can start Tuesday and we'll see how the job works out" is a highly intelligent response to uncertainty.) To be sure, employment relationships are more personal and hence often stormier than those that exist in financial markets, but that is no warrant for replacing the contract at will with a for-cause contract provision. The proper question is: will the shift in methods of control work a change for the benefit of both parties, or will it only make a difficult situation worse? . . .

1. *Administrative Costs*. There is one last way in which the contract at will has an enormous advantage over its rivals. It is very cheap to administer. Any effort to use a for-cause rule will in principle allow all, or at least a substantial fraction of, dismissals to generate litigation. Because motive will be a critical element in these cases, the chances of either side obtaining summary judgment will be negligible. Similarly, the broad modern rules of discovery will allow exploration into every aspect of the employment relation. Indeed, a little imagination will allow the plaintiff's lawyer to delve into the general employment policies of the firm, the treatment of similar cases, and a review of the individual file. The employer for his part will be able to examine every aspect of the employee's performance and personal life in order to bolster the case for dismissal. . . .

Conclusion

The recent trend toward expanding the legal remedies for wrongful discharge has been greeted with wide approval in judicial, academic, and popular circles. In this paper, I have argued that the modern trend rests in large measure upon a misunderstanding of the contractual processes and the ends served by the contract at will. No system of regulation can hope to match the benefits that the contract at will affords in employment relations. The flexibility afforded by the contract at will permits the ceaseless marginal adjustments that are necessary in any ongoing productive activity conducted, as all activities are, in conditions of technological and business change. The strength of the contract at will should not be judged by the occasional cases in which it is said to produce unfortunate results, but rather by the vast run of cases where it provides a sensible private response to the many and varied problems in labor contracting. All too often the case for a wrongful discharge doctrine rests upon the identification of possible employer abuses, as if they were all that mattered. But the proper goal is to find the set of comprehensive arrangements that will minimize the frequency and severity of abuses by employers and employees alike. Any effort to drive employer abuses to zero can only increase the difficulties inherent in the employment relation. Here, a full analysis of the relevant costs and benefits shows why the constant minor imperfections of the market, far from being a reason to oust private agreements, offer the most powerful reason for respecting them. The doctrine of wrongful discharge is the problem and not the solution. This is one of the many situations in which courts and legislatures should leave well enough alone.

Notes

1. Act of July 5, 1935, ch. 372, 49 Stat. 449 (codified as amended at 29 U.S.C. §§ 151–169 (1982)).

2. Pub. L. No. 88–352, 78 Stat. 253 (codified as amended at 42 U.S.C. §§ 2000e to 2000e–17 (1982)).

3. Payne v. Western & Atl. R.R., 81 Tenn. 507, 518–19 (1884), *overruled on other grounds,* Hutton v. Waters, 132 Tenn. 527, 544, 179 S.W. 134, 138 (1915). The passage continues as follows:

    He may refuse to work for a man or company, that trades with any obnoxious person, or does other things which he dislikes. He may persuade his fellows and the employer may lose all his hands and be compelled to close his doors; or he may yield to the demand and withdraw his custom or cease his dealings, and the obnoxious person be thus injured or wrecked in business.

    81 Tenn. at 519. It should be noted that *Payne* did not itself involve the discharge of an employee for a bad reason or no reason at all. As the last two quoted sentences indicate, the question of the status of the contract arose obliquely, in a defamation suit by a merchant against a railroad. The railroad's yard master had posted a sign that read: "Any employee of this company on Chattanooga pay-roll who trades with L. Payne from this date will be discharged. Notify all in your department." *Payne,* 81 Tenn. at 510.

    The plaintiff Payne claimed that his business, which had been heavily dependent upon the trade of railroad workers, had thereby been ruined. The court held for the defendant on the grounds that (a) there was no defamation implicit in the announcement and (b) the employer's notice to its employees was within its rights because all the contracts with its workers were terminable at will. *Hutton* overruled *Payne,* not on the ground that contracts at will were against public policy, but on an abuse-of-rights theory according to which an employer cannot use his right to discharge employees for the sole purpose of harming third-party interests. The propriety of the *Hutton* theory is a difficult question, but my views tend toward those of the *Payne* court. *See* Epstein, *A Common Law for Labor Relations: A Critique of the New Deal Labor Legislation,* 92 YALE L.J. 1357, 1367–69, 1381 (1983).

4. *E.g.,* Blackburn, *Restricted Employer Discharge Rights: A Changing Concept of Employment at Will,* 17 AM. BUS. L.J. 467, 491–92 (1980); Blades, **Employment at Will** *v. Individual Freedom: On Limiting the Abusive Exercise of Employer Power,* 67 COLUM. L. REV. 1404, 1405–06, 1413–14, 1435 (1967); Blumrosen, *Employer Discipline: United States Report,* 18 RUTGERS L. REV. 428, 428–34 (1964); Feinman, *The Development of the **Employment at Will** Rule,* 2 AM. J. LEGAL HIST. 118, 131–35 (1976); Murg & Scharman, **Employment at Will:** *Do the Exceptions Overwhelm the Rule?,* 23 B.C.L. REV. 329, 338–40, 383–84 (1982); Peck, *Unjust Discharges from Employment: A Necessary Change in the Law,* 40 OHIO ST. L.J. 1, 1–10 (1979); Summers, *Individual Protection Against Unjust Dismissal: Time for a Statute,* 62 VA. L. REV. 481, 484 (1976); Weynard, *Present Status of Individual Employee Rights,* PROC. N.Y.U. 22D ANN. CONF. ON LAB. 171, 214–16 (1970); Note, *Guidelines for a Public Policy Exception to the **Employment at Will** Rule,* 13 CONN. L. REV. 617, 641–42 (1980); Note, *Protecting Employees at Will Against Wrongful Discharge: The Public Policy Exception,* 96 HARV. L. REV. 1931, 1931–35 (1983); Note, *Protecting At Will Employees Against Wrongful Discharge: The Duty to Terminate Only in Good Faith,* 93 HARV. L. REV. 1816, 1824–28 (1980) [hereinafter cited as Note, *Wrongful Discharge*]; Note, *A Common Law Action for the Abusively Discharged Employee,* 26 HASTINGS L.J. 1435, 1443–46 (1975); Note, *Implied Contract Rights to Job Security,* 26 STAN. L. REV. 335, 337–40 (1974); Note, *California's Controls on Employer Abuse of Employee Political Rights,* 22 STAN. L. REV. 1015, 1015–20 (1970).

5. The traditional rule has been codified under current California law: "An employment, having no specified term, may be terminated at the will of either party on notice to the other." CAL. LAB. CODE § 2922 (West 1971). Indeed, this should mean, as it now does, that where a contract speaks of "permanent" employment, the presumption should again be that the contract is terminable at will, for all that "permanent" connotes is the absence of any definite termination date. It does not imply one in which there is a lifetime engagement by either employer or employee, especially where none of the subsidiary terms for such a long-term relationship is identified by the parties. The proper rule of construction should be that the contract is terminable at will by either side.

6. Kronman, *Paternalism and the Law of Contracts,* 92 YALE L.J. 763, 777 (1983). The point is especially important in connection with the law of undue influence, where there is a long historical dispute over the relationship between the adequacy of consideration received and the procedural soundness of the underlying transaction. *See* Simpson, *The Horwitz Thesis and the History of Contracts,* 46 U. CHI. L. REV. 533, 561–80 (1979). Nonetheless, paternalistic explanations, whatever their force elsewhere, have little power in connection with employment relations. Indeed, if one thought it appropriate to restrict the powers of workers to make their own decisions during negotiations over the terms of employment, it might follow that restrictions on their right to participate in unions could be justified as well, for in both instances workers have proven that they often need to be protected against their own folly.

John J. McCall

NO

A Defense of Just Cause Dismissal Rules

I. Introduction

. . . Discussion of business practices often proceeds as if market principles are the only criteria needed in order to assess whether a practice is wise and reasonable. However, purely market-based analyses fail to acknowledge an indisputable fact: all markets operate in a social space that is defined by the moral values of the culture in which they are embedded. An example that illustrates this fact is the difference between U.S. and European practices governing the dismissal of individual employees. If we understand the legal differences between the U.S. and Europe, as well as management's response to those differences, we can see how differences in particular accepted moral norms give a different shape to the marketplace.

In dismissal policy, U.S. law follows a modified Employment at Will (EAW) approach. Corporations have wide discretion in both the procedures and reasons governing an individual employee's termination. For example, except for a handful of reasons identified as illegitimate by statute or past judicial precedent, employers may terminate for any or even for no reason. (Legally prohibited reasons include firings based on race or those in violation of clear public policy.) Employees who successfully press a wrongful discharge case through the courts may stand to recover very sizable awards (in the millions of dollars). However, winning a suit requires that the employee bear the initial burden of establishing that the discharge was for one of the identified illegitimate reasons.

Most European corporations operate in a much different legal environment. There, the legal systems usually mandate a Just Cause approach to dismissal. Under this approach, corporations must notify non-probationary employees of intent to dismiss. They are also significantly limited in the reasons the law will accept as adequate grounds for dismissal. Corporations must supply the employee with the reason for intended dismissal and the employee has the right to challenge the reason, usually in a pre-termination hearing and always before an external, easily accessible, and independent arbiter. Further, the initial burden of proof is on the employer. If, say, an employer wishes to dismiss an employee for poor productivity, the employer must have both clear, previously announced performance standards and evidence that the particular

From *Business Ethics Quarterly*, vol. 13, issue 2, April 2003, pp. 151–153, 161–175. Copyright © 2003 by Business Ethics Quarterly. Reprinted by permission of The Philosophy Documentation Center, publisher of Business Ethics Quarterly. References omitted employee has failed to meet those standards. If successful, aggrieved employees can receive remedies such as some small multiple of wages or re-instatement (though the latter happens in a very small minority of cases). This Just Cause approach places substantially greater limits on the power of European employers to dismiss a worker.

Legal differences, though, are only part of the difference between the U.S. and European dismissal policies. Interviews I have conducted with executives from across the European Community revealed a strong and almost universal moral endorsement of Just Cause requirements. Senior managers in a wide variety of firms (from small local manufacturers to mega-firms whose products are recognizable in the international marketplace, from large national retailers to EC-wide food distributors) expressed the same sentiment when responding to questions about their attitude towards legally mandated Just Cause: The employee deserves not only an in-house hearing but also an external "court of appeal" where he/she can challenge the reasons for dismissal. Management sometimes mentioned the difficulties encountered under such a system but also often described those difficulties as a cost of doing business, a cost that was required by the moral values to which they were committed.

This commitment seems to extend beyond the few managers that I interviewed. No concerted efforts by business specifically to repeal Just Cause dismissal rules has been part of recent European legal reform. There has been a significant change, however, in that the percentage of temporary and part-time work has grown substantially in Europe over the past decade as regulations governing fixed-term employment contracts have been relaxed. Some attribute this change to corporate desires for a more flexible labor law. There is some truth to this. However, we need to be careful in identifying just what flexibility employers desire. Is it, for example, in rules governing individual dismissal or in rules governing severance in cases of collective dismissals? My interviews found the latter to be more a source of complaint.

In the U.S., on the other hand, corporate lobbying efforts historically have resisted legally mandated Just Cause dismissal rules. Just Cause proposals have been introduced in the legislatures of any number of states over the last decades, but only in the case of Montana has the proposal been enacted into law. While quite a number of large U.S. corporations have adopted internal appeals mechanisms and have promised workers that they will be dismissed only for cause, those systems are voluntary and without the easily accessible external appeals mechanisms available to Europeans. (Non-unionized U.S. workers usually must make their case in the court system, a potentially expensive and daunting proposition.) And recently, many U.S. corporations, in a move to prevent costly wrongful firing suits, are requiring workers to sign waiver statements that indicate acceptance of Employment at Will. Even some corporations that have extensive, voluntarily adopted grievance systems have done this. In the U.S., notwithstanding the common cultural heritage with Western Europe, the traditional emphases on economic liberty, competition, and individualism have given a different shape to the labor market. It would appear, at least at first blush, that the U.S. and Europe have sharply different values that are reflected in how employees are treated.

What are the possible responses for ethicists confronted by circumstances where markets are shaped by such conflicting value assumptions? One response, of course, is to retreat into an easy moral and cultural relativism that views cultural differences as simply brute, irresolvable disagreement. That would be too easy, however. For while some disagreements between cultures may be incapable of rational resolution, others might be settled by careful argument. For instance, it may be that analysis could show that one of the conflicting opinions is inadequate even on the basis of its own foundational assumptions. It is always possible that a given particular normative commitment is not justified by the fundamental principles of its own value system. To assume, without analysis, that any particular extant cultural norm is coherent with the basic values espoused by the culture is to assume too much.

Another response is available, then, for ethicists who wish to analyze cultural difference. It is to assess the degree to which the specific conflicting judgments of the cultures are (or are not) reasonable given their respective supporting arguments and underlying principles. In the pages that follow, I suggest that such an analysis will find fault with the arguments advanced in the U.S. against Just Cause. I want to argue that, given the underlying principles revealed by those arguments, the U.S. should drop its opposition and, instead, institute Just Cause protections for workers.

Typically, the arguments against Just Cause divide into two broad categories: those based on predicted dire social consequences and those based on individual right claims. For instance, the more *laissez faire* U.S approach is often defended as both a) more productive, and b) required by the rights to property and freedom of contract. I want to argue, however, that: 1) the empirical prediction of productivity losses with Just Cause is not supported by the evidence; 2) the economic arguments based on ideal market analyses are fraught with difficulties; and 3) the appeals to property or contract rights are insufficient to trump the claimed right of employees to freedom from arbitrary dismissal. Accordingly, I will propose that a Just Cause legal regime is preferable to the current U.S. model.

II. Consequences

Consequentialist objections to Just Cause themselves fall into two broad categories. One is associated with practical management and organizational behavior worries; the other comes from the ideal market analyses of law and economics theorists. Both types of argument are substantially speculative and I believe both have serious shortcomings. . . .

A. Market Arguments

. . . The claims that job security provisions are costly to workers themselves can also be challenged. In order to determine whether workers are better off with job security, we need to identify, in the words of a classic jazz tune, "Compared to What?" Even if, for the sake of argument, we accept that there is a wage premium for workers without job security under EAW rules (contrary to some suggestions above), we need to ask whether workers with job security under a legal EAW regime are economically worse off, not only than workers without job security in that EAW system, but also than workers under a Just Cause regime that grants job security as the initial entitlement (Hager, 1991). Under the latter approach, of course, it is management that must buy the right to terminate at will from employees. Once again, the judgment will likely be influenced by the starting assumptions one makes about the distribution of entitlements.

The previously cited experimental evidence in Millon (1998) about the outcomes of parallel bargaining circumstances where entitlements were reversed is relevant here as well. The evidence cited concerning waivable employment default rules (rules that establish initial legal rules that the parties are free to negotiate around) showed that those persons favored by a default rule do better in negotiations than if the default rule were the opposite. Millon argues that this evidence indicates that workers both with and without job security under a job security default rule will be better off than workers employed at will under an EAW default rule.

Finally, Epstein's argument about the probability of error and the attendant possible harms has fatal flaws. His claim that employer abuse is improbable is discredited by problems noted above. The claim that unfairly dismissed but competent employees are unlikely to suffer serious harm may be an inaccurate description of potential employers' criteria of evaluation. There are reasons for suspecting that an employee who was dismissed, even unfairly, is permanently seen as suspect goods. Additionally, the ease with which even competent employees can find replacement work is overstated. Finally, his appeal to the potential damage to the corporation of large jury verdicts is a red herring, at least as an argument against Just Cause. For, recall that Just Cause policies typically give increased job security for employees in exchange for decreased corporate exposure to the "litigation lottery." For example, in the U.K. there was a limit of £11,000 on unfair dismissal awards (Donkin, 1994). Under Montana's Unfair Dismissal From Employment Act, the maximal award is four times earnings less what one could reasonably have been expected to earn since the termination (Bierman et al., 1993). The potential for large jury awards is irrelevant when assessing the costs of Just Cause.

The preceding theoretical market-based arguments against Just Cause thus fare no better than do those driven by practical management concern for worker productivity. In neither case is there a preponderance of argument to establish that Just Cause damages productivity. And so, these speculative concerns about the potential harmful consequences cannot lead to a rejection of Just Cause.

This final paragraph on the consequential arguments against Just Cause may be an appropriate place to note a tension between the two broad categories of consequential argument we have identified. The motivation argument claimed that workers needed to be motivated by fear of job loss. Such motivation can only be effective if job loss is perceived as both a real possibility and a serious harm. However, some market-based arguments claim that job security provisions are unnecessary and that unfairly dismissed employees are not seriously damaged. But these claims cannot both be true. For if the market already deters abuse, provides for job security, and minimizes the harm of unfair discharge, then the motivational argument loses all force since job loss is unlikely and not harmful. Alternatively, if, as I suspect is more likely, the motivational argument is correct in holding that workers see job loss as a serious harm, then that would disclose the absolute unreality of some of the law and economics objections to Just Cause.

We need now to move to a consideration of the rights based objections to Just Cause policies.

III. Rights

A. Rights Objections

Typically, rights arguments against Just Cause appeal to two members of the generally recognized pantheon of rights—property and freedom of contract (Werhane, 1985; Werhane and Radin, 1999).

Property rights are traditionally understood to involve an owner's entitlement to control goods in specific ways. Owners are entitled, among other things, to possess, to use, to benefit from, to dispose of, and to limit others' use of, benefit from, and access to the thing owned. If we take one's house or car as paradigmatic examples, ownership entitles one to deny access or use rights to others and to revoke previously granted access and use rights. Concretely, I have a right to control who enters my house and a right to ask any guest to leave. Opponents of Just Cause treat corporate property analogously. They argue that owners (or more usually, the agents of owners—managers) retain the right to deny employees further access to the work site, that is, to terminate employment. Legally mandated job security policies are thus unjust interferences with owners' property rights.

The second rights argument against Just Cause sees it as a violation of the right of free individuals to engage in voluntary exchanges with others. By prohibiting contracts with terms that specify employment at will, Just Cause policies interfere with persons' abilities to negotiate for themselves whatever contract provisions they find most desirable. For instance, under some Just Cause regimes, workers may be prohibited from choosing at will employment in exchange for greater income. As such, this second argument claims that Just Cause policies are unjust limits on market agents' freedoms of contract and association (Maitland, 1984; Narveson, 1992; Nozick, 1974). (This claim may not be true, of course. It is possible that Just Cause merely functions as the default interpretation when contracts are silent about dismissal terms, or it could make the job security entitlement one that is waivable by the right holder but only in exchange for at least a statutorily guaranteed minimum consideration.)

B. Method

These arguments are not easily dismissed. The rights they appeal to have powerful rhetorical force, especially in the U.S. But before we accept them as cogent objections, we need to clarify the circumstances of the debate. The debate over Just Cause is a case of conflicting right claims. Management and owners claim rights to property and freedom of contract. Workers claim conflicting rights to freedom from arbitrary and unfair discharge. It is true that the first two rights have existing recognition while, in the U.S. at least, the third is at best what Joel Feinberg calls a manifesto right, one claimed to be supported by good reasons but not yet socially sanctioned. However, its manifesto status is not a reason for allowing property and freedom of contract rights immediately to "trump" job security. For it may be that, on analysis, we decide that our current understanding of rights fails in not recognizing a right to job security.

A more reasonable method for resolving conflicts between rights claims must directly assess the merits of the competing claims. Moreover, a reasonable method will do more than consider the relative importance of the conflicting rights in some general and abstract way. Rather, resolving conflicts between rights requires us to focus on the particular cases where the conflict arises since the conflict between rights typically occurs in defined marginal areas. Recognizing job security rights, for example, will not interfere with conceptions of non-corporate property rights, nor will it impact other aspects of corporate property rights, such as the right freely to sell one's shares in the market.

We can satisfy these requirements for a reasonable assessment of rights conflicts if we ask two questions of each of the competing claims: 1) What are the justifying or foundational reasons for this right (why is it a right)? 2) What harm would be done to those underlying values if we recognized a conflicting right claim and thus marginally constrained the scope of a particular right? Here, for instance, we need to ask what are the foundations of property, freedom of contract, and job security rights, and what harm would be done to those respective values if we denied a right to job security and gave owners the right to terminate at will or, alternatively, if we denied owners that right and instituted a Just Cause policy.

C. Response to Property Objections

What are the foundations of property rights? There is a very clear historical tradition of argument justifying rights to private ownership of property (that is rights privately to control goods, to benefit from them, to exclude others from using them, etc). In the modern period, individual rights to possess property privately have three significant foundations: autonomy, fairness, and utility. First, private control over property has been presented as instrumentally advancing an owner's autonomy by providing her a secure base of material possessions that frees her from over-reliance on the decisions of others. Second, it has been upheld as the only approach that fairly rewards the effort expended or the risk assumed in a productive activity. Finally, it has been urged as providing incentive for people to work and invest, thus raising the total amount of economic production and, in turn, the net standard of living.

Interestingly, the claimed right of employees to job security can be argued to rest on the same grounds: Dismissals can be arbitrary (fairness). They can damage the worker's ability to gain a wage, and thus make life both less happy (utility) and less within his/her control (autonomy). Workers who are no longer able to rely on secure income will have many significant life choices foreclosed (autonomy). Just Cause, then, can be defended on the same grounds of autonomy, fairness, and utility that are the traditional supports for private property rights.

What harm to these three underlying values would be done if corporations were required by Just Cause rules to extend job security to their workers? Would constraining the scope of an owner's right to deny access to corporate property hamper fairness or autonomy for owners? Would overall social utility be decreased if workers had a right to be free from arbitrary and unfair dismissal?

1. Fairness

First, consider the question about relative impacts on fairness. As was previously noted, property rights, and the associated rights to benefit from and to control goods, are historically justified, in part, on fairness grounds. But fairness, as the parent of any young child will attest, is often simultaneously both an overused and underdefined moral concept. Nonetheless, appeals to fairness can be more reasonably grounded than the simple assertion of "That's not fair!" if clear criteria are available. Criteria for assessing the fairness of a distribution, for example, typically will refer to three considerations: contribution, risk, and/or arbitrariness. Fair treatment requires that allocations of goods (and entitlements over them) be proportional to a person's contribution or risk assumed in creating the goods. It also requires that goods and benefits not be allocated to (or removed from) a person for arbitrary reasons. Since investors bear risk and make a contribution, risk and contribution are intuitively good, not arbitrary, moral reasons for allocating to them rights to privately control corporate property.

However, Just Cause rules do not erase owners' control over corporate property; they merely alter the right to control at the margins. Owners, even under Just Cause, still retain substantial control over assets—they can sell their shares freely; they can collectively dictate to management (with some limits) corporate policy, they retain rights to residual income, etc. This marginal decrease in an owner's control over property under Just Cause seems, whether on grounds of contribution or risk, insufficient to override an employee claim to job security because employees can also point to past contribution and risk as well. In addition, they can assert that they ought not be removed from employment without good cause, that is, for arbitrary reasons. Thus, recognizing an employee claim of dismissal only for good cause simply reduces the owner's marginal control. Moreover, evidence above also suggests that the Just Cause may have small impact on the owner's return/benefit.

Some, of course, will object to this analysis by arguing that the wages paid by the market assure fair treatment of workers (presumably because the wage rate is consensual). In this argument, so long as employees are paid for their past work, they have been fully compensated for their effort, risk, and contributions. They thus have no claim on future employment.

A number of points can be made in response to this argument that wages are full and fair compensation. The assumption (that past wages are adequate compensation for past contribution) may be challenged. Consider, for example, evidence from some analyses of internal labor markets (the labor market as it operates within a firm). These analyses claim that employees are paid less than their marginal contribution to the firm in the earlier years of their career and more than their marginal contribution later in their career (because wages and benefits tend to rise over time in a way that is not based purely on increased productivity). This deferred compensation of the early years is recouped only gradually. Employers can also use the deferral as a mechanism to reduce monitoring costs and to bind a worker to the firm, thus also reducing turnover costs (since a voluntary quit means foregoing deferred wages). Employers reap benefits from this aspect of the internal labor market. However, when an employee is fired without good cause, employers can also opportunistically and unfairly seize the promised future wages. (Blair, 1995; Lazear, 1992; Osterman, 1992; and Weiler, 1990) Thus, it is not necessarily the case that past wages can be assumed to be full and fair compensation for previous contribution. Terminating without good cause may instead be a paradigmatically unfair seizure.

However, even if we assume that the wage already paid is fair compensation for one's past risk and contribution, the issue here is whether terminating a relationship without good cause is acceptable on fairness grounds. It may not be if certain conditions are present. For example, even where pay for past contributions is morally adequate, it is possible that management actions created an expectation of future employment, expectations upon which employees relied. (See, for instance, Kim, 1999 and Singer, 1988, for discussions of ways in which reliance is elicited by particular firms and by economic institutions more broadly. It is worth noting that such reliance has historically been to the firm's advantage, allowing it to secure long term labor and to reduce monitoring costs.) What is fair can be a function not only of wages agreed to but also of promises made (explicitly and implicitly) and of consequent patterns of reliance.

Moreover, the fact that representations upon which employees relied were made by the firm's agents is not the only relevant consideration here. Such representations may be sufficient to raise questions of fairness but they are not necessary. Fairness norms can be implicated as well when, even without clear representations that created reliance, one party has come to depend in basic ways on a relationship or practice. When others crucially depend on and expect continued participation in a cooperative enterprise, it appears patently unfair to abruptly end the relationship without notice and without good reason, an idea we reflect in our common moral assessments of contexts as varied as marriage, housing, and access to traditional routes of public passage through private property. (See Singer, 1989 and Beerman and Singer, 1988 for extended discussions of how these moral assessments are reflected in much of our settled law in areas other than employment.) Thus, giving either party in an employment relationship the power to terminate the relationship without due process and good cause violates commonly held norms of fairness where there is long-standing dependence and expectation. It is especially unfair when one party has the preponderance of power.

The preceding point is merely an instance of a more general point: fair treatment in employment relationships often involves more than consensual monetary exchange. Employees clearly can be paid adequately but nonetheless treated unfairly if subjected to harassment or merely to ridicule. Thus there is clear need to consider when termination, even when past wages were adequate, is compatible with reasonable criteria of fairness. It is presumptively not when corporate actions create expectations of future employment. Dismissal without good reason from one's source of income, from one's social network, and from all the other goods associated with employment would seem to run afoul of this reliance criterion of fairness as well. So, even if past wages were adequate, it is still possible that a dismissal is unfair if it is based on arbitrary reasons.

We have, then, strong reasons for suggesting that firing without good cause, and thus removing a person from a source of income upon which he/she crucially depends, is inherently arbitrary and unfair. We need however to become more precise about what constitutes good cause and whether the set of reasons described as "good cause" is equivalent to the set of reasons accepted under Just Cause policies. It may, of course, be the case that Just Cause rules are more substantively restrictive than merely requiring that dismissal be for morally acceptable, good cause. We can evaluate whether this is the case by identifying the cases where Just Cause rules differ from EAW in the substantive grounds for permissible discharge. Recall that both Just Cause and EAW allow dismissal on grounds of inadequate performance, theft, absenteeism, etc. There are, though, at least three main scenarios where Just Cause is more restrictive than EAW. These are its prohibitions on dismissal for no reason, for personal reasons that are unrelated to productivity, and for the reason that there is a more productive replacement available for a currently adequate employee.

The first and second of these reasons seem to be paradigmatic examples of unfair treatment. Terminating a person's employment for no reason or for purely personal reasons is the epitome of arbitrary treatment. The third reason seems more defensible, however. Maintaining a current employee who merely performs adequately when there are others available who project to be superior performers certainly appears to damage the interests of the firm, as well as the interests of owners and, indeed, of other workers. Dismissing such an employee and replacing him with the predicted superior performer could, from that perspective, be argued as neither arbitrary nor unfair. Under this analysis, cause for termination exists whenever the firm possesses any competitive economic reason for dismissal.

We should reiterate here the previous point about the systemic effects of a firm's labor practices. Allowing the contemplated replacement policy is not a simple exchange of two workers, one for the other. Instead, it alters the entire system of employee relations. As noted above, it is not obvious that the potential gain of the more productive worker is greater than the opportunity costs inherent in adopting this replacement policy. Here, however, the question is not the productivity impact of the replacement but its fairness. At least two serious questions may be raised about the fairness of a policy that allows the replacement of an adequate performer whenever another is available who projects to be superior.

First, we need to ask which persons might be placed at greater risk by allowing such replacement. Arguably, allowing an adequate performer to be replaced would differentially impact more mature workers who might have both higher wages and declining productivity. The removal of longer-term employees whose loyalty has been a benefit to the firm in the past would seem to run counter to notions of fair treatment (for reasons of both contribution and expectation), and would seem to impose unreasonable demands for productivity over the course of a working career. A replacement policy of the sort under discussion here conjures the image of persons (human resources) being used up and disposed of.

Of course, the current American structure is not strict EAW but rather an EAW modified by numerous pieces of employment legislation, legislation that includes a prohibition on age discrimination. Thus, the fact that strict EAW might have this differential impact on mature workers is not to say that current U.S. legal standards would have this impact. This is true enough. But nonetheless, Just Cause would differ from even the modified U.S. version of EAW in that it places the burden of proof in termination on the employer rather than on the employee (as the U.S. law does). This fact is not insignificant given the substantial hurdles faced by plaintiffs under U.S. law and given the attitudinal sea change that would be indicated by adoption of Just Cause policy.

Second, and more importantly, allowing the replacement of an adequate performer has unacceptable implications for ideas about what corporations are entitled to. If we assume that a corporation has set reasonable standards of adequate performance, an open-ended policy permitting replacement of adequate performers essentially entails that employers can threaten dismissal unless ever-increasing productivity demands are satisfied. This demand for optimal, "110%" productivity goes beyond what any partner to an economic relationship is morally entitled. Employers are entitled to reasonable productivity and may morally threaten dismissal if a worker fails to meet that standard. Of course, a necessary condition for a reasonable demand is that a worker could meet it but being able to meet a demand is not sufficient to establish its reasonableness. For a demand to be reasonable, it must be one that can be met, not at any cost, but at a reasonable cost. That is, what is a reasonable demand must be seen in light of what we believe a decent human life to include. Demands that jeopardize goods that are constitutive of such a life are demands that are unreasonable. (Consider, from a wholly different context, Judith Thomson's (1971) analysis of what demands can reasonably be placed on a woman in order for her to avoid having to accept responsibility for pregnancy.) Workplace productivity demands that have seriously damaging impacts on family and social existence are, on any account of a decent human life, demands that are unreasonable. More generally, workplace demands that so exhaust a person's energy or time that other central aspects of life must be neglected are demands that go beyond what a corporation is reasonably entitled to. Given the unavoidable and central role that employment plays in contemporary life, a policy that allows employers to demand ever-increasing productivity under threat of dismissal is an unreasonable policy.

We have, then, grounds for believing that the set of morally good reasons for dismissal map on to that set of reasons for dismissal allowed under Just Cause rules. We can also see that some of the reasons for dismissal allowed under even the limited EAW of the U.S. are reasons that fall outside the set of morally good reasons. And, as argued above, firing without good reasons is arbitrary and, hence, unfair. Thus, the very considerations of fairness that are used in the American tradition to justify private property suggest that corporate property rights be limited by the adoption of Just Cause constraints on dismissal.

2. Autonomy

A private property right justified by appeal to autonomy seems a similarly unlikely candidate for overriding a right to be free from arbitrary dismissal. In Locke's original formulation of the argument, private property gave landowners some autonomy because it conferred on them an economic independence, especially from the powers of the crown. In the contemporary environment, most workers have whatever measure of economic independence they possess, not from landed estates, but from the security of the income gained by selling their labor on the market. To the degree that income is at risk from job loss, then to that degree workers have lost independence. Arbitrary dismissal, therefore, can substantially damage the ability of a worker to control important aspects of his/her life. On the other hand, precluding arbitrary dismissal through a Just Cause policy does not seriously decrease the degree to which the share-holders' investment in stock provides for economic independence and, hence, does not impact the ability of investors to have control over their lives. (For a more complete version of this analysis of the relation between autonomy, property, and employee rights, see McCall, 2001.)

Of course, someone might argue that Just Cause policies decrease the owner's autonomy and independence because they would decrease value of the investment. That presupposes that productivity and/or profits will decline as a result of job security. As was noted above, that assumption has not been shown to be warranted. But even if stock value or investment income did marginally decline, proponents of job security could respond by arguing that owners are entitled not to maximal return but merely to returns compatible with a requirement to treat others fairly. An invocation of the preceding fairness argument, then, has the potential to blunt even the speculative concern that job security would decrease share value or return.

It should be noted that the preceding analyses have been assuming as a context a moderately large, publicly traded corporation. Analyzing the impact of Just Cause on fairness and autonomy might be different for smaller ventures or ones that are owned by individuals or small numbers of partners. Citibank and the mom and pop corner grocery are at different extremes and may require different policies in practice. Requiring the corner grocer, or for that matter a regular employer of a household worker, to follow the same dismissal procedures as Citibank may more seriously damage the employer's control over his/her life. There may then be an argument for limiting the scope of Just Cause policies to businesses over a certain threshold size. We need to be aware, however, that even in small firms, arbitrary dismissal can still have a devastating impact on the employee and his/her family. Perhaps some mandatory severance but without the procedural requirements would be in order even for the smaller employer. If that were a known requirement, it could be planned for and calculated into the total cost of a person's employment, just as employer Social Security payments already are.

3. Utility

The analysis of the impact of mandated job security on net utility is perhaps less clear, partly because projections about future social consequences are so speculative. But some have claimed, as we have seen, that job security requirements will lower return to investors (thus depressing investment and production), reduce productivity, lower wages for employees, and depress overall employment. A number of points have been made in rebuttal of these charges above. These will not be repeated here. As for the impact on total employment, Just Cause would seem to have little net effect. It does not commit employers to keep workers who are unproductive, nor does it require them to keep workers when there is a downturn in demand. Just Cause may have an impact on the care and speed with which firms select permanent employees but it should not affect total employment levels. (See a similar analysis even for the more costly requirements of severance and restrictions on layoffs in Abraham and Houseman, 1993 and 1994, as well as Houseman, 1990.)

An item to watch, however, is whether Just Cause will increase the incentive of companies to hire temporary workers in order to avoid the process requirements for discharging employees who have completed the probationary period. This would be a significant effect given the income, benefits, and security differences between permanent and temporary work. Recent revisions in European law might provide a test case for this; the evidence is still out. I suspect, moreover, that the evidence of increased use of temporary workers is not clearly due to Just Cause rather than to other, more expensive requirements attaching to treatment of fulltime employees (e.g., other benefits or layoff provisions).

Whether the wages of other workers would decline and thus have an impact on overall utility will depend on whether there really is a wage premium for workers employed at will. This may not be the case since Just Cause appears to have little impact on net corporate income and, therefore, little effect on the employers' wage bargaining stance. Moreover, the evidence cited by Millon (1998) and discussed above makes the assumption of a wage premium problematic. However, if there nonetheless *is* a wage premium and workers under Just Cause are precluded from gaining that premium (which of course would only occur under non-waivable Just Cause rules), a utilitarian justification of Just Cause will depend in part on the benefits and costs of job security to workers, and on the relative size of the employee populations interested respectively in security or the potentially greater income gained without security. Pursuit of these questions will be left for the next section's discussion of freedom of contract.

D. Response to the Freedom of Contract Argument

In order to assess the conflict between freedom of contract rights and rights to job security, we need to ask about the foundations of freedom of contract just as we have asked about the foundations of property and job security rights. Freedom of contract has been defended on grounds of utility in that each person, as best judge of his/her own interests, is also in the best position to optimize the satisfaction of those interests. Allowing each person in the competitive marketplace to determine which goods he/she desires and how much he/she is willing to pay for them will, it is claimed, maximize the net satisfaction of interests.

A second defense of freedom of contract is on grounds of individual autonomy in that freedom of contract will obviously allow persons more direct control over their lives than if the ability to negotiate one's own terms were restricted. For instance, some will argue that employees should have the freedom to choose the job rules they prefer rather than be forced by legal mandates to accept "benefits" they do not wish to have. (Compare Narveson's (1992) argument on mandated worker participation.)

Of course, our commitment to autonomy does not result in absolute freedom of contract, as those in favor of Just Cause will be quick to note. In employment law in particular, we already accept a myriad of limits on the power of parties to set the terms of contracts. Laws governing discrimination, workplace safety, minimum wage, and sexual harassment are just a few instances where we constrain both employers and employees in negotiating contract terms. Since freedom of contract is not equivalent to absolute freedom of contract, the argument against Just Cause is incomplete unless it can show that Just Cause limits are inappropriate while other limits are acceptable. (I do not mean to suggest that all current legal limits on contracts, or even all those just mentioned, must be accepted. Rather, the point is that if one accepts any limits on contracts then one needs to distinguish those from the limits one does not accept. I also take it that a position which rejects all limits is *prima facie* an unreasonable one.)

Some might respond that acceptable limits are ones that are needed to correct for clear market failures. But, the argument continues, there are no clear failures with respect to job security. We have already discussed in Section II the reasons for suspecting that market failures of knowledge, power, and mobility might explain the relative absence of job security provisions in U.S. contracts. To the degree that those points are telling, then this attempt fails to distinguish job security from other market correcting limits on contracts.

However, even if there are no market failures with respect to job security, the response is problematic for other reasons. Not every justifiable limit on freedom of contract exists merely to remedy market failure. It would be odd indeed to claim that Civil Rights protections against discrimination and sexual harassment are responses to classic market failures. Rather, it is more natural to see such laws as expressing the belief that jeopardizing a person's employment for these morally arbitrary reasons is degrading and simply wrong.

So, some limits on contract freedoms can be defended on grounds other than correction of market failures. This is true of job security protections as well. If we accept the preceding fairness arguments, we might use Just Cause limits on employment contracts to underscore social opposition to the serious, avoidable, and arbitrary harms caused by at-will dismissals. Or, if we modeled an autonomy argument on traditional utility analysis, we might construct a "net autonomy" case for Just Cause as follows. Workers dismissed without cause suffer at least temporary loss of income, the stress that comes with that and, in all probability, loss of seniority and firm specific investment. These harms are proportionally greater the more that the dismissal would impact one's future employment applications. All of these economic losses will have serious impacts on the real life choices available to the dismissed worker. There is significant impact, then, on autonomy. The limits caused by job security requirements on the autonomy of other workers who might wish to trade security for increased income are not nearly so great. They merely lose the (speculative) marginal wage increase that might be available under at-will contracts. Moreover, this loss is not a necessary consequence of Just Cause rules. It occurs only when those rules are mandated as un-waivable; they need not be. Constraining freedom of contract, then, might produce more net autonomy for workers than would a discharge at will rule.

So, job security protections may be a rational choice for society either because workers who want them are unable to negotiate for them successfully (the market failure explanation) or because we simply want, as part of a commitment to fairness, institutionally to express an opposition to dismissals without just cause, or because we believe such protections maximize net autonomy.

Finally, we should note the following with respect to utility claims. Some provision prohibiting firing without cause is one of the first demands of union contracts. It would be surprising if unorganized workers somehow desired job security less. More reasonable is the assumption that they desire it but have been unable to secure individually for themselves what organized workers have secured. If this is true and workers generally want security, then perhaps net satisfaction would be also increased by legally proscribed protections against unfair dismissal.

IV. Conclusion

A review of the objections to Just Cause, both on grounds of consequences and rights, reveals them to be seriously deficient. Most seriously, the very foundational values of the rights commonly used in the U.S. to oppose Just Cause suggest, instead, that job security should be pursued. Concerns for fairness and autonomy arguably ought to drive the U.S. toward Just Cause requirements rather than away from them. The American resistance to Just Cause seems unwarranted on its own grounds once one recognizes that the American system of private property and freedom of contract depend on fairness and autonomy.

There is, however, a reason for resisting the introduction of Just Cause requirements that we have not yet addressed. It may be, despite the rhetoric, that Just Cause policies are simply ineffective at protecting workers from unfair dismissals. That is, while a Just Cause mechanism may be necessary for protecting workers, it may be that it alone is not sufficient. After all, most extant Just Cause policies place significant limits on the compensation available to employees when arbitrators judge them to have been unfairly dismissed. So, some might argue that current Just Cause policies cannot achieve their stated goals because they provide disincentives that are insufficient to deter arbitrary dismissals.

In fact, a survey of the Montana Bar Association completed in 1993 suggests that the Montana Wrongful Discharge from Employment Act may not adequately protect workers. More than half of the attorney respondents claimed that they personally declined to represent a plaintiff in a wrongful discharge suit. Most who said this cited as their reason the inadequate compensation available under the act given the complexity and hours involved in such suits. Perhaps more strikingly, a number of respondents reported that they believed that the act's reduction in liability for corporations had made some corporations more likely to discharge unfairly since they were no longer concerned about large damage awards (Bierman et al., 1993).

It might be that, since punishments under some extant Just Cause regimes, particularly in Montana and the U.K., are relatively small, employers who are not already committed to principles of fair dismissal will have little reason not to discharge without cause. If that is the case, what could the advantage of Just Cause be over the current American approach that at least poses the threat of the litigation lottery? There may still be two reasons for preferring Just Cause. First, a smaller, but highly probable, award for cases of unjust dismissal seems preferable to a litigation lottery where only some unfairly dismissed workers are even eligible for compensation (e.g., if they have been subject to the few unacceptable grounds enumerated under the U.S. approach). Unfairly dismissed workers are treated more equitably as a class and in relation to each other under Just Cause. And, the greater probability of an award might still serve as a disincentive for unjust termination, especially were the maximum awards more generous than those in the U.K. and Montana.

Second, the adoption of a Just Cause approach serves as a statement of public opposition to dismissal without cause. Law, in addition to its deterrence function, can also be a vehicle for educating and for creating or re-enforcing publicly important values. Law can serve the purpose of public notice of society's basic value commitments. The Civil Rights laws of the 1960s may be an historical example of how law can play a role in reshaping extant social norms that are incompatible with the espoused foundational values of the culture. So, while some currently extant Just Cause approaches may not alone guarantee protection for workers against unfair dismissal, properly constructed and publicized Just Cause laws can assist in readjusting a value system so that employers are more likely to be socialized to accept the principles of Just Cause. This would be a benefit in that it would make American employment practice more adequately reflect the espoused foundational values of its own culture.

Precisely how any U.S. Just Cause protections ought to be codified requires more debate than is possible here. Three distinct possibilities suggest themselves. (See Sunstein, 2001 and 2002, Eastlund 2002, Millon 1998.) One is that Just Cause merely be made the default rule when employment contracts fail to specify dismissal rules. This approach would allow employers and employees to contract around the default rules by adopting specific alternate provisions in the employment contract. Another approach is to make Just Cause the default but also mandate that any opting out of the default rule will provide both for some specified minimum level of compensation and some specific remaining employment protection. A third option would be to follow the lead of most of the industrialized world and to mandate non-waivable Just Cause protections for workers in all firms exceeding a small minimum size. Which of these approaches fits best with the moral values underlying the modern American commitment to private property is a matter for further argument. That argument will have to wait for another article. However, even without that analysis, we can conclude that some Just Cause protections for employees have very strong presumptive support.

Note

I would like to thank George Brenkert for some helpful comments that made this paper more cogent and more clear. I would also like to hold him responsible for any serious argumentative gaffes—but I doubt I can get away with that.

Bibliography

Abraham, Katherine, and Susan Houseman. 1993. *Job Security in America*. Washington, D.C.: The Brookings Institute.

_____. 1994. "Does Employment Protection Inhibit Labor Market Flexibility?" In *Social Protection versus Economic Flexibility*. Rebecca Blank, ed. Chicago: University of Chicago Press.

Beerman, Jack, and William Singer. 1989. "Baseline Questions in Legal Reasoning: The Case of Property in Jobs." *Georgia Law Review* 23: 911.

Bierman, Leonard, et at. 1993. "Montana's Wrongful Discharge from Employment Act: The Views of the Montana Bar." *Montana Law Review* 54: 367.

Blair, Margaret M. 1995. *Ownership and Control: Rethinking Corporate Governance for the Twenty-First Century*. Washington, D.C.: The Brookings Institute.

Donkin, Richard. 1994. "Making Fairness Work." *The Financial Times,* Management Section. September 7, 1994, p. 12.

Dworkin, Ronald. 1977. *Taking Rights Seriously*. Cambridge, Mass.: Harvard University Press.

Eastlund, Cynthia. 2002. "How Wrong Are Employees about Their Rights, and Why Does it Matter?" *New York University Law Review* 77: 6.

Epstein, Richard. 1984. "In Defense of Contract at Will." *University of Chicago Law Review* 51: 947.

Hager, Mark. 1991. "The Emperor's Clothes Are Not Efficient." *American University Law Review* 41: 7.

Houseman, Susan. 1990. "The Equity and Efficiency of Job Security." In *New Developments in the Labor Market*. K. Abraham and R. McKersie, eds. Cambridge, Mass: MIT Press.

Kim, Pauline T. 1997. "Bargaining with Imperfect Information: A Study of Worker Perceptions of Legal Protection in an At-Will World." *Cornell Law Review* 83: 105.

_____. 1999. "Norms, Learning and Law: Exploring the Influences on Workers' Legal Knowledge." *University of Illinois Law Review* 1999: 447.

Lazear, Edward P. 1992. "Compensation, Productivity and the New Economics of Personnel." In *Research Frontiers in Industrial Relations and Human Resources*. D. Lewin et al., eds. Madison, Wis.: Industrial Relations Research Association.

Maitland, Ian. 1989. "Rights in the Workplace." *Journal of Business Ethics* 8: 951.

McCall, John J. 2001. "Employee Voice in Corporate Governance: A Defense of Strong Participation Rights." *Business Ethics Quarterly* 11: 1.

Millon, David. 1998. "Default Rules, Wealth Distribution and Corporate Law Reform." *University of Pennsylvania Law Review* 146: 975.

Narveson, Jan. 1992. "Democracy and Economic Rights." In *Economic Rights.* E. Paul et al., eds. Cambridge: Cambridge University Press.

Nozick, Robert. 1974. *Anarchy, State and Utopia.* New York, N.Y.: Basic Books.

Osterman, Paul. 1992. "Internal Labor Markets in a Changing Environment." In *Research Frontiers in Industrial Relations and Human Resources.* D. Lewin et al., eds. Madison, Wis.: Industrial Relations Research Association.

Singer, Joseph William. 1988. "The Reliance Interest in Property." *Stanford University Law Review* 40: 614.

Sunstein, Cass R. 2001. "Human Behavior and the Law of Work." *Virginia Law Review* 87: 205.

_____. 2002. "Switching the Default Rule." *New York University Law Review* 77: 106.

Thomson, Judith Jarvis. 1971. "In Defense of Abortion." *Philosophy and Public Affairs* 1: 1.

Weiler, Paul. 1990. *Governing the Workplace.* Cambridge, Mass.: Harvard University Press.

Werhane, Patricia. 1985. *Persons, Rights and Corporations.* Englewood Cliffs, N.J.: Prentice Hall.

Werhane, Patricia, and Tara Radin. 1999. "Employment at Will and Due Process." In *Ethical Issues in Business: A Philosophical Approach,* 6th ed. Thomas Donaldson and Patricia Werhane, eds. Upper Saddle River, N.J.: Prentice Hall.

POSTSCRIPT

Is "Employment-at-Will" Good Social Policy?

Ultimately, the rights of Americans are determined by law. In Europe, as McCall points out, the laws are much more protective of the employee than they are in the United States. Epstein and others claim that European-style laws lead to less "efficiency"; that it is more difficult in Europe for investors to make money quickly. McCall and others argue that we should not be trampling fundamental notions of justice in order to achieve trifles more of efficiency. What do you think?

Suggested Reading

If the subject interests you, you might find interesting the following readings:

Cynthia Eastlund, "How Wrong Are Employees about Their Rights, and Why Does It Matter?" *New York University Law Review* 77:6, 2002.

Richard Green et al., "On the Ethics of At-Will Employment in the Public Sector," Public Integrity, vol.8, no.4, Fall 2006.

Edward P. Lazear, "Compensation, Productivity and the New Economics of Personnel," in D. Lewin et al., eds., *Research Frontiers in Industrial Relations and Human Resources* (Madison, WI: Industrial Relations Research Association).

Thomas Donaldson and Thomas Dunfee, *Ties That Bind* (Boston: Harvard University Press, 1999).

ISSUE 11

Is CEO Compensation Justified by Performance?

YES: Ira T. Kay, from "Don't Mess with CEO Pay," *Across the Board* (January/February 2006)

NO: Edgar Woolard, Jr., from "CEOs Are Being Paid Too Much," *Across the Board* (January/February 2006)

ISSUE SUMMARY

YES: Ira Kay, a consultant on executive compensation for Watson Wyatt Worldwide, argues that in general the pay of the CEO tracks the company's performance, so in general CEOs are simply paid to do what they were hired to do–bring up the price of the stock to increase shareholder wealth.

NO: Edgar Woolard, a former CEO himself, holds that the methods by which CEO compensation is determined are fundamentally flawed, and suggests some significant changes.

"CEOs are paid a lot to face facts, however unpleasant," writes Geoffrey Colvin in *Fortune*, "so it's time they faced this one: The issue of their pay has finally landed on the national agenda and won't be leaving soon." He ticks off the sources of national discontent with the enormous sums (and stocks, etc.) paid to the corporate chiefs: that layoffs continue, that the lowest-paid workers advance only slowly, that Japanese CEOs are paid much less for much more productivity—but mostly, just that paying one person more money than he can ever spend on anything worthwhile for himself or his family, while the world's millions struggle, suffer, and starve, just seems to be wrong.

For the fifth edition of this text (1998), the "No" side of the debate was carried by John Cassidy's 1997 *New Yorker* article "Gimme." Even then we could not use Colvin's 1992 article. For since Colvin wrote, Cassidy pointed out, chief executive compensation had gone much higher—by a factor of four for the average compensation, up to factors of fifteen and twenty for fortunate individuals. Colvin had clucked at annual compensation from $1.5 million to as high as $3 million a year; Cassidy observed compensation already at the $18 million and $20 million level. For the sixth edition of this text (2000), Cassidy no longer sufficed. Compensation had gone up to $60, $70, $90 million. The reason for the increase is clear enough—stock prices have gone up, shareholder wealth has increased enormously, and for reasons detailed in both of the selections that follow, shareholders wish to compensate management of their companies according to the increase in the price of the stock. Two questions arise immediately: First, if that's the system, what are we to do with compensation "insurance" policies that guarantee the same compensation no matter where the stock goes? Don't those arrangements kind of miss the point? And the second question is, Is this right? The shareholders' interests legitimately dictate some aspects of corporate policy, and the salaries have been agreed upon by the legally appropriate parties, but if the result is substantially unjust, should not the people as a whole step in and rectify the situation?

Urgency was added to the issue in the recession that followed the election of George W. Bush in 2000. As the computers rolled in early April 2001, stocks had undergone a sudden "correction," read, gone very far south, and shareholder wealth decreased substantially. Do we find CEO compensation humbly bowing to the facts of the ROI? Not in the least. "While typical investors lost 12 percent of their portfolios last year [2000], based on the Wilshire 5000 total market index, and profits for the Standard & Poor's 500 companies rose at less than half their pace in the 1990's, chief executives received an average 22 percent raise in salary and bonus." So we found out from a Special Report on Executive Pay from the *New York Times* on April 1, 2001 (First Business Page), and that was no April Fool. Not much had changed in 2005, according to *Forbes,* when Peter Cartwright of Calpine, which runs gas-fired power plants, took home (over the last six years) average annual compensation of $13 million while the ROI of the company over the same period was—7 percent. Average compensation over the last five years for Terry Semel of Yahoo came to $258.3 million; for Barry Diller of IAC/InterActiveCorp, $239.9 million; for William McGuire of UnitedHealth Group, $342.3 million. That last is cause for pause: your health care dollars and mine fueled that income. We knew the doctors weren't getting rich; now we know who is. You see how these 2005 figures dwarfed those that so bothered Geoffrey Colvin.

Should the American people step in and claim the right to set limits in the name of justice to the outsized amounts lavished on the fortunate sons of capitalism? That possibility is precisely what troubles Colvin. If CEOs will not regulate their own compensation, Congress and the SEC could surely step in and do a bit of regulating on their own. The prospect is not enticing to the business community. On the other hand, is this not exactly why we have government—so that when private motives get out of hand, the people as a whole can step in and defend their long-term interests?

Bear in mind, as you read the following selections, that the corporation was set up as a private enterprise, literally: a voluntary contract among investors to increase their wealth by legal means. But it is chartered and protected by the state, in the service of the state's long-term interest in a thriving economy. Adam Smith would be pleased; he argued that leaving investors to make money as best they could for their own selfish interests would best increase the welfare of the whole body of the people. The question that confronts us is, At what point do we conclude that the legal means set up for private parties to serve our interests by serving their own have failed in their purported effect and should be modified or revised? Or do we have any right to do that at this point? What do you think?

YES ↵

Ira T. Kay

Don't Mess with CEO Pay

For years, headlines have seized on dramatic accounts of outrageous amounts earned by executives—often of failing companies—and the financial tragedy that can befall both shareholders and employees when CEOs line their own pockets at the organization's expense. Images of lavish executive lifestyles are now engraved in the popular consciousness. The result: public support for political responses that include new regulatory measures and a long list of demands for greater shareholder or government control over executive compensation.

These images now overshadow the reality of thousands of successful companies with appropriately paid executives and conscientious boards. Instead, fresh accusations of CEOs collecting huge amounts of undeserved pay appear daily, fueling a full-blown mythology of a corporate America ruled by executive greed, fraud, and corruption.

This mythology consists of two related components: the myth of the failed pay-for-performance model and the myth of managerial power. The first myth hinges on the idea that the link between executive pay and corporate performance—if it ever existed—is irretrievably broken. The second myth accepts the idea of a failed pay-for-performance model and puts in its service the image of unchecked CEOs dominating subservient boards as the explanation for decisions resulting in excessive executive pay. The powerful combination of these two myths has captured newspaper headlines and shareholder agendas, regulatory attention and the public imagination.

This mythology has spilled over into the pages of *Across the Board*, where the September/October cover story links high levels of CEO pay to the country's growing income inequality and wonders why U.S. workers have not taken to the streets to protest "the blatant abuse of privilege" exercised by CEOs. In "The Revolution That Never Was," James Krohe Jr. manages to reference Marie Antoinette, Robespierre, Adam Smith, Alexis de Tocqueville, Andrew Jackson, Kim Jong II, Jack Welch, guerrilla warfare, "economic apartheid," and police brutality in Selma, Ala., in an article that feeds virtually every conceivable element of the myth of executive pay and wonders why we have not yet witnessed calls for a revolution to quash the "financial frolics of today's corporate aristocrats."

In a very different *Across the Board* feature story published a few months earlier, the myth of managerial power finds support in an interview with one of the myth's creators, Harvard professor Lucian Bebchuk, who believes that the pay-for-performance model is broken and that executive control over boards is to blame. Bebchuk is a distinguished scholar who has significant insights into the executive-pay process, but he greatly overestimates the influence of managerial power in the boardroom and ignores empirical evidence that most companies still operate under an intact and explicit pay-for-performance model. And although he acknowledges in his interview with *ATB* editor A.J. Vogl that "American companies have been successful and executives deserve a great deal of credit," his arguments about managerial power run counter to the realities of this success.

Fueling the Fiction

These two articles, in different ways, contribute to what is now a dominant image of executives collecting unearned compensation and growing rich at the expense of shareholders, employees and the broader community. In recent years, dozens of reporters from business magazines and the major newspapers have called me and specifically asked for examples of companies in which CEOs received exorbitant compensation, approved by the board, while the company performed poorly. Not once have I been asked to comment on the vast majority of companies—those in which executives are appropriately rewarded for performance or in which boards have reduced compensation or even fired the CEO for poor performance.

I have spent hundreds of hours answering reporters' questions, providing extensive data and explaining the pay-for-performance model of executive compensation, but my efforts have had little impact: The resulting stories feature the same anecdotal reporting on those corporations for which the process has gone awry. The press accounts ignore solid research that shows that annual pay for most executives moves up and down significantly with the company's performance, both financial and stock-related. Corporate wrongdoings and outlandish executive pay packages make for lively headlines, but the reliance on purely anecdotal reporting and the highly prejudicial language adopted are a huge disservice to the companies, their executives and employees, investors, and the public. The likelihood of real economic damage to the U.S. economy grows daily.

For example, the mythology drives institutional investors and trade unions with the power to exert enormous pressure on regulators and executive and board practices. The California Public Employees' Retirement System—the nation's largest public pension fund—offers a typical example in its Nov. 15, 2004, announcement of a new campaign to rein in "abusive compensation practices in corporate America and hold directors and compensation committees more accountable for their actions."

The AFL-CIO's website offers another example of the claim that managerial power has destroyed the efficacy of the pay-for-performance model: "Each year, shocking new examples of CEO pay greed are made public. Investors are concerned not just about the growing size of executive compensation packages, but the fact that CEO pay levels show little apparent relationship to corporate profits, stock prices or executive performance. How do CEOs do it? For years, executives have relied on their shareholders to be passive absentee owners. CEOs have rigged their own compensation packages by packing their boards with conflicted or negligent directors."

The ROI of the CEO

As with all modern myths, there's a grain of truth in all the assumptions and newspaper stories. The myths of managerial power and of the failed pay-for-performance model find touchstones in real examples of companies where CEOs have collected huge sums in cash compensation and stock options while shareholder returns declined. (You know the names—there's no need to mention them again here.) Cases of overstated profits or even outright fraud have fueled the idea that executives regularly manipulate the measures of performance to justify higher pay while boards default on their oversight responsibilities. The ability of executives to time the exercise of their stock options and collect additional pay through covert means has worsened perceptions of the situation both within and outside of the world of business.

These exceptions in executive pay practices, however, are now commonly mistaken for the rule. And as Krohe's article demonstrates, highly paid CEOs have become the new whipping boys for social critics concerned about the general rise in income inequality and other broad socioeconomic problems. Never mind that these same CEOs stand at the center of a corporate model that has generated millions of jobs and trillions of dollars in shareholder earnings. Worse, using CEOs as scapegoats distracts from the real causes of and possible solutions for inequality.

The primary determinant of CEO pay is the same force that sets pay for all Americans: relatively free—if somewhat imperfect—labor markets, in which companies offer the levels of compensation necessary to attract and retain the employees who generate value for shareholders. Part of that pay for most executives consists of stock-based incentives. A 2003 study by Brian J. Hall and Kevin J. Murphy shows that the ratio of total CEO compensation to production workers' average earnings closely follows the Dow Jones Industrial Average. When the Dow soars, the gap between executive and non-executive compensation widens. The problem, it seems, is not that CEOs receive too much performance-driven, stock-based compensation, but that non-executives receive too little.

The key question is not the actual dollar amount paid to a CEO in total compensation or whether that amount represents a high multiple of pay of the average worker's salary but, rather, whether that CEO creates an adequate return on the company's investment in executive compensation. In virtually every area of business, directors routinely evaluate and adjust the amounts that companies invest in all inputs, and shareholders directly or indirectly endorse or challenge those decisions. Executive pay is no different.

Hard Realities

The corporate scandals of recent years laid bare the inner workings of a handful of public companies where, inarguably, the process for setting executive pay violated not only the principle of pay-for-performance but the extensive set of laws and regulations governing executive pay practices and the role of the board. But while I condemn illegal actions and criticize boards that reward executives who fail to produce positive financial results, I know that the vast majority of U.S. corporations do much better by their shareholders and the public. I have worked directly with more than a thousand publicly traded companies in the United States and attended thousands of compensation-committee meetings, and I have *never* witnessed board members straining to find a way to pay an executive more than he is worth.

In addition, at Watson Wyatt I work with a team of experts that has conducted extensive research at fifteen hundred of America's largest corporations and tracked the relationship between these pay practices and corporate performance over almost twenty years. In evaluating thousands of companies annually, yielding nearly twenty thousand "company years" of data, and pooling cross-sectional company data over multiple years, we have discovered that for both most companies and the "typical" company, there is substantial pay-for-performance sensitivity. That is, high performance generates high pay for executives and low performance generates low pay. Numerous empirical academic studies support our conclusions.

Our empirical evidence and evidence from other studies have produced the following key findings:

1. Executive pay is unquestionably high relative to low-level corporate positions, and it has risen dramatically over the past ten to fifteen years, faster than inflation and faster than average employee pay. But executive compensation generally tracks total returns to shareholders—even including the recent rise in pay.
2. Executive stock ownership has risen dramatically over the past ten to fifteen years. High levels of CEO stock ownership are correlated with and most likely the cause of companies' high financial and stock-market performance.
3. Executives are paid commensurate with the skills and talents that they bring to the organization. Underperforming executives routinely receive pay reductions or are terminated—far more often than press accounts imply.
4. CEOs who are recruited from outside a company and have little influence over its board receive compensation that is competitive with and often higher than the pay levels of CEOs who are promoted from within the company.
5. At the vast majority of companies, even extraordinarily high levels of CEO compensation represent a tiny fraction of the total value created by the corporation under that CEO's leadership. (Watson Wyatt has found that U.S. executives receive approximately 1 percent of the net income generated by the corporations they manage.) Well-run companies, it bears pointing out, produce significant shareholder returns and job security for millions of workers.

Extensive research demonstrates a high and positive correlation between executive pay and corporate performance. For example, high levels of executive stock ownership in 2000, created primarily through stock-option awards, correlated with higher stock-market valuation and long-term earnings per share over the subsequent five-year period. In general, high-performing companies are led by highly paid executives—with pay-for-performance in full effect. Executives at low-performing companies receive lower amounts of pay. Reams of data from other studies confirm these correlations.

Why CEOs Are Worth the Money

The huge gap between the realities of executive pay and the now-dominant mythology surrounding it has become even more evident in recent years. Empirical studies show that executive compensation has closely tracked corporate performance: Pay rose during the boom years of the 1990s, when U.S. corporations generated huge returns, declined during the 2001–03 profit slowdown, and increased in 2004 as profits improved. The myth of excessive executive pay continued to gain power, however, even as concrete, well-documented financial realities defied it.

The blind outrage over executive pay climbed even during the slowdown, as compensation dropped drastically. During this same period, in the aftermath of the corporate scandals, Congress and the U.S. regulatory agencies instituted far-reaching reforms in corporate governance and board composition, and companies spent millions to improve their governance and transparency. But the critics of executive pay and managerial power were only encouraged to raise their voices.

It might surprise those critics to learn that CEOs are not interchangeable and not chosen by lot; they are an extremely important asset to their companies and generally represent an excellent investment. The relative scarcity of CEO talent is manifested in many ways, including the frenetic behavior of boards charged with filling the top position when a CEO retires or departs. CEOs have significant, legitimate, market-driven bargaining power, and in pay negotiations, they use that power to obtain pay commensurate with their skills. Boards, as they should, use their own bargaining power to retain talent and maximize returns to company shareholders.

Boards understand the imperative of finding an excellent CEO and are willing to risk millions of dollars to secure the right talent. Their behavior is not only understandable but necessary to secure the company's future success. Any influence that CEOs might have over their directors is modest in comparison to the financial risk that CEOs assume when they leave other prospects and take on the extraordinarily difficult task of managing a major corporation, with a substantial portion of their short- and long-term compensation contingent on the organization's financial success.

Lucian Bebchuk and other critics underestimate the financial risk entailed in executive positions when they cite executives' large severance packages, derided as "golden parachutes." Top executive talent expects and can command financial protections commensurate with the level of risk they assume. Like any other element of compensation, boards should and generally do evaluate severance agreements as part of the package they create to attract and retain talent. In recent years, boards have become more aware of the damage done when executive benefits and perquisites are excessive and not aligned with non-executive programs, and are now reining in these elements.

Properly designed pay opportunities drive superior corporate performance and secure it for the future. And most importantly, many economists argue, the U.S. model of executive compensation is a significant source of competitive advantage for the nation's economy, driving higher productivity, profits, and stock prices.

Resetting the Debate

Companies design executive pay programs to accomplish the classic goals of any human-capital program. First, they must attract, retain, and motivate their human capital to perform at the highest levels. The motivational factor is the most important, because it addresses the question of how a company achieves the greatest return on its human-capital investment and rewards executives for making the right decisions to drive shareholder value. Incentive-pay and pay-at-risk programs are particularly effective, especially at the top of the house, in achieving this motivation goal.

Clearly, there are exceptions to the motivational element—base salaries, pensions, and other benefits, for example—that are more closely tied to retention goals and are an essential part of creating a balanced portfolio for the employee. The portfolio as a whole must address the need for income and security and the opportunity for creating significant asset appreciation.

A long list of pressures, including institutional-investor pushback, accounting changes, SEC investigations, and scrutiny from labor unions and the media, are forcing companies to rethink their executive-compensation programs, especially their stock-based incentives. The key now is to address the real problems in executive compensation without sacrificing the performance-based model and the huge returns that it has generated. Boards are struggling to achieve greater transparency and more rigorous execution of their pay practices—a positive move for all parties involved.

The real threat to U.S. economic growth, job creation, and higher living standards now comes from regulatory overreach as proponents of the mythology reject market forces and continue to push for government and institutional control over executive pay. To the extent that the mythology now surrounding executive pay leads to a rejection of the pay-for-performance model and restrictions on the risk-and-reward structure for setting executive compensation, American corporate performance will suffer.

There will be more pressure on boards to effectively reduce executive pay. This may meet the social desires of some constituents, but it will almost surely cause economic decline, for companies and the U.S. economy. We will see higher executive turnover and less talent in the executive suite as the most qualified job candidates move into other professions, as we saw in the 1970s, when top candidates moved into investment banking, venture-capital firms, and consulting, and corporate performance suffered as a result.

Our research demonstrates that aligning pay plans, incentive opportunities, and performance measures throughout an organization is key to financial success. Alignment means that executives and non-executives alike have the opportunity to increase their pay through performance-based incentives. As new regulations make it more difficult to execute the stock-based elements of the pay-for-performance model, for example, by reducing broad-based stock options, we will see even less alignment between executives' compensation and the pay packages of the rank-and-file. We are already witnessing the unintended consequences of the new requirement for stock-option expensing as companies cut the broad-based stock-option plans that have benefited millions of workers and given them a direct stake in the financial success of the companies for which they work.

Instead of changing executive pay plans to make them more like pay plans for employees, we should be reshaping employee pay to infuse it with the same incentives that drive performance in the company's upper ranks. A top-down regulatory approach to alignment will only damage the entire market-based, performance-management process that has worked so well for most companies and the economy as a whole. Instead of placing artificial limits on executive pay, we should focus squarely on increasing performance incentives and stock ownership for both executive and non-executive employees and rewarding high performers throughout the organization, from top to bottom. Within the context of a free-market economy, equal opportunity—not income equality by fiat—is the goal.

The short answer to James Krohe's question of why high levels of executive pay have not sparked a worker revolution is that the fundamental model works too well. Workers vote to support that model every day when they show up for work, perform well, and rely on corporate leadership to pursue a viable plan for meeting payroll and funding employee benefits. Shareholders vote to support the model every time they purchase shares or defeat one of the dozens of proposals submitted in recent years to curb executive compensation. Rejecting the pay-for-performance model for executive compensation means returning to the world of the CEO as caretaker. And caretakers—as shown by both evidence and common sense—do not create high value for shareholders or jobs for employees.

In some ways, the decidedly negative attention focused on executive pay has increased the pressure that executives, board members, HR staffs, and compensation consultants all feel when they enter into discussions about the most effective methods for tying pay to performance and ensuring the company's success. The managerial-power argument has contributed to meaningful discussions about corporate governance and raised the level of dialogue in boardrooms. These are positive developments.

When the argument is blown into mythological proportions, however, it skews thinking about the realities of corporate behavior and leads to fundamental misunderstandings about executives, their pay levels, and their role in building successful companies and a flourishing economy. Consequently, the mythology now surrounding executive compensation leads many to reject a pay model that works well and is critical to ongoing growth at both the corporate and the national economic level. We need to address excesses in executive pay without abandoning the core model, and to return the debate to a rational, informed discussion. And we can safely leave Marie Antoinette out of it.

Edgar Woolard, Jr.,

→ NO

CEOs Are Being Paid Too Much

There's a major concern out there for all of us. I personally am extremely saddened by the loss of the respect that this country's corporate leaders have experienced. We've had a double blow in the last ten years or so. The first one we know way too much about—the fraud at Enron, Tyco, Adelphia, World-Com, and many others.

The CEOs say there were a few rotten apples in that barrel, and maybe that's the answer—but there are a hell of lot more rotten apples than I would have ever guessed. But that's just the base of one of the issues that has eroded the trust and confidence in American business leaders.

The second one is the perception of excess compensation received by CEOs getting worse year by year. And if directors agree, they can be the leaders in making a very important change. I'd like to deal with it by describing several myths about compensation and trying to undermine them.

Myth #1: CEO Pay by Competition

The first is the myth that CEO pay is driven by competition—and to that I say "bull." CEO pay is driven today primarily by outside consultant surveys, and by the fact that many board members have bought into the concept that your CEO has to be at least in the top half, and maybe in the top quartile. So we have the "ratchet, ratchet, ratchet" concept. We all understand it well enough to know that if everybody is trying to be in the top half, everybody is going to get a hefty increase every year. If Bill and Sally get an increase in their total compensation, I have to get an increase so that I will stay in the top half.

How can we change that?

In 1990, we addressed this issue at DuPont. I became CEO in 1989, and I was concerned about what was evident even then. A 1989 *Business Week* article talked about executive pay—who makes the most and are they worth it: Michael Eisner, $40 million in 1988; Ross Johnson, $20 million; and others. I don't know Eisner, but I know that even fifteen years later he's one of the most criticized CEOs in the country.

What we did at DuPont was go to a simple concept: internal pay equity. I went to the board and the compensation committee and said, "We're going to look at the people who run the businesses, who make decisions on prices and new products with guidance from the CEO—the executive vice presidents— and we're going to set the limit of what a CEO in this company can be paid at 1.5 times the pay rate for the executive vice president—50 percent."

From *Across the Board,* January/February 2006. Copyright © 2006 by Conference Board, Inc. Reprinted by permission.

That to me seemed equitable. It had been anywhere from 30 to 50 percent in the past. I said, "Let's set it at 50 percent, and we're not going to chase the surveys." And this is the way DuPont has done it ever since. I think we have tweaked it up a little bit since then, but using a multiple still is the right way to go.

Board members can do this by suggesting that the HR and compensation people look at what's happened to internal pay equity, and seriously consider going in that direction. That will solve this problem in a great way.

Myth #2: Compensation Committees Are Independent

I give a "double bull" to this one. It could be that committees are becoming more independent, but over the last fifteen years they certainly haven't been.

Let me describe how it works: The compensation committee talks to an outside consultant who has surveys that you could drive a truck through and that support paying anything you want to pay. The consultant talks to the HR vice president, who talks to the CEO. The CEO says what he'd like to receive—enough so he will be "respected by his peers." It gets to the HR person, who tells the consultant, and the CEO gets what he's implied he deserves. The members of the compensation committee are happy that they're independent, the HR person is happy, the CEO is happy, and the consultant gets invited back next year.

There are two ways to change that as well. Here's the first one. When John Reed came back to the New York Stock Exchange to try to clean up the mess after Dick Grasso, he made the decision—which I admire him for—that the board was going to have its own outside consultant, one who was not going to be allowed to talk to internal people—not to the HR vice president, not to the CEO.

I'm the head of the comp committee at the NYSE, and when I talk with our outside consultant, he gives us his ideas of what he thinks the pay package ought to be. Then, with the consultant there, I talk to the compensation committee, and we make a decision. I talk to the HR vice president to see if he has any other thoughts, but the committee is totally independent.

The other way to change things is to truly insist on pay-for-performance, which everyone likes to talk about but no one does. Boards pay everybody in the top quartile whether they have good performance or bad performance—or even if they're about to be fired.

Well, I was on a board fifteen years ago, and four CEOs were on the compensation committee, and for two consecutive years, we gave the CEO and the executives there no bonus, no salary increase, and modest stock options, because their performance was lousy those years. After that, they did extremely well, and we paid them extremely well. That's how pay-for-performance should work.

Myth #3: Look How Much Wealth I Created

This one is really a joke. It was born in the 1980s and '90s during the stock-market bubble, when all CEOs were beating their chest about how much wealth they were creating for shareholders. And I'd look to the king, Jack Welch. Jack's the best CEO of the last fifty years, and I've told him this. But he likes to say, "I created $400 billion worth of wealth." No, Jack—no, you didn't. He said that when GE's stock was at 60, but when the bubble burst it went to 30, and it's in the low 30s now. So he created $150 to $200 billion.

But besides the actual figure, there are two things wrong with his claim. Now, I don't care how much money Jack Welch made. God bless him; I think he's terrific. But what did it do? It set a new level for CEO pay based on the stock-market bubble; all the other CEOs were saying, "Look how much wealth I created."

So you've got this more recent high level of executive pay, and then you've got the ratcheting effect in the system. Those things have to change.

Myth #4: Severance for Failing

The last one is the worst of all. Any directors who agree to give these huge severance pay packages to CEOs who fail—Philip Purcell of Morgan Stanley got $114 million, Carly Fiorina of Hewlett-Packard got $20 million—why are you doing that? No one else gets paid excessively when they fail. They get fired; they get fair severance.

All of this is killing the image of CEOs and corporate executives. When it comes to our image, we're in the league with lawyers and politicians. I don't want to be there, and I don't think you do either. We need the respect of our employees and the general public. And there's a lot of skepticism about leaders in politics and in churches and in the military—but we can't have it in the business community, because we're the backbone of the market system that has made this country great and created so many opportunities for people. We can't be seen as either dishonest or greedy.

What can you do about it?

Some of you CEOs need to show leadership and say, "We're going to do internal pay equity." It's easy to get the data, and then you can decide what you think is fair and how much you think the CEO contributes versus the other business leaders who make their companies so strong.

Compensation committees need to seriously consider implementing internal pay equity. Pay only for outstanding performance. Quit giving people money just because Bill and Sally are getting it. Consider going to an independent consultant that deals only with the board while you deal with HR and the CEO.

Last, take a look at stock-option packages. Not just for one year but the mega-grants that built up in the 1980s and '90s. If you've given huge stock-option packages for the last five years, look at their value. There's nothing in the Bible that says that you have to give increased stock options every year. Give a smaller grant; give a different kind of grant; put some kind of limits on.

There are many ways to do it, but it's important to get the system back under control. It's important for our image, for our reputation, for integrity, for trust, and for our leadership in this country.

POSTSCRIPT

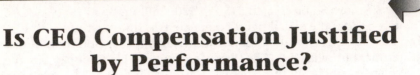

Is CEO Compensation Justified by Performance?

In 1992, when Geoffrey Colvin wrote the article bringing the problem of CEO compensation to public attention, he was worried about the country's perception of annual outlays of $1.7 million average total CEO compensation for almost 300 large companies, with pay going up to a whopping $3.2 million annually for the really big companies. By 1995, the CEO of a multibillion-dollar company received an average of $4.37 million in compensation, up 23 percent from 1994. And it got worse from there, with 1996 figures going through the roof: how on earth could Jack Welch, CEO of General Electric, spend the $21.4 million in salary and performance bonuses (and about $18 million in stock options) that he received in 1996, or Green Tree Financial Corporation's Lawrence Coss spend his $102.4 million in salary and bonus (plus stock options worth at least $38 million)? The Business Section of *The New York Times* at the end of 1997 glowed with projected bonuses of $11 billion for Wall Street that year—that was over and above salary, and before stock options. Two years later, Jack Welch was pulling in $68 million. As per the introduction to this issue, the amounts then tripled, quadrupled, into amounts per individual that dwarf the annual health budgets of most of the world. The situation is not correcting itself.

The political impact of these salaries is muted for the present, probably due to the failure of the American left, or liberal political orientation, to find a powerful spokesperson who might gain the confidence of the American people. The moral dimensions of the problem have not changed since the days of the prophet Amos of the Hebrew Scriptures: What right have the rich to enjoy their warm palaces and mansions, dining plentifully on the best food from all the world, while the poor suffer from hunger and cold? But the political dimensions are volatile, and dependent upon the rest of the system to provide context and opportunity. This issue will be with us for a while.

Suggested Reading

For further information on this subject, look into the following:

The Bible: Books of Amos and Hosea, Gospel according to Matthew.

AP dispatch, April 21, Cleveland. "Welch Defends Pay: Ratio Proposal Rejected by Shareholders," *Connecticut Post*, Thursday, April 22, 1999, C1-C2.

Thomas A. Stewart, "CEO Pay: Mom Wouldn't Approve," *Fortune*, vol. 135 (March 31, 1997), pp. 119–20.

Mike Maharry, "AFL-CIO Launches Web Site to Expose CEO Pay Levels." *The New Tribune*, Tacoma, Washington (April 11, 1997).

The New York Times Special Report on Executive Pay, First Business Page (April 1, 2001).

Peter Truell, "Another Year, Another Bundle: Billions in Bonuses Are Expected to Fall on Wall Street," *The New York Times*, Business Day (December 5, 1997), pp. D1–4.

John A. Byrne, "Gross Compensation?" *Business Week* (March 18, 1996), pp. 32–33.

Jack Lederer and Carl R. Weinberg, "CEO Compensation: Share the Wealth," *Chief Executive*, vol. 116, (September 1996), pp. 30–47.

Dana Wechsler Linden and Vicki Contavespi, "Incentivize Me, Please," *Forbes* (May 27, 1991), pp. 208–12.

Frederick Schmitt, "Study Finds CEO Salaries Tracking Performance," *National Underwriter* (October 21, 1996), p. 48.

Peter Passell, "A Theory of Capitalism: Lonely, and Rich at the Top," *The New York Times* (August 27, 1995), p. E5.

Jean McGuire, Sandra Dow and Kamal Argheyd, "CEO Incentives and Corporate Social Performance," *Journal of Business Ethics,* vol. 45, no. 4 (July 2003).

Internet References . . .

Advertising World

Advertising World, maintained by the Department of Advertising at the University of Texas at Austin, links to numerous sites on marketing and advertising. Among the many indexed topics are ethics and self-regulation, consumer interest, public relations, and market research.

http://advertising.utexas.edu/world/

Overlawyered.com

Overlawyered.com explores an American legal system that too often turns litigation into a weapon against guilty and innocent alike, erodes individual responsibility, rewards sharp practice, enriches its participants at the public's expense, and resists even modest efforts at reform and accountability. This page focuses on litigation over auto safety.

http://overlawyered.com/topics/auto.html

The Pew Initiative on Food and Biotechnology

The Pew Initiative on Food and Biotechnology was established as an independent and objective source of information that encourages research and debate on agricultural biotechnology. It is the purpose of this site to provide a resource that would enable consumers as well as policymakers to make their own informed decisions on the subject.

http://pewagbiotech.org

Consumer Issues

*W*hat does the customer have a right to expect from the maker of the products that he buys? The answer, essentially, is quality and honesty. It sounds simple, but somehow we cannot be sure that the manufacturers are giving us good products and the salesmen are telling the truth about them; the controversies have never ceased.

- Is Direct-to-Consumer Advertising of Pharmaceuticals Bad for Our Health?
- Was Ford to Blame in the Pinto Case?
- Should We Require Labeling of Genetically Modified Food?

ISSUE 12

Is Direct-to-Consumer Advertising of Pharmaceuticals Bad for Our Health?

YES: Sidney M. Wolfe, from "Direct-to-Consumer Advertising—Education or Emotion Promotion?" *The New England Journal of Medicine* (February 14, 2002)

NO: Alan F. Holmer, from "Direct-to-Consumer Advertising—Strengthening Our Health Care System," *The New England Journal of Medicine* (February 14, 2002)

ISSUE SUMMARY

YES: In this powerful debate, invited by *The New England Journal of Medicine*, two students of current pharmaceutical practices square off: Sidney Wolfe, M.D., of the Public Citizen Health Research Group in Washington, D.C., cites the dangers of overpromoting cures to the consumer.

NO: Alan Holmer, J.D., of the Pharmaceutical Research and Manufacturers of America, also in Washington, insists that more information for consumers can only improve the health of Americans.

There is a work in the Hippocratic corpus, in fact, *The Decorum,* in which the physician, while treating the patient, is advised "to perform all this quickly and adroitly, always concealing from the patient what you are doing." The patient is to be told nothing of the diagnosis or prognosis, "for much harm has come from this in the past." Of patients, it was assumed that they knew little of the conditions of their bodies, and that they knew even less about treatments and drugs. All the patients needed to do was to follow the doctor's orders. As for the reasons for those orders, there was no point in trying to explain within the compass of a visit what it had taken the physician four years of medical school to learn.

The prevailing doctrine on sharing information with patients followed the Hippocratic author exactly: Patients need to be cheered with optimistic forecasts that would set their minds at rest, for if they heard bad news, they would surely take a turn for the worse. Medical ethics, then, which forbids the physician to "do harm" to the patient, required deception and concealment.

Naturally, the same ethic was applied to any drugs that might be prescribed. The physician was to give patients medicine, or prescribe it for the local pharmacist, with the same cheery optimism evidenced in the treatment to that point: Patients were assured that the medicine would surely help their condition, whether or not the physician felt any such confidence.

The consumer movement of the 1960s and 1970s produced different patients and eventually, different physicians. Informed consent became the rule in medicine: The physician had to tell the patient everything that a reasonable patient might want to know about the treatment proposed, especially about its risks, or risk liability if anything went wrong. Consumers were also asking hard questions about the cars and food that they bought; it was only a matter of time before they started asking about the medications they bought at the pharmacy. Especially as drugs became more expensive, consumers wanted to know what they were really buying, and soon, whether there might be a less expensive alternative—a knockoff or generic version of the medicine. It was an earth-shaking change: A culture that had tamely bought Bayer for headaches and Phillips for constipation all through the century suddenly discovered supermarket brands and many other choices. Pharmaceutical companies became understandably concerned for their future.

Advertising was not new to the pharmaceutical industry. Drug reps had gone from physician's office to physician's office promoting their brands, sometimes using highly suspect means to get physicians to prescribe them. But direct-to-consumer advertising was very rare. It has been legal for some time, so long as adequate provision was made for disclosing risks and contraindications, but the FDA tended to be very strict about what constituted "adequate provision"—until the 1997 FDA guidelines that simplified and clarified the methods of creating an acceptable marketing campaign. Since then, the ads have blanketed TV land, extolling the virtues of brand X and the wondrous relief it will bring to the suffering viewers, but always concluding, "Ask your doctor if brand X is right for you."

Is this right? Note that the placebo effect cuts two ways in direct-to-consumer advertising: If the drug is in fact right for the patient's condition, and the physician prescribes it, the TV aura will do most of the work of the physician in boosting the confident hope of the patient that will lead to healing. It can speed the work of the drug and shorten the patient's illness. On the other hand, if the drug is not in fact right for the patient's condition and the physician refuses to prescribe it, the patient leaves the office half convinced that whatever the physician did prescribe is inferior to the drug he has already convinced himself he needs, and the TV aura will have a *negative* placebo effect, retarding the effectiveness of the treatment adopted. It may simply drive the patient to another physician who might be more cooperative.

Bear in mind, as you read these selections, that the practice of medicine is very old, and this controversy, like the medicines around which it swirls, are very new. Where, in this field, does consumer choice really fit? Do the advertisements really convey enough information to constitute informed consent? Should the ads be banned—or voluntarily forgone by the pharmaceutical industry?

YES ↵

Sidney M. Wolfe

Direct-to-Consumer Advertising— Education or Emotion Promotion?

During the past two decades, there has been an irreversible change in the nature of the doctor-patient relationship. Patients are seeking much more medical information and are actively participating in decisions affecting their health. Intruding into this trend has been the rise of direct-to-consumer promotion, which, in its initial thrust, bypasses primary care doctors and other physicians. Although increased access by patients to accurate, objective information about tests to diagnose and drugs to treat illnesses is an important advance, confusion arises when commercially driven promotional information is represented as educational. Two articles in this issue of the *Journal* address the direct-to-consumer promotion of medical products and services. Rosenthal et al.[1] describe the resources allocated to direct-to-consumer advertising of prescription drugs, as compared with other forms of promotion. Lee and Brennan[2] examine issues arising from the direct-to-consumer marketing of high-technology medical screening tests. These articles raise several questions. Is direct-to-consumer advertising educational or emotional? How often is it misleading? Is enforcement by the Food and Drug Administration (FDA) of advertising regulations adequate? What can be done to neutralize the negative effect of this type of advertising?

In an excellent review of direct-to-consumer promotion, Mintzes stated that "the question is not whether consumers should obtain information about treatment options; the question is whether drug promotion—whose aim is to sell a product—can provide the type of information consumers need."[3] Addressing the issue of pharmaceutical advertising more generally 30 years ago in the *Journal*, Ingelfinger[4] argued that "advertisements should be overtly recognized for what they are—an unabashed attempt to get someone to buy something, although some useful information may be provided in the process." He suggested that such advertising should be divested of its "pseudo-educational character."

Serious deficiencies have been documented in the educational value of advertising for prescription drugs. In a survey of 1872 viewers of television advertisements, 70 percent thought they had learned little or nothing more about the health condition requiring treatment, and 59 percent thought they

From *The New England Journal of Medicine*, vol. 346, no. 7, February 14, 2002, pp. 524–526. Copyright © 2002 by Massachusetts Medical Society. All rights reserved. Reprinted by permission.

knew little or nothing more about the drug being advertised.[5] Another study found that whereas many advertisements provided information about the name and symptoms of the disease for which the drug was being promoted, few educated patients about the success rate of the drug, the necessary duration of use, alternative treatments (including behavioral changes) that could improve their health, or misconceptions about the disease to be treated. The average number of "educational codes" (i.e., specific learning points relating to a medical condition or a treatment) present in the advertisements was only 3.2 out of a possible 11.[6]

None of these deficiencies should be surprising in the light of the characterization of advertising by the Canadian economist Stephen Leacock as "the science of arresting the human intelligence long enough to get money from it." Leacock also thought that, for the purpose of selling, advertising "is superior to reality."[7] An advertisement, aimed at the marketers of pharmaceutical products, from an agency that creates drug advertisements provides some revealing insights about how the process works. The promotional material describes the hippocampus as the "prescription-writing center of the brain"—the part that "processes information by connecting new concepts with the parts of the brain where gut instincts are formed, areas that influence emotional behavior and form memories." The advertising agency asserts that its "communications are focused on making the hippocampus respond positively to your product . . . [by demonstrating] how your product is superior and unique."[8] An executive of a company that focuses on direct-to-consumer advertising commented that "consumers react emotionally, so you want to know how they feel about your message and what emotional triggers will get them to act. . . . We want to identify the emotions we can tap into to get that customer to take the desired course of action."[9] Another article, describing problems the drug industry has had in adapting to direct-to-consumer marketing, said that companies "are overly focused on communicating rational attributes to customers. But consumers often choose a product on [the basis of] emotional attributes. . . . How an emotional appeal fits into fair balance in advertising prescription drugs under the requirements and approval process of FDA is not clear."[10]

Patients have dangerous misperceptions about direct-to-consumer advertising. According to one study, a substantial proportion of people incorrectly believed that only the safest and most effective drugs could be advertised directly to consumers and that the FDA required that it be allowed to review advertisements before they were published.[11] According to another study, consumers rated the safety and appeal of drugs described with an incomplete statement of risks more positively than similar drugs described with a more complete statement of risks.[12]

Defenses of direct-to-consumer advertising by the pharmaceutical industry inevitably mention that the real gatekeeper is the doctor, since only the doctor can write a prescription. Even Rosenthal et al. state that doctors will only write a prescription for a drug when they are "familiar with it and comfortable prescribing it."[1] Although it is beyond the scope of this editorial, it is important to examine studies assessing the accuracy of sources of information that physicians use to learn about new drugs or devices. There is evidence that many

Figure 1

FDA Actions Enforcing Drug Advertising Regulations and Drug-Industry Expenditures for Promotion.

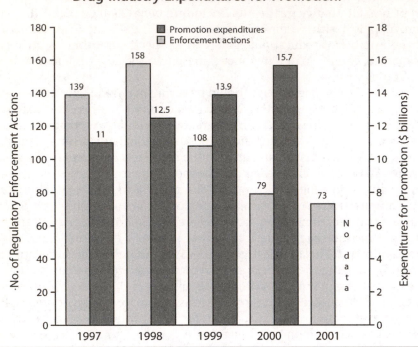

Data on promotion are as reported by Rosenthal et al.[1] Data on enforcement actions (warning letters and notices of violation) are from the FDA Web site.[15] FDA enforcement data for 2001 were extrapolated from data for the first 11 months.

drug advertisements are not balanced or accurate,[13, 14] and duped gatekeepers may not adequately resist patients' exhortations to write a prescription.

Since a ban on the advertising of pharmaceutical agents is incompatible with the First Amendment, much stricter control by the FDA of misleading advertising is necessary. Although expenditures for the promotion of drugs increased from $11 billion in 1997 to $15.7 billion in 2000 (Fig. 1), there was a significant decrease in the number of actions taken by the FDA to enforce advertising regulations—from 139 letters of warning to companies or notices of violation in 1997 to 79 in 2000 and an estimated 73 in 2001. The FDA is grossly understaffed for this important oversight function: the entire Division of Drug Marketing, Advertising, and Communications has had only 28 to 30 employees since 1997 (Abrams T: personal communication). A further handicap for the FDA is that it lacks the legal authority to impose civil monetary penalties on companies, even when they repeatedly violate the law. An editorial in a December 2001 issue of *Business Week* commented that "pharmaceutical company advertising on TV promotes high-priced new drugs with marginal improvement over cheaper generic versions. The FDA should crack down harder on misleading ads."[16] In the realm of screening with the use of computed tomography, analyzed by Lee and Brennan,[2] enforcement is beginning to occur. The FDA recently sent a notice of violation to a company, CAT-scan2000, for illegally promoting screening for heart disease in asymptomatic people: this form of technology has not been approved for such screening.[17]

Beyond increased enforcement by the FDA, the issue of better information for patients must be addressed. The irritation felt by many physicians when patients approach them after seeing a direct-to-consumer advertisement may derive from the fact that such advertisements, with their powerful, emotion-arousing images and frequently unbalanced information on safety and effectiveness, mislead patients into believing that drugs are better than they actually are. There is a hollow ring to the statement by Pharmaceutical Research and Manufacturers of America president Alan Holmer that "direct-to-consumer advertising is an excellent way to meet the growing demand for medical information, empowering consumers by educating them about health conditions and possible treatments."[18]

The education of patients—or physicians—is too important to be left to the pharmaceutical industry, with its pseudoeducational campaigns designed, first and foremost, to promote drugs. Public Health Service agencies such as the National Institutes of Health and the FDA, along with medical educators in schools and residency programs, must move much more forcefully to replace tainted drug company "education" with scientifically based, useful information that will stimulate better conversations between doctors and patients and lead to true empowerment.

References

1. Rosenthal M. B., Berndt E. R., Donohue J. M., Frank R. G, Epstein A. M. Promotion of prescription drugs to consumers. N Engl J Med 2002; 346:498–505.

2. Lee T. H., Brennan T. A. Direct-to-consumer marketing of high-technology screening tests. N Engl J Med 2002;346:529–31.

3. Mintzes B. Blurring the boundaries: new trends in drug promotion. Amsterdam: HAI-Europe, 1998. (Accessed January 25, 2002, at . . .)

4. Ingelfinger F. J. Advertising: informational but not educational. N Engl J Med 1972;286:1318–9.

5. Understanding the effects of direct-to-consumer prescription drug advertising. Menlo Park, Calif.: The Henry J. Kaiser Family Foundation, November 2001.

6. Bell R. A., Wilkes M. S., Kravitz R. L. The educational value of consumer-targeted prescription drug print advertising. J Fam Pract 2000; 49:1092–8.

7. Leacock S. The garden of folly. New York: Dodd Mead, 1924:122–31.

8. Wolfe S. Drug advertisements that go straight to the hippocampus. Lancet 1996;348:632.

9. Why Rubin-Ehrenthal sticks exclusively to DTC accounts. Medical Marketing and Media. September 1999:136–46.

10. Liebman M. Return on TV advertising isn't a clear picture. Medical Marketing and Media. November 2001:81–4.

11. Bell R. A., Kravitz R. L., Wilkes M. S. Direct-to-consumer prescription drug advertising and the public. J Gen Intern Med 1999;14:651–7.

12. Davis J. J. Riskier than we think? The relationship between risk statement completeness and perceptions of direct to consumer advertised prescription drugs. J Health Commun 2000;5:349–69.

13. Stryer D, Bero L. A. Characteristics of materials distributed by drug companies: an evaluation of appropriateness. J Gen Intern Med 1996;11:575–83.

14. Wilkes M. S., Doblin B. H., Shapiro M. F. Pharmaceutical advertisements in leading medical journals: experts' assessments. Ann Intern Med 1992;116:912–9.

15. Center for Drug Evaluation and Research. Compliance activities: warning letters and notice of violation letters to pharmaceutical companies. Rockville, Md.: Food and Drug Administration, 2002. (Accessed January 25, 2002, at . . .)

16. How to control drug costs, simply. Business Week. December 10, 2001.

17. Letter to CATscan 2000 President/CEO Gina Johnson. Rockville, Md.: Food and Drug Administration, January 3, 2002.

18. Holmer A. F. Direct-to-consumer prescription drug advertising builds bridges between patients and physicians. JAMA 1999;281:380–2.

Alan F. Holmer **NO**

Direct-to-Consumer Advertising— Strengthening Our Health Care System

It has been almost five years since the Food and Drug Administration (FDA) issued guidelines clarifying the agency's broadcast requirements for the advertising of specific pharmaceutical agents directly to consumers on television.[1] Previously, most direct-to-consumer advertising had been confined to newspapers and magazines. We think this expansion to television has been a positive step.

Does direct-to-consumer advertising strengthen or weaken the physician–patient relationship? Physicians should and do remain in control of prescribing medicines. As the article by Rosenthal et al. in this issue of the *Journal*[2] makes clear, pharmaceutical companies recognize this fact by directing a large proportion of their promotional activities toward physicians. Moreover, survey data consistently show that when patients ask a physician to prescribe a specific medicine that has been advertised directly to consumers, many receive a different medicine or an alternative, nonpharmaceutical treatment. Among respondents to an FDA survey who said advertisements had caused them to talk with a physician and ask for a particular drug, about half said their doctor recommended a nondrug therapy or a different medicine.[3]

We disagree with the assertion that direct-to-consumer advertising bypasses physicians. The purpose of this advertising is to encourage patients to talk to their physicians about their medical conditions and treatment options. In fact, every television advertisement for a prescription drug must include the message that viewers should ask their physician or pharmacist about the product. Such discussions are beneficial— to the patient, who gains a better understanding of the physician's recommendation for treatment, and to the physician, who gains a better understanding of the patient's needs. In the FDA survey, most patients who had been prompted by direct-to-consumer advertising to discuss a drug with their doctor stated that their doctor welcomed the question (81 percent), discussed the drug with them (79 percent), and reacted as if the question were an ordinary part of the visit (71 percent).

The physician–patient relationship is strengthened, not weakened, when, as surveys show, direct-to-consumer advertising prompts a patient to talk with

From *The New England Journal of Medicine*, vol. 346, no. 7, February 14, 2002, pp. 526–528.

a physician for the first time about a previously undiscussed condition. A 1999 survey by *Prevention* magazine found that since 1997, as many as 24 million Americans had been prompted by a direct-to-consumer advertisement to talk to a doctor about a medical condition they had previously not discussed.[4] This type of advertising also adds to the information available to patients about the risks, side effects, and treatment profile of a particular drug. For example, 82 percent of the respondents to the FDA survey[3] reported seeing information on risks or side effects in direct-to-consumer advertising, and 81 percent reported seeing information on who should not take a drug.

Moreover, direct-to-consumer advertising appears to encourage compliance with physician-prescribed treatment regimens. Lack of compliance is a critical problem in achieving efficacious medical care. In the 2000 *Prevention* survey,[5] 22 percent of consumers said direct-to-consumer advertising made it more likely—whereas only 3 percent said it made it less likely—that they would take their medicine regularly; 33 percent of respondents to the 1999 survey reported that such advertising had reminded them to refill a prescription.[4] A study by Pfizer and RxRemedy from June 2001 found that the percentage of patients with diabetes, depression, elevated cholesterol levels, arthritis, or allergies who continued with therapy after six months was substantially higher when the patient asked for a medicine after being prompted by direct-to-consumer advertising than when the patient was given a prescription for a medicine without such prompting.[6]

Direct-to-consumer advertising is concentrated among a few therapeutic classes. These classes include agents for the treatment of conditions whose symptoms are easily recognized by consumers (such as arthritis, seasonal allergies, and obesity), agents for the treatment of chronic diseases that are often undiagnosed (such as high cholesterol, osteoporosis, and depression), and agents for the enhancement of the quality of life (such as those for skin conditions or hair loss). These advertisements may help consumers to recognize symptoms and encourage them to seek appropriate care.

What accounts for the emergence of direct-to-consumer advertising? Patients are turning to the growing volume of publicly accessible health care information. Dr. Nancy Ostrove, deputy director of the FDA's Division of Drug Marketing, Advertising, and Communications, Center for Drug Evaluation and Research, has argued that direct-to-consumer advertising of pharmaceuticals "is consistent with the whole trend toward consumer empowerment" and has asserted her belief that "there is a certain public health benefit associated with letting people know what's available."[7] In keeping with this trend, direct-to-consumer advertising is used throughout our health care system: managed care organizations, hospitals, and doctors all advertise to consumers. Unlike other health care information, direct-to-consumer advertising of drugs is subject to intense scrutiny by FDA regulators, who evaluate it for accuracy and balance.

In today's health care marketplace, there are numerous financial factors that influence the delivery of medical care. There are payment incentives that are linked to patterns of prescribing and dispensing of medications, formularies that are typically structured at least partially on the basis of financial considerations, and variable cost-sharing arrangements with patients for certain types of medicines. In the light of these strategies designed to influence decisions about the medicines that patients receive, the provision of information to patients about their treatment options through direct-to-consumer advertising is a healthy development that helps balance the system. With so many parties using such financial incentives and encouraging patients to assume increased responsibility for their medical care, it is surprising that the transmission of FDA-regulated information to consumers has engendered controversy.

Direct-to-consumer advertising does not affect the prices of drugs[8]: price increases of drugs are the least important factor contributing to the increase in pharmaceutical spending. In 2000, price inflation accounted for approximately one fifth of the growth.[9] Such advertising may increase the rate of use of prescription drugs by prompting the treatment of patients for previously untreated conditions and by improving compliance with treatment among those with known conditions. If so, this increase is a positive development. The proper use of prescription drugs is often the most effective and least expensive form of health care. Ostrove testified to a Senate subcommittee in July 2001 that there is no evidence that direct-to-consumer advertising is increasing inappropriate prescribing,[10] and an unpublished industry-supported study on cholesterol-lowering statins, which are the subject of a substantial amount of direct-to-consumer advertising, found no tendency toward less appropriate prescribing as the rate of use increased.[11] As John Calfee of the American Enterprise Institute has observed, "On the whole, increases in drug utilization seem to be driven primarily by the fact that health care organizations, physicians, and patients find many of the newer drugs to be extremely valuable. In fact, there is strong evidence that many of the most effective drugs are underused, rather than overused."[12]

Direct-to-consumer advertising is clearly here to stay. Given this reality, physicians must, as Rosenthal et al. note, "develop strategies for helping their patients evaluate this information and make appropriate and informed choices about treatment."[2] With such a diversity of treatment options available for acute and chronic diseases, patients need the guidance that only a trusted health care professional can provide. The health care system is stronger as a consequence. Direct-to-consumer advertising does not replace the physician–patient relationship; its purpose is rather to encourage an informed discussion between patient and physician.

References

1. Center for Drug Evaluation and Research. Guidance for Industry: consumer-directed broadcast advertisements. Rockville, Md.: Food and Drug Administration, August 1999. (Accessed January 25, 2002, at . . .)

2. Rosenthal MB, Berndt ER, Donohue JM, Frank RG, Epstein AM. Promotion of prescription drugs to consumers. N Engl J Med 2002;346:498–505.

3. Center for Drug Evaluation and Research. Attitudes and behaviors associated with direct-to-consumer (DTC) promotion of prescription drugs: main survey results. Rockville, Md.: Food and Drug Administration, 1999. (Accessed January 25, 2002, at . . .)

4. Year two: a national survey of consumer reactions to direct-to-consumer advertising. Emmaus, Pa.: Rodale, 1999.

5. International survey on wellness and consumer reactions to DTC advertising of Rx drugs. Emmaus, Pa.: Rodale, 2000.

6. Drug ads help people take their medicines. New York: Pfizer, November 29, 2001. (Accessed January 28, 2002, at . . .)

7. Stolberg SG. The Nation: ads that circumvent doctors: want a new drug? Plenty to choose from on TV. New York Times. January 23, 2000.

8. Manning R, Keith A. The economics of direct-to-consumer advertising of prescription drugs. Economic Realities in Health Care Policy 2001;2(1):3–9.

9. Pharmaceutical industry profile 2001: a century of progress. Washington, D.C.: Pharmaceutical Research and Manufacturers of America, 2001.

10. Teinowitz I. DTC regulation by FDA debated; agency says it has no evidence ads prompt unnecessary prescriptions. Advertising Age. July 30, 2001:6.

11. Calfee J, Winston C, Stempski R. Statin drug advertising effects. Presented at the University of Chicago Conference on the Regulation of Medical Innovation and Pharmaceutical Markets, Chicago, April 20–21, 2001.

12. Calfee JE. Public hearings on direct-to-consumer advertising of prescription drugs. Testimony before the Senate Subcommittee on Consumer Affairs, Foreign Commerce, and Tourism, Committee on Commerce, Science and Transportation, Washington, D.C., July 24, 2001:2–3.

POSTSCRIPT

Is Direct-to-Consumer Advertising of Pharmaceuticals Bad for Our Health?

It is worth noticing that the disagreements between Wolfe and Holmer go well beyond the single issue they are discussing. They disagree most on the nature of human autonomy—on whether consumers should be allowed, even encouraged, to make mistakes that may hurt them, *by the health care system, of which the FDA forms a part, and by the business community, the economic engine of the country.* Consumers have often made less-than-optimal choices, and the economic system, viewed as an extension of the rights of the citizen, certainly permits these choices. It is the duty of the storekeeper, as a citizen, to respect the autonomy of the consumer. But we have also always insisted that our professionals have a different duty to the people, because of their expertise: They have a duty to deep their clients/patients from harm, and to oppose any economic regimes that systematically harm the citizens in professional areas. Well, where is our duty to the health care consumer, the buyer of pharmaceuticals? Is he (analytically) closer to the doctor's patient, or to the storekeeper's customer? Can the physician, in an increasingly competitive insurance-driven profession, be counted on to hold the line against patient demands that stem from inappropriate advertising? How much do we care if he cannot?

Suggested Reading

If you want to pursue the subject, you might consider the following readings:

Judith Andre, "The Alleged Incompatibility of Business and Medical Ethics," *Business Ethics,* 1999.

Meredith B. Rosenthal, Ernst R. Berndt, Julie M. Donohue, Richard G. Frank and Arnold M. Epstein, "Promotion of Prescription Drugs to Consumers," *The New England Journal of Medicine,* 346(7): 498–505 (February 14, 2002).

Thomas H. Lee and Troyen A. Brennan, "Sounding Board: Direct-to-Consumer Marketing of High-Technology Screening Tests," *The New England Journal of Medicine,* 346(7): 529–31.

Jeffrey M. Drazen, Lead Editorial: "The Consumer and the Learned Intermediary in Health Care," *The New England Journal of Medicine,* 346(7): 523–24 (February 14, 2002).

ISSUE 13

Was Ford to Blame in the Pinto Case?

YES: Mark Dowie, from "Pinto Madness," *Mother Jones* (September–October 1977)

NO: Ford Motor Company, from Closing Argument by Mr. James Neal, Brief for the Defense, *State of Indiana v. Ford Motor Company*, U.S. District Court, South Bend, Indiana (January 15, 1980)

ISSUE SUMMARY

YES: Mark Dowie's article broke a new kind of scandal for American manufacturing, alleging that Ford Motor Company had deliberately put on the road an unsafe car—the Pinto—in which hundreds of people suffered burn deaths and horrible disfigurement. The accusations gave rise to a series of civil suits and one criminal proceeding, in which Ford was charged with criminal homicide.

NO: James Neal, who was chief attorney for the Ford Motor Company's defense against the charge of criminal homicide in connection with the burn deaths, persuaded the jury that Ford could not be held responsible for deaths which were actually caused by others—the driver of the van that struck the victims, for example—and which resulted from Ford's patriotic efforts to produce a competitive small car.

Some cases in business ethics become "classics" in their own time. By 1980 we were considering "the Pinto Case" in our classes, wondering how safe "safe" had to be where the automobile was concerned, wondering how much management might be held accountable for, wondering if criminal penalties were appropriate for respectable businessmen, no matter what they or their product might be doing. This is arguably not the Pinto Case's own time. Almost thirty years has passed since the accident and what followed from it. But we still teach the case. We still don't know how "safe" a vehicle has to be; we still don't know how much responsibility for product failures to assign to corporations, and what the appropriate way might be to force a corporation to take that responsibility. The doubts remain, and the case retains its interest.

There is no doubt about the case that occasioned the criminal prosecution. Three girls died horribly in an automobile accident on August 10, 1978.

They had stopped their car, a 1973 Ford Pinto, on U.S. Highway 33 near Goshen, Indiana, and were about to get under way again when they were struck from the rear, at high speed, by a van with a possibly impaired driver. The car immediately burst into flames, and the girls had no chance to escape the accident before the flames reached them.

The van driver should have been watching where he was going. Beyond that obvious comment, what was wrong with the car? Why did it burst into flames so quickly? Mark Dowie, general manager of business operations of the magazine *Mother Jones*, had argued a year earlier that there was a great deal wrong with the Ford Pinto. He had put together the story printed here from data obtained for him by some very disaffected Ford engineers. The data suggested that the Pinto had been rushed into production without adequate testing; that it had a very vulnerable fuel system that would rupture with any rear-end collision; that even though the vulnerability was discovered before production, Ford had hurried the Pinto to the market anyway; and that successful lobbying thereafter had prevented the government regulators from catching up with them and requiring a safer gas tank.

Most suggestive from the public's point of view was a document supplied by one of the engineers, an estimate of the probable costs of refitting valves to prevent fire in a rollover accident. It was a cost-benefit analysis that placed a dollar value on a human life, estimated the probability of fatal accident, estimated the amount of money needed to settle a lawsuit for loss of life, estimated the amount of money needed to do the refitting so that there would not be that loss of life—and concluded that it was more economical to let the people die and settle the suits afterward. For sheer bottom-line-oriented cynicism, the document was unparalleled in the history of business enterprise, and Ford Motor Company will never live it down.

When reading these selections, pause to enjoy not only the interesting case, but also the finely directed passion of the contestants. Mark Dowie's trenchant prose is a fine example of investigative reporting, muckraking at its best. And nothing can compare with the superb lawyering of James Neal. Who is to blame for anything, if you are a lawyer? Not your client! Anything else! Blame the van driver, marijuana, the government, professors, the service station, the highway, society at large, anything, but not your client. Then ask yourself: Does Neal give the wealthy corporation an unfair advantage in such proceedings? Does the public have the money to hire such advocates? Would you have that kind of money? The jury had a difficult task of sorting out the situation: Was this deliberate malfeasance by Ford? Was it a series of unlucky decisions made in good faith? Or was this just a very unfortunate accident?

Do we know what constitutes sufficient reason to attribute "responsibility" to any person, company, or set of conditions? What kinds of risks do we assume when buying a car, or a motorcycle, or a can of tuna fish? For what is the manufacturer responsible? Should we be willing to assume more risks in the enormously competitive market that prevails among small automobiles? Does the product liability suit unjustly cripple American efforts to compete in highly competitive industries? Is this something we should worry about?

YES ↰   **Mark Dowie**

Pinto Madness

One evening in the mid-1960s, Arjay Miller was driving home from his office in Dearborn, Michigan, in the four-door Lincoln Continental that went with his job as president of the Ford Motor Company. On a crowded highway, another car struck his from the rear. The Continental spun around and burst into flames. Because he was wearing a shoulder-strap seat belt, Miller was unharmed by the crash, and because his doors didn't jam he escaped the gasoline-drenched, flaming wreck. But the accident made a vivid impression on him. Several months later, on July 15, 1965, he recounted it to a U.S. Senate subcommittee that was hearing testimony on auto safety legislation. "I still have burning in my mind the image of that gas tank on fire," Miller said. He went on to express an almost passionate interest in controlling fuel-fed fires in cars that crash or roll over. He spoke with excitement about the fabric gas tank Ford was testing at that very moment. "If it proves out," he promised the senators, "it will be a feature you will see in our standard cars."

Almost seven years after Miller's testimony, a woman, whom for legal reasons we will call Sandra Gillespie, pulled onto a Minneapolis highway in her new Ford Pinto. Riding with her was a young boy, whom we'll call Robbie Carlton. As she entered a merge lane, Sandra Gillespie's car stalled. Another car rear-ended hers at an impact speed of 28 miles per hour. The Pinto's gas tank ruptured. Vapors from it mixed quickly with the air in the passenger compartment. A spark ignited the mixture and the car exploded in a ball of fire. Sandra died in agony a few hours later in an emergency hospital. Her passenger, 13-year-old Robbie Carlton, is still alive; he has just come home from another futile operation aimed at grafting a new ear and nose from skin on the few unscarred portions of his badly burned body. (This accident is real; the details are from police reports.)

Why did Sandra Gillespie's Ford Pinto catch fire so easily, seven years after Ford's Arjay Miller made his apparently sincere pronouncements—the same seven years that brought more safety improvements to cars than any other period in automotive history? An extensive investigation by *Mother Jones* over the past six months has found these answers:

- Fighting strong competition from Volkswagen for the lucrative small-car market, the Ford Motor Company rushed the Pinto into production in much less than the usual time.

- Ford engineers discovered in pre-production crash tests that rear-end collisions would rupture the Pinto's fuel system extremely easily.
- Because assembly-line machinery was already tooled when engineers found this defect, top Ford officials decided to manufacture the car anyway—exploding gas tank and all—*even though Ford owned the patent on a much safer gas tank.*
- For more than eight years afterwards, Ford successfully lobbied, with extraordinary vigor and some blatant lies, against a key government safety standard that would have forced the company to change the Pinto's fire-prone gas tank.

By conservative estimates Pinto crashes have caused 500 burn deaths to people who would not have been seriously injured if the car had not burst into flames. The figure could be as high as 900. Burning Pintos have become such an embarrassment to Ford that its advertising agency, J. Walter Thompson, dropped a line from the end of a radio spot that read "Pinto leaves you with that warm feeling."

Ford knows the Pinto is a firetrap, yet it has paid out millions to settle damage suits out of court, and it is prepared to spend millions more lobbying against safety standards. With a half million cars rolling off the assembly lines each year, Pinto is the biggest-selling subcompact in America, and the company's operating profit on the car is fantastic. Finally, in 1977, new Pinto models have incorporated a few minor alterations necessary to meet that federal standard Ford managed to hold off for eight years. Why did the company delay so long in making these minimal, inexpensive improvements?

- Ford waited eight years because its internal "cost-benefit analysis," *which places a dollar value on human life,* said it wasn't profitable to make the changes sooner.

Before we get to the question of how much Ford thinks your life is worth, let's trace the history of the death trap itself. Although this particular story is about the Pinto, the way in which Ford made its decision is typical of the U.S. auto industry generally. There are plenty of similar stories about other cars made by other companies. But this case is the worst of them all.

⋯◈⋯

The next time you drive behind a Pinto (with over two million of them on the road, you shouldn't have much trouble finding one), take a look at the rear end. That long silvery object hanging down under the bumper is the gas tank. The tank begins about six inches forward of the bumper. In late models the bumper is designed to withstand a collision of only about five miles per hour. Earlier bumpers may as well not have been on the car for all the protection they offered the gas tank.

Mother Jones has studied hundreds of reports and documents on rear-end collisions involving Pintos. These reports conclusively reveal that if you ran into that Pinto you were following at over 30 miles per hour, the rear end of the car would buckle like an accordion, right up to the back seat. The tube leading to the gas-tank cap would be ripped away from the tank itself, and gas would immediately begin sloshing onto the road around the car. The buckled gas tank would be jammed up against the differential housing (that big bulge in the middle of your rear axle), which contains four sharp, protruding bolts likely to gash holes in the tank and spill still more gas. Now all you need is a spark from a cigarette, ignition, or scraping metal, and both cars would be engulfed in flames. If you gave that Pinto a really good whack—say, at 40 mph—chances are excellent that its doors would jam and you would have to stand by and watch its trapped passengers burn to death.

This scenario is no news to Ford. Internal company documents in our possession show that Ford has crash-tested the Pinto at a top-secret site more than 40 times and that *every* test made at over 25 mph without special structural alteration of the car has resulted in a ruptured fuel tank. Despite this, Ford officials denied under oath having crash-tested the Pinto.

Eleven of these tests, averaging a 31-mph impact speed, came before Pintos started rolling out of the factories. Only three cars passed the test with unbroken fuel tanks. In one of them an inexpensive light-weight plastic baffle was placed between the front of the gas tank and the differential housing, so those four bolts would not perforate the tank. (Don't forget about that little piece of plastic, which costs one dollar and weighs one pound. It plays an important role in our story later on.) In another successful test, a piece of steel was placed between the tank and the bumper. In the third test car the gas tank was lined with a rubber bladder. But none of these protective alterations was used in the mass-produced Pinto.

In pre-production planning, engineers seriously considered using in the Pinto the same kind of gas tank Ford uses in the Capri. The Capri tank rides over the rear axle and differential housing. It has been so successful in over 50 crash tests that Ford used it in its Experimental Safety Vehicle, which withstood rear-end impacts of 60 mph. So why wasn't the Capri tank used in the Pinto? Or, why wasn't that plastic baffle placed between the tank and the axle—something that would have saved the life of Sandra Gillespie and hundreds like her? Why was a car known to be a serious fire hazard deliberately released to production in August of 1970?

⚜

Whether Ford should manufacture subcompacts at all was the subject of a bitter two-year debate at the company's Dearborn headquarters. The principals in this corporate struggle were the then-president Semon "Bunky" Knudsen, whom Henry Ford II had hired away from General Motors, and Lee Iacocca, a spunky Young Turk who had risen fast within the company on the enormous success of the Mustang. Iacocca argued forcefully that Volkswagen and the Japanese were going to capture the entire American subcompact market unless Ford put out its own alternative to the VW Beetle. Bunky Knudsen said, in effect: let them have the small-car market; Ford makes good money on medium and large models. But he lost the battle and later resigned. Iacocca became president and almost immediately began a rush program to produce the Pinto.

Like the Mustang, the Pinto became known in the company as "Lee's car." Lee Iacocca wanted that little car in the showrooms of America with the 1971 models. So he ordered his engineering vice president, Bob Alexander, to oversee what was probably the shortest production planning period in modern automotive history. The normal time span from conception to production of a new car model is about 43 months. The Pinto schedule was set at just under 25.

. . . Design, styling, product planning, advance engineering and quality assurance all have flexible time frames, and engineers can pretty much carry these on simultaneously. Tooling, on the other hand, has a fixed time frame of about 18 months. Normally, an auto company doesn't begin tooling until the other processes are almost over: you don't want to make the machines that stamp and press and grind metal into the shape of car parts until you know all those parts will work well together. *But Iacocca's speed-up meant Pinto tooling went on at the same time as product development.* So when crash tests revealed a serious defect in the gas tank, it was too late. The tooling was well under way.

When it was discovered the gas tank was unsafe, did anyone go to Iacocca and tell him? "Hell no," replied an engineer who worked on the Pinto, a high company official for many years, who, unlike several others at Ford, maintains a necessarily clandestine concern for safety. "That person would have been fired. Safety wasn't a popular subject around Ford in those days. With Lee it was taboo. Whenever a problem was raised that meant a delay on the Pinto, Lee would chomp on his cigar, look out the window and say 'Read the product objectives and get back to work.'"

The product objectives are clearly stated in the Pinto "green book." This is a thick, top-secret manual in green covers containing a step-by-step production plan for the model, detailing the metallurgy, weight, strength and quality of every part in the car. The product objectives for the Pinto are repeated in an article by Ford executive F. G. Olsen published by the Society of Automotive Engineers. He lists these product objectives as follows:

1. TRUE SUBCOMPACT
   - Size
   - Weight
2. LOW COST OF OWNERSHIP
   - Initial price
   - Fuel consumption
   - Reliability
   - Serviceability
3. CLEAR PRODUCT SUPERIORITY
   - Appearance
   - Comfort
   - Features
   - Ride and Handling
   - Performance

Safety, you will notice, is not there. It is not mentioned in the entire article. As Lee Iacocca was fond of saying, "Safety doesn't sell."

Heightening the anti-safety pressure on Pinto engineers was an important goal set by Iacocca known as "the limits of 2,000." The Pinto was not to weigh an ounce over 2,000 pounds and not to cost a cent over $2,000. "Iacocca enforced these limits with an iron hand," recalls the engineer quoted earlier. So, even when a crash test showed that that one-pound, one-dollar piece of plastic stopped the puncture of the gas tank, it was thrown out as extra cost and extra weight.

People shopping for subcompacts are watching every dollar. "You have to keep in mind," the engineer explained, "that the price elasticity on these subcompacts is extremely tight. You can price yourself right out of the market by adding $25 to the production cost of the model. And nobody understands that better than Iacocca."

Dr. Leslie Ball, the retired safety chief for the NASA manned space program and a founder of the International Society of Reliability Engineers, recently made a careful study of the Pinto. "The release to production of the Pinto was the most reprehensible decision in the history of American engineering," he said. Ball can name more than 40 European and Japanese models in the Pinto price and weight range with safer gas-tank positioning. Ironically, many of them, like the Ford Capri, contain a "saddle-type" gas tank riding over the back axle. *The patent on the saddle-type tank is owned by the Ford Motor Co.*

Los Angeles auto safety expert Byron Bloch has made an in-depth study of the Pinto fuel system. "It's a catastrophic blunder," he says. "Ford made an extremely irresponsible decision when they placed such a weak tank in such a ridiculous location in such a soft rear end. It's almost designed to blow up—premeditated."

A Ford engineer, who doesn't want his name used, comments: "This company is run by salesmen, not engineers; so the priority is styling, not safety." He goes on to tell a story about gas-tank safety at Ford.

Lou Tubben is one of the most popular engineers at Ford. He's a friendly, outgoing guy with a genuine concern for safety. By 1971 he had grown so concerned about gas-tank integrity that he asked his boss if he could prepare a presentation on safer tank design. Tubben and his boss had both worked on the Pinto and shared a concern for its safety. His boss gave him the go-ahead, scheduled a date for the presentation and invited all company engineers and key production planning personnel. When time came for the meeting, a grand total of two people showed up—Lou Tubben and his boss.

"So you see," continued the anonymous Ford engineer ironically, "there *are* a few of us here at Ford who are concerned about fire safety." He adds: "They are mostly engineers who have to study a lot of accident reports and look at pictures of burned people. But we don't talk about it much. It isn't a popular subject. I've never seen safety on the agenda of a product meeting and, except for a brief period in 1956, I can't remember seeing the word safety in an advertisement. I really don't think the company wants American consumers to start thinking too much about safety—for fear they might demand it, I suppose."

Asked about the Pinto gas tank, another Ford engineer admitted: "That's all true. But you miss the point entirely. You see, safety isn't the issue, trunk space is. You have no idea how stiff the competition is over trunk space. Do you realize that if we put a Capri-type tank in the Pinto you could only get one set of golf clubs in the trunk?"

Blame for Sandra Gillespie's death, Robbie Carlton's unrecognizable face and all the other injuries and deaths in Pintos since 1970 does not rest on the shoulders of Lee Iacocca alone. For, while he and his associates fought their battle against a safer Pinto in Dearborn, a larger war against safer cars raged in Washington. One skirmish in that war involved Ford's successful eight-year lobbying effort against Federal Motor Vehicle Safety Standard 301, the rear-end provisions of which would have forced Ford to redesign the Pinto.

But first some background:

During the early '60s, auto safety legislation became the *bête-noire* of American big business. The auto industry was the last great unregulated business, and if *it* couldn't reverse the tide of government regulation, the reasoning went, no one could.

People who know him cannot remember Henry Ford II taking a stronger stand than the one he took against the regulation of safety design. He spent weeks in Washington calling on members of Congress, holding press conferences and recruiting business cronies like W. B. Murphy of Campbell's Soup to join the anti-regulation battle. Displaying the sophistication for which today's American corporate leaders will be remembered, Murphy publicly called auto safety "a hula hoop, a fad that will pass." He was speaking to a special luncheon of the Business Council, an organization of 100 chief executives who gather periodically in Washington to provide "advice" and "counsel" to government. The target of their wrath in this instance was the Motor Vehicle Safety Bills introduced in both houses of Congress, largely in response to Ralph Nader's *Unsafe at Any Speed.*

By 1965, most pundits and lobbyists saw the handwriting on the wall and prepared to accept government "meddling" in the last bastion of free enterprise. Not Henry. With bulldog tenacity, he held out for defeat of the legislation to the very end, loyal to his grandfather's invention and to the company that makes it. But the Safety Act passed the House and Senate unanimously, and was signed into law by Lyndon Johnson in 1966.

While lobbying for and against legislation is pretty much a process of high-level back-slapping, press-conferencing and speech-making, fighting a regulatory agency is a much subtler matter. Henry headed home to lick his wounds in Grosse Pointe, Michigan, and a planeload of the Ford Motor Company's best brains flew to Washington to start the "education" of the new federal auto safety bureaucrats.

Their job was to implant the official industry ideology in the minds of the new officials regulating auto safety. Briefly summarized, that ideology states that auto accidents are caused not by *cars,* but by 1) people and 2) highway conditions.

This philosophy is rather like blaming a robbery on the victim. Well, what did you expect? You were carrying money, weren't you? It is an extraordinary experience to hear automotive "safety engineers" talk for hours without ever mentioning cars. They will advocate spending billions educating youngsters, punishing drunks and redesigning street signs. Listening to them, you can momentarily begin to think that it is easier to control 100 million drivers than a handful of manufacturers. They show movies about guardrail design and advocate the clear-cutting of trees 100 feet back from every highway in the nation. If a car is unsafe, they argue, it is because its owner doesn't properly drive it. Or, perhaps, maintain it.

In light of an annual death rate approaching 50,000, they are forced to admit that driving is hazardous. But the car is, in the words of Arjay Miller, "the safest link in the safety chain."

Before the Ford experts left Washington to return to drafting tables in Dearborn they did one other thing. They managed to informally reach an agreement with the major public servants who would be making auto safety decisions. This agreement was that "cost-benefit" would be an acceptable mode of analysis by Detroit and its new regulators. And as we shall see, cost-benefit analysis quickly became the basis of Ford's argument against safer car design.

◄◊►

Cost-benefit analysis was used only occasionally in government until President Kennedy appointed Ford Motor Company President Robert McNamara to be Secretary of Defense. McNamara, originally an accountant, preached cost benefit with all the force of a Biblical zealot. Stated in its simplest terms, cost-benefit analysis says that if the cost is greater than the benefit, the project is not worth it—no matter what the benefit. Examine the cost of every action, decision, contract, part, or change, the doctrine says, then carefully evaluate the benefits (in dollars) to be certain that they exceed the cost before you begin a program or—and this is the crucial part for our story—pass a regulation.

As a management tool in a business in which profits matter over everything else, cost-benefit analysis makes a certain amount of sense. Serious problems come, however, when public officials who ought to have more than corporate profits at heart apply cost-benefit analysis to every conceivable decision. The inevitable result is that they must place a dollar value on human life.

Ever wonder what your life is worth in dollars? Perhaps $10 million? Ford has a better idea: $200,000.

Remember, Ford had gotten the federal regulators to agree to talk auto safety in terms of cost-benefit analysis. But in order to be able to argue that various safety costs were greater than their benefits, Ford needed to have a dollar value figure for the "benefit." Rather than be so uncouth as to come up with such a price tag itself, the auto industry pressured the National Highway

Table 1

What's Your Life Worth? Societal Cost Components for Fatalities, 1972 NHTSA Study

Component	1971 Costs
Future productivity losses	
Direct	$132,000
Indirect	41,300
Medical Costs	
Hospital	700
Other	425
Property damage	1,500
Insurance administration	4,700
Legal and court	3,000
Employer losses	1,000
Victim's pain and suffering	10,000
Funeral	900
Assets (lost consumption)	5,000
Miscellaneous accident costs	200
Total per fatality: $200,725	

Here is a chart from a federal study showing how the National Highway Traffic Safety Administration has calculated the value of a human life. The estimate was arrived at under pressure from the auto industry. The Ford Motor Company has used it in cost-benefit analyses arguing why certain safety measures are not "worth" the savings in human lives. The calculation above is a breakdown of the estimated cost to society every time someone is killed in a car accident. We were not able to find anyone, either in the government or at Ford, who could explain how the $10,000 figure for "pain and suffering" had been arrived at.

Traffic Safety Administration to do so. And in a 1972 report the agency decided a human life was worth $200,725. (For its reasoning, see [Table 1].) Inflationary forces have recently pushed the figure up to $278,000.

Furnished with this useful tool, Ford immediately went to work using it to prove why various safety improvements were too expensive to make.

Nowhere did the company argue harder that it should make no changes than in the area of rupture-prone fuel tanks. Not long after the government arrived at the $200,725-per-life figure, it surfaced, rounded off to a cleaner $200,000, in an internal Ford memorandum. This cost-benefit analysis argued that Ford should not make an $11-per-car improvement that would prevent 180 fiery deaths a year. (This minor change would have prevented gas tanks from breaking so easily both in rear-end collisions, like Sandra Gillespie's, and in rollover accidents, where the same thing tends to happen.)

Ford's cost-benefit table [Table 2] is buried in a seven-page company memorandum entitled "Fatalities Associated with Crash-Induced Fuel Leakage and Fires." The memo argues that there is no financial benefit in complying with proposed safety standards that would admittedly result in fewer auto fires, fewer burn deaths and fewer burn injuries. Naturally, memoranda that speak so casually of "burn deaths" and "burn injuries" are not released to the

Table 2

$11 vs a Burn Death: Benefits and Costs Relating to Fuel Leakage Associated With the Static Rollover Test Portion of FMVSS 208

Benefits

Savings: 180 burn deaths, 180 serious burn injuries, 2,100 burned vehicles.
Unit cost: $200,000 per death, $67,000 per injury, $700 per vehicle.
Total benefit: 180 × ($200,000) + 180 × ($67,000) + 2,100 × ($700) = $49.5 million.

Costs

Sales: 11 million cars, 1.5 million light trucks.
Unit cost: $11 per car, $11 per truck.
Total cost: 11,000,000 × ($11) + 1,500,000 × ($11) = $137 million.

From Ford Motor Company internal memorandum: "Fatalities Associated with Crash-Induced Fuel Leakage and Fires."

public. They are very effective, however, with Department of Transportation officials indoctrinated in McNamarian cost-benefit analysis.

All Ford had to do was convince men like John Volpe, Claude Brinegar and William Coleman (successive Secretaries of Transportation during the Nixon-Ford years) that certain safety standards would add so much to the price of cars that fewer people would buy them. This could damage the auto industry, which was still believed to be the bulwark of the American economy. "Compliance to these standards," Henry Ford II prophesied at more than one press conference, "will shut down the industry."

The Nixon Transportation Secretaries were the kind of regulatory officials big business dreams of. They understood and loved capitalism and thought like businessmen. Yet, best of all, they came into office uninformed on technical automotive matters. And you could talk "burn injuries" and "burn deaths" with these guys, and they didn't seem to envision children crying at funerals and people hiding in their homes with melted faces. Their minds appeared to have leapt right to the bottom line—more safety meant higher prices, higher prices meant lower sales and lower sales meant lower profits.

So when J. C. Echold, Director of Automotive Safety (which means chief anti-safety lobbyist) for Ford, wrote to the Department of Transportation—which he still does frequently, at great length—he felt secure attaching a memorandum that in effect says it is acceptable to kill 180 people and burn another 180 every year, *even though we have the technology that could save their lives for $11 a car.*

Furthermore, Echold attached this memo, confident, evidently, that the Secretary would question neither his low death/injury statistics nor his high cost estimates. But it turns out, on closer examination, that both these findings were misleading.

First, note that Ford's table shows an equal number of burn deaths and burn injuries. This is false. All independent experts estimate that for each person who dies by an auto fire, many more are left with charred hands, faces and limbs. Andrew McGuire of the Northern California Burn Center estimates the ratio of burn injuries to deaths at ten to one instead of the one to one Ford shows here. Even though Ford values a burn at only a piddling $67,000 instead of the $200,000 price of life, the true ratio obviously throws the company's calculations way off.

The other side of the equation, the alleged $11 cost of a fire-prevention device, is also a misleading estimation. One document that was *not* sent to Washington by Ford was a "Confidential" cost analysis *Mother Jones* has managed to obtain, showing that crash fires could be largely prevented for considerably *less* than $11 a car. The cheapest method involves placing a heavy rubber bladder inside the gas tank to keep the fuel from spilling if the tank ruptures. Goodyear had developed the bladder and had demonstrated it to the automotive industry. We have in our possession crash-test reports showing that the Goodyear bladder worked well. On December 2, 1970 (*two years before* Echold sent his cost-benefit memo to Washington), Ford Motor Company ran a rear-end crash test on a car with the rubber bladder in the gas tank. The tank ruptured, but no fuel leaked. On January 15, 1971, Ford again tested the bladder and again it worked. The total purchase and installation cost of the bladder would have been $5.08 per car. That $5.08 could have saved the lives of Sandra Gillespie and several hundred others.

⚜

When a federal regulatory agency like the National Highway Traffic Safety Administration (NHTSA) decides to issue a new standard, the law usually requires it to invite all interested parties to respond before the standard is enforced—a reasonable enough custom on the surface. However, the auto industry has taken advantage of this process and has used it to delay lifesaving emission and safety standards for years. In the case of the standard that would have corrected that fragile Pinto fuel tank, the delay was for an incredible eight years.

The particular regulation involved here was Federal Motor Vehicle Safety Standard 301. Ford picked portions of Standard 301 for strong opposition back in 1968 when the Pinto was still in the blueprint stage. The intent of 301, and the 300 series that followed it, was to protect drivers and passengers *after* a crash occurs. Without question the worst postcrash hazard is fire. So Standard 301 originally proposed that all cars should be able to withstand a fixed barrier impact of 20 mph (that is, running into a wall at that speed) without losing fuel.

When the standard was proposed, Ford engineers pulled their crash-test results out of their files. The front ends of most cars were no problem—with minor alterations they could stand the impact without losing fuel. "We were already working on the front end," Ford engineer Dick Kimble admitted. "We knew we could meet the test on the front end." But with the Pinto particularly, a 20-mph rear-end standard meant redesigning the entire rear end of the car. With the Pinto scheduled for production in August of 1970, and with $200 million worth of tools in place, adoption of this standard would have created a minor financial disaster. So Standard 301 was targeted for delay, and, with some assistance from its industry associates, Ford succeeded beyond its wildest expectations: the standard was not adopted until the 1977 model year. Here is how it happened:

There are several main techniques in the art of combating a government safety standard: a) make your arguments in succession, so the feds can be working on disproving only one at a time; b) claim that the real problem is not X but Y (we already saw one instance of this in "the problem is not cars but people"); c) no matter how ridiculous each argument is, accompany it with thousands of pages of highly technical assertions it will take the government months or, preferably, years to test. Ford's large and active Washington office brought these techniques to new heights and became the envy of the lobbyists' trade.

The Ford people started arguing against Standard 301 way back in 1968 with a strong attack of technique b). Fire, they said, was not the real problem. Sure, cars catch fire and people burn occasionally. But statistically auto fires are such a minor problem that NHTSA should really concern itself with other matters.

Strange as it may seem, the Department of Transportation (NHTSA's parent agency) didn't know whether or not this was true. So it contracted with several independent research groups to study auto fires. The studies took months which was just what Ford wanted.

The completed studies, however, showed auto fires to be more of a problem than Transportation officials ever dreamed of. Robert Nathan and Associates, a Washington research firm, found that 400,000 cars were burning up every year, burning more than 3,000 people to death. Furthermore, auto fires were increasing five times as fast as building fires. Another study showed that 35 per cent of all fire deaths in the U.S. occurred in automobiles. Forty per cent of all fire department calls in the 1960s were to vehicle fires—a public cost of $350 million a year, a figure that, incidentally, never shows up in cost-benefit analyses.

Another study was done by the Highway Traffic Research Institute in Ann Arbor, Michigan, a safety think-tank funded primarily by the auto industry (the giveaway there is the words "highway traffic" rather than "automobile" in the group's name). It concluded that 40 per cent of the lives lost in fuel-fed fires could be saved if the manufacturers complied with proposed Standard 301. Finally, a third report was prepared for NHTSA by consultant Eugene Trisko entitled "A National Survey of Motor Vehicle Fires." His report indicates that the Ford Motor Company makes 24 per cent of the cars on the American road, yet these cars account for 42 per cent of the collision-ruptured fuel tanks.

Ford lobbyists then used technique a)—bringing up a new argument. Their line then became: yes, perhaps burn accidents do happen, but rear-end collisions are relatively rare (note the echo of technique b) here as well). Thus Standard 301 was not needed. This set the NHTSA off on a new round of analyzing accident reports. The government's findings finally were that rear-end collisions were seven and a half times more likely to result in fuel spills than were front-end collisions. So much for that argument.

By now it was 1972; NHTSA had been researching and analyzing for four years to answer Ford's objections. During that time, nearly 9,000 people burned to death in flaming wrecks. Tens of thousands more were badly burned and scarred for life. And the four-year delay meant that well over 10 million new unsafe vehicles went on the road, vehicles that will be crashing, leaking fuel and incinerating people well into the 1980s.

Ford now had to enter its third round of battling the new regulations. On the "the problem is not X but Y" principle, the company had to look around for something new to get itself off the hook. One might have thought that, faced with all the latest statistics on the horrifying number of deaths in flaming accidents, Ford would find the task difficult. But the company's rhetoric was brilliant. The problem was not burns, but . . . impact! Most of the people killed in these fiery accidents, claimed Ford, would have died whether the car burned or not. They were killed by the kinetic force of the impact, not the fire.

And so once again, as in some giant underwater tennis game, the ball bounced into the government's court and the absurdly pro-industry NHTSA began another slow-motion response. Once again it began a time-consuming round of test crashes and embarked on a study of accidents. The latter, however, revealed that a large and growing number of corpses taken from burned cars involved in rear-end crashes contained no cuts, bruises or broken bones. They clearly would have survived the accident unharmed if the cars had not caught fire. This pattern was confirmed in careful rear-end crash tests performed by the Insurance Institute for Highway Safety. A University of Miami study found an inordinate number of Pintos burning on rear-end impact and concluded that this demonstrated "a clear and present hazard to all Pinto owners."

Pressure on NHTSA from Ralph Nader and consumer groups began mounting. The industry-agency collusion was so obvious that Senator Joseph Montoya (D-N.M.) introduced legislation about Standard 301. NHTSA waffled some more and again announced its intentions to promulgate a rear-end collision standard.

Waiting, as it normally does, until the last day allowed for response, Ford filed with NHTSA a gargantuan batch of letters, studies and charts now arguing that the federal testing criteria were unfair. Ford also argued that design changes required to meet the standard would take 43 months, which seemed like a rather long time in light of the fact that the entire Pinto was designed in about two years. Specifically, new complaints about the standard involved the weight of the test vehicle, whether or not the brakes should be engaged at the moment of impact and the claim that the standard should only apply to cars, not trucks or buses. Perhaps the most amusing argument was that the engine should not be idling during crash tests, the rationale being that an idling engine meant that the gas tank had to contain gasoline and that the hot lights needed to film the crash might ignite the gasoline and cause a fire.

Some of these complaints were accepted, others rejected. But they all required examination and testing by a weak-kneed NHTSA, meaning more of those 18-month studies the industry loves so much. So the complaints served their real purpose—delay; all told, an eight-year delay, while Ford manufactured more than three million profitable, dangerously incendiary Pintos. To justify this delay, Henry Ford II called more press conferences to predict the demise of American civilization. "If we can't meet the standards when they are published," he warned, "we will have to close down. And if we have to close down some production because we don't meet standards we're in for real trouble in this country."

⋅◈⋅

While government bureaucrats dragged their feet on lifesaving Standard 301, a different kind of expert was taking a close look at the Pinto—the "recon man." "Recon" stands for reconstruction; recon men reconstruct accidents for police departments, insurance companies and lawyers who want to know exactly who or what caused an accident. It didn't take many rear-end Pinto accidents to demonstrate the weakness of the car. Recon men began encouraging lawyers to look beyond one driver or another to the manufacturer in their search for fault, particularly in the growing number of accidents where passengers were uninjured by collision but were badly burned by fire.

Pinto lawuits began mounting fast against Ford. Says John Versace, executive safety engineer at Ford's Safety Research Center, "Ulcers are running pretty high among the engineers who worked on the Pinto. Every lawyer in the country seems to want to take their depositions." (The Safety Research Center is an impressive glass and concrete building standing by itself about a mile from Ford World Headquarters in Dearborn. Looking at it, one imagines its large staff protects consumers from burned and broken limbs. Not so. The Center is the technical support arm of Jack Echold's 14-person anti-regulatory lobbying team in World Headquarters.)

When the Pinto liability suits began, Ford strategy was to go to a jury. Confident it could hide the Pinto crash tests, Ford thought that juries of solid American registered voters would buy the industry doctrine that drivers, not cars, cause accidents. It didn't work. It seems that juries are much quicker to see the truth than bureaucracies, a fact that gives one confidence in democracy. Juries began ruling against the company, granting million-dollar awards to plaintiffs.

"We'll never go to a jury again," says Al Slechter in Ford's Washington office. "Not in a fire case. Juries are just too sentimental. They see those charred remains and forget the evidence. No sir, we'll settle."

Settlement involves less cash, smaller legal fees and less publicity, but it is an indication of the weakness of their case. Nevertheless, Ford has been settling when it is clear that the company can't pin the blame on the driver of the other car. But, since the company carries $2 million deductible product-liability insurance, these settlements have a direct impact on the bottom line. They must therefore be considered a factor in determining the net operating profit on the Pinto. It's impossible to get a straight answer from Ford on the profitability of the Pinto and the impact of lawsuit settlements on it—even when you have a curious and mildly irate shareholder call to inquire, as we did. However, financial officer Charles Matthews did admit that the company establishes a reserve for large dollar settlements. He would not divulge the amount of the reserve and had no explanation for its absence from the annual report.

Until recently, it was clear that, whatever the cost of these settlements, it was not enough to seriously cut into the Pinto's enormous profits. The cost of retooling Pinto assembly lines and of equipping each car with a safety gadget like that $5.08 Goodyear bladder was, company accountants calculated, greater than that of paying out millions to survivors like Robbie Carlton or to widows and widowers of victims like Sandra Gillespie. The bottom line ruled, and inflammable Pintos kept rolling out of the factories.

In 1977, however, an incredibly sluggish government has at last instituted Standard 301. Now Pintos will have to have rupture-proof gas tanks. Or will they?

⌭

To everyone's surprise, the 1977 Pinto recently passed a rear-end crash test in Phoenix, Arizona, for NHTSA. The agency was so convinced the Pinto would fail that it was the first car tested. Amazingly, it did not burst into flame.

"We have had so many Ford failures in the past," explained agency engineer Tom Grubbs, "I felt sure the Pinto would fail."

How did it pass?

Remember that one-dollar, one-pound plastic baffle that was on one of the three modified Pintos that passed the pre-production crash tests nearly ten years ago? Well, it is a standard feature on the 1977 Pinto. In the Phoenix test it protected the gas tank from being perforated by those four bolts on the differential housing.

We asked Grubbs if he noticed any other substantial alterations in the rear-end structure of the car. "No," he replied, "the [plastic baffle] seems to be the only noticeable change over the 1976 model."

But was it? What Tom Grubbs and the Department of Transportation didn't know when they tested the car was that it was manufactured in St. Thomas, Ontario. Ontario? The significance of that becomes clear when you learn that Canada has for years had extremely strict rear-end collision standards.

Tom Irwin is the business manager of Charlie Rossi Ford, the Scottsdale, Arizona, dealership that sold the Pinto to Tom Grubbs. He refused to explain why he was selling Fords made in Canada when there is a huge Pinto assembly plant much closer by in California. "I know why you're asking that question, and I'm not going to answer it," he blurted out. "You'll have to ask the company."

But Ford's regional office in Phoenix has "no explanation" for the presence of Canadian cars in their local dealerships. Farther up the line in Dearborn, Ford people claim there is absolutely no difference between American and Canadian Pintos. They say cars are shipped back and forth across the border as a matter of course. But they were hard pressed to explain why some Canadian Pintos were shipped all the way to Scottsdale, Arizona. Significantly, one engineer at the St. Thomas plant did admit that the existence of strict rear-end collision standards in Canada "might encourage us to pay a little more attention to quality control on that part of the car."

The Department of Transportation is considering buying an American Pinto and running the test again. For now, it will only say that the situation is under investigation.

Whether the new American Pinto fails or passes the test, Standard 301 will never force the company to test or recall the more than two million pre-1977 Pintos still on the highway. Seventy or more people will burn to death in those cars every year for many years to come. If the past is any indication, Ford will continue to accept the deaths.

According to safety expert Byron Bloch, the older cars could quite easily be retrofitted with gas tanks containing fuel cells. "These improved tanks would add at least 10 mph improved safety performance to the rear end," he estimated, "but it would cost Ford $20 to $30 a car, so they won't do it unless they are forced to." Dr. Kenneth Saczalski, safety engineer with the Office of Naval Research in Washington, agrees. "The Defense Department has developed virtually fail-safe fuel systems and retrofitted them into existing vehicles. We have shown them to the auto industry and they have ignored them."

Unfortunately, the Pinto is not an isolated case of corporate malpractice in the auto industry. Neither is Ford a lone sinner. There probably isn't a car on the road without a safety hazard known to its manufacturer. And though Ford may have the best auto lobbyists in Washington, it is not alone. The anti-emission control lobby and the anti-safety lobby usually work in chorus form, presenting a well-harmonized message from the country's richest industry, spoken through the voices of individual companies—the Motor Vehicle Manufacturers Association, the Business Council and the U.S. Chamber of Commerce.

Furthermore, cost-valuing human life is not used by Ford alone. Ford was just the only company careless enough to let such an embarrassing calculation slip into the public records. The process of willfully trading lives for profits is built into corporate capitalism. Commodore Vanderbilt publicly scorned George Westinghouse and his "foolish" air brakes while people died by the hundreds in accidents on Vanderbilt's railroads.

The original draft of the Motor Vehicle Safety Act provided for criminal sanction against a manufacturer who willfully placed an unsafe car on the market. Early in the proceedings the auto industry lobbied the provision out of the bill. Since then, there have been those damage settlements, of course, but the only government punishment meted out to auto companies for non-compliance to standards has been a minuscule fine, usually $5,000 to $10,000. One wonders how long the Ford Motor Company would continue to market lethal cars were Henry Ford II and Lee Iacocca serving 20-year terms in Leavenworth for consumer homicide.

 **NO**

Closing Argument by Mr. Neal

If it please the Court, Counsel, ladies and gentlemen:

Not too many years ago our broad American Industry straddled the world like a giant.

It provided us with the highest standards of living ever known to man.

It was ended, eliminated, no more. Now it is an Industry weakened by deteriorating plants and equipment, weakened by lack of products, weakened by lack of manpower, weakened by inadequate capital, weakened by massive Government controls, weakened by demands on foreign oil and reeling from competition from foreign manufacturers.

I stand here today to defend a segment of that tattered Industry.

One company that saw the influx of foreign, small-made cars in 1967 and '68 and tried to do something about it, tried to build a small car with American labor that would compete with foreign imports, that would keep Americans employed, that would keep American money in America.

As State's witness, Mr. Copp, admitted, Ford Motor Company would have made more profit sticking to the bigger cars where the profit is.

That would have been the easiest way.

It was not the way Ford Motor Company took.

It made the Ford to compete. And this is no easy effort, members of the jury.

As even Mr. Copp admitted, the Automobile Industry is extremely regulated.

It has to comply with the Clean Air Act, the Safety Act, the Emissions Control Act, the Corporate Average Fuel Economy Act, the Safety Act, and OSHA as well as a myriad of Statutes and Regulations applicable to large and small businesses generally, and, again, as Mr. Copp admitted, it now takes twice as many Engineers to make a car as it did before all the massive Government controls.

Nevertheless, Ford Motor Company undertook the effort to build a subcompact, to take on the imports, to save jobs for Americans and to make a profit for its stockholders.

This rather admirable effort has a sad ending.

On August 10, 1978, a young man gets into a van weighing over 4,000 pounds and heads towards Elkhart, Indiana, on a bad highway called "U.S. 33."

He has a couple of open beer bottles in his van, together with his marijuana which he may or may not have been smoking. . . .

From *U. S. District Court*, South Bend, Indiana, State of Indiana v. Ford Motor Company (January 15, 1980).

As he was cruising along on an open stretch of highway in broad daylight at at least 50 to 55 miles per hour, he drops his "smoke," ignores his driving and the road, and fails to see a little Pinto with its emergency flashers on stopped on the highway ahead.

He plows into the rear of the Pinto with enormous force and three young girls are killed.

Not the young man, but Ford Motor Company is charged with reckless homicide and arraigned before you.

I stand here to defend Ford Motor Company, and to tell you that we are not killers. . . .

Mr. Cosentino gave you the definition of "reckless homicide" as "plain, conscious and unjustifiable disregard of harm, which conduct involves substantial deviation from acceptable standards of conduct."

This case and the elements of this case, strictly speaking, involve 40 days, July 1, 1978 to August 10, 1978, and the issue is whether, during that period of time, Ford Motor Company recklessly, as that term is defined, omitted to warn of a danger and repair, and that reckless omission caused the deaths involved. . . .

[I]n my opening statement, I asked you to remember nine points, and I asked you to judge me, my client, by how well or how poorly we supported those nine points.

Let me run through briefly and just tick them off, the nine points, with you, and then let me get down to discussing the evidence and record with respect to those nine points.

One, I said this was a badly-designed highway, with curbs so high the girls couldn't get off when they had to stop their car in an emergency.

Two, I said that the girls stopped there with their emergency flashers on, and this boy in a van weighing more than 4,000 pounds, with his eyes off the road, looking down trying to find the "smoke," rammed into the rear of that Pinto at at least 50 miles an hour, closing speed.

And by "closing speed," I mean the differential speed.

That is Points 1 and 2.

Point 3, I said the 1973 Pinto met every fuel-system integrity standard of any Federal, State or Local Government.

Point No. 4, I said, Ford Motor Company adopted a mandatory standard dealing with fuel-system integrity on rear-impact of 20 miles per hour moving-barrier, 4,000 pound moving-barrier, and I said that no other manufacturer in the world had adopted any standard, only Ford Motor Company.

Five, I said that the Pinto, it is not comparable to a Lincoln Continental, a Cadillac, a Mercedes Benz or that Ascona, or whatever that exotic car was that Mr. Bloch called—but I did say No. 5, it is comparable to other 1973 subcompacts.

No. 6, I said that . . . we would bring in the Engineers who designed and manufactured the Pinto, and I brought them from the stand, and they would tell you that they thought the Pinto was a good, safe car, and they bought it for themselves, their wives and their children to drive.

No. 7, I told you that we would bring in the statistics that indicated to us as to our state of mind that the Pinto performed as well or better than other subcompacts.

And, No. 8, I said we would nevertheless tell you that we decided to recall the Pinto in June of 1978, and having made that decision for the reasons that I—that I told you I would explain, we did everything in our power to recall that Pinto as quickly as possible, that there was nothing we could have done between July 1, 1978 and 8-10-1978, to recall the Pinto any faster.

And finally, No. 9, I said we would demonstrate that any car, any subcompact, any small car, and even some larger cars, sitting out there on Highway 33 in the late afternoon of August 10, 1978 and watching that van roar down that highway with the boy looking for his "smoke"—any car would have suffered the same consequences.

Those are the nine points I ask you to judge me by, and let me touch on the evidence, now, with respect to those nine points. . . .

The van driver, Duggar, took his eyes off the road and off driving to look around the floor of the van for a "smoke."

Duggar had two open beer bottles in the car and a quantity of marijuana.

Duggar was not prosecuted for reckless homicide or for possession of marijuana, even though his prior record of conviction was:

November, '73, failure to yield right-of-way;

April, '76, speeding 65 miles an hour in a 45 mile an hour zone;

July, '76, running stop sign;

June, '77, speeding 45 in a 25 zone;

August, '77, driver's license suspended;

September, '77, driving with suspended license;

December, '77, license suspended again.

Mr. Cosentino, you got up in front of this jury and you cried.

Well, I cry, too, because Mr. Duggar is driving, and you didn't do anything about him with a record like that except say, "Come in and help me convict Ford Motor Company, and I will help you get probation."

We all cry.

But crying doesn't do any good, and it doesn't help this jury.

The big disputed fact in this case regarding the accident, ladies and gentlemen, is the closing speed. The differential speed, the difference between the speed the Pinto was going, if any, and the speed the van was going.

That is the big disputed fact in regard to this accident.

And whether the Pinto was stopped or not is relevant only as it affects closing speed. . . .

Mr. Duggar testified—I guess he is great about speed, because while he's looking down there for his "smoke," he knows he is going 50 miles per hour in the van.

But he said he was going 50 miles per hour at the time of impact, and he said the Pinto was going 15.

But here is the same man who admits he was going at least 50 miles per hour and looking around down "on a clear day," trying to find the "smoke" and looked up only to see the Pinto ten feet ahead of him.

Here is a witness willing to say under oath that the Pinto was going 15 miles per hour, even though he had one-sixth of a second—one-sixth of a second to make the judgment on the speed.

Here is a witness who says he had the time to calculate the speed of the Pinto but had no time even to try to apply brakes because there were no skid marks.

And here is a witness who told Dr. Galen Miller, who testified here, that—told him right after the accident that in fact the Pinto was stopped.

And here was a witness who made a deal with the State.

And here was a witness who's not prosecuted for recklessness.

And here is a witness who is not prosecuted for possession of marijuana.

So the State's proof from Mr. Alfred Clark through Mr. Duggar is kind of a smorgasbord or a buffet—you can go in and take your choice.

You can pick 15—5 miles per hour, if you want to as to differential speed, or you can take 35 miles per hour.

And the State, with the burden of proof says, "Here," "Here," "Here. I will give you a lot of choice."

"You want choices? I will give you choices. Here. Take 5. Take 15. 10, 15, 20, 25, 30, 35."

Because, ladies and gentlemen of the jury,—and I'm sure you are—the alternatives the State offers you are closing speeds of anywhere from 5 miles—on the low side—to 35 miles on the high side as a differential speed in this accident. . . .

Mr. Toms, the former National Highway Traffic Safety Administrator, told you that in his opinion the 20 mile per hour rear-impact moving-barrier was a reasonable and acceptable standard of conduct for 1973 vehicles.

Why didn't Ford adopt a higher standard?

Mr. MacDonald, a man even Mr. Copp—do you remember this? Mr. Mac-Donald sitting on the stand, the father of the Pinto, as Mr. Cosentino called him—and he didn't deny it.

He says, "Yes, it is my car."

Mr. MacDonald, a man even Mr. Copp—on cross examination I asked him, I said:

"Q Mr. Copp, isn't it a fact that you consider Harold MacDonald an extremely safety-conscious Engineer?"

And he said:

"A Yes, sir."

Mr. MacDonald, that extremely safety-conscious Engineer, told you he did not believe a higher standard could be met for 1973 cars without greater problems, such as handling, where more accidents and death occur.

Mr. Copp, let's take the State's witness, Copp.

Mr. Copp admitted that even today, seven years later, the Federal Government Standard is only 30 miles per hour, 10 miles higher than what Ford adopted—voluntarily adopted for itself for 1973.

And Mr. Copp further testified that a 30 mile an hour would be equivalent only to a 31.5 or 32 mile car-to-car.

So, ladies and gentlemen of the jury, Mr. Cosentino tells you about, "Oh, isn't it terrible to put these cars out there, wasn't it awful—did you know?"

Well, do you know that today, the—today, 1980 model cars are required to meet only a 30 mile an hour rear-impact moving-barrier standard? 1980 cars.

And that that is equivalent to a 32 mile an hour car-to-car, and yet Ford Motor Company, the only company in the world, imposed upon itself a standard and made a car in 1973, seven years ago, that would meet 26 to 28 miles an hour, within 5, 6 or 7 miles of what the cars are required by law to meet today.

Mr. Cosentino will tell you, frankly, the cars today, in his judgment, are defective and he will prosecute.

What a chaos would evolve if the Government set the standard for automobiles and says, "That is reasonable," and then Local Prosecutors in the fifty states around the country start saying, "I am not satisfied, and I am going to prosecute the manufacturer."

Well, Mr. Cosentino may say that the standard should be 40.

The Prosecutor in Alabama may say, "No, it should be 50."

The Prosecutor in Alaska may say, "No, it should be 60."

And the Prosecutor in Tennessee—they say—you know, "I am satisfied—I am satisfied with 30," or, "I think it should be 70."

How can our companies survive?

Point 5, the 1973 Pinto was comparable in design and manufacture to other 1973 subcompacts.

I say again, ladies and gentlemen, we don't compare the Pinto with Lincolns, Cadillacs, Mercedes Benz—we ask you to compare the Pinto with the other three subcompacts.

Let's take the State's witnesses on this point first.

Mr. Bloch—Mr. Cosentino didn't mention Mr. Bloch, but I don't want him to be forgotten.

Mr. Bloch and Mr. Copp complain about the Pinto, and that is easy.

Let's descend to the particulars. Let's see what they really said.

Well, they complain about the metal, the gage of the metal in the fuel tank; you remember that?

And then on cross examination it was brought out that the general range of metal in fuel tanks ranged between twenty-three-thousandths of an inch and forty-thousandths of an inch.

That is the general range. Twenty-three-thousandths on the low to forty-thousandths on the high, and lo and behold, what is the gage of metal in the Pinto tank?

Thirty-five-thousandths.

And Mr. Bloch admits that it is in the upper third of the general range.

And they complain about the bumper on the Pinto.

And, remember, I said we would show that the Pinto was comparable to other '73 subcompacts.

They complain about the bumper, but then they admit on cross examination the Vega, the Gremlin, the Colt, the Pinto and the Toyota had about the same bumper.

And they complain of a lack of a protective shield between the tank and the axle, but they admitted on cross examination that no other 1973 car had such a shield, and Mr. Copp admits that there was no significant puncture in the 1973—in the Ulrich accident caused by the axle, and you remember I had him get up here and say, "Point out where this protective shield would have done something, where this puncture source we are talking about—" and you remember, it is so small—I can't find it now.

So much for the protective shield.

And then they complained about the insufficient rear structure in the Pinto, but they both admit that the Pinto had a left side rail hat section and that the Vega had none, nothing on either side, that the Pinto had shear plates, these plates in the trunk, and that neither the Vega, the Gremlin or the Colt or Toyota had any of these.

And the Vega used the coil-spring suspension, when the Pinto had a leaf-spring, and that was additional structure.

I am not going through all those—well, I will mention one more thing.

They talked about puncture sources, there is a puncture source there, puncture source here, but on cross examination, they end up by admitting that the puncture sources on all subcompacts have about the same—and in about the same space. . . .

Mr. MacDonald testified, "Yes, I thought the Pinto was a reasonably safe car. I think the '73 Pinto is still a reasonably safe car, and I bought one, I drove it for years for myself."

Mr. Olsen—you remember little Mr. Frank Olsen?

He came in here, has his little eighteen-year-old daughter—he said, "I am an Engineer responsible for the Pinto. I think it is a safe car. I bought one for my little eighteen-year-old daughter, and she drove it for several years."

And Mr. Freers, the man who Mr. Cosentino objected to going over the fact that he was from Rose-Hullman, and on the Board of Trustees there—Mr. Freers said, "I like the Pinto. I am an Engineer responsible for the Pinto, and I bought a '73 Pinto for my young son and he drove it several years."

And then Mr. Feaheny says, "I am one of the Engineers responsible for the Pinto, and I bought one for my wife, the mother of my six children, and she drove it for several years."

Now, when Mr. Cosentino tried to say there was something phoney about that—he brought out their salaries.

And I—I don't know how to deal with the salary question.

It just seems to me to be so irrelevant, like some other things I am going to talk about in a minute that I am just going to simply say, "It is irrelevant," and go on.

But he said to these people—he suggested to you, suggested to these people, "Well, you make a lot of money, you can afford better than a Pinto."

Like, "You don't really mean you had a Pinto?"

And Mr. Feaheny says, "Yes, I could afford a more expensive car, but, you know, I—all of us, we have been fighting, we come out with something we thought would fight the imports, and we were proud of it, and our families were proud of it."

Do you think, ladies and gentlemen of the jury, that Mr. MacDonald was indifferent, reckless, when he bought and drove the Pinto?

He drives on the same roads, he has the—subject to the same reckless people that Mr. Cosentino didn't prosecute.

Do you think that Mr. Olsen was reckless and indifferent when he gave a Pinto to his eighteen-year-old daughter, a '73 Pinto?

Do you think that Mr. Freers was reckless when he gave one to his young son? . . .

Finally, ladies and gentlemen—not "finally," but Point No. 8: Notwithstanding all I have said, Ford Motor Company decided on June 8th, 1978, to recall the Pintos to improve fuel systems and did everything in its power to recall it as quickly as possible.

This is really what this case, I guess, is all about, because that period of time involved is July 1, 1978 until August 10, 1978.

And the Court will charge you, as I said, the elements are whether we recklessly failed to warn and repair during that period of time.

And whether that reckless omission, if any, caused the deaths.

And you may ask—and I think it is fair to ask—why recall the Pinto, the '73 Pinto, if it is comparable to other subcompacts, if statistics say it is performing as well as other '73 subcompacts?

And if Ford had a standard for '73 that no other manufacturer had?

And Feaheny and Mr. Misch told you why.

The Federal Government started an investigation. The publicity was hurting the Company.

They thought the Government was wrong, but they said, "You can't fight City Hall."

"We could fight and fight and we could go to Court and we could fight, but it's not going to get us anywhere. If we can improve it, let's do it and let's don't fight the Federal Government."

Maybe the Company should not have recalled the '73 Pinto.

Douglas Toms did not think, as he told you on the stand under oath, that the '73 Pinto should have been recalled.

He had information that the Pinto did as well as other cars;

That Pinto fire accidents equaled the total Pinto population or equaled the percentage of Pinto population to all car population.

And Mr. Bloch, on the other hand, says, "All of them should be recalled."

He said, "The Pinto should have been recalled."

He said, "The Vega should have been recalled."

He said, "The Gremlin should be recalled."

And he didn't know about the Dodge Colt.

Nevertheless, the Company did decide to recall the Pinto. And they issued widely-disseminated Press Releases on June 9, 1978.

It was in the newspapers, TV, radio, according to the proof in this case.

And thereafter the Government regulated what they did in the recall.

That is what Mr. Misch told you.

He said, "From the time we started—June 9, 1978—to August 10, Mr.—the Federal Government regulated what we did."

Now, Mr. Cosentino is prosecuting us.

And the Federal Government has regulated us.

Mr. Misch said, "The Federal Government reviewed what kind of Press Releases we should issue, what kind of Recall Letter we should issue, what kind of a Modification Kit that they would approve."

Even so—it is undisputed, absolutely undisputed that we did everything in our power to recall as fast as possible—nights, days, weekends.

And notwithstanding all of that, the first kit—the first complete kit was assembled August 1, 1978.

And on August 9, 1978, there were only 20,000 kits available for 1,600,000 cars.

And this was not Ford's fault. Ford was pushing the suppliers, the people who were outside the Company doing work for them.

And Mr. Vasher testified that he got the names of the current owners from R. L. Polk on July 17;

That the Ulrich name was not among them;

That he sent the Recall Letter in August to the original owner because he had no Ulrich name.

Now,—and he said he couldn't have gotten the Ulrich name by August 10.

Now, Mr. Cosentino said, "Well, the Ulrich Registration was on file with the State of Indiana and it is open to the public."

Well, Ford Motor Company doesn't know where these 1,600,000 cars are. It has to use R. L. Polk because they collect the information by the VIN Numbers.

If Ford Motor Company went to each state, they would go to fifty states and they would have each of the fifty states run through its files 1,600,000 VIN Numbers.

And Mr. Vasher, who is the expert in there, said it would take months and months to do that.

And, finally, ladies and gentlemen, the Government didn't approve the Modification Kit until August 15, 1978.

But the State says that we should have warned—we should have warned 1973 Pinto owners not to drive the car.

But the Government never suggested that.

Based on our information, and confirmed by the Toms testimony, our cars were performing as well—or better than—other '73 subcompacts.

As Mr. Misch so succinctly stated, "We would have been telling the Pinto owners to park their Pintos and get into another car no safer—and perhaps even less safe—than the Pinto." . . .

Well, we submit that the physical facts, the placement of the—the placement of the gasoline cap, where it is found, the testimony of Levi Woodard, and Nancy Fogo—demonstrate the closing speed in this case was at least 50 to 60 miles per hour.

Mr. Copp, the State's witness, testified that no small car made in America in 1973 would withstand 40 to 50 miles per hour—40 to 50 rear-impact. No small car made in America in 1973 would withstand a 40-plus mile per hour rear-impact.

The Dodge Colt would not have; the Vega could not have; the Gremlin would not have; and certainly even the Toyota would not have.

Mr. Habberstad told you that no small car—and some big cars—would have withstood this crash.

And he established by the crash-tests you have seen that the Vega could not withstand 50;

That the Gremlin could not withstand 50;

That the Toyota Corolla with the tank over the axle could not withstand 50;

And that even a full-sized Chevrolet Impala cannot withstand 50 miles per hour.

If it made no difference what kind of car was out there, members of the jury, how can Ford Motor Company have caused the deaths? . . .

I am not here to tell you that the 1973 Pinto was the strongest car ever built.

I'm not here to tell you it is equal to a Lincoln, a Cadillac, a Mercedes— that funny car that Mr. Bloch mentioned.

I'm not here to tell you a stronger car couldn't be built.

Most of us, however, learn early in life that there is "no Santa Claus," and, "There's no such thing as a free lunch."

If the public wanted it, and could pay for it, and we had the gasoline to drive it, Detroit could build a tank of a car—a car that would withstand practically anything, a car that would float if a careless driver drove it into the water.

A car that would be invulnerable even to the "Duggars" of the world.

But, members of the jury, only the rich could afford it and they would have to stop at every other gasoline station for a refill.

I am here to tell you that the 1973 Pinto is comparable to other '73 subcompacts, including that Toyota, that Corolla with the tank over the axle.

I am here to tell you it was not designed by some mysterious figure you have never seen.

It was designed and manufactured by Harold MacDonald, Frank Olsen and Howard Freers.

I am here to tell you these are the decent men doing an honorable job and trying to do a decent job.

I am here to tell you that Harold MacDonald, Frank Olsen, and Howard Freers are not reckless killers.

Harold MacDonald is the same man, State's witness, Copp, called an "extremely safety-conscious individual."

Frank Olsen is the same "Frank Olsen" Mr. Copp said was a "good Engineer."

And Howard Freers is the same "Howard Freers" Mr. Copp said was a "man of honesty and integrity."

I am here to tell you that these men honestly believe and honestly believed that the 1973 Pinto was—and is—a reasonably safe car—so safe they bought it for their daughters, sons and family.

Do you think that Frank Olsen believed he was acting in plain, conscious, unjustifiable disregard of harm?

When he bought a '73 Pinto for his eighteen-year-old daughter?

Or Howard Freers, when he bought one for his young son?

I am here to tell you that the design and manufacture of an automobile is not an easy task;

That it takes time to know whether a change in one part of the 14,000 parts of a car will or will not cause greater problems elsewhere in the car or its performance.

I am here to tell you that safety is a matter of degree;

That no one can say that a car that will meet a 26 to 28 mile per hour rear-impact is unsafe and one that will meet a 30 to 32 impact is safe.

I am here to tell you that if this country is to survive economically, it is really time to stop blaming Industry or Business, large or small, for our own sins.

I am here to tell you that no car is now or ever can be safe when reckless drivers are on the road.

I am here to tell you that Ford Motor Company may not be perfect, but it is not guilty of reckless homicide.

Thank you, members of the jury.

And God bless you in your deliberations.

POSTSCRIPT

Was Ford to Blame in the Pinto Case?

Well, is Ford guilty? The jury said no, but the larger issue remains open: How shall we allot responsibility, where many factors combine to bring about an injury?

Consider the following: Ford Motor Company obeyed the law, but the law was not all it should have been. The reason it was not is that the Ford Motor Company spent a great deal of money lobbying Congress to put obstacles in front of new and higher legal safety standards, in order to be able to sell the Pinto for a lower price and thus increase its market share and yes, its profits. Is not the government, through its agencies, just as guilty as Ford for not fulfilling its role as protector of the consumer?

What was the government's duty at this point? To protect those consumers of the automobile? To protect the workers in the Ford Motor Company factories? To protect the American manufacturers against further encroachments from foreign competition? Does government have some absolute duty in these cases, or are our legislators asked only to bring about the greatest good for the greatest number? How would they have done *that*, in this case? Three girls aren't very many. Could it not be shown that all the people who innocently and safely enjoyed their Pintos at the lower cost outweigh, in their happiness, the enormous unhappiness of the very few who got burned? Or is that the sort of thinking that we take ethics courses to learn not to do?

Ford Motor Company found new structural allies when the criminal negligence case was brought against it. Under our Constitution, the legal system joins in to protect the defendant in these cases. When we enter the courtroom, and The People stand at the bar training all Its accusatory weight against an individual, the traditions weigh in heavily on the side of the individual—and in general, that is as we want it to be. It seems odd that the same traditions apply when the "individual" is one of the largest corporations in the world. If you are very large and rich, you can hire lawyers like James Neal, who knows how to discount every bit of evidence against his client, how to introduce every piece of evidence in favor, and then also knows how to discredit witnesses, how to argue by suggestion, and above all how to deflect attention from his client's wrongdoing. His facts are correct, his presentation is inherently plausible—*of course* the driver of the van was at fault—and his style is immensely entertaining. Could The People hire such a lawyer? Not on your life.

Have we lost perspective on risk? We know how to make a safe car. We build it like a tank and rig it to go no faster than 30 miles per hour. But no one would buy it. So we make unsafe cars that people will buy—lighter, faster, more likely to crumple and burn in an accident. Is this trade-off acceptable to a trading nation that is used to making choices? Or should we be more diligent about eliminating the last threats to safety?

Suggested Reading

For more information regarding the Pinto case and its subsequent effects, try some of the following readings:

Lawrence A. Benningson and Arnold I. Benningson, "Product Liability: Manufacturers Beware!" *Harvard Business Review* 53(3): 122–32 (May–June 1974).

Richard DeGeorge, "Ethical Responsibilities of Engineers in Large Organizations: The Pinto Case." *Business and Professional Ethics Journal* 1(1): 4–14 (Fall 1981).

Richard A. Epstein, "Is Pinto a Criminal?" *Regulation* (March–April 1980), pp. 16–17.

Niles Howard and Susan Antilla, "What Price Safety? The 'Zero-Risk' Debate." *Dun's Review* (September 1979), pp. 47–57.

David G. Owen, *Products Liability in a Nutshell,* Eighth Edition, Eagan: MN: West, 2008.

Mark B. Fuller and Malcolm S. Salter, "Ford Motor Company (A)" (Boston: Case Study, Harvard Business School, 1982), p. 4.

ISSUE 14

Should We Require Labeling for Genetically Modified Food?

YES: Philip L. Bereano, from "The Right to Know What We Eat," *Seattle Times* (October 11, 1998)

NO: Joseph A. Levitt, from Statement before the Health, Education, Labor, and Pensions Committee, United States Senate (September 26, 2000)

ISSUE SUMMARY

YES: The consumer's interest in knowing where his food comes from does not necessarily have to do with the chemical and nutritional properties of the food. Kosher pastrami, for instance, is identical to the nonkosher product, and dolphin-safe tuna is still tuna. But we have a real and important interest in knowing the processes by which our foods arrived on the table, Bereano argues, and the demand for a label for bioengineered foods is entirely legitimate.

NO: Levitt points out that as far as the law is concerned, only the nutritional traits and characteristics of foods are subject to safety assessment. Labeling has been required only where health risks exist, or where there is danger that a product's marketing claims may mislead the consumer as to the food's characteristics. Breeding techniques have never been subject to labeling, nor should genetic engineering techniques.

How much weight can a little label bear? We have seen a profound change in the function of the label over the course of the last century. At first, the label, if such there was, said only what the container contained and the brand name. "Carter's Little Liver Pills." "Argo Cornstarch." With advances in packaging, the labels became more attractive, brighter, eye-catching, and began to carry marketing claims. That was the label's purpose: to sell the product, by featuring a trusted brand name (logo, trademark) and an advertisement for the product, in a design aimed at capturing attention.

Poisons, of course, had to be labeled as such, to warn consumers to use them carefully—and to warn off the vulnerable. Remember the frightening skull and crossbones?

The consumer movement changed all that. Calling upon the police power of the state (the right and obligation of the state to protect the health, safety, and morals of the citizens), the Food and Drug Administration began requiring labels to fulfill serious informational functions. Now actual weights have to be listed on the package, a list of ingredients in order of weight must appear on any complex product, and the real nutritional content has to be listed in a plainly visible uniform panel on the back of the package (even for little candy bars). Even nonfood items have labeling requirements; garments and bedding must state the materials from which they are made, and bedding labels must warrant that those materials are new.

Those who would like genetically modified (GM) foods to be labeled as such do not conceal their interest in the same agenda. They would like to see all GM foods (corn, for instance) and all processed foods containing GM ingredients (vegetable oil, for instance) labeled as such, so that consumers will be worried by the labels, so that eventually GM foods will be taken off the market. In the light of the general profitability of GM foods, it seems politically more feasible to get a labeling requirement than a prohibition. Besides, in some polls, up to 70 percent of consumers have said that they would want to know if the product they bought was genetically modified. Who could object to full information about a product, the process by which it was produced as well as its content, being given to the consumer?

As it turns out, there are many objections. One is the sheer mass of effort required to sort out foods that contain GM products (practically ubiquitous at this point), especially processed foods like cereals and bake mixes. More important, whether or not a label designates a difference in a product, the consumer must assume it does and must assume, unless there is proof to the contrary, that it designates a dangerous difference. There was no doubt as to the intention or the effect of the requirement of labeling for tobacco products. There is every reason to think that a required label, "Contains Genetically Modified Products," would be read as a skull and crossbones.

Not every political agenda justifies labeling, after all. How would we react to a request to label as such all boxes of tampons or sanitary pads that were packed by African Americans? Suppose we could come up with a survey that showed that up to 70 percent of white women in a particular area would want to have that information. Would that influence our reaction? Ask yourself, as you read the following selections, just what political agenda or secondary purposes we want attached to the police power of the state. Is the demand for "labeling" justified or not?

YES ↵

Philip L. Bereano

The Right to Know What We Eat

"I personally have no wish to eat anything produced by genetic modification, nor do I knowingly offer this sort of produce to my family or guests. There is increasing evidence that many people feel the same way."

—Prince Charles, *London Telegraph,* June 8, 1998.

Genetic engineering is a set of new techniques for altering the basic makeup of plants and animals. Genes from insects, animals, and humans have been added to crop plants; human genes have been added to pigs and cattle.

Although genetic-engineering techniques are biologically novel, the industry and government are so eager to achieve financial success that they say the products of the technologies are pretty much the same ("substantially equivalent") as normal crops. Despite the gene tinkering, the new products are not being tested extensively to find out how they differ and to be sure that any hazards are within acceptable limits.

These foods are now appearing in the supermarkets and on our dinner plates, but the industry and government have been vigorously resisting consumer attempts to label these "novel foods" in order to distinguish them from more traditional ones.

The failure of the U.S. government to require that genetically engineered foods (GEFs) be labeled presents consumers with quandaries: issues of free speech and consumers' right to know, religious rights for those with dietary restrictions, and cultural rights for people, such as vegetarians, who choose to avoid consuming foods of certain origins.

The use of antibiotic-resistant genes engineered into crop plants as "markers" can contribute to the spread of antibiotic-tolerant disease bacteria; this resistance is a major public-health problem, as documented by a recent study of the National Academy of Sciences. Some genetic recombinations can lead to allergic or auto-immune reactions. The products of some genes which are used as plant pesticides have been implicated in skin diseases in farm and market workers.

The struggle over labeling is occurring because industry knows that consumers do not want to eat GEFs; labeled products will likely fail in the marketplace. However, as the British publication *The Economist* noted, "if Monsanto cannot persuade us, it certainly has no right to foist its products on us." Labels would counter "foisting" and are legally justifiable.

The Government's Rationale

In 1992, the government abdicated any supervision over GEFs. Under Food and Drug Administration's rules, the agency does not even have access to industry information about a GEF unless the company decides voluntarily to submit it. Moreover, important information on risk-assessment questions is often withheld as being proprietary, "confidential business information." So "safety" cannot be judged in a precautionary way; we must await the inevitable hazardous event.

According to a former FDA official, the genetic processes used in the development of a new food are "NOT considered to be material information because there is no evidence that new biotech foods are different from other foods in ways related to safety."

James Maryanski, FDA biotechnology coordinator, claims that whether a food has been genetically engineered is not a "material fact" and FDA would not "require things to be on the label just because a consumer might want to know them."

Yet a standard law dictionary defines "material" as "important," "going to the merits," "relevant." Since labeling is a form of speech from growers and processors to purchasers, it is reasonable, therefore, to interpret "material" as comprising whatever issues a substantial portion of the consuming public defines as "important." And all the polls show that whether food is genetically engineered falls into such a category.

Last May, several religious leaders and citizen groups sued the FDA to change its position and to require that GEFs be labeled.

Process Labels

Some government officials have said that labeling should be only about the food product itself, not the process by which it is manufactured. Yet, the U.S. has many process food labels: kosher, dolphin-free, Made in America, union-made, free-range (chickens, for example), irradiated, and "green" terms such as "organic."

For many of these products, the scientific difference between an item which can carry the label and that which cannot is negligible or nonexistent. Kosher pastrami is chemically identical to non-kosher meat. Dolphin-free tuna and tuna caught by methods which result in killing of dolphins are the same, as are many products which are "made in America" when compared to those made abroad, or those made by unionized as opposed to nonunion workers.

These labeling rules recognize that consumers are interested in the processes by which their purchases are made and have a legal right to such knowledge. In none of these labeling situations has the argument been made that if the products are substantially equivalent, no label differentiation is permissible. It is constitutionally permissible for government rules to intrude slightly on the commercial speech of producers in order to expand the First Amendment rights of consumers to know what is of significant interest to them.

Substantial Equivalence

In order to provide an apparently rational basis for its refusal to exercise regulatory oversight in this regard, the U.S. government has adopted the industry's position that genetically engineered foods are "substantially equivalent" to their natural counterparts. The FDA ignores the contradictory practice of corporations in going to another government agency, the Patent Office, where they argue that a GEF is novel and different (in order to justify receiving monopoly protection).

"Substantial equivalence" is used as a basis for both eliminating regulatory assessment and failing to require labels on GEFs. However, the concept of substantial equivalence is subjective and imprecise.

Most genetic engineering is designed to meet corporate—not consumer—needs. Foods are engineered, for instance, to produce "counterfeit freshness." Consumers believe engineered characteristics such as color and texture indicate freshness, flavor and nutritional quality. Actually the produce is aging and growing stale, and nutritional value is being depleted. So much for "substantial equivalence."

The Precautionary Principle

Consumers International, a global alliance of more than 200 consumer groups, has suggested that "because the effects (of GEFs) are so difficult to predict, it is vital to have internationally agreed and enforceable rules for research protocols, field trials and post-marketing surveillance." This approach has become known as the "precautionary principle" and has entered into the regulatory processes of the European Union.

The principle reflects common-sense aphorisms such as "Better safe than sorry" and "An ounce of prevention is worth a pound of cure." It rests on the notion that parties who wish to change the social order (often while making money or gaining power and influence) should not be able to slough the costs and risks onto others. The new procedure's proponents should have to prove it is safe rather than forcing regulators or citizens to prove a lack of safety.

Look Before You Eat

For GEFs, labeling performs important functions in carrying out the precautionary principle. It places a burden on industry to show that genetic manipulations are socially beneficial and provides a financial incentive for them to do research to reduce uncertainty about the consequences of GEFs.

Democratic notions of free speech include the right to receive information as well as to disseminate it. It is fundamental to capitalist market theory that for transactions to be most efficient all parties must have "perfect information." The realities of modern food production create a tremendous imbalance of knowledge between producer and purchaser. Our society has relied on the government to redress this imbalance and make grocery shopping a fairer and more efficient—as well as safer—activity.

In an economic democracy, choice is the fundamental prerogative of the purchaser.

As some biologists have put it, "The risk associated with genetically engineered foods is derived from the fact that, although genetic engineers can cut and splice DNA molecules with precision in the test tube, when those altered DNA molecules are introduced into a living organism, the full range of effects on that organism cannot be predicted or known before commercialization. The introduced DNA may bring about unintended changes, some of which may be damaging to health."

Numerous opinion polls in the U.S. and abroad in the past decade have shown great skepticism about genetic alteration of foods; a large proportion of respondents, usually majorities, are reluctant to use such products. Regardless of whether they would consume GEFs, consumers feel even more strongly that they should be labeled.

In a *Toronto Star* poll reported on June 2, 98 percent favored labeling. Bioindustry giant Novartis surveyed U.S. consumers and found 93 percent of them wanted information about genetic engineering of food.

Alice Waters, originator of the legendary Berkeley restaurant Chez Panisse and recently selected to organize a new restaurant at the Louvre in Paris, has said, "The act of eating is very political. You buy from the right people, you support the right network of farmers and suppliers who care about the land and what they put in the food. If we don't preserve the natural resources, you aren't going to have a sustainable society."

However, the U.S. government has been resisting attempts to label GEFs. Despite the supposed environmentalist and consumer sympathies of the Clinton-Gore administration, the government believes nothing should impede the profitability of biotech as a mainstay to the future U.S. economy.

The administration's hostility to labeling may also be coupled to political contributions made to it by the interested industries.

Regulation and Free Speech

The government is constrained by the First Amendment from limiting or regulating the content of labels except for the historic functions of protecting health and safety and eliminating fraud or misrepresentation.

The American Civil Liberties Union has noted that "a simple distinction between noncommercial and commercial speech does not determine the extent to which the guarantees of the First Amendment apply to advertising and similar communications relating to the sale or other disposition of goods and services."

Supreme Court decisions have warned against attaching "more importance to the distinction between commercial and noncommercial speech than our cases warrant." Can the government prohibit certain commercial speech, such as barring a label saying "this product does not contain genetically engineered components"?

In several recent cases, the Court has restricted government regulation of commercial speech, in effect allowing more communication. The First Amendment directs us to be skeptical of regulations that seek to keep people in the dark for what the government perceives to be their own good. Thus, it would be hard to sustain the government if it tried to prohibit labeling foods as "free from genetically engineered products," if the statement were true.

In 1995, the FDA's Maryanski took the position that "the FDA is not saying that people don't have a right to know how their food is produced. But the food label is not always the most appropriate method for conveying that information." Is it acceptable for a government bureaucrat to make decisions about what are appropriate methods of information exchange among citizens?

The government and the industry suggest that labels on GEFs might amount to "misrepresentation" by implying that there is a difference between the genetically engineered and nongenetically engineered foods. It is hard, however, to understand how a truthful statement can ever amount to a "misrepresentation." (And of course, they are different, by definition.)

The first food product bearing a label "No GE Ingredients," a brand of corn chips, made its appearance this summer.

Some states have laws creating a civil cause of action against anyone who "disparages" an agricultural product unless the defendant can prove the statements were based on "reasonable and reliable scientific" evidence.

A Harvard analysis suggests that "at stake in the dispute about food-safety claims is scientific uncertainty in an uncertain and unpredictable world. Agricultural disparagement statutes are supposed to regulate the exchange of ideas in that gray area between science and the public good. The underlying approach of these statutes is to regulate speech by encouraging certain kinds of exchanges and punishing others. . . ."

According to the ACLU, "these so-called 'veggie libel' laws raise obvious First Amendment problems and threaten to chill speech on important issues of public concern." Consumers Union argues that "such laws, we believe, give the food and agriculture industry the power to choke off concerns and criticism about food quality and safety."

Such enactments did not prevail in the suit by Texas cattle ranchers against Oprah Winfrey and her guest Howard Lyman (of the Humane Society) for their on-air conversations about "mad-cow disease" possibilities in the United States. The lawsuit was widely seen as a test of the First Amendment constitutionality of such state statutes, although the case was actually resolved on much narrower grounds.

Consequences of Regulation

As Prince Charles noted in his essay, "we cannot put our principles into practice until there is effective segregation and labeling of genetically modified products. Arguments that this is either impossible or irrelevant are simply not credible."

Nonetheless, the biotech industry (and many governments, including our own) make the argument that it is impossible to keep genetically engineered foodstuffs separate from naturally produced ones. However, the same industries actually require rigorous segregation (for example, of seeds) when they are protecting their monopolies on patented food items.

Although it undoubtedly has related costs, the segregation of kosher food products from non-kosher ones, for example, has been routine in this country for decades. The only difference for GEFs appears to be one of scale, not technique, in monitoring the flow of foodstuffs, spot-testing and labeling them appropriately.

In Support of Mandatory Labeling

Can the government mandate commercial speech—for example, requiring GEFs to bear a label proclaiming their identity?

The government does require some label information which goes beyond consumer health effects; not every consumer must need mandated information in order for it to be required by law. These requirements have never been judged an infringement of producers' constitutional rights. For example:

- Very few consumers are sensitive to sulfites, although all wine must be labeled.
- The burden is put on tobacco manufacturers to carry the surgeon general's warning, even though the majority of cigarette smokers will not develop lung cancer and an intended effect of the label is to reinforce the resolve of nonconsumers to refrain from smoking.
- Labeling every processed food with its fat and calorie analysis is mandated, even though vast numbers of Americans are not overweight or suffering from heart disease.
- Irradiated foods (other than spices) must carry a specific logo.
- Finally, the source of hydrolyzed proteins in foods must be on a label to accommodate vegetarian cultural practices and certain religious beliefs.

These legal requirements are in place because many citizens want such information, and a specific fraction need it. An identifiable fraction of consumers actually need information about genetic modification—for example, as regards allergenicity—as the FDA itself has recognized in the Federal Register, and almost all want it.

Foods which are comprised, to any but a trace extent, of genetically altered components or products should be required to be labeled. This can be justified in some instances on scientific and health grounds, and for other foods on the social, cultural, religious and political interest consumers may have in the processes by which their food is produced.

Consumers' right to know is an expression of an ethical position which acknowledges individual autonomy; it is also a social approach which helps to rectify the substantial imbalance of power which exists in a modern society where commercial transactions occur between highly integrated and well-to-do corporations, on the one hand, and atomized consumers on the other.

We should let labeled GEFs run the test of the marketplace.

Statement of Joseph A. Levitt

Introduction

Mr. Chairman and members of the Committee, thank you for giving the Food and Drug Administration (FDA or the Agency) the opportunity to testify today on its regulatory program for foods derived from plants using the tools of modern biotechnology—also known as genetically engineered, or bioengineered, foods. I am Joseph A. Levitt, Director of FDA's Center for Food Safety and Applied Nutrition (CFSAN). Within FDA, CFSAN oversees bioengineered plant products or ingredients intended for human consumption. Our Center for Veterinary Medicine oversees bioengineered plant products used as or in animal feed, as well as bioengineered products used to improve the health or productivity of animals (including fish).

We believe it is very important for the public to understand how FDA is regulating the new bioengineered foods being introduced into the marketplace and to have confidence in that process. To that end, I appreciate this opportunity to describe our policies and procedures to the Committee and to the public.

First, let me state that FDA is confident that the bioengineered plant foods on the U.S. market today are as safe as their conventionally bred counterparts. This conclusion was echoed by a report by the National Resource Council of the National Academy of Sciences which stated, "The committee is not aware of any evidence that foods on the market are unsafe to eat as a result of genetic modification." Since FDA's 1994 evaluation of the Flavr Savr tomato, the first genetically-engineered plant food to reach the U.S. market, FDA has reviewed the data on more than 45 other products, ranging from herbicide resistant soybeans to a canola plant with modified oil content. To date, there is no evidence that these plants are significantly different in terms of food safety from crops produced through traditional breeding techniques.

The topic of bioengineering has generated much controversy, particularly about whether these foods should be labeled or not. As I discuss in more detail later in my testimony, FDA held three public meetings on bioengineered foods late last year, the second one of which I chaired. We wanted to hear the views from all, and importantly, we wanted to discuss and obtain feedback on ways in which information on bioengineered foods could be most appropriately and helpfully conveyed.

From *U. S. Senate Health, Education, Labor, and Pensions Committee*. The Future of Food: Biotechnology and Consumer Confidence. Hearing, September 26, 2000. Washington, DC: U.S. Government Printing Office, 2000.

Partly in response to information gained from the public meetings and comments received by the Agency, FDA announced on May 3, 2000, that it will be taking steps to modify our current voluntary process for bioengineered foods to establish mandatory premarket notification and make the process more transparent. Further, we will be developing guidance for food manufacturers who wish voluntarily to label their products regarding whether or not they contain bioengineered ingredients. To ensure that the Agency has the best scientific advice, we also are adding experts in this field to our foods and veterinary medicine advisory committees. FDA is taking these steps to help provide consumers with continued confidence in the safety of the U.S. food supply and to ensure that the Agency's oversight procedures will meet the challenges of the future. The proposed notification rule and draft guidance are currently under development. . . .

Legal and Regulatory Issues

FDA regulates bioengineered plant food in conjunction with the United States Department of Agriculture (USDA) and the Environmental Protection Agency (EPA). FDA has authority under the Federal Food, Drug, and Cosmetic (FD&C) Act to ensure the safety of all domestic and imported foods for man or other animals in the United States market, except meat, poultry and egg products which are regulated by USDA. (Note that the safety of animal drug residues in meat and poultry is regulated by FDA's Center for Veterinary Medicine.) Pesticides are regulated primarily by EPA, which reviews safety and sets tolerances (or establishes exemptions from tolerance) for pesticides. FDA enforces the pesticide tolerances set by EPA. USDA's Animal & Plant Health Inspection Service (APHIS) oversees the agricultural and environmental safety of planting and field testing of bioengineered plants.

Bioengineered foods and food ingredients must adhere to the same standards of safety under the FD&C Act that apply to their conventionally-bred counterparts. This means that these products must be as safe as the traditional foods in the market. FDA has broad authority to initiate regulatory action if a product fails to meet the standards of the FD&C Act.

FDA relies primarily on two sections of the FD&C Act to ensure the safety of foods and food ingredients:

1. The adulteration provisions of section 402(a)(1). Under this postmarket authority, FDA has the power to remove a food from the market (or sanction those marketing the food) if the food poses a risk to public health. It is important to note that the FD&C Act places a legal duty on developers to ensure that the foods they market to consumers are safe and comply with all legal requirements.
2. The food additive provisions (section 409). Under this section, a substance that is intentionally added to food is a food additive, unless the substance is generally recognized as safe (GRAS) or is otherwise exempt (e.g., a pesticide, the safety of which is overseen by EPA).

The FD&C Act requires premarket approval of any food additive—regardless of the technique used to add it to food. Thus, substances introduced into food are either (1) new food additives that require premarket approval by FDA or (2) GRAS, and are exempt from the requirement for premarket review (for example, if there is a long history of safe use in food). Generally, foods such as fruits, vegetables, and grains, are not subject to premarket approval because they have been safely consumed over many years. Other than the food additive system, there are no premarket approval requirements for foods generally.

In 1992, knowing that bioengineered products were on the horizon, FDA published a policy explaining how existing legal requirements would apply to products developed using the tools of biotechnology (57 FR 22984; May 29, 1992; "Statement of Policy: Foods Derived from New Plant Varieties"). The 1992 policy was designed to answer developers' questions about these products prior to marketing to assist them in meeting their legal duty to provide safe and wholesome foods to consumers. The basic principle of the 1992 policy is that the traits and characteristics of the foods should be the focus of safety assessment for all new varieties of food crops, no matter which techniques are used to develop them.

Under FDA policy, a substance that would be a food additive if it were added during traditional food manufacturing is also treated as a food additive if it is introduced into food through bioengineering of a food crop. Our authority under section 409 permits us to require premarket approval of any food additive and thus, to require premarket review of any substance intentionally introduced via bioengineering that is not generally recognized as safe.

Generally, substances intentionally introduced into food that would be reviewed as food additives include those that have unusual chemical functions, have unknown toxicity, or would be new major dietary components of the food. For example, a novel sweetener bioengineered into food would likely require premarket approval. In our experience with bioengineered food to date, however, we have reviewed only one substance under the food additive provisions, an enzyme produced by an antibiotic resistance gene, and we approved that one. In general, substances intentionally added to food via biotechnology to date have been well-characterized proteins and fats, and are functionally very similar to other proteins and fats that are commonly and safely consumed in the diet and thus are presumptively GRAS.

In 1994, for the first bioengineered product planned for introduction into the market, FDA moved deliberately, following the 1992 policy. We conducted a comprehensive scientific review of Calgene's data on the Flavr Savr™ tomato and the use of the kanamycin resistance marker gene. FDA also held a public meeting of our Food Advisory Committee (the Committee) to examine applicability of the 1992 policy to products such as the Flavr Savr™ tomato. The Committee members agreed with FDA that the scientific approach presented in the 1992 policy was sound and that questions regarding the Flavr Savr™ had been addressed. The Committee members also suggested that we remove unnecessary reviews to provide an expedited decision process on the marketing of bioengineered foods that do not raise substantive scientific issues.

In response, that same year, FDA established a consultative process to help companies comply with the FD&C Act's requirements for any new food, including a bioengineered food, that they intend to market. Since that time, companies have used the consultative process more than 45 times as they sought to introduce genetically altered plants representing ten different crops into the U.S. market. We are not aware of any bioengineered food product on the market under FDA's jurisdiction that has not been evaluated by FDA through the current consultation process.

Typically, the consultation begins early in the product development stage, before it is ready for market. Company scientists and other officials will meet with FDA scientists to describe the product they are developing. In response, the Agency advises the company on what tests would be appropriate for the company to assess the safety of the new food.

After the studies are completed, the data and information on the safety and nutritional assessment are provided voluntarily to FDA for review. The Agency evaluates the information for all of the known hazards and also for potential unintended effects on plant composition and nutritional properties, since plants may undergo changes other than those intended by the breeders. Specifically, FDA scientists are looking to assure that the newly expressed compounds are safe for food consumption, there are no allergens new to the food, no increased levels of natural toxicants, and no reduction of important nutrients. They are also looking to see whether the food has been changed in any substantive way such that the food would need to be specially labeled to reveal the nature of the change to consumers.

Some examples of the information reviewed by FDA include: the name of the food and the crop from which it is derived; the uses of the food, including both human food and animal feed uses; the sources, identities, and functions of introduced genetic material and its stability in the plant; the purpose or intended technical effect of the modification and its expected effect on the composition or characteristic properties of the food or feed; the identity and function of any new products encoded by the introduced genetic material, including an estimate of its concentration; comparison of the composition or characteristics of the bioengineered food to that of food derived from the parental variety or other commonly consumed varieties with special emphasis on important nutrients, anti-nutrients, and toxicants that occur naturally in the food; information on whether the genetic modification altered the potential for the bioengineered food to induce an allergic response; and, other information relevant to the safety and nutritional assessment of the bioengineered food.

It should be noted that if a plant developer used a gene from a plant whose food is commonly allergenic, FDA would presume that the modified food may be allergenic unless the developer could demonstrate that the food would not cause allergic reactions in people allergic to food from the source plant. If FDA scientists have more questions about the safety data, the company either provides more detailed answers or conducts additional studies. Our experience has been that no bioengineered product has gone on the market until FDA's questions about the product have been answered.

Labeling

Labeling, either mandatory or voluntary, of bioengineered foods is a controversial issue. Section 403 of the FD&C Act sets labeling requirements for all foods. All foods, whether derived using bioengineering or not, are subject to these labeling requirements.

Under section 403(a)(1) of the FD&C Act, a food is misbranded if its labeling is false or misleading in any particular way. Section 201(n) of the FD&C Act provides additional guidance on how labeling may be misleading. It states that labeling is misleading if it fails to reveal all facts that are "material in light of such representations (made or suggested in the labeling) or material with respect to consequences which may result from the use of the article to which the labeling or advertising relates under the conditions of use prescribed in the labeling or advertising thereof or under such conditions of use as are customary or usual."

While the legislative history of section 201(n) contains little discussion of the word "material," there is precedent to guide the Agency in its decision regarding whether information on a food is in fact material within the meaning of 201(n). Historically, the Agency has generally limited the scope of the materiality concept to information about the attributes of the food itself. FDA has required special labeling on the basis of it being "material" information in cases where the absence of such information may: 1) pose special health or environmental risks (e.g., warning statement on certain protein diet products); 2) mislead the consumer in light of other statements made on the label (e.g., requirement for quantitative nutrient information when certain nutrient content claims are made about a product); or 3) in cases where a consumer may assume that a food, because of its similarity to another food, has nutritional, organoleptic, or functional characteristics of the food it resembles when in fact it does not (e.g., reduced fat margarine not suitable for frying).

FDA does not require labeling to indicate whether or not a food or food ingredient is a bioengineered product, just as it does not require labeling to indicate which breeding technique was used in developing a food plant. Rather, any significant differences in the food itself have to be disclosed in labeling. If genetic modifications do materially change the composition of a food product, these changes must be reflected in the food's labeling. This would include its nutritional content (for example, more folic acid or greater iron content) or requirements for storage, preparation, or cooking, which might impact the food's safety characteristics or nutritional qualities. For example, one soybean variety was modified to alter the levels of oleic acid in the beans; because the oil from this soybean is significantly different when compared to conventional soybean oil, we advised the company to adopt a new name for that oil, a name that reflects the intended change.

If a bioengineered food were to contain an allergen not previously found in that food, information about the presence of the allergen would be material as to the potential consequences of consumption of the food. If FDA determined that labeling would be sufficient to enable the food to be safely marketed, the Agency would require that the food be labeled to indicate the presence of the allergen.

FDA has received comments suggesting that foods developed through modern biotechnology should bear a label informing consumers that the food was produced using bioengineering. While we have given careful consideration to these comments, we do not have data or other information that would form a basis for concluding under the FD&C Act that the fact that a food or its ingredients was produced using bioengineering is material within the meaning of 201(n) and thus, is a fact that must be disclosed in labeling. Hence, we believe that we have neither a scientific nor legal basis to require such labeling. We are developing, however, draft guidance for those that wish voluntarily to label either the presence or absence of bioengineered food in food products.

Public Outreach

Although FDA is confident that its current science-based approach to regulating bioengineered foods is protecting the public health, we realized we had been quietly looking at and reviewing these products and making decisions related to their safety while the public was largely unaware of what we were doing. When trade issues erupted last summer with Europe—and in the World Trade Organization meetings in Seattle—it raised public concern that there might be safety issues with these foods.

New technologies typically raise complex questions—scientific, policy, and even ethical. In light of the newness of this technology and the apparent concern, FDA held the three public meetings I previously mentioned. The public meetings had three purposes: to determine whether there were any new scientific or labeling issues that the Agency should consider; to help the public understand FDA's current policy and become familiar with what we are already doing; and to explore the ways in which information on bioengineered foods could be most appropriately and helpfully conveyed.

FDA asked specific questions on both scientific and safety issues as well as about public information issues. We heard from 35 panelists and over 250 additional speakers in the three meetings. More than 50,000 written comments have been submitted.

What did we learn at these meetings?

First and foremost, no information was presented that indicates there is a safety problem with any bioengineereed food or feed now in the marketplace.

In general, we heard support for strengthening FDA's premarket review process for bioengineered foods, in varying degrees. Views on labeling were very strong and much more polarized. Overall, we heard from many points of view that FDA needs to take additional steps to increase consumer confidence in these products.

As to specific concerns, there were four basic points of view:

1. One group was concerned primarily with anything that could possibly harm the environment, with food safety being a secondary concern.
2. A second group was concerned about the possibility that there might be unknown long-term food safety problems, despite the absence of any scientific information that would support the existence of such problems.

3. A third group said they were not so concerned about food safety—they would eat bioengineered foods—but still wanted to know what technologies and ingredients were involved in producing their food.
4. A fourth group speaking for developing countries, said they need this technology and do not want it limited or taken away.

New Initiatives

As I mentioned, FDA announced on May 3, as part of an Administration initiative, that we will be taking steps to strengthen the premarket notification program for bioengineered foods. We also intend to provide guidance to food manufacturers who wish voluntarily to label their products regarding whether or not they contain bioengineered ingredients. Our goal is to enhance public confidence in the way in which FDA is regulating bioengineered foods. We want the public to know, loud and clear, that FDA stands behind the safety of these products.

As part of this initiative, we will be proposing regulations to make it mandatory that developers of bioengineered plant varieties notify FDA at least 120 days before they intend to market such products. FDA will require that specific information be submitted to help determine whether the foods pose any safety or labeling concerns. The Agency will be providing further guidance to industry on the scientific data needed to ensure that foods developed through bioengineering are safe for human consumption. To help make the process more transparent, the Agency has made a commitment to ensuring that, consistent with information disclosure laws, consumers have access to information submitted to FDA as part of the notification process and to FDA's responses in a timely fashion.

The proposed rule on premarket notification and the draft labeling guidance are both high priorities for the Agency, and we intend to publish each of these later this fall. Both will provide a full opportunity for public comment before final policies are established. Let me assure you that when we come to a decision regarding these matters, FDA will operate in an open, transparent manner so that the public can understand our regulatory approach and continue to provide us with feedback about its impact. As a scientific organization we are comfortable with debate over complex scientific issues, and welcome the discussions that have occurred at public meetings to date. It is important that the public, including the scientific community, clearly understand FDA's policy on bioengineered foods.

Additional Activities

Before closing, let me briefly describe a few other activities of Agency involvement in the food biotechnology subject area. In our May 3 announcement, FDA stated our intention to augment our food and veterinary medicine advisory committees by adding scientists with agricultural biotechnology expertise. FDA will use these committees to address over-arching scientific questions pertaining to bioengineered foods and animal feed. More specifically, I am restructuring the Food Advisory Committee so that it will contain several special focus subcommittees. One of those subcommittees will have scientists with expertise in bioengineering, and will focus on issues pertaining to food biotechnology.

As I am sure you are aware, the National Academy of Sciences has formed a new standing Committee on Agricultural Biotechnology. FDA has participated in several of its meetings, including one just last week, on September 18, in which two FDA experts made presentations. We think the work of this committee is very important. We are formalizing our relationship with it, particularly with regard to exploring what the potential is for any unknown long-term health effects to result from consumption of bioengineered food.

FDA is actively participating in the work of the U.S. Codex Committee on food labeling, which is considering issues on policies for possible labeling of foods derived using bioengineering. In addition, FDA is participating in the newly formed "Ad Hoc Committee on Foods Derived from Biotechnology." This committee is especially important because its initial focus is to develop principles and guidelines for the evaluation of the safety of bioengineered foods. FDA is providing an international leadership role in this committee to develop harmonized policies for assessing the safety of bioengineered food.

Let me comment briefly on the recall announced by Kraft Foods this past Friday. FDA commends Kraft Foods for acting responsibly in light of testing showing the possibility that the products contained a bioengineered protein that had not been approved for human consumption. This reinforces the importance of FDA, EPA and other interested parties to be vigilant in assuring that the rules pertaining to bioengineered foods are being fully adhered to. FDA's investigation is continuing in this case.

Mr. Chairman, thank you again for the opportunity to address these issues. I am happy to answer any questions you might have.

POSTSCRIPT

Should We Require Labeling for Genetically Modified Food?

William Safire, a journalist often amused by popular trends in the use of the English language, at one point titled his weekly essay "Franken-: A Terrifying New Prefix is Stalking Europe." His point was not that many European nations, acting in fear, have banned or restricted the import of genetically modified foods, but that language had evolved to express that fear. "Franken-," from Mary Godwin Shelley's nineteenth-century book *Frankenstein*, has come to characterize the product of any human "tampering" with nature that displeases the speaker. The fact that we have modified breeds of plants and animals for centuries, in fact millennia, through selective breeding or other methods of assisting evolution, tends to get lost in the scuffle. The language helps the scuffling.

Labeling is another way to use language to affect policy. It simply is not politically neutral to attach a label to something, especially when on our usual understandings, it should not need one. Every required addition to the labels on our food has been made in response to a public agenda, usually concerning public health, but occasionally (as in the case of the tuna and the pastrami) concerning public causes that have nothing to do with the quality of the food. Do we want genetically engineered products to follow that route?

Suggested Reading

If you would like to think further on this topic, you may profit from the following:

Michael Fumento, "Crop Busters," *Reason* (January 2000). This article criticizes opponents of genetically engineered foods.

Kristi Coale, "Mutant Food," *Salon* (January 12, 2000). This article looks at how a lawsuit filed against the Food and Drug Administration reveals FDA internal doubts of genetic engineering safety.

Jon Luoma, "Pandora's Pantry," *Mother Jones* (January/February 2000).

Frederic Golden, "Who's Afraid of Frankenfood?" *Time* (November 29, 1999).

Food and Drug Administration Biotechnology Home Page. This FDA site explains federal policies on bioengineered foods.

U. S. Department of Agriculture (USDA) Biotechnology home page. This site answers frequently asked questions about biotechnology and provides information on regulatory oversight of biotechnology.

Center for Food Safety, International Food Information Council, Greenpeace: Biotechnology and Better Foods and Industry Web site.

Internet References . . .

U.S. Business Cycle Indicators Data

This site leads to the 256 data series known as the U.S. Business Cycle Indicators, which are used to track and predict U.S. business activity. The subjects of the data groups are clearly listed.

http://www.economagic.com/bci-97.htm

Voice of the Shuttle: Postindustrial Business Theory Page

This site links to a variety of resources on many subjects related to business theory, including restructuring, reengineering, downsizing, flattening, the team concept, outsourcing, business and globalism, human resources management, labor relations, statistics, and history, as well as information and resources on job searches, careers, working from home, and business start-ups.

http://vos.ucsb.edu/browse.asp?id=2727

Society, Religion, and Technology Project

This is the home page on patenting living organisms of the Society, Religion, and Technology Project (SRT) of the Church of Scotland. It provides a simple introduction to the issues involved, other SRT pages on patenting, and links to related pages.

http://www.srtp.org.uk.patent.shtml

Global Objectives

*O*ur business is increasingly carried on in distant waters and foreign villages. The corporation of the future is a global enterprise, difficult to track, avoiding the jurisdiction of any national government. What sorts of ethical obligations attend their operations? Are there products we should not buy because of the way they were manufactured? Are there products we should not sell because of their potential to cause harm to the citizens of other lands (who willingly buy them)?

- Are Multinational Corporations Free from Moral Obligation?
- Are Sweatshops an Inhumane Business Practice?
- Should Patenting Life Be Forbidden?

ISSUE 15

Are Multinational Corporations Free from Moral Obligation?

YES: Manuel Velasquez, from "International Business, Morality, and the Common Good," *Business Ethics Quarterly* (January 1992)

NO: John E. Fleming, from "Alternative Approaches and Assumptions: Comments on Manuel Velasquez," *Business Ethics Quarterly* (January 1992)

ISSUE SUMMARY

YES: In the absence of accepted enforcement agencies, there is little probability that any multinational corporation will suffer for violation of rules restricting business for the sake of the common good. Since any business that tried to conform to moral rules in the absence of enforcement would unjustifiably cease to be competitive, it must be the case, Velasquez argues, that moral strictures are not binding on such companies.

NO: Velasquez's logic is impressive, replies Fleming, but conditions on the ground in the multinational corporation are not as he describes. Real corporations tend to deal with long-term customers and suppliers in the goldfish bowl of international media exposure and must adhere to moral standards or lose business.

In three ways, this issue is not what it seems.

First, to hear Velasquez tell it, it seems to be an issue between the hard-headed realists of Hobbesian persuasion—those who realize that business is business and the bottom line is all that really counts—and the liberal idealists, who'd like to think that high moral thoughts really influence world affairs. Velasquez concludes, very regretfully, that a Hobbesian realist, knowing all the worst about human nature, must acknowledge that moral obligations simply do not apply in the absence of moral community. Yet Fleming does not answer in the tone of lofty idealism, but in that of the practitioner who has to keep an enterprise afloat from day to day. Realism and hardheadedness seem to have switched sides in the course of the debate, apparently; realistically, the only way to serve the bottom line is by (tolerably) moral behavior. Velasquez, it now appears, is the lofty idealist, sacrificing moral principles at the altar of an abstract egoism that could never be put into practice on the multinational scene.

Second, to hear Velasquez tell it, right action is on trial: Can morality justify itself with regard to profit? Can we show that acting for the common good will not damage the profit picture or detract from the increase in shareholder wealth? For if not, we will have to forgo morality. Fleming appears to answer Velasquez's question in the affirmative: Yes, we can show that right action is compatible with (in fact necessary for) the health of the bottom line and the corporate enterprise in general. But in reality, his answer goes much further than that. It is not the behavior that is in question but the theory—not the conclusions of the syllogism but the major premise. For if Fleming is right, the major premise of Hobbesian capitalism—that the sole social responsibility of business is to increase its profits, as Milton Friedman put it so succinctly—is simply incorrect, or unworkable. For any activity that might be expected to follow from the injunction to serve the bottom line and increase profits, activity in total disregard of the moral persuasions of all others in your society, is not only morally wrong on some eternal scale but also self-defeating: Business will plunge and the shareholders will be left with valueless promises. So the theory—not, in this reading, a normative theory, but an empirical generalization about the way things happen in fact—fails to predict the data. It is a flawed theory, and needs, based on this reading, to be replaced.

Third, to hear both Velasquez and Fleming tell it, the dispute is over human behavior—both about the way humans *will* behave and the way they *should* behave—in business situations. But both of them condition their predictions and advice on the nature of the international business community. Fleming is claiming centrally that the international business scene is not at all as Velasquez thinks it is—strangers interacting in strange lands, on a one-time basis only—but is a place of custom, regular habits, and familiar people, where memories are long, word gets around, and tolerance for being taken advantage of is very short. It sounds like a small town. And indeed, that is what the world is coming to be.

Ask yourself, as you read these selections, how international dealings differ from domestic dealings. Does it stretch the imagination to consider folks abroad rather like the folks at home, after getting used to time zone changes and differences in manners? What are the real controls on human behavior—enforcement of laws or the simple social expectations of peers and colleagues?

YES

Manuel Velasquez

International Business, Morality, and the Common Good

During the last few years an increasing number of voices have urged that we pay more attention to ethics in international business, on the grounds that not only are all large corporations now internationally structured and thus engaging in international transactions, but that even the smallest domestic firm is increasingly buffeted by the pressures of international competition. . . .

Can we say that businesses operating in a competitive international environment have any moral obligations to contribute to the international common good, particularly in light of realist objections? Unfortunately, my answer to this question will be in the negative. . . .

International Business

. . . When speaking of international business, I have in mind a particular kind of organization: the multinational corporation. Multinational corporations have a number of well known features, but let me briefly summarize a few of them. First, multinational corporations are businesses and as such they are organized primarily to increase their profits within a competitive environment. Virtually all of the activities of a multinational corporation can be explained as more or less rational attempts to achieve this dominant end. Secondly, multinational corporations are bureaucratic organizations. The implication of this is that the identity, the fundamental structure, and the dominant objectives of the corporation endure while the many individual human beings who fill the various offices and positions within the corporation come and go. As a consequence, the particular values and aspirations of individual members of the corporation have a relatively minimal and transitory impact on the organization as a whole. Thirdly, and most characteristically, multinational corporations operate in several nations. This has several implications. First, because the multinational is not confined to a single nation, it can easily escape the reach of the laws of any particular nation by simply moving its resources or operations out of one nation and transferring them to another nation. Second, because the multinational is not confined to a single nation, its interests are not aligned

From *Business Ethics Quarterly*, vol. 2, no. 1, January 1992, pp. 41–43. Copyright © 1992 by Business Ethics Quarterly. Reprinted by permission of The Philosophy Documentation Center, publisher of Business Ethics Quarterly. References omitted with the interests of any single nation. The ability of the multinational to achieve its profit objectives does not depend upon the ability of any particular nation to achieve its own domestic objectives. . . .

The Traditional Realist Objection in Hobbes

The realist objection, of course, is the standard objection to the view that agents—whether corporations, governments, or individuals—have moral obligations on the international level. Generally, the realist holds that it is a mistake to apply moral concepts to international activities: morality has no place in international affairs. The classical statement of this view, which I am calling the "traditional" version of realism, is generally attributed to Thomas Hobbes. . . .

In its Hobbsian form, as traditionally interpreted, the realist objection holds that moral concepts have no meaning in the absence of an agency powerful enough to guarantee that other agents generally adhere to the tenets of morality. Hobbes held, first, that in the absence of a sovereign power capable of forcing men to behave civilly with each other, men are in "the state of nature," a state he characterizes as a "war . . . of every man, against every man." Secondly, Hobbes claimed, in such a state of war, moral concepts have no meaning:

> To this war of every man against every man, this also is consequent; that nothing can be unjust. The notions of right and wrong, justice and injustice have there no place. Where there is no common power, there is no law: where no law, no injustice.

Moral concepts are meaningless, then, when applied to state of nature situations. And, Hobbes held, the international arena is a state of nature, since there is no international sovereign that can force agents to adhere to the tenets of morality.

The Hobbsian objection to talking about morality in international affairs, then, is based on two premises: (1) an ethical premise about the applicability of moral terms and (2) an apparently empirical premise about how agents behave under certain conditions. The ethical premise, at least in its Hobbsian form, holds that there is a connection between the meaningfulness of moral terms and the extent to which agents adhere to the tenets of morality: If in a given situation agents do not adhere to the tenets of morality, then in that situation moral terms have no meaning. The apparently empirical premise holds that in the absence of a sovereign, agents will not adhere to the tenets of morality: they will be in a state of war. This appears to be an empirical generalization about the extent to which agents adhere to the tenets of morality in the absence of a third-party enforcer. Taken together, the two premises imply that in situations that lack a sovereign authority, such as one finds in many international exchanges, moral terms have no meaning and so moral obligations are nonexistent. . . .

Revising the Realist Objection: The First Premise

. . . The neo-Hobbsian or realist . . . might want to propose this premise: When one is in a situation in which others do not adhere to certain tenets of morality, and when adhering to those tenets of morality will put one at a significant competitive disadvantage, then it is not immoral for one to like-wise fail to adhere to them. The realist might want to argue for this claim, first, by pointing out that in a world in which all are competing to secure significant benefits and avoid significant costs, and in which others do not adhere to the ordinary tenets of morality, one risks significant harm to one's interests if one continues to adhere to those tenets of morality. But no one can be morally required to take on major risks of harm to oneself. Consequently, in a competitive world in which others disregard moral constraints and take any means to advance their self-interests, no one can be morally required to take on major risks of injury by adopting the restraints of ordinary morality.

A second argument the realist might want to advance would go as follows. When one is in a situation in which others do not adhere to the ordinary tenets of morality, one is under heavy competitive pressures to do the same. And, when one is under such pressures, one cannot be blamed—i.e., one is excused—for also failing to adhere to the ordinary tenets of morality. One is excused because heavy pressures take away one's ability to control oneself, and thereby diminish one's moral culpability.

Yet a third argument advanced by the realist might go as follows. When one is in a situation in which others do not adhere to the ordinary tenets of morality it is not fair to require one to continue to adhere to those tenets, especially if doing so puts one at a significant competitive disadvantage. It is not fair because then one is laying a burden on one party that the other parties refuse to carry.

Thus, there are a number of arguments that can be given in defense of the revised Hobbsian ethical premise that when others do not adhere to the tenets of morality, it is not immoral for one to do likewise. . . .

Revising the Realist Objection: The Second Premise

Let us turn to the other premise in the Hobbsian argument, the assertion that in the absence of a sovereign, agents will be in a state of war. As I mentioned, this is an apparently empirical claim about the extent to which agents will adhere to the tenets of morality in the absence of a third-party enforcer.

Hobbes gives a little bit of empirical evidence for this claim. He cites several examples of situations in which there is no third party to enforce civility and where, as a result, individuals are in a "state of war." Generalizing from these few examples, he reaches the conclusion that in the absence of a third-party enforcer, agents will always be in a "condition of war." . . .

Recently, the Hobbsian claim . . . has been defended on the basis of some of the theoretical claims of game theory, particularly of the prisoner's dilemma. Hobbes' state of nature, the defense goes, is an instance of a prisoner's dilemma, and *rational* agents in a Prisoner's Dilemma necessarily would choose not to adhere to a set of moral norms. . . .

A Prisoner's Dilemma is a situation involving at least two individuals. Each individual is faced with two choices: he can cooperate with the other individual or he can choose not to cooperate. If he cooperates and the other individual also cooperates, then he gets a certain payoff. If, however, he chooses not to cooperate, while the other individual trustingly cooperates, the noncooperator gets a larger payoff while the cooperator suffers a loss. And if both choose not to cooperate, then both get nothing.

It is a commonplace now that in a Prisoner's Dilemma situation, the most rational strategy for a participant is to choose not to cooperate. For the other party will either cooperate or not cooperate. If the other party cooperates, then it is better for one not to cooperate and thereby get the larger payoff. On the other hand, if the other party does not cooperate, then it is also better for one not to cooperate and thereby avoid a loss. In either case, it is better for one to not cooperate.

. . . In Hobbes' state of nature each individual must choose either to cooperate with others by adhering to the rules of morality (like the rule against theft), or to not cooperate by disregarding the rules of morality and attempting to take advantage of those who are adhering to the rules (e.g., by stealing from them). In such a situation it is more rational . . . to choose not to cooperate. For the other party will either cooperate or not cooperate. If the other party does not cooperate, then one puts oneself at a competitive disadvantage if one adheres to morality while the other party does not. On the other hand, if the other party chooses to cooperate, then one can take advantage of the other party by breaking the rules of morality at his expense. In either case, it is morally rational to not cooperate.

Thus, the realist can argue that in a state of nature, where there is no one to enforce compliance with the rules of morality, it is more rational from the individual's point of view to choose not to comply with morality than to choose to comply. Assuming—and this is obviously a critical assumption—that agents behave rationally, then we can conclude that agents in a state of nature will choose not to comply with the tenets of ordinary morality. . . .

Can we claim that it is clear that multinationals have a moral obligation to pursue the global common good in spite of the objections of the realist?

I do not believe that this claim can be made. We can conclude from the discussion of the realist objection that the Hobbsian claim about the pervasiveness of amorality in the international sphere is false when (1) interactions among international agents are repetitive in such a way that agents can retaliate against those who fail to cooperate, and (2) agents can determine the trustworthiness of other international agents.

But unfortunately, multinational activities often take place in a highly competitive arena in which these two conditions do not obtain. Moreover, these conditions are noticeably absent in the arena of activities that concern the global common good.

First, as I have noted, the common good consists of goods that are indivisible and accessible to all. This means that such goods are susceptible to the free rider problems. Everyone has access to such goods whether or not they do their part in maintaining such goods, so everyone is tempted to free ride on the generosity of others. Now governments can force domestic companies to do their part to maintain the national common good. Indeed, it is one of the functions of government to solve the free rider problem by forcing all to contribute to the domestic common good to which all have access. Moreover, all companies have to interact repeatedly with their host governments, and this leads them to adopt a cooperative stance toward their host government's objective of achieving the domestic common good.

But it is not clear that governments can or will do anything effective to force multinationals to do their part to maintain the global common good. For the governments of individual nations can themselves be free riders, and can join forces with willing multinationals seeking competitive advantages over others. Let me suggest an example. It is clear that a livable global environment is part of the global common good, and it is clear that the manufacture and use of chlorofluorocarbons is destroying that good. Some nations have responded by requiring their domestic companies to cease manufacturing or using chlorofluorocarbons. But other nations have refused to do the same, since they will share in any benefits that accrue from the restraint others practice, and they can also reap the benefits of continuing to manufacture and use chlorofluorocarbons. Less developed nations, in particular, have advanced the position that since their development depends heavily on exploiting the industrial benefits of chlorofluorocarbons, they cannot afford to curtail their use of these substances. Given this situation, it is open to multinationals to shift their operations to those countries that continue to allow the manufacture and use of chlorofluorocarbons. For multinationals, too, will reason that they will share in any benefits that accrue from the restraint others practice, and that they can meanwhile reap the profits of continuing to manufacture and use chlorofluorocarbons in a world where other companies are forced to use more expensive technologies. Moreover, those nations that practice restraint cannot force all such multinationals to discontinue the manufacture or use of chlorofluorocarbons because many multinationals can escape the reach of their laws. An exactly parallel, but perhaps even more compelling, set of considerations can be advanced to show that at least some multinationals will join forces with some developing countries to circumvent any global efforts made to control the global warming trends (the so-called "greenhouse effect") caused by the heavy use of fossil fuels.

The realist will conclude, of course, that in such situations, at least some multinationals will seek to gain competitive advantages by failing to contribute to the global common good (such as the good of a hospitable global environment). For multinationals are rational agents, i.e., agents bureaucratically structured to take rational means toward achieving their dominant end of increasing their profits. And in a competitive environment, contributing to the common good while others do not, will fail to achieve this dominant end. Joining this conclusion to the ethical premise that when others do not adhere to the requirements of morality it is not immoral for one to do likewise, the realist can conclude that multinationals are not morally obligated to contribute to such global common goods (such as environmental goods).

Moreover, global common goods often create interactions that are not iterated. This is particularly the case where the global environment is concerned. As I have already noted, preservation of a favorable global climate is clearly part of the global common good. Now the failure of the global climate will be a one-time affair. The breakdown of the ozone layer, for example, will happen once, with catastrophic consequences for us all; and the heating up of the global climate as a result of the infusion of carbon dioxide will happen once, with catastrophic consequences for us all. Because these environmental disasters are a one-time affair, they represent a non-iterated prisoner's dilemma for multinationals. It is irrational from an individual point of view for a multinational to choose to refrain from polluting the environment in such cases. Either others will refrain, and then one can enjoy the benefits of their refraining; or others will not refrain, and then it will be better to have also not refrained since refraining would have made little difference and would have entailed heavy losses.

Finally, we must also note that although natural persons may signal their reliability to other natural persons, it is not at all obvious that multinationals can do the same. As noted above, multinationals are bureaucratic organizations whose members are continually changing and shifting. The natural persons who make up an organization can signal their reliability to others, but such persons are soon replaced by others, and they in turn are replaced by others. What endures is each organization's single-minded pursuit of increasing its profits in a competitive environment. And an enduring commitment to the pursuit of profit in a competitive environment is not a signal of an enduring commitment to morality.

John E. Fleming

→ **NO**

Alternative Approaches and Assumptions: Comments on Manuel Velasquez

Introduction

I feel that Professor Velasquez has written a very interesting and thought-provoking paper on an important topic. His initial identification with a "strong notion of the common good" raises the level of analysis to a high but very complex plane. The author introduces the interesting and, from my view, unusual *realist objection* in the Hobbsian form. After a rigorous analysis of this concept Professor Velasquez reaches what I find to be a disturbing conclusion: "It is not obvious that we can say that multinationals have an obligation to contribute to the global common good. . . ." He then finishes the paper with a strong plea for the establishment of "an international authority capable of forcing everyone to contribute toward the global good."

It would be presumptuous of me to question the fine ethical reasoning that appears in the paper. I am impressed with its elegance. However, in a topic of this complexity I would like to think that there might be alternative approaches and assumptions that would lead us to a different conclusion. The presentation of such alternatives will be the path that I will take, examining the conceptual and empirical underpinnings of the argument from a management viewpoint.

The Model of a Multinational Corporation

The profit-maximizing, rational model of a multinational corporation presented in the paper is consistent with traditional economics and serves as a useful approximation of the firm from a theoretical viewpoint. But it falls somewhat short in less than purely competitive environments and was never intended to describe the decision processes of actual managers. Empirical studies of firms can lead to a profit-sacrificing, bounded rational model. The importance of profit is still there, but the stockholder does not get all the benefits. Other stakeholders are considered and rewarded. Out of all this can come the important concept of corporate social responsibility, which can

From *Business Ethics Quarterly*, vol. 2, no. 1, January 1992, pp. 41–43. Copyright © 1992 by Business Ethics Quarterly. Reprinted by permission of The Philosophy Documentation Center, publisher of Business Ethics Quarterly. References omitted include such topics as concerns for the environment and for host country governments.

I also find the faceless and interchangeable bureaucrat a poor model for business executives, particularly the chief executive officers of large corporations. Many of these individuals have a personal impact on the organization, including such areas as business ethics and corporate responsibility. There are also important behavioral aspects of management, such as pride in the firm and corporate culture, that are fertile soil for the nurture of ethics.

Most large American multinational corporations have codes of ethics and some have well-developed programs concerned with ethical behavior worldwide. A number of these firms emphasize that their one code of conduct applies everywhere that they do business. At the GTE Corporation its vision and values statements have been translated into nine different languages and distributed to all its employees to ensure this world-wide understanding of how it conducts its business. This is a far cry from the situational ethics described in the model used by Professor Velasquez.

Model of the International Business Climate

The planning and decision environment of the managers conducting international business is different from that described in the paper. There is the very real problem of a lack of an overarching global government and enforceable laws for the international arena. Nevertheless, there are other very strong restraining forces on companies that prevent the "state of nature" (or law of the jungle) described in the paper. For example, the national governments that do exist influence the ethical behavior of companies acting within their boundaries and beyond. The Foreign Corrupt Practices Act of the United States has set a new standard of behavior in the area of bribery that dictates how American companies will behave worldwide. The financial practices of large banks and securities markets have added major constraints to global corporate behavior. There are also a number of regional and functional organizations in the areas of trade and monetary issues that provide limitations to managerial decision making.

The decisions of multinational executives are also constrained by such factors as public opinion and the pressures of special interest groups. In this area the media also plays a strong role. Examples of these forces are the actions of interest groups that forced marketing changes on infant formula manufacturers and the strong "green" movement that is affecting business decisions throughout many parts of the world. My own view is that considerable progress has been made in the area of limiting the manufacture and release of chlorofluorocarbons. This is a very complex issue involving tremendous social and economic changes that are far more critical, widespread and controlling than the profits of the producing companies. Even with the existence of an enforcing government there is no guarantee that the problem would be solved speedily. An example in point is the acid rain problem of the United States.

Model of the Prisoner's Dilemma

From the standpoint of managerial decision making the Prisoner's Dilemma model does not simulate a situation that is frequently found in international business. An executive generally would not be negotiating or making mutually beneficial decisions with competitors. I would see the greatest amount of effort of multinational decision makers devoted to the development of repeat customers. Such an accomplishment comes about through solving customer problems with better product/service at a lower cost. An emphasis on efficiency and excellence is a far more effective use of executive time than questionable negotiations with a competitor. I believe that the weakness Professor Velasquez identifies in the Prisoner's Dilemma model as a one-time event with competitors applies even more to negotiations with customers.

The author also points out a major weakness of the model in the signaling of intent that goes on between individuals. He then states that this same signaling is not found to any great extent between companies. I would disagree with this thought. An important part of corporate strategic planning is analyzing market signals. United States antitrust forbids direct contact between competitors on issues relating to the market. But there is no limitation on independent analysis of competitive actions and the interpretation of actions by competitors. When Kodak introduced its instant camera, both Kodak and Polaroid watched the other's actions to determine whether it signaled detente or fight.

Conclusion

For the reasons enumerated above I tend to question the models and assumptions that Professor Velasquez has used in his ethical analysis. And, with these underpinnings in jeopardy, I also tend to question the tentative conclusion of his moral reasoning as it relates to the managerial aspects of international business. I feel that multinationals *do* have a strong obligation to contribute to the global common good.

POSTSCRIPT

Are Multinational Corporations Free from Moral Obligation?

As we write, international business has sunk into a sea of troubles: The once-booming Asian economies seem to have gone into self-destruct mode, movie stars and athletes spend air time defending their products from accusations of exploitation and sweatshop abuses, trade in securities has gone global and gone wild. What are the possibilities for the comprehensive set of international laws, guidelines, and the committees to enforce them, as suggested by Velasquez?

Is national sovereignty an idea whose time has come, gone, and gone south? While boundaries between peoples—which may or may not correspond to anyone's idea of settled "national" boundaries—are the subject of violent disputes worldwide, while the economy goes global with blinding speed, unable to recognize any national boundaries at all, can we say that national boundaries make any sense at all? But then, how would we know what each central government controls? What is the reason for the centrality of national sovereignty?

We have, as Velasquez mentions, international conventions on certain subjects—ozone-depleting substances, for example. But on more immediate, and expensive, environmental issues, agreement is hard to reach and harder to monitor (witness the global warming conference in Kyoto).

Suggested Reading

For further exploration of this issue, read any of the following:

Nader Asgary and Mark C. Mitschow, "Toward a Model for International Business Ethics," *Journal of Business Ethics,* vol. 36 no. 3, March 2002.

Muel Kaptein, "Business Codes of Multinational Firms: What Do They Say?" *Journal of Business Ethics,* vol. 50 no. 1, March 2004.

Thomas Friedman, *The Lexus and the Olive Tree* (Revised and Updated Ed. Farrar, Straus and Giroux, 2000).

ISSUE 16

Are Sweatshops an Inhumane Business Practice?

YES: Denis G. Arnold and Norman E. Bowie, "Respect for Workers in Global Supply Chains: Advancing the Debate over Sweatshops." *Business Ethics Quarterly*, January 2001.

NO: Gordon G. Sollars and Fred Englander, "Sweatshops: Kant and Consequences." *Business Ethics Quarterly*, January 2001.

ISSUE SUMMARY

YES: Philosophers Arnold and Bowie argue that managers of multinational enterprises have a duty to ensure that workers in their supply chains are treated with dignity and respect, which includes paying a living wage to those who work in factories with which they contract.

NO: Sollars and Englander contend that this work is needed for the very survival of individuals, and the multinational enterprises are not participating directly in the coercion of the workers in sweatshops.

According to the World Bank, about one-fifth of the world's population lives below the international poverty line. Economic success in China and India has decreased world poverty, but economic inequality is still extremely high. There are still many individuals in Third World countries receiving very low wages from either multinational companies themselves or subcontractors for those companies. This creates ethical problems for the parent company, the consumer, the supplier, and the worker. Critics hold that workers should have basic rights of dignity and safety, as well as a living wage in a job. What if these conditions are not met? Should we do away with the jobs because of these poor working conditions? Are bad jobs preferable to no jobs at all?

Creative approaches are needed if workers' rights are to be respected and commercial success and survival are to be fostered at the same time. Often, today's sweatshops violate the very tenets of business ethics and yet they continue to flourish. This is the case because companies and corporations have not settled on criteria that would condemn sweatshops. These criteria should be used to examine the impoverished and underdeveloped living conditions in regions where the companies locate their factories/sweatshops.

From a Kantian perspective, should multinational corporations do more to promote the dignity of the individuals they employ or rely upon? Top-brand manufacturers have been embarrassed by their sweatshop practices or by the practices of a subcontractor. Some corporations claim to have made changes to address these problems, but that has sometimes meant pulling their factories out of impoverished countries altogether rather than changing the working conditions there. They then trumpet that their products are sweatshop-free. The impoverished workers, meanwhile, are unemployed and may not find another job to sustain their meager quality of life—thus they become worse off than they were working in the substandard conditions in the first place. Other multinational corporations remain in the impoverished countries and claim to have changed their practices, but allegedly their subcontractors still use poor workers in sweatshop conditions.

YES ↵

Denis G. Arnold and
Norman E. Bowie

Respect for Workers in Global Supply Chains: Advancing the Debate over Sweatshops

One of the principal human rights victories in recent years has been the transformation of the factories of many large multinational enterprises (MNEs) from sweatshops into safe and healthy places to work. Prompted by public outrage over the widespread abuse of worker rights in these factories, MNEs such as Nike, Adidas-Salamon, Mattel, and the Gap have implemented numerous measures to help ensure that the workers who manufacturer goods in their supply chains are treated with dignity and respect. In so doing, they have joined companies with longstanding policies of respect for workers in their supply chains, such as Levi Strauss and Motorola. In both their own factories, and in those of their contractors, these MNEs have enhanced compliance with local labor laws, implemented new and improved health and safety standards, improved wages, and created a variety of additional benefits such as after-hours educational opportunities and microenterprise loan programs.

For the past several years we have argued that MNEs' managers have duties, both in their own factories and in their contract factories, to ensure that the dignity of workers is respected. In "Sweatshops and Respect for Persons" we argued that these duties include the following: to adhere to local labor laws, to refrain from coercion, to meet minimum health and safety standards, and to pay workers a living wage. We are gratified that many MNEs, especially those in the apparel and footwear sector, are now meeting these duties (though we claim no responsibility for these changes). In their commentary on our paper, Gordon Sollars and Fred Englander challenge some of our conclusions. In what follows we argue that several of their criticisms are based on an inaccurate reading of our paper, and that none of their remaining criticisms successfully challenges our main arguments.

1. The Obligations of MNEs Regarding Subcontractors

In many cases, MNEs do not directly employ some or all of the workers who manufacture the goods that they design, market, and sell. For example, none of the 10,000 workers in the Tae Kwang Vina factory—discussed in "Sweatshops

From *Business Ethics Quarterly*, Vol. 17, Issue 1, 2007, pp. 135–145. Copyright © 2007 by Business Ethics Quarterly. Reprinted by permission of The Philosophy Documentation Center, publisher of Business Ethics Quarterly. References omitted.

and Respect for Persons"—work for Nike, although Nike is the only MNE that the factory supplies. In our paper we argued that MNEs have a duty to ensure that the dignity of such workers is respected. Sollars and Englander dispute this conclusion, but they misunderstand our line of argument. We began by endorsing Michael Santoro's claim that the moral duty of MNEs in this regard is similar to the legal doctrine of *respondeat superior.* We then argued that this duty has a two-fold justification. First, we argued that MNE managers are constrained by the categorical imperative in general, and the doctrine of respect for persons in particular. Second, we argued that individuals have unique duties as a result of their unique circumstances.

In reply to our first argument, Sollars and Englander rightly point out that much depends on the implications of respecting others. We addressed that issued in some detail in "Sweatshops and Respect for Persons." In that essay, after quoting Kant on human dignity, we summarized an argument by Hill regarding the implications of this, and then provided our own elaboration of the issue as based on Kant's *Metaphysics of Morals*:

> Thomas Hill Jr. has discussed the implication of Kant's arguments concerning human dignity at length. Hill argues that treating persons as ends in themselves requires supporting and developing certain human capacities, including the capacity to act on reason; the capacity to act on the basis of prudence or efficiency; the capacity to set goals; the capacity to accept categorical imperatives; and the capacity to understand the world and reason abstractly. *Based on Kant's writings in the* Metaphysics of Morals, *we would make several additions to the list. There Kant argues that respecting people means that we cannot be indifferent to them. Indifference is a denial of respect. He also argues that we have an obligation to be concerned with the physical welfare of people and their moral well being. Adversity, pain, and want are temptations to vice and inhibit the ability of individuals to develop their rational and moral capacities. It is these rational and moral capacities that distinguish people from mere animals. People who are not free to develop these capacities may end up leading lives that are closer to animals than to moral beings. Freedom from externally imposed adversity, pain, and want facilitate the cultivation of one's rational capacities and virtuous character. Thus, treating people as ends in themselves means ensuring their physical well being and supporting and developing their rational and moral capacities.* [Italics added]

Sollars and Englander's criticism of our interpretation of Kantian respect for persons is constituted mainly by a long exegesis of the passage from Hill, together with the claim that the passage from Hill does not support our position. They ignore our discussion of the *Metaphysics of Morals* (partially quoted above in italics) and Bowie's discussion of the issue in *Business Ethics: A Kantian Perspective.* Since we do not believe Sollars and Englander engage the first part of our argument in a substantive manner, we will put aside their remarks on that part of argument and instead turn our attention to their comments on the second part of our argument.

We argued that MNEs have distinct duties regarding the employees of their contract factories because of the power they have over the owners and managers of such factories, and because of the substantial resources at their disposal. MNEs typically dictate to their contractors such terms as price, quality, quantity, and date of delivery. This imbalance in power means that they have the ability to either hinder or enhance the ability of contract factory managers to respect employees. For example, if MNE supply chain managers know, or have reason to know, that the factory cannot meet the terms of the contract while adhering to local labor laws, providing safe working conditions, or paying a living wage, then they are properly regarded as partially responsibe for those disrespectful practices. Sollars and Englander's main criticism of this position is stated as follows:

> Our point is that the subcontractor or supplier has done *something* via the bargain to reduce pain, adversity, or poverty, while other actors may have done *nothing*. It is unreasonable to expect any bargain struck between two parties to redress every issue of fairness or desert that may apply to one party. MNEs are in some sense "taking advantage" of background conditions in the Third World when they outsource their production, but this alone does not make them responsible for the poverty that makes their sourcing decisions profitable.

So, because the subcontractor has improved the situation of employees by employing them via their contract with the MNE, and because the contract between the supplier and the MNE cannot reasonably be expected to "redress every issue of fairness or desert" that may apply to one party, MNEs have no distinctive duties regarding subcontractors of their employees. Note that on this account, if an MNE's management knew that the terms of the contract made it impossible for an employer to pay even the legally mandated wages and benefits of workers while fulfilling the contract, the MNE would not be responsible, partly or entirely, for the failure to pay such wages and benefits, nor would the MNE or its managers have violated any duties. The only justification that Sollars and Englander provide for this claim is the implicit reference to a reasonable person standard in the passage quoted above—a standard that we find unreasonable. By contrast, in our view, any ethically justifiable contract between two parties must be consistent with respect for the dignity of the two parties and those they represent. We acknowledge that this is a *prima facie* moral standard, one that could be superseded under special circumstances, or with the genuine consent of relevant parties. However, Sollars and Englander have provided no reason for thinking that this standard ought not apply when MNEs negotiate contracts with their suppliers.

Nonetheless, we do think that there are good objections to the brief argument regarding the duties of MNEs to subcontractors that we provided in "Sweatshops and Respect for Persons." But these are not Sollars and Englander's arguments. For example, some companies are too small to contract for use of all of a subcontractor's capacity, but must instead place orders that represent a small percentage of a supplier's capacity. In such cases, it is unreasonable to believe that the company can exert the sort of influence over the subcontractor that we assume above. This is especially true if the subcontractor is dealing with multiple companies at the same time, each with somewhat different standards or codes for the treatment of workers. Our response to such an objection would be to point out that companies genuinely interested in ensuring that workers in their supply chains are treated with dignity at work can collaborate with one another in order to ensure that uniform standards are adapted and implemented. Indeed, such collaborative efforts have been in place for several years.

Universalizability

At the conclusion of their discussion of the obligations of MNEs regarding sub-contractors. Sonars and Englander attempt to undermine our Kantian analysis of MNEs' obligations regarding subcontractors by deploying Korsgaard's interpretation of the conceptual contradiction test of the first formulation of the categorical imperative. This interpretation holds that conceptual contradictions are best understood "by imagining, in effect, that the action you propose to perform in order to carry out your purpose is the standard procedure for carrying out that purpose." Their argument, in essence, is that demonstrating respect for workers by providing them with a living wage constitutes a conceptual contradiction. It does so, in their view, because living wages always increase unemployment, thus harming the class of persons that living wages are intended to benefit. First, we note that Korsgaard's interpretation of the categorical imperative has been persuasively criticized by Barbara Herman, but for present purposes we will ignore this. Second, in developing this argument, Sollars and Englander do not accurately characterize the position we defend in "Sweatshops and Respect for Persons." This is evident when they describe the maxim necessary for their position: "The maxim of paying a subsistence wage could have the purpose of helping persons, whose lot is among the very worst, have some means to use their rationality to achieve 'moral perfection.'" In "Sweatshops and Respect for Persons" we argued that MNE managers have duties regarding adherence to local laws, coercion, health and safety standards, and wages. However, in seeking to undermine our position Sollars and Englander focus only on the wage issue. Our position regarding wages is as follows:

> It is our contention that, at a minimum, respect for employees entails that MNEs and their suppliers have a moral obligation to ensure that employees do not live under conditions of overall poverty by providing adequate wages for a forty-eight hour work week to satisfy both basic food needs and basic non-food needs. Doing so helps to ensure the physical well-being and independence of employees, contributes to the development of their rational capacities, and provides them with opportunities for moral development. This in turn allows for the cultivation of self-esteem.

We argued further that employers should voluntarily raise wages to this level, and that they should do so without laying-off employees, seeking instead to cover any increased costs in other ways:

> Our contention is that it is economically feasible for MNEs to voluntarily raise wages in factories in developing economics without causing increases in unemployment. MNEs may choose to raise wages while maintaining existing employment levels. Increased labor costs that are

not offset by greater productivity may be passed on to consumers, or, if necessary, absorbed through internal cost cutting measures such as reductions in executive compensation.

A maxim that would correspond to our position is as follows.

> In order to satisfy the basic food needs and basic non-food needs of employees and provide them with opportunities for the development of their rational capacities and moral development, we will ensure that all employees are paid the following wage for a forty-eight-hour work week (whichever is greater): The minimum wage required by law, or the wage necessary to allow them to live above the overall poverty line, for a forty-eight-hour work week, covering any additional costs by means other than employee layoffs.

Sollars and Englander provide no reason for thinking that such a maxim is not universalizable. Indeed, their *only* basis for challenging the universalizability of such a maxim is the stipulation that improving employee wages *must* cause increased unemployment. While they never take up a maxim that corresponds precisely to our view, even their truncated version of a maxim regarding wages is consistent with Korsgaard's interpretation of the conceptual contradiction test of the categorical imperative if one allows that voluntarily raising wages while maintaining existing employment levels does not lead to greater unemployment. Their retort at this stage must be that one cannot raise wages without increasing unemployment, but as we shall argue below, such a view is untenable.

In concluding this section it is worth noting that in seeking to undermine our position regarding wages, Sollars and Englander ignore our arguments in "Sweatshops and Respect for Persons" regarding the rule of law and health and safety conditions. However, since adhering to local labor laws and ensuring decent health and safety conditions can be costly, we find their implicit acceptance of our defense of the duties of MNEs regarding the rule of law and decent health and safety standards puzzling. In other words, if, as they suppose, raising wages will cause inevitable increases in unemployment, isn't the same true of adhering to local labor laws and improving working conditions? Why focus on the wage issue alone? A more consistent view would seem to be that MNE managers have duties to ignore local labor laws, ignore working conditions, and pay the lowest possible wages, so long as none of these practices deterred employees from working in MNE factories. We have argued that such a view is indefensible on Kantian grounds.

II. Coercion

In "Sweatshops and Respect for Persons" we argued that MNE managers have a moral obligation to prevent the use of coercion for certain purposes within factories. In particular, we argued that "[u]sing coercion as a means of compelling employees to work overtime, to meet production quotas despite injury, or to remain at work while in need of medical attention, is incompatible with respect for persons because the coercers treat their victims as mere tools." On our account, psychological coercion is properly understood to take place when three conditions hold:

First, the coercer must have a desire about the will of his or her victim. However, this is a desire of a particular kind because it can only be fulfilled through the will of another person. Second, the coercer must have an effective desire to compel his or her victim to act in a manner that makes efficacious the coercer's other regarding desire. The distinction between an other regarding desire and a coercive will is important because it provides a basis for delineating between cases of coercion and, for example, cases of rational persuasion. In both instances a person may have an other regarding desire, but in the case of coercion that desire will be supplemented by an effective first-order desire which seeks to enforce that desire on the person, and in cases of rational persuasion it will not. What is of most importance in such cases is that P intentionally attempts to compel Q to comply with an other regarding desire of P's own. These are necessary, but not sufficient conditions of coercion. In order for coercion to take place, the coercer must be successful in getting his or her victim to conform to his or her other regarding desire. In all cases of coercion P attempts to violate the autonomy of Q. When Q successfully resists P's attempted coercion, Q retains his or her autonomy. In such cases P retains a coercive will.

Sollars and Englander accept this account of psychological coercion, but deny that we have provided a clear example of coercion. In their view, what we described as coercion is merely a case of an employer enforcing a job requirement. They claim that "In the case of a routine job practice X, the supervisor need not have a desire to compel a worker to do X, although the supervisor might well prefer that the worker do X to save the expense of finding a new worker. The desire of the supervisor may simply be that some worker or other do X." It is unclear what further point they are attempting to make about coercion or sweatshops, but one might read them as maintaining that coercion seldom, if ever, takes place in sweatshops.

In making their case, Sollars and Englander refer to only one of the three examples of coercion that we offered (example one, below). Since the explicit point of their discussion of coercion is to deny that we provided a persuasive example of coercion in sweatshops, we think it reasonable to consider each of the three examples of coercion that we provided.

[1] Bangladesh, El Salvador, and other developing economies lack the social welfare programs that workers in North America and Europe take for granted. If workers lose their jobs, they may end up without any source of income. Thus, workers are understandably fearful of being fired for noncompliance with demands to work long overtime hours. When a worker is threatened with being fired by a supervisor unless she agrees to work overtime, and when the supervisor's intention in making the threat is to ensure compliance, then the supervisor's actions are properly understood as coercive.

[2] Similar threats are used to ensure that workers meet production quotas, even in the face of personal injury. . . .
    We do not claim that production quotas are inherently coercive. Given a reasonable quota, employees can choose whether or not to

work diligently to fill that quota. Employees who choose idleness over industriousness and are terminated as a result are not coerced. However, when a supervisor threatens workers who are ill or injured with termination unless they meet a production quota that either cannot physically be achieved by the employees, or can only be achieved at the cost or further injury to the employee, the threat is properly understood as coercive. In such cases the employee will inevitably feel compelled to meet the quota.

[3] [W]orkers report being threatened with termination if they seek medical attention. For example, when a worker in El Salvador who was three months pregnant began hemorrhaging she was not allowed to leave the factory to receive medical attention. She subsequently miscarried while in the factory, completed her long work day, and took her fetus home for burial. Other workers have died because they were not allowed to leave the factory to receive medical attention. In cases where workers suffer miscarriages or death, rather than risk termination, we believe that it [is] reasonable to conclude that the workers are coerced into remaining at work.

We think these examples illustrate well our account of coercion, and nothing Sollars and Englander have written undermines that judgment. It may well be that the practices described in each of these examples are routinely found in sweatshops. However, such a claim by itself does not constitute an objection to our view, for coercion may well be routine. What Sollars and Englander seem to be claiming is that overtime (i.e., hours worked beyond the forty-eight-hour work week we specify in our essay), quotas, and a strict attendance policy (one banning absence for medical reasons) are conditions of employment that employees may accept or reject, rather than informal practices coercively enforced by callous supervisors.

There are numerous problems with such a view. First, Sollars and Englander provide no reasons that would lead one to believe that coercion is not routinely used by supervisors in the ways that we describe. Indeed, all that need be the case is that the supervisors intend to compel the worker to, e.g., remain at work longer than forty-eight hours in a week and that the worker acquiesce to the supervisors' threat. One can easily imagine a scenario in which an employee who thought she was signing on for a forty-eight-hour work week freely chooses to work many additional hours in order to improve her earnings. However, one can also easily imagine a working mother declining to work overtime so that she can care for her children, and a supervisor coercing her into working overtime. It is equally easy to imagine scenarios in which quotas are met despite the exacerbation of an employee's work related disability, or in which an employee attends work despite a grave illness, only because they are coerced into doing so.

Second, Sollars and Englander seem to regard coercion as morally unjustified in all circumstances. This is why, one suspects, they object to the idea that employees can be coerced into working overtime. In their view, overtime of any length and duration appears to be a reasonable expectation of factory owners and managers, especially when the worker is fortunate to have the job at all. However, coercion is only *prima facie* objectionable. For example, if a supervisor threatens an employee with termination unless he stops sexually harassing fellow employees, the supervisor is coercing the harasser. However, such coercion is morally justified insofar as the supervisor is seeking to stop one employee from disrespecting other employees in an especially harmful manner. A claim that might be more consistent with the view of Sollars and Englander is that supervisors coerce employees into working overtime, meeting production quotas, and attending work despite serious illnesses, but that such coercion is justifiable. In "Sweatshops and Respect for Persons" we argued that such coercion is *not* morally justifiable on Kantian grounds. It remains up to Sollars and Englander to argue the contrary thesis. Without such an argument, their position is untenable insofar as those types of coercion occur in the workplace.

III. Wages and the Inadequacy of Mere Economic Analysis

In "Sweatshops and Respect for Persons" we advanced the thesis that employers have a duty to pay workers the minimum wage required by law, or the wage necessary to allow them to live above the overall poverty line, for a forty-eight-hour work week, covering any additional costs by means other than employee layoffs. We did not take a position on whether or not such a duty should be enforced via legislation. Instead, we argue that such a duty should be voluntarily embraced by MNEs and their contractors. In reply to this thesis, Sollars and Englander argue that the body of empirical research in economics supports the following conclusions: (1) that there is significant controversy over whether or not legally mandated minimum wages cause increases in unemployment; and (2) that the effect of efficiency wages on worker productivity is indeterminate. For the sake of argument, we grant these conclusions. Neither claim undermines our main thesis regarding wages. Sollars and Englander's fundamental mistake is their failure to distinguish between legally mandated wages and the voluntary fulfillment of duties regarding wages. In particular, they fail to link their discussion of the literature on minimum wages, and the controversy among economists on that issue, to the claim that MNE managers have an obligation to pay a living wage without covering additional costs via layoffs. Furthermore, they ignore our claim that if enhanced efficiency alone cannot compensate for increased labor costs, other strategies can and should be utilized.

We suspect that Sollars and Englander would respond by arguing that even if living wages were implemented via voluntary actions on the part of MNE managers, rather than via minimum wage legislation, the result would still be increased unemployment. While we recognize the relevance of economic analysis to this debate, their analysis of wages appears to be grounded in the attribution of a purely instrumental account of practical reasoning to MNEs managers. In their discussion of wages, at least, they seem to view managers as subject to overwhelming economic forces such that if wages are increased, employees must be laid off in order to compensate for increased costs. However, once it is acknowledged that MNE managers are capable of acting on their duties to a variety of stakeholders, it is not difficult to see how competent managers could meet their duties to workers by voluntarily raising wages without laying off employees. Indeed, one recent study found that when wages were voluntarily increased in the Indonesian apparel and footwear sector as a result of anti-sweatshop campaigns, employment levels actually *increased* resulting in a "win-win" situation. The increased wage costs for MNEs were so small that they appear to simply have been absorbed as operating expenses. In cases where such increased costs cannot be easily absorbed as operating expenses, and where increased productivity and loyalty do not completely offset increased labor costs, available evidence demonstrates that these costs may be passed on to consumers. If cases arise where this is not possible, internal cost-cutting measures, such as reductions in executive compensation and perks, are an attractive means of compensating for the cost of treating workers with dignity. In our view, the costs of respecting workers must be regarded as a necessary condition of doing business.

IV. Conclusion

In "Sweatshops, and Respect for Persons" we argued that MNEs have duties to adhere to local labor laws, to refrain from coercion, to meet minimum health and safety standards, and to pay workers a living wage. All, or nearly all, of these duties are now being fulfilled by many MNEs. Sollar and Englander have, in our judgment, failed to undermine any of our main theses. We acknowledge that much work yet remains to be done in order to advance theoretical discussion of the "sweatshop" problem. We hope that by demonstrating the shortcomings of the arguments discussed above, we have made modest progress toward that goal.

Gordon G. Sollars and Fred
Englander

NO

Sweatshops:
Kant and Consequences

Introduction

Arnold and Bowie (2003) attempt to derive ethical constraints on the actions of the managers of multinational enterprises (MNEs) or the MNEs themselves from a Kantian perspective. In particular, they adopt the Formula of Humanity version of Kant's categorical imperative, which they interpret in terms of respect for persons. Arnold and Bowie use other elements from Kant's system of ethics, but state that even "sympathetic readers" (Arnold & Bowie 2003: 222) who do not accept Kant's full system should be responsive to Kant's argument for the Formula of Humanity. From this starting point, Arnold and Bowie claim to reach the conclusions that MNEs or their managers have duties not to tolerate or encourage violations of the rule of law,[1] use coercion, allow unsafe working conditions, or pay wages that are below subsistence levels.

We contest Arnold and Bowie's claims, in particular, that they have established that MNEs have a duty to pay a subsistence wage above market levels.[2] Although we try to be sympathetic readers, we conclude that even within Arnold and Bowie's Kantian framework such a duty does not emerge. Regarding coercion, we agree with Arnold and Bowie that coercion is wrong on Kantian (and, of course, other) grounds. No doubt instances of coercion exist, but we disagree that Arnold and Bowie's example of a requirement to work overtime constitutes an example of coercion even by their own definition. Thus, a supposed paradigm case regarding sweatshops and overtime hours fails.

Finally, although we applaud Arnold and Bowie for addressing economic issues in an attempt to establish the feasibility of their subsistence-wage duty within a Kantian framework, we find that the weight of economic argument goes against them. As we discuss below, the best reading of current economic literature is that the raising of wages above market levels should be expected to increase unemployment, and, in particular, unemployment among the least skilled workers. Thus, if Kantian arguments actually could establish a subsistence-wage duty, concern for the well-being of the least-advantaged should be expected to lead to the classic tension between deontological and consequentialist concerns. Perhaps a strict Kantian perspective clearly favors the duty, trumping issues of consequences. However, Arnold and Bowie have broadened their audience

From *Business Ethics Quarterly*, Vol. 17, Issue 1, 2007, pp. 115–133. Copyright © 2007 by Business Ethics Quarterly. Reprinted by permission of The Philosophy Documentation Center, publisher of Business Ethics Quarterly. References omitted.

beyond strict Kantians, by arguing that any persons sympathetic to the Formula of Humanity should accept the subsistence-wage duty. A pluralist view could both have such sympathy and be concerned about well being. Arnold and Bowie's argument does not address how conflicts between these perspectives should be resolved.

1. Subcontractors and Suppliers

Typically, MNEs do not employ workers under sweatshop conditions; rather the sweatshop workers are employed by subcontractors or suppliers of an MNE. This has led sweatshop critics to argue that such MNEs inherit responsibility for the actions of these other entities. Arnold and Bowie (2003: 226) present three arguments in favor of the idea that MNEs are responsible for the practices of their subcontractors or suppliers.

The first argument is actually quoted from Santoro (2000: 161). Santoro asserts that the standard for judging MNE responsibility for the treatment of sweatshop workers by subcontractor or supplier companies "is similar" to the legal doctrine of *respondeat superior*. First, we note that neither Santoro nor Arnold and Bowie give an argument that provides a moral justification for this legal doctrine, which is part of the law dealing with master-servant relationships. In particular, Arnold and Bowie do not attempt to derive it from the Formula of Humanity, which is their acknowledged Kantian touchstone. However, illustrating the usefulness of a Kantian perspective is only one of Arnold and Bowie's goals, and so for the sake of the argument we will assume the moral legitimacy of *respondeat superior*. The law distinguishes between a "servant," for whose actions the master may be liable under *respondeat superior*, and an "independent contractor," for whose actions the master is not liable. We claim that for an argument to be "similar" to *respondeat superior*, the argument should retain the distinction between servant and independent contractor. Thus, the question becomes whether subcontractors and suppliers are properly construed as servants rather than contractors.

Gifis defines a "contractor" as "one who makes an agreement with another to do a piece of work, retaining for himself the control of the means, method and manner of producing the result to be accomplished, neither party having the right to terminate the contract at will" (Gifis 1984: 97). The same source defines a "servant" as a person who "with respect to the physical conduct in the performance of the services is subject to" the control of another (Gifis 1984: 438). The commonsense meanings of "subcontractor" and "supplier" clearly favor the first definition over the second; indeed, a "subcontractor" is a kind of contractor, and thus not a servant. Further, as a factual matter, we claim that subcontractors and suppliers are not typically subject to the control of MNEs in their "physical conduct." Finally, the Restatement of Agency (2d) states that "service under an agreement to use care and skill in accomplishing results" marks an independent contractor.[3] Such service is the essence of the outsourcing relationships that MNEs have with subcontractors.

It might be said in defense of Arnold and Bowie's gesturing at *respondeat superior* that they simply mean to claim that subcontractors or suppliers are agents of MNEs, and that this agency confers responsibility on the MNEs.[4] We do not wish to deny that it is logically possible for such responsibility to be conferred on MNEs in some fashion, in some circumstances. However, the *respondeat superior* doctrine is all that Arnold and Bowie offer in this regard, and this very doctrine clearly illustrates that the principal/agent relationship does not necessarily confer responsibility for an agent's action on the principal. Indeed, it seems designed to exclude the very agents at issue in the sweatshop debate. The blanket statement that MNEs are responsible for the actions of their subcontractors and suppliers might be true, but it is simply not supported by the invocation of *respondeat superior.*

The second argument is that managers of MNEs are simply individuals who are constrained to show respect to others, including the employees of subcontractors or suppliers, as required by the categorical imperative in its Formula of Humanity interpretation. The challenge here is to unpack what is meant by "respect." Arnold and Bowie begin with the straightforward Kantian claim that showing respect means treating persons as ends in themselves. Next, they approvingly cite Hill (1992) regarding the implication of Kant's arguments concerning the treatment of persons as ends. According to Arnold and Bowie, Hill argues that treating persons as ends in themselves requires "supporting and developing certain human capabilities" (Arnold & Bowie 2003: 223). They add that Kant also argues that mere indifference fails to show respect, and that there is "an obligation to be concerned with the physical welfare of people and their moral well-being" (Arnold & Bowie 2003: 223). Finally, Arnold and Bowie's second argument incorporates by reference the argument in Bowie (1999).[5] All of this is in preparation for Arnold and Bowie's claim that, with regard to wages, respect for persons requires a forty-eight hour per week wage level that is sufficient to satisfy basic food and non-food needs:

> Doing so helps to ensure the physical well-being and independence of employees, contributes to the development of their rational capabilities, and provides them with opportunities for moral development. (Arnold & Bowie 2003: 234)

We find a number of difficulties with this argument. First, we simply do not read Hill's discussion of human capabilities as making the claim that these capabilities require development and support. The references given in both Arnold and Bowie (2003) and Bowie (1999) to Hill's capability discussion are to a description of the capabilities that Kant includes in the notion of "humanity": acting on principles; following hypothetical imperatives; setting goals; accepting categorical imperatives independently of reward or punishment; and some ability to understand the world and reason abstractly (Hill 1992: 40–41). Hill himself says nothing about a requirement to "develop and support" these capabilities in that discussion, and he makes it clear that Kant believed that this degree of humanity belongs to even "the most foolish and depraved persons" (Hill 1992: 41). These are capabilities that ordinary human beings possess as a matter of course.

Second, Hill's own discussion demonstrates that it is not an easy matter to be sure what Kant meant by "always treating humanity as an end."

Hill reviews a number of things that Kant says about ends, in particular, that objective ends are to be "conceived only negatively—that is, as an end against which we should never act" (Hill 1992: 44), The straightforward reading of this, Hill allows, is that treating humanity as an end can be achieved simply by restraint—no positive effort to help others by "development and support" is required. In light of Kant's various other remarks, Hill himself finds this statement about ends "puzzling" (Hill 1992: 44). In an attempt to resolve this puzzle (and other difficulties), Hill turns to Kant's distinction between personal ends—which only have a price—and ends in themselves—which have a dignity, that is, an "unconditional and incomparable worth" (Hill 1992: 47). It is at this point that Hill begins to prescribe what respect for persons entails, rather than simply describe the constituent capabilities of humanity possessed by any ordinary person. He lists seven items:

1. refusing to damage a person's rational capacities (*e.g.,* via drugs or lobotomy);
2. refusing to destroy a person;
3. attempting to develop and improve rational capabilities;
4. attempting to exercise these capabilities as far as possible;
5. appealing to reason rather than use manipulation;
6. leaving freedom for others to pursue their (rational) ends; and
7. requiring that humanity should be honored or at least not "mocked, dishonored, or degraded" (Hill 1992: 50–51).

We note that the first, second, sixth, and seventh items are consistent with the idea that only restraint, not any positive "developing" or "supporting" action, is required. Indeed, if we identify, as seems plausible here, "manipulation" with "coercion," then item five can be viewed in the same way.[6] Now it is clear on Kantian grounds that workers ought not to be coerced.[7] From the discussion of *respondeat superior* above, we do not see how managers of MNEs are responsible for such coercion of workers as might occur, initiated by subcontractor or supplier companies. However, while the status of subcontractors and suppliers as independent contractors insulates MNEs from responsibility for coercion, MNEs certainly ought not endorse or acquiesce in the use of coercion by their subcontractors or suppliers. Our concern is with imperfect duties, not the violation of perfect ones.

Items three and four deal with rational capacities. With regard to item three, the development of rational capacities, Kant, perhaps surprisingly, does not hold that we have a duty to develop the rational capabilities of others (Hill 1992: 52; Kant 1964: 44). Hill does note that Kant was, nevertheless, "in his own life" committed to the idea that "one should at least provide opportunities for others' rational development" (Hill 1992: 53). This brings us to item four, which deals with each person's own exercise of these capacities. Here, Hill points out that reason is to be exercised in order to attain "moral perfection," not happiness, either one's own or others. Standing in the way of such perfection is pain, adversity, and poverty, since these are temptations to vice (Hill 1992: 53). However, assuming that coercion and deception are not present, the bargain between employer and employee improves the situation of the employee from her own perspective, that is, in terms of her own plans and projects. The bargain acts to lessen the pain, adversity, or poverty present in a pre-existing situation. To the extent that MNEs contracting with various companies that employ sweatshop workers create jobs for workers, MNEs are assisting in the exercise of reasoning by workers. Thus, they contribute to the provision of item three, even though Kant, at least, did not consider it a duty to do so.

Now, Arnold and Bowie might argue that managers of MNEs could do more for the employees of their subcontractors and suppliers. This is true, but then so could anyone. We must be careful not to implicitly turn the ethical principle that "ought implies can" into "can implies ought."[8] There is any number of things that could be done to remove pain, adversity, or poverty. The bargain (excluding coercion or fraud) between employer and employee is one of those things, and it is perverse to fault it in particular because it might have done more for one party. Note that we do not imply here that a sweatshop worker has no moral grounds for complaint against *some party or other* simply because she makes a bargain with a subcontractor or supplier of an MNE. Rather, our point is that the subcontractor or supplier has done *something* via the bargain to reduce pain, adversity, or poverty, while other actors may have done *nothing*. It is unreasonable to expect any bargain struck between two parties to redress every issue of fairness or desert that may apply to one party. MNEs are in some sense "taking advantage" of background conditions in the Third World when they outsource their production, but this alone does not make them responsible for the poverty that makes their sourcing decisions profitable. It would be a different matter if, for example, particular MNEs conspired with host governments to keep sweatshop workers impoverished. However, Arnold and Bowie provide no examples of this. With regard to MNEs taken as a group, considerable evidence of their salutary effect on Third World poverty comes from a wide variety of sources such as those cited in Maitland (2001) and Brown, Deardorff, and Stern (2004).

Arnold and Bowie point out that Kant argued that a rich person has a duty of charity that a poor person lacks, and that Kant acknowledged that individuals have particular duties as a result of particular circumstances.[9] However, they do not attempt to derive either of these claims from the Formula of Humanity interpretation of the categorical imperative, so it is not clear how central a position these claims hold in their approach.[10] In any event, the duty of charity is a "wide" or "imperfect" duty. Thus, according to Hill's analysis, there is not only freedom to choose to do or not do some act of charity on some occasion, but also latitude for judgment in deciding if a given principle is relevant to a particular situation and freedom to choose various ways of satisfying a principle (Hill 1992: 155). The decision to increase wages is precisely a matter of such judgment. The effect of such a decision could well be to increase unemployment, which would presumably increase pain, adversity, or poverty for those unemployed. Further, the employer could have other duties, in particular a duty to investors or other stakeholders that, given these freedoms of judgment, may mitigate any duty to ameliorate pain, adversity, or poverty beyond the contribution the bargain already makes.

We are not directly challenging the Kantian framework. Rather, we are pointing out that the framework itself does not provide support for the selection of a wage level (or working hours) apart from the knowledge of a myriad of factors that are purely contingent. Indeed, Hayek has argued that market institutions are the best we have for dealing with the severe constraints that human beings face in bringing our necessarily fragmented knowledge to bear in a way that will improve our welfare (Hayek 1945). A market wage, even one that is insufficient for meeting basic food and non-food needs, can still be the best alternative to unemployment. As a result of this item-by-item examination of Hill's claims, we conclude that a reliance on market-determined wages—absent coercion or deception—is fully consistent with the Kantian duties of individuals.

Arnold and Bowie's third argument has already been touched on: the claim that individuals can have unique duties as a result of unique circumstances.[11] We have previously raised the question of how this principle might be tied to the categorical imperative. However, we prefer not to propose and then critique such attempted ties ourselves. Rather, we will point out that Arnold and Bowie have switched the focus from persons as moral agents to MNEs as moral agents. Arnold and Bowie stress the resources that MNEs have to "ensure that the employees of its business partners are respected" (Arnold & Bowie 2003: 227). However, the resources of MNEs are not the same as the resources freely available to any person who might be an MNE manager. We have dealt with the case of individuals above. Arnold and Bowie make a separate point about MNEs with their third argument only to the extent that MNEs, as opposed to the individuals that comprise them, can have duties.

We favor the view that organizations are not moral agents, but this contentious issue need not be explored here. Within a Kantian approach, viewing the corporation as a moral agent has the radical consequence that the corporation has a dignity, not a price. Thus, it would be wrong to buy or sell corporations or shares in corporations. Such a view would completely invalidate any present form of capitalism, and Arnold and Bowie give no indication that they endorse such a view. Given the obvious problem with viewing the corporation as a moral agent from a Kantian perspective, we do not find that Arnold and Bowie provide sufficient detail for us to be confident that we understand exactly what they are claiming in their third argument. In any event, we do not see how to make sense of a claim that an organization has a duty to do some action X without also claiming that at least some individual in the organization has a duty to do some action Y. We have argued above that individuals do not have a duty to do such things Y as Arnold and Bowie suggest would discharge such purported Kantian obligations. As such, MNEs (or their managers) cannot be faulted for the wage levels of their subcontractors or suppliers.

This completes our critique of Arnold and Bowie's attempt to derive a subsistence-wage duty from the Formula of Humanity. We believe that the attempt fails. However, Kantian arguments are famously recondite, and we do not wish to express overconfidence in our rebuttal. Kant states that the various interpretations he gives for the categorical imperative are equivalent (Kant 1997: 43); therefore, each interpretation should yield the same answer regarding a putative duty. As an alternative check of our conclusion, we offer some additional analysis using the Formula of Universal Law interpretation of the categorical imperative:

> act only in accordance with that maxim through which you can at the same time will that it become a universal law. (Kant 1997: 31)

This is to be understood in terms of what can be willed without contradiction, and Kant explains that there are two ways in which contradictions can arise. The first is that some actions have as their maxim something that could not even be conceived as a universal law without contradiction in the conception; the second is that some actions have as their maxim something that, although conceivable, could not be willed without that will contradicting itself. Korsgaard notes that there have been at least three different interpretations of what Kant meant by "contradiction" in the literature (Korsgaard 1996: 78). We cannot hope to do better than to follow the one favored by Korsgaard herself, the Practical Contradiction Interpretation.

Korsgaard states:

> [T]he contradiction that is involved in the universalization of an immoral maxim is that the agent would be unable to act on the maxim in a world in which it were universalized so as to achieve his own purpose—that is the purpose that is specified in the maxim. Since he wills to act on his maxim, this means that his purpose will be frustrated. If this interpretation is correct, then it is essential that in testing maxims of actions the purpose always be included in the formulation of the maxim. (Korsgaard 1996: 92)

The maxim of paying a subsistence wage could have the purpose of helping persons, whose lot is among the very worst, have some means to use their rationality to achieve "moral perfection" (as discussed above). (Other purposes might also be plausible, but any such purpose would seem to be directed at assisting these persons in some way.) Will this very purpose be frustrated by the universalization of the maxim to pay a subsistence wage?

There are three cases to consider: the subsistence wage is below, equal to, or above the market-determined wage. In the first two cases, the purpose can be met by universalizing the maxim, but acting on the maxim has no independent effect. The wage arrived at by the market is already meeting the purpose. The only interesting case is when the subsistence wage is above market levels. When a minimum or subsistence wage is set above the market wage, we argue below (section 4) that the best understanding of the economic literature is that some increased amount of unemployment will result. Assuming, then, that some unemployment will result when a wage above the market level is paid, persons who are unemployed will have even fewer means provided to them under the maxim than they would if they were employed at the market wage. Thus, the maxim contradicts its own purpose, at least with regard to those who remain or become unemployed. It is open to Arnold and Bowie to argue that the maxim should apply only to those who do manage to get employment under it, but we see no reason why those who cannot find work or who lose their jobs should be excluded from consideration.

To conclude this section we note that the concept of respect can be explicated in a variety of ways, and there is no obvious limit on the number of ways that respect can be given or withheld. Arnold and Bowie argue for an expansive concept of respect; however, persons also show respect when they decide to rely upon agreements to further their life plans and projects rather than on the use of force, and when they reach agreements without deception. Since this minimalist concept of respect is consistent with Hill's arguments, it should be both plausible and attractive to Arnold and Bowie's "sympathetic readers" as an alternative. Further, adopting this view of respect keeps the conclusions drawn from the Formula of Humanity consistent with those drawn from the Formula of Universal Law.

2. Coercion

Arnold and Bowie distinguish between physical and psychological coercion, and they report evidence of both in sweatshop environments. Physical coercion need not detain us. We agree with Arnold and Bowie that workers should not be physically coerced on Kantian (or, for that matter, various other) grounds. MNEs and their subcontractors and suppliers should not use physical coercion; and we accept that there are Kantian reasons for MNEs not to contract under circumstances in which the employees of their subcontractors and suppliers are physically coerced. Regarding psychological coercion, Arnold and Bowie give three conditions as definitional: (1) the coercer must have a desire about the will of the victim; (2) the coercer must have a desire to compel the victim to act in a way that makes the coercer's first desire efficacious; and (3) the coercer must be successful in getting the victim to conform (Arnold & Bowie 2003: 229). They make clear that a person who simply makes a choice that is not very desirable is not coerced by the lack of good options. Thus choosing to work in a sweatshop because the only alternatives are worse does not, by itself, on Arnold and Bowie's account constitute psychological coercion. However, Arnold and Bowie hold that psychological coercion does occur when:

> a worker is threatened with being fired by a supervisor unless she agrees to work overtime, and when the supervisor's intention in making the threat is to ensure compliance. (Arnold & Bowie 2003: 230)

We will accept this account of psychological coercion (if only for the sake of the argument), but not that Arnold and Bowie have given a clear example of such coercion. For some action X, it could well be the case that a supervisor making such a threat is acting coercively, but this does not fit well when X is replaced by "overtime" (or even "extensive overtime") in the context of sweatshops. We assume that the practice of overtime is understood by prospective workers; they might prefer not to work overtime and especially not the overtime that is actually demanded of them. However, this simply makes their choice of a sweatshop that requires overtime less desirable than it might otherwise be. To the extent that overtime is routine, the supervisor's request is not a threat, but simply a statement of the conditions of employment. Workers who are acceptable to management are those who will work overtime, and unacceptable workers may be fired (or are never hired in the first place). Failure to observe this distinction would collapse Arnold and Bowie's account of coercion into a "bad-alternatives" account, which they seem to reject.

In the case of a routine job practice X, the supervisor need not have a desire to compel a worker to do X, although the supervisor might well prefer that the worker do X to save the expense of finding a new worker. The desire of the supervisor may simply be that some worker or other do X. Now, a particular—less ethical—supervisor might find more satisfaction or enjoyment in a situation in which overtime was routine than one in which it was not. Perhaps such a supervisor satisfies Arnold and Bowie's conditions for psychological coercion—we are not sure. However, in the case of a routine practice, this would simply mean that their definition of psychological coercion was at odds with their claim not to accept a "bad-alternatives" account of coercion.

Conclusion

We have explored Arnold and Bowie's claim regarding a duty of MNEs or their managers to ensure the payment of subsistence wages by their subcontractors and suppliers, and concerning the use of coercion by these same groups. With the exception of physical coercion, we find that their rationale, based on the Formula of Humanity, is insufficient to establish the duty they state. In particular, a duty to pay above-market wages does not follow from the arguments they present. Nor, even if it did, should the reader, based on current economic research, be unconcerned that such a duty would not work to worsen the situation of the least advantaged workers.

Notes

1. We do not contest this claim.
2. We will not treat working conditions separate from wages. Our justification, apart from space limitations, is that many attempts to improve working conditions would increase costs of labor, and so have much the same effects as raising wage levels. However, we have no intention to argue that working conditions should not be improved if this can be done at no cost or at a net economic benefit.
3. The Restatement of Agency (2d) lists ten conditions to be considered when determining if an agent is a servant or an independent contractor. We believe that these conditions clearly mark subcontractors and suppliers of MNEs as independent contractors, but since Arnold & Bowie do not attempt to support their claim regarding *respondeat superior* in any detail, we spare the reader an item by item examination of the conditions in favor of the commonsense argument in the text. See American Law Institute (1958).
4. This point was suggested by an anonymous reviewer.
5. See especially chapter two. We will not treat the argument in Bowie (1999) separately. We find it most persuasive in dealing with the prohibitions on

coercion and deception, which can be observed negatively. Bowie's argument for duties to take some positive action is on a par with the one we discuss below.

6. We will discuss "psychological" coercion, another element of Arnold and Bowie's argument, below.

7. See the "Coercion" section below.

8. Arnold and Bowie's concern with consequences at the end of their paper could perhaps be viewed as intended to rebut a claim that the principle "ought implies can" would be violated by their conclusions regarding duties. However, at this stage in their argument, the duties (oughts) they call for have not yet been established.

9. This claim actually constitutes their third argument, which we handle here in terms of individuals. The implications for companies are treated below.

10. Since Arnold and Bowie are not urging that we adopt Kant's complete system of philosophy, but only drawing out what they take to be implications of the Formula of Humanity, their argument is convincing only to the extent that any ethical elements they introduce are linked to this formulation.

11. We do not contest that persons can have special obligations as the result of voluntary choice, such as the choice to make a promise. Employers should of course keep their promises; many reasons, Kantian and non-Kantian, can be given for this. The challenge is to show that simply being in a certain (unchosen) circumstance can create a duty. Even here, we do not necessarily claim that there are no such duties, but only that Arnold and Bowie owe the reader an explanation of how such duties follow from the Formula of Humanity.

References

American Law Institute. 1958. Restatement of Agency (2d). St. Paul, MN: American Law Institute Publishers.

Arnold, D. G., & Bowie, N. E. 2003. Sweatshops and respect for persons. *Business Ethics Quarterly*, 13: 221–42.

Baker, M., Benjamin, D., & Stranger, S. 1999. The highs and lows of the minimum wage effect: A time-series cross-section study of the Canadian law. *Journal of Labor Economics*, 17 (2): 318–50.

Bellante, D., & Picone, G. 1999. Fast food and unnatural experiments: Another perspective on the New Jersey minimum wage. *Journal of Labor Research*, 20 (4): 463–77.

Bliss, C., & Stern, N. H. 1978. Productivity, wages and nutrition, parts i and ii. *Journal of Development Economics*, 5: 331–98.

Borjas, G. J. 2005. Labor economics. New York: McGraw-Hill.

Bowie, N. E. 1999. Business ethics: A Kantian perspective. Oxford: Blackwell Publishers Inc.

Brown, D. K., Deardorff, A. V., & Stern, R. M. 2004. The effects of multinational production on wages and working conditions in developing countries. In R. E.

Baldwin & L. A. Winters (Eds.), *Challenges to globalization: Analyzing the economics.* Chicago: The University of Chicago Press.

Burkhauser, R. V., Couch, K. A., & Wittenburg, D. C. 2000a. A reassessment of the new economics of the minimum wage literature with monthly data from the current population survey. *Journal of Labor Economics,* 18 (4): 653–701.

———. 2000b. Who minimum wage increases bite: an analysis using monthly data from the sipp and the cps. *Southern Economic Journal,* 67 (1): 16–40.

Campbell, C. M., III. 1993. Pay efficiency wages? Evidence with data at the firm level. *Journal of Labor Economics,* 11 (3): 442–70.

Cappelli, P., & Chauvin, K. 1991. An interplant test of the efficiency wage hypothesis. *The Quarterly Journal of Economics,* 106 (3): 769–87.

Card, D., & Krueger, A. B. 1994. Minimum wages and employment: A case study of the fast-food industry in New Jersey and Pennsylvania. *The American Review,* 84 (4): 772–93.

———. 1995. Myth and measurement: The economics of the minimum wage. Princeton, NJ: Princeton University Press.

Castillo-Freeman, A. J., & Freeman, R. B. 1992. When the minimum wage really bites: The effect of the U.S.-level minimum wage on Puerto Rico. In G. J. Borjas & R. B. Freeman (Eds.), *Immigration and the work force: Economic consequences for the United States and source areas:* 177–211. Chicago: University of Chicago Press.

Ehrenberg, R. G., & Smith, R. S. 2003. Labor economics: Theory and public policy (8th ed.). Boston: Addison Wesley, Inc.

Freeman, R. B. 1997. Honor of David Card: Winner of the John Bates Clark medal. *Journal of Economic Perspectives,* 11 (2): 161–78.

Gera, S., & Grenier, G. 1994. Interindustry wage differentials and efficiency wages: Some Canadian evidence. *Canadian Journal of Economics,* 27 (1): 81–100.

Gifis, S. H. 1984. Law dictionary (2nd ed.). New York: Barron's Educational Series.

Hayek, F. A. 1945. The use of knowledge in society. *The American Economic Review,* 35 (4).

Hill, T. E., Jr. 1992. Dignity and practical reasoning in Kant's moral theory. Ithaca, NY: Cornell University Press.

Huang, T.-L., Hallam, A., Orazem, P. F., & Paterno, E. M. 1998. Empirical tests of efficiency wage models. *Economica,* 65: 125–43.

Kant, I. 1964. The metaphysical principles of virtue (J. Ellington, Trans.). Indianapolis: The Bobbs-Merrill Company, Inc.

———. 1997. Groundwork of the metaphysics of morals (M. Gregor, Trans.). Cambridge: Cambridge University Press.

Karz, L. F., & Krueger, A. B. 1992. The effects of the minimum wage on the fast-food industry. *Industrial and Labour Relations Review,* 46 (1): 6–21.

Keane, M. P. 1993. Individual heterogeneity and interindustry wage differentials. *Journal of Human Resources,* 28 (1): 134–61.

Korsgaard, C. M. 1996. Creating the kingdom of ends. Cambridge: Cambridge University Press.

Krueger, A. B. 1991. Ownership, agency, and wages: An examination of franchising in the fast food industry. *The Quarterly Journal of Economics,* 106 (1): 75–101.

Leonard, J. S. 1987. Carrots and Sticks: Pay, supervision and turnover. *Journal of Labor Economics*, 5 (4): S136–S151.

Maitland, I. 2001. The great non-debate over international sweatshops. In T. L. Beauchamp, & N. E. Bowie (Eds.), *Ethical theory and business,* 6th ed. Englewood Cliffs, NJ: Prentice Hall.

Maloney, W. F., & Mendez, J. N. 2003. Measuring the impact of minimum wages: Evidence from Latin America, *NBER Working Papers 9800:* National Bureau of Economic Research.

Michl, T. 2000. Can rescheduling explain the New Jersey minimum wage studies? *Eastern Economic Journal*, 26 (3): 265–76.

Neumark, D., & Wascher, W. 1995. Minimum wage effects on school and work transitions of teenagers. *American Economic Review*, 85 (2): 244–49.

———. 2004. Minimum wages, labor market institutions, and youth employment: A cross-national analysis. *Industrial and Labor Relations Review*, 57 (2): 223–48.

Partridge, M. D., & Partridge, J. S. 1999a. Do minimum wage hikes raise US long term unemployment? Evidence using state minimum wage rates. *Regional Studies,* 33 (8): 713–26.

———. 1999b. Do minimum wage hikes reduce employment? State-level evidence from the low-wage retail sector. *Journal of Labor Research,* 20 (3): 393–414.

Republic of El Salvador. 2000. Monitoring report on maguilas and bonded areas: Ministry of Labor, Monitoring and Labor Relations Unit.

Ressler, R. W., Watson, J. K., & Mixon, F. 1996. Full wages, part-time employment, and the minimum wage. *Applied Economics*, 28 (11): 1415–19.

Santoro, M. A. 2000. Profits and Principles: Global capitalism and human rights in China. Ithaca, NY: Cornell University Press.

Spriggs, W., & Schmitt, J. 1996. The minimum wage. In T. Schafer & J. Faux (Eds.), *Reclaiming Prosperity: A blueprint for progressive economic reform:* 166–73. Armonk, NY: M. E. Sharpe.

Strauss, J., & Thomas, D. 1998. Health, nutrition, and economic development. *Journal of Economic Literature*, 36 (2): 766–817.

Walsh, F. 1999. A multisector model of efficiency wages. *Journal of Labor Economics*, 17 (2): 351–75.

Zavodny, M. 2000. Effect of the minimum wage on employment and hours. *Labour Economics*, 7 (6): 729–50.

POSTSCRIPT

Are Sweatshops an Inhumane Business Practice?

Consumers are thinking about the people who make the products they purchase and the conditions in which they work. American retailers and name brands have produced clothing, shoes, toys, and more. Store shelves are filled with merchandise made in sweatshops, where the workers often conduct their labor in unsafe conditions with little pay. Many of these retailers say that they are following strict codes of conduct and performing on-site monitoring. However, business ethicists believe that some factories have found ways to conceal abuses and to keep double sets of books to fool auditors. At some factories, individuals are tutored with a script to recite to auditors, but this script does not accurately reflect the real conditions at the sweatshop. What can Americans ethically believe about what they wear and use? Is a Kantian ideal being followed in the production of these goods? Should it be?

Suggested Reading

Ronald J. Adams "Retail profitability and sweatshops: a global dilemma," *Journal of Retailing and Consumer Services* (vol. 9, no. 3, May 2002).

John Miller "Why Economists Are Wrong About Sweatshops and the Anti-sweatshop Movement," *Challenge,* vol. 46, no. 1, January-February 2003.

Ellen Israel Rosen, *Making Sweatshops: The Globalization of the U.S. Apparel Industy,* First Ed (University of California Press, 2002)

ISSUE 17

Should Patenting Life Be Forbidden?

YES: Jeremy Rifkin, from "Should We Patent Life?" *Business Ethics* (March/April 1998)

NO: William Domnarski, from "Dire New World," *Intellectual Property Magazine* (January 1999)

ISSUE SUMMARY

YES: Jeremy Rifkin, a persistent critic of unreflective support of "scientific progress," fears that genetic engineering extends human power over the rest of nature in ways that are unprecedented and whose consequences cannot be known. He urges a halt to research along these lines, especially research whose aim is no more than profit for the company that "owns" the results.

NO: William Domnarski, an intellectual property lawyer, finds the patenting of genes or genetic discoveries no different from patenting any other ideas. The purpose of patents is to reward and encourage useful invention, and there is no doubt that the modifications we introduce to the genetic material of plants and animals are useful to feed a starving world.

There is an apocryphal story that at a meeting of a gentlemanly scientific society in the seventeenth century, one of the members proposed a toast to the next scientific discovery, to which another of the members immediately added a fervent wish "that it may be of no use to anyone." The story illustrates well the ambivalence of scientific research that informs this issue.

Why do we seek knowledge? A sufficient reason might be that the Lord created our minds, and a fascinating world to study, and that in seeking wisdom and insight into the ways of nature we honor our creator and raise our minds closer to the divine mind. Something of that sort seems to have informed Aristotle's praise for the life of contemplation in the tenth book of the *Nicomachean Ethics*. But Francis Bacon, an early-seventeenth-century philosopher of science, suggested another reason altogether: "The end of our foundation is the knowledge of causes, and secret motions of things; and the enlarging of the bounds of human empire, to the effecting of all things possible." Knowledge is power, and the reason we pursue knowledge is to increase the power of human beings. It was the mission of science to expand the domain of human understanding precisely so that in knowing all things, we might do all things.

Shall we pursue knowledge of the genetic factors in animal and plant life, including possibly knowledge of the human genome? As we reflect on the problem, Monsanto Inc. is going forward with genetically engineered agricultural plant germ lines for export. Europe has firmly said, no genetically modified organisms (GMOs) on our tables, and in many places farmers have refused to grow them. Already a controversy has exploded in the grocery market: May GMOs grown without fertilizers or pesticides be labeled "organic"? Enthusiasts point out that GMOs, because they are better plants, often don't need any fertilizers or pesticides, so that should make organic farmers and their customers very happy. Critics point out that the reason they don't need chemical fertilizers or pesticides is that they have the bug repellent and heaven only knows what other chemicals engineered into their skins.

Why is Monsanto investing all this time and money to develop new lines of plants? One obvious reason is to make money. But if they are going to make money, they have to have patents on the new seeds they develop, or they will immediately be outflanked and undersold by similar firms that can duplicate their seeds without all the expensive investment. So patents are necessary in order to protect the enterprise. Meanwhile, Monsanto claims that all it wants to do is provide more food for a hungry world, a goal that we can only applaud, and that it needs the protection of patents to keep up the good work.

Where is technology taking us in this case? Can we separate out the genuine altruism (they really do want to feed the world) from the scientific curiosity (a universal human motive) from the selfish desire to make a very large amount of money very quickly?

Bear in mind, as you read these selections, that you are looking at a real cutting-edge issue. For most of biotechnology, we don't even know the empirical consequences ten years down the road—that's how recent the science is. Should we calculate costs versus benefits, as far as they may be known? Or should we adopt the precautionary principle and put off all introduction of this technology (where it has not altogether taken over already)? Shall we allow the entrepreneur inventor to reap the fortunes associated with a good patent or two on the most recent developments? Or shall we decide that life in all its forms is sacred, not open to private claim or profit?

YES ↰   Jeremy Rifkin

Should We Patent Life?

A handful of companies are engaged in a race to patent all 100,000 human genes. In less than a decade, the race will be over. The genetic legacy of our species will be held in the form of private intellectual property. The genes inside your cells will belong not to you, but to global corporations. Welcome to the world of the biotech revolution.

While the 20th century was shaped by breakthroughs in physics and chemistry, the 21st century will belong to the biological sciences. Scientists are deciphering the genetic code, unlocking the mystery of millions of years of evolution. Global life science companies, in turn, are beginning to exploit these new advances. The raw resources of the new economic epoch are genes— already being used in businesses ranging from agriculture and bioremediation to energy and pharmaceuticals.

By 2025, we may be living in a world remade by a revolution unmatched in history. The biotech revolution raises unprecedented ethical questions we've barely begun to discuss. Will the artificial creation of cloned and transgenic animals mean the end of nature and the substitution of a bio-industrial world? Will the release of genetically engineered life forms into the biosphere cause catastrophic genetic pollution? What will it mean to live in a world where babies are customized in the womb—and where people are stereotyped and discriminated against on the basis of their genotype? What risks do we take in attempting to design more "perfect" human beings?

At the heart of this new commercial revolution is a chilling question of great ethical impact, whose resolution will affect civilization for centuries to come: *Should we patent life?* The practice has already gotten a green light, through a controversial Supreme Court decision and a subsequent ruling by the Patent and Trademark Office in the 1980s. But if the question were put directly to the American people, would they agree? If you alter one gene in a chimpanzee, does that make the animal a human "invention"? If you isolate the gene for breast cancer, does that give you the right to "own" it? Should a handful of global corporations be allowed to patent all human genes?

On the eve of the Biotech Century, we do still have an opportunity to raise ethical issues like these—although the window is rapidly closing.

We've only completed the first decade of a revolution that may span several centuries. But already there are 1,400 biotech companies in the U.S., with a total of nearly $13 billion in annual revenues and more than 100,000 employees. Development is proceeding in an astonishing number of areas:

At Harvard University, scientists have grown human bladders and kidneys in laboratory jars. Monsanto hopes to have a plastic-producing plant on the market by the year 2003—following up on the work of Chris Sommerville at the Carnegie Institution of Washington, who inserted a plastic-making gene into a mustard plant. Another biotech company, the Institute of Genomic Research, has successfully sequenced a microbe that can absorb large amounts of radioactivity and be used to dispose of deadly radioactive waste. The first genetically engineered insect, a predator mite, was released in 1996 by researchers at the University of Florida, who hope it will eat other mites that damage strawberries and similar crops.

At the University of Wisconsin, scientists have genetically altered brooding turkey hens to increase their productivity, by eliminating the "brooding" instinct: the desire to sit on and hatch eggs. Other researchers are experimenting with the creation of sterile salmon who will not have the suicidal urge to spawn, but will remain in the open sea, to be commercially harvested. Michigan State University scientists say that by breaking the spawning cycle of chinook salmon, they can produce seventy-pound salmon, compared to less than eighteen pounds for a fish returning to spawn. In short, the mothering instinct and the mating instinct are being bred out of animals.

With genetic engineering, humanity is extending its reach over the forces of nature far beyond the scope of any previous technology—with the possible exception of the nuclear bomb. At the same time, corporations are assuming ownership and control over the hereditary blueprints of life itself. Can any reasonable person believe such power is without risk?

Genes are the "green gold" of the biotech century, and companies that control them will exercise tremendous power over the world economy. Multinational corporations are already scouting the continents in search of this new precious resource, hoping to locate microbes, plants, animals, and humans with rare genetic traits that might have future market potential. Having located the desired traits, biotech companies are modifying them and seeking patent protection for their new "inventions."

The worldwide race to patent the gene pool is the culmination of a 500-year-odyssey to enclose the ecosystems of the Earth. That journey began in feudal England in the 1500s, with the passage of the great "enclosure acts," which privatized the village commons—transforming the land from a community trust to private real estate. Today, virtually every square foot of landmass on the planet is under private ownership or government control.

But enclosure of the land was just the beginning. Today, the ocean's coastal waters are commercially leased, the air has been converted into commercial airline corridors, and even the electromagnetic spectrum is considered commercial property—leased for use by radio, TV, and telephone companies. Now the most intimate commons of all—the gene pool—is being enclosed and reduced to private commercial property.

The enclosure of the genetic commons began in 1971, when an Indian microbiologist and General Electric employee, Ananda Chakrabarty, applied to the U.S. Patents and Trademark Office (PTO) for a patent on a genetically engineered microorganism designed to consume oil spills. The PTO rejected the request, arguing that living things are not patentable. The case was appealed all the way to the Supreme Court, which in 1980—by a slim margin of five to four—ruled in favor of Chakrabarty. Speaking for the majority, Chief Justice Warren Burger argued that "the relevant distinction was not between living and inanimate things," but whether or not Chakrabarty's microbe was a "human-made invention."

In the aftermath of that historic decision, bioengineering technology shed its pristine academic garb and bounded into the marketplace. On Oct. 13, 1980—just months after the court's ruling—Genentech publicly offered one million shares of stock at $35 per share. By the time the trading bell had rung that first day, the stock was selling at over $500 per share. And Genentech had yet to introduce a single product.

Chemical, pharmaceutical, argribusiness, and biotech startups everywhere sped up their research—mindful that the granting of patent protection meant the possibility of harnessing the genetic commons for vast commercial gain. Some observers, however, were not so enthused. Ethicist Leon Kass asked:

> "What is the principled limit to this beginning extension of the domain of private ownership and dominion over living nature . . . ? The principle used in Chakrabarty says that there is nothing in the nature of being, not even in the patentor himself, that makes him immune to being patented."

While the Supreme Court decision lent an air of legal legitimacy to the emerging biotech industry, a Patent Office decision in 1987 opened the floodgates. In a complete about-face, the PTO ruled that all genetically engineered multicellular living organisms—including animals—are potentially patentable. The Commissioner of Patents and Trademarks at the time, Donald J. Quigg, attempted to calm a shocked public by asserting that the decision covered every creature except human beings—because the Thirteenth Amendment to the Constitution forbids human slavery. On the other hand, human embryos and fetuses as well as human genes, tissues, and organs were now potentially patentable.

What makes the Supreme Court decision and Patent Office ruling suspect, from a legal point of view, is that they defy previous patent rulings that say one cannot claim a "discovery of nature" as an invention. No one would suggest that scientists who isolated, classified, and described the properties of chemical elements in the periodic table—such as oxygen and helium—ought to be granted a patent on them. Yet someone who isolates and classifies the properties of human genes can patent them.

The European Patent Office, for example, awarded a patent to the U.S. company Biocyte, giving it ownership of all human blood cells which have come from the umbilical cord of a newborn child and are being used for any therapeutic purposes. The patent is so broad that it allows this one company to refuse the use of any blood cells from the umbilical cord to any individual unwilling to pay the patent fee. Blood cells from the umbilical cord are particularly important for marrow transplants, making it a valuable commercial asset. It should be emphasized that this patent was awarded simply because Biocyte was able to isolate the blood cells and deep-freeze them. The company made no change in the blood itself.

A similarly broad patent was awarded to Systemix Inc. of Palo Alto, Calif., by the U.S. Patent Office, covering all human bone marrow stem cells. This extraordinary patent on a human body part was awarded despite the fact that Systemix had done nothing whatsoever to alter or engineer the cells. Dr. Peter Quisenberry, the medical affairs vice chairman of the Leukemia Society of America, quipped, "Where do you draw the line? Can you patent a hand?"

⚜

The life patents race is gearing up in the wake of government and commercial efforts to map the approximately 100,000 human genes that make up the human genome—a project with enormous commercial potential. As soon as a gene is tagged its "discoverer" is likely to apply for a patent, often before knowing the function of the gene. In 1991, J. Craig Venter, then head of the National Institute of Health Genome Mapping Research Team, resigned his government post to head up a genomics company funded with more than $70 million in venture capital. At the same time, Venter and his colleagues filed for patents on more than 2,000 human brain genes. Many researchers on the Human Genome Project were shocked and angry, charging Venter with attempting to profit off research paid for by American taxpayers.

Nobel laureate James Watson, co-discoverer of the DNA double helix, called the Venter patent claims "sheer lunacy." Still, it's likely that within less than ten years, all 100,000 or so genes that comprise the genetic legacy of our species will be patented—making them the exclusive intellectual property of global corporations.

The patenting of life is creating a firestorm of controversy. Several years ago, an Alaskan businessman named John Moore found his own body parts had been patented, without his knowledge, by the University of California at Los Angeles (UCLA), and licensed to the Sandoz Pharmaceutical Corp. Moore had been diagnosed with a rare cancer and underwent treatment at UCLA. A researcher there discovered that Moore's spleen tissue produced a blood protein that facilitates the growth of white blood cells valuable as anti-cancer agents. The university created a cell line from Moore's spleen tissue and obtained a patent on the "invention." The cell line is estimated to be worth more than $3 billion.

Moore subsequently sued, claiming a property right over his own tissue. But in 1990, the California Supreme Court ruled against him, saying Moore had no such ownership right. Human body parts, the court argued, could not be bartered as a commodity in the marketplace.

The irony of the decision was captured by Judge Broussard, in his dissenting opinion. The ruling "does *not* mean that body parts may not be bought or sold," he wrote. "[T]he majority's holding simply bars *plantiff*, the source of the cells, from obtaining the benefit of the cell's value, but permits *defendants*, who allegedly obtained the cells from plaintiff by improper means, to retain and exploit the full economic value of their ill-gotten gains."

❦

A battle of historic proportions has also emerged between the high-technology nations of the North and the developing nations of the South, over ownership of the planet's genetic treasures. Some Third World leaders say the North is attempting to seize the biological commons, most of which is in the rich tropical regions of the Southern Hemisphere, and that their nations should be compensated for use of genetic resources. Corporate and governmental leaders in the North maintain that the genes increase in value only when manipulated using sophisticated gene-splicing techniques, so there's no obligation to compensate the South.

To ease growing tensions, a number of companies have proposed sharing a portion of their gains. Merck & Co., the pharmaceutical giant (often considered a leader in social responsibility), entered into an agreement recently with a research organization in Costa Rica, the National Biodiversity Institute, to pay the organization a paltry $1 million to secure the group's plant, microorganism, and insect samples. Critics liken the deal to European settlers giving American Indians trinkets in return for the island of Manhattan. The recipient organization, on the other hand, is granting a right to bio-prospect on land it has no historic claim to in the first place—while indigenous peoples are locked out of the agreement.

Such agreements are beginning to meet with resistance from countries and non-governmental organizations (NGOs) in the Southern Hemisphere. They claim that what Northern companies are calling "discoveries" are really the pirating of the indigenous knowledge of native peoples and cultures. To defuse opposition, biotech corporations are seeking to impose a uniform intellectual property regime worldwide. And they've gone a long way toward achieving that with the passage of the Trade Related Aspects of Intellectual Property Agreements (TRIPS) at the Uruguay Round of the General Agreement on Tariffs and Trade (GATT). Sculpted by companies like Bristol Myers, Merck, Pfizer, Dupont, and Monsanto, the TRIPS agreement makes no allowance for indigenous knowledge, and grants companies free access to genetic material from around the world.

Suman Sahai, director of the Gene Campaign—an NGO in New Delhi—makes the point, "God didn't give us 'rice' or 'wheat' or 'potato.'" These were once wild plants that were domesticated over eons of time and patiently bred by generations of farmers. Sahai asks, "Who did all of that work?" Groups like his argue that Southern countries should be compensated for their contribution to biotech.

Still others take a third position: that neither corporations nor indigenous peoples should claim ownership, because the gene pool ought not to be for sale, at any price. It should remain an open commons and continue to be used freely by present and future generations. They cite precedent in the recent historic decision by the nations of the world to maintain the continent of Antarctica as a global commons free from commercial exploitation.

The idea of private companies laying claim to human genes as their exclusive intellectual property has resulted in growing protests worldwide. In May of 1994, a coalition of hundreds of women's organizations from more than forty nations announced opposition to Myriad Genetics's attempt to patent the gene that causes breast cancer in some women. The coalition was assembled by The Foundation on Economic Trends. While the women did not oppose the screening test Myriad developed, they opposed the claim to the gene itself. They argued that the breast cancer gene was a product of nature and not a human invention, and should not be patentable. Myriad's exclusive rights to such a gene could make screening more expensive, and might impede research by making access to the gene too expensive.

The central question in these cases—Can you patent life?—is one of the most important issues ever to face the human family. Life patenting strikes at the core of our beliefs about the very nature of life and whether it is to be conceived as having sacred and intrinsic value, or merely utility value. Surely such a fundamental question deserves to be widely discussed by the public before such patents become a ubiquitous part of our daily lives.

The biotech revolution will force each of us to put a mirror to our most deeply held values, making us ponder the ultimate question of the purpose and meaning of existence. This may turn out to be its most important contribution. The rest is up to us.

William Domnarski → **NO**

Dire New World

With an authorial voice that only a conspiracy maven such as Oliver Stone could love, Jeremy Rifkin is back, this time to warn us about the dangers inherent in our idea of so-called "progress," as Rifkin puts it.

Rifkin—the president of the Foundation of Economic Trends and the author of many books on economic trends relating to science, technology, and culture—is especially worried about the implications of the biotech century that will not wait two years to begin. It's here now, and unless we heed Rifkin's warnings and keep ourselves from temptation by agreeing with him that progress is too fraught for mischief to be acceptable, we'll end up in a genetically polluted world in which genetic discrimination reigns—though you will be able to go down to your local laboratory when the time comes to be fitted with that new vital organ you've had cloned in the expectation that you might need it.

The advances in genetic engineering in medicine—to say nothing of the advances in plant genetics—have been staggering. Now knowing most of the code, we can identify and even act on various types of diseases and disabilities before birth. We have added a range of new treatments in which genetically engineered cells are introduced into the body to take hold and combat disease. Alzheimer's disease and Parkinson's disease are not on the verge of being conquered, but we are closer to victory than ever because of genetic research.

But where some see the advances that genetic engineering has produced, Rifkin sees a new wave of eugenic zealots eager to use our genetic makeup as even more revealing of our true nature than the SAT.

Ripped from the Headlines

Rifkin relies primarily on national news magazines and newspapers to sketch both the developments in and the predictions for various aspects of this scientific revolution, and, in that sense, his story is one ripped from the headlines. His persistent complaint is that journalists fail to present balanced coverage because of a delight in describing the often dazzling possible uses of the technology at issue. What's left out, he argues, are the myriad ethical issues that coalesce around the question of whether progress, by itself, is a good thing.

Trying to interpret the scientific breakthroughs that are changing the way we think of both ourselves as individuals and the dominant species on the

From *Intellectual Property*, January 1999, pp. 1–4. Copyright © 1999 by Incisive Media Ltd. Reprinted by permission.

planet, Rifkin details seven strands of what he calls the new operational matrix of the biotech century. It's not the evil that men do that outlives them; it's the mischief that computers and genetic research can get us into when they are spliced together that we need to worry about.

Four strands of the biotech century's matrix encompass recombinant DNA techniques; the wholesale reseeding of the planet with genetically enhanced and devised plants; gene mapping; and computers that can probe and manage the vast genetic resources of our bodies and our planet. The other strands include the ideological, philosophical, and cultural structures supporting the new research and its application.

In Rifkin's view, the courts are primarily to blame for this state of affairs because they have allowed for the patenting of genetically altered cells, thus creating a slippery slope that we will be unable to negotiate. Going further, however, he argues that a new cultural context has emerged that favors the new biotechnologies. Underpinning all of this is a new cosmological narrative that sees evolution as an improvement in information processing, rather than as a random process of selection winnowing its way through passive natural elements.

They Know Not What They Do

Rifkin complains that the scientists know not what they do, unwittingly creating Frankensteins at every turn. He objects that their sheer ability to do something seems to them justification enough to just do it. They are too little concerned with the collateral effects of genetic engineering.

It's clear that Rifkin is writing for an audience already persuaded by his general thesis and by his credentials as a prophet of doom. And he wants us to know that he was right in all the predictions on genetic engineering that he began making 20 years ago. But the world still hasn't caught on to the issue as he has framed it—that progress is generally bad—so he's back for more hectoring. What Rifkin does not want to accept is that as a culture we desire and embrace progress.

The press does not seem guilty of the one-sided reporting that Rifkin ascribes to it. Recently, for example, *The New York Times* featured two reports on a new technique in genetic engineering that allows scientists to take embryonic human stem cells before they have distinguished themselves as the type of cell they will be, such as a brain cell or heart cell; the technique then coaxes those cells to morph into the type of cell that is needed. The result is that heart cells can be grown and then used to heal the heart when it fails—all rather heady—or should I say hearty—stuff.

The use of such new cell technology has been condemned by some because it comes perilously close to infringing on our notion of what constitutes an individual. As opponents see it, there is a great difference between using stem cells from miscarried fetuses, which a spokesperson for the Catholic Church finds acceptable, and using cells derived from pre-implantation embryos that were created in fertility clinics. To use the latter cells is to use humans for research, the opponents stress.

Annoying Disingenuousness

One senses, however, that Rifkin would not have been satisfied with the coverage that the ethical issues received, because the heart of the story emphasizes that scientists are all but dancing with excitement over this new technology. There is, at the core of Rifkin's book, an annoying disingenuousness. He poses himself in a neutral posture that pretends to provide us with the information we need to decide if this biotech century is for us; at the same time, Rifkin urges us to think that the problems created by the new technologies outweigh the possible benefits.

Two lines of reasoning in particular show how, despite his good intentions, Rifkin seems out of touch with reality, at least as it is defined by law. The first is the supposed exploitation of indigenous peoples by agribusiness and pharmaceutical companies that search the world, especially the world in the southern hemisphere, for new plants that yield new drugs or new strains of foodstuffs. The indigenous peoples, the argument goes, have done all the work in cultivating the plants over time, which makes the genetic manipulations of the big companies a negligible contribution at best, certainly not one entitling them to patent protection and profits. What Rifkin does not want to acknowledge is that patents are hard earned and necessary for research to continue. Rifkin wants a world that does not privilege the capacity of science to make productive what otherwise wouldn't be. His is a politically correct world, blissfully ignorant of law's contribution to society.

The second and perhaps more revealing line of misguided reasoning is Rifkin's unwillingness to accept patent law for what it is. The Supreme Court has recognized that the distinction is not between living and inanimate things, but between products of nature, whether living or not, and human-made inventions. Rifkin's argument is that scientists cannot be said to create anything patentable because the life they manipulate was already there. That is a narrow and misguided view of both the law and of what scientists do. The law sides with progress; Rifkin sides against it. What Rifkin cannot accept is what Justice William O. Douglas wrote in *The Great A&P Tea Co. v. Supermarket Corp.*, 340 U.S. 147 (1950)—30 years before the celebrated oil-eating bacteria case of 1980: That the inventions that most benefit mankind are those that "push back the frontiers of chemistry, physics and the like."

As his book makes all too clear, Rifkin does not want to explore the frontier. He wants to circle the wagons and hold off, through the pouting in his book, that which cannot be held back. Those concerned with the ethical implications of genetic research are with us and are heard. That we as a society want to search the frontier should not be dismissed, as Rifkin so keenly wants to dismiss them, as ignorant, selfish or misguided.

POSTSCRIPT

Should Patenting Life Be Forbidden?

In general, we in the United States have adopted the cost-benefit approach to problems with new products. If we cannot foresee the consequences of a new technology, we tend to make an educated guess about the benefits of all kinds, another educated guess about probable costs of all kinds, and balance the one against the other. Engineered seeds seem to have the potential to increase crop yields, cut labor costs, and, not inconsequentially, lower the use of fertilizers and pesticides. Those are benefits. As for costs—well, we don't know, there might not be any. So go ahead with the new life forms, and allow the companies the patents they need to make them profitable.

On the other hand, in Europe, the custom is to use the precautionary approach toward new technology. If we don't know what the costs might be, try the seeds in a small controlled area for a long time and see what the costs are. If we don't like them, kill the technology. Only after the seeds are proved safe over generations will we make them publicly available.

Suggested Reading

Which approach do you think is better for such new technologies? If you want more to read on the subject, consider the following:

Phillip Bereano "Does Genetic Research Threaten Our Civil Liberties?" http://www.actionbioscience.org/genomic/bereano.html

D.L. Dickenson "Patently Paradoxical? Public Order and genetic patents," 2004 www.nature.com/nrg/journal/v5/n2/full/nrg1278.html

G. Tyler Miller, *Living in the Environment*, 11th ed. (Belmont, CA: Brooks/ Cole Publishing, 2000).

Internet References . . .

FAQs about Free-Market Environmentalism

Sponsored by the Thoreau Institute, this site lists and answers frequently asked questions about free-market environmentalism. It is the Institute's position that a free-market system can solve many environmental problems better than more government regulation can.

http://ti.org/faqs.html

Pennsylvania Department of Environmental Protection

This home page of the Pennsylvania Department of Environmental Protection monitors environmental responsibility.

http://www.dep.state.pa.us

Rainforest Facts

This Rainforest Facts site contains statistics on the rain forest as well as information on rain forest products, worldwide rain forest protection efforts, the tropical timber industry, and more.

http://www.pbs.org/tal/costa_rica/rainfacts.html

Environmental Policy and Corporate Responsibility

*T*here is a powerful new initiative to enlist business in the enterprise of saving the natural environment, a direction that traditionally private enterprise has left to the government and the NGOs. How should the corporation respond to this new set of demands on its resources?

- Do Environmental Restrictions Violate Basic Economic Freedoms?

- Is Bottling Water a Good Solution to Problems of Water Purity and Availability?

- Should the World Continue to Rely on Oil as a Major Source of Energy?

ISSUE 18

Do Environmental Restrictions Violate Basic Economic Freedoms?

YES: John Shanahan, from "Environment," in Stuart M. Butler and Kim R. Holmes, eds. *Issues '96: The Candidate's Briefing Book* (Heritage Foundation, 1996)

NO: Paul R. Ehrlich and Anne H. Ehrlich, from "Brownlash: The New Environmental Anti-Science," *The Humanist* (November/December 1996)

ISSUE SUMMARY

YES: John Shanahan, vice president of the Alexis de Tocqueville Institution in Arlington, Virginia, argues that many government environmental policies are unreasonable and infringe on basic economic freedoms. He concedes that environmental problems exist but denies that there is any environmental "crisis."

NO: Environmental scientists Paul R. Ehrlich and Anne H. Ehrlich, whose 1974 book *The End of Affluence* first outlined the consequences of environmental mismanagement, argue that many objections to environmental protections are self-serving and based on bad or misused science.

Which would you think is more important, if you had to choose: Profitability in the corporation, yielding return on investment to the shareholder, good products reliably supplied for the customer, a tax base for the public sector, jobs for the workers, and, in short, the fundamentals of American life? Or the protection of the natural environment, the protection of our fragile ecosystems for the generations to follow us? This is not an easy choice to make, and it confronts our legislatures on a daily basis.

Take pesticides, for example. They form a profitable part of the chemicals manufacturing industry all by themselves, precisely because they increase agricultural production, by orders of magnitude, wherever they are used.

On the other hand, as Rachel Carson pointed out in 1962 (*Silent Spring*, Houghton Mifflin), pesticides don't know enough to poison only crop-eating insects. They poison every living thing that consumes them. They poison the insects that eat the crops, the predator insects that used to keep the crop-eaters' numbers under control, the birds that eat the insects that fall to earth, the fish that eat the insects that land in the water (or that live in the water into which the spray falls, or is washed), and us who eat the fish. When it poisons the birds, their eggs no longer are viable, and the species starts to die out. Which is more important—the present profits of the industry and the present low prices in the vegetable aisle, or the future of the birds? What do you say? What would your grandchildren say?

Since the 1960s, successive administrations in this nation have attempted, with more or less enthusiasm, to adopt regulations that will limit economic freedoms in order to protect the environment. As our knowledge of ecology has increased, so have the regulations, and predictably, so have the objections to them. It seems that every plant manager, every developer, and even every homeowner bumps into environmental regulations every time they turn around—or try to get something done to improve the value of their property or enterprise. We have as a very close national memory, that America was founded for freedom: the freedom to do what you want to do without monarchs and bishops hovering over you telling you how to think and what you can and cannot build. All this regulation rankles.

Where will this controversy end? Compromise is the great American tradition, but it is no compromise for the environmentalists. If you want to save a stretch of open space for future generations, and I want to build a subdivision on it, I will argue that we must compromise, and you let me build on half of it. But now that half is gone for good. What timber harvester would not gladly accept a compromise that gave him 90 percent of the forest, leaving only 10 percent to be preserved? He would happily promise that he would never ask for any more. But the great redwood forests of the Pacific Northwest are more than 90 percent gone, and the lumbermen want more.

Are there ways that humans can live harmoniously with nature, profiting from relationships that mimic those that existed prior to the Industrial Revolution (only smarter)? The Rocky Mountain Institute has published a powerful argument that such relationships are entirely possible and even more economical than the business arrangements we have now. (See *Natural Capitalism*, by Amory and Hunter Lovins and Paul Hawken, Rocky Mountain Institute 1999.)

Ask yourself, as you read these selections, which orientation toward the environment is likely to result in a stronger world in the next generation. John Shanahan's selection is from the Heritage Foundation's 1996 *Candidate's Briefing Book,* supplying arguments for conservative candidates to help them get elected; the Ehrlichs insist that the environmental crisis is very real and that the "brownlash" opponents of environmentalism are peddling worthless ideology in the face of the facts.

YES

John Shanahan

Environment

The Issues

Americans want a clean, healthy environment. They also want a strong economy. But environmental protection is enormously expensive, costs jobs, and stifles economic opportunity. On the other hand, before government stepped in, robust economic activity such as manufacturing led to a deteriorating and unhealthy environment. The challenge is how to achieve both a strong economy and a healthy environment. After all, what Americans actually want is a high overall quality of life.

Three decades ago, as people perceived that their quality of life was beginning to deteriorate, they began to support aggressive policies to reduce pollution. These policies frequently failed to live up to their sponsors' claims; they also became increasingly and unnecessarily expensive. But the environment did improve, especially in the early years. Now, however, Americans are becoming aware that many of these policies are unreasonable and that, even when they work, they result only in small improvements at a heavy cost in jobs and freedom. Americans also are beginning to recognize that there often is no sound scientific basis for assertions of environmental harm or risk to the public. The pendulum finally has begun to swing the other way.

Conservatives, like Americans generally, have no wish to return to the days of black smoke billowing out of smokestacks. But they do believe common sense can be brought to bear in dealing with the environment: that it is possible to protect the environment without sacrificing the freedoms for which America stands. Conservative candidates and legislators therefore should stress the following themes:

Examples of regulatory abuse It is important to show that "good intentions" often are accompanied by oppressive, senseless regulations.

An ethic of conservation Candidates need to explain that conserving or efficiently using natural resources is not in dispute. The debate is over how best to do this: through markets or through government controls.

Economic freedom Candidates need to point out that many government "solutions" to environment problems conflict with basic economic freedoms.

Property-based solutions Candidates need to explain that environmental objectives can be achieved best not by issuing thousands of pages of rules that people will try to circumvent, but by capitalizing on the incentives associated with owning property.

Sound science Candidates need to argue that we need policies based on sound science, not "tabloid science."

Priority setting Candidates must explain that not all problems are of the same importance or urgency, and that regulating all risks equally means fewer lives are saved for the dollars spent than would be saved if priorities were set.

The Facts

While pollution levels have fallen dramatically since 1970, most reductions were achieved early and at relatively low cost. From 1970 to 1990, total emission levels fell 33.8 percent. Over the same period, lead levels in the air fell 96.5 percent, and carbon monoxide levels in the air fell 40.7 percent. But reductions have slowed dramatically. . . .

Unworkable Regulations

Environmental regulation does more than just cost too much. Candidates also should use the growing litany of horror stories to demonstrate how ill-conceived environmental regulations, while delivering little benefit, lead to unintended consequences for businesses especially small businesses, which are disproportionately minority-owned and minority-run.

- Larry Mason's family owned a sawmill employing 40 workers in Beaver, Washington. In the mid-1980s, based on harvest assurances from the U.S. Forest Service and loan guarantees from the Small Business Administration, the family invested $1 million in its business. Then, says Mason, "in 1990, the spotted owl injunctions closed our mill, made my equipment worthless, and my expertise obsolete. The same government that encouraged me to take on business debt then took away my ability to repay."
- While the Clean Water Act (CWA) requires a waste treatment facility to submit a simple form stating that a fence restricts access by the public, the Resource Conservation and Recovery Act (RCRA) requires an additional 25 pages detailing the fence design, the location of the posts and gates, a cross section of the wire mesh, and other minor technical matters. RCRA is so wasteful that one plant, whose CWA permit application was only 17 pages long, had to file a seven-foot stack of supporting documents with its applications.
- Ronald Cahill, a disabled Wilmington, Massachusetts, dry cleaner, purchased expensive dry-cleaning equipment to comply with EPA regulations governing the use of trichlorotrifluoroethane (CFC-113). But the EPA levied a tax on all chlorofluorocarbons (CFCs), making

> CFC-113 hard to find and extremely expensive. In 1995, Cahill's business went under. Washington, says Cahill, "has put me out of business with excessive taxes and regulations."

Regulatory abuses like these usually are a direct result of the way government bureaucracies attack environmental problems. Typically, these agencies regulate without regard to the cost imposed on individuals and businesses. Yet it makes no sense to issue a regulation for which the burden far outweighs any benefit that might be conferred. In fact, it often is unclear whether there will be any benefit at all because the science on which many regulations are based is so poor.

Also, instead of setting realistic performance standards and giving businesses the freedom to develop innovative ways of meeting them, agencies typically rely on inflexible command-and-control regulations that, for example, specify what technologies companies must use. Since businesses differ in their operating structures, this one-size-fits-all approach rarely leads to cost-effective solutions compared to more flexible and dependable performance standards. Moreover, by eliminating the incentive for companies to seek out these cost-effective solutions, it stifles innovative technologies or techniques that reduce costs. In the end, of course, the consumer is the one who pays.

Perhaps the most troublesome aspect of current environmental policy is the fact that bureaucrats and liberal lawmakers generally consider regulation the only option. Creative solutions shown to be less expensive, more effective, and more respectful of human liberty are rejected out of hand. Instead of setting up a system of incentives to lure businesses into operating with environmental impact in mind, the system relies on punishment regardless of whether this accomplishes the desired goal or creates unintended consequences.

Rejecting Property Rights

Regulations have become increasingly unfair. The Environmental Protection Agency (EPA), Department of the Interior (DOI), Army Corps of Engineers, and other federal agencies operate on the premise that property should be used to satisfy government's needs and objectives without regard to who owns the property or the financial burden imposed on them. It is this mentality that leads government reflexively to reject the creative solutions advanced by free-market advocates, including incentive-based approaches to protecting endangered species. By ignoring property rights, establishment environmentalists, bureaucrats, and liberal legislators also ignore the benefits to be derived from free trade and free markets.

The most unfair and burdensome hardship inflicted by government "regulatory takings" is that property owners are not compensated for their losses. For instance, if an elderly husband and wife spend a large portion of their retirement savings to buy land on which to build their dream home and that land subsequently is designated a wetland, they lose the value of their property as well as their savings. They are stuck with property they cannot use and the government does nothing to reimburse them for their loss. Unfortunately, tales of financial hardship caused by government designation of land as wetland or endangered-species habitat have become common. For instance:

- Bill Stamp's family in Exeter, Rhode Island, has been blocked from farming or developing its 70 acres of land for 11 years, yet has been assessed taxes at rates determined by the land's industrial value up to $72,000 annually. As a result, this fifth-generation farm family may lose its life savings. The government, however, appears unmoved. Stamp relates what one Army Corps of Engineers enforcement officer told him: "We know that this is rape, pillage, and plunder of your farm, but this is our job."
- A small church in Waldorf, Maryland, was told by the Army Corps of Engineers that one-third of its land, on which it planned to build a parking lot, was a wetland and could not be used. Part of this so-called wetland is a bone-dry hillside which almost never collects water. Says Reverend Murray Southwell of the Freewill Baptists, "this obvious misinterpretation of wetland law made it necessary for us to purchase an additional lot [for $45,000, which] has been a heavy financial burden on this small missions church."
- Developer Buzz Oates wants to develop less than 4 percent of the Sutter Basin in Sacramento, California, where an estimated 1,000 giant garter snakes live. But the federal government mandated that he pay a "mitigation" fee of nearly $3.8 million for the 40 or fewer snakes he might disturb: $93,950 per snake. Says Oates, in an age of "depleted [fiscal] resources and deteriorating school infrastructure, this is a very tough pill to swallow."

Hundreds of such stories have surfaced over the past few years, and many analysts suspect that far more are never made public. According to Bob Adams, Project Director for Environmental and Regulatory Affairs at the National Center for Public Policy Research, "the stories we have compiled are just the tip of the iceberg, but many people are simply too scared to come forward or feel powerless against the government."

Ironically, federal agencies and the Clinton Administration argue that it would cost too much money to compensate landowners. Leon Panetta, then Director of the Office of Management and Budget, told the House Committee on Public Works and Transportation's Subcommittee on Water Resources and the Environment on May 26, 1994, that paying compensation for wetlands regulation would be "an unnecessary and unwise use of taxpayer dollars" and a drain on the federal budget.

Property owners counter that regulatory takings are a drain on the family budget. Nancie Marzulla, President of Defenders of Property Rights, points out that "what people don't realize is that these landowners typically are not wealthy and powerful corporations, but normal Americans schoolteachers and elderly couples whose lives are destroyed by stretched interpretations of a single environmental law." Moreover, the federal government already owns about one out of every three acres in the country (with even more owned by state and local governments). If the federal government can afford to maintain one-third of the nation's land, it should be able to pay landowners for regulatory confiscation of their property. If not, maybe it should consider selling the least ecologically sensitive land from its vast holdings to pay for the land it wants.

Lost Opportunities, Lost Lives

Ask the average American how much a human life is worth, and the answer likely will be that "no amount is too much." This is how Congress and federal agencies justify imposing sometimes staggering costs on businesses to reduce the risks of death by infinitesimal amounts. What policymakers fail to understand is that wasting resources in this way means not being able to use them in other ways that might well produce better results and save even more lives.

If lawmakers ever did consider which environmental policies actually save the most lives, they would scrap many existing rules, freeing up resources to be used in other ways. This commonsense approach would lead to regulation that is very different, in its scope and fundamental assumptions, from that which burdens America today. . . .

What America Thinks about the Environment

When asked by the media, pollsters, or politicians, Americans routinely answer that they want a clean and healthy environment. Indeed, the majority of Americans consider themselves "environmentalists." This does not translate, however, into automatic acceptance of the environmental lobby's agenda. Conservative candidates need to make this clear to discourage voters from supporting policies they do not believe in simply because they are portrayed as "pro-environment."

The dichotomy in public opinion shows up in polling data. When respondents are asked general or theoretical questions that involve little personal sacrifice, or that do not identify those burdened, government intervention fares well. In one poll, for instance, 60 percent of respondents agreed that we must protect the environment even if it costs jobs in the community. In another, 72 percent of respondents said they would pay somewhat higher taxes if the money was used to protect the environment and prevent water and air pollution.

On the other hand, when respondents are asked questions that are more specific, that involve greater sacrifice, or that identify the people losing jobs, government intervention is less popular. When respondents are asked to pay much higher taxes to protect the environment, support drops by almost half. By the same token, only one-third would be willing to accept cuts in their standard of living. When asked to pick between spotted owls and Northwest workers who stand to lose their jobs because of efforts to protect the owls, respondents choose jobs by a margin of 3 to 2. . . .

Perhaps the most refreshing change in attitudes in recent years is the recognition that the country can have economic growth and environmental protection simultaneously. Vice President Al Gore has made the point that economic growth and environmental protection are not incompatible. This is true, but only if America's environmental laws are structured correctly to encourage responsible behavior as part of the business decision-making process. Gore advocates stringent command-and-control regulations that are inconsistent with growth and lead to little real gains in environmental protection.

Whenever this question comes up, Americans must be told that the way to promote both environmental protection and economic growth is to allow them to work hand in hand. The government must stop regarding them as mutually exclusive and stop pitting economic freedom against the environment. Laws must be based on, and work with, a free market. Only then can Americans maximize their economic and environmental quality of life.

The Need for Common Sense

Given Americans' ambivalence on the question of environmental protection, it is all the more important for conservatives to approach the issue in a commonsense way. People must understand that environmental protection need not come at the expense of jobs, but will cost jobs if the socialist model of centralized control for protecting the environment is not set aside. It doesn't work. Rather, the country should adopt a reasonable, commonsense approach to environmental protection that is based on:

Freedom with responsibility Conservatives traditionally have stressed economic growth while ignoring the importance of environmental problems. Thus, they have fought environmentalists step by step and have lost step by step. The reason, while unpleasant, is not complicated. Environmentalists have had the moral high ground, even though they typically have not provided the most beneficial solutions. In short, conservatives have been on the wrong side of an emotional issue.

Two lessons demonstrate why:

- **First**, leftists and the public at large understand that publicly owned goods, free of constraints on usage, will be depleted over time. Garrett Hardin, Professor Emeritus of Human Ecology at the University of California, in his seminal 1968 work *The Tragedy of the Commons* showed that when a good is publicly owned, or "owned" in common, no one has an incentive to conserve or to manage it. In fact, there is a perverse incentive to use the good inefficiently to deplete it. This fact is at the heart of most environmental problems, such as air and water pollution and species extinction.
- **Second**, if there are incentives to conserve resources, people will conserve out of self-interest. People with a vested interest in providing environmental benefits through property ownership or other positive incentives will provide them voluntarily, without coercion.

. . . "Freedom with responsibility for one's actions" should be the conservative message. Responsibility restrains wasteful behavior. Ironically, the old environmentalist slogan "Make the polluter pay" is consistent with this message. But when they say this, conservatives and liberals mean different things. As Al Cobb, then Director of Environment and Energy at the National Policy Forum, has said, "What the environmental lobby means by that phrase is that corporate polluters should be punished severely for any pollution whatsoever. What conservatives mean, however, is that polluters should bear the full cost of environmental degradation, but no more." At the same time, individuals and corporations also should be rewarded for conservation and other environmentally sound practices.

Conservation through property rights   The free market reflects the conservation ethic better than any command-and-control regulation from Washington. A free market can occur, however, only when private citizens engage in trade, and people can trade only what they own: some form of property. Thus, property is the cornerstone of a free market. If property rights are insecure or publicly owned, a market cannot function effectively. Some critics misleadingly call this "market failure," but it is really a failure to use markets and their main engine: property rights. As a result, both environmental protection and personal liberty suffer. A resource that is not owned will deteriorate or be depleted because neither protection of nor damage to that resource is part of the individual's usual decision-making process. Others, however, are still forced to bear the consequences.

Conservative candidates should concentrate on explaining the innovative ways in which property rights can be used to protect the environment. The most efficient method and the most protective of individual rights and freedoms is to enlist self-interest in the service of environmental protection.

Consider [two] examples of how the principle of property rights-based environmentalism works: . . .

- In Scotland and England, the popularity of fishing has burgeoned in recent decades. Property rights to fishing sites have developed as the building block for markets to provide access to prime fishing spots. As a result, many private, voluntary associations have been formed to purchase fishing rights access. In Scotland, "virtually every inch of every major river and most minor ones is privately owned or leased. . . ." Owners of fishing rights on various stretches of the rivers charge others for the right to fish. These rivers are not overfished because it is not in the owner's best interest to allow the fish population to be depleted. Because he wants to continue charging fishermen for the foreseeable future, the owner conserves his fish stock, allowing them to reproduce, and prevents pollution from entering his stretch of the river. If a municipality pollutes the water upstream, the owner of the fishing rights can sue for an injunction. Everyone wins, including fishermen looking for quality fishing with some privacy.
- One group's approach to wetland protection has shown the power of property rights to achieve environmental goals. Ducks Unlimited,

a group consisting of hunters and non-hunters alike, is dedicated to enhancing duck populations. To do this, it has purchased property or conservation easements with privately raised funds. Unlike other groups (for example, the National Wildlife Federation) that began as organizations of hunters and outdoorsmen but later lost much of their original focus and joined forces with the more extreme elements of the environmental lobby, Ducks Unlimited still focuses on protecting duck habitat. In the last 58 years, it has raised and invested $750 million to conserve 17 million acres in Canada alone, an effort which benefits other wildlife as well as ducks. In 1994, it restored or created about 50,000 acres of wetlands. Since Ducks Unlimited itself pays for the habitat it protects, in many ways it embodies the essence of the conservative message: that the market should be allowed to determine the best and highest use of a good or resource in this case, duck habitat.

Unfortunately, property rights are under attack from the environmental lobby. The Fifth Amendment to the U.S. Constitution states, "nor shall private property be taken for public use, without just compensation," but this has been interpreted as protection primarily against the physical taking of property. Most infringements, however, involve federal decrees that deny owners the right to use their property as they see fit, for example, to continue farming. Since the courts have been unclear on the degree of protection property owners should have from such intrusions, legislative protection is needed.

Sound science, not tabloid science Before issuing regulations to protect health, regulators should ask whether the science behind a measure justifies the often enormous expenditures involved. Unfortunately, however, the federal government often acts in response to strong environmentalist-generated public pressure without adequate scientific justification. . . .

- In 1992, the National Aeronautics and Space Administration (NASA) reported that [the] hole in the Earth's protective ozone layer might open up over North America that spring. This hypothetical hole, which would have been in addition to the annual Antarctic hole, would be caused by chlorofluourocarbons (CFCs), a refrigerant. After widespread media coverage on the threat of CFCs, the White House moved a production ban, scheduled for the year 2000, up to 1996, raising the cost of the ban by tens of billions of dollars. Unfortunately, NASA held its press conference before it had finished the study or subjected it to even cursory peer review. The hypothesized ozone hole over North America never materialized. Nor could it have. According to Patrick Michaels of the Climatology Department at the University of Virginia, "The only way you could produce an ozone hole in the high latitudes of the Northern Hemisphere that resembles what occurs in the Southern Hemisphere (where the ozone hole occurs) would be to flatten our mountains and submerge our continents. Then you would have airflow patterns similar to those that occur in the Southern Hemisphere, and are the ones that are required to create an ozone hole." One would think NASA would know this as well. Now, although no information other than a thoroughly discredited hypothesis justifies dramatically stepping up the phaseout, the country is redirecting its limited economic resources at an extra cost of hundreds of dollars per household because of the ban, which is now in place.

Instead of merely responding to tabloid claims or politically motivated studies by federal agencies and environmental organizations trying to justify their budgets, regulations should be based on credible scientific findings open to public scrutiny. For instance, agencies should use consistent methodologies to determine risks. Currently, they use different methods. Thus, for example, risk assessments by different agencies may turn up different answers as to whether a chemical at a particular dose level causes cancer. Theoretically, exposure to some level of a chemical could be found to be both deadly and perfectly safe.

Government assessments also should reveal the assumptions and uncertainties in their analyses. Typically, because of missing data, most studies use certain assumptions to estimate these uncertainties. These assumptions, sometimes unreasonably gloomy, usually determine the conclusion reached. For instance, sometimes an estimate of the likely risk from some chemical is multiplied thousands, or even millions, of times just to be "conservative." Yet the analyses used to justify these enormously expensive regulations often are obscure as to their assumptions. Moreover, the reports rarely reveal the level of uncertainty involved in arriving at their conclusions.

Whenever regulations that address risks are considered, each agency should be required to conduct risk assessments if only to aid in intelligent decision-making that are consistent, that are transparent to public scrutiny, and that fully detail their assumptions and levels of uncertainty. Moreover, each study should be reviewed before a regulation is published to ensure that scientific guidelines are strictly followed. If federal agencies cannot meet even this very limited standard, it is unconscionable for them to impose costly standards on others.

The need to set priorities   The economy has a limited capacity to absorb environmental regulations. Simply put, the country cannot afford to eliminate every risk. Thus, there is a trade-off: Attempting to regulate one risk out of existence may mean that another risk (or other risks) will have to be tolerated. In most cases, the cure is worse than the disease. Misguided and excessive regulation can cost lives, so it is critical that regulators recognize the costs of their actions. Spending enormous amounts of money to eradicate small or even hypothetical risks means that those dollars cannot be used in other productive ways public or private that might be of greater benefit to the nation.

. . . [I]t is essential that policymakers develop a priority list of environmental problems, based on the extent of the possible risk each appears to pose and the cost of reducing that risk to acceptable levels. With such a list, policymakers can know just how much protection is being bought for every dollar spent. Americans finally will get the maximum environmental "bang for the buck." Conversely, the federal government will be able to achieve environmental objectives at the lowest cost, and thus with the fewest "pink slips" for American workers.

Is There an Environmental Crisis?

Is there an environmental crisis? The answer is a resounding "No." Certainly the country and planet have environmental problems that need to be addressed. But overall, the environment has been improving. Unfortunately, the public is subjected only to the "Chicken Little" version of the situation, and reports of environmental progress and refutations of environmental alarmists are rarely covered in the press.

In his 1995 book *A Moment on the Earth,* which details many of the improvements that have taken place in the last three decades, *Newsweek* editor Gregg Easterbrook notes that reports of positive environmental developments, such as significantly lower air pollution in major U.S. cities, are buried inside the newspapers. Negative news, meanwhile, gets front-page attention, and the news that is reported often contains numerous misleading "facts."

The truth is that threats to the environment have lessened considerably. Lead has been almost eliminated. Even in Los Angeles, the most polluted city in the country, levels of Volatile Organic Compounds (VOCs) have fallen by more than half since 1970. In other formerly polluted cities, such as Atlanta, the air is now considered relatively clean as VOCs are down by almost two-thirds and Nitrous Oxide is down 15 percent.

In area after area so-called global warming, endangered species, wetlands, pesticides, hazardous waste, and automotive fuel economy, for example, the problem is the same: only rarely are the facts heard by the American people.

**Paul R. Ehrlich and
Anne H. Ehrlich**

NO

Brownlash: The New Environmental Anti-Science

Humanity is now facing a sort of slow-motion environmental Dunkirk. It remains to be seen whether civilization can avoid the perilous trap it has set for itself. Unlike the troops crowding the beach at Dunkirk, civilization's fate is in its own hands; no miraculous last-minute rescue is in the cards. Although progress has certainly been made in addressing the human predicament, far more is needed. Even if humanity manages to extricate itself, it is likely that environmental events will be defining ones for our grandchildren's generation—and those events could dwarf World War II in magnitude.

Sadly, much of the progress that has been made in defining, understanding, and seeking solutions to the human predicament over the past 30 years is now being undermined by an environmental backlash. We call these attempts to minimize the seriousness of environmental problems the *brownlash* because they help to fuel a backlash against "green" policies. While it assumes a variety of forms, the brownlash appears most clearly as an outpouring of seemingly authoritative opinions in books, articles, and media appearances that greatly distort what is or isn't known by environmental scientists. Taken together, despite the variety of its forms, sources, and issues addressed, the brownlash has produced what amounts to a body of anti-science—a twisting of the findings of empirical science—to bolster a predetermined worldview and to support a political agenda. By virtue of relentless repetition, this flood of anti-environmental sentiment has acquired an unfortunate aura of credibility.

It should be noted that the brownlash is not by any means a coordinated effort. Rather, it seems to be generated by a diversity of individuals and organizations. Some of its promoters have links to right-wing ideology and political groups. And some are well-intentioned individuals, including writers and public figures, who for one reason or another have bought into the notion that environmental regulation has become oppressive and needs to be severely weakened. But the most extreme—and most dangerous—elements are those who, while claiming to represent a scientific viewpoint, misstate scientific findings to support their view that the U.S. government has gone overboard with regulation, especially (but not exclusively) for environmental protection, and that subtle, long-term problems like global warming are nothing to worry about. The words and sentiments of the brownlash are profoundly troubling to us and many of our colleagues. Not only are the underlying agendas seldom revealed but, more important, the confusion and distraction created among the public and policy-makers by brownlash pronouncements interfere with and prolong the already difficult search for realistic and equitable solutions to the human predicament.

Anti-science as promoted by the brownlash is not a unique phenomenon in our society; the largely successful efforts of creationists to keep Americans ignorant of evolution is another example, which is perhaps not entirely unre-lated. Both feature a denial of facts and circumstances that don't fit religious or other traditional beliefs; policies built on either could lead our society into serious trouble.

Fortunately, in the case of environmental science, most of the public is fairly well informed about environmental problems and remains committed to environmental protection. When polled, 65 percent of Americans today say they are willing to pay good money for environmental quality. But support for environmental quality is sometimes said to be superficial; while almost everyone is in favor of a sound environment—clean air, clean water, toxic site cleanups, national parks, and so on—many don't feel that environmental deterioration, especially on a regional or global level, is a crucial issue in their own lives. In part this is testimony to the success of environmental protection in the United States. But it is also the case that most people lack an apprecia-tion of the deeper but generally less visible, slowly developing global prob-lems. Thus they don't perceive population growth, global warming, the loss of biodiversity, depletion of groundwater, or exposure to chemicals in plastics and pesticides as a personal threat at the same level as crime in their neighbor-hood, loss of a job, or a substantial rise in taxes.

So anti-science rhetoric has been particularly effective in promoting a series of erroneous notions, including:

- Environmental scientists ignore the abundant good news about the environment.
- Population growth does not cause environmental damage and may even be beneficial.
- Humanity is on the verge of abolishing hunger; food scarcity is a local or regional problem and not indicative of overpopulation.
- Natural resources are superabundant, if not infinite.
- There is no extinction crisis, and so most efforts to preserve species are both uneconomic and unnecessary.
- Global warming and acid rain are not serious threats to humanity.
- Stratospheric ozone depletion is a hoax.
- The risks posed by toxic substances are vastly exaggerated.
- Environmental regulation is wrecking the economy.

How has the brownlash managed to persuade a significant segment of the public that the state of the environment and the directions and rates in which it is changing are not causes for great concern? Even many individuals who are sensitive to local environmental problems have found brownlash dis-tortions of global issues convincing. Part of the answer lies in the overall lack of scientific knowledge among United States citizens. Most Americans readily grasp the issues surrounding something familiar and tangible like a local dump site, but they have considerably more difficulty with issues involving genetic variation or the dynamics of the atmosphere. Thus it is relatively easy to rally support against a proposed landfill and infinitely more difficult to impose a carbon tax that might help offset global warming.

Also, individuals not trained to recognize the hallmarks of change have difficulty perceiving and appreciating the gradual deterioration of civilization's life-support systems. This is why record-breaking temperatures and violent storms receive so much attention while a gradual increase in annual global temperatures—measured in fractions of a degree over decades—is not considered newsworthy. Threatened pandas are featured on television, while the constant and critical losses of insect populations, which are key elements of our life-support systems, pass unnoticed. People who have no meaningful way to grasp regional and global environmental problems cannot easily tell what information is distorted, when, and to what degree.

Decision-makers, too, have a tendency to focus mostly on the more obvious and immediate environmental problems—usually described as "pollution"—rather than on the deterioration of natural ecosystems upon whose continued functioning global civilization depends. Indeed, most people still don't realize that humanity has become a truly global force, interfering in a very real and direct way in many of the planet's natural cycles.

For example, human activity puts ten times as much oil into the oceans as comes from natural seeps, has multiplied the natural flow of cadmium into the atmosphere eightfold, has doubled the rate of nitrogen fixation, and is responsible for about half the concentration of methane (a potent greenhouse gas) and more than a quarter of the carbon dioxide (also a greenhouse gas) in the atmosphere today—all added since the industrial revolution, most notably in the past half-century. Human beings now use or co-opt some 40 percent of the food available to all land animals and about 45 percent of the available freshwater flows.

Another factor that plays into brownlash thinking is the not uncommon belief that environmental quality is improving, not declining. In some ways it is, but the claim of uniform improvement simply does not stand up to close scientific scrutiny. Nor does the claim that the human condition in general is improving everywhere. The degradation of ecosystem services (the conditions and processes through which natural ecosystems support and fulfill human life) is a crucial issue that is largely ignored by the brownlash. Unfortunately, the superficial progress achieved to date has made it easy to label ecologists doomsayers for continuing to press for change. At the same time, the public often seems unaware of the success of actions taken at the instigation of the environmental movement. People can easily see the disadvantages of environmental regulations but not the despoliation that would exist without them. Especially resentful are those whose personal or corporate ox is being gored when they are forced to sustain financial losses because of a sensible (or occasionally senseless) application of regulations.

Of course, it is natural for many people to feel personally threatened by efforts to preserve a healthy environment. Consider a car salesperson who makes a bigger commission selling a large car than a small one, an executive of a petrochemical company that is liable for damage done by toxic chemicals released into the environment, a logger whose job is jeopardized by enforcement of the Endangered Species Act, a rancher whose way of life may be threatened by higher grazing fees on public lands, a farmer about to lose the farm because of environmentalists' attacks on subsidies for irrigation water, or a developer who wants to continue building subdivisions and is sick and tired of dealing with inconsistent building codes or U.S. Fish and Wildlife Service bureaucrats. In such situations, resentment of some of the rules, regulations, and recommendations designed to enhance human well-being and protect life-support systems is understandable.

Unfortunately, many of these dissatisfied individuals and companies have been recruited into the self-styled "wise-use" movement, which has attracted a surprisingly diverse coalition of people, including representatives of extractive and polluting industries who are motivated by corporate interests as well as private property rights activists and right-wing ideologues. Although some of these individuals simply believe that environmental regulations unfairly distribute the costs of environmental protection, some others are doubtless motivated more by a greedy desire for unrestrained economic expansion.

At a minimum, the wise-use movement firmly opposes most government efforts to maintain environmental quality in the belief that environmental regulation creates unnecessary and burdensome bureaucratic hurdles which stifle economic growth. Wise-use advocates see little or no need for constraints on the exploitation of resources for short-term economic benefits and argue that such exploitation can be accelerated with no adverse long-term consequences. Thus they espouse unrestricted drilling in the Arctic National Wildlife Refuge, logging in national forests, mining in protected areas or next door to national parks, and full compensation for any loss of actual or potential property value resulting from environmental restrictions.

In promoting the view that immediate economic interests are best served by continuing business as usual, the wise-use movement works to stir up discontent among everyday citizens who, rightly or wrongly, feel abused by environmental regulations. This tactic is described in detail in David Helvarg's book, *The War Against the Greens:*

> To date the Wise Use/Property Rights backlash has been a bracing if dangerous reminder to environmentalists that power concedes nothing without a demand and that no social movement, be it ethnic, civil, or environmental, can rest on its past laurels. . . . If the anti-enviros' links to the Farm Bureau, Heritage Foundation, NRA, logging companies, resource trade associations, multinational gold-mining companies, [and] ORV manufacturers . . . proves anything, it's that large industrial lobbies and transnational corporations have learned to play the grassroots game.

Wise-use proponents are not always candid about their motivations and intentions. Many of the organizations representing them masquerade as groups seemingly attentive to environmental quality. Adopting a strategy biologists call "aggressive mimicry," they often give themselves names resembling those of genuine environmental or scientific public-interest groups: National Wetland Coalition, Friends of Eagle Mountain, the Sahara Club, the Alliance for Environment and Resources, the Abundant Wildlife Society of North America, the Global Climate Coalition, the National Wilderness Institute, and the American Council on Science and Health. In keeping with aggressive mimicry, these organizations often actively work *against* the interests implied in their names—a practice sometimes called *greenscamming.*

One such group, calling itself Northwesterners for More Fish, seeks to limit federal protection of endangered fish species so the activities of utilities, aluminum companies, and timber outfits utilizing the region's rivers are not hindered. Armed with a $2.6 million budget, the group aims to discredit environmentalists who say industry is destroying the fish habitats of the Columbia and other rivers, threatening the Northwest's valuable salmon fishery, among others.

Representative George Miller, referring to the wise-use movement's support of welfare ranching, overlogging, and government giveaways of mining rights, stated: "What you have . . . is a lot of special interests who are trying to generate some ideological movement to try and disguise what it is individually they want in the name of their own profits, their own greed in terms of the use and abuse of federal lands."

Wise-use sentiments have been adopted by a number of deeply conservative legislators, many of whom have received campaign contributions from these organizations. One member of the House of Representatives recently succeeded in gaining passage of a bill that limited the annual budget for the Mojave National Preserve, the newest addition to the National Parks System, to one dollar—thus guaranteeing that the park would have no money for upkeep or for enforcement of park regulations.

These same conservative legislators are determined to slash funding for scientific research, especially on such subjects as endangered species, ozone depletion, and global warming, and have legislated for substantial cutbacks in funds for the National Science Foundation, the U.S. Geological Survey, the National Aeronautics and Space Administration, and the Environmental Protection Agency. Many of them and their supporters see science as self-indulgent, at odds with economic interests, and inextricably linked to regulatory excesses.

The scientific justifications and philosophical underpinnings for the positions of the wise-use movement are largely provided by the brownlash. Prominent promoters of the wise-use viewpoint on a number of issues include such conservative think tanks as the Cato Institute and the Heritage Foundation. Both organizations help generate and disseminate erroneous brownlash ideas and information. Adam Myerson, editor of the Heritage Foundation's journal *Policy Review,* pretty much summed up the brownlash perspective by saying: "Leading scientists have done major work disputing the current hennypennyism about global warming, acid rain, and other purported environmental catastrophes." In reality, however, most "leading" scientists support what Myerson calls henny-pennyism; the scientists he refers to are a small group largely outside the mainstream of scientific thinking.

In recent years, a flood of books and articles has advanced the notion that all is well with the environment, giving credence to this anti-scientific "What, me worry?" outlook. Brownlash writers often pepper their works with code phrases such as *sound science* and *balance*—words that suggest objectivity while in fact having little connection to what is presented. *Sound science* usually means science that is interpreted to support the brownlash view. *Balance* generally means giving undue prominence to the opinions of one or a handful of contrarian scientists who are at odds with the consensus of the scientific community at large.

Of course, while pro-environmental groups and environmental scientists in general may sometimes be dead wrong (as can anybody confronting environmental complexity), they ordinarily are not acting on behalf of narrow economic interests. Yet one of the remarkable triumphs of the wise-use movement and its allies in the past decade has been their ability to define public-interest organizations, in the eyes of many legislators, as "special interests"—not different in kind from the American Tobacco Institute, the Western Fuels Association, or other organizations that represent business groups.

But we believe there is a very real difference in kind. Most environmental organizations are funded mainly by membership donations; corporate funding is at most a minor factor for public-interest advocacy groups. There are no monetary profits to be gained other than attracting a bigger membership. Environmental scientists have even less to gain; they usually are dependent upon university or research institute salaries and research funds from peer-reviewed government grants or sometimes (especially in new or controversial areas where government funds are largely unavailable) from private foundations.

One reason the brownlash messages hold so much appeal to many people, we think, is the fear of further change. Even though the American frontier closed a century ago, many Americans seem to believe they still live in what the great economist Kenneth Boulding once called a "cowboy economy." They still think they can figuratively throw their garbage over the backyard fence with impunity. They regard the environmentally protected public land as "wasted" and think it should be available for their self-beneficial appropriation. They believe that private property rights are absolute (despite a rich economic and legal literature showing they never have been). They do not understand, as Pace University law professor John Humbach wrote in 1993, that "the Constitution does not guarantee that land speculators will win their bets."

The anti-science brownlash provides a rationalization for the short-term economic interests of these groups: old-growth forests are decadent and should be harvested; extinction is natural, so there's no harm in overharvesting economically important animals; there is abundant undisturbed habitat, so human beings have a right to develop land anywhere and in any way they choose; global warming is a hoax or even will benefit agriculture, so there's no need to limit the burning of fossil fuels; and so on. Anti-science basically claims we can keep the good old days by doing business as usual. But the problem is we can't.

Thus the brownlash helps create public confusion about the character and magnitude of environmental problems, taking advantage of the lack of consensus among individuals and social groups on the urgency of enhancing environmental protection. A widely shared social consensus, such as the United States saw during World War II, will be essential if we are to maintain environmental quality while meeting the nation's other needs. By emphasizing dissent, the brownlash works against the formation of any such consensus; instead it has helped thwart the development of a spirit of cooperation mixed with concern for society as a whole. In our opinion, the brownlash fuels conflict by claiming the environmental problems are overblown or nonexistent and that unbridled economic development will propel the world to new levels of prosperity with little or no risk to the natural systems that support society. As a result, environmental groups and wise-use proponents are increasingly polarized.

Unfortunately, some of that polarization has led to ugly confrontations and activities that are not condoned by the brownlash or by most environmentalists, including us. As David Helvarg stated, "Along with the growth of Wise Use/Property Rights, the last six years have seen a startling increase in intimidation, vandalism, and violence directed against grassroots environmental activists." And while confrontations and threats have been generated by both sides—most notably (but by no means exclusively) over the northern spotted owl protection plan—the level of intimidation engaged in by wise-use proponents is disturbing, to say the least. . . .

Fortunately, despite all the efforts of the brownlash to discourage it, environmental concern in the United States is widespread. Thus a public-opinion survey in 1995 indicated that slightly over half of all Americans felt that environmental problems in the United States were "very serious." Indeed, 85 percent were concerned "a fair amount" and 38 percent "a great deal" about the environment. Fifty-eight percent would choose protecting the environment over economic growth, and 65 percent said they would be willing to pay higher prices so that industry could protect the environment better. Responses in other rich nations have been similar, and people in developing nations have shown, if anything, even greater environmental concerns. These responses suggest that the notion that caring about the environment is a luxury of the rich is a myth. Furthermore, our impression is that young people care especially strongly about environmental quality—a good omen if true.

Nor is environmental concern exclusive to Democrats and "liberals." There is a strong Republican and conservative tradition of environmental protection dating back to Teddy Roosevelt and even earlier. Many of our most important environmental laws were passed with bipartisan support during the Nixon and Ford administrations. Recently, some conservative environmentalists have been speaking out against brownlash rhetoric. And public concern is rising about the efforts to cripple environmental laws and regulations posed by right-wing leaders in Congress, thinly disguised as "deregulation" and "necessary budget-cutting." In January 1996, a Republican pollster, Linda Divall, warned that "our party is out of sync with mainstream American opinion when it comes to the environment."

Indeed, some interests that might be expected to sympathize with the wise-use movement have moved beyond such reactionary views. Many leaders in corporations such as paper companies and chemical manufacturers, whose activities are directly harmful to the environment, are concerned about their firms' environmental impacts and are shifting to less damaging practices. Our friends in the ranching community in western Colorado indicate their concern to us every summer. They want to preserve a way of life and a high-quality environment—and are as worried about the progressive suburbanization of the area as are the scientists at the Rocky Mountain Biological Laboratory. Indeed, they have actively participated in discussions with environmentalists and officials of the Department of the Interior to set grazing fees at levels that wouldn't force them out of business but also wouldn't subsidize overgrazing and land abuse.

Loggers, ranchers, miners, petrochemical workers, fishers, and professors all live on the same planet, and all of us must cooperate to preserve a sound environment for our descendants. The environmental problems of the planet can be solved only in a spirit of cooperation, not one of conflict. Ways must be found to allocate fairly both the benefits and the costs of environmental quality.

POSTSCRIPT

Do Environmental Restrictions Violate Basic Economic Freedoms?

The dilemmas that face us as we attempt to adjust our lifestyles to the needs of a suddenly threatened environment are the hardest that this generation will know. It is not just that we are being asked to refrain in the future from certain profitable activities in order to preserve some part of the environment, like building hotels on barrier beaches, for instance. We will be asked—told—to cut back on portions of our lives that we have taken for granted. We will be told to stop driving our cars except in direst emergency, cancel travel plans, forget the vacation house, and pay astronomical prices for goods and services that have always been reasonable. We will be told to separate our trash scrupulously, into plastics, glass, metals, paper, and organic waste, and to take it to five different receiving stations for recycling and reusing. Daily life will be poorer, and it will take up much more of our time and labor. Most of these burdens will be chosen by us, through democratically conducted elections and legislation. But there will be no real choice, for the alternative may be the death of the biosphere, including its human component.

Suggested Reading

It sounds terrible. But it doesn't have to be. Some writers are optimistic, most currently the Rocky Mountain Institute's Amory and Hunter Lovins and Paul Hawken, who argue, in *Natural Capitalism*, that we have the technology on board now to save the planet and provide Americans *and the rest of the world* with a really pleasant lifestyle. We suggest that you read it. In addition to *Natural Capitalism*, you may profit from consulting some of the following:

J. Baird Callicott and Michael Nelson, eds. *The Great, New, Wilderness Debate* (Athens: University of Georgia Press, 1998).

Daniel Etsy and Andrew Winston, *Green to Gold: How Smart Companies Use Environmental Strategy to Innovate, Create Value, and Build Competitive Advantage,* Hoboken: NJ: Wiley, 2009.

Simon Swaffield *Theory in Landscape Architecture: A Reader,* Illustrated Ed., Philadelphia, PA: University of Pennsylvania Press, 2002.

ISSUE 19

Is Bottling Water a Good Solution to Problems of Water Purity and Availability?

YES: Julie Stauffer, from "Water," *Body + Soul* (April/May 2005)

NO: Brian Howard, from "Message in a Bottle," *E: The Environment Magazine* (September/October 2003)

ISSUE SUMMARY

YES: Julie Stauffer presents a good argument for care in the selection and use of drinking water, while recognizing that guarantees are few and far between in the bottled water industry. The commonly available information on bottled water certainly conveys the impression that it is purer and better than mere tap water; all the ads conjure up a vigorous and healthy outdoor lifestyle amid forests, lakes, and pure flowing springs.

NO: Brian Howard argues that bottling water is environmentally disastrous because of the huge drains on scarce aquifers and the haphazard disposal of the plastic bottles and that tap water is often superior to bottled in purity.

We are a nation in love with our bottled water. In 2007, Americans spent about $15 billion on bottles of water, some with very sophisticated labels. Why, when tap water is safe? Possibly this is a habit we picked up from the Europeans, who have never considered their tap water fit to drink. (They may be right; the last time I was in St. Petersburg, Russia, I was firmly warned not only not to drink the gray water that emerged from the tap but to keep my mouth and eyes closed while showering to prevent any contact with mucous membranes.) But with its wide open spaces to filter our groundwater, contamination of tap water has never really been America's problem; by all accounts and measures and tests, the public water supply in the United States is perfectly fit for all purposes, and until recently, that's what we used it for. Has there been some sudden revelation that American tap water is contaminated, poisoned, whatever?

Apparently not, but that has not stopped the consumer enthusiasm. Bottled water continues to be seen as a healthy product of choice among consumers looking to quench their thirst. Globally, sales have increased a whopping 17.8 percent over the past year. In North America alone, sales have jumped from $8.4 billion to $13.3 billion in a year, accounting for 68 percent of the total growth. In 2004 in the United States, the average person consumed 18.2 gallons of bottled water, by 2007 the average person consumed 29 gallons of bottled water per year.

There are three problems with this trend, as the *E* magazine selection points out. First, there are no guarantees on the provenance of the water in the bottle; while your tap water comes from upstate reservoirs in the country, tested and verified, your bottled water company could have its wells in the middle of the landfill. Second, if the water is really being drained from some pure aquifer somewhere, that's water that will be unavailable to local farmers and wildlife. Water does not go to waste, anywhere on earth; it's keeping something alive, and that something is going to have to struggle with a lowered water table if we pump it into plastic bottles and ship it east and west. Third, where do those plastic bottles come from, and where do they go? They start life as scarce petrochemicals (driving up the price of oil), and they tend to end up in landfills.

Bottled water is not safer or purer than tap water, even its defenders point out. Somewhere between 40 and 70 percent of bottled water is simply the tap water of the area where it is bottled, possibly purified with some mechanical filters. As such, it often contains the same "chemicals" that some aficionados insist they wish to eliminate. This is not all bad; the chlorine in most tap water is crucial for removing lethal pathogens, and the fluorides are really good for children's teeth. But isn't the whole enterprise sort of pointless? It isn't as though bottled water tasted better, to the extent that pure water can be said to have taste at all; in every blind test we've tried, consumers have not been able to distinguish bottled from tap water. To be sure, the little bottles are enormously convenient. But couldn't we just refill them when we're done?

Ask yourself, as you read these selections, why we do what we do—not just concerning bottled water but concerning the ten thousand choices we make as consumers every month. How much is style worth? How much is value? How much of our choice depends on market, advertising, pure hype? How much does the environment count in our consumer choices?

YES ↰

Julie Stauffer

Water

We can't live without water—lots of it. The crisp, clear liquid—which makes up about 60 percent of our body weight—carries nourishment to our cells, regulates our body temperature, and helps our kidneys detoxify, among other tasks. Yet water itself may introduce toxins into our systems. So what's the healthiest way to replenish the 10 to 12 cups we lose daily?

A lot of us are wondering: More than one in four Americans are concerned about the quality and safety of their tap water, according to a recent Gallup survey, and tens of millions are reaching for bottled or filtered water instead, creating a billion-dollar business. Is that mistrust justified?

The answer isn't simple. On the one hand, 92 percent of U.S. public drinking-water systems meet federal health standards, which are quite rigorous, though perhaps not updated recently enough. On the other hand, the nonprofit Physicians for Social Responsibility estimates that thousands of people each year get sick because of pathogens in their drinking water, contracting everything from mild stomach upsets to hepatitis. And scientists are only beginning to discover the impact of the many chemicals that find their way into water sources, some of which are not monitored.

Yet there's no need to be alarmed. Taking the worry out of water is a lot simpler than you may think, requiring just a few steps. Most crucial among them: understanding your public water supplier's Consumer Confidence Report and, if necessary, properly filtering your drinking water.

Think of it as tapping into a fresh start. . . .

Fix the Problems

Using a water filter is the easiest and most comprehensive way to clean up your tap water. If you choose to use bottled water, follow our guidelines to pick a good one. At the least, be sure to run your tap for a couple of minutes in the morning to flush out any lead that's accumulated overnight. And never drink or cook with *hot* water from the tap, because hot water dissolves lead far more than cold water does.

Water filters Whether you use a stand-alone jug or an installed system that hooks directly to your tap, make sure your filter meets the standards of the independent American National Standards Institute and National Sanitation Foundation (ANSI/NSF). And remember that different filters remove different contaminants, so read the tiny print on the package before you go to the checkout counter to make sure that your concerns are addressed. Not all water filters remove lead, for example, so if lead is an issue, be sure to buy a filter that has been ANSI/NSF certified to remove lead.

Stand-alone jug filters   Jug filters, the pitchers or small tanks that you fill from your tap, cost about $20 and are by far the most common and affordable option. They're a little more work than installed systems because you must regularly refill and clean the jug as well as change the filter. Keep your filtered water in the fridge to prevent bacteria from growing, and make sure that you replace your filter according to the manufacturer's instructions—don't just rely on the various signaling systems, which can be inaccurate. A filter that's been used too long can actually release all the contaminants it has accumulated back into your water.

Installed filtering systems   These are more convenient than jug filters and they treat larger volumes of water, but they're pricier, running from $200 to $500, including installation. Their filters, too, must be changed regularly. Some systems hook directly to the faucet, while others attach from under the sink. If you plan to buy one of the latter, by sure to pass up any with brass components. Several years ago, the Center for Environmental Health found that brass alloys in a number of under-the-sink filters sold in California leached lead into the water, though all the manufacturers that were implicated agreed to reformulate their filters.

Bottled water   Americans spend more than $8.3 billion a year on bottled water, but what they're drinking may not be any safer or better regulated than tap water. A bottle of water that sports an image of a pure mountain glacier may actually be municipal tap water that has undergone an extra purification process. In fact, 60 to 70 percent of bottled water sold in the United States is exempt from federal regulations because it's packaged and sold in the same state, not crossing state lines. Moreover, if a product is recalled because it fails to comply with federal regulations, it's generally left up to the bottler to voluntarily make the recall.

Follow these tips to choose a safe bottled water:

Check affiliations   Look for manufacturers that belong to the International Bottled Water Association (IBWA), which requires its members to test their water daily and to have their bottling plants inspected annually by an independent third party. You can find a listing of IBWA member companies on the group's Web site . . .

Scrutinize labels   Labels will reveal the water's source. When a bottled water fails to meet federal regulations, the label must also state that it contains "excessive levels" of the contaminant in question. If you want water that's closer to nature, stick with brands labeled "natural spring water" or "natural mineral water." And make sure the brand's ingredients match your needs. For example, if you're on a salt-restricted diet, choose a water with less than 10 mg of sodium per liter. If you have any questions about what's inside the container, contact the manufacturer. (By agreement, all IBWA members list their phone numbers or addresses on their labels.)

Assess packaging   Water in clear bottles made from polyethylene terephthalate tastes better than water in soft, cloudy jugs made from high-density polyethylene plastic. Avoid polycarbonate (the strong rigid plastic used in five-gallon water-cooler jugs) because it can leach bisphenol-A, a potential carcinogen and hormone mimic.

Chances are, your water—whether from the tap or bottled—is perfectly safe. But you won't know for sure until you do a little investigating. In this case, an ounce of prevention is worth a gallon of cure. Given that a woman of average size should consume 64 ounces of liquid a day, the peace of mind gained by doing a little homework could be enormous.

HOT-BUTTON CONTAMINANTS

The Environmental Protection Agency's (EPA) Safe Drinking Water Act, now 30 years old, is quite strict. But even so, there are dozens of common drinking-water contaminants it does not cover, and some regulations may be too lax.

These are some of the hot-button contaminants you may want to test for yourself or use a filter to eliminate.

Arsenic
Arsenic, which occurs naturally in rock and soil, is widely recognized as a carcinogen, but it's expensive to remove from drinking water, whether tap or bottled. In 2006, the current EPA standard of 50 parts per billion (ppb) will be changed to 10 parts per billion (ppb). However, scientists believe there is no safe level of arsenic.

Disinfection by-Products (DBPs)
Water suppliers often use chlorine to kill disease-causing bugs. Unfortunately, the chlorination process releases by-products that have been linked to cancers in humans, and chlorinated water has been linked to spontaneous abortions and stillbirths. Another common method of disinfection, ozonation, creates by-products, including formaldehyde and acetaldehyde, that have been linked to cancer. The EPA is considering strengthening regulations for DBPs.

Methyl Tertiary-Butyl Ether (MTBE)
This common gasoline additive, found in the water supplies of 36 states, may cause cancer. There is currently no health standard for MTBE in drinking water, although the EPA is studying the possibility of developing one.

Perchlorate

This rocket-fuel ingredient, which has contaminated hundreds of water sources in California as well as the Colorado River, interferes with the function of the thyroid gland, which in adults can lead to problems with metabolism and in children and developing fetuses can affect brain development. There is currently no national standard for perchlorate in drinking water.

Radon

A naturally occurring radioactive gas that can leach into drinking water from the surrounding soil and rocks, radon increases the risk of lung cancer and cancer of the gastrointestinal tract. The EPA is investigating regulations for radon, but nothing has been finalized.

BOTTLED-WATER BREAKDOWN

There are several categories of bottled water, each reflecting the water's source. Check labels to see which type you're buying.

Spring Water

This water comes from an underground source and flows naturally to the Earth's surface. Bottlers can add carbon dioxide to make it sparkling. Some representative brands: Evian, Poland Spring, Dannon, Crystal Geyser, Trinity.

Mineral Water

This is water that contains at least 250 parts per million (ppm) of naturally occurring dissolved minerals such as calcium, magnesium, sodium, potassium, silica, and bicarbonates. Like spring water, it also comes from an underground source and flows naturally to the earth's surface. Some representative brands: Vittel, Perrier.

Purified Drinking Water

A lot of bottled water has been treated by distillation, deionization, or reverse osmosis. The source of the water doesn't need to be named, and it may even be municipal tap water, but the label must say how the water was purified. Some representative brands: Aquafina, Dasani.

Artesian Water

In artesian wells underground pressure is high enough to push the water to the surface once the well is drilled, making it something like spring water. Some representative brands: Fiji, Avita.

Well Water

Wells are underground water reserves that can be pumped to the surface. Typically, bottled well water is sold locally or regionally.

Brian Howard

→ **NO**

Message in a Bottle: Despite the Hype, Bottled Water Is Neither Cleaner Nor Greener Than Tap Water

"**Y**ou drink tap water? Are you crazy?" asks a 21-year-old radio producer from the Chicago area. "I *only* drink bottled water." In a trendy nightclub in New York City, the bartender tells guests they can *only* be served bottled water, which costs $5 for each tiny half-pint container. One outraged clubber is stopped by the restroom attendant as she tries to refill the bottle from the tap. "You can't do that," says the attendant. "New York's tap water isn't safe."

Whether a consumer is shopping in a supermarket or a health food store, working out in a fitness center, eating in a restaurant or grabbing some quick refreshment on the go, he or she will likely be tempted to buy bottled water. The product comes in an ever-growing variety of sizes and shapes, including one bottle that looks like a drop of water with a golden cap. Some fine hotels now offer the services of "water sommeliers" to advise diners on which water to drink with different courses.

A widening spectrum of bottled water types are crowding the market, including spring, mineral, purified, distilled, carbonated, oxygenated, caffeinated and vitamin-enriched, as well as flavors, such as lemon or strawberry, and specific brands aimed at children. Bottled water bars have sprung up in the hipper districts, from Paris to Los Angeles.

The message is clear: Bottled water is "good" water, as opposed to that nasty, unsafe stuff that comes out of the tap. But in most cases tap water adheres to stricter purity standards than bottled water, whose source—far from a mountain spring—can be wells underneath industrial facilities. Indeed, 40 percent of bottled water began life as, well, tap water.

A 2001 World Wildlife Fund (WWF) study confirmed the widespread belief that consumers associate bottled water with social status and healthy living. Their perceptions trump their objectivity, because even some people who claim to have switched to bottled water "for the taste" can't tell the difference: When *Good Morning America* conducted a taste test of its studio audience, New York City tap water was chosen as the heavy favorite over the oxygenated water O2, Poland Spring and Evian. Many of the "facts" that bottled water

From *E/The Environmental Magazine*, September/October 2003, pp. 27–31, 34, 36–39. Copyright © 2003 by E/The Environmental Magazine. Reprinted by permission of Featurewell.

drinkers swear by are erroneous. Rachele Kuzma, a Rutgers student, says she drinks bottled water at school because "it's healthier" and "doesn't have fluoride," although much of it does have fluoride.

Bottled water is so ubiquitous that people can hardly ask for water anywhere without being handed a bottle. But what is the cost to society and the environment?

Largely Self-Regulated

The bottled water industry has exploded in recent years, and enjoys annual sales of more than $35 billion worldwide. In 2002, almost six billion gallons of bottled water were sold in the U.S., representing an increase of nearly 11 percent over 2001. Americans paid $7.7 billion for bottled water in 2002, according to the consulting and research firm Beverage Marketing Corporation. Bottled water is the fastest-growing segment of the beverage industry, and the product is expected to pass both coffee and milk to become the second-most-consumed beverage (behind soft drinks) by 2004. According to the Natural Resources Defense Council (NRDC), "More than half of all Americans drink bottled water; about a third of the public consumes it regularly." While most people would argue that bottled water is healthier than convenient alternatives like sugared sodas or artificially flavored drinks, are the third of bottled water consumers who claim they are motivated by promises of purity (according to a 2000 survey) getting what they pay for?

While the Environmental Protection Agency (EPA) regulates the quality of public water supplies, the agency has no authority over bottled water. Bottled water that crosses state lines is considered a food product and is overseen by the Food and Drug Administration (FDA), which does mandate that it be bottled in sanitary conditions using food-grade equipment. According to the influential International Bottled Water Association (IBWA), "By law, the FDA Standard of Quality for bottled water must be as stringent as the EPA's standards for public drinking water."

However, the FDA is allowed to interpret the EPA'S regulations and apply them selectively to bottled water. As Senior Attorney Erik Olson of the NRDC explains, "Although the FDA has adopted some of the EPA's regulatory standards, it has decided not to adopt others and has not even ruled on some points after several years of inaction." In a 1999 report, the NRDC concludes that bottled water quality is probably not inferior to average tap water, but Olson (the report's principal author) says that gaps in the weak regulatory framework may allow careless or unscrupulous bottlers to market substandard products. He says that may be of particular concern to those with compromised immune systems.

The IBWA urges consumers to trust bottled water in part because the FDA requires water sources to be "inspected, sampled, analyzed and approved." However, the NRDC argues that the FDA provides no specific requirements—such as proximity to industrial facilities, underground storage tanks or dumps—for bottled water sources. That's looser monitoring than occurs at the EPA, which requires more specific assessments of tap water sources. Olson says one brand of "spring water," which had a graphic of mountains and a lake on the label, was actually taken from a well in Massachusetts in the parking lot of an industrial facility. The well, which is no longer used for bottled water, was near hazardous waste and had experienced contamination by industrial chemicals.

According to Olson, the FDA has no official procedure for rejecting bottled water sources once they become contaminated. He also says a 1990 government audit revealed that 25 percent of water bottlers had no record of source approval. Further, in contrast to the EPA, which employs hundreds of staffers to protect the nation's tap water systems, the FDA doesn't have even one full-time regulator in charge of bottled water.

Scott Hoober of the Kansas Rural Water Association says that although municipal system managers have to pay a certified lab to test samples weekly, monthly and quarterly for a long list of contaminants, water bottlers can use any lab they choose to perform tests as infrequently as once a year. Unlike utilities, which must publish their lab results in a public record, bottlers don't have to notify anyone of their findings, including consumers who inquire. The FDA has the authority to ask for a company's data, although test results can be destroyed after two years.

Olson adds, "Unlike tap water violations, which are directly enforceable, if a company exceeds bottled water standards, it is not necessarily a violation—they can just say so on the label, and may be insulated from enforcement." Further, while EPA rules specify that no confirmed *E. coli* or fecal coliform (bacteria that indicate possible contamination by fecal matter) contamination is allowed in tap water, the FDA merely set a minimum level for *E. coli* and fecal coliform presence in bottled water. Tap water from a surface source must be tested for cryptosporidium, giardia and viruses, unlike bottled water, and must also be disinfected, unlike bottled water. Hoober also notes that food products such as "carbonated water," "soda water" and "seltzer water"—in addition to most flavored waters—are held to even looser standards than "true" bottled water.

The EPA concludes, "Some bottled water is treated more than tap water, while some is treated less or not at all." Henry Kim, consumer safety officer for the FDA, asserts, "We want bottled water to have a comparable quality to that of tap water"—which, of course, runs counter to the widely held public belief that bottled water is *better*. The situation is similar in the European Union and in Canada, where there are more regulations on tap than bottled water. That New York restroom attendant would be surprised to learn that her city's tap water was tested some 560,000 times in 2002.

Environmentalists also point out that if a brand of bottled water is wholly packaged and sold within the same state, it is technically not regulated by the FDA, and is therefore only legally subject to state standards, which tend to vary widely in scope and vigor. Coop America reports that 43 states have one or fewer staff members dedicated to bottled water regulation. On the other hand, California enforces strict regulations on bottled water contaminants, and Fort Collins, Colorado tests bottled water sold in town and posts the results online. The NRDC estimates that 60 to 70 percent of bottled water brands sold in the U.S. are single-state operations. Stephen Kay, vice president of communications of the IBWA, says he doubts the percentage is that high.

Kay is adamant that "no bottled water escapes regulation," and he points out that all members of the IBWA (which are responsible for 80 percent of U.S. bottled water sales) must also adhere to the organization's mandatory Model Code. This code does close some of the FDA's regulatory gaps, including setting a zero tolerance for coliform contamination, and it requires members to follow certain standards and undergo an annual, unannounced plant inspection. However, Olson stresses that, except in a few states, this Model Code is not legally binding or enforceable. Members of the much smaller National Spring Water Association follow their own guidelines, and must get their water from free-flowing springs.

One result of such Byzantine bottled water standards has been the widespread use of disinfection to reduce possible contaminants. Although the FDA does not require it, disinfection is mandatory in several states, including New York, California and Texas. However, chemicals commonly used to disinfect water, including chlorine and ozone gas, may react unpredictably, forming potentially carcinogenic byproducts. Opponents also argue that disinfection destroys naturally beneficial bacteria, creating a blank slate. Further, Mark Johnson of bottler Trinity Springs—which taps a spring in Idaho so pure it doesn't need any treatment—concludes, "If you don't disinfect, you must protect the source and increase environmental awareness so the source stays protected."

What's Really in that Bottle?

Even with widespread disinfection, consumer groups have raised numerous warnings about a host of different microorganisms and chemicals that have been found in bottled water. In a four-year scientific study, the NRDC tested more than 1,000 bottles of 103 brands of bottled water. The group concluded, "Although most bottled water tested was of good quality, some brands' quality was spotty." A third of the tested brands were found to contain contaminants such as arsenic and carcinogenic compounds in at least some samples at levels exceeding state or industry standards.

An earlier NRDC-commissioned study tested for hundreds of different chemicals in 38 brands of California bottled water. Two samples had arsenic contamination, six had chemical byproducts of chlorination, and six had measurable levels of the toxic chemical toluene. Several samples violated California's bottled water standards. In a study published in the *Archives of Family Medicine,* researchers at Case Western Reserve University and Ohio State University compared 57 samples of bottled water to Cleveland's tap water. While 39 of the bottled water samples were purer than the tap water, 15 of the bottles had significantly higher bacteria levels. The scientists concluded that although all of the water they tested was safe to drink, "use of bottled water on the assumption of purity can be misguided."

Another area of potential concern is the fact that no agency calls for testing of bottled water after it leaves its initial packaging plant, leaving some to wonder what happens during months of storage and transport. To begin to examine this question, the Kansas Department of Health and Environment tested 80 samples of bottled water from retail stores and manufacturers. All 80 of the samples had detectable levels of chlorine, fluoride and sodium. Seventy-eight of the 80 contained some nitrate (which can cause methemoglobinemia, or blue-baby syndrome, in higher doses), 12 had nitrite, 53 had chloroform, 33 contained bromodichloro-methane, 25 had arsenic and 15 tested positive for lead.

Forty-six of the samples contained traces of some form of the carcinogen (and hormone disrupter) phthalate, while 12 of those exceeded federal safety levels for that chemical. According to Olson, phthalates may leach out of some plastic bottles into water. "Phthalates are not legally regulated in bottled water because of intense industry pressure," says Olson. Although Co-op America concludes that there is little evidence of a link between phthalate exposure from bottled water and any health problems, the group suggests using glass over plastic bottles as a precaution. Similarly, if your office cooler is made of polycarbonate, it may be releasing small amounts of the potential hormone disrupter bisphenol A into the water.

Idaho's Pure Health Solutions, a water purification company, also conducted its own study that concluded certain bacteria grow significantly in bottled water over a 12-day period. Bacteria will normally grow in tap water within a few days if it is kept bottled up at room temperature. Most municipal water managers leave a residual amount of chlorine in tap water after treatment specifically to inhibit the growth of bacteria as the water runs through pipes and sits in tanks.

The IBWA argues that the presence of benign bacteria in bottled water has no bearing on public health, since the treatment processes used by manufacturers ensure the death of any potentially harmful organisms. The group's website claims that there have been no confirmed cases of illness in the U.S. as a result of bottled water. The IBWA does mention an instance in 1994 in the Northern Mariana Islands, in which bottled well water was linked to a disease outbreak. The NRDC argues that no U.S. government agency actively searches for incidents of illness from bottled water.

On the Internet, one can find testimonials and news reports about people who claim to have gotten sick from tainted bottled water. One man writes that he and his fiancee became ill after drinking bottled water in the Dominican Republic. The Allegheny County Health Department in Pennsylvania reports discovering high levels of coliform in bottled water samples that were taken "after a man reported that he became sick from drinking the water."

Misleading Labels

Another complaint commonly levied against the bottled water industry is that many of the myriad product labels are misleading. Not long ago, New York-based artist Nancy Drew began collecting water bottles for a project. She concluded, "In a culture so inundated with images solely designed for promotion and profit, water is the most absurd element to see being used in this context." Drew's subsequent art views water labels' ubiquitous depictions of pristine landscapes as a stark contrast to the "gluttonous consumption and sense of status that they represent."

The IBWA states, "The labeling requirements ensure that the source and purity of the bottled water are identified and that, if the label is false or misleading, the supplier is subject to civil or criminal sanctions." Even so, the FDA technically requires that bottled water labels disclose only three variables: the class of water (such as spring or mineral), the manufacturer, and the volume. That brand of Massachusetts "spring water" exposed by NRDC was so-named because the source occasionally bubbled up to the surface in the industrial parking lot.

As ABC News put it, "Ad campaigns touting spring-fed or glacier-born H_2O are winning over a population increasingly skeptical of taps and willing to shell out big bucks for what they consider a purer, tastier and safer drink." Water bottlers use product names such as More Precious Than Gold, Ice Mountain, Desert Quench, Pure American, Utopia and Crystal Springs. The Environmental Law Foundation has sued eight bottlers on the basis that they used words like "pure" to market water containing bacteria, arsenic and chlorine breakdown products.

Co-op America advises consumers "to be wary of words like 'pure,' 'pristine,' 'glacial,' 'premium,' 'natural' or 'healthy.' They're basically meaningless words added to labels to emphasize the alleged purity of bottled water over tap water." The group points out that, in one case, bottled water labeled as "Alaska Premium Glacier Drinking Water: Pure Glacier Water from the Last Unpolluted Frontier" was actually drawn from Public Water System #111241 in Juneau. The FDA now requires this bottler to add "from a municipal source" on the label. According to Co-op America, "as much as 40 percent of bottled water is actually bottled tap water, sometimes with additional treatment, sometimes not." So-called purified water can be drawn from any source as long as it is subsequently treated, which leaves some to wonder how that differs from good old tap water.

The number one (Aquafina) and two (Dasani) top-selling brands of bottled water in the U.S. both fall in the category of purified water. Dasani is sold by Coca-Cola, while Aquafina is a Pepsi product. As *U.S. News & World Report* explains, "Aquafina is municipal water from spots like Wichita, Kansas." The newsmagazine continues, "Coke's Dasani (with minerals added) is taken from the taps of Queens, New York, Jacksonville, Florida, and elsewhere." Everest bottled water originates from southern Texas, while Yosemite brand is drawn from the Los Angeles suburbs.

In June, a lawsuit was filed against Poland Spring, the nation's largest bottled spring water company. Poland Spring is a brand of Nestlé Waters North America, which used to be called Perrier Group of America. Nestlé Waters is owned by the Switzerland-based Nestlé S.A., the world's largest food company. Nestlé's 14 other brands of U.S. bottled water include Arrowhead, Deer Park, Aberfoyle, Zephyrhills, Ozarka and Ice Mountain.

The plaintiffs charged that Nestlé duped consumers by advertising that Poland Spring water comes from "some of the most pristine and protected sources deep in the woods of Maine." The lawsuit alleges that ever since the original Poland Spring was shut down in 1967, the company has used man-made wells, at least one of which is in a parking lot along a busy road. "Poland

Spring is exactly what we say it is—natural spring water," responded a Nestlé spokesperson.

Mistrusting the Tap

Despite all the hype, the NRDC concludes, "While much tap water is indeed risky, having compared available data, we conclude that there is no assurance that bottled water is any safer than tap water." Scientists at the University of Geneva arrived at the same conclusion, and add that, in 50 percent of the cases they studied, the only difference between tap and bottled water was that the latter contained added minerals and salts, "which do not actually mean the water is healthier." In 1997, the United Nations Food and Agriculture Organization concluded that bottled water does not have greater nutritional value than tap water.

So why do so many of us trust and prefer bottled water to the liquid that is already piped directly into our homes? For the price of one bottle of Evian, a person can use 1,000 gallons of tap water in the home. Americans spend around $10,700 on bottled water every minute, reports Co-op America, and many consumers think nothing of paying three times as much per gallon of bottled H_2O as they do for gasoline.

Kay says the IBWA does not intend to promote bottled water as a replacement for tap water, except maybe during emergencies. "Since bottled water is considered a food product by law, it doesn't make sense to single it out as needing more regulations than other foods," says Kay. He also stresses that IBWA guidelines strictly prevent members from trying to capitalize on fears over tap water, or from directly advertising that their products are more pure than municipal water.

Bottled water's competition is soft drinks, not tap water, says Kay. Karen from Ames, Iowa posted on the 2000days web diary: "In the summer I buy bottled water more often so I'll have something to drink that's not loaded with syrup and stuff."

Some critics have also found it ironic that many people who purchase bottled water end up refilling the containers from a tap. Clearly, some consumers may be more interested in buying the product for its packaging than for the water itself—or they impulsively purchased a bottle where there was no immediate access to a tap.

The Green Response

More and more environmentalists are beginning to question the purpose of lugging those heavy, inefficient, polluting bottles all over the Earth. The parent organization of the World Wildlife Fund, the Switzerland-based World Wide Fund for Nature, argues strongly that the product is a waste of money and is very environmentally unfriendly. Co-op America concludes: "By far the cheapest—and often the safest—option is to drink water from a tap. It's also the most environmentally friendly option." Friends of the Earth says, "We might as well drink water from the tap and save all this waste."

The WWF argues that the distribution of bottled water requires substantially more fuel than delivering tap water, especially since over 22 million tons of the bottled liquid is transferred each year from country to country. Instead of relying on a mostly preexisting infrastructure of underground pipes and plumbing, delivering bottled water—often from places as far-flung as France, Iceland or Maine—burns fossil fuels and results in the release of thousands of tons of harmful emissions. Since some bottled water is also shipped or stored cold, electricity is expended for refrigeration. Energy is likewise used in bottled water processing. In filtration, an estimated two gallons of water is wasted for every gallon purified.

When most people think of bottled water, they probably envision the single-serve plastic bottle, which has exploded in popularity and is now available almost anywhere food products are sold. The WWF estimates that around 1.5 million tons of plastic are used globally each year in water bottles, leaving a sizable manufacturing footprint. Most water bottles are made of the oil-derived polyethylene terephthalate, which is known as PET. While PET is less toxic than many plastics, the Berkeley Ecology Center found that manufacturing PET generates more than 100 times the toxic emissions—in the form of nickel, ethylbenzene, ethylene oxide and benzene—compared to making the same amount of glass. The Climate Action Network concludes, "Making plastic bottles requires almost the same energy input as making glass bottles, despite transport savings that stem from plastic's light weight."

Andrew Swanander, owner of Mountain Town Spring Water, says, "I'm embarrassed and appalled to see my bottled water products discarded on the side of the road." In fact, a considerable number of used water bottles end up as litter, where they can take up to 1,000 years to biodegrade. A 2002 study by Scenic Hudson reported that 18 percent by volume of recovered litter from the Hudson River (and 14 percent by weight) was comprised of beverage containers.

Pat Franklin, the executive director of the Container Recycling Institute (CRI), says nine out of 10 plastic water bottles end up as either garbage or litter—at a rate of 30 million per day. According to the Climate Action Network, when some plastic bottles are incinerated along with other trash, as is the practice in many municipalities, toxic chlorine (and potentially dioxin) is released into the air while heavy metals deposit in the ash. If plastics are buried in landfills, not only do they take up valuable space, but potentially toxic additives such as phthalates may leak into the groundwater. "It's ironic that many people drink bottled water because they are afraid of tap water, but then the bottles they discard can result in more polluted water," says Franklin. "It's a crazy cycle."

Franklin also acknowledges that although her group is a strong advocate of recycling, the very concept may encourage people to consume more plastics. Replacing used water bottles with new containers made from virgin resources consumes energy and pollutes the air, land and water. CRI estimates that supplying thirsty Americans with water bottles for one year consumes more than 1.5 million barrels of oil, which is enough to generate electricity for more than 250,000 homes for a year, or enough to fuel 100,000 cars for a year.

Big Footprint

Despite such a sizable environmental footprint, the push to recycle plastic water bottles has not been as successful as many consumers might like to think as they faithfully toss their used containers into those blue bins. As *Utne* magazine recently reported, "Despite the ubiquitous arrow symbol, only five percent of plastic waste is currently recycled in America and much of that must be fortified with huge amounts of virgin plastic." One limitation is that recycling plastic causes it to lose strength and flexibility, meaning the process can only be done a few times with any given sample.

Another problem is that different types of plastics are very difficult to sort, even though they can't be recycled together. Common plastic additives such as phthalates or metal salts can also thwart recycling efforts as can too high a ratio of colored bottles (such as Dasani's blue containers) to clear bottles. Because of the challenges, many recycling centers refuse to accept plastics. In fact, a fair amount of America's plastic recycling is done in Asia, where laxer environmental laws govern polluting factories and fuel is spent in international transport.

According to a report recently released by the California Department of Conservation (CDOC), more than one billion water bottles are ending up in the state's trash each year, representing enough plastic to make 74 million square feet of carpet or 16 million sweaters. Darryl Young, the director of CDOC, says only 16 percent of PET water bottles sold in California are being recycled, compared to much higher rates for aluminum and glass. "It's good people are drinking water, but we need to do more outreach to promote recycling," says Young.

Franklin says one potential deterrent to recycling may be that water bottles are often used away from home, meaning they aren't likely to make it into curbside bins. Young advises people to ask for recycling bins in retail and public spaces.

Industry analysts point out that demand exceeds supply in the market for recycled PET plastic, which is used in a range of goods from flowerpots to plastic lumber. Franklin says deposit systems, or so-called bottle bills, would go a long way to improving the collection of used water bottles, especially since only half the country has curbside recycling available. But only a few states have bottle bills, largely because of strong opposition from the container, beverage and retail industries (and their front group, Keep America Beautiful). While Kay stresses that the IBWA urges consumers to recycle, he says his organization opposes bottle bills because "food retailers shouldn't have to devote any money-making floor space to storing and sorting recyclables, especially as that may lead to unsanitary conditions."

The WWF says alternatives to bottled water such as boiling and filtering are cheaper and more sustainable in areas that have contaminated tap sources. Co-op America and CRI advise consumers to fill their own bottles to take with them on the go. Glass doesn't leach chemicals, and sturdy plastics can be repeatedly washed, so consumers don't have to worry about breeding bacteria. For a lessened environmental impact, spring and other specialty waters can be purchased in bulk. But as BBC News concluded, "The conservationists are fighting an uphill battle. The bottled water market is booming . . . and shows no signs of drying up."

Battling the Bottlers

Numerous environmental and social activists have recently begun to put up a fight against the expanding bottled water industry, which they claim threatens local wells, streams, wetlands and ways of life. Bottling companies may pump up to 500 gallons per minute, or even more, out of each well, and many wells run 24 hours a day, 365 days a year. Such operations have drawn intense opposition in Florida, New Hampshire, Pennsylvania, Texas, Michigan and Wisconsin. Many residents of these states depend heavily on groundwater for residential, agricultural and fishery use. In Wisconsin, for example, three out of four homes and 97 percent of municipalities obtain their water from the ground.

"Resistance against water bottlers is a classic NIMBY (not-in-my-backyard) issue," says Kay. The IBWA claims bottlers wouldn't pump aquifers to depletion because that wouldn't make good business sense. But civil engineer and hydrologist Tom Ballestero of the University of New Hampshire cautions that surrounding wells and the environment can be negatively impacted before an aquifer is severely depleted. "The groundwater they are pumping and exporting was going somewhere where it had an environmental benefit," says Ballestero. Geologist David Bainbridge of Alliant International University also points out that there are scant few penalties against users who draw down water tables or deplete aquifers. Due to the long amount of time it takes to naturally replenish aquifers, most scientists consider groundwater a nonrenewable resource.

Much of the opposition to water bottlers has been directed at Nestlé Waters North America, which taps around 75 different U.S. spring sites. A spokesperson for the corporation, Jane Lazgin, says most communities welcome the jobs and revenue brought by bottling operations. Even so, Nestlé lost several bids to set up bottling plants in the Midwest due to intense opposition. Eventually, for its Ice Mountain brand, Nestlé built a $100 million plant capable of bottling 260 million gallons of water a year from an aquifer in Michigan's rural Mecosta County, which is about 60 miles north of Grand Rapids. Nestlé paid around $150 for permits and received substantial tax breaks.

Local activists, mobilized by the newly formed Michigan Citizens for Water Conservation, protested the plant on the grounds that the facility would take too heavy a toll on the surrounding environment and quality of life. Although Nestlé claims it conducted "exhaustive studies for nearly two years to ensure that the plant does not deplete water sources or harm the ecosystem," the activists pointed out that the state has no authority to limit the amount of water that is actually removed.

Three Native American tribes sued the state on the basis that rivers, and ultimately, the Great Lakes, would be affected. Michigan Citizens for Water Conservation and a few local residents also filed a lawsuit, claiming that the Mecosta operations violate state and federal water rights. The controversy became a hot topic during the 2002 gubernatorial election. As *Grist* reported, "Both major party candidates publicly and repeatedly expressed their resolve to modernize state water policy to block other multinational corporations from privatizing, bottling and selling hundreds of millions of gallons of Michigan's groundwater annually across state lines." A ruling on the case is expected soon, and is believed to have far-reaching ramifications.

In Florida, Nestlé angered many people, including the group Save Our Springs, when it took over Crystal Spring, which is near Tampa. The company fenced out the public, which had enjoyed the water for generations. After five years of bottling operations, the spring level has dropped. Some officals are worried, since the spring feeds the source of Tampa's water. Nestlé blames the change on dry spells and local development.

Local residents have also fought Nestlé in rural northeast Texas, where they complain that a well across the street front the company's bottling site went dry five days after Nestlé began operations. Nestlé's Lazgin claims that well dried up because it was old and shallow, and that it was not on the same aquifer as the bottling plant. Critics counter that aquifer geology is a fairly subjective science. The Texas Supreme Court ruled in favor of Nestlé under the state's "rule of capture." Save Our Springs President Terri Wolfe told *The Northwestern,* "The poor people whose wells run dry because of [bottlers] can't afford that water."

What's the Quencher?

A host of environmental groups are joining resource managers in the call for Americans to cut back on bottled water and instead look to tap systems to provide our daily needs. As the NRDC points out, incidents of chemical or microbial contamination in tap water are actually relatively rare. In a recent review of the nation's public drinking water infrastructure, researchers at the Harvard School of Public Health concluded, "Reasonably reliable water is currently available to nearly all 270 million U.S. residents."

Writing in *The Kansas Lifeline,* Scott Hoober expresses frustration on the part of municipal water managers, who are increasingly shackled with negative reputations despite their actual accomplishments. Hoober advises managers sarcastically, "What are you waiting for? Turn a few valves, install a bottling plant and begin to make the big bucks. You could sell your water for half of what the other bottler down the road is charging and still make a bundle. With no meters or mains to maintain, no monthly billing, lower lab bills, why, you could afford a top-dollar advertising campaign telling folks how much better your water is than the stuff that used to come out of the tap."

It's true that tap water does face numerous threats, including possible contamination from the potentially harmful byproducts of chlorination, the specter of pollution and a lack of adequate funding. Stresses from global warming, urban sprawl and population increase also must be factored in, as well as the looming threat of terrorism. The WWF argues that governments should focus their limited energies on repairing current tap water infrastructures and on protecting watersheds from harmful farm, industry and urban pollutants.

Many public water supply advocates feel that tax dollars should be paying to deal with tap water's challenges. We certainly need to think twice before handing off the public water trust to private companies that put it in attractive bottles at a high price. CONTACT: International Bottled Water Association, (800)WATER-11, . . . Natural Resources Defense Council, (212)727-2700, . . .

POSTSCRIPT

Is Bottling Water a Good Solution to Problems of Water Purity and Availability?

Ultimately, bottled water is the poster child for the consumer society. Although it is not safer than tap water and it doesn't taste better, it looks neat—makes us feel European, and slim and athletic (runners and cyclists drink water while exercising). But it really is no more exciting than, well, a drink of water. There is damage to the environment, but right at this point in U.S. history, the environment does not seem to be a selling point for the American consumer. (Witness the sales of SUVs and trucks to people who don't need them.)

Suggested Reading

If you want to pursue water further, the following sources might be valuable:

Elizabeth Royte *Bottlemania: How Water Went on Sale and Why We Bought It,* First U.S. Edition, New York: Bloomsbury USA, 2008.

Arthur von Weisenberger, "Reading Between the Lines of Bottled Water Labels," http://www.botledwaterweb.com/articles/avw-002.htm.

Janet L. Sawin, "Water Scarcity Could Overwhelm the Next Generation," from *World Watch* (vol. 16, no. 4 2003), by Worldwatch Institute, www.worldwatch.org.

Barbara Whitaker, "For Town, Water Is a Fighting Word," from *The New York Times,* (March 23, 2003), p. A23.

ISSUE 20

Should the World Continue to Rely on Oil as a Major Source of Energy?

YES: Red Cavaney, from "Global Oil Production about to Peak? A Recurring Myth," *Worldwatch* (January–February 2006)

NO: James Howard Kunstler, from *The Long Emergency* (Grove/ Atlantic, 2005)

ISSUE SUMMARY

YES: Red Cavaney, president and chief executive officer of the American Petroleum Institute, argues that recent revolutionary advances in technology will yield sufficient quantities of available oil for the foreseeable future.

NO: James Howard Kunstler contends that the peak of oil production, Hubbert's Peak, was itself the important turning point in our species' relationship to petroleum. Unless strong conservation measures are put in place, the new scarcity will destroy much that we have come to expect in our lives.

We might begin with the fact that the idea of an "oil crisis" has become part of our lives in the last half century. Suddenly gasoline prices are higher, there are lines at the gas stations, political commentators suddenly discover international affairs, and a mood of panic pervades the country. Resolutions are made, actions begun, but then the whole crisis seems to peter out. What's happening?

First, is oil "running out"? Since the 1930s, energy prognosticators have used a model called Hubbert's Curve (named for geologist M. King Hubbert, who first projected it) that predicted the end of oil as an available resource. As oil recovery technology has progressed, the curve has been lengthened; Red Cavaney's selection relies heavily on this fact. But the curve is still there, and even a major contraction in the oil supply will have a very significant effect on the way America continues to grow and develop; James Kunstler calls our attention to some of the changes we may expect.

There are two major dimensions to the "oil crisis," both of which affect the business community. The first is a management dilemma, stemming from the interaction of the U.S. economy and a global monopoly: how to control the impact of the decisions of international business consortia in the energy business. Business is all about supply and demand (see the selection by Adam Smith in Issue 1). In the case of petroleum, the lion's share of the supply is controlled by energy consortia that as Smith would approve, consider their own economic interests first, with the result that they rarely have the interests of the people of the United States as a priority. The logic of economic success for the industry, as all oil producers know, requires that the producers reduce the supply available for purchase, causing the price to rise, for an interval of time that will be limited by the customer's perception that he is spending too much for oil, and has recourse to other methods of obtaining energy—for instance, by developing solar energy as a source of power or placing restrictions on the amount of gasoline that automobiles sold in the United States can consume in a mile. At that point, production is raised dramatically, oil prices drop precipitously, and as a result, all investments in alternatives to oil consumption are abandoned. After that point, enough time is allowed to elapse so that investments will have been liquidated and the alternative workforce scattered; then the squeeze begins again. American consumers, on this understanding, are at the mercy of a foreign monopoly in complete control of the price of gasoline and heating oil, and would be well advised to use the periods of inexpensive oil to assemble the capital needed to solve the energy problem once and for all. That gathering of capital can only be done by heavy taxation of oil alone, or of all carbon, sufficient to keep the price of oil level for the consumer while the capital accumulates. The American public dislikes taxes in general, and the oil industry dislikes oil taxes even more.

The second dimension is an industry crisis caused by an environmental threat: how to adjust our automotive industry, traditionally the heart and pride of our manufacturing capacity, to minimize the damage done to the environment by the burning of all fossil fuels, especially the burning of gasoline in the use of automobiles and trucks for transportation. Our automotive industry is set up like all the others—to provide a healthy return to the shareholders by producing products that the consumers want and will buy and that yield a high profit margin. That requirement does not well describe small, fuel-efficient cars, but it does describe the large, low-fuel-mileage sport utility vehicles (SUVs) introduced in the 1990s and now flooding our highways. As the American public contemplates images of polar bears stranded on vanishing ice, hurricanes in the Caribbean, and expanding deserts in Africa, it becomes increasingly likely that each new administration will insist on conservation measures, starting with the all-too-visible SUVs. How should the automotive industry—and the advertisers, the oil companies, and the consumers—respond?

Bear in mind, as you read these selections, that global business will suffer major disruptions in any initiative to end oil dependence; what advantages might make the sacrifices worth their cost?

YES ↵

Red Cavaney

Global Oil Production about to Peak? A Recurring Myth

Once again, we are hearing that world oil production is "peaking," and that we will face a steadily diminishing oil supply to fuel the global economy. These concerns have been expressed periodically over the years, but have always been at odds with energy and economic realities. Such is the case today.

Let's look at some history: In 1874, the chief geologist of Pennsylvania predicted we would run out of oil in four years—just using it for kerosene. Thirty years ago, groups such as the Club of Rome predicted an end of oil long before the current day. These forecasts were wrong because, nearly every year, we have found more oil than we have used, and oil reserves have continued to grow.

The world consumes approximately 80 million barrels of oil a day. By 2030, world oil demand is estimated to grow about 50 percent, to 121 million barrels a day, even allowing for significant improvements in energy efficiency. The International Energy Agency says there are sufficient oil resources to meet demand for at least the next 30 years.

The key factor here is technology. Revolutionary advances in technology in recent years have dramatically increased the ability of companies to find and extract oil—and, of particular importance, recover more oil from existing reservoirs. Rather than production peaking, existing fields are yielding markedly more oil than in the past. Advances in technology include the following:

Directional Drilling. It used to be that wellbores were basically vertical holes. This made it necessary to drill virtually on top of a potential oil deposit. However, the advent of miniaturized computers and advanced sensors that can be attached to the drill bit now allows companies to drill directional holes with great accuracy because they can get real-time information on the subsurface location throughout the drilling process.

Horizontal Drilling. Horizontal drilling is similar to directional drilling, but the well is designed to cut horizontally through the middle of the oil or natural gas deposit. Early horizontal wells penetrated only 500 to 800 feet of reservoir laterally, but technology advances recently allowed a North Slope operator to penetrate 8,000 feet of reservoir horizontally. Moreover, horizontal wells can operate up to 10 times more productively than conventional wells.

From *World Watch*, January/February 2006, pp. 13–15. Copyright © 2006 by Worldwatch Institute. Reprinted by permission. www.worldwatch.org

404

3-D Seismic Technology.   Substantial enhancements in computing power during the past two decades have allowed the industry to gain a much clearer picture of what lies beneath the surface. The ability to process huge amounts of data to produce three-dimensional seismic images has significantly improved the drilling success rate of the industry.

Primarily due to these advances, the U.S. Geological Survey (USGS), in its 2000 *World Petroleum Assessment,* increased by 20 percent its estimate of undiscovered, technically recoverable oil. USGS noted that, since oil became a major energy source about 100 years ago, 539 billion barrels of oil have been produced outside the United States. USGS estimates there are 649 billion barrels of undiscovered, technically recoverable oil outside the United States. But, importantly, USGS also estimates that there will be an *additional* 612 billion barrels from "reserve growth"—nearly equaling the undiscovered resources. Reserve growth results from a variety of sources, including technological advancement in exploration and production, increases over initially conservative estimates of reserves, and economic changes.

The USGS estimates reflected several factors:

- As drilling and production within discovered fields progresses, new pools or reservoirs are found that were not previously known.
- Advances in exploration technology make it possible to identify new targets within existing fields.
- Advances in drilling technology make it possible to recover oil and gas not previously considered recoverable in the initial reserve estimates.
- Enhanced oil recovery techniques increase the recovery factor for oil and thereby increase the reserves within existing fields.

Here in the United States, rather than "running out of oil," potentially vast oil and natural gas reserves remain to be developed. According to the latest published government estimates, there are more than 131 billion barrels of oil and more than 1,000 trillion cubic feet of natural gas remaining to be discovered in the United States. However, 78 percent of this oil and 62 percent of this gas are expected to be found beneath federal lands—much of which are non-park and non-wilderness lands—and coastal waters. While there is plenty of oil in the ground, oil companies need to be allowed to make major investments to find and produce it.

The U.S. Energy Information Administration has projected that fossil fuels will continue to dominate U.S. energy consumption, with oil and natural gas providing almost two-thirds of that consumption in the year 2025, even though energy efficiency and renewables will grow faster than their historical rates. However, renewables in particular start from a very small base; and the major shares provided by oil, natural gas, and coal in 2025 are projected to be nearly identical to those in 2003.

Those who block oil and natural gas development here in the United States and elsewhere only make it much more difficult to meet the demand for oil, natural gas, and petroleum products. Indeed, it is not surprising that some of the end-of-oil advocates are the same people who oppose oil and natural gas development everywhere.

Failure to develop the potentially vast oil and natural gas resources that remain in the world will have a high economic cost. We must recognize that we live in a global economy, and that there is a strong link between energy and economic growth. If we are to continue to grow economically, here in the United States, in Europe, and the developing world, we must be cost-competitive in our use of energy. We need *all* sources of energy. We do not have the luxury of limiting ourselves to one source to the exclusion of others. Nor can we afford to write off our leading source of energy before we have found cost-competitive and readily available alternatives.

Consider how oil enhances our quality of life—fueling growth and jobs in industry and commerce, cooling and warming our homes, and getting us where we need to go. Here in the United States, oil provides about 97 percent of transportation fuels, which power nearly all of the cars and trucks traveling on our nation's highways. And plastics, medicines, fertilizers, and countless other products that extend and enhance our quality of life are derived from oil.

In considering our future energy needs, we also need to understand that gasoline-powered automobiles have been the dominant mode of transport for the past century—and the overwhelming preference of hundreds of millions of people throughout the world. Regardless of fuel, the automobile—likely to be configured far differently from today—will remain the consumer's choice for personal transport for decades to come. The freedom of mobility and the independence it affords consumers is highly valued.

The United States—and the world—cannot afford to leave the Age of Oil before realistic substitutes are fully in place. It is important to remember that man left the Stone Age not because he ran out of stones—and we will not leave the Age of Oil because we will run out. Yes, someday oil will be replaced, but clearly not until substitutes are found—substitutes that are proven more reliable, more versatile, and more cost-competitive than oil. We can rely on the energy marketplace to determine what the most efficient substitutes will be.

As we plan for our energy future, we also cannot afford to ignore the lessons of recent history. In the early 1970s, many energy policymakers were sure that oil and natural gas would soon be exhausted, and government policy was explicitly aimed at "guiding" the market in a smooth transition away from these fuels to new, more sustainable alternatives. Price controls, allocation schemes, limitations on natural gas, massive subsidies to synthetic fuels, and other measures were funded heavily and implemented.

Unfortunately, the key premises on which these programs were based, namely that oil was nearing exhaustion and that government guidance was desirable to safely transition to new energy sources, are now recognized as having been clearly wrong—and to have resulted in enormously expensive mistakes.

Looking into the distant future, there will be a day when oil is no longer the world's dominant energy source. We can only speculate as to when and how that day will come about. For example, there is an even bigger hydrocarbon resource that can be developed to provide nearly endless amounts of energy: methane hydrates (methane frozen in ice crystals). The deposits of methane hydrates are so vast that when we develop the technology to bring them to market, we will have clean-burning energy for 2,000 years. It's just one of the exciting scenarios we may see in the far-off future. But we won't be getting there anytime soon, and until we do, the Age of Oil will continue.

The Long Emergency

A few weeks ago, the price of oil ratcheted above fifty-five dollars a barrel, which is about twenty dollars a barrel more than a year ago. The next day, the oil story was buried on page six of the *New York Times* business section. Apparently, the price of oil is not considered significant news, even when it goes up five bucks a barrel in the span of ten days. That same day, the stock market shot up more than a hundred points because, CNN said, government data showed no signs of inflation. Note to clueless nation: Call planet Earth.

Carl Jung, one of the fathers of psychology, famously remarked that "people cannot stand too much reality." What you're about to read may challenge your assumptions about the kind of world we live in, and especially the kind of world into which events are propelling us. We are in for a rough ride through uncharted territory.

It has been very hard for Americans—lost in dark raptures of nonstop infotainment, recreational shopping and compulsive motoring—to make sense of the gathering forces that will fundamentally alter the terms of everyday life in our technological society. Even after the terrorist attacks of 9/11, America is still sleepwalking into the future. I call this coming time the Long Emergency.

Most immediately we face the end of the cheap-fossil-fuel era. It is no exaggeration to state that reliable supplies of cheap oil and natural gas underlie everything we identify as the necessities of modern life—not to mention all of its comforts and luxuries: central heating, air conditioning, cars, airplanes, electric lights, inexpensive clothing, recorded music, movies, hip-replacement surgery, national defense—you name it.

The few Americans who are even aware that there is a gathering global-energy predicament usually misunderstand the core of the argument. That argument states that we don't have to run out of oil to start having severe problems with industrial civilization and its dependent systems. We only have to slip over the all-time production peak and begin a slide down the arc of steady depletion.

The term "global oil-production peak" means that a turning point will come when the world produces the most oil it will ever produce in a given year and, after that, yearly production will inexorably decline. It is usually represented graphically in a bell curve. The peak is the top of the curve, the halfway point of the world's all-time total endowment, meaning half the world's oil will be left. That seems like a lot of oil, and it is, but there's a big catch: It's the half that is much more difficult to extract, far more costly to get, of much poorer quality and located mostly in places where the people hate us. A substantial amount of it will never be extracted.

The United States passed its own oil peak—about 11 million barrels a day—in 1970, and since then production has dropped steadily. In 2004 it ran just above 5 million barrels a day (we get a tad more from natural-gas condensates). Yet we consume roughly 20 million barrels a day now. That means we have to import about two-thirds of our oil, and the ratio will continue to worsen.

The U.S. peak in 1970 brought on a portentous change in geoeconomic power. Within a few years, foreign producers, chiefly OPEC, were setting the price of oil, and this in turn led to the oil crises of the 1970s. In response, frantic development of non-OPEC oil, especially the North Sea fields of England and Norway, essentially saved the West's ass for about two decades. Since 1999, these fields have entered depletion. Meanwhile, worldwide discovery of new oil has steadily declined to insignificant levels in 2003 and 2004.

Some "cornucopians" claim that the Earth has something like a creamy nougat center of "abiotic" oil that will naturally replenish the great oil fields of the world. The facts speak differently. There has been no replacement whatsoever of oil already extracted from the fields of America or any other place.

Now we are faced with the global oil-production peak. The best estimates of when this will actually happen have been somewhere between now and 2010. In 2004, however, after demand from burgeoning China and India shot up, and revelations that Shell Oil wildly misstated its reserves, and Saudi Arabia proved incapable of goosing up its production despite promises to do so, the most knowledgeable experts revised their predictions and now concur that 2005 is apt to be the year of all-time global peak production.

It will change everything about how we live.

To aggravate matters, American natural-gas production is also declining, at five percent a year, despite frenetic new drilling, and with the potential of much steeper declines ahead. Because of the oil crises of the 1970s, the nuclear-plant disasters at Three Mile Island and Chernobyl and the acid-rain problem, the U.S. chose to make gas its first choice for electric-power generation. The result was that just about every power plant built after 1980 has to run on gas. Half the homes in America are heated with gas. To further complicate matters, gas isn't easy to import. Here in North America, it is distributed through a vast pipeline network. Gas imported from overseas would have to be compressed at minus-260 degrees Fahrenheit in pressurized tanker ships and unloaded (re-gasified) at special terminals, of which few exist in America. Moreover, the first attempts to site new terminals have met furious opposition because they are such ripe targets for terrorism.

Some other things about the global energy predicament are poorly understood by the public and even our leaders. This is going to be a permanent energy crisis, and these energy problems will synergize with the disruptions of climate change, epidemic disease and population overshoot to produce higher orders of trouble.

We will have to accommodate ourselves to fundamentally changed conditions.

No combination of alternative fuels will allow us to run American life the way we have been used to running it, or even a substantial fraction of it. The wonders of steady technological progress achieved through the reign of cheap oil have lulled us into a kind of Jiminy Cricket syndrome, leading many Americans to believe that anything we wish for hard enough will come true. These days, even people who ought to know better are wishing ardently for a seamless transition from fossil fuels to their putative replacements.

The widely touted "hydrogen economy" is a particularly cruel hoax. We are not going to replace the U.S. automobile and truck fleet with vehicles run on fuel cells. For one thing, the current generation of fuel cells is largely designed to run on hydrogen obtained from natural gas. The other way to get hydrogen in the quantities wished for would be electrolysis of water using power from hundreds of nuclear plants. Apart from the dim prospect of our building that many nuclear plants soon enough, there are also numerous severe problems with hydrogen's nature as an element that present forbidding obstacles to its use as a replacement for oil and gas, especially in storage and transport.

Wishful notions about rescuing our way of life with "renewables" are also unrealistic. Solar-electric systems and wind turbines face not only the enormous problem of scale but the fact that the components require substantial amounts of energy to manufacture and the probability that they can't be manufactured at all without the underlying support platform of a fossil-fuel economy. We will surely use solar and wind technology to generate some electricity for a period ahead but probably at a very local and small scale.

Virtually all "biomass" schemes for using plants to create liquid fuels cannot be scaled up to even a fraction of the level at which things are currently run. What's more, these schemes are predicated on using oil and gas "inputs" (fertilizers, weed-killers) to grow the biomass crops that would be converted into ethanol or bio-diesel fuels. This is a net energy loser—you might as well just burn the inputs and not bother with the biomass products. Proposals to distill trash and waste into oil by means of thermal depolymerization depend on the huge waste stream produced by a cheap oil and gas economy in the first place.

Coal is far less versatile than oil and gas, extant in less abundant supplies than many people assume and fraught with huge ecological drawbacks—as a contributor to greenhouse "global warming" gases and many health and toxicity issues ranging from widespread mercury poisoning to acid rain. You can make synthetic oil from coal, but the only time this was tried on a large scale was by the Nazis under wartime conditions, using impressive amounts of slave labor.

If we wish to keep the lights on in America after 2020, we may indeed have to resort to nuclear power, with all its practical problems and eco-conundrums. Under optimal conditions, it could take ten years to get a new generation of nuclear power plants into operation, and the price may be beyond our means. Uranium is also a resource in finite supply. We are no closer to the more difficult project of atomic fusion, by the way, than we were in the 1970s.

The Long Emergency is going to be a tremendous trauma for the human race. We will not believe that this is happening to us, that 200 years of modernity can be brought to its knees by a world-wide power shortage. The survivors will have to cultivate a religion of hope—that is, a deep and comprehensive belief that humanity is worth carrying on. If there is any positive side to stark changes coming our way, it may be in the benefits of close communal relations, of having to really work intimately (and physically) with our neighbors, to be part of an enterprise that really matters and to be fully engaged in meaningful social enactments instead of being merely entertained to avoid boredom. Years from now, when we hear singing at all, we will hear ourselves, and we will sing with our whole hearts.

POSTSCRIPT

Should the World Continue to Rely on Oil as a Major Source of Energy?

"Twixt the optimist and the pessimist, the difference is droll: the optimist sees the donut, and the pessimist sees the hole" (Anonymous). The selections you have just finished represent the optimistic and the pessimistic sides of the "oil reserves conflict" as we know it. There is more to this subject. We might ask the optimist if the availability of oil is really the heart of this question. Burning fossil fuels hurts the earth; should we cut back on our consumption of oil just to save the earth, now, even if oil supplies are abundant? But there is a question for the pessimist, too: Granted that our "lifestyles" this minute require lots of oil, does our happiness depend on it, too? What would it be like to live in a way that consumes lots less oil because it consumes lots less of any kind of energy? Outside of the field of business ethics (and sometimes inside it, too) explorations into the notions of "simplicity" and "the simple life" continue. The less consumption-oriented life suggested in these explorations does not seem to be significantly lower in quality than our own—in many ways, it seems better. Should some ambitious entrepreneurs be looking into these possibilities, as the wave of America's economic future? Think about it.

Suggested Reading

Hawken, Paul, Amory B. Lovins and L. Hunter Lovins. *Natural Capitalism: Creating the Next Industrial Revolution*. New York: Little, Brown (1999).

Newton, Lisa, *Ethics and Sustainability*. New York, NY: Prentice Hall, 2002.

Newton, Lisa. Business Ethics and the Natural Environment. Hoboken, NJ: Wiley, John and Sons, Incorporated, 2005.

Newton, Lisa *Business Ethics and the Natural Environment* Blackwood, NY: Blackwell Publishers, 2005.

Contributors to This Volume

EDITORS

ELAINE E. ENGLEHARDT is a Distinguished Professor of Ethics and Professor of Philosophy at Utah Valley University (UVU). She has taught ethics, philosophy and communication classes at UVU for the past thirty years. For the past twenty years, she has written and directed seven multi-year, national grants. Four large grants are in ethics across the curriculum from the Department of Education; and three are from the National Endowment for the Humanities. She is the author of five books and the co-editor of *Teaching Ethics*. She has also written numerous articles. She received her Ph.D. from the University of Utah.

LISA H. NEWTON is a Professor of Philosophy at Fairfield University. She joined the faculty in 1969 and teaches courses in ethics, applied ethics, environmental studies, health care ethics and several other areas. She is the Director of the Applied Ethics Center at Fairfield University. She is also the Director of the Program in Environmental Studies at Fairfield University. Dr. Newton received her PhD in Philosophy from Columbia University in New York City. She is currently on the Executive Committee of the Association for Professional and Practical Ethics. She is the author of fifteen books and articles. She received her Ph.D. from Columbia University.

MICHAEL S. PRITCHARD is Willard A. Brown Professor of Philosophy and Co-Director of the Center for the Study of Ethics in Society at Western Michigan University. He is Co-Editor of *Teaching Ethics*, the official journal of the Society for Ethics Across the Curriculum. He also serves on the Executive Committee of the Association for Practical and Professional Ethics. His areas of teaching include: ethical theory; practical ethics; ethics in engineering; and philosophy for children. He is the author ten books and umerous articles. He received his Ph.D. from the University of Wisconsin.

AUTHORS

DENIS G. ARNOLD received his Ph.D. in philosophy from the University of Minnesota in 1997 and is a past fellow of the National Endowment for the Humanities. His work in ethics and business ethics has appeared in *History of Philosophy Quarterly, American Philosophical Quarterly,* and other publications. Arnold is co-editor with Laura Hartman and Richard Wokutch of *Rising Above Sweatshops: Innovative Management Approaches to Global Labor Challenges* (New York: Praeger, 2004). He teaches philosophy and chairs the legal studies program at Pacific Lutheran University. His current research focuses on the ethical dimensions of global capitalism.

THOMAS A. BASS is a professor of English and journalism at the State University of New York–Albany. He has taught literature and history at Hamilton College and at the University of California. Mr. Bass has published numerous books, the most recent being *The Spy Who Loved Us* (Public Affairs, February 2009).

PHILIP L. BEREANO is a professor in the College of Engineering, Department of Technical Communication, University of Washington, Seattle. For over 30 years he has worked on issues regarding technologies and public policies and is widely published in these areas. He chairs the national Committee on Databases and Civil Liberties of the American Civil Liberties Union, and is a co-founder of the Council for Responsible Genetics. He participated in the development of the UN Cartagena Biosafety protocol. He is active in the American Civil Liberties Union, the Council for Responsible Genetics, and the Washington Biotechnology Action Council.

SISSELA BOK is a philosopher, author, and teacher who is well known for the books *Lying* (New York: Pantheon, 1978) and *Secrets* (New York: Pantheon Books, 1982). She received her B.A. and M.A. in psychology from George Washington University in 1957 and 1958, and her Ph.D. in philosophy from Harvard University in 1970. Formerly a Professor of Philosophy at Brandeis University, she is currently a Senior Visiting Fellow at the Harvard Center for Population and Development Studies, Harvard School of Public Health.

NORMAN E. BOWIE is the Elmer L. Andersen Chair in Corporate Responsibility at the University of Minnesota, where he holds a joint appointment in the departments of Philosophy and Strategic Management and Organization. He is a frequent contributor to scholarly journals in business ethics. His most recently edited book is *Blackwell Guide to Business Ethics*. His co-edited text *Ethical Theory and Business* is in its sixth edition. He has held a position as Dixon's Professor of Business Ethics and Social Responsibility at the London Business School and has been a fellow at Harvard's Program in Ethics and the Professions.

RED CAVANEY has served as President and Chief Executive Officer of the American Petroleum Institute. He was President, Chief Executive Officer and a director of the American Plastics Council from 1994 to 1997, immediately following service as President of the American Forest & Paper Association and President of its predecessor, the American Paper Institute. He is a past Chairman of the American Society of Association Executives and the current Chairman of the American Council on Capital Formation.

CHRISTOPHER L. CULP is adjunct professor of finance at the Graduate School of Business at the University of Chicago, a principal at Chicago Partners LLC, and senior fellow in financial regulation at the Competitive Enterprise Institute.

CHAUNCEY M. DEPREE, JR., is the author of several articles including "Who's Reading Your Office E-mail? Is That Legal?", and "Coping With Environmental and Tort Claims." He has published in *ABACUS, Journal of Accounting and Public Policy, Issues in Accounting Education, the CPA Journal, the CPCU Journal, and the Professional Lawyer* (ABA). He is a Professor in the School of Professional Accountancy, College of Business Administration, at the University of Southern Mississippi.

JOE DESJARDINS is Professor in the philosophy department formed jointly by the College of St. Benedict and St. John's University in Minnesota. He presently serves as the Executive Director of the Society for Business Ethics. Among his publications are: *An Introduction to Business Ethics* (McGraw Hill), *Environmental Ethics: An Introduction to Environmental Philosophy* (Wadsworth), of *Contemporary Issues in Business Ethics,* co-editor, with John McCall, (5th Ed, Wadsworth) He received his Ph.D. from the University of Notre Dame and taught for many years at Villanova University before moving to Minnesota.

WILLIAM DOMNARSKI is an attorney in private practice in Minneapolis, Minnesota. His articles have appeared in such journals as *American Scholar* and *Virginia Quarterly,* and he is the author of *In the Opinion of the Court* (Champaign, IL: University of Illinois Press, 1995).

MARK DOWIE is an investigative journalist and a former editor of *Mother Jones* magazine. He is the author of *Losing Ground: American Environmentalism at the Close of the Twentieth Century* (Cambridge, MA: MIT Press, 1996) and coauthor, with David T. Hanson and Wendell Berry, of *Waste Land: Meditations on a Ravaged Landscape* (New York: Aperture Foundation, 1997).

PAUL AND ANNE EHRLICH are environmental writers who are best known for *Healing the Planet: Strategies for Resolving the Environmental Crisis* (Boston: Addison-Wesley, 1991) and *Betrayal of Science and Reason: How Anti-Environmental Rhetoric Threatens Our Future* (Washington, D.C.: Island Press, 1996). Paul Ehrlich launched a major sector of the environmental movement with his *The Population Bomb* (New York: Ballantine Books, 1971).

FRED ENGLANDER is a Professor of Economics in the Economics and Finance Department at Farleigh Dickinson University at the Silberman College of Business. He holds M.A. and Ph.D. degrees from Rutgers University. His research includes, "the role of government in the economy, and "ethical dimensions of public policy issues."

FRIEDRICH ENGELS (1820–1895), a German socialist, was the closest collaborator of Karl Marx in the foundation of modern communism. The official Marxism of the Soviet Union relied heavily on Engels's contribution to Marxist theory. After the death of Marx in 1883, Engels served as the foremost authority on Marx and Marxism, and he edited volumes 2 and 3 of *Das Kapital* on the basis of Marx's incomplete manuscripts and notes. Two major works by Engels are *Anti-Duhring* and *The Dialectics of Nature.*

RICHARD A. EPSTEIN is a James Parker Hall Professor of Law at the University of Chicago. He authored "Unconscionability: A Critical Reappraisal" in 1975.

MILTON FRIEDMAN (1912–2006), U.S. laissez-faire economist, emeritus professor at the University of Chicago, and senior research fellow at the Hoover Institution, was one of the leading modern exponents of liberalism in the nineteenth-century European sense. He was the author of *Capitalism and Freedom* and coauthor of *A Monetary History of the United States* and *Free to Choose*. He was awarded the Nobel Prize for Economics in 1976.

STEVE H. HANKE is professor of applied economics at the Johns Hopkins University, a principal at Chicago Partners LLC, and a senior fellow at the Cato Institute.

GILBERT HARMAN is Stuart Professor of Philosophy at Princeton University. He regularly co-teaches interdisciplinary courses in "The Philosophy and Psychology of Rationality" and "The Psychology and Philosophy of Ethics." He has been co-director (with George Miller) of the Princeton University Cognitive Science Laboratory and is chair of the Faculty Committee for Cognitive Studies. He is author of *Explaining Value and Other Essays in Moral Philosophy* and *Reasoning, Meaning and Mind,* both published by Oxford University Press.

ALAN F. HOLMER has served as President and Chief Executive Officer of the Pharmaceutical Research and Manufacturers of America (PhRMA), where for nearly ten years he led the organization that represents the interests of leading pharmaceutical and biotechnology companies. In addition to his pharmaceutical industry experience, Mr. Holmer has significant expertise in handling legal, international trade and governmental issues, having held various positions within the Office of the U.S. Trade Representative, the Commerce Department and the White House, including serving as Deputy U.S. Trade Representative with rank of Ambassador. He received an A.B. degree from Princeton University and a J.D. from Georgetown University Law Center.

BRIAN HOWARD is managing editor of *E* and turns on the tap when he wants a glass of water.

REBECCA K. JUDE is an attorney, at Jude & Jude, and PLLC. She has published several journal articles with Chauncey M. DePree including, "Ten Practical Suggestions for Terminating an Employee and "Who's Reading Your Office E-mail? Is That Legal?"

IRA T. KAY is the director of Watson Wyatt's compensation practice. He works closely with U.S., public, international and private companies on long-term incentive plans to increase shareholder value. He conducts research on stock option overhang, executive pay and performance, and CEO stock ownership. He is a co-author of *The Human Capital Edge, CEO Pay and Shareholder Value: Helping the U.S. Win the Global Economic War;* and *Value at the Top: Solutions to the Executive Compensation Crisis.* He holds a Ph.D. in economics from Wayne State University.

JAMES HOWARD KUNSTLER is best known for his books *The Geography of Nowhere* (1994), a history of American suburbia and urban development, and the more recent *The Long Emergency* (2005). He has written a science fiction novel describing a future culture, *World Made by Hand* (2008). He is a leading proponent of the movement known as "New Urbanism." He has also written *Home From Nowhere,* and *The City in Mind.*

ROBERT A. LARMER, B.A., M.A., Ph.D., is associate professor of philosophy at the University of New Brunswick. His responsibilities include courses in philosophy of religion and ethics. He is the author of various articles in philosophy of religion and of *Water Into Wine: An Investigation of the Concept of Miracle.*

JOSEPH A. LEVITT, Esq. is the director of the Center for Food Safety and Applied Nutrition, Food and Drug Administration, Department of Health and Human Services, Washington D.C.

IAN MAITLAND teaches business ethics and international business at the University of Minnesota. He is author of the *Causes of Industrial Disorder* (Oxford, UK: Routledge, 1983) and has published in the *Journal of Business Ethics, Journal of Politics, Academy of Management Review, British Journal of Industrial Relations, California Management Review, Business and the Contemporary World,* and elsewhere.

KARL MARX (1818–1883) was a student of philosophy and economics and author of *Das Kapital* and the *Communist Manifesto,* 1848.

JOHN McCALL is a professor in the departments of Philosophy and Management at St. Joseph's University. He has also taught at Georgetown University's McDonough School of Business and at the Wharton School of the University of Pennsylvania. He is coauthor (with Joe DesJardins) of *Contemporary Issues in Business Ethics,* now in its fourth edition. He has published on welfare reform, corporate responsibility, product liability, and especially on employee rights issues.

JAMES NEAL is a lawyer who has served in many mass disaster and product liability cases, including the Ford Pinto suit and the Exxon Valdez environmental suit.

LISA H. NEWTON is a program director in Applied Ethics and philosophy professor at Fairfield University, Fairfield, Connecticut.

JEREMY RIFKIN is president of the Foundation on Economic Trends and a long-time critic of innovative technology. He is the author of *The End of*

Work: The Decline of the Global Labor Force and the Dawn of the Post-Market Era (New York: Tarcher, 1996) and *The Biotech Century: Harnessing the Gene and Remaking the World* (New York: Putnam, 1998).

RICHARD ROSEN is a writer for *The American Prospect.*

JOHN SHANAHAN is vice president of the Alexis de Tocqueville Institution in Arlington, VA.

ADAM SMITH (1723–1790) was a Scottish philosopher and economist. Author of *An Inquiry into the Nature and Causes of the Wealth of Nations,* first edition, London, 1776.

JEREMY SNYDER is an Assistant Professor at Simon Fraser University in Burnaby, Canada.

GORDON G. SOLLARS is an Associate Professor of Management at Farleigh Dickinson University at the Silberman College of Business. He has an M.B.A. from the Wharton School, University of Pennsylvania and a Ph.D. from the University of Virginia.

ROBERT C. SOLOMON is Quincy Lee Centennial Professor of Business and Philosophy and Distinguished Teaching Professor at the University Texas at Austin. He has authored six books in business ethics, *Above the Bottom Line, It's Good Business, Ethics and Excellence, New World of Business, A Better Way to Think About Business,* and *Building Trust* (with Fernando Flores). He has written many articles and essays, and he lectures and consults world-wide for a variety of institutions and corporations.

JULIE STAUFFER, a published author on environmental issues and a contributor to many environmental publications, researched and published a book on water: its pollution in underdeveloped countries as well as in the United States and the scarcity of water worldwide due to pollution.

JUSTIN WELBY is Sub Dean and Canon for Reconciliation Ministry at Coventry Cathedral, working on interfaith relations, reconciliation, and conflict resolution in the United Kingdom, Africa, and the Middle East. He lectures on ethics and finance in the United Kingdom and Switzerland and is on the Board of the International Association for Catholic Social Teaching.

JOSEPH WIELAND is director of the Centre for Business Ethics associated with the German Business Ethics Network. He is also professor of economic and business ethics in Konstanz, Germany. He previously lectured in economics at the University of Witten/Herdecke. His book, *The Ethics of Governance,* is published in Marburg, Germany, by Metropolis.

SIDNEY M. WOLFE is a physician and presently the director of Public Citizen, a consumer and health advocacy lobbying group. Wolfe is also the editor of the book and website, *Worst Pills, Best Pills*. He has publicly crusaded against some pharmaceutical drugs he deemed as dangerous. Some of these drugs include: Phenacetin, Darvon, Oraflex, Zomax Vioxx, and Baycol.

EDGAR WOOLARD, JR., is a member of the Board of Telex Communications, Inc. He is a former director of the New York Stock Exchange, Inc., Citigroup Inc., IBM, Apple Computer, Inc. and Bell Atlantic Delaware. He is also a former Chairman of the Business Council. He is a member of the Board of Trustees of the Christiana Care Health System and the North Carolina Textile Foundation., Inc., and a member of the National Academy of Engineering, and the American Philosophical Society.

MATT ZWOLINSKI is an assistant professor of philosophy at the University of San Diego and a co-director of the University of San Diego's Institute for Law and Philosophy. He has written numerous articles on ethics, law, and economics. He is also the author of *Arguing About Political Philosophy* (Routledge, January 2009).